Effective AI, Blockchain, and E-Governance Applications for Knowledge Discovery and Management

Rajeev Kumar
Infrastructure University, Kuala Lumpur, Malaysia

Abu Bakar Abdul Hamid
Infrastructure University, Kuala Lumpur, Malaysia

Noor Inayah Binti Ya'akub
Infrastructure University, Kuala Lumpur, Malaysia

A volume in the Advances in Computational
Intelligence and Robotics (ACIR) Book Series

Published in the United States of America by
　IGI Global
　Engineering Science Reference (an imprint of IGI Global)
　701 E. Chocolate Avenue
　Hershey PA, USA 17033
　Tel: 717-533-8845
　Fax: 717-533-8661
　E-mail: cust@igi-global.com
　Web site: http://www.igi-global.com

Library of Congress Cataloging-in-Publication Data

Names: Kumar, Rajeev, 1985- editor. | Abdul Hamid, Abu Bakar, 1967- editor.
　| Noor Inayah Yaakub, editor.
Title: Effective AI, blockchain, and e-governance applications for
　knowledge discovery and management / edited by: Rajeev Kumar, Abu Bakar
　Abdul Hamid, and Noor Inayah Binti Ya'akub.
Description: Hershey, PA : Engineering Science Reference, [2023] | Includes
　bibliographical references and index. | Summary: "Effective AI,
　Blockchain, and E-Governance Applications for Knowledge Discovery and
　Management provides a global perspective on current and future trends
　concerning the integration of intelligent systems with cybersecurity
　applications, including recent advances and challenges related to the
　concerns of security and privacy issues in deep learning with an
　emphasis on the current state-of-theart methods, methodologies and
　implementation, attacks, and countermeasures. The book also discusses
　the challenges that need to be addressed for implementing DL-based
　security mechanisms that should have the capability of collecting or
　distributing data across several applications. Topics covered include
　skill development and tools for intelligence systems, deep learning,
　machine learning, blockchain, IoT, cloud computing, data ethics, and
　infrastructure. It is ideal for independent researchers, research
　scholars, scientists, libraries, industry experts, academic students,
　business associations, communication and marketing agencies,
　entrepreneurs, and all potential audiences with a specific interest in
　these topics"-- Provided by publisher.
Identifiers: LCCN 2023011126 (print) | LCCN 2023011127 (ebook) | ISBN
　9781668491515 (hardcover) | ISBN 9781668491522 (paperback) | ISBN
　9781668491539 (ebook)
Subjects: LCSH: Information technology--Economic aspects. | Knowledge
　economy. | Artificial intelligence--Economic aspects. | Information
　technology--Economic aspects. | Information technology--Social aspects.
Classification: LCC HC79.I55 E38 2023 (print) | LCC HC79.I55 (ebook) |
　DDC 303.48/33--dc23/eng/20230324
LC record available at https://lccn.loc.gov/2023011126
LC ebook record available at https://lccn.loc.gov/2023011127

This book is published in the IGI Global book series Advances in Computational Intelligence and Robotics (ACIR) (ISSN: 2327-0411; eISSN: 2327-042X)

British Cataloguing in Publication Data
A Cataloguing in Publication record for this book is available from the British Library.

All work contributed to this book is new, previously-unpublished material. The views expressed in this book are those of the authors, but not necessarily of the publisher.

For electronic access to this publication, please contact: eresources@igi-global.com.

Advances in Computational Intelligence and Robotics (ACIR) Book Series

Ivan Giannoccaro
University of Salento, Italy

ISSN:2327-0411
EISSN:2327-042X

MISSION

While intelligence is traditionally a term applied to humans and human cognition, technology has progressed in such a way to allow for the development of intelligent systems able to simulate many human traits. With this new era of simulated and artificial intelligence, much research is needed in order to continue to advance the field and also to evaluate the ethical and societal concerns of the existence of artificial life and machine learning.

The **Advances in Computational Intelligence and Robotics (ACIR) Book Series** encourages scholarly discourse on all topics pertaining to evolutionary computing, artificial life, computational intelligence, machine learning, and robotics. ACIR presents the latest research being conducted on diverse topics in intelligence technologies with the goal of advancing knowledge and applications in this rapidly evolving field.

COVERAGE

- Agent technologies
- Computational Intelligence
- Cognitive Informatics
- Natural Language Processing
- Adaptive and Complex Systems
- Fuzzy Systems
- Pattern Recognition
- Artificial Life
- Intelligent Control
- Evolutionary Computing

IGI Global is currently accepting manuscripts for publication within this series. To submit a proposal for a volume in this series, please contact our Acquisition Editors at Acquisitions@igi-global.com or visit: http://www.igi-global.com/publish/.

Titles in this Series

For a list of additional titles in this series, please visit: www.igi-global.com/book-series

Advanced Interdisciplinary Applications of Machine Learning Python Libraries for Data Science
Soly Mathew Biju (University of Wollongong in Dubai, UAE) Ashutosh Mishra (Yonsei University, South Korea) and Manoj Kumar (University of Wollongong in Dubai, UAE)
Engineering Science Reference • © 2023 • 304pp • H/C (ISBN: 9781668486962) • US $275.00

Recent Developments in Machine and Human Intelligence
S. Suman Rajest (Dhaanish Ahmed College of Engineering, India) Bhopendra Singh (Amity University, Dubai, UAE) Ahmed J. Obaid (University of Kufa, Iraq) R. Regin (SRM Institute of Science and Technology, Ramapuram, India) and Karthikeyan Chinnusamy (Veritas, USA)
Engineering Science Reference • © 2023 • 359pp • H/C (ISBN: 9781668491898) • US $270.00

Advances in Artificial and Human Intelligence in the Modern Era
S. Suman Rajest (Dhaanish Ahmed College of Engineering, India) Bhopendra Singh (Amity University, Dubai, UAE) Ahmed J. Obaid (University of Kufa, Iraq) R. Regin (SRM Institute of Science and Technology, Ramapuram, India) and Karthikeyan Chinnusamy (Veritas, USA)
Engineering Science Reference • © 2023 • 409pp • H/C (ISBN: 9798369313015) • US $300.00

Handbook of Research on Advancements in AI and IoT Convergence Technologies
Jingyuan Zhao (University of Toronto, Canada) V. Vinoth Kumar (Jain University, India) Rajesh Natarajan (University of Applied Science and Technology, Shinas, Oman) and T.R. Mahesh (Jain University, India)
Engineering Science Reference • © 2023 • 372pp • H/C (ISBN: 9781668469712) • US $380.00

Scalable and Distributed Machine Learning and Deep Learning Patterns
J. Joshua Thomas (UOW Malaysia KDU Penang University College, Malaysia) S. Harini (Vellore Institute of Technology, India) and V. Pattabiraman (Vellore Institute of Technology, India)
Engineering Science Reference • © 2023 • 286pp • H/C (ISBN: 9781668498040) • US $270.00

Handbook of Research on Thrust Technologies' Effect on Image Processing
Binay Kumar Pandey (Department of Information Technology, College of Technology, Govind Ballabh Pant University of Agriculture and Technology, India) Digvijay Pandey (Department of Technical Education, Government of Uttar Pradesh, India) Rohit Anand (G.B. Pant DSEU Okhla-1 Campus, India & Government of NCT of Delhi, New Delhi, India) Deepak S. Mane (Performance Engineering Lab, Tata Research, Development, and Design Center, Australia) and Vinay Kumar Nassa (Rajarambapu Institute of Technology, India)
Engineering Science Reference • © 2023 • 542pp • H/C (ISBN: 9781668486184) • US $350.00

701 East Chocolate Avenue, Hershey, PA 17033, USA
Tel: 717-533-8845 x100 • Fax: 717-533-8661
E-Mail: cust@igi-global.com • www.igi-global.com

Table of Contents

Detailed Table of Contents

Chapter 1

Parvataneni Rajendra Kumar, Department of Computer Science and Engineering(AI&ML),
NRI Institute of Technology, India

S. Meenakshi, Department of Science and Humanities (General Engineering), R.M.K.
Engineering College, India

S. Shalini, Department of Computer Science and Engineering, Dayananda Sagar Academy
of Technology, India

S. Rukmani Devi, Department of Computer Science and Applications, Saveetha College of
Liberal Arts and Sciences, SIMATS University (Deemed), India

S. Boopathi, Department of Mechanical Engineering, Muthayammal Engineering College,
India

The integration of deep learning and blockchain technologies has the potential to revolutionize soil quality prediction in smart agriculture. Deep learning models, like neural networks and convolutional neural networks, enable accurate predictions of soil properties by considering intricate relationships within data. Contextual learning approaches, including embeddings and data fusion, enrich the prediction process by incorporating external factors like weather conditions and land management practices. Blockchain technology ensures secure storage of predictions and data, while smart contracts facilitate automated model execution. This integrated system empowers farmers with accurate predictions for optimal resource allocation and fosters collaboration through decentralized data sharing. Future directions include advancements in deep learning algorithms, blockchain applications, and potential integration with IoT and remote sensing technologies.

Chapter 2

Lakshmana Phaneendra Maguluri, Department of Computer Science and Engineering,
Koneru Lakshmaiah Education Foundation, India

A. N. Arularasan, Department of Artificial Intelligence and Data Science, Panimalar
Engineering College, India

S. Boopathi, Department of Mechanical Engineering, Muthayammal Engineering College,
India

This chapter investigates security concerns involving AI-powered drones in smart cities, emphasising the importance of secure deployment. It discusses topics like data privacy, cybersecurity risks, physical security, and ethical repercussions. Security precautions such encrypted communication channels, intrusion detection systems, collision avoidance systems, and observance of moral and legal norms are discussed. The chapter offers case studies of successful AI-based drone deployments as well as recommendations for best practises for upcoming operations. The chapter addresses challenges and embraces ethical concerns in an effort to support the moral integration of AI-based drones in smart city scenarios.

Chapter 3

In recent years, the business landscape has experienced significant shifts due to technological advancements and the abundance of data. These changes have not spared human resource management (HRM), as it too has undergone a profound transformation. Capitalizing on the integration of advanced business analytics techniques with HRM practices, organizations have gained invaluable insights to optimize their workforce management, augmented decision-making processes, and elevated overall organizational performance. This chapter embarks on an exploration of the boundless potential that advanced business analytics holds for HRM. It delves into a comprehensive examination of the diverse applications of advanced analytics techniques, encompassing predictive analytics, prescriptive analytics, and machine learning, within HRM processes, thereby discerning their profound impact on organizational outcomes. Additionally, the chapter elucidates the intricacies of implementing advanced analytics in HRM, elucidating both the challenges that may arise and the opportunities that lie ahead.

Chapter 4

Solar radiation, Earth's main energy source, affects surface radiation balance, hydrological cycles, plant photosynthesis, weather, and climatic extremes. A stacking model based on the best of 12 machine learning models predicted and compared daily and monthly sun radiation levels. The results suggest machine learning algorithms use climatic parameters. A trend study of high land surface temperatures and solar radiation showed how solar radiation compounds catastrophic climatic events. GBRT, XG Boost, GPR, and random forest models better predicted daily and monthly sun radiation. The stacking model, which comprises the GBRT, XG Boost, GPR, and random forest models, exceeded the single models in daily solar radiation prediction but did not outperform the XGBoost model in monthly prediction. Stacking and XG Boost models estimate sun radiation best.

Chapter 5

Human resources have always been the company's most significant asset. Employees should be viewed as resources to acquire a competitive edge, and MSMEs (micro, small, and medium enterprises) and startups may succeed in a competitive market by aligning human resource activities with fundamental company objectives. With the advent of technology and the expansion of business, HR analytic tools can now be used to manage personnel and monitor their performance online. The application of HR analytics has enhanced employee performance and boosted corporate efficiency in areas such as recruiting quality, talent management, employee productivity, and employee attrition. Human resource analytics are critical for connecting HR strategy with overall company strategy. HR analytics helps HR managers design strategies that provide startups with a competitive edge. HR analytics, according to a new study, are revolutionizing the human resources department and HR managers.

Smart street light systems are being used more frequently in modern communities because they offer an effective and economical way to illuminate roads while reducing energy use and carbon emissions. Now, wireless networks can connect to and manage streetlights. With the aid of this technology, streetlights may be remotely monitored and controlled depending on variables such as traffic flow, weather, and the time of day. Energy is used as efficiently as possible, and maintenance costs are decreased. A smart streetlight system powered by IoT and LoRa can improve a city's efficiency and sustainability while also improving the quality of life for its residents. To maximize energy efficiency and reduce maintenance costs, the system may automatically adjust the streetlights' brightness and scheduling based on the data. This chapter provides a LoRa and IoT-based smart streetlight system with a cost-effective solution for modern smart cities.

Chapter 7

Emerging technologies are distinct in that they stimulate the creation of automated and intelligent businesses at a quick pace. Business processes are being reimagined and reinvented by these companies. When blockchain was initially introduced to the world in 2008, it was touted as the next great digital revolution. This chapter seeks to offer an overview of blockchain technology by defining it and explaining how it works. However, because blockchain technology is still in its infancy, nothing is known about how this new technology may be used to practical applications. As a result, the chapter highlights its distinct characteristics that set it apart from other technologies. Despite government intervention and an environment that promotes entrepreneurship, MSMEs, which have long been the backbone of any economy, continue to face the same difficulties that small businesses face. This chapter demonstrates how blockchain may assist in resolving these challenges in the hopes of spurring greater research and development in the field of blockchain, particularly in the context of MSMEs.

Chapter 8

The rising volume of data in our networked world is a huge problem that necessitates practical and user-friendly solutions. Computational approaches may be useful, but we must recognize that problem-solving knowledge is stored in the human mind, not in robots. A strategic goal for finding answers to data-intensive problems might be to combine two domains that provide optimal preconditions: human-computer interaction (HCI) and knowledge discovery (KDD). HCI is concerned with human vision, cognition, intelligence, decision-making, and interactive visualization approaches; hence, it focuses mostly on supervised methods. KDD is primarily concerned with intelligent machines and data mining, namely the creation of scalable algorithms for discovering previously undiscovered associations in data, and hence focuses on automatic computational approaches. A proverb illustrates this perfectly: "Computers are incredibly fast, accurate, but stupid. Humans are incredibly slow, inaccurate, but brilliant."

Vandana Madaan, Maharishi Markandeswar (Deemed), India
Ram Singh, Maharishi Markandeswar (Deemed), India
Anil Dhawan, Mukand Lal National College, India

Organizations from different sectors are using blockchain technology, but still it is only 0.5% of the world population that is using blockchain technology in 2019, but there is a steady increase in its demand, and it is anticipated that this demand will increase to 80% of the population using it. HR is becoming an inevitable strategic function of the organizations, and blockchain is helping the organizations to overhaul the HR functioning. HR managers are using blockchain in various processes such as recruitment and selection, validation, mapping skills, processing payroll, security of data, and prevention of frauds. This chapter attempts to identify the characteristics and uses of blockchain technology and scope of its application in human resource management. The study would be conducted by reviewing the extant literature from various secondary sources of data collection. The study will assist in providing an insight about implementation of blockchain in HRM and also facilitate in organizational decision making about the implementation of technology.

Somendra Tripathi, Faculty of Engineering and Technology, Rama University, India
Hari Om Sharan, Rama University, India
C. S. Raghuvanshi, Rama University, India

Attacks targeting cybersecurity are getting more widespread and complex over time. Additional innovation and rapid application development methodology within combative tactics have been required due to the increasing complexity and technological sophistication that have been developing. While still extensively used and encouraged, previous approaches to penetration detection and packet inspection are not sufficient for meeting the preferences of changing security threats. Machine learning is being touted as a supplementary justification for keyloggers, trojan horses, and other cyberattacks as computational capabilities and affordability keep on increasing. The total amount of information gathered by electronic objects has drastically increased in recent years as a consequence of the fast and easy efficiency innovations in some of those peripherals and their use in a range of applications.

Chapter 11

Smart parking models and approaches aim to optimize the use of parking spaces, reduce traffic congestion, and provide a more efficient parking experience. There are various models, and approaches are used like sensor-based parking, IoT-based parking, mobile-based parking, automatic parking systems, and shared parking. Overall, these models and approaches aim to optimize parking usage, reduce traffic congestion, and improve the overall parking experience for users. By leveraging new technologies and innovative approaches, smart parking solutions can help make urban areas more efficient and sustainable.

Chapter 12

Blockchain encourages artificial intelligence towards intelligence while also increasing its autonomy and credibility. In this chapter, the authors examine the relationship between blockchain technology and artificial intelligence from a more thorough and three-dimensional standpoint. One of the greatest problems with blockchain implementations in IoV is that they cannot meet the computational and energy needs of conventional blockchain systems since IoV nodes are limited in their ability to use resources. A marketplace that enables stakeholders (CSPs, asset suppliers, service providers, regulators, etc.) to interact and exchange value with confidence based on smart provenance and governance may be developed using blockchain and distributed ledger technologies (DLT). These innovations offer a decentralised audit architecture that is safe. Such transactions (who uses what) can be kept on a distributed ledger marketplace in an immutable setting. A decentralised consensus process that does not need mining or incentivization in a permissionless architecture ensures data integrity.

Chapter 13

Artificial intelligence (AI) has been a growing field in recent years, with the development of deep learning (DL) techniques providing new opportunities for plant disease classification. Convolutional neural networks (CNNs) and other advanced techniques such as transfer learning, deep ensemble learning, and others have been used to classify plant diseases with high accuracy. However, these techniques are not only complex but also challenging to implement, making it important to provide a comprehensive understanding of their use in plant disease classification. This chapter aims to explore the use of deep learning techniques for plant disease classification. It will provide an overview of the various DL techniques and their applications in the classification of plant diseases. It will also provide a comprehensive understanding of transfer learning, deep ensemble learning, and other advanced methods in plant disease classification. Additionally, the chapter will provide case studies to illustrate the practical applications of DL techniques in plant disease classification.

Chapter 14

Jorge Vareda Gomes, Universidade Lusófona, Portugal
Mario Romão, ISEG, Universidade de Lisboa, Portugal

The main objective of investments in information systems and technology is to increase operational efficiency, reduce costs, and improve the quality levels provided by organizations. In the last decades, IS/IT has positioned itself as a strategic tool that, through innovative combinations, has allowed the flexibility that organizations need to respond to current challenges. The health sector has sought to improve its effectiveness and efficiency through the adoption of IS/IT solutions to enhance quality of services, i.e., patient safety, organizational efficiency, and end-user satisfaction. Hospitals are complex organizations, and this complexity increases the opportunity for unavoidable human error. A poorly integrated system can decrease operational efficiency and reduce the quality of health services. The issue remains controversial. This study aims to review the literature on the topic and explore the trends and challenges that arise today. The study concludes that emerging technologies can offer opportunities for all organizations that effectively know how to better exploit them.

Chapter 15

Olena Korzhyk, Universidade Autónoma de Lisboa, Portugal
Jorge Vareda Gomes, Universidade Lusófona, Lisboa, Portugal
Gonçalo João, CICEE, Universidade Autónoma de Lisboa, Portugal

Digitalization is nowadays one of the fastest developing processes. The adoption of digital technologies can provide innumerous opportunities for the organizations to evolve and gain competitive advantage by leveraging technologies to respond to dynamic expectations and demands. Information about the country's digitalization level is essential to decision makers in both public and private organizations. It can present insights into which areas need the most investment, and furthermore to gain feedback on the outcomes of these investments. To assess the evolution of this process in different countries, various indexes were proposed and employed by different corporations. Indexes are analyzed thoroughly by their structure, coverage, weights, methodology, and ranking. The result of the practical work is an equivalence table which shows the percentage of their similarity. Additionally, a new digitalization index is proposed, based on the result of the previous comparison, which can be applied to analyze both public and private sector of the country's digitalization level.

Chapter 16

Pedro Azevedo, tb.lx, Portugal
Jorge Vareda Gomes, Universidade Lusófona, Portugal
Mario Romão, ISEG, Universidade de Lisboa, Portugal

Supply chains can span a huge number of countries, cross many borders, and require interoperation of a multitude of organizations. This vastness impacts business competitiveness since it adds complexity and can difficult securing traceability, chain of custody, and transparency. The authors propose that assuring chain of custody and traceability via blockchain allows organizations to demonstrate product provenance, integrity, and compliance. This work proposes that to effect true traceability the more complete approach is to connect both the supply chain actors (SCAs) and products identifications using digital certificates. A blockchain is used to manage the traceability of products and validation of the identities. Importing, verifying, and storing the certificates uses an off-chain data storage solution for products certificates. To create, validate the certificates, and setup the chain of trust, a public key infrastructure (PKI) was designed as part of the proposal. The results were architectural artifacts, including an Ethereum smart contract and a PKI-based certificate authentication system.

Chapter 17

Pradeep Kumar, Teerthanker Mahaveer University, India
Rajeev Kumar, G.L. Bajaj Institute of Technology and Management, India
Kumar Balwant Singh, L.S. College, Muzaffarpur, India
Madhurendra Kumar, Centre for Development of Advanced Computing, India

Internet and applications have become an essential part of life nowadays. We are now at the stage where we can think about future smart cities as we are having various driving forces in the form of web-based applications. The main phenomena behind data-computing can be considered as for keeping data persistent, secure, available, and relevant for the information in real time. In the chapter, the authors proposed blockchain representation-based application process that is a low cost and efficient application for true sense ubiquitous usage that is also the demand of current time. The implemented application is providing a huge data security scenario for a web application system, and it is dealing with the efficient information processing towards storage, processing, and access of the information in a real time. In this chapter, the authors provided various schemes for high availability of on-demand data with proper asymmetric algorithms techniques.

Chapter 18

Mohammad Daradkeh, University of Dubai, UAE & Yarmouk University, Jordan

Despite the potential benefits of knowledge sharing in these communities, the process of knowledge sharing is complex and unique within the metaverse. Therefore, a comprehensive understanding of the knowledge sharing dynamics in virtual communities within the metaverse domain is crucial. This chapter provides a comprehensive overview of the knowledge sharing landscape in metaverse virtual communities and outlines a roadmap for more efficient knowledge sharing and innovation in these communities. Based on a review of relevant practices and previous research, a knowledge sharing model is formulated to account for the unique impact of the metaverse on these communities. The process of knowledge sharing involves gathering community knowledge, internalizing situational knowledge, and sharing it through broadcasting and diffusion. The chapter offers valuable insights for researchers, practitioners, and policymakers in the field of virtual communities and knowledge sharing and provides a foundation for future research in this area.

    R. Abilasha, Hindusthan College of Arts and Sciences, India
    A. V. Senthil Kumar, Hindusthan College of Arts and Sciences, India
    Ibrahiem M. M. El Emary, King Abdulaziz University, Saudi Arabia
    Namita Mishra, I.T.S. School of Management, India
    Veera Talukdar, RNB Global University, India
    Rohaya Latip, Universiti Putra Malaysia, Malaysia
    Ismail Bin Musirin, Universiti Teknologi MARA, Malaysia
    Meenakshi Sharma, University of Petroleum and Energy Studies, India

There is an increase in the number of vehicles in last two decades. So, it becomes important to make effective use of technology to enable free parking in public and private places. In conventional parking systems, drivers face complexity in finding vacant parking slots. It requires more human involvement in the parking zone. To deal with the issue, the authors propose a smart parking system based on IoT and machine learning techniques to manage the real time management of parking and qualms. The proposed solution makes use of smart sensors, cloud computing, cyber physical system. It is victorious in addressing the challenges such as demonstrating status of parking slot in advance to end-user, use of reserved and unreserved parking slots, erroneous parking, real-time analysis of engaged slots, detecting numerous objects in a parking slot such as bike in car slot, error recognition in more mechanism, and traffic management during crest hours. This minimizes the individual interference, saves time, money, and liveliness.

Preface

Artificial intelligence, blockchain, machine learning, deep learning is a fascinating area to work in: from detecting anomalous events in live streams of sensor data to identifying emergent topics involving text collection, exciting problems are never too far away.

Deep learning models usually have sensitive information of the users and these models should not be vulnerable and expose to security and privacy. However, Artificial Intelligence, Blockchain models are still susceptible to various security attacks perturbed by imperceptible noise which allow these models to forecast/ predict inaccurately with high degree of confidence. Therefore, it is important to look into the security aspects and related counter measure techniques of Artificial Intelligence, Blockchain models. This edited book focuses on the recent advances and challenges related to the concerns of security and privacy issues in Artificial Intelligence, Blockchain and deep learning with an emphasis on the current state-of-art methods, methodologies and implementation, attacks, and their countermeasures. This edited book also discusses the challenges that need to be addressed for implementing Artificial Intelligence, Blockchain and DL-based security mechanisms that should have the capability in collecting or distributing data across several applications.

Every effort has been made to make the concepts simple and comprehensive. This edited book is divided into sixteen chapters by different authors.

The organization of these chapters are:

Chapter 1: Soil Quality Prediction in Context Learning Approaches Using Deep Learning and Blockchain for Smart Agriculture

Chapter 2: Assessing Security Concerns for AI-Based Drones in Smart Cities

Chapter 3: Transformation Human Resource Management Using Advanced Business Analytics

Chapter 4: Solar Radiation Analysis for Predicting Climate Change Using Deep Learning Techniques

Chapter 5: Transformation of Indian MSME (Micro, Small, and Medium Enterprises) and Start-Ups Using Advance HR Analytics

Chapter 6: Smart Street Light System for Smart City Using IoT (LoRa)

Chapter 7: Overcoming MSME Challenges With Blockchain

Chapter 8: Human Computer Interaction for Knowledge Discovery for Management

Chapter 9: Use and Applications of Blockchain Technology in Human Resource Management Functions

Chapter 10: Intelligent Data Encryption Classifying Complex Security Breaches Using Machine Learning Technique

Chapter 11: Machine Learning Methods and IoT for Smart Parking Models and Approaches

Chapter 12: Blockchain Methods and Data-Driven Decision Making With Autonomous Transportation

Chapter 13: Plant Disease Classification Using Deep Learning Techniques

Rajeev Kumar
Infrastructure University Kuala Lumpur, Malaysia

Abu Bakar Abdul Hamid
Infrastructure University Kuala Lumpur, Malaysia

Noor Inayah Binti Ya'akub
Infrastructure University Kuala Lumpur, Malaysia

Chapter 1
Soil Quality Prediction in Context Learning Approaches Using Deep Learning and Blockchain for Smart Agriculture

Parvataneni Rajendra Kumar

Department of Computer Science and Engineering(AI&ML), NRI Institute of Technology, India

S. Meenakshi

ⓘ https://orcid.org/0000-0001-5075-6808

Department of Science and Humanities (General Engineering), R.M.K. Engineering College, India

S. Shalini

Department of Computer Science and Engineering, Dayananda Sagar Academy of Technology, India

S. Rukmani Devi

Department of Computer Science and Applications, Saveetha College of Liberal Arts and Sciences, SIMATS University (Deemed), India

S. Boopathi

ⓘ https://orcid.org/0000-0002-2065-6539

Department of Mechanical Engineering, Muthayammal Engineering College, India

ABSTRACT

The integration of deep learning and blockchain technologies has the potential to revolutionize soil quality prediction in smart agriculture. Deep learning models, like neural networks and convolutional neural networks, enable accurate predictions of soil properties by considering intricate relationships within data. Contextual learning approaches, including embeddings and data fusion, enrich the prediction process by incorporating external factors like weather conditions and land management practices. Blockchain technology ensures secure storage of predictions and data, while smart contracts facilitate automated model execution. This integrated system empowers farmers with accurate predictions for optimal resource allocation and fosters collaboration through decentralized data sharing. Future directions include advancements in deep learning algorithms, blockchain applications, and potential integration with IoT and remote sensing technologies.

DOI: 10.4018/978-1-6684-9151-5.ch001

INTRODUCTION

In recent years, the field of agriculture has undergone a profound transformation driven by technological advancements and the pressing need for sustainable practices. With a growing global population and changing climate patterns, there is an increasing demand for innovative solutions that can enhance agricultural productivity while minimizing resource depletion and environmental degradation (Hanumanthakari et al., 2023; Koshariya, Khatoon, et al., 2023; Selvakumar et al., 2023). Smart agriculture, often referred to as precision agriculture, is emerging as a key paradigm that leverages technology to address these challenges. Within the realm of smart agriculture, one critical aspect is the accurate assessment of soil quality – a fundamental determinant of crop yields and ecosystem health (Durai & Shamili, 2022a).

Soil quality, defined as the ability of soil to perform its functions within an ecosystem, is influenced by a myriad of factors including physical, chemical, and biological properties. Assessing soil quality traditionally involves labour-intensive methods that often yield limited insights due to the spatial and temporal variability of soil conditions (Boopathi et al., 2023; Gnanaprakasam et al., 2023; Jeevanantham et al., 2022). Moreover, conventional methods are time-consuming, expensive, and may not provide real-time data crucial for making informed agricultural decisions. As a result, there is a growing interest in exploring novel approaches that can provide more efficient and precise soil quality predictions (Shahbazi & Byun, 2021).

This chapter sets out to explore the synergy between deep learning techniques and blockchain technology in the context of soil quality prediction for smart agriculture. Deep learning, a subset of machine learning, has demonstrated remarkable success in various domains such as image recognition, natural language processing, and medical diagnosis. Its ability to automatically learn complex patterns from large datasets makes it an attractive candidate for solving intricate problems, including soil quality assessment (Babu & Supriya, 2022; Vyas et al., 2022). Meanwhile, blockchain technology, initially popularized as the underlying technology for cryptocurrencies, offers a decentralized and tamper-resistant platform for secure data storage and sharing. The immutable and transparent nature of blockchain can contribute to enhancing the reliability and integrity of soil quality data (Hossain et al., n.d.; Jadav et al., 2023a). This chapter explores the integration of deep learning and blockchain for soil quality prediction, aiming to bridge the gap between theoretical foundations and real-world applications. It provides insights into technical intricacies, challenges, and potential benefits of this innovative approach. By examining relevant literature, case studies, and conceptual frameworks, readers can gain a holistic understanding of how this amalgamation of technologies can revolutionize soil quality assessment and agriculture (Hossain et al., n.d.; Sumathi et al., 2022).

Agriculture, the backbone of global food production, faces mounting challenges in the 21st century due to factors such as rapid population growth, changing climate patterns, and the need for sustainable resource management. In response to these challenges, modern agriculture is evolving into a data-driven and technology-enhanced domain, with smart agriculture (SA) emerging as a transformative approach (Hassija et al., 2021; Sumathi et al., 2022). At the heart of SA lies the integration of cutting-edge technologies that empower farmers with accurate insights, enabling them to make informed decisions for optimal land management, resource allocation, and sustainable crop production. Among these technologies, deep learning (DL) and blockchain (BC) stand out as pivotal tools that, when harmonized, offer a synergistic solution for one of the fundamental aspects of agriculture: soil quality prediction (Hassija et al., 2021; Jabbar et al., 2020).

Soil quality assessment is paramount for effective agricultural practices. Traditionally, farmers relied on subjective observations or labour-intensive laboratory analyses to understand soil properties. However, these methods are often time-consuming, expensive, and limited in spatial coverage. The advent of DL, a subset of machine learning, has brought forth a paradigm shift in how soil quality assessment is approached (Bhandary et al., 2020; Chenthara et al., 2020). DL algorithms, such as neural networks, can learn intricate relationships within massive datasets, enabling accurate predictions of soil properties. Furthermore, contextual learning approaches within DL empower models to incorporate external factors that influence soil quality, such as weather conditions, crop types, and land management practices. Contextual learning involves the fusion of contextual data with soil data, which enriches the predictions by considering the complex interplay of variables affecting soil properties (Chenthara et al., 2020; William et al., 2022). While DL revolutionizes soil quality prediction, the integration of BC complements it by ensuring data security, transparency, and collaboration. BC is a decentralized and immutable digital ledger that records transactions securely. In the context of SA, BC guarantees the integrity of soil quality predictions, prevents data tampering, and fosters trust among stakeholders. Smart contracts, self-executing code on the BC, automate processes such as model execution and data sharing permissions (Koshariya, Khatoon, et al., 2023; P. Kumar et al., 2023). These contracts eliminate intermediaries and enable the execution of complex, trustless agreements, enhancing the efficiency and reliability of the integrated system (Arora et al., 2019; Emadi et al., 2020; William et al., 2022).

The convergence of DL and BC presents a holistic approach to soil quality prediction in the context of SA. This chapter delves into the intricacies of this integration, highlighting its significance, methodologies, and implications. It aims to explore how these technologies collectively revolutionize soil quality assessment and set the stage for a sustainable agricultural future (A. N. Ahmed et al., 2019; Arora et al., 2019; Emadi et al., 2020). The subsequent sections of this chapter will delve into the background of soil quality assessment, the objectives and scope of the study, and the importance of contextual learning approaches within the framework. Additionally, the chapter will elucidate the potential of the integrated system through case studies in both small-scale farming in developing countries and large-scale commercial farming operations. Moreover, the future directions and opportunities for advancements in DL algorithms, expanding BC applications, and integration with the Internet of Things (IoT) and remote sensing technologies will be discussed (Du et al., 2019; Janizadeh et al., 2019; Van Klompenburg et al., 2020).

In essence, this chapter serves as a comprehensive exploration of how the amalgamation of DL and BC transcends traditional soil quality assessment methods. By leveraging DL's predictive power and BC's security and transparency, the integrated system brings data-driven decision-making to the forefront of agriculture. As global challenges continue to reshape the agricultural landscape, the fusion of these technologies offers a transformative solution that empowers farmers, promotes sustainability, and lays the foundation for a more efficient and resilient food production system.

BACKGROUND

Agriculture has been the backbone of human civilization, providing sustenance and livelihoods for millennia. However, as the world's population continues to grow and environmental challenges become more pronounced, traditional agricultural practices are proving inadequate to meet modern demands (Gnanaprakasam et al., 2023; Koshariya, Kalaiyarasi, et al., 2023; Sankar et al., 2023). In this context, the concept of smart agriculture has emerged as a transformative approach that employs cutting-edge technologies to optimize resource utilization, increase productivity, and minimize environmental impact. One of the fundamental aspects of smart agriculture is the accurate assessment of soil quality (Bhandary et al., 2020; Chenthara et al., 2020).

Soil quality serves as the foundation for agricultural productivity. It encompasses a range of physical, chemical, and biological properties that determine the soil's ability to support plant growth, retain water, and cycle nutrients. Ensuring optimal soil quality is paramount for achieving high crop yields, sustainable land use, and ecosystem health. Historically, soil quality assessment has relied on labor-intensive and time-consuming methods, often involving manual sampling and laboratory analysis. These approaches, while informative, are constrained by their limited spatial and temporal coverage, impeding their effectiveness in supporting real-time decision-making (Janizadeh et al., 2019; Van Klompenburg et al., 2020).

OBJECTIVES

The primary objective of this chapter is to explore the synergistic potential of deep learning and blockchain technologies in advancing soil quality prediction for smart agriculture. Specifically, the chapter aims to:

Provide an overview of the critical role soil quality plays in agricultural productivity, resource conservation, and environmental sustainability.

Present a comprehensive review of various deep learning techniques, such as neural networks, CNNs, RNNs, and transfer learning, and their application to soil quality assessment.

Introduce the concept of context learning and its relevance to improving the accuracy of soil quality predictions by incorporating contextual information.

Discuss the potential of blockchain technology to address challenges related to data security, transparency, and integrity in soil quality assessment.

Detail the integration of deep learning and blockchain to create a robust and secure framework for soil quality prediction, highlighting the technical and practical considerations.

Present case studies that exemplify the implementation of the proposed approach in diverse agricultural scenarios, emphasizing its effectiveness and adaptability.

Outline potential advancements in deep learning algorithms, blockchain applications, and their integration with other emerging technologies such as IoT and remote sensing.

SCOPE OF THE CHAPTER

The scope of this chapter encompasses a multidisciplinary exploration of the integration of deep learning and blockchain technologies for soil quality prediction in the context of smart agriculture. The chapter does not seek to exhaustively cover every aspect of deep learning or blockchain, but rather to provide an in-depth understanding of their relevance and application to soil quality assessment. The focus is on conceptual clarity, practical implementation, and the potential impact of this integration on agricultural practices.

While the chapter primarily centers on the integration of deep learning and blockchain, it also acknowledges the broader context by discussing the importance of soil quality in agriculture, the limitations of conventional methods, and the evolving landscape of smart agriculture. Real-world case studies are included to illustrate the feasibility and advantages of the proposed approach in different agricultural settings.

The chapter aims to bridge the gap between theoretical understanding and practical application, offering insights that cater to researchers, practitioners, and policymakers interested in leveraging technology for sustainable agricultural development. Additionally, it paves the way for further research and collaboration in this burgeoning field where technology meets the soil, nurturing the growth of smarter and more resilient agricultural systems.

SOIL QUALITY ASSESSMENT IN AGRICULTURE

Importance of Soil Quality

Soil quality serves as the foundation of agricultural productivity and ecosystem health, making its accurate assessment a pivotal factor in modern agriculture. The concept of soil quality goes beyond traditional measures of soil fertility and encompasses a broader array of attributes that determine the soil's ability to support plant growth, sustain biodiversity, and maintain ecological balance. As agricultural practices become more sophisticated and global food security remains a paramount concern, understanding and managing soil quality has gained significant prominence (Alessandrino et al., 2023; Bui et al., 2020; Singh et al., 2023).

Optimal Nutrient Availability: Soil quality directly influences the availability and cycling of essential nutrients for plant growth. A soil's nutrient-holding capacity and its capacity to release nutrients based on plant demands are critical for achieving healthy and high-yielding crops. Proper nutrient management, informed by accurate soil quality assessment, minimizes the excessive use of fertilizers, reducing environmental pollution and improving resource efficiency.

Water Retention and Drainage: Soil quality affects water retention and drainage characteristics. Soil with good water-holding capacity ensures consistent moisture availability to plants, even during dry periods. Conversely, soils with inadequate drainage can lead to waterlogging, which hampers root growth and can result in plant stress and reduced yields. Precise assessment of soil quality aids in designing irrigation strategies that conserve water and optimize plant water uptake.

Soil Structure and Compaction: The physical structure of soil impacts root penetration, aeration, and water movement. Soil compaction, often caused by heavy machinery and improper land management, can lead to restricted root growth and decreased water infiltration. Accurate soil quality assessment enables farmers to identify compacted areas, implement soil conservation practices, and enhance root zone development.

Erosion Prevention and Soil Health: Soil quality assessment is crucial for identifying erosion-prone areas. Healthy soils with well-developed structure and organic matter are more resistant to erosion, preserving topsoil and minimizing sediment runoff into water bodies. Soil quality assessment can guide erosion control measures, contributing to long-term soil health and sustainable land use.

Biodiversity and Ecosystem Services: Healthy soil is a habitat for a diverse range of microorganisms, insects, and small animals that contribute to nutrient cycling, disease suppression, and overall ecosystem resilience. Accurate assessment of soil quality aids in maintaining these essential ecosystem services that underpin agricultural sustainability.

Climate Change Mitigation and Adaptation: Soil quality assessment plays a role in both mitigating and adapting to climate change. Soils rich in organic matter sequester carbon, helping to mitigate greenhouse gas emissions. Furthermore, understanding soil quality assists in selecting crop varieties that are resilient to changing climatic conditions, enhancing agricultural resilience.

Precision Agriculture: Soil quality assessment is a cornerstone of precision agriculture, enabling farmers to tailor their management practices to specific soil characteristics within fields. This leads to optimized resource allocation, reduced input waste, and improved crop performance.

Sustainable Land Use Planning: Governments and policymakers rely on accurate soil quality assessments for land use planning and policy formulation. Zoning agricultural land based on soil quality can help prevent soil degradation, urban encroachment on fertile land, and unsustainable land management practices (Demattê et al., 2019; Lal, 2020).

The soil quality assessment is an indispensable tool for modern agriculture. As the world grapples with the challenges of feeding a growing population while preserving natural resources, the accurate evaluation of soil quality becomes a linchpin in achieving sustainable and resilient agricultural systems. The integration of advanced technologies, such as deep learning and blockchain, holds the promise of revolutionizing soil quality assessment, paving the way for more efficient, informed, and ecologically sound agricultural practices.

Traditional Soil Analysis Methods

Traditionally, soil analysis has been conducted using a combination of laboratory-based tests and field observations to assess various physical, chemical, and biological properties of soil (Figure 1). These methods have provided valuable insights into soil characteristics and have guided agricultural practices for decades. However, they often suffer from limitations in terms of time, cost, and spatial coverage, which can hinder their effectiveness in supporting real-time decision-making in modern agriculture (Demattê et al., 2019; Lal, 2020).

Figure 1. Traditional soil analysis methods

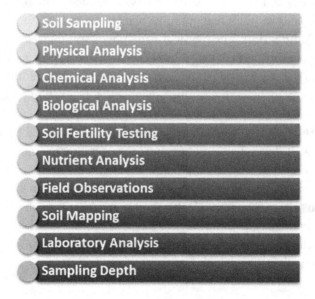

Soil Sampling: Soil samples are collected from different points within a field to capture its variability. These samples are then analyzed to determine soil properties. However, this process can be labor-intensive, and the number of samples collected may not represent the entire field adequately.

Physical Analysis: Physical properties, such as soil texture, structure, and porosity, are assessed through methods like sieve analysis, sedimentation, and texture by feel. These properties influence water holding capacity, drainage, and root penetration.

Chemical Analysis: Chemical properties like pH, nutrient content, and cation exchange capacity (CEC) are determined through laboratory tests. Soil pH affects nutrient availability, and nutrient levels impact plant health and growth.

Biological Analysis: Biological properties, including microbial activity and soil organic matter content, are indicators of soil health and fertility. These properties are often assessed through indirect methods that measure microbial respiration or estimate organic carbon content.

Nutrient Analysis: Nutrient availability is determined through tests such as the Mehlich-3 extraction method, which extracts nutrients from the soil for analysis. These tests help in adjusting nutrient management practices to optimize crop yields.

Soil Fertility Testing: Soil fertility tests evaluate nutrient levels in the soil to guide fertilizer application. This involves assessing macronutrients like nitrogen, phosphorus, and potassium.

Field Observations: Visual observations of soil conditions, such as color, structure, and compaction, provide qualitative insights into soil quality and potential issues.

Soil Mapping: Soil maps are created by analyzing the spatial distribution of soil properties across a landscape. These maps guide land management decisions, but they often lack fine-scale accuracy.

Laboratory Analysis: Samples collected from the field are sent to laboratories for analysis, which can take time. This delay limits the timeliness of decision-making for planting, irrigation, and nutrient application.

Sampling Depth: Soil properties can vary significantly with depth. Traditional methods often focus on the topsoil, potentially missing important information from deeper layers.

While traditional soil analysis methods have been instrumental in guiding agricultural practices, their limitations in terms of spatial coverage, timeliness, and labor intensiveness have spurred the exploration of more advanced and innovative approaches. The integration of deep learning and blockchain, as explored in this chapter, offers the potential to overcome some of these limitations, enabling more accurate and efficient soil quality assessment for smart agriculture.

DEEP LEARNING TECHNIQUES FOR SOIL QUALITY PREDICTION

Deep learning techniques have revolutionized various domains by enabling machines to learn complex patterns and representations from data. In the context of soil quality prediction, these techniques offer the potential to capture intricate relationships among soil properties, leading to more accurate and efficient predictions (Bui et al., 2020; Du et al., 2019; Ferrag et al., 2021).

Neural Networks for Regression

Neural networks are foundational deep learning models that consist of interconnected layers of nodes, or neurons, which process and transform data. In the context of soil quality prediction, neural networks can be employed for regression tasks, where the objective is to predict a continuous numerical output (e.g., nutrient levels, pH) based on input features (e.g., soil texture, organic matter content) (Boopathi, 2023b; Boopathi, Arigela, et al., 2022; Jeevanantham et al., 2022).

Convolutional Neural Networks (CNNs) for Soil Image Analysis

Soil images captured through remote sensing or on-site cameras can provide valuable insights into soil quality. CNNs, a specialized type of neural network, excel at processing image data. They use convolutional layers to automatically learn hierarchical features from images, enabling them to detect patterns and structures relevant to soil properties. CNNs can analyze soil images to identify soil erosion, texture variations, or organic matter distribution (Durai & Shamili, 2022b; Jadav et al., 2023b).

Recurrent Neural Networks (RNNs) for Temporal Soil Data

Soil conditions often exhibit temporal variations influenced by factors such as weather patterns and crop growth stages. RNNs are suited for sequential data analysis, making them valuable for predicting soil quality over time. By capturing temporal dependencies in the data, RNNs can model how soil properties evolve and interact with changing environmental conditions.

Transfer Learning and Pretrained Models

Deep learning models often require large amounts of data for training. Transfer learning leverages pretrained models, trained on massive datasets for related tasks, and fine-tunes them for specific applications. For soil quality prediction, transfer learning can expedite model development and improve predictive performance, especially when limited soil data is available (Boopathi, 2023a; Hema et al., 2023; Syamala et al., 2023). These deep learning techniques offer advantages such as automatic feature extraction, nonlinear modeling, and adaptability to various data types. They can handle diverse soil data sources, including sensor readings, imagery, and historical data. However, the successful application of deep learning relies on data quality, quantity, and appropriate model architectures.

As discussed in this chapter, integrating deep learning with context learning and blockchain can further enhance the accuracy, robustness, and transparency of soil quality predictions. The combination of these technologies allows for the inclusion of contextual factors, secure data sharing, and tamper-resistant data storage, contributing to a comprehensive and innovative approach to soil quality assessment in smart agriculture.

CONTEXT LEARNING APPROACHES

Context learning approaches are emerging paradigms in machine learning that aim to enhance the accuracy and relevance of predictions by considering the contextual information surrounding data points. In the context of soil quality prediction, context learning techniques can provide deeper insights into the relationships between soil properties and external factors, resulting in more precise and adaptable models (Durai & Shamili, 2022b; Ferrag et al., 2021; Singh et al., 2023). This section delves into the fundamental concepts of context learning and explores two key strategies within this framework: contextual embeddings and contextual data fusion.

Definition and Concepts

Context learning acknowledges that data points are not isolated entities but are interconnected and influenced by their surroundings. In soil quality prediction, contextual information can encompass a wide range of factors such as weather conditions, crop types, land management practices, and spatial relationships. By incorporating context, models can capture dependencies and patterns that traditional approaches might overlook.

Contextual Embeddings

Contextual embeddings involve transforming input data, often text or categorical features, into numerical representations that capture their contextual meaning. In the soil quality context, textual descriptions of soil types, crop varieties, or weather conditions can be converted into embeddings that capture semantic relationships. This enables models to understand and exploit contextual nuances for prediction.

For instance, embedding techniques like Word2Vec or GloVe can be applied to convert qualitative descriptions of soil texture (e.g., sandy, loam, clay) into numerical vectors. These embeddings reflect the semantic relationships between different textures, allowing the model to recognize patterns in soil quality associated with specific textures.

Contextual Data Fusion

Contextual data fusion involves integrating information from multiple sources to provide a more comprehensive view of the data. In soil quality prediction, this means combining various data types, such as soil sensor measurements, satellite imagery, weather data, and historical records. By fusing diverse data sources, models can capture complex interactions between soil properties and external factors.

For example, combining soil moisture readings from sensors with satellite imagery showing land cover changes can provide insights into how changes in vegetation affect soil moisture levels. By incorporating these external factors, models can refine their predictions of soil quality indicators affected by moisture, such as nutrient availability.

Contextual data fusion can be particularly powerful when used alongside deep learning techniques. Convolutional neural networks (CNNs) can process satellite imagery to extract spatial features, while recurrent neural networks (RNNs) can capture temporal patterns in weather data. By integrating these diverse features, models can create a more holistic representation of soil quality dynamics (Bui et al., 2020; Du et al., 2019).

Incorporating context learning into soil quality prediction not only improves prediction accuracy but also increases the interpretability of models by providing insights into why certain predictions are made. These techniques enable a more sophisticated understanding of the complex interactions between soil properties and external variables, paving the way for more informed and adaptive agricultural practices.

BLOCKCHAIN TECHNOLOGY FOR DATA SECURITY AND INTEGRITY

Overview of Blockchain

Blockchain technology is a decentralized and distributed digital ledger that records transactions in a secure, transparent, and immutable manner. Originally popularized as the underlying technology for cryptocurrencies like Bitcoin, blockchain has found applications across various industries, including agriculture (Babu & Supriya, 2022; Jadav et al., 2023a). In the context of soil quality prediction and smart agriculture, blockchain offers several key features:

- **Decentralization**: Unlike traditional centralized systems, blockchain operates on a network of computers (nodes) that collectively maintain and validate the ledger. This decentralized nature enhances security and prevents a single point of failure.
- **Transparency and Immutability**: Transactions recorded on the blockchain are visible to all participants and cannot be altered once confirmed. This immutability ensures data integrity and prevents tampering.
- **Security**: Cryptographic techniques secure data stored on the blockchain. Transactions are linked and secured through cryptographic hashes, ensuring the authenticity and integrity of the data.
- **Consensus Mechanisms**: Blockchain networks use consensus mechanisms to agree on the validity of transactions. This prevents fraudulent or conflicting data from being added to the blockchain.
- **Smart Contracts**: Smart contracts are self-executing code stored on the blockchain. They automatically execute predefined actions when certain conditions are met, eliminating the need for intermediaries.

Smart Contracts for Soil Data Management

Smart contracts play a pivotal role in managing soil data in a blockchain-based system. In the context of soil quality prediction, smart contracts can automate data collection, validation, and compensation processes. For instance, when sensors collect soil quality measurements, smart contracts can trigger automatic verification and payment mechanisms. These contracts ensure that only valid and accurate data is recorded, enhancing the reliability of the data stored on the blockchain (R. A. Ahmed et al., 2022; Jadav et al., 2023b; Khan et al., 2022).

Smart contracts can also facilitate agreements between various stakeholders in the agricultural ecosystem. Farmers, researchers, and data providers can define rules and conditions for accessing and using soil quality data. Smart contracts enforce these rules, enabling secure and transparent data sharing while maintaining the privacy of sensitive information (Koshariya, Kalaiyarasi, et al., 2023; Kumara et al., 2023; Sankar et al., 2023; Syamala et al., 2023).

Decentralized Data Sharing and Privacy

Blockchain's decentralized nature supports secure and controlled data sharing among stakeholders. In the context of soil quality prediction, different parties, such as farmers, researchers, and regulatory authorities, can access relevant soil data while maintaining control over their own data.

Blockchain's cryptographic techniques enable selective data sharing, ensuring that only authorized participants can access specific data. Private keys and encryption mechanisms provide an additional layer of security, protecting sensitive data from unauthorized access. This is particularly important when sharing proprietary information about soil management practices or crop yields (R. A. Ahmed et al., 2022; Jadav et al., 2023b; Khan et al., 2022). Furthermore, blockchain's transparency and auditability enable traceability of data usage. Data transactions are recorded on the blockchain, making it possible to track who accessed the data and for what purpose. This accountability fosters trust among stakeholders and ensures responsible data handling. Incorporating blockchain technology into soil quality prediction and smart agriculture addresses challenges related to data security, privacy, and accountability. The integration of blockchain and deep learning, as explored in this chapter, offers a comprehensive solution for accurate, secure, and context-aware soil quality assessment, paving the way for more sustainable and efficient agricultural practices.

INTEGRATION OF DEEP LEARNING AND BLOCKCHAIN FOR SOIL QUALITY PREDICTION

The integration of deep learning and blockchain technologies for soil quality prediction presents a powerful paradigm for accurate, secure, and context-aware agricultural practices (Figure 2). This section outlines the architectural design that harmonizes these technologies, offering a comprehensive solution for enhanced soil quality assessment in the context of smart agriculture (Demattê et al., 2019; Singh et al., 2023).

Figure 2. Process of integration: Deep learning and blockchain for soil quality prediction

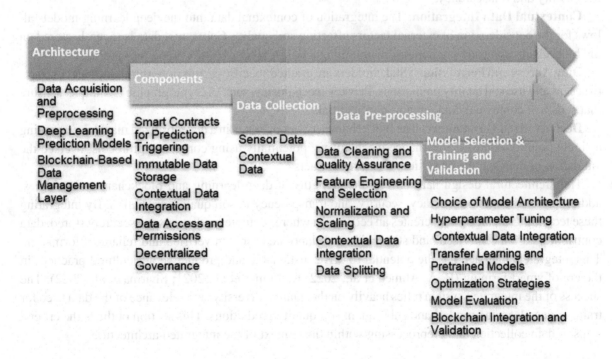

Architecture

At its core, the integrated system consists of three main components: data acquisition and pre-processing, deep learning prediction models, and the blockchain-based data management layer (Alessandrino et al., 2023; Emadi et al., 2020).

Data Acquisition and Preprocessing: Sensors, satellite imagery, weather APIs, and other data sources collect soil-related and contextual information. Data is preprocessed to clean noise, handle missing values, and standardize features. Contextual data, such as weather conditions and land management practices, are integrated with soil data to form comprehensive input for the deep learning models.

Deep Learning Prediction Models: Deep learning models, including neural networks, CNNs, RNNs, or hybrid architectures, are trained on the enriched dataset. Models learn complex relationships between soil properties and contextual factors, enabling accurate predictions of soil quality indicators.

Blockchain-Based Data Management Layer: Validated soil quality predictions are securely stored on the blockchain. Smart contracts manage data transactions, ensuring the validity of incoming data, triggering predictions, and rewarding data contributors. Data sharing permissions are enforced using blockchain's transparency and cryptographic techniques.

Components

Smart Contracts for Prediction Triggering: Smart contracts automate the execution of deep learning models when new soil data is added. Triggered by the arrival of new data, the smart contract ensures that the data is valid, initiates the prediction process, and records the outcome on the blockchain.

Immutable Data Storage: Validated soil quality predictions are stored on the blockchain in an immutable and tamper-proof manner. Each prediction is linked to its corresponding data inputs, ensuring traceability and transparency.

Contextual Data Integration: The integration of contextual data into the deep learning models allows for the consideration of external factors affecting soil quality. Contextual data is securely stored on the blockchain alongside predictions, maintaining a holistic record of the prediction process.

Data Access and Permissions: Stakeholders are granted specific permissions through smart contracts to access and use soil quality predictions. Privacy mechanisms, such as cryptographic techniques, ensure that sensitive contextual data remains confidential.

Decentralized Governance: The blockchain network operates in a decentralized manner, preventing a single point of control. Governance mechanisms, potentially using consensus protocols, oversee the validation of data and the execution of smart contracts.

The architectural design harmonizes the strengths of deep learning and blockchain technologies, addressing challenges of accuracy, security, and transparency in soil quality prediction. By integrating these technologies, the system creates an ecosystem where accurate predictions are securely stored, data contributors are incentivized, and stakeholders collaborate based on verified and reliable information. This integrated approach has the potential to drive sustainable and productive agricultural practices in the era of smart farming (R. A. Ahmed et al., 2022; R. Kumar et al., 2021; Sharma et al., 2022). The success of the integrated system relies heavily on the quality, diversity, and relevance of the data used for training deep learning models and subsequent soil quality predictions. This section outlines the crucial steps of data collection and preprocessing within the context of the integrated architecture.

Data Collection

Sensor Data: Soil quality data is collected through sensors placed in agricultural fields. These sensors measure properties such as nutrient levels, pH, moisture content, and temperature. Sensors might include soil moisture sensors, pH meters, and nutrient probes.

Contextual Data: External factors like weather conditions, crop type, irrigation schedules, and historical data are collected to provide contextual information. Weather APIs, satellite imagery, and IoT devices can contribute to this data.

Data Pre-Processing

Data Cleaning and Quality Assurance: Remove outliers, noise, and errors that may distort predictions. Address missing data points using techniques like interpolation, imputation, or considering their impact on predictions (Jadav et al., 2023b; Khan et al., 2022; Sakthi & DafniRose, 2022).

Feature Engineering and Selection: Select relevant features that have a significant impact on soil quality. Engineer new features that capture interactions between soil properties and context.

Normalization and Scaling: Standardize features to ensure they have similar scales, preventing dominance by features with larger values.

Contextual Data Integration: Combine soil data with contextual information like weather conditions or crop type to create enriched input for deep learning models. Contextual embeddings can transform qualitative context into numerical representations.

Data Splitting: Divide the dataset into training, validation, and testing subsets. Cross-validation may also be employed to assess model performance.

Data Security and Privacy Considerations

- **Anonymization**: Personal or sensitive information within the dataset should be anonymized to protect individuals' privacy.
- **Data Encryption**: Data, especially contextual information, can be encrypted before storage on the blockchain to ensure privacy.
- **Access Control**: Smart contracts can define permissions for accessing data, ensuring that only authorized parties can view or use specific datasets.

Data Integrity and Blockchain Integration

- **Data Validation**: Before data is added to the blockchain, it undergoes validation through smart contracts to verify its authenticity and quality.
- **Immutable Storage**: Validated soil quality predictions are stored on the blockchain, providing an immutable record of the prediction process and inputs.
- **Timestamping**: Blockchain's inherent timestamping feature ensures the chronological order of data transactions, contributing to traceability.

The data collection and preprocessing phase forms the bedrock of the integrated system. Accurate, diverse, and well-preprocessed data fuels the deep learning models' ability to make reliable predictions.

Furthermore, the integration of blockchain ensures the security, transparency, and accountability of the data, enhancing the overall robustness and credibility of soil quality assessment in the realm of smart agriculture (Bui et al., 2020; Sumathi et al., 2022). Once the data has been collected, preprocessed, and enriched with contextual information, the next critical phase involves training and optimizing deep learning models for accurate soil quality prediction. This section outlines the key steps in model training and optimization within the context of the integrated architecture.

Model Selection

Choice of Model Architecture: Select appropriate deep learning architectures based on the nature of the data and the prediction task. This could involve neural networks, CNNs, RNNs, or hybrid models (Babu & Supriya, 2022; Mohanta et al., 2021).

Hyperparameter Tuning: Adjust hyperparameters like learning rate, batch size, and regularization parameters to optimize model performance.

Training and Validation

Data Splitting: Use the training subset to train the model and the validation subset to fine-tune hyper-parameters and prevent overfitting.

Loss Function Selection: Choose an appropriate loss function that aligns with the prediction task, such as mean squared error for regression tasks.

Mini-Batch Training: Utilize mini-batch training to update model weights in smaller increments, facilitating convergence and efficient use of resources.

Contextual Data Integration

Concatenation or Fusion: Combine contextual information with soil data as inputs to the model. Consider architectural modifications, like attention mechanisms, to ensure the model effectively uses the contextual cues (Arora et al., 2019; Du et al., 2019).

Transfer Learning and Pretrained Models

Pretrained Embeddings: If contextual data includes text or categorical information, leverage pretrained embeddings to capture semantic relationships.

Transfer Learning: Employ transfer learning if relevant pretrained models exist in related domains, adapting them to the soil quality prediction task.

Optimization Strategies

Regularization Techniques: Apply techniques like dropout, L1/L2 regularization to prevent overfitting and improve model generalization.

Early Stopping: Monitor the validation loss during training and halt training when the loss plateaus or starts increasing, preventing overfitting.

Gradient Descent Variants: Utilize gradient descent optimization variants like Adam, RMSprop, or SGD to accelerate convergence.

Model Evaluation

Testing Subset: Test the trained model on the independent testing subset to assess its generalization performance (Awan et al., 2019; Demattê et al., 2019).

Evaluation Metrics: Use appropriate metrics for the prediction task, such as mean absolute error (MAE) for regression or accuracy for classification.

Contextual Performance Analysis: Analyze how well the model utilizes contextual information by comparing predictions with and without context.

Blockchain Integration and Validation

Smart Contract Execution: Smart contracts are triggered to execute the trained model when new soil data is added, ensuring predictions are generated securely.

Transaction Recording: The prediction outcome and associated contextual information are recorded on the blockchain as an immutable transaction.

The model training and optimization phase involves fine-tuning deep learning models to accurately predict soil quality indicators while harnessing the power of contextual information. The integration with blockchain ensures that predictions are securely stored, transparently accessible, and traceable (Anitha et al., 2023; Boopathi, Sureshkumar, et al., 2022; Koshariya, Kalaiyarasi, et al., 2023; Koshariya, Khatoon, et al., 2023; Vanitha et al., 2023). By uniting these technologies, the integrated system becomes a robust tool for informed decision-making in smart agriculture.

Soil Quality Prediction using Context Learning

Incorporating context learning into soil quality prediction enriches the accuracy and relevance of predictions by considering contextual factors that influence soil properties. This section outlines the process of utilizing context learning techniques within the integrated architecture for soil quality prediction (Bui et al., 2020; Emadi et al., 2020; Janizadeh et al., 2019; Van Klompenburg et al., 2020).

Contextual Embeddings: Convert qualitative contextual information, such as weather conditions or land management practices, into numerical embeddings. Apply techniques like Word2Vec, GloVe, or contextual embeddings based on transformer architectures to capture semantic relationships.

Contextual Data Fusion: Integrate contextual data with soil quality data to form enriched input for deep learning models. Combine different types of data, such as sensor readings, satellite imagery, and weather data, to capture complex interactions.

Model Architecture

Deep Learning Model Selection: Choose a suitable deep learning architecture that aligns with the prediction task and incorporates contextual information. Depending on the data, consider using neural networks, CNNs, RNNs, or hybrid models.

Contextual Integration: Design the model to accept both soil quality data and contextual embeddings or fused contextual data as inputs.

Attention Mechanisms: Implement attention mechanisms to enable the model to focus on different contextual factors based on their relevance to the prediction.

Training and Optimization

Enriched Data Training: Train the model using the enriched dataset containing both soil quality data and contextual features.

Hyperparameter Tuning: Fine-tune hyperparameters to ensure the model effectively learns from contextual cues without overfitting.

Prediction Process

- **Smart Contract Triggering**: When new soil data is added, smart contracts are triggered to execute the trained model with the accompanying contextual information (A. N. Ahmed et al., 2019; Janizadeh et al., 2019).
- **Context-Aware Predictions**: The model utilizes the contextual embeddings or fused data to make context-aware predictions.
- **Blockchain Record**: Record the prediction outcome, contextual information, and corresponding soil data on the blockchain.

Evaluation and Continuous Learning

- **Performance Assessment**: Evaluate the model's performance using appropriate metrics, considering the improvements gained from context learning.
- **Feedback Loop**:Continuously collect new contextual data and soil quality measurements to update the model and enhance its predictive capabilities.

By incorporating context learning techniques, the integrated system elevates soil quality prediction to a more sophisticated level, where predictions are influenced not only by inherent soil properties but also by external factors that play a crucial role in shaping soil conditions. This holistic approach empowers agricultural stakeholders with more accurate and actionable insights for optimal land management and sustainable farming practices.

CASE STUDIES AND PRACTICAL IMPLEMENTATIONS

Case Study: Small-Scale Farming in Developing Countries

In the context of small-scale farming in developing countries, where limited resources and uncertain weather patterns pose significant challenges, the integration of deep learning and blockchain technologies for soil quality prediction can have a transformative impact. This case study illustrates how the integrated system can be applied to enhance agricultural practices in such settings (Alessandrino et al., 2023; Lal, 2020; Singh et al., 2023).

Challenge: Small-scale farmers lack access to advanced soil analysis techniques and struggle to make informed decisions about irrigation, fertilizer application, and crop selection due to unreliable soil quality information.

Solution: The integrated system combines deep learning and blockchain to provide accurate, context-aware predictions for soil quality indicators, enabling farmers to optimize resource utilization and increase yields sustainably.

Implementation

Figure 3 shows integrated system combining deep learning and blockchain in small-scale manufacturing.

Figure 3. Implementation of integrated system combines deep learning and blockchain in small scale forming process

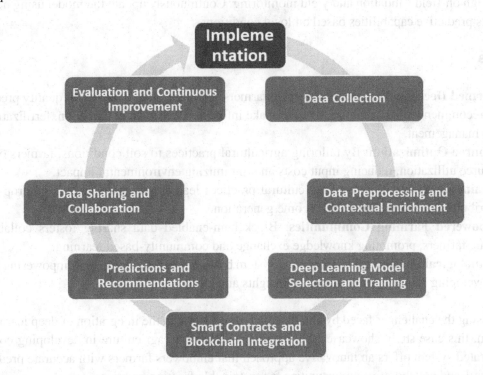

Data Collection: Deploy low-cost soil sensors in fields to collect soil quality data, including nutrient levels, pH, and moisture content. Gather contextual data, such as weather forecasts, crop types, and historical yield data, through partnerships with local weather stations and agricultural organizations (Arora et al., 2019; William et al., 2022).

Data Preprocessing and Contextual Enrichment: Clean and preprocess soil and contextual data, handling missing values and outliers. Transform qualitative contextual information into embeddings using language models, capturing local farming practices and weather patterns.

Deep Learning Model Selection and Training: Choose a neural network architecture that accommodates the small-scale dataset and incorporates contextual embeddings. Train the model using both soil quality data and enriched contextual features(Boopathi & Kanike, 2023; Ramudu et al., 2023; Sengeni et al., 2023).

Smart Contracts and Blockchain Integration: Develop smart contracts that trigger the model execution when new soil data is acquired. Implement blockchain to record predictions, contextual information, and corresponding soil measurements in an immutable ledger.

Predictions and Recommendations: When a farmer adds new soil data, the model executes through the smart contract and provides predictions for soil quality indicators. Recommendations are generated based on predicted soil properties, guiding farmers on irrigation schedules, nutrient application, and crop selection.

Data Sharing and Collaboration:Blockchain ensures secure and transparent data sharing among farmers, cooperatives, and local agricultural experts. Farmers can exchange knowledge and practices, collectively benefiting from the integrated system's insights.

Evaluation and Continuous Improvement: Assess the accuracy of predictions and recommendations through on-field validation and yield monitoring. Continuously update the model using new data, refining its predictive capabilities based on local conditions.

Benefits

- **Informed Decision-Making**: Small-scale farmers gain access to accurate soil quality predictions and recommendations, enabling them to make informed decisions on irrigation, fertilization, and crop management.
- **Resource Optimization**: By tailoring agricultural practices to soil conditions, farmers optimize resource utilization, reducing input costs and minimizing environmental impact.
- **Sustainable Yields**: Improved agricultural practices lead to increased yields and crop quality, contributing to food security and income generation.
- **Empowered Farming Communities**: Blockchain-enabled data sharing fosters collaboration among farmers, promoting knowledge exchange and community-based learning.
- **Technological Inclusion**: The integrated system bridges the technology gap, empowering farmers in developing countries with advanced insights and tools.

By addressing the challenges faced by small-scale farmers through the integration of deep learning and blockchain, this case study showcases the potential to transform agriculture in developing countries. The integrated system offers an innovative approach that empowers farmers with accurate predictions, data security, and collaborative opportunities for sustainable farming practices.

Case Study 2: Large-Scale Commercial Farming

In the context of large-scale commercial farming operations, where efficiency, precision, and yield optimization are paramount, the integration of deep learning and blockchain technologies for soil quality prediction can revolutionize agricultural practices. This case study demonstrates how the integrated system can enhance productivity in such settings (Awan et al., 2019; Sharma et al., 2022).

Scenario

Challenge: Large-scale commercial farms need to manage vast areas of land efficiently, optimize resource allocation, and minimize environmental impact while maximizing yields. Traditional soil analysis methods are time-consuming and may not provide the required spatial and temporal granularity.

Solution: The integrated system combines deep learning and blockchain to provide accurate, real-time predictions for soil quality indicators across the entire farm, enabling data-driven decision-making and precision agriculture.

Implementation

- **Data Collection**: Deploy a network of advanced soil sensors, drones, and satellite imagery to collect high-resolution soil quality and contextual data across the farm. Utilize IoT devices for real-time weather monitoring, machinery data, and irrigation information.
- **Data Preprocessing and Contextual Fusion**: Process and normalize the high-volume data collected from sensors, drones, and satellites. Fuse the various data sources, including soil data, weather data, and machinery data, to create comprehensive inputs for the deep learning model.
- **Deep Learning Model Selection and Training**: Choose a deep learning architecture, such as CNNs or hybrid models, capable of processing multi-modal and high-dimensional data. Train the model on historical data, incorporating both soil measurements and contextual features.
- **Smart Contracts and Blockchain Integration**: Develop smart contracts that initiate model execution when new data is gathered from sensors or other devices. Employ blockchain to securely store and timestamp predictions, sensor data, and other relevant information.
- **Real-time Predictions and Automation**: As new data streams in, smart contracts trigger real-time predictions for soil quality indicators, allowing for quick adjustments to farming practices. Automation systems adjust irrigation, fertilization, and machinery operations based on predictions and recommendations.
- **Data Sharing and Supply Chain Transparency**: Blockchain-enabled data sharing ensures that stakeholders across the supply chain have access to accurate soil quality information, promoting transparency and traceability.
- **Performance Monitoring and Continuous Learning**: Continuously monitor the accuracy of predictions through ground-truth validation and yield monitoring.
- Regularly update the model with new data to adapt to changing environmental conditions.

Benefits

- **Precision Agriculture**: Accurate, real-time predictions enable precise and targeted application of resources, reducing waste and optimizing crop yields.
- **Resource Efficiency**: Data-driven decision-making minimizes resource use, including water and fertilizers, while maintaining optimal plant health.
- **Yield Enhancement**: Tailored cultivation practices lead to increased yields and crop quality, contributing to profitability.
- **Sustainability**: Data-based optimization reduces environmental impact, promoting sustainable farming practices.

- **Supply Chain Confidence**: Transparent data sharing via blockchain assures downstream stakeholders of product quality and origin, fostering trust.

By integrating deep learning and blockchain technologies, this case study illustrates how large-scale commercial farms can transition towards data-driven and precision-based agriculture. The integrated system offers a sophisticated approach that harnesses real-time insights to enhance productivity, sustainability, and supply chain transparency in large-scale farming operations.

FUTURE DIRECTIONS AND OPPORTUNITIES

As the fields of deep learning and blockchain continue to evolve, the integration of these technologies for soil quality prediction in agriculture presents promising future directions and opportunities. This section highlights potential advancements and expansions in various aspects of the integrated system (Demattê et al., 2019; Sharma et al., 2022; Singh et al., 2023).

Advancements in Deep Learning Algorithms

- XAI enables deep learning models with improved interpretability, improving stakeholder understanding and trust in agricultural decision-making scenarios, particularly in complex scenarios.
- Ensemble Learning combines multiple deep learning models to enhance prediction accuracy and reduce biases, resulting in robust predictions.
- Federated learning enables collaborative model training across farms, maintaining data privacy and a broader dataset while ensuring data privacy.

Expanding Blockchain Applications in Agriculture

- Blockchain-enabled agricultural supply chain tracking for transparency and traceability from farm to consumer.
- Develop blockchain-based certification systems for organic and sustainable farming practices, ensuring consumer verifiability.
- Blockchain enhances agricultural product authenticity, origin verification, and reduces fraud risk.

Potential Integration With IoT and Remote Sensing

- IoT integration improves real-time data collection for agriculture and drone predictions.
- Utilize satellite imagery, remote sensing, and aerial drones for high-resolution prediction insights.

Contextual Learning Enhancement

- Develop models for temporal context learning, capturing long-term patterns like weather cycles and soil properties.
- Implement dynamic contextual weighting mechanisms to dynamically weigh contextual factors based on relevance to prediction scenarios.

Edge Computing and On-Device Predictions

- Edge AI deployment optimizes deep learning models for IoT devices, reducing latency and improving real-time predictions.
- Implement on-device predictions for enhanced data privacy and security by processing sensitive data locally.

Collaboration and Data Sharing Ecosystem

- Agricultural Consortia: collaborative efforts between stakeholders, researchers, and tech companies to develop and share data and models.
- Develop decentralized data marketplaces for farmers to securely share and receive compensation.

The future of the integrated system lies in the continuous evolution of deep learning algorithms, expanding the applications of blockchain in agriculture, and leveraging emerging technologies like IoT and remote sensing. These advancements will enable more accurate predictions, enhanced collaboration, and sustainable agricultural practices, ultimately contributing to a more efficient and resilient global food supply (Boopathi, 2023a; Hema et al., 2023; Syamala et al., 2023; Venkateswaran et al., 2023).

CONCLUSION

The integration of deep learning and blockchain technologies for soil quality prediction in smart agriculture presents a transformative approach that addresses critical challenges in modern farming practices. This chapter has explored the synergies between these technologies and their potential to revolutionize soil quality assessment, enabling more informed decision-making, resource optimization, and sustainable agricultural practices.

By combining deep learning's capability to learn complex patterns from diverse data sources with blockchain's attributes of data security, transparency, and decentralized data sharing, the integrated system offers a comprehensive solution for accurate and context-aware soil quality prediction. Deep learning techniques improve accuracy and relevance by capturing relationships between soil properties and contextual factors. Contextual embeddings and fusion enhance predictions, while blockchain technology ensures secure storage and transparency. Smart contracts enable automated execution and transparent outcomes. Accurate soil quality predictions enable farmers to optimize resource allocation, reducing input costs and environmental impact, making precision agriculture feasible. Blockchain-based data sharing fosters collaboration among stakeholders, fostering a community of farmers, researchers, and experts. Data marketplaces enable secure and compensated exchange. The integrated system promotes sustainable agricultural practices, enhances supply chain transparency, and builds consumer trust. Future directions include advancements in deep learning algorithms, IoT integration, and blockchain applications for continued innovation in soil quality prediction.

In conclusion, the integration of deep learning and blockchain technologies presents a holistic solution that transcends traditional soil analysis methods. As agriculture adapts to the demands of a growing population and changing environmental conditions, this integrated approach has the potential to usher in a new era of data-driven, efficient, and sustainable agricultural practices, fostering a brighter future for both farmers and the global food supply.

LIST OF ABBREVIATIONS

DL: Deep Learning
   BC: Blockchain
   QA: Soil Quality Assessment
   SA: Smart Agriculture
   CNN: Convolutional Neural Network
   RNN: Recurrent Neural Network
   IoT: Internet of Things
   XAI: Explainable Artificial Intelligence
   MAE: Mean Absolute Error
   IoT: Internet of Things

REFERENCES

Ahmed, A. N., Othman, F. B., Afan, H. A., Ibrahim, R. K., Fai, C. M., Hossain, M. S., Ehteram, M., & Elshafie, A. (2019). Machine learning methods for better water quality prediction. *Journal of Hydrology (Amsterdam)*, *578*, 124084. doi:10.1016/j.jhydrol.2019.124084

Ahmed, R. A., Hemdan, E. E.-D., El-Shafai, W., Ahmed, Z. A., El-Rabaie, E.-S. M., & Abd El-Samie, F. E. (2022). Climate-smart agriculture using intelligent techniques, blockchain and Internet of Things: Concepts, challenges, and opportunities. *Transactions on Emerging Telecommunications Technologies*, *33*(11), e4607. doi:10.1002/ett.4607

Alessandrino, L., Pavlakis, C., Colombani, N., Mastrocicco, M., & Aschonitis, V. (2023). Effects of graphene on soil water-retention curve, van Genuchten parameters, and soil pore size distribution—A comparison with traditional soil conditioners. *Water (Basel)*, *15*(7), 1297. doi:10.3390/w15071297

Anitha, C., Komala, C., Vivekanand, C. V., Lalitha, S., & Boopathi, S. (2023). Artificial Intelligence driven security model for Internet of Medical Things (IoMT). *IEEE Explore*, 1–7.

Arora, D., Gautham, S., Gupta, H., & Bhushan, B. (2019). Blockchain-based security solutions to preserve data privacy and integrity. *2019 International Conference on Computing, Communication, and Intelligent Systems (ICCCIS)*, 468–472. 10.1109/ICCCIS48478.2019.8974503

Awan, S. H., Ahmed, S., Safwan, N., Najam, Z., Hashim, M. Z., & Safdar, T. (2019). Role of internet of things (IoT) with blockchain technology for the development of smart farming. *Journal of Mechanics of Continua and Mathematical Sciences*, *14*(5), 170–188.

Babu, A. S., & Supriya, M. (2022). Blockchain Based Precision Agriculture Model Using Machine Learning Algorithms. *2022 International Conference on Breakthrough in Heuristics And Reciprocation of Advanced Technologies (BHARAT)*, 127–132. 10.1109/BHARAT53139.2022.00036

Bhandary, M., Parmar, M., & Ambawade, D. (2020). A blockchain solution based on directed acyclic graph for IoT data security using IoTA tangle. *2020 5th International Conference on Communication and Electronics Systems (ICCES)*, 827–832.

Boopathi, S. (2023a). Deep Learning Techniques Applied for Automatic Sentence Generation. In Promoting Diversity, Equity, and Inclusion in Language Learning Environments (pp. 255–273). IGI Global. doi:10.4018/978-1-6684-3632-5.ch016

Boopathi, S. (2023b). Internet of Things-Integrated Remote Patient Monitoring System: Healthcare Application. In *Dynamics of Swarm Intelligence Health Analysis for the Next Generation* (pp. 137–161). IGI Global. doi:10.4018/978-1-6684-6894-4.ch008

Boopathi, S., Arigela, S. H., Raman, R., Indhumathi, C., Kavitha, V., & Bhatt, B. C. (2022). Prominent Rule Control-based Internet of Things: Poultry Farm Management System. *IEEE Explore*, 1–6.

Boopathi, S., & Kanike, U. K. (2023). Applications of Artificial Intelligent and Machine Learning Techniques in Image Processing. In *Handbook of Research on Thrust Technologies' Effect on Image Processing* (pp. 151–173). IGI Global. doi:10.4018/978-1-6684-8618-4.ch010

Boopathi, S., Kumar, P. K. S., Meena, R. S., Sudhakar, M., & Associates. (2023). Sustainable Developments of Modern Soil-Less Agro-Cultivation Systems: Aquaponic Culture. In Human Agro-Energy Optimization for Business and Industry (pp. 69–87). IGI Global.

Boopathi, S., Sureshkumar, M., & Sathiskumar, S. (2022). Parametric Optimization of LPG Refrigeration System Using Artificial Bee Colony Algorithm. *International Conference on Recent Advances in Mechanical Engineering Research and Development*, 97–105.

Bui, D. T., Tsangaratos, P., Nguyen, V.-T., Van Liem, N., & Trinh, P. T. (2020). Comparing the prediction performance of a Deep Learning Neural Network model with conventional machine learning models in landslide susceptibility assessment. *Catena*, *188*, 104426. doi:10.1016/j.catena.2019.104426

Chenthara, S., Ahmed, K., Wang, H., Whittaker, F., & Chen, Z. (2020). Healthchain: A novel framework on privacy preservation of electronic health records using blockchain technology. *PLoS One*, *15*(12), e0243043. doi:10.1371/journal.pone.0243043 PMID:33296379

Demattê, J. A. M., Dotto, A. C., Bedin, L. G., Sayão, V. M., & Souza, A. B. (2019). Soil analytical quality control by traditional and spectroscopy techniques: Constructing the future of a hybrid laboratory for low environmental impact. *Geoderma*, *337*, 111–121. doi:10.1016/j.geoderma.2018.09.010

Du, S., Li, T., Yang, Y., & Horng, S.-J. (2019). Deep air quality forecasting using hybrid deep learning framework. *IEEE Transactions on Knowledge and Data Engineering*, *33*(6), 2412–2424. doi:10.1109/TKDE.2019.2954510

Durai, S. K. S., & Shamili, M. D. (2022). Smart farming using machine learning and deep learning techniques. *Decision Analytics Journal*, *3*, 100041. doi:10.1016/j.dajour.2022.100041

Emadi, M., Taghizadeh-Mehrjardi, R., Cherati, A., Danesh, M., Mosavi, A., & Scholten, T. (2020). Predicting and mapping of soil organic carbon using machine learning algorithms in Northern Iran. *Remote Sensing (Basel)*, *12*(14), 2234. doi:10.3390/rs12142234

Ferrag, M. A., Shu, L., Djallel, H., & Choo, K.-K. R. (2021). Deep learning-based intrusion detection for distributed denial of service attack in agriculture 4.0. *Electronics (Basel)*, *10*(11), 1257. doi:10.3390/electronics10111257

Gnanaprakasam, C., Vankara, J., Sastry, A. S., Prajval, V., Gireesh, N., & Boopathi, S. (2023). Long-Range and Low-Power Automated Soil Irrigation System Using Internet of Things: An Experimental Study. In Contemporary Developments in Agricultural Cyber-Physical Systems (pp. 87–104). IGI Global.

Hanumanthakari, S., Gift, M. M., Kanimozhi, K., Bhavani, M. D., Bamane, K. D., & Boopathi, S. (2023). Biomining Method to Extract Metal Components Using Computer-Printed Circuit Board E-Waste. In *Handbook of Research on Safe Disposal Methods of Municipal Solid Wastes for a Sustainable Environment* (pp. 123–141). IGI Global. doi:10.4018/978-1-6684-8117-2.ch010

Hassija, V., Batra, S., Chamola, V., Anand, T., Goyal, P., Goyal, N., & Guizani, M. (2021). A blockchain and deep neural networks-based secure framework for enhanced crop protection. *Ad Hoc Networks*, *119*, 102537. doi:10.1016/j.adhoc.2021.102537

Hema, N., Krishnamoorthy, N., Chavan, S. M., Kumar, N., Sabarimuthu, M., & Boopathi, S. (2023). A Study on an Internet of Things (IoT)-Enabled Smart Solar Grid System. In *Handbook of Research on Deep Learning Techniques for Cloud-Based Industrial IoT* (pp. 290–308). IGI Global. doi:10.4018/978-1-6684-8098-4.ch017

Hossain, M. M., Rahman, M. A., Chaki, S., Ahmed, H., Haque, A., Tamanna, I., Lima, S., Ferdous, M. J., & Rahman, M. S. (n.d.). *Smart-Agri: A Smart Agricultural Management with IoT-ML-Blockchain Integrated Framework*. Academic Press.

Jabbar, R., Fetais, N., Krichen, M., & Barkaoui, K. (2020). Blockchain technology for healthcare: Enhancing shared electronic health record interoperability and integrity. *2020 IEEE International Conference on Informatics, IoT, and Enabling Technologies (ICIoT)*, 310–317. 10.1109/ICIoT48696.2020.9089570

Jadav, N. K., Rathod, T., Gupta, R., Tanwar, S., Kumar, N., & Alkhayyat, A. (2023). Blockchain and artificial intelligence-empowered smart agriculture framework for maximizing human life expectancy. *Computers & Electrical Engineering*, *105*, 108486. doi:10.1016/j.compeleceng.2022.108486

Janizadeh, S., Avand, M., Jaafari, A., Phong, T. V., Bayat, M., Ahmadisharaf, E., Prakash, I., Pham, B. T., & Lee, S. (2019). Prediction success of machine learning methods for flash flood susceptibility mapping in the Tafresh watershed, Iran. *Sustainability (Basel)*, *11*(19), 5426. doi:10.3390u11195426

Jeevanantham, Y. A., Saravanan, A., Vanitha, V., Boopathi, S., & Kumar, D. P. (2022). Implementation of Internet-of Things (IoT) in Soil Irrigation System. *IEEE Explore*, 1–5.

Khan, A. A., Shaikh, Z. A., Belinskaja, L., Baitenova, L., Vlasova, Y., Gerzelieva, Z., Laghari, A. A., Abro, A. A., & Barykin, S. (2022). A blockchain and metaheuristic-enabled distributed architecture for smart agricultural analysis and ledger preservation solution: A collaborative approach. *Applied Sciences (Basel, Switzerland)*, *12*(3), 1487. doi:10.3390/app12031487

Koshariya, A. K., Kalaiyarasi, D., Jovith, A. A., Sivakami, T., Hasan, D. S., & Boopathi, S. (2023). AI-Enabled IoT and WSN-Integrated Smart Agriculture System. In *Artificial Intelligence Tools and Technologies for Smart Farming and Agriculture Practices* (pp. 200–218). IGI Global. doi:10.4018/978-1-6684-8516-3.ch011

Koshariya, A. K., Khatoon, S., Marathe, A. M., Suba, G. M., Baral, D., & Boopathi, S. (2023). Agricultural Waste Management Systems Using Artificial Intelligence Techniques. In *AI-Enabled Social Robotics in Human Care Services* (pp. 236–258). IGI Global. doi:10.4018/978-1-6684-8171-4.ch009

Kumar, P., Sampath, B., Kumar, S., Babu, B. H., & Ahalya, N. (2023). Hydroponics, Aeroponics, and Aquaponics Technologies in Modern Agricultural Cultivation. In Trends, Paradigms, and Advances in Mechatronics Engineering (pp. 223–241). IGI Global.

Kumar, R., Kumar, P., Tripathi, R., Gupta, G. P., Gadekallu, T. R., & Srivastava, G. (2021). SP2F: A secured privacy-preserving framework for smart agricultural Unmanned Aerial Vehicles. *Computer Networks*, *187*, 107819. doi:10.1016/j.comnet.2021.107819

Kumara, V., Mohanaprakash, T., Fairooz, S., Jamal, K., Babu, T., & Sampath, B. (2023). Experimental Study on a Reliable Smart Hydroponics System. In *Human Agro-Energy Optimization for Business and Industry* (pp. 27–45). IGI Global. doi:10.4018/978-1-6684-4118-3.ch002

Lal, R. (2020). Soil quality and sustainability. In *Methods for assessment of soil degradation* (pp. 17–30). CRC Press. doi:10.1201/9781003068716-2

Mohanta, B. K., Chedup, S., & Dehury, M. K. (2021). Secure trust model based on blockchain for internet of things enable smart agriculture. *2021 19th OITS International Conference on Information Technology (OCIT)*, 410–415.

Ramudu, K., Mohan, V. M., Jyothirmai, D., Prasad, D., Agrawal, R., & Boopathi, S. (2023). Machine Learning and Artificial Intelligence in Disease Prediction: Applications, Challenges, Limitations, Case Studies, and Future Directions. In Contemporary Applications of Data Fusion for Advanced Healthcare Informatics (pp. 297–318). IGI Global.

Sakthi, U., & DafniRose, J. (2022). Blockchain-enabled smart agricultural knowledge discovery system using edge computing. *Procedia Computer Science*, *202*, 73–82. doi:10.1016/j.procs.2022.04.011

Sankar, K. M., Booba, B., & Boopathi, S. (2023). Smart Agriculture Irrigation Monitoring System Using Internet of Things. In *Contemporary Developments in Agricultural Cyber-Physical Systems* (pp. 105–121). IGI Global. doi:10.4018/978-1-6684-7879-0.ch006

Selvakumar, S., Adithe, S., Isaac, J. S., Pradhan, R., Venkatesh, V., & Sampath, B. (2023). A Study of the Printed Circuit Board (PCB) E-Waste Recycling Process. In Sustainable Approaches and Strategies for E-Waste Management and Utilization (pp. 159–184). IGI Global.

Sengeni, D., Padmapriya, G., Imambi, S. S., Suganthi, D., Suri, A., & Boopathi, S. (2023). Biomedical Waste Handling Method Using Artificial Intelligence Techniques. In *Handbook of Research on Safe Disposal Methods of Municipal Solid Wastes for a Sustainable Environment* (pp. 306–323). IGI Global. doi:10.4018/978-1-6684-8117-2.ch022

Shahbazi, Z., & Byun, Y.-C. (2021). Smart manufacturing real-time analysis based on blockchain and machine learning approaches. *Applied Sciences (Basel, Switzerland)*, *11*(8), 3535. doi:10.3390/app11083535

Sharma, V., Tripathi, A. K., & Mittal, H. (2022). Technological revolutions in smart farming: Current trends, challenges & future directions. *Computers and Electronics in Agriculture*, *201*, 107217. doi:10.1016/j.compag.2022.107217

Singh, A., Gaurav, K., Sonkar, G. K., & Lee, C.-C. (2023). Strategies to measure soil moisture using traditional methods, automated sensors, remote sensing, and machine learning techniques: Review, bibliometric analysis, applications, research findings, and future directions. *IEEE Access : Practical Innovations, Open Solutions*, *11*, 13605–13635. doi:10.1109/ACCESS.2023.3243635

Sumathi, M., Rajkamal, M., Raja, S., Venkatachalapathy, M., & Vijayaraj, N. (2022). A crop yield prediction model based on an improved artificial neural network and yield monitoring using a blockchain technique. *International Journal of Wavelets, Multresolution, and Information Processing*, *20*(06), 2250030. doi:10.1142/S0219691322500308

Syamala, M., Komala, C., Pramila, P., Dash, S., Meenakshi, S., & Boopathi, S. (2023). Machine Learning-Integrated IoT-Based Smart Home Energy Management System. In *Handbook of Research on Deep Learning Techniques for Cloud-Based Industrial IoT* (pp. 219–235). IGI Global. doi:10.4018/978-1-6684-8098-4.ch013

Van Klompenburg, T., Kassahun, A., & Catal, C. (2020). Crop yield prediction using machine learning: A systematic literature review. *Computers and Electronics in Agriculture*, *177*, 105709. doi:10.1016/j.compag.2020.105709

Vanitha, S., Radhika, K., & Boopathi, S. (2023). Artificial Intelligence Techniques in Water Purification and Utilization. In *Human Agro-Energy Optimization for Business and Industry* (pp. 202–218). IGI Global. doi:10.4018/978-1-6684-4118-3.ch010

Venkateswaran, N., Vidhya, R., Naik, D. A., Raj, T. M., Munjal, N., & Boopathi, S. (2023). Study on Sentence and Question Formation Using Deep Learning Techniques. In *Digital Natives as a Disruptive Force in Asian Businesses and Societies* (pp. 252–273). IGI Global. doi:10.4018/978-1-6684-6782-4.ch015

Vyas, S., Shabaz, M., Pandit, P., Parvathy, L. R., & Ofori, I. (2022). Integration of artificial intelligence and blockchain technology in healthcare and agriculture. *Journal of Food Quality*, *2022*, 2022. doi:10.1155/2022/4228448

William, P., Yogeesh, N., Vimala, S., Gite, P., & Associates. (2022). Blockchain technology for data privacy using contract mechanism for 5G networks. *2022 3rd International Conference on Intelligent Engineering and Management (ICIEM)*, 461–465.

Chapter 2
Assessing Security Concerns for AI–Based Drones in Smart Cities

Lakshmana Phaneendra Maguluri
Department of Computer Science and Engineering, Koneru Lakshmaiah Education Foundation, India

A. N. Arularasan
Department of Artificial Intelligence and Data Science, Panimalar Engineering College, India

S. Boopathi
ⓘD https://orcid.org/0000-0002-2065-6539
Department of Mechanical Engineering, Muthayammal Engineering College, India

ABSTRACT

This chapter investigates security concerns involving AI-powered drones in smart cities, emphasising the importance of secure deployment. It discusses topics like data privacy, cybersecurity risks, physical security, and ethical repercussions. Security precautions such encrypted communication channels, intrusion detection systems, collision avoidance systems, and observance of moral and legal norms are discussed. The chapter offers case studies of successful AI-based drone deployments as well as recommendations for best practises for upcoming operations. The chapter addresses challenges and embraces ethical concerns in an effort to support the moral integration of AI-based drones in smart city scenarios.

INTRODUCTION

AI-based drones are unmanned aerial vehicles (UAVs) that use artificial intelligence to enhance autonomy and perform complex tasks. These autonomous drones, equipped with AI algorithms, can adapt to changing environments without human intervention. The integration of AI-based drones in smart cities has the potential to revolutionize urban life, including surveillance, transportation, delivery services, and emergency response. These autonomous devices gather real-time data, analyze it, and make informed decisions, enabling efficient and proactive actions in urban environments(Do et al., 2021). AI-based drone deployment in smart cities raises security concerns due to sensitive data, cyber threats, physical

DOI: 10.4018/978-1-6684-9151-5.ch002

safety risks, and ethical implications. This chapter provides a comprehensive understanding of security challenges and vulnerabilities, enabling the development of strategies and frameworks for evaluating and mitigating these concerns. This analysis contributes to the development of guidelines and best practices for stakeholders involved in deploying and managing AI-driven drone systems(Vashisth et al., 2021).

This chapter explores security concerns for AI-based drones in smart cities, including data privacy, cybersecurity, physical safety, and ethical implications. It proposes a framework for assessing and managing these issues, incorporating risk assessment methodologies and mitigation strategies. The chapter also presents case studies and best practices from real-world scenarios. Addressing security concerns with AI-based drones in smart cities is crucial for protecting personal privacy, preventing malicious activities, mitigating risks, and promoting ethical decision-making. This chapter is valuable for policymakers, urban planners, drone operators, and researchers seeking to harness the potential of AI-based drones while maintaining a secure and trustworthy urban environment. Smart cities aim to improve urban challenges and quality of life by addressing urban challenges. AI-based drones play a crucial role in urban planning, public safety, traffic management, and environmental monitoring. However, these advanced technologies raise security concerns that require careful evaluation and attention (Rawat et al., 2022). AI-based drones collect vast amounts of data, including sensitive information about individuals, activities, and surroundings. To maintain privacy rights and prevent harm, it is crucial to safeguard this data from unauthorized access, misuse, and breaches. Establishing robust protection mechanisms, encryption techniques, and compliance with privacy regulations are essential steps in addressing these concerns.

Cybersecurity risks are a significant concern in AI-based drones, as they are interconnected within smart city ecosystems. To mitigate these risks, securing communication channels, implementing strong authentication protocols, and regularly updating software and firmware are essential measures. Physical safety is crucial for preventing accidents and protecting both drones and citizens. Collision avoidance systems, advanced sensors, and integration with air traffic management systems can help mitigate mid-air collision risks and ensure safe operations (Alqurashi et al., 2022; Kumar & Mohanty, 2021). Establishing fail-safe mechanisms and emergency procedures minimizes system failures and enables timely response in critical situations. Ethical implications in AI-based drones are crucial, as they can impact societal values, individual rights, and fairness. Bias in AI algorithms can lead to discriminatory outcomes or profiling. Addressing these concerns requires transparency, accountability, and adherence to legal and ethical frameworks. A comprehensive framework for assessing and managing risks is essential, including risk assessment methodologies, vulnerability identification, impact evaluation, and mitigation strategies. This systematically evaluates and addresses security concerns, fostering a secure and trustworthy environment for AI-based drone operations in smart cities (Mohammed et al., 2014; Rawat et al., 2022).

This chapter presents case studies and best practices for secure AI-based drones in smart cities, offering insights into practical challenges and lessons learned. It emphasizes the importance of addressing security concerns to ensure responsible and secure use of these technologies. By exploring and measuring concerns, proposing a comprehensive assessment framework, and highlighting case studies, this chapter aims to contribute to the establishment of secure AI-based drone operations, enhancing safety, efficiency, and sustainability in urban environments. AI-based drones have diverse applications in smart cities, including (Rawat et al., 2022):

- AI-based drones enhance surveillance and security in smart cities by autonomously monitoring areas, detecting suspicious activities, and sending real-time alerts to authorities. They are essential for crowd monitoring, perimeter security, disaster response, and crime prevention.

- Drones with AI can efficiently manage urban traffic by collecting real-time data on flow, congestion, and accidents. AI algorithms analyze this data to identify patterns, predict congestion, and suggest alternative routes, enabling authorities to make informed decisions and optimize traffic management strategies.
- AI-based drones are revolutionizing the delivery and logistics industry in smart cities by navigating urban landscapes, avoiding obstacles, and delivering packages efficiently. They optimize routes based on real-time traffic information, reducing costs and improving speed.
- Drones with AI sensors and cameras monitor environmental parameters in smart cities, collecting data on air quality, noise, temperature, and pollution. AI algorithms analyze this data to identify patterns, assess risks, and support sustainable urban planning decision-making.
- AI-based drones are used for infrastructure inspection, capturing high-resolution images and performing automated analysis to detect structural defects, identify maintenance requirements, and ensure urban infrastructure safety and integrity.
- AI-based drones aid in emergency response by assessing and responding quickly, surveying disaster areas, identifying survivors, and relaying real-time information. They also aid in search and rescue operations, helping locate missing persons in urban environments.

AI-based drones in smart cities are gaining popularity due to advancements in technologies, sensor capabilities, and regulatory frameworks. These drones offer potential for improving efficiency, safety, and sustainability, transforming urban operations and enhancing residents' quality of life.

Integration of Drones in Smart City Infrastructure

Drones' integration in smart city infrastructure involves seamlessly integrating drone systems into urban frameworks, addressing challenges and enhancing efficiency. Key aspects include seamless integration, efficient utilization, and addressing challenges (McEnroe et al., 2022; Mohammed et al., 2014).

- Regulatory frameworks are crucial for drone operations in smart cities, defining rules and guidelines like flight restrictions, licensing, privacy, and safety standards. These frameworks work with stakeholders to ensure responsible and compliant drone operations in the smart city environment.
- Smart city infrastructure must adapt to drone operations by creating designated takeoff and landing zones, charging stations, and storage facilities. Communication networks and sensors may also be necessary for drone connectivity and data transmission.
- Communication and Connectivity: Seamless communication and connectivity are crucial for efficient drone operations in smart cities. Drones rely on robust wireless networks to transmit real-time data, receive commands, and communicate with other devices within the smart city ecosystem. Integration with existing communication infrastructure ensures reliable and secure connectivity for drone operations.
- The data collected by drones can be integrated with smart city platforms and data analytics systems. This allows for the efficient processing and analysis of drone-generated data, enabling insights and actionable intelligence for decision-making. Integration with data management systems facilitates data sharing, visualization, and integration with other urban data sources.
- Integrating drones into the smart city infrastructure requires collaboration among various stakeholders. This includes cooperation between government agencies, drone operators, technology

providers, and citizens. Collaboration fosters the exchange of knowledge, data, and expertise, promoting effective drone deployment and maximizing the benefits of their integration.

- Drones can contribute to urban planning and design by providing valuable data and insights. They can capture aerial imagery and generate 3D maps, helping urban planners visualize and analyze the city's physical features. This data aids in identifying areas for development, assessing infrastructure needs, and optimizing resource allocation.
- Ensuring public acceptance and education is crucial for successful drone integration in smart cities. Public awareness campaigns and educational initiatives help citizens understand the benefits, safety measures, and privacy considerations associated with drone operations. Engaging the public and addressing their concerns fosters trust and acceptance of drones as part of the smart city infrastructure.

Drones can enhance urban services, efficiency, and address challenges in smart cities by integrating them into infrastructure, data integration, collaboration, and public acceptance. This transformation transforms urban environments and improves residents' quality of life.

SECURITY CONCERNS IN AI-BASED DRONES

Data Privacy and Protection

Data privacy and protection are crucial security concerns for AI-based drones operating in smart city environments. These drones collect vast amounts of data, including images, videos, and sensor readings. Ensuring privacy rights and addressing these concerns is essential (Haider et al., 2022; Yahuza et al., 2021).

- **Data Collection and Storage:** AI-based drones collect a wide range of data during their operations. It is essential to clearly define what types of data are collected, the purpose of collection, and the duration for which the data is stored. Minimizing the collection of unnecessary data can help reduce privacy risks.
- **Anonymization and Encryption:** To protect individual privacy, drone data should be anonymized and encrypted. Anonymization techniques, such as removing personally identifiable information or using pseudonyms, can help ensure that the data cannot be directly linked to specific individuals. Encryption methods, including secure protocols and algorithms, can safeguard the data during transmission and storage, preventing unauthorized access.
- **Access Control and Authorization:** Implementing strict access control mechanisms is crucial for protecting drone data. Only authorized personnel should have access to the data, and access privileges should be granted based on the principle of least privilege. Strong authentication protocols, such as two-factor authentication, can help prevent unauthorized access to the drone's data storage and control systems.
- **Data Sharing and Consent:** When sharing drone data with third parties, explicit consent should be obtained from individuals whose data is being shared. Clear and transparent data sharing policies should be established, outlining the purpose, recipients, and duration of data sharing. Individuals should have the right to revoke their consent at any time.

- **Compliance with Privacy Regulations:** AI-based drone operations should adhere to applicable privacy regulations and standards. This includes compliance with data protection laws, such as the General Data Protection Regulation (GDPR) in the European Union, which governs the collection, processing, and storage of personal data. Compliance ensures that privacy rights of individuals are respected, and appropriate safeguards are in place to protect their data.
- **Data Retention and Deletion:** Establishing clear guidelines for data retention and deletion is essential to minimize privacy risks. Drone data should be retained only for as long as necessary to fulfill the purpose for which it was collected. Once the data is no longer needed, it should be securely deleted to prevent unauthorized access or unintended use.
- **Security Audits and Monitoring:** Regular security audits and monitoring of drone systems and data infrastructure help identify potential vulnerabilities and ensure compliance with security measures. Monitoring can detect unauthorized access attempts, data breaches, or any suspicious activities related to the drone's data storage and transmission.

Cybersecurity Risks and Vulnerabilities

Cybersecurity risks and vulnerabilities are significant concerns for AI-based drones operating in smart city ecosystems, as they are connected to networks and systems, making them potential targets for cyberattacks (Nandutu et al., 2023).

- **Unauthorized Access:** AI-based drones are vulnerable to unauthorized access by malicious actors, potentially compromising sensitive data, manipulating operations, or even hijacking. To prevent this, strong authentication mechanisms like secure login credentials and multi-factor authentication are essential.
- **Malware and Software Exploitation:** Drones are vulnerable to malware and software vulnerabilities, allowing attackers to gain control and extract sensitive data. Regular software updates, firmware patches, and security audits are crucial to address these issues and protect against malware attacks.
- **Communication Interception:** The drone's communication channels must be secured to prevent cyber attackers from intercepting and manipulating them, resulting in unauthorized commands or sensitive data theft. Encryption techniques, secure protocols, and communication channels help mitigate this risk.
- **GPS Spoofing and Jamming:** GPS spoofing and jamming are attacks on drone navigation systems, causing incorrect positioning and disrupting the drone's signal. To protect against these attacks, anti-spoofing measures like signal validation and backup navigation systems are implemented.
- **Data Integrity and Tampering:** Cyber attackers can manipulate AI-based drone data, potentially causing false information or incorrect analysis. Ensuring data integrity through cryptographic measures, validation techniques, and secure storage mechanisms protects against data tampering.
- **Supply Chain Risks:** AI-based drones' supply chain poses vulnerabilities and risks, as malicious actors can compromise components or software. To mitigate these risks, thorough security assessments, integrity assurance, and secure development practices are crucial.
- **Insider Threats:** Insider threats pose a risk to AI-based drone security, as authorized individuals, like operators or maintenance personnel, can misuse privileges and introduce vulnerabilities.

Addressing these risks involves proper access controls, background checks, and cybersecurity training for personnel.

AI-based drones can operate securely by addressing cybersecurity risks and vulnerabilities. Regular security assessments, vulnerability management, and adherence to best practices are essential for safeguarding drone systems and maintaining stakeholder trust in smart city operations.

Physical Safety and Collision Avoidance

AI-based drones in smart cities pose a security concern due to their shared airspace with aircraft, pedestrians, vehicles, and infrastructure. Key aspects to consider include physical safety, collision avoidance, and minimizing collisions (Yu & Carroll, 2021).

- **Collision Detection and Avoidance Systems:** AI-based drones should be equipped with robust collision detection and avoidance systems. These systems use sensors, such as cameras, lidar, radar, or ultrasonic sensors, to detect obstacles in the drone's flight path. Real-time data processing and AI algorithms enable the drone to make informed decisions to avoid collisions.
- **Sense and Avoid Technologies:** Drones can incorporate sense and avoid technologies to enhance their ability to detect and avoid obstacles. These technologies may include computer vision, object recognition, and machine learning algorithms that enable the drone to identify and react to objects in its vicinity, ensuring safe navigation.
- **Integration with Air Traffic Management Systems:** Integration with air traffic management systems is crucial to ensure the safe integration of drones into airspace. Collaborative efforts between drones, traditional aircraft, and air traffic control systems can help establish communication protocols, traffic flow management, and airspace allocation to prevent collisions and maintain safe operations.
- **Fail-Safe Mechanisms and Emergency Procedures:** AI-based drones should be equipped with fail-safe mechanisms and emergency procedures to handle system failures or critical situations. These mechanisms may include automated return-to-home functions, emergency landing protocols, or parachutes to ensure the safe recovery of the drone and mitigate risks to people and property.
- **Compliance with Aviation Regulations:** AI-based drones must comply with aviation regulations and guidelines established by relevant authorities. These regulations may include altitude restrictions, flight paths, and operational limitations to ensure safe drone operations in urban airspace. Compliance with these regulations helps minimize risks and maintain the overall safety of smart city environments.

Ethical Implications and Bias

AI-based drones in smart cities raise ethical concerns about fairness, accountability, transparency, and potential biased decision-making. Key aspects to consider include fairness, accountability, transparency, and potential bias (Lv et al., 2021; Yu & Carroll, 2021).

- AI algorithms used by drones should be designed and trained to ensure fairness and avoid biases. Biases can arise due to the data used for training the algorithms or the inherent biases in the algorithms themselves. Continuous monitoring and evaluation of the algorithms can help detect and mitigate biases to ensure fair and unbiased decision-making.
- Stakeholders involved in AI-based drone operations should establish accountability and transparency mechanisms. This includes clear guidelines on how decisions are made, who is responsible for those decisions, and mechanisms for addressing complaints or concerns. Transparent decision-making processes and accountability frameworks foster trust and mitigate the risks of unethical practices.
- The deployment of AI-based drones should adhere to legal and ethical frameworks governing drone operations. These frameworks may include guidelines on data protection, privacy rights, human rights, and ethical considerations. Compliance with these frameworks helps ensure that drone operations align with societal values and respect the rights and well-being of individuals.
- Despite the autonomy of AI-based drones, human oversight and intervention are crucial to address ethical implications and biases. Humans should have the ability to intervene or override automated decisions made by the drones, particularly in critical or ethically sensitive situations. Human operators should be trained to make ethical judgments and exercise discretion when necessary.

AI-based drones can operate responsibly and ethically in smart cities by addressing safety concerns, ethical decision-making, collision avoidance systems, aviation regulations compliance, AI algorithm biases, and ethical frameworks. This contributes to a safe, fair, and trustworthy environment.

DATA PRIVACY AND PROTECTION FOR DRONES

Collection, Storage, and Usage of Drone Data

Data privacy and protection are crucial for AI-based drone data collection, storage, and usage. Ensuring secure handling and safeguarding individual privacy is essential (Finn & Wright, 2016).

- Clearly define the purpose for collecting drone data and ensure that it is collected only for legitimate and specific purposes. Avoid collecting unnecessary or excessive data that is not directly relevant to the intended objectives.
- Obtain informed consent from individuals whose data is being collected by the drones. Inform them about the purpose, duration, and scope of data collection, and provide an opt-out mechanism if possible. Individuals should have the right to understand and control how their data is being used.
- Anonymize the collected drone data by removing personally identifiable information or using encryption techniques to ensure that individual identities cannot be easily traced. Aggregating the data can further protect individual privacy while still allowing for analysis and insights.
- Implement robust security measures to protect the storage and transmission of drone data. Encrypt the data both at rest and in transit to prevent unauthorized access. Utilize secure storage systems and communication protocols that adhere to industry best practices.

- Establish clear guidelines for data retention and deletion. Retain the data only for as long as necessary to fulfill the purpose for which it was collected, and then securely delete it. Regularly review and update retention policies to ensure compliance with privacy regulations.
- Implement access controls to restrict data access to authorized personnel only. Apply encryption to sensitive drone data to ensure that even if unauthorized access occurs, the data remains protected and unreadable.
- Adhere to applicable privacy regulations, such as the General Data Protection Regulation (GDPR) in the European Union or other local data protection laws. Familiarize yourself with the legal requirements regarding data privacy and protection and ensure compliance throughout the entire data lifecycle.
- When sharing drone data with third parties, establish clear agreements and contracts that outline the purpose, scope, and security measures to be followed. Ensure that the third parties adhere to privacy and security standards and have appropriate safeguards in place.
- Conduct regular security audits and assessments to identify and address any vulnerabilities or risks related to the collection, storage, and usage of drone data. This includes reviewing access controls, encryption practices, and compliance with privacy policies.

AI-based drones can respect privacy rights, safeguard sensitive data, and comply with regulations by implementing robust data privacy measures. Prioritizing secure drone data handling throughout its lifecycle is essential for maintaining trust and responsible data practices in smart city environments.

Anonymization and Encryption Techniques

AI-based drones use anonymization and encryption techniques for data privacy and protection, ensuring confidentiality and integrity (Bentotahewa et al., 2021; Chen & Wang, 2019; Yang et al., 2022). Anonymization and Encryption Techniques for Drones is illustrated in Figure 1.

Figure 1. Anonymization and encryption techniques for drones

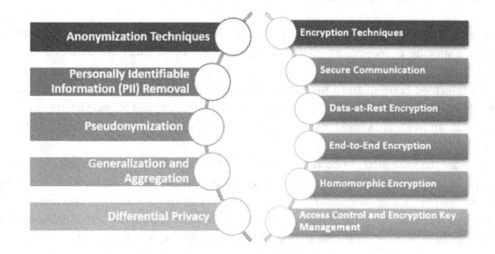

Anonymization Techniques

- **Personally Identifiable Information (PII) Removal:** Anonymization starts with the removal of PII, such as names, addresses, social security numbers, or any other data that can directly identify individuals. By eliminating these identifiers, the data is dissociated from specific individuals, enhancing privacy protection.
- **Pseudonymization:** Instead of completely removing identifiers, pseudonymization replaces them with pseudonyms or unique identifiers that cannot be directly linked to specific individuals. This approach allows for data analysis while still protecting individual privacy.
- **Generalization and Aggregation:** Generalizing or aggregating data involves reducing the level of detail or granularity in the dataset. For example, age ranges instead of exact ages or combining data into larger groups. This helps prevent re-identification of individuals while preserving the usefulness of the data for analysis.
- **Differential Privacy:** Differential privacy adds noise or perturbation to the dataset, making it difficult to identify individual records or extract sensitive information. This technique provides a quantifiable measure of privacy protection and helps protect against re-identification attacks.

Encryption Techniques

- **Secure Communication:** Encryption is applied to the communication channels between the drone and the ground control station to protect data transmission. Secure protocols like SSL/TLS ensure that the data is encrypted during transit, preventing unauthorized access or eavesdropping.
- **Data-at-Rest Encryption:** Drone data stored on internal storage devices or external servers should be encrypted to protect against unauthorized access in case of physical theft or data breaches. Strong encryption algorithms and secure key management practices should be employed to ensure the confidentiality and integrity of the stored data.
- **End-to-End Encryption:** End-to-end encryption provides protection to the data throughout its entire lifecycle, from collection to storage and transmission. This ensures that only authorized parties with the proper encryption keys can access and decrypt the data.
- **Homomorphic Encryption:** Homomorphic encryption allows for computations on encrypted data without requiring decryption, providing a way to perform operations on sensitive data while preserving privacy. This technique can be useful when performing analysis on drone data while keeping it encrypted.
- **Access Control and Encryption Key Management:** Access control mechanisms should be implemented to control who can access the encrypted data. Strong encryption key management practices, such as key rotation, secure key storage, and access controls for encryption keys, are vital to maintain the integrity and security of the encrypted data.

Anonymization and encryption techniques significantly improve data privacy and protection in AI-based drones. These techniques minimize re-identification, unauthorized access, and data breaches while enabling analysis and insights. It's crucial to apply these techniques in compliance with privacy regulations and regularly assess their effectiveness in protecting sensitive information.

CYBERSECURITY FOR AI-BASED DRONES

Cybersecurity for AI-based drones requires secure communication channels and protection against hacking and unauthorised access, as illustrated in Figure 2.

Figure 2. Cybersecurity for AI-based drones

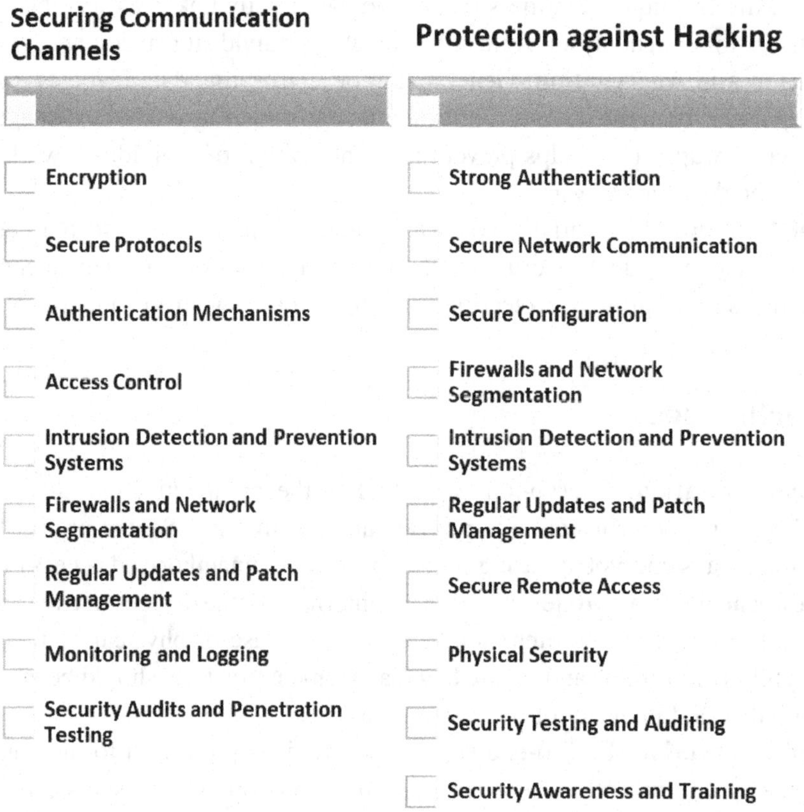

Securing Communication Channels	Protection against Hacking
Encryption	Strong Authentication
Secure Protocols	Secure Network Communication
Authentication Mechanisms	Secure Configuration
Access Control	Firewalls and Network Segmentation
Intrusion Detection and Prevention Systems	Intrusion Detection and Prevention Systems
Firewalls and Network Segmentation	Regular Updates and Patch Management
Regular Updates and Patch Management	Secure Remote Access
Monitoring and Logging	Physical Security
Security Audits and Penetration Testing	Security Testing and Auditing
	Security Awareness and Training

Securing Communication Channels

Cybersecurity for AI-based drones requires secure communication channels between the drone and ground control station to prevent unauthorized access, data interception, and manipulation (Pooyandeh et al., 2022).

- **Encryption:** Encrypting the communication channels between the drone and the ground control station is essential to protect the confidentiality and integrity of the transmitted data. Strong encryption algorithms, such as AES (Advanced Encryption Standard), should be used to encrypt the data in transit. This prevents unauthorized individuals from intercepting and understanding the transmitted information.

- **Secure Protocols:** Utilize secure communication protocols, such as Secure Socket Layer/Transport Layer Security (SSL/TLS), to establish a secure and encrypted connection between the drone and the ground control station. These protocols provide secure authentication, data encryption, and integrity verification to protect against unauthorized access and data tampering.
- **Authentication Mechanisms:** Implement robust authentication mechanisms to ensure that only authorized entities can establish a connection with the drone. This can include password-based authentication, digital certificates, or token-based authentication. Two-factor authentication can add an extra layer of security by requiring multiple forms of verification.
- **Access Control:** Restrict access to the drone's control systems and communication channels to authorized personnel only. Use access control mechanisms, such as role-based access control (RBAC), to enforce proper user privileges and prevent unauthorized individuals from accessing the drone's communication channels.
- **Intrusion Detection and Prevention Systems:** Deploy intrusion detection and prevention systems (IDPS) to monitor the communication channels for any suspicious activities or attempts to compromise the security of the drone. IDPS can detect and alert against potential cyber threats, such as network intrusions, malware, or unauthorized access attempts.
- **Firewalls and Network Segmentation:** Implement firewalls and network segmentation to separate the drone's communication network from other networks. Firewalls help filter and control network traffic, while network segmentation ensures that the drone's communication channels are isolated from other potentially insecure networks, reducing the attack surface.
- **Regular Updates and Patch Management:** Keep the drone's communication systems up to date with the latest security patches and updates. Regularly update the firmware and software of the drone's communication components to address any identified vulnerabilities and ensure that known security weaknesses are remediated.
- **Monitoring and Logging:** Monitor and log network traffic and communication activities to detect any abnormal or suspicious behavior. Centralized logging and real-time monitoring systems enable timely detection and response to potential security incidents.
- **Security Audits and Penetration Testing:** Conduct regular security audits and penetration testing to identify vulnerabilities in the drone's communication channels. This helps identify potential weaknesses and allows for proactive measures to be taken to mitigate security risks.

Implementing cybersecurity measures to secure AI-based drone communication channels ensures data integrity and confidentiality, preventing unauthorized access, data interception, and manipulation, ensuring overall security and trustworthiness in drone operations.

Protection against Hacking and Unauthorized Access

Cybersecurity for AI-based drones involves safeguarding against hacking and unauthorized access to prevent malicious actors from gaining control or accessing sensitive data (Kumar & Mohanty, 2021).

- **Strong Authentication**: Implement strong authentication mechanisms to ensure that only authorized personnel can access the drone's control systems and data. This may include the use of complex passwords, two-factor authentication, or biometric authentication methods. Strong authentication helps prevent unauthorized individuals from gaining access to the drone.

- **Secure Network Communication**: Employ secure communication protocols, such as Secure Shell (SSH) or Virtual Private Networks (VPNs), for remote access and communication with the drone's control systems. These protocols establish encrypted and authenticated connections, protecting against eavesdropping and unauthorized access.
- **Secure Configuration**: Configure the drone's systems and network components securely. Change default passwords, disable unnecessary services and ports, and apply the principle of least privilege to limit access privileges to essential functions only. Regularly update firmware and software to patch known vulnerabilities.
- **Firewalls and Network Segmentation**: Utilize firewalls to monitor and control incoming and outgoing network traffic. Implement network segmentation to isolate the drone's control systems from other networks, preventing unauthorized access from other devices or systems.
- **Intrusion Detection and Prevention Systems**: Deploy intrusion detection and prevention systems (IDPS) to monitor the drone's network traffic for suspicious activities. IDPS can detect and alert against potential intrusion attempts, malware infections, or unauthorized access. Real-time monitoring helps identify and respond to security incidents promptly.
- **Regular Updates and Patch Management**: Keep the drone's software, firmware, and operating systems up to date with the latest security patches and updates. Regularly check for vulnerabilities and apply patches to address any identified security weaknesses.
- **Secure Remote Access**: If remote access to the drone's control systems is necessary, implement secure remote access solutions. This may include VPNs, secure remote desktop protocols, or secure remote management tools. Use strong encryption and authentication mechanisms to protect remote access connections.
- **Physical Security**: Protect the physical access to the drone's hardware and control systems. Ensure that physical access points, such as ports and connectors, are secure and inaccessible to unauthorized individuals. Store the drone in a secure location when not in use.
- **Security Testing and Auditing**: Conduct regular security testing, vulnerability assessments, and penetration testing to identify weaknesses in the drone's systems and infrastructure. Engage third-party security experts to evaluate the drone's security posture and identify potential vulnerabilities that may be missed internally.
- **Security Awareness and Training**: Educate drone operators and personnel about cybersecurity best practices, including strong password management, recognizing phishing attacks, and avoiding suspicious downloads or attachments. Regular training and awareness programs help cultivate a security-conscious culture and reduce the risk of human errors or insider threats.

Implementing cybersecurity measures protects AI-based drones from hacking and unauthorized access, mitigating malicious risks. Proactive measures ensure integrity, confidentiality, and availability, while ongoing vigilance protects sensitive data.

Software and Firmware Updates

Cybersecurity for AI-based drones requires timely and secure software and firmware updates to address vulnerabilities, patch security flaws, and maintain system security (Ferrag et al., 2021).

- Regularly update the drone's software and firmware, staying informed about security patches and updates from manufacturers or vendors. Apply updates promptly to ensure the drone runs on secure, stable versions.
- Implement a robust patch management process for secure software and firmware updates, identifying vulnerabilities, assessing impact, testing in controlled environments, and deploying them promptly.
- Verify software and firmware updates' authenticity by downloading from official sources or trusted repositories, and verifying digital signatures or checksums to prevent tampering or malicious software installation.
- Secure distribution channels for software and firmware updates use encrypted connections or trusted servers, ensuring no compromise during transit and reducing the risk of malware or unauthorized modifications.
- Stay connected with drone manufacturers and software vendors for security updates, patches, and vulnerabilities. Engage with support channels for guidance, assistance, and resolving issues related to updating and resolving issues.
- Perform controlled environment testing before deploying software and firmware updates to ensure compatibility with drone hardware and systems. Check for adverse effects on performance, functionality, and critical components.
- Implement rollback procedures and maintain backups of previous software and firmware versions to restore functionality and mitigate risks in case of issues or failures after updates.
- Conduct regular security audits and vulnerability assessments to identify drone software and firmware weaknesses, involving professionals or independent auditors to evaluate security posture, identify vulnerabilities, and recommend mitigation measures.
- Educate drone operators and personnel on the significance of software and firmware updates in cybersecurity, fostering a culture of awareness and emphasizing their role in protecting against evolving threats and vulnerabilities.

AI-based drones can maintain robust security by following software and firmware updates, addressing vulnerabilities and protecting against emerging threats. Regular updates enhance cybersecurity, reliability, performance, and functionality.

Intrusion Detection and Response

Cybersecurity for AI-based drones involves intrusion detection and response mechanisms to detect and respond to potential security breaches. Key considerations include identifying suspicious activities, unauthorized access attempts, and anomalous behavior, ensuring a secure and reliable drone (Kharchenko et al., 2022; van Waveren et al., 2023).

- Deploy intrusion detection systems to monitor the drone's network traffic and systems for potential security breaches. IDS can analyze network packets, log files, and system behavior to detect patterns or indicators of malicious activities. IDS can be signature-based, behavior-based, or anomaly-based, and they generate alerts or notifications when suspicious activities are detected.

- Continuously monitor the drone's network, communication channels, and systems in real time to promptly detect and respond to potential intrusions. Monitor logs, network traffic, system events, and other relevant indicators to identify any abnormal or unauthorized activities.

- Security Information and Event Management (SIEM): Implement a SIEM system to collect and analyze security events from various sources within the drone's infrastructure. SIEM enables the correlation of events and logs, providing a centralized view of the security landscape. It helps detect patterns, identify potential threats, and initiate appropriate response actions.

- Integrate threat intelligence feeds into the intrusion detection and response systems. These feeds provide up-to-date information about known threats, attack vectors, and malicious indicators. Leveraging threat intelligence enhances the capability to detect and respond to emerging threats effectively.

- Develop an incident response plan that outlines the steps to be taken in the event of a security incident. Define roles and responsibilities, establish communication channels, and specify the actions to be taken to mitigate and recover from a security breach. Regularly test and update the incident response plan to ensure its effectiveness.

- Implement automated response mechanisms to minimize the impact of security incidents. Automated actions can include isolating compromised systems, blocking malicious IP addresses, or shutting down unauthorized access attempts. Automated responses can be based on predefined rules or triggered by specific security events.

- Conduct forensic analysis following a security incident to understand the nature and extent of the breach, identify the attack vectors, and gather evidence for further investigation. Forensic analysis helps in understanding the attack's impact and strengthening defenses to prevent similar incidents in the future.

- Educate drone operators and personnel about the importance of intrusion detection and response, and train them on recognizing and reporting potential security incidents. Foster a culture of cybersecurity awareness and encourage a proactive approach to security monitoring and incident response.

- Conduct regular security assessments, vulnerability scanning, and penetration testing to identify potential weaknesses in the drone's systems and infrastructure. Engage security professionals or independent auditors to evaluate the effectiveness of intrusion detection and response mechanisms and recommend improvements.

AI-based drones utilize robust intrusion detection and response mechanisms to quickly identify and respond to security breaches, reducing cyber attacks' impact. This enhances system security, protects sensitive data, and ensures safe operation in smart city environments.

ENSURING PHYSICAL SAFETY OF DRONES

Collision Avoidance Systems and Sensors

To ensure drone safety, collision avoidance systems and sensors are implemented to detect and prevent potential collisions with objects or obstacles in flight paths (Altawy & Youssef, 2017; Galvane et al.,

2018). These systems play a crucial role in preventing accidents and ensuring safe drone operation as shown in Figure 3.

Figure 3. Collision avoidance systems and sensors

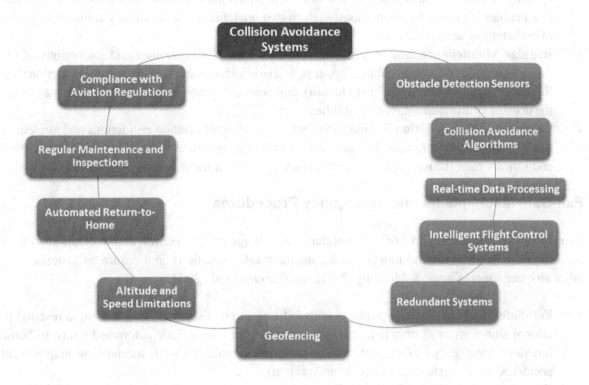

- **Obstacle Detection Sensors:** Drones can use obstacle detection sensors like cameras, lidar, radar, or ultrasonics to provide real-time data on their surroundings, detecting objects or obstacles in the flight path.
- **Collision Avoidance Algorithms:** Implement collision avoidance algorithms using obstacle detection sensors to analyze data and adjust drone's path, speed, or altitude.
- **Real-time Data Processing:** Real-time sensor data processing in the drone's collision avoidance system enables timely decision-making and responsiveness to dynamic environments and unexpected obstacles.
- **Intelligent Flight Control Systems:** Integrate collision avoidance systems with drone's flight control systems, allowing autonomously adjusted trajectory and speed based on detected obstacles, reducing collision risk.
- **Redundant Systems:** Require redundant obstacle detection and collision avoidance systems to improve reliability and reduce system failure risk. Redundancy ensures backup mechanisms for monitoring and avoiding obstacles in case of failure.
- **Geofencing:** Geofencing techniques create virtual boundaries or no-fly zones for drones, preventing them from entering restricted areas and reducing collision risks with critical infrastructure, sensitive locations, or manned aircraft.

- **Altitude and Speed Limitations:** Set altitude and speed limitations for drones to ensure safe operation and reduce the risk of collisions. Establishing maximum altitude and speed limits helps maintain a safe separation between drones and other objects in the airspace.
- **Automated Return-to-Home:** Implement an automated return-to-home function in the drone's system to ensure safe navigation in case of critical situations or loss of communication. This feature enables the drone to autonomously return to a predefined safe location, minimizing the risk of collisions or accidents.
- **Regular Maintenance and Inspections:** Conduct regular maintenance and inspections of the drone's sensors, collision avoidance systems, and overall hardware to ensure proper functionality. Regular calibration and testing help identify any potential issues or malfunctions that may affect the drone's collision avoidance capabilities.
- **Compliance with Aviation Regulations:** Adhere to relevant aviation regulations and guidelines that govern drone operations. Compliance ensures that the drone's collision avoidance systems and sensors meet the required standards and are operated in a safe and responsible manner.

Fail-Safe Mechanisms and Emergency Procedures

Drones' physical safety requires fail-safe mechanisms, emergency procedures, and integration with air traffic management systems to mitigate risks, maintain safe operations, and ensure coexistence with other airspace users (Kumar & Mohanty, 2021; van Waveren et al., 2023).

- **Fail-Safe Mechanisms**: Equip drones with fail-safe mechanisms that enable them to respond to critical situations or system failures. These mechanisms can include automated return-to-home functions, emergency landing protocols, or parachute systems. Fail-safe mechanisms help prevent accidents and mitigate risks to people and property.
- **Emergency Procedures**: Establish clear emergency procedures for drone operators to follow in case of unexpected situations, such as loss of control, battery failure, or communication disruptions. These procedures should outline the appropriate actions to take to minimize risks and ensure the safe recovery or landing of the drone.
- **Integration with Air Traffic Management Systems**: Facilitate integration between drones and air traffic management systems to ensure the safe integration of drones into airspace shared with manned aircraft. Collaborative efforts between drones and traditional air traffic control systems can help establish communication protocols, traffic flow management, and airspace allocation to prevent collisions and maintain safe operations.
- **Communication and Information Exchange**: Enable communication and information exchange between drones and air traffic management systems to enhance situational awareness. This can include sharing real-time position data, flight plans, or status updates to ensure effective coordination and avoidance of potential conflicts with other airspace users.
- **Compliance with Aviation Regulations**: Adhere to aviation regulations and guidelines governing drone operations, including those related to airspace usage, altitude restrictions, flight paths, and operational limitations. Compliance with these regulations ensures that drones operate within defined safety parameters and adhere to the established rules and procedures.
- **Collision Avoidance Systems**: Implement robust collision avoidance systems and sensors, as discussed earlier, to detect and avoid potential collisions with objects or other aircraft. Integration

of these systems with air traffic management systems allows for coordinated collision avoidance measures and enhances overall airspace safety.

- **Pilot Training and Certification**: Ensure that drone operators undergo appropriate training and certification programs that cover airspace regulations, emergency procedures, collision avoidance techniques, and safe operating practices. Well-trained operators have a better understanding of safety considerations and can make informed decisions to prevent accidents.
- **Continuous Monitoring and Assessment**: Continuously monitor and assess the performance and effectiveness of fail-safe mechanisms, emergency procedures, and integration with air traffic management systems. Regular evaluation helps identify any shortcomings, update procedures as needed, and improve the overall safety of drone operations.

Addressing Ethical Implications

Addressing ethical implications in AI-based drones involves considerations such as fairness and bias in AI algorithms, accountability and transparency, and adherence to legal and ethical frameworks for drone operations. By addressing these aspects, the ethical challenges associated with the use of AI-based drones can be mitigated (Kumar & Mohanty, 2021; McEnroe et al., 2022).

- Ensure fair AI algorithms in drones by regularly evaluating and auditing algorithms, implementing techniques like data augmentation, diverse training data, and algorithmic fairness measures, and establishing guidelines for handling biased data.
- Establish accountability and transparency in AI-based drone decision-making processes by defining responsible parties, providing explanations, and documenting data, algorithms, and decisions. This helps build trust and facilitates better understanding and scrutiny.
- Adhere to legal and ethical frameworks for drone operations in smart cities. Familiarize yourself with regulations, privacy laws, aviation laws, and guidelines. Establish internal policies and procedures that cover data protection, privacy rights, human rights, and ethical considerations. Engage with stakeholders to address concerns and conflicts.
- Ethical impact assessments evaluate AI-based drone operations, considering privacy, human rights, safety, social impact, and biases. Engage diverse stakeholders, inform drone development, identify risks, and implement mitigation measures.

Case Study: Zipline - Medical Supply Delivery in Rwanda

Zipline successfully uses AI-based drones for secure medical supply delivery in Rwanda, transporting essentials like blood and vaccines to remote areas with limited healthcare access (Gangwal et al., 2019; Griffith et al., 2023; Mateen et al., 2020).

Secure Communication: Zipline utilizes secure communication channels between the ground control station and the drones, ensuring the confidentiality and integrity of the data transmitted during the delivery process.

Collision Avoidance Systems: The drones are equipped with advanced collision avoidance systems that use sensors and AI algorithms to detect and avoid obstacles in their flight path, ensuring the physical safety of the drones and the people on the ground.

Regulatory Compliance: Zipline works closely with regulatory authorities to obtain the necessary permits and comply with aviation regulations, ensuring the safe and legal operation of their drones. Compliance with regulations contributes to maintaining security standards and minimizing risks.

Robust Data Privacy and Protection: Zipline prioritizes data privacy and protection. They anonymize and encrypt sensitive data, ensuring the confidentiality and integrity of medical information during transportation. They also adhere to data retention and deletion policies to comply with privacy regulations.

Redundancy and Fail-Safe Mechanisms: Zipline incorporates redundancy in their systems, including backup drones and multiple communication channels, to ensure uninterrupted operations and mitigate risks in case of system failures or emergencies.

Best Practices

- Secure AI drone implementation requires collaboration among stakeholders, including operators, regulators, cybersecurity experts, and community representatives.
- Implement robust security architecture with communication protocols, encryption, intrusion detection, and access controls for drone protection.
- Regular security assessments, vulnerability scanning, and penetration testing help identify and address system weaknesses, maintaining a strong security posture.
- Train drone operators, ground staff on cybersecurity best practices, incident response, data privacy, fostering security-conscious behavior.
- Continuously monitor drone systems, software, firmware, and apply security patches and updates to enhance system security.
- Integrate ethical considerations in AI-based drone design, operation, ensuring fairness, transparency, and accountability.

Case study highlights holistic approach for secure AI-based drone implementation, involving technical, regulatory, and ethical considerations to harness potential in smart city environments (Gangwal et al., 2019).

CONCLUSION

AI-based drones in smart cities offer benefits but raise security, ethical, and safety concerns. This chapter explores data privacy, cybersecurity risks, physical safety, ethical implications, and legal frameworks for secure usage.

- AI drones face security challenges like cyber threats, data breaches, and unauthorized access; measures include encryption, intrusion detection, and audits.
- Drone data privacy requires practices like anonymization, encryption, informed consent, secure storage, and compliance with regulations, ensuring responsible handling and safeguarding sensitive data.
- AI-based drones face cybersecurity risks, including securing communication channels, protecting against hacking, and ensuring system integrity. Strong authentication, encryption, network segmentation, and continuous monitoring are crucial to mitigate these risks.

- Physical safety of drones requires collision avoidance, obstacle detection, fail-safe mechanisms, integration with air traffic management, compliance with aviation regulations, regular maintenance, and emergency procedures for safe operations.
- Ethical implications of AI-based drones require fairness, accountability, transparency, and adherence to legal frameworks. Ethical impact assessments, stakeholder engagement, and training promote responsible use.

Future Directions and Challenges

AI-based drones in smart cities face challenges in standardization, advanced AI capabilities, interoperability, public acceptance, regulatory adaptation, and ethical AI development. Standardization promotes consistency and interoperability among systems and operators, while advanced AI algorithms and machine learning techniques enhance drone operations. Interoperability and integration are crucial for safe and efficient operations. Public acceptance and trust require transparent communication, addressing privacy, safety, and security concerns. Regulatory adaptation requires balancing innovation with public safety and security.

AI-based drones in smart cities require a multidimensional approach involving technological advancements, regulatory frameworks, ethical considerations, and stakeholder collaboration to ensure safety, security, and well-being.

ACRONYMS

PII - Personally Identifiable Information
SSL - Secure Socket Layer
TLS - Transport Layer Security
RBAC - Role-Based Access Control
IDPS - Intrusion Detection and Prevention Systems
SIEM - Security Information and Event Management
VPN - Virtual Private Network
AI - Artificial Intelligence
UAV - Unmanned Aerial Vehicle
Lidar - Light Detection and Ranging
AES - Advanced Encryption Standard
IDS - Intrusion Detection Systems

REFERENCES

Alqurashi, F. A., Alsolami, F., Abdel-Khalek, S., Sayed Ali, E., & Saeed, R. A. (2022). Machine learning techniques in internet of UAVs for smart cities applications. *Journal of Intelligent & Fuzzy Systems*, *42*(4), 3203–3226. doi:10.3233/JIFS-211009

Altawy, R., & Youssef, A. M. (2017). Security, privacy, and safety aspects of civilian drones: A survey. *ACM Transactions on Cyber-Physical Systems*, *1*(2), 1–25. doi:10.1145/3001836

Bentotahewa, V., Hewage, C., & Williams, J. (2021). Solutions to Big Data Privacy and Security Challenges Associated With COVID-19 Surveillance Systems. *Frontiers in Big Data*, *4*, 645204. doi:10.3389/fdata.2021.645204 PMID:34977562

Chen, Y. J., & Wang, L. C. (2019). Privacy protection for internet of drones: A network coding approach. *IEEE Internet of Things Journal*, *6*(2), 1719–1730. doi:10.1109/JIOT.2018.2875065

Do, H. T., Truong, L. H., Nguyen, M. T., Chien, C. F., Tran, H. T., Hua, H. T., Nguyen, C. V., Nguyen, H. T. T., & Nguyen, N. T. T. (2021). Energy-Efficient Unmanned Aerial Vehicle (UAV) Surveillance Utilizing Artificial Intelligence (AI). *Wireless Communications and Mobile Computing*, *2021*, 1–11. doi:10.1155/2021/8615367

Ferrag, M. A., Friha, O., Maglaras, L., Janicke, H., & Shu, L. (2021). Federated Deep Learning for Cyber Security in the Internet of Things: Concepts, Applications, and Experimental Analysis. *IEEE Access : Practical Innovations, Open Solutions*, *9*, 138509–138542. doi:10.1109/ACCESS.2021.3118642

Finn, R. L., & Wright, D. (2016). Privacy, data protection and ethics for civil drone practice: A survey of industry, regulators and civil society organisations. *Computer Law & Security Report*, *32*(4), 577–586. doi:10.1016/j.clsr.2016.05.010

Galvane, Q., Lino, C., Christie, M., Fleureau, J., Servant, F., Tariolle, F. L., & Guillotel, P. (2018). Directing cinematographic drones. *ACM Transactions on Graphics*, *37*(3), 1–18. doi:10.1145/3181975

Gangwal, A., Jain, A., & Mohanta, S. (2019). Blood Delivery by Drones: A Case Study on Zipline. *International Journal of Innovative Research in Science, Engineering and Technology*, *8*(8), 8760–8766.

Griffith, E. F., Schurer, J. M., Mawindo, B., Kwibuka, R., Turibyarive, T., & Amuguni, J. H. (2023). The Use of Drones to Deliver Rift Valley Fever Vaccines in Rwanda: Perceptions and Recommendations. *Vaccines*, *11*(3), 605. doi:10.3390/vaccines11030605 PMID:36992189

Haider, M., Ahmed, I., & Rawat, D. B. (2022). Cyber Threats and Cybersecurity Reassessed in UAV-assisted Cyber Physical Systems. *International Conference on Ubiquitous and Future Networks, ICUFN, 2022-July*, 222–227. 10.1109/ICUFN55119.2022.9829584

Kharchenko, V., Illiashenko, O., Fesenko, H., & Babeshko, I. (2022). AI Cybersecurity Assurance for Autonomous Transport Systems: Scenario, Model, and IMECA-Based Analysis. *Communications in Computer and Information Science*, *1689 CCIS*, 66–79. doi:10.1007/978-3-031-20215-5_6

Kumar, C. R. S., & Mohanty, S. (2021). Current trends in cyber security for drones. *Proceedings - International Carnahan Conference on Security Technology, 2021-October*, 1–5. 10.1109/ICCST49569.2021.9717376

Lv, Z., Qiao, L., Hossain, M. S., & Choi, B. J. (2021). Analysis of Using Blockchain to Protect the Privacy of Drone Big Data. *IEEE Network*, *35*(1), 44–49. doi:10.1109/MNET.011.2000154

Mateen, F. J., Leung, K. H. B., Vogel, A. C., Cissé, A. F., & Chan, T. C. Y. (2020). A drone delivery network for antiepileptic drugs: A framework and modelling case study in a low-income country. *Transactions of the Royal Society of Tropical Medicine and Hygiene, 114*(4), 308–314. doi:10.1093/trstmh/trz131 PMID:31943110

McEnroe, P., Wang, S., & Liyanage, M. (2022). A Survey on the Convergence of Edge Computing and AI for UAVs: Opportunities and Challenges. *IEEE Internet of Things Journal, 9*(17), 15435–15459. doi:10.1109/JIOT.2022.3176400

Mohammed, F., Idries, A., Mohamed, N., Al-Jaroodi, J., & Jawhar, I. (2014). UAVs for smart cities: Opportunities and challenges. *2014 International Conference on Unmanned Aircraft Systems, ICUAS 2014 - Conference Proceedings*, 267–273. 10.1109/ICUAS.2014.6842265

Nandutu, I., Atemkeng, M., & Okouma, P. (2023). Integrating AI ethics in wildlife conservation AI systems in South Africa: A review, challenges, and future research agenda. *AI & Society, 38*(1), 245–257. doi:10.100700146-021-01285-y

Pooyandeh, M., Han, K. J., & Sohn, I. (2022). Cybersecurity in the AI-Based Metaverse: A Survey. *Applied Sciences (Basel, Switzerland), 12*(24), 12993. doi:10.3390/app122412993

Rawat, B., Bist, A. S., Apriani, D., Permadi, N. I., & Nabila, E. A. (2022). AI Based Drones for Security Concerns in Smart Cities. [ATM]. *APTISI Transactions on Management, 7*(2), 125–130. doi:10.33050/atm.v7i2.1834

van Waveren, S., Rudling, R., Leite, I., Jensfelt, P., & Pek, C. (2023). Increasing Perceived Safety in Motion Planning for Human-Drone Interaction. *Proceedings of the 2023 ACM/IEEE International Conference on Human-Robot Interaction*, 446–455. 10.1145/3568162.3576966

Vashisth, A., Singh Batth, R., & Ward, R. (2021). Existing Path Planning Techniques in Unmanned Aerial Vehicles (UAVs): A Systematic Review. *Proceedings of 2nd IEEE International Conference on Computational Intelligence and Knowledge Economy, ICCIKE 2021*, 366–372. 10.1109/ICCIKE51210.2021.9410787

Yahuza, M., Idris, M. Y. I., Ahmedy, I., Wahab, A. W. A., Nandy, T., Noor, N. M., & Bala, A. (2021). Internet of Drones Security and Privacy Issues: Taxonomy and Open Challenges. *IEEE Access : Practical Innovations, Open Solutions, 9*, 57243–57270. doi:10.1109/ACCESS.2021.3072030

Yang, W., Wang, S., Yin, X., Wang, X., & Hu, J. (2022). A Review on Security Issues and Solutions of the Internet of Drones. *IEEE Open Journal of the Computer Society, 3*, 96–110. doi:10.1109/OJCS.2022.3183003

Yu, S., & Carroll, F. (2021). Implications of AI in National Security: Understanding the Security Issues and Ethical Challenges. In *Advanced Sciences and Technologies for Security Applications* (pp. 157–175). Springer. doi:10.1007/978-3-030-88040-8_6

Chapter 3
Transformation Human Resource Management Using Advanced Business Analytics

Rashi Shukla

Rama University, Kanpur, India

ABSTRACT

In recent years, the business landscape has experienced significant shifts due to technological advancements and the abundance of data. These changes have not spared human resource management (HRM), as it too has undergone a profound transformation. Capitalizing on the integration of advanced business analytics techniques with HRM practices, organizations have gained invaluable insights to optimize their workforce management, augmented decision-making processes, and elevated overall organizational performance. This chapter embarks on an exploration of the boundless potential that advanced business analytics holds for HRM. It delves into a comprehensive examination of the diverse applications of advanced analytics techniques, encompassing predictive analytics, prescriptive analytics, and machine learning, within HRM processes, thereby discerning their profound impact on organizational outcomes. Additionally, the chapter elucidates the intricacies of implementing advanced analytics in HRM, elucidating both the challenges that may arise and the opportunities that lie ahead.

INTRODUCTION

Definition of Transformation in Human Resource Management

Transformation Human Resource Management (THRM) refers to the process of implementing significant changes to traditional HR practices within an organization. It involves the adoption of new technologies, systems, and strategies that are designed to enhance the efficiency and effectiveness of HR operations. THRM is a critical aspect of organizational development, as it helps businesses adapt to changing market conditions and remain competitive. In this article, we will explore the key principles and practices of THRM and how they can be applied to achieve organizational success (Cooke & Saini, 2010). Example:

DOI: 10.4018/978-1-6684-9151-5.ch003

An example of THRM would be a company that decides to implement a new HRIS (Human Resource Information System) to streamline their HR processes. This system would allow employees to access their personal information and benefits online, reducing the workload of HR staff and improving overall efficiency. The company could also implement a performance management system that provides real-time feedback and coaching to employees, enabling them to develop their skills and contribute more effectively to the organization. These changes would not only enhance the employee experience but also improve the company's bottom line by reducing costs and increasing productivity. However, if the new technologies and systems are not properly integrated or if employees are not adequately trained on their use, they may actually hinder HR operations and create more problems than solutions. For example, if the HRIS is not properly maintained or updated, it may lead to inaccuracies in employee records or delays in processing time-off requests. Similarly, if employees do not receive adequate training on the performance management system, they may feel overwhelmed and confused by the new process, leading to lower morale and productivity.

The Importance of Advanced Business Analytics in HR

Another example of THRM is the use of advanced business analytics in HR. With the help of analytics tools, HR professionals can gather and analyze data on various aspects of employee performance, such as attendance, productivity, and engagement. This data can then be used to identify trends and patterns as well as develop strategies for improving employee performance and retention. For instance, analytics can help HR teams identify which employees are at risk of leaving the organization and take proactive steps to retain them. They can also help identify areas where employees may improve their performance. Overall, the use of advanced business analytics in HR can lead to more informed decision-making and, ultimately, better outcomes for both employees and the organization as a whole. need additional training or support, and to provide targeted interventions. However, a detailed counterexample could be that relying too heavily on data and analytics may overlook the human element of HR. Data can be biased or incomplete, and decisions based solely on data may not take into account individual circumstances or emotions. Additionally, employees may feel uncomfortable or devalued if their performance is reduced to numbers and metrics. Therefore, it is important for HR professionals to balance the use of advanced analytics with empathy and understanding toward employees.

Purpose of the HR Analytics

HR analytics is not to replace human judgment but rather to enhance it. By leveraging data and analytics, HR professionals can gain deeper insights into workforce trends and patterns, which can inform strategic planning and resource allocation. For example, analytics can help identify which departments or teams are experiencing high turnover rates and enable HR to take proactive measures to address the underlying causes. Similarly, analytics can help identify skills gaps and training needs, allowing HR to design targeted learning and development programs that improve employee performance and retention. Ultimately, the purpose of HR analytics is to drive better business outcomes by empowering HR professionals with the insights and tools they need to make informed decisions that positively impact the organization and its employees. For instance, HR analytics can help identify top-performing employees and determine the best ways to reward and retain them, such as by offering career development opportunities or competitive compensation packages.

ADVANCED BUSINESS ANALYTICS IN HR

Definition and Explanation of Advanced Business Analytics

Advanced business analytics in HR refers to the use of advanced statistical and machine learning techniques to analyze complex data sets related to HR functions. This includes analyzing data on employee demographics, performance, engagement, turnover, and compensation, among others. Advanced business analytics goes beyond traditional HR analytics by using predictive modeling and data mining to identify patterns and trends that may not be immediately apparent ("HR Analytics Methodical Measurement of Hr Processes," 2021; Nolan, 2011). By using these advanced techniques, HR professionals can make more accurate predictions and identify opportunities for improvement that may have been missed using traditional methods. The goal of advanced business analytics in HR is to provide HR professionals with the tools and insights they need to make data-driven decisions that can lead to improved business outcomes.

For example, advanced business analytics in HR can help organizations identify the root causes of high turnover rates and develop targeted retention strategies. By analyzing data on employee demographics, performance, engagement, and compensation, HR professionals can identify patterns and trends that may be contributing to turnover. They can then use this information to develop more effective retention programs, such as by offering career development opportunities or adjusting compensation packages to better align with market standards.

The Importance of Advanced Business Analytics in HR

Another area where advanced business analytics in HR can be beneficial is in predicting future workforce needs. By analyzing data on current workforce demographics, skills, and performance, HR professionals can identify potential gaps in the workforce and develop strategies to address them before they become a problem (Schwalje, 2012). This can include identifying areas where additional training or recruitment may be necessary or even predicting which employees are most likely to leave the organization in the near future and developing strategies to retain them. Overall, advanced business analytics in HR is a powerful tool for organizations looking to make data-driven decisions and improve their overall business outcomes. For instance, using advanced business analytics in marketing can help companies target their advertisements to specific demographics. By analyzing data such as customer age, location, and interests, businesses can create personalized ads that are more likely to resonate with their target audience. They can also track the success of their ads in real-time and adjust their strategies accordingly. This approach has been particularly effective in the e-commerce industry, where personalized product recommendations based on customer data have been shown to increase conversion rates and drive sales.

Benefits of Advanced Business Analytics in HR

Extend beyond just recruitment and retention. One area where it can be particularly useful is in identifying patterns of employee behavior that may indicate potential issues with workplace culture or management practices. By analyzing data such as employee survey responses, turnover rates, and performance metrics, organizations can gain insights into areas where they may need to make improvements to create a more positive and productive work environment (Sev, 2017). This can lead to higher levels of employee engagement and satisfaction and, ultimately, better business outcomes. Additionally, advanced business analytics can help HR professionals identify the most effective training and development programs for their employees based on data-driven insights into employee skill gaps and performance. For example, a company may use data analysis to identify which employees struggle with a particular task or process and then tailor training programs to address those specific needs. This can result in more efficient and effective training, leading to improved job performance and increased productivity.

TRANSFORMATIONAL HR USING ADVANCED BUSINESS ANALYTICS

Can also enable organizations to make data-driven decisions about workforce planning and resource allocation. By analyzing data on employee performance, turnover, and other factors, HR professionals can identify areas where additional resources or staffing may be needed, as well as areas where they may be able to reallocate resources to improve overall efficiency (Snell, 2007). This can help organizations better align their workforce with their business goals and objectives, ultimately leading to improved performance and profitability. Furthermore, advanced business analytics can help HR professionals track and measure the impact of their initiatives over time, allowing them to continuously refine and improve their strategies for maximum impact. Overall

Definition and Explanation of Transformational HR Using Advanced Business Analytics

Transformational HR using advanced business analytics refers to the use of data-driven insights to transform HR practices and strategies (DiClaudio, 2019). This approach involves leveraging data analytics tools and techniques to gain a deeper understanding of the workforce, identify areas for improvement, and make data-driven decisions about talent management. By harnessing the power of advanced business analytics, HR professionals can gain a competitive advantage by improving recruitment, retention, training, and resource allocation. This ultimately leads to improved performance, productivity, and profitability for the organization.

Role of Advanced Business Analytics in Transformational HR

Advanced business analytics play a crucial role in the transformation of HR practices by providing HR professionals with real-time data and insights that can inform their decision-making. With the help of advanced analytics tools, HR professionals can analyze large volumes of data to identify patterns, trends, and correlations that can help them make data-driven decisions about talent management. This includes everything from identifying the most effective recruitment channels to understanding which training programs are most effective for different employee groups. By leveraging advanced business analytics, HR professionals can create a more agile and responsive HR function that is better able to meet the needs of the organization and its employees (Gupta, 2020).

For example, a HR team may use advanced analytics to analyze their recruitment process and identify areas for improvement. They may find that certain job postings are not attracting the right candidates or that certain recruitment channels are more effective than others. With this information, they can make data-driven decisions to improve their recruitment strategy and attract top talent. Additionally, they may use analytics to identify which training programs are most effective for different employee groups, leading to improved employee performance and retention. However, relying solely on data-driven decision-making can lead to overlooking important qualitative factors such as cultural fit and individual preferences, which can ultimately impact employee satisfaction and retention. Overall, while advanced analytics tools can provide valuable insights and help HR professionals make data-driven decisions, it is important to balance this with qualitative factors and individual preferences to ensure a well-rounded approach to talent management.

Benefits of Transformational HR using Advanced Business Analytics

Furthermore, HR professionals can also use advanced analytics to gain a deeper understanding of employee engagement and sentiment. By analyzing data from employee surveys, social media, and other sources, HR teams can identify trends and patterns in employee feedback and take action to address any areas of concern. This can lead to improved employee satisfaction and a more positive workplace culture. In addition, analytics can help HR professionals predict future workforce needs and identify potential skill gaps, allowing them to proactively develop talent and plan for future growth. Overall, the use of advanced business analytics in HR can lead to a more efficient, effective, and strategic approach to talent management.

For example, a company may use analytics tools to analyze employee feedback and identify patterns of dissatisfaction related to the company's culture. They may discover that employees value a strong sense of community and collaboration but feel that the company's current policies and practices do not support these values. HR professionals can then take action to address these concerns, such as implementing team-building activities or revising policies to better align with employee preferences. This can lead to increased employee satisfaction and retention, ultimately improving the company's bottom line (Kotamena et al., 2021). However, it is important to note that analytics can also perpetuate biases and lead to discriminatory hiring practices if not used properly. For example, if HR teams rely solely on analytics to determine which candidates to hire, they may unintentionally exclude diverse candidates who do not fit into a predetermined mold based on previous hiring patterns.

HOW TO IMPLEMENT TRANSFORMATIONAL HR USING ADVANCED BUSINESS ANALYTICS

Implementing transformational HR using advanced business analytics requires a thoughtful and strategic approach. First, HR teams must ensure that they have access to high-quality data and analytics tools that can provide meaningful insights into the workforce. This may require investing in new technology or partnering with external vendors who specialize in HR analytics. Next, HR professionals must work closely with other departments, such as IT and finance, to ensure that they have the resources and support needed to implement data-driven initiatives. Finally, HR teams must be prepared to adapt and evolve their strategies over time as new data becomes available and business needs change (Chatrakul Na Ayudhya et al., 2015). By taking Steps to Implement Transformational HR Using Advanced Business Analytics Organizations can unlock the full potential of their workforce and create a more diverse and inclusive workplace. It is important to note that while analytics can be a valuable tool in the hiring process, it should not be the sole determining factor. HR teams must also consider other factors such as cultural fit, soft skills, and potential for growth when making hiring decisions. By combining data-driven insights with a holistic approach to talent management, organizations can create a workforce that is both high-performing and inclusive. For example, a company may use HR analytics to identify patterns in employee turnover and determine the underlying causes. They may discover that a lack of career development opportunities is causing employees to leave and use this insight to create new training and advancement programs. Additionally, they may partner with IT to implement a new HR information system that allows for real-time tracking of employee performance and engagement, enabling them to proactively address potential issues before they become major problems.

Key Considerations before Implementing Transformational HR Using Advanced Business Analytics include ensuring data privacy and security, establishing clear goals and objectives, and providing adequate training and support for HR teams to effectively utilize analytics tools. It is also important to involve stakeholders from across the organization, including senior leadership, to ensure buy-in and alignment with the overall strategy. By carefully considering these factors and leveraging the power of advanced analytics, HR teams can drive meaningful change and unlock the full potential of their workforce. For example, a company may use HR analytics to identify patterns in employee turnover and determine the underlying causes. They may discover that a lack of career development opportunities is causing employees to leave and use this insight to create new training and advancement programs. Additionally, they may partner with IT to implement a new HR information system that allows for real-time tracking of employee performance and engagement, enabling them to proactively address potential issues before they become major problems ("Remote Workforce, Virtual Team Tasks, and Employee Engagement Tools in a Real-Time Interoperable Decentralized Metaverse," 2022). Best Practices for Implementing Transformational HR Using Advanced Business Analyticsinclude establishing a strong data governance framework, selecting the right analytics tools and technologies, and building a team with the necessary skills and expertise. It is also important to continuously evaluate and refine the analytics strategy to ensure it is delivering the desired outcomes and driving positive change. Ultimately, organizations that successfully leverage advanced analytics in HR will be better equipped to attract, retain, and develop top talent, driving improved performance and business results. For instance, a company may use HR analytics to identify which job positions have the highest turnover rate and what factors contribute to this trend. They may find that low job satisfaction is the leading cause and use this information to improve employee engagement through initiatives like flexible work arrangements and wellness programs (Wheatley, 2016). Moreover, they may partner with external vendors to integrate their HR analytics tools with other business systems, such as finance and operations, to gain a more holistic view of organizational performance.

CHALLENGES AND SOLUTIONS

Challenges in Implementing Transformational HR Using Advanced Business Analytics include data quality and availability issues, resistance to change from employees and stakeholders, and a lack of understanding of how to effectively use analytics to drive decision-making. To overcome these challenges, organizations can invest in data management and governance processes, provide training and education to employees on the benefits of analytics, and engage in change management initiatives to ensure a smooth transition to the new approach. Additionally, partnering with experienced analytics vendors and consultants can provide valuable guidance and support throughout the implementation process. By addressing these challenges head-on, organizations can unlock the full potential of advanced analytics in HR and achieve significant improvements in workforce performance and business outcomes. For example, a company may invest in data cleansing and integration tools to improve the quality and availability of their HR data while also providing training programs that educate employees on how to use analytics to make data-driven decisions. They may also engage in communication campaigns that highlight the benefits of the new approach and address any resistance or concerns from stakeholders. Ultimately, by taking a proactive and strategic approach, organizations can successfully implement transformational HR using advanced analytics and drive positive change throughout their workforce. However, a counterexample to this approach is when organizations rely too heavily on data analytics and overlook the importance of human judgment and intuition in decision-making. This can lead to a lack of diversity in perspectives and potentially biased outcomes. Additionally, data privacy concerns can arise if sensitive employee information is not properly protected and managed.

Solutions to Overcome the Challenges

To mitigate these risks, organizations can establish clear guidelines and policies for the ethical use of data analytics in HR decision-making. This can include involving a diverse range of stakeholders in the analytics process and regularly reviewing and auditing the data to ensure accuracy and fairness. It is also important to invest in robust data security measures and adhere to relevant regulations and compliance standards. By taking a balanced approach that leverages the strengths of both data analytics and human judgment, organizations can effectively navigate these challenges and drive positive outcomes for their workforce and business as a whole. For example, a company may use advanced analytics to identify patterns of employee turnover and develop strategies to retain top talent. They may also launch a communication campaign to address concerns from employees about the new approach and emphasize the benefits of staying with the company. However, if the company solely relies on the data without taking individual circumstances and employee feedback into account, they may end up offering retention incentives to employees who are already planning to leave while neglecting those who are considering leaving for other reasons. This can result in a waste of resources and a failure to address the root causes of turnover.

Benefits to Organizations Using Advanced Business Analytics In HR

One of the key benefits of using advanced business analytics in HR is the ability to identify trends and patterns in employee data that may not be immediately apparent through other means. For example, analytics can help identify specific groups of employees that may be at higher risk of turnover or disengagement, allowing organizations to implement targeted interventions to address those issues. Additionally, analytics can help organizations track the effectiveness of various HR initiatives and identify areas for improvement, leading to more informed decision-making and better outcomes overall. Ultimately, the use of advanced business analytics in HR can help organizations optimize their workforce and improve employee retention, engagement, and productivity. For instance, a company may use data to analyze the impact of offering wellness programs on employee health and well-being, resulting in decreased absenteeism and increased job satisfaction. However, there is a risk of relying too heavily on data and overlooking the importance of individualized approaches. For example, if an organization solely relies on data to determine promotions or pay raises, it may overlook the unique skills and contributions of each employee and create a demotivating work environment. Additionally, there may be ethical concerns around the collection and use of employee data, such as privacy violations or discrimination. It is important for organizations to consider these potential challenges and approach the use of advanced business analytics in HR with caution and a balanced perspective, taking into account both the benefits and potential drawbacks. Overall, when used appropriately, advanced business analytics can be a powerful tool for optimizing HR practices and improving organizational outcomes (McCartney & Fu, 2022).

The Future of HR With Advanced Business Analytics

To mitigate these risks, organizations can combine data-driven insights with a human-centered approach that values individual experiences and perspectives. For example, HR professionals can use data to identify trends and patterns in employee feedback but also engage in open and honest conversations with employees to better understand their needs and preferences. Additionally, organizations can establish clear guidelines and protocols for data collection, storage, and use to ensure that employee privacy is protected and ethical standards are upheld. By leveraging the strengths of both data analytics and human expertise, organizations can create a more inclusive and effective HR strategy that drives success for both employees and the business as a whole. For instance, a company could use advanced business analytics to track employee performance and identify areas for improvement, but then work with individual employees to develop personalized development plans that align with their goals and interests. This approach not only helps the organization achieve its objectives but also fosters a culture of trust and collaboration among employees. However, a counterexample to this approach can be seen in instances where organizations prioritize data over human experiences and perspectives. This can lead to a lack of empathy and understanding towards employees, resulting in disengagement and decreased morale (Jackson & Culbertson, 2013). For example, if an organization solely relies on data to assess employee performance without taking individual circumstances or subjective factors into account, it may lead to demotivation and dissatisfaction among employees who feel their efforts are not recognized or valued. In conclusion, the future of HR lies in the integration of advanced business analytics with a human-centered approach. By combining data-driven insights with open and honest conversations with employees, organizations can create a more inclusive and effective HR strategy that drives success for both employees and the business as a whole. However, it is important for organizations to prioritize human experiences and perspectives over data to avoid disengagement and decreased morale among employees. By striking a balance between data analytics and human expertise, organizations can foster a culture of collaboration and trust and ultimately achieve their goals while empowering their workforce.

CONCLUSION

In conclusion, the use of advanced business analytics in HR decision-making can bring significant benefits to organizations, including increased efficiency, improved decision-making, and enhanced employee experiences. However, it is important to recognize and address the potential challenges and risks associated with this approach, such as data privacy concerns and the need for human judgment and individualized approaches. By adopting a balanced and ethical approach to data analytics, organizations can drive positive outcomes for their workforce and business as a whole. It is clear that transformational HR using advanced business analytics is an essential component of modern HR practices, and organizations that embrace this approach are better equipped to succeed in today's rapidly changing business environment. For instance, a company that uses advanced analytics to analyze employee engagement data can identify areas where employees are dissatisfied and implement targeted interventions to address those issues.

This can lead to increased employee satisfaction, reduced turnover, and improved business outcomes overall. Ultimately, the use of advanced business analytics in HR is a powerful tool for organizations looking to optimize their workforce and stay ahead of the competition. However, it is important to note that relying solely on data analytics can also lead to oversimplified solutions and a lack of consideration for individual employee needs and experiences. For example, a company may use data to determine that offering more flexible work hours will increase employee retention but fail to recognize that some employees may prefer more structure in their schedules. It is crucial for organizations to balance the insights gained from data with human judgment and personalized approaches in order to truly enhance the employee experience and drive positive business outcomes. In conclusion, while the use of advanced business analytics in HR can bring numerous benefits, it is important for organizations to approach it in a balanced and ethical manner. This involves recognizing and addressing potential challenges and risks while also leveraging the insights gained from data to drive positive outcomes for both the workforce and the business as a whole. By balancing data with human judgment and individualized approaches, organizations can optimize their workforce and stay ahead of the competition.

REFERENCES

Chatrakul Na Ayudhya, U., Prouska, R., & Lewis, S. (2015, July 13). Work-life balance can benefit business during financial crisis and austerity. *Human Resource Management International Digest*, *23*(5), 25–28. doi:10.1108/HRMID-05-2015-0078

Cooke, F. L., & Saini, D. S. (2010, May). (How) Does the HR strategy support an innovation oriented business strategy? An investigation of institutional context and organizational practices in Indian firms. *Human Resource Management*, *49*(3), 377–400. doi:10.1002/hrm.20356

DiClaudio, M. (2019, April 8). People analytics and the rise of HR: How data, analytics and emerging technology can transform human resources (HR) into a profit center. *Strategic HR Review*, *18*(2), 42–46. doi:10.1108/SHR-11-2018-0096

Gupta, M. (2020, April 20). HR Analytics: Trend from Data to Predictive Analysis for HR Professionals. *International Journal of Psychosocial Rehabilitation*, *24*(5), 2674–2682. doi:10.37200/IJPR/V24I5/PR201969

Hr, A. M. M. O. H. P. (2021, January 1). HR Analytics Methodical Measurement Of Hr Processes. *Elementary Education Online*, *20*(1). Advance online publication. doi:10.17051/ilkonline.2021.01.713

Jackson, A., & Culbertson, S. (2013). Bad employees or bad policies: What can organizations do to stop misuse of information technology resources? *The Academy of Management Perspectives*, *27*(1). Advance online publication. doi:10.5465/amp.2013.0026

Kotamena, F., Senjaya, P., Putri, R. S., & Andika, C. B. (2021, March 14). Competence or communication: from HR professionals to employee performance via employee satisfaction. *Jurnal Manajemen Dan Kewirausahaan*, *22*(1), 33–44. doi:10.9744/jmk.22.1.33-44

McCartney, S., & Fu, N. (2022, January 12). Bridging the gap: Why, how and when HR analytics can impact organizational performance. *Management Decision*, *60*(13), 25–47. doi:10.1108/MD-12-2020-1581

Nolan, S. (2011, February 22). HR analytics. *Strategic HR Review*, *10*(2). Advance online publication. doi:10.1108hr.2011.37210baa.001

Normalini, R., Ramayah, T., & Kurnia, S. (2012, July 20). Antecedents and outcomes of human resource information system (HRIS) use. *International Journal of Productivity and Performance Management*, *61*(6), 603–623. doi:10.1108/17410401211249184

Remote Workforce, Virtual Team Tasks, and Employee Engagement Tools in a Real-Time Interoperable Decentralized Metaverse. (2022). *Psychosociological Issues in Human Resource Management*, *10*(1), 78. doi:10.22381/pihrm10120226

Schwalje, W. (2012). Rethinking How Establishment Skills Surveys Can More Effectively Identify Workforce Skills Gaps. SSRN *Electronic Journal*. doi:10.2139/ssrn.2017556

Sev, J. T. (2017, January 25). Stress Management Strategies: An Approach For Productive Employee Performance In The Nigerian Banking Organizations A Survey Of Commercial Banking Firms In Nigeria. *Archives of Business Research*, *5*(1). Advance online publication. doi:10.14738/abr.51.2526

Snell, A. (2007, January 1). Measuring the financial impact of HR: Defining and controlling the areas where HR adds cost and value. *Strategic HR Review*, *6*(2), 28–31. doi:10.1108/14754390780000954

Wheatley, D. (2016, April 1). Employee satisfaction and use of flexible working arrangements. *Work, Employment and Society*, *31*(4), 567–585. doi:10.1177/0950017016631447

Chapter 4
Solar Radiation Analysis for Predicting Climate Change Using Deep Learning Techniques

Rajendra Kumar
Rama University, Kanpur, India

ABSTRACT

Solar radiation, Earth's main energy source, affects surface radiation balance, hydrological cycles, plant photosynthesis, weather, and climatic extremes. A stacking model based on the best of 12 machine learning models predicted and compared daily and monthly sun radiation levels. The results suggest machine learning algorithms use climatic parameters. A trend study of high land surface temperatures and solar radiation showed how solar radiation compounds catastrophic climatic events. GBRT, XG Boost, GPR, and random forest models better predicted daily and monthly sun radiation. The stacking model, which comprises the GBRT, XG Boost, GPR, and random forest models, exceeded the single models in daily solar radiation prediction but did not outperform the XGBoost model in monthly prediction. Stacking and XG Boost models estimate sun radiation best.

INTRODUCTION

The largest source of energy on Earth is solar radiation, and the quantity of solar radiation reaching the Earth's surface is influenced by the atmosphere, hydrosphere, and biosphere (Budyko, 1969; Islam et al., 2009). Solar radiation also plays an important influence in global climate, and even little variations in the Sun's energy output induce significant changes in the Earth's temperature (Beer et al., 2010; Siingh et al., 2011). The Sun's irradiance has the largest impact on Earth's high atmosphere, while the lower atmosphere protects the planet from the increasing heat. If the Sun is causing Earth's warming, one would anticipate the upper atmosphere to get more heated. Variations in solar radiation influence global temperatures, global mean sea level, and the occurrence of severe weather events

DOI: 10.4018/978-1-6684-9151-5.ch004

(Bhargawa & Singh, 2019). These variables are accountable for climate change. Accurate measurements and assessments of solar radiation's temporal and geographical variability are therefore critical in research on solar energy, construction materials, and severe weather and climate events (Cline et al., 1998; Garland et al., 1990; Grant & Tuohimaa, 2004; Hoogenboom, 2000). The warming caused by growing quantities of man-made greenhouse gases is several times higher than any impacts caused by recent fluctuations in solar activity. Many approaches for predicting solar radiation have been developed, including theoretical parameter models, empirical models, artificial intelligence algorithms, and satellite retrieval data (Halabi et al., 2018; Li et al., 2008; Lu et al., 2011; Makade et al., 2019; Mellit, 2008; Wild, 2009). The A-P model, initially suggested by Angstrom (1924) and Prescott (1940), is commonly used to estimate solar radiation. The BCM model was developed by Bristow and Campbell (1984) by examining the connection between solar radiation and daily maximum and minimum temperatures. Yang et al. (2001) created a hybrid model (YHM) to improve the A-P model by investigating the influence of meteorological factors before evaluating the model's accuracy in Japan. Salazar (2011) contrasted the YHM with a climatological solar radiation model to determine the horizontal direct and diffuse components of solar radiation, resulting in the CYHM (corrected YHM). Gueymard (2003) investigated sun irradiance forecasts using 19 solar radiation models, indicating that detailed transmittance models outperform bulk models. Many academics have been motivated by the advancement of machine learning algorithms to create solar radiation prediction models (Azadeh et al., 2009; Chen et al., 2011; Jiang, 2009; Voyant et al., 2012). Fadare (2009) and Linares-Rodrguez et al. (2011) built solar radiation prediction models using artificial neural network (ANN) technology and tested their predictive capacity. Xue (2017) developed a solar radiation prediction model using a back-propagation algorithm and demonstrated that the forecast accuracy was dependent on the combination and configuration of the input parameters. Chen et al. (2011) built a solar radiation prediction model utilizing the support vector machine (SVM) approach and demonstrated that the SVM-based algorithm had varying predicted accuracy while employing various kernel functions. Both Olatomiwa et al. (2015) and Shamshirband et al. (2016) optimized the SVM algorithm and produced accurate predictions. Tree techniques, such as the random forest approach and the gradient boosting regression tree (GBRT), have been utilized to build solar radiation prediction models with promising results (Fan et al., 2018; Persson et al., 2017; Sun et al., 2016; Zeng et al., 2020). Some researchers have conducted comparative analyses of a range of machine learning algorithms in recent years (Meenal & Selvakumar, 2018; Pang et al., 2020; Shamshirband et al., 2016), and all of these studies reveal that the ANN algorithm does not provide excellent prediction outcomes but does suggest a path for algorithm development. Deep learning algorithms have been used in several research to estimate solar radiation. Shamshir Rahman et al. (2019), for example, analyze several forms of deep learning algorithms used in the area of solar, and the findings demonstrate that hybrid networks outperform single networks. Mishra et al. (2020) suggested and got excellent results using a short-term solar radiation prediction model based on WT-LSTM, demonstrating that deep learning technology has significant promise in solar radiation. Gao et al. (2020) propose a CEEMDAN-CNN-LSTM model for hourly multi-region solar irradiance estimation, and the results show that the model can achieve more accurate prediction performance than existing models.

Machine learning has had notable success as an investigative tool in a variety of fields, including natural language processing and image recognition (Angra & Ahuja, 2017).

Figure 1. The geographical location of solar radiation monitoring station in India

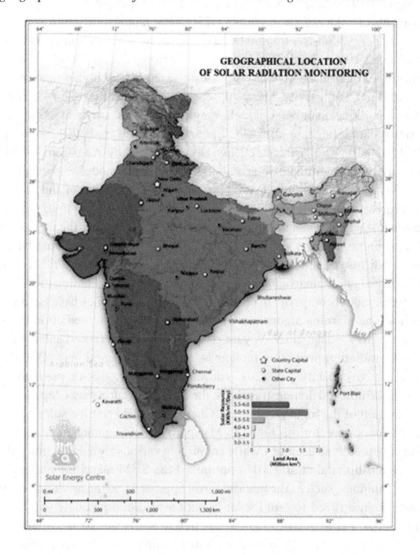

Machine learning has risen to prominence in the development of solar radiation models and is a major study area. However, many researchers have concentrated on the development of one or more machine learning approaches, and there have been few in-depth examinations of the distinctions between these models. To investigate the differences in solar radiation forecast models, we utilized a daily dataset of meteorological elements and fundamental radiation elements for India and China from 1980 to 2016. Following data processing, we used the random forest technique to chosen variables and retrieved a monthly dataset from the daily dataset. We used 12 machine learning approaches to build a solar radiation forecast model. We discovered the top solar radiation prediction methods by comparing the forecast outcomes of these 12 machine learning models. The models with the strongest prediction abilities were then layered in a linear model. A stack model was created, and the projected outcomes were examined.

Figure 2. The frame work of the stacking model

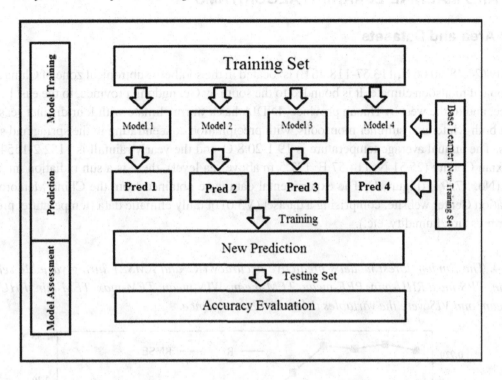

Figure 3. Flow chart of the machine learning models used to estimate solar radiation

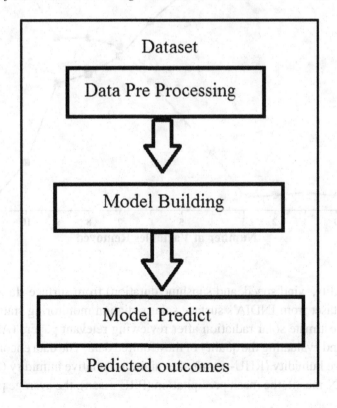

DATA AND MACHINE LEARNING ALGORITHMS

Study Area and Datasets

India city (24.48-30.06 N, 113.57-118.46 E) is located in the southern subtropical zone of China and has a subtropical monsoon climate. It is bounded to the south by Guangdong province, to the east by Fujian province, and to the west by Hunan province. INDIA has a warm climate with four distinct seasons including both winter and summer monsoons, with precipitation concentrating in the spring and summer seasons. The annual average temperature is 19.1-20.8 C, and the yearly rainfall is 1152.2-1554.9 mm. In Ganxian County (25.51 N, 114.57 E, 137.5 m above sea level), there is a sun radiation monitoring station (No. 57993) (Figure 1). The experimental data were obtained from the China Meteorological Information Center website, comprising a dataset (V3.0) of daily climatic data (temperature, precipitation, air pressure, humidity, etc.).

Figure 4. The random forest model's predictive accuracy (R2 and RMSE) during variable selection. PRS-min, PRS-max, RHU-min, PRE-mean, TEM-mean, WIN-mean, TEM-max, TEM-min, RHU-mean, PRS-mean, and VIS were the variables deleted in that sequence.

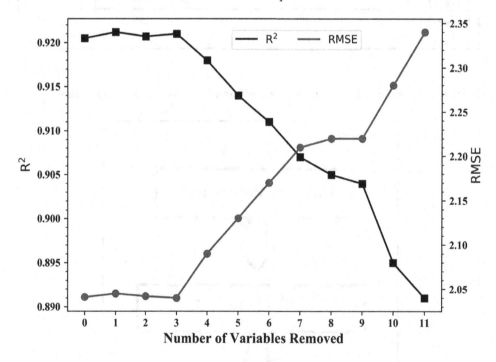

Temperature, visibility, wind speed, and sunshine duration) from surface stations in China, as well as a daily radiation dataset from INDIA's surface solar radiation monitoring station. We selected data from 1980 to 2016 to estimate solar radiation after reviewing relevant papers (Angra & Ahuja, 2017; Jiang & Wang, 2017) and evaluating the quality of the acquired data. The data encompassed the visibility (VIS), the mean relative humidity (RHU-mean), the minimum relative humidity (RHU-min), the mean speed of the wind (WIN-mean), the mean precipitation (PRE-mean), the average pressure (PRS-mean), the highest pressure (PRS-max), the minimum pressure (PRS-min), the sunshine duration (SSD), the average temperature (TEM-mean), the maximum temperature (TEM-max), the minimum temperature (TEM-min),

Given the duration of the research period and the inherent inaccuracies in instrument-based observations, data quality control was critical. We removed missing and anomalous values from the meteorological data before applying the standards for solar radiation data quality control suggested by Younes et al. (2005). There were 13,100 daily data recordings and 432 monthly average data records collected in total. The dataset was then separated into training and test sets and normalized, with the training set accounting for 90% of total data and the test set accounting for 10%. There were 11,790 per day training sets, 1,310 daily test sets, 388 monthly training sets, and 44 monthly test sets in our final sample.

Prediction of the Flow of Solar Radiation

Our experiment was divided into three sections (Figure 3): data preparation, model construction, and model prediction. Data preparation included four steps: data quality check, dataset splitting, data scaling, and variable selection. Data quality control, dataset segmentation, and data scaling are all covered in Section "Study Area and Datasets," while variable selection is covered in Section "Variable Selection." The following were the primary model-building processes: algorithm selection, parameter selection, model creation, and model saving. In the parameter selection stage, we employed the 10-fold cross-validation approach (Jiang & Wang, 2017). We may get a thorough description of the model building under Section "Model Building." In the model prediction stage, the stored model from the model construction step was utilized to estimate solar radiation using the test dataset. Then we store the projected findings and analysis. The particular experimental stages were as follows:

(1) Gather and preprocess data;
(2) Choose a machine learning method from the 12 available to forecast solar radiation;
(3) Compare solar radiation predicting abilities based on various factors;
(4) Save the model if the greatest prediction ability is attained.
(5) Return to step (2) and choose another machine learning algorithm, repeating this process until all 12 methods have been exposed to machine learning model development.
(6) Input the preprocessing dataset (we produced daily and monthly datasets to measure the solar radiation prediction performance of the 12 machine learning models) and utilize the 12 stored machine learning models to forecast solar radiation and get the anticipated results;
(7) Save predicted results and analyze.

Variable Selection

The parameter selection stage is critical for building machine learning models. The genetic algorithm (Huang et al., 2015), the Tabu search (Corazza et al., 2013), particle swarm optimization (Khatibi Bardsiri et al., 2013), and the random forest algorithm (Kapwata & Gebreslasie, 2016) are the current popular variable selection techniques. We chose data variables using the random forest technique (Zeng et al., 2020). Normalized daily data were utilized to build and train the random forest model, as well as to determine the model's significance.

The data preprocessing experiment was designed to validate the relevance of variables in a given model and to investigate the influence of variable modifications on the model's predictive performance. The experiment went as follows:

(1) After finishing the data quality control procedure, split the dataset into a training set and a test set;

(2) use the training set to train and store the model, then compute the correlation coefficient (R2) and root mean square error (RMSE) of the saved model;

(3) Remove the least important variable depending on the order of relevance of the variables in the model;

(4) Repeat procedures (2) and (3) until there are only two variables left (the bare minimum for computation).

Model Building

Experiments were carried out in Python 3.6 with the use of third-party libraries such as Pandas, NumPy, the scikit-learn machine learning library (Sklearn), and the Xgb library. The models were built using twelve machine learning methods. Each algorithm's initial parameter values were established based on the algorithm's properties. For example, the number of hidden layers and neurons in a neural network model were established using empirical calculations and neural network design principles (Basheer & Hajmeer, 2000). The parameter adjustment techniques for distinct machine learning algorithms were then used to establish the relevant selection ranges of the adjustment parameters and other parameters. To choose parameters for each of the 12 machine learning models, we utilized Sklearn's Grid Search CV approach, finally saving the best model. The initial layer of the stacking model is made up of numerous models with high predictive potential. The first layer model's parameters are the parameters chosen before, while the second layer is built using repeated linear regressions. The train set was used to train the model after determining the optimal parameters, and the final model was stored. The model creation time is the time spent training the model, and the final model size is the model memory. When the model was built, the test set was used to get the forecast result.

RESULTS

Description and Selection of Variables

The RAD had an average yearly range of 1-30.48 MJ/m2, with a mean of 12.02 MJ/m2 and a standard deviation of 6.28 MJ/m2 (Table 1). The yearly mean (standard deviation) data were VIS 16.02 (6.21) km, RHU-mean 74.46 (11.04)%, WIN-mean 1.45 (0.78) m/s, PRE-mean 39.5 (98.9) mm, PRS- mean 999.51 (4.86) hPa, TEM-mean 19.66 (4.46)∘C, TEM- max 24.28 (5.46)∘C, TEM-min 16.39 (4.2)∘C, GST-mean 22.29 (5.56)∘C, and SSD 4.79 (3.92) h. Aside from the RHU-mean, PRE-mean, and PRS-mean, the variable mean values were greatest in summer, followed by spring and autumn, and lowest in winter.

Predictive Performance for Daily Solar Radiation

Figure 5 depicts how the 12 machine learning models performed in forecasting solar radiation for the provided daily dataset. According to the statistical data, the majority of the machine learning models utilized to estimate solar radiation produced good results. The 12 machine learning models' R2 scores varied from 0.840 to 0.930. The top machine learning models for predicting solar radiation were the GBRT, GPR, XGBoost, and random forest models, with R2 values of 0.930, 0.9255, 0.924, and 0.923, respectively. The extreme learning machine and decision tree models had R2 values of 0.876 and 0.840, respectively, indicating that these models had the lowest accuracy for predicting solar radiation. The RMSE values of the 12 machine learning models ranged from 1.989 to 2.997 MJ/m2. The GBRT model has the lowest RMSE (1.989 MJ/m2) value.

Figure 5. Description and selection of variables

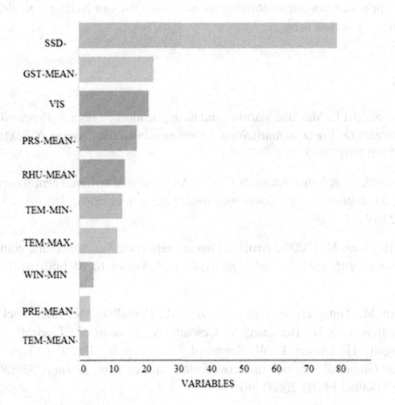

CONCLUSION

We used meteorological components and solar radiation data to do data preprocessing and variable selection for the INDIA station in China from 1995 to 2022. Then, 12 machine learning models were developed using Sklearn and the Xgb library. The XGBoost, GPR, GBRT, and random forest models were chosen as the first layer, and multiple linear regression was chosen as the second layer, to construct a stacking model to predict solar radiation using R2, RMSE, MAE, and BIAS indices to compare and evaluate the predictive ability of the 12 machine learning models.

The SSD was determined as the most critical variable after using the random forest climate change technique to pick the variables. From 1995 to 2022, the time series of the yearly maximum GST-mean and the accompanying sun radiation value revealed that the maximum GTS-max rises with solar radiation, confirming the relevance of solar radiation in compound severe climatic events. For the daily and monthly datasets, the GBRT, XGBoost, random forest, and GPR models outperformed the other models. The GBRT model predicted the most accurately for daily datasets, whereas the XGBoost model predicted the most accurately for monthly datasets. The random forest climate change model took the longest to build, followed by the GBRT and GPR models, while the XGBoost model took the quickest. This behavior is connected to the model principles.

The daily solar radiation climate change prediction model enhanced the stacking model's prediction abilities, but the monthly model performed badly, which might be attributed to insufficient monthly training data. We determined that the XGBoost model is the best solar radiation climate change value prediction model, while we recommend utilizing the stacking fusion or XGBoost model to develop the model when the quantity of data is big.

REFERENCES

Angra, S., & Ahuja, S. (2017). Machine learning and its applications: a review. *Proceedings of the 2017 International Conference On Big Data Analytics and Computational Intelligence, ICBDACI 2017*, 57–60. 10.1109/ICBDACI.2017.8070809

Azadeh, A., Maghsoudi, A., & Sohrabkhani, S. (2009). An integrated artificial neural networks approach for predicting global radiation. *Energy Conversion and Management*, *50*(6), 1497–1505. doi:10.1016/j. enconman.2009.02.019

Basheer, I. A., & Hajmeer, M. (2000). Artificial neural networks: Fundamentals, computing, design, and application. *Journal of Microbiological Methods*, *43*(1), 3–31. doi:10.1016/S0167-7012(00)00201-3 PMID:11084225

Beer, C., Reichstein, M., Tomelleri, E., Ciais, P., Jung, M., Carvalhais, N., Rödenbeck, C., Arain, M. A., Baldocchi, D., Bonan, G. B., Bondeau, A., Cescatti, A., Lasslop, G., Lindroth, A., Lomas, M., Luyssaert, S., Margolis, H., Oleson, K. W., Roupsard, O., ... Papale, D. (2010). Terrestrial gross carbon dioxide uptake: Global distribution and covariation with climate. *Science*, *329*(5993), 834–838. doi:10.1126cience.1184984 PMID:20603496

Bhargawa, A., & Singh, A. K. (2019). Solar irradiance, climatic indicators and climate change – An empirical analysis. *Advances in Space Research*, *64*(1), 271–277. doi:10.1016/j.asr.2019.03.018

Budyko, M. I. (1969). The effect of solar radiation variations on the climate of the Earth. *Tellus. Series A, Dynamic Meterology and Oceanography*, *21*(5), 611–619. doi:10.3402/tellusa.v21i5.10109

Chen, J. L., Liu, H. B., Wu, W., & Xie, D. T. (2011). Estimation of monthly solar radiation from measured temperatures using support vector machines – A case study. *Renewable Energy*, *36*(1), 413–420. doi:10.1016/j.renene.2010.06.024

Cline, D. W., Bales, R. C., & Dozier, J. (1998). Estimating the spatial distribution of snow in mountain basins using remote sensing and energy balance modeling. *Water Resources Research, 34*(5), 1275–1285. doi:10.1029/97WR03755

Corazza, A., Di Martino, S., Ferrucci, F., Gravino, C., Sarro, F., & Mendes, E. (2013). Using tabu search to configure support vector regression for effort estimation. *Empirical Software Engineering, 18*(3), 506–546. doi:10.100710664-011-9187-3

Fan, J., Wang, X., Wu, L., Zhou, H., Zhang, F., Yu, X., Lu, X., & Xiang, Y. (2018). Comparison of support vector machine and extreme gradient boosting for predicting daily global solar radiation using temperature and precipitation in humid subtropical climates: A case study in China. *Energy Conversion and Management, 164*, 102–111. doi:10.1016/j.enconman.2018.02.087

Garland, F. C., Garland, C. F., Gorham, E. D., & Young, J. F. (1990). Geographic variation in breast cancer mortality in the United States: A hypothesis involving exposure to solar radiation. *Preventive Medicine, 19*(6), 614–622. doi:10.1016/0091-7435(90)90058-R PMID:2263572

Grant, W. B., & Tuohimaa, P. (2004). Geographic variation of prostate cancer mortality rates in the United States: Implications for prostate cancer risk related to vitamin D (Beer et al., 2010) (multiple letters). *Int. J. Cancer, 111*, 470–471. doi: .20220 doi:10.1002/ijc

Halabi, L. M., Mekhilef, S., & Hossain, M. (2018). Performance evaluation of hybrid adaptive neuro-fuzzy inference system models for predicting monthly global solar radiation. *Appl. Energy, 213*, 247–261. doi: .01.035 doi:10.1016/j.apenergy.2018

Hoogenboom, G. (2000). Contribution of agrometeorology to the simulation of crop production and its applications. *Agricultural and Forest Meteorology, 103*(1-2), 137–157. doi:10.1016/S0168-1923(00)00108-8

Huang, G., Huang, G. B., Song, S., & You, K. (2015). Trends in extreme learning machines: A review. *Neural Networks, 61*, 32–48. doi:10.1016/j.neunet.2014.10.001 PMID:25462632

Islam, M. D., Kubo, I., Ohadi, M., & Alili, A. A. (2009). Measurement of solar energy radiation in Abu Dhabi, UAE. *Appl. Energy, 86*, 511–515. doi: .apenergy.2008.07.012 doi:10.1016/j

Jiang, G., & Wang, W. (2017). Error estimation based on variance analysis of k-fold cross-validation. *Pattern Recognit., 69*, 94–106. doi: .2017.03.025 doi:10.1016/j.patcog

Jiang, Y. (2009). Computation of monthly mean daily global solar radiation in China using artificial neural networks and comparison with other empirical models. *Energy, 34*(9), 1276–1283. doi:10.1016/j.energy.2009.05.009

Kapwata, T., & Gebreslasie, M. T. (2016). Random forest variable selection in spatial malaria transmission modelling in Mpumalanga Province,South Africa. *Geospatial Health, 11*(3), 251–262. doi:10.4081/gh.2016.434 PMID:27903050

Khatibi Bardsiri, V., Jawawi, D. N. A., Hashim, S. Z. M., & Khatibi, E. (2013). A PSO-based model to increase the accuracy of software development effort estimation. *Software Quality Journal, 21*(3), 501–526. doi:10.100711219-012-9183-x

Li, X., Wang, L., & Sung, E. (2008). AdaBoost with SVM-based component classifiers. *Engineering Applications of Artificial Intelligence, 21*(5), 785–795. doi:10.1016/j.engappai.2007.07.001

Lu, N., Qin, J., Yang, K., & Sun, J. (2011). A simple and efficient algorithm to estimate daily global solar radiation from geostationary satellite data. *Energy, 36*(5), 3179–3188. doi:10.1016/j.energy.2011.03.007

Makade, R. G., Chakrabarti, S., & Jamil, B. (2019). Prediction of global solar radiation using a single empirical model for diversified locations across India. *Urban Climate, 29*, 100492. doi:10.1016/j.uclim.2019.100492

Meenal, R., & Selvakumar, A. I. (2018). Assessment of SVM, empirical and ANN based solar radiation prediction models with most influencing input parameters. *Renewable Energy, 121*, 324–343. doi:10.1016/j.renene.2017.12.005

Mellit, A. (2008). Artificial Intelligence technique for modelling and forecasting of solar radiation data: A review. *Int. J. Artif. Intell. Soft Comput., 1*(1), 52. doi:10.1504/IJAISC.2008.021264

Pang, Z., Niu, F., & O'Neill, Z. (2020). Solar radiation prediction using recurrent neural network and artificial neural network: A case study with comparisons. *Renewable Energy, 156*, 279–289. doi:10.1016/j.renene.2020.04.042

Persson, C., Bacher, P., Shiga, T., & Madsen, H. (2017). Multi-site solar power forecasting using gradient boosted regression trees. *Solar Energy, 150*, 423–436. doi:10.1016/j.solener.2017.04.066

Shamshirband, S., Mohammadi, K., Tong, C. W., Zamani, M., Motamedi, S., & Ch, S. (2016). A hybrid SVM-FFA method for prediction of monthly mean global solar radiation. *Theoretical and Applied Climatology, 125*(1-2), 53–65. doi:10.100700704-015-1482-2

Siingh, D., Singh, R. P., Singh, A. K., Kulkarni, M. N., Gautam, A. S., & Singh, A. K. (2011). Solar activity, lightning and climate. *Surveys in Geophysics, 32*(6), 659–703. doi:10.100710712-011-9127-1

Sun, H., Gui, D., Yan, B., Liu, Y., Liao, W., & Zhu, Y. (2016). Assessing the potential of random forest method for estimating solar radiation using air pollution index. *Energy Convers. Manag., 119*, 121–129. doi: .enconman.2016.04.051 doi:10.1016/j

Voyant, C., Muselli, M., Paoli, C., & Nivet, M. L. (2012). Numerical weather prediction (NWP) and hybrid ARMA/ANN model to predict global radiation. *Energy, 39*(1), 341–355. doi:10.1016/j.energy.2012.01.006

Wild, M. (2009). Global dimming and brightening: A review. *Journal of Geophysical Research, 114*, D00D16. Advance online publication. doi:10.1029/2008JD011470

Zeng, Z., Wang, Z., Gui, K., Yan, X., Gao, M., & Luo, M. (2020). Daily global solar radiation in China estimated from high-density meteorological observations: A random forest model framework. *Earth Space Sci., 7*. doi:10.1029/2019EA001058

Chapter 5
Transformation of Indian MSMEs (Micro, Small, and Medium Enterprises) and Startups Using Advanced HR Analytics

Rashi Dubey

Rama University, India

ABSTRACT

Human resources have always been the company's most significant asset. Employees should be viewed as resources to acquire a competitive edge, and MSMEs (micro, small, and medium enterprises) and startups may succeed in a competitive market by aligning human resource activities with fundamental company objectives. With the advent of technology and the expansion of business, HR analytic tools can now be used to manage personnel and monitor their performance online. The application of HR analytics has enhanced employee performance and boosted corporate efficiency in areas such as recruiting quality, talent management, employee productivity, and employee attrition. Human resource analytics are critical for connecting HR strategy with overall company strategy. HR analytics helps HR managers design strategies that provide startups with a competitive edge. HR analytics, according to a new study, are revolutionizing the human resources department and HR managers.

INTRODUCTION

Human resource management is concerned with maximizing the utilization of people to meet organizational and personal goals. It largely focuses on the tasks of recruiting, managing, and departing in enterprises. HR departments review employee performance and develop new training programs for them in order to keep staff engaged and productivity high. Human resource management originated as a separate profession in the early twentieth century, influenced by Frederick Winslow Taylor (1856-1915).

DOI: 10.4018/978-1-6684-9151-5.ch005

John R. Commons, an American institutional economist, popularized the phrase "human resource" in his book "The Distribution of Wealth," published in 1893. Human resource departments, however, were not founded until the twentieth century to handle the interactions between businesses and workers. Because it is a continual communication process between managers and workers to accomplish Enterprise objectives and enhance employee personnel skills, performance management is an essential part of human resources. The communication process includes defining clear precise expectations, creating objectives, offering ongoing feedback, and reviewing outcomes. Performance management provides a communication channel between a manager and an employee that is maintained throughout the year in the hopes of reaching both organizational and individual objectives.

Examine all of the obtained data and fix performance gaps utilizing the data offered to better understand employee managers. One of the technologies used to acquire such data is HR Analytics. The collecting and utilization of talent data to enhance essential talent is known as human resource analytics. It is generally used to make data-driven choices, such as anticipating staff turnover and recognizing top performers, or predicting skills that need to be developed. HR Analytics is also known as people analytics. It allows your organization to evaluate the influence of HR KPIs on overall business performance and make data-driven choices.

There are four types of HR Analytics:

- Descriptive Statistics
- Diagnostics Analytics
- Predictive Analytics
- Prescriptive Analytics

Descriptive Statistics: Statistics that are descriptive Gathering raw data does not make sense and is not always beneficial, but it may be useful if sorted and structured. Descriptive analysis (also known as observing and reporting) is the most prevalent sort of analysis. It essentially collects all accessible historical data and condenses it into something comprehensible. A headcount of personnel in Enterprises or a single department would be included in Descriptive Analytics. Descriptive analytics also includes more complicated indicators, such as turnover rates. They look at previous data to figure out what happened.

Diagnostic Analytics: Diagnostic analytics explains why something occurred while descriptive analytics tells you what happened. We go beyond what is occurring to see why it is occurring. Make an observation, then determine the descriptive analysis before moving on to the diagnostic analysis. Data drilling and data mining are two diagnostic analytics methodologies. In order to analyze the fundamental reasons and identify solutions, businesses must first understand why issues emerge.

Predictive Analytics: What exactly is Predictive Analytics? Descriptive analytics is based on past data or takes a step back. Predictive analytics anticipates. Various statistical models and projections are utilized in these analytics to anticipate what could happen. The goal of this study is to identify the demands of companies. Patterns uncovered via descriptive analytics are used to build models. It may aid the talent acquisition team in identifying whether an employee is a suitable cultural fit for the Startups by predicting how long an employee will remain in the Enterprises. Following the prediction of the future, the next question is what can be done about it.

Prescriptive Analytics: Prescriptive Analytics produces suggestions based on past and forecasted data. This study is especially beneficial to organizations that experience seasonal demand. For instance, a business could want to determine how many staff to recruit for the holidays. Prescriptive analytics might also help determine how to correctly recruit a new employee based on required skills and expertise, as well as throughout the employee life cycle. You decide what to do based on all of the facts presented on previous levels. What should happen next is indicated by the data itself. Professional HR Analytical tools like as PowerBi, Tableau, SPSS, and Microsoft Excel are employed in today's enterprises.

LITERATURE REVIEW

Keerthi P. Lakshmi and Dr. P. Reddy Raghunadha (2017) in their study Article titled "HR Analytics' - An Efficient Evidence Based HRM Tool," they observed that human resources are important to organizations and should be focused. According to them, the ideal method for an Enterprise to make choices is via an evidence-based approach, and HR Analytics not only aids in this process but also encourages Startups to maintain good data to demonstrate ROI in HR investments.

In their study "HR analytics and performance assessment system: A conceptual framework for employee performance improvement," Sharma Anshu and Sharma Tanuja (2017) discovered the influence of HR analytics on the PA system and its impact on employees' willingness to improve performance by offering a conceptual model. In this situation, HR analytics was used as a solution to increase the accuracy of the assessment process by using expert data analysis tools. This Article, along with other assumptions for performance management academics, provided alternate pathways for future research to further advance this subject.

Dr. Sumathi R. Anita (2019), in their article, "A study on the assessing the factors of HR analytics on performances management in the services sector of chosen organizations in Chennai," they revealed how the performance management system affects employee performance. And how may the different phases of the performance management system influence employee performance? The initial purpose is to investigate the performance management system, as well as the relationship between the two. The second purpose is to use the WERS 2004 dataset to investigate performance management systems and their link to employee performance. The ultimate aim is to identify and suggest the nature of the link between the performance management system and employee performance.

In their research article, "HR Analytics Methodical Measurement of HR Processes," Kailash Udhay and Prathyusha M (2020) discovered that HR Analytics is more important because it assesses how employees contribute to the Enterprises, predicts workforce requirements, and links workforce utilization to strategic goals to improve business performance. In his instance, the HR Analytics technique is well recognized in the pharmaceutical sector and might be replicated by other firms in the same industry.

H.H.D.P.J. Opatha (2020) discovered in their research Article titled "HR Analytics: A Literature Review and New Conceptual Model" that HR analytics provides a data-driven framework for solving workforce problems by analyzing data with a combination of software and methods that apply statistical models, providing new insights for smarter decision making, and allowing managers to optimize human resource management.

Dr. Khan Imran, Dr. Said Muhammad, and Dr. Hameed Filza (2021) observed in their study Article, "The Impact of Performance Management Systems on Employee Performance," that any Enterprise's management should enhance their performance management system practices to make them more continuous. It is suggested that management investigate and investigate employee problems, acknowledge them, and aid workers in addressing them as a unified team. Startups should utilize employee recognition initiatives to promote and motivate employees. Employees strive to meet the objectives because their efforts are valued and recognized. Startups should include their employees in goal creation and reward them for their efforts in meeting those objectives.

Fu Na and McCartney (2022), in their study report titled "Bridging the Gap: Why, How, and When HR Analytics Can Impact Enterprise Performance," observed that HR Analytics is still a new concept and that academics are currently emphasizing how HR analytics may enhance decision making and accomplish Enterprise objectives. This research created a chain model in which access to HR technology allows HR analytics, which encourages Evidence Based Management and so enhances corporate performance.

STATEMENT OF THE ISSUE

HRIS, LMS, ATS, and other comparable systems are brimming with tasty, useful, and regularly up-to-date data. Nonetheless, HR seldom provides high-impact reports to stakeholders. Big Data is the focus on measurements that are too massive to examine. For example, statistics on voluntary vs. involuntary termination. What if the appropriate persons willingly leave? What if the wrong personnel continue to work? Here's another example: EEO statistics are provided to the Department of Labor on an annual basis (for the vast majority of MSME (Micro, Small, and Medium Enterprises) and Startups), but data pertaining to specific managers is also required if an MSME (Micro, Small, and Medium Enterprises) and Startups is charged with discrimination. Is this information verified?

Analytical Skills: In MSME (Micro, Small, and Medium Enterprises) and Startups, the analytical expert is often the CFO, Engineering, or Quality team. Some human resource professionals may opt to concentrate their professional development efforts on enhancing their data analysis and assessment abilities.

Big Data and Not-So-Big Data: If the number of MSME (Micro, Small, and Medium Businesses) and Startups is large, collecting big data on recruiting, training, succession planning, and turnover is straightforward. Small MSME (Micro, Small, and Medium Enterprises) and startups, on the other hand, seldom have access to large data. Analysis and critical thinking regarding smaller data demand various techniques when little samples are used to make big conclusions.

Assessments in Hiring: According to the Department of Labor's Uniform Guidelines on Employee Selection Procedures, all processes/practices used to hire/promote employees must be legitimate. Too frequently, assessments or procedures that have not been internally verified (tests, assessments, interview practices, application screening) are used.

Curiosity: Inquire, "What is the most important thing(s) that needs to be reviewed in order to have an impact on the business and help executives make informed decisions?"

OBJECTIVES OF THE STUDY

- The study's goals are to investigate how HR Analytics helps MSME (Micro, Small, and Medium Enterprises) and Startups manage their performance.
- Understanding the factors that contribute to staff turnover and retention in startups
- Understanding business employee behavior
- Understanding how HR data may be linked to obtain relevant conclusions regarding turnover.
- To take a closer look at how the accuracy of HR data might help you make more accurate decisions.
- To investigate how HR data can aid in improving employee performance.

SIGNIFICANCE/RATIONALE OF THE STUDY

HR analytics help MSME (Micro, Small, and Medium Enterprises) and Startups acquire, retain, and maintain personnel. As a consequence, MSME (Micro, Small, and Medium Businesses) and startups have made significant investments in IT solutions that support a broad range of HR operations, such as manpower planning, recruiting, performance management, legal, employee engagement, and talent development. Analytics has been defined as a 'must have' capacity for the HR profession, a tool for producing value from people, and a means of expanding the HR function's strategic impact (CIPD, 2013). Availability, acquisition, development, and retention of key talent was cited as the most important business challenge their companies face in 2016, regardless of geography, by nearly three-quarters (72%) of CEOs polled by PWC, demonstrating the global significance of delivering business results through talent and validating the importance of HR in business operations PWC 2014. CEOs are reading about it in the business press and placing pressure on their CHROs to learn it. Understanding the business environment, the CHRO has been investing heavily in HR analytics to keep ahead of the competition Deloitte (2016). It is not enough to recognize the need and make investments; it is also important to create a competent ecosystem capable of generating genuine value via the effective and efficient use of analytics. As a consequence, it is vital for MSME (Micro, Small, and Medium Businesses) and Startups to identify the need, acquire relevant technology, and develop the skills necessary to properly use the technology.

SIGNIFICANCE OF HR-ANALYTICS

- Due to its predictive nature, HR analytics assists in identifying and exposing defective practices that become the major cause of attrition, hence aiding in the retention and retention of high-value personnel.
- It allows HR to show efficiency and responsibility in order to meet business goals.
- HR analytics can help you arrange your human resources in the most cost-effective way possible.
- It enables more precise forecasting of labor requirements and skill sets in order to meet the objectives of MSME (Micro, Small, and Medium Enterprises) and Startups.
- It assists in the objective procurement of the finest possible talent for MSME (Micro, Small, and Medium Enterprises) and Startup personnel needs for particular jobs.
- It helps MSME (Micro, Small, and Medium Enterprises) and Startups improve their performance by making better choices, notably in talent acquisition.
- It facilitates in the simple description of essential performance components and bits that may have a major influence on the performance of MSME and Startups.
- HR analytics help with the administration and categorization of all HR tasks.

RECOMMENDATIONS FOR FURTHER RESEARCH

- Increased understanding of exponential technologies has been connected to more effective application of HR analytics in MSME (Micro, Small, and Medium Enterprises) and Startups.
- Adopting modern HR analytics methodologies and technologies may help process and project-based MSME (Micro, Small, and Medium Enterprises) and Startups be more effective.

- User-generated data on social networking sites may be integrated into sophisticated human resource appraisal algorithms.
- Advanced HR analytics may be applied more effectively in MSME and Startups that have a high degree of maturity in terms of business intelligence and integrated reporting methodologies.
- HR analytics may improve employee job engagement and motivation in the workplace.
- HR analytics maturity may be associated with greater MSME (Micro, Small, and Medium Enterprises) and Startups agility and overall operational success.

EXPECTED OUTCOME OF THE STUDY

The study's findings show that HR Analytics can help HR professionals understand business capabilities and develop plans that optimize ability speculations while actually observing and improving in various HR functions such as talent acquisition, employee engagement, performance management, compensation and benefits, and others.

EIGHT EXPECTED OUTCOMES OF THE STUDY

1. Using evidence-based HR practices
2. Improving talent acquisition and recruitment
3. Managing employee performance and productivity
4. Assisting in the development of equitable compensation and benefit packages
5. Making effective workforce planning possible
6. Conducting skill gap analyses is simple.
7. Improving candidate and employee experience by increasing learning and development, up skilling, and re-skilling.
8. Recognizing inefficiencies

HR has a huge impact on company results, and utilising information gives you a competitive edge in corporate decision making. MSME and Startups are developing groups of analytics professionals, fast supplanting old administrative frameworks, and implementing analytics into HR to make better-informed judgments and strategies. Human resource work is now evolving from an administrative role to a collaborative system, meaning that innovation is having a big influence on how HR engages with representatives and partners. The use of analytics, on the other hand, is not new; in the past two years, a growing number of firms have realized that information may assist enhance both HR skills and company processes in general. According to the report, there are many benefits and drawbacks to reforming human resource management using HR analytics, including a lack of interest and support from the company and management. HR Analytics collects and deciphers employee-related data to help them perform better, and HR Analytics handle difficult jobs and assist in the development of future initiatives. Transforming Human Resource Management using HR Analytics has also been found to have a substantial influence on MSME (Micro, Small, and Medium Enterprises) and Startups.

RESEARCH METHODOLOGY

Types of Data

The researcher would use both primary and secondary data to conduct this study and effectively demonstrate its goal.

Primary Source of Data

An open-ended and closed-ended questionnaire, a structured interview, and personnel resumes would be used to gather primary data by the researcher. The questionnaire is delivered to workers in MSME (Micro, Small, and Medium Enterprises) and Startups, and the researcher will conduct interviews and deploy Data Analytics utilizing data supplied by employees for any job in MSME and Startups to analyze, train, and evaluate its efficacy.

Secondary Source of Data

Secondary data sources would be regarded a significant aspect of the research to support the numerous points stated in the study. These data would originate from a variety of sources, including Kaggle, Github, the IIMS research center, MSME, and numerous companies.

Sampling Size and Sampling Techniques

Because the population is so large, the researcher used census techniques as a sampling method in this study to examine the role of employees in MSME and Startups from the specified section and to express their ideas about the importance of training on employee performance for the MSME. The research will concentrate on and split MSME (Micro, Small, and Medium Enterprises) employees into two groups: those who work in startups and those who work in MSMEs.

Method of Data Analysis

In this research, we will use a quantitative, qualitative, and data science approach to assess the influence of training on employee performance at MSME (Micro, Small, and Medium Enterprises) and Startups. The questionnaires that will be sent to respondents will produce quantitative data, and the replies of the managers to the MSME questions will produce qualitative data that will improve this research. I will organize the data gathering in tabular form and interpret all of the data in theoretical form in order to examine this research.

Scope of the Study

The research solely takes into account the influence of training on employee performance in respect to the challenges and possible remedies. Despite the fact that the influence of training on employee performance in MSME (Micro, Small, and Medium Enterprises) and startups may be impacted by a range of circumstances, the research will solely address this impact.

Methodological Scope

The methodological scope will include the use of a census research design, data gathering through primary and secondary data collecting, data interpretation via tabulation and theoretical analysis, and data interpretation via tabulation and theoretical analysis.

CONCLUSION

The facts presented in the study demonstrate that HR Analytics can provide a comprehension of business capacities and assist HR professionals in developing plans that effective and speculations while actually observing and making improvements in various HR functions such as talent acquisition, employee engagement, performance management, compensation and benefits, and several others. HR plays a vital role in corporate outcomes, and leveraging information provides a critical advantage in business decision making. MSME (Micro, Small, and Medium Enterprises) and startups are developing groups of analytics professionals, fast supplanting old administrative frameworks, and incorporating analytics into HR to make better-informed judgements and plans. Human Resource work is currently transitioning from an administrative role to a collaborative system, meaning that innovation is having a big influence on how HR engages with representatives as well as partners. However, the use of analytics is far from new in the last two years, an increasing number of businesses have recognized that information may help to enhance both HR capacities and company processes in general. The study concludes that there are a number of benefits and challenges to transforming human resource management with HR Analytics, such as a lack of interest and support from the business and management, a lack of training skill development programme to handle HR Analytics, HR Analytics gathers and deciphers employee related information and helps them perform better, and HR Analytics carry out complex tasks and help them perform better. It has also been shown that transforming human resource management using HR analytics has a substantial influence on a startups.

REFERENCES

Anita, R., & Sumathi, N. (2019). A study on the measuring the factors of HR analytics on performances management in services sector of selected companies in Chennai. *Journal of Advanced Composition, 12*(12).

Deloitte. (2016). *Global Human Capital Trends 2016. The new MSME (Micro, Small, and Medium Enterprises) and Startups: Different by design.* Author.

Fairhurst, P. (2014). Big data and HR analytics. *IES Perspectives on HR, 2014,* 7–13.

Gardner, N., McGranahan, D., & Wolf, W. (2011). *Question for your HR chief: Are we using our people.* Academic Press.

Kailash & Prathyusha. (2020). HR Analytics Methodical Measurement of HR Processes. *International Journal of Innovative Science and Research Technology, 5*(11).

King, Z. (2010). *Human Capital Reporting: What information counts in the city*. Academic Press.

KPMG. (2015). *Evidence-based HR. The bridge between your people and delivering business strategy*. Author.

Lawler, E. E., Levenson, A., & Boudreau, J. (2004). *HR Metrics and Analytics Uses and Impacts*. Academic Press.

Levenson, A. (2011). Using targeted analytics to improve talent decisions. *People and Strategy, 34*(2), 34.

McCartney, S., & Fu, N. (2022). Bridging the gap: Why, how and when HR analytics can impact Enterprisesal performance. *Management Decision, 60*(13), 25–47. doi:10.1108/MD-12-2020-1581

Opatha. (2020). HR Analytics: A Literature Review and New Conceptual Model. *International Journal of Scientific and Research Publications, 10*(6).

Reddy & Keerthi. (2017). HR Analytics - An Effective Evidence Based HRM Tool. *International Journal of Business and Management Invention, 6*(7).

Said, Khan, & Hameed. (2021). The impact of performance management system on employees' performance. *International Journal of Business and Management Sciences, 2*.

Sharma, A., & Sharma, T. (2017). HR analytics and performance appraisal system: A conceptual framework for employee performance improvement. *Management Research Review, 40*(6), 684–697. doi:10.1108/MRR-04-2016-0084

van Dooren. (2012). *HR Analytics in practice*. Academic Press.

Chapter 6
Smart Street Lighting System for Smart Cities Using IoT (LoRa)

C. V. Suresh Babu
iD https://orcid.org/0000-0002-8474-2882
Hindustan Institute of Technology and Science, India

R. Monika
iD https://orcid.org/0009-0004-2185-597X
Hindustan Institute of Technology and Science, India

T. Dhanusha
iD https://orcid.org/0009-0000-5499-6833
Hindustan Institute of Technology and Science, India

K. Vishnuvaradhanan
iD https://orcid.org/0009-0002-8261-5086
Hindustan Institute of Technology and Science, India

A. Harish
Hindustan Institute of Technology and Science, India

ABSTRACT

Smart street light systems are being used more frequently in modern communities because they offer an effective and economical way to illuminate roads while reducing energy use and carbon emissions. Now, wireless networks can connect to and manage streetlights. With the aid of this technology, streetlights may be remotely monitored and controlled depending on variables such as traffic flow, weather, and the time of day. Energy is used as efficiently as possible, and maintenance costs are decreased. A smart streetlight system powered by IoT and LoRa can improve a city's efficiency and sustainability while also improving the quality of life for its residents. To maximize energy efficiency and reduce maintenance costs, the system may automatically adjust the streetlights' brightness and scheduling based on the data. This chapter provides a LoRa and IoT-based smart streetlight system with a cost-effective solution for modern smart cities.

DOI: 10.4018/978-1-6684-9151-5.ch006

INTRODUCTION

The concept of a "smart street" is to employ technology to enhance urban streets' sustainability, effectiveness, and safety. It is a crucial component of the concept of the smart city, which seeks to use technology to improve urban efficiency, livability, and environmental friendliness. The primary features of smart lights include automated ON-OFF, automatic brightness management, free Wi-Fi, and emergency control. Smart street applications utilizing LoRa technology are a tool for building more livable, sustainable, and effective cities. Cities may raise the standard of living for their citizens by utilizing the power of data and cutting-edge communication technology to increase safety, lessen congestion, and improve quality of life.

A cost-effective and long-lasting solution for street lighting in metropolitan areas that increases safety and lowers energy use and light pollution is a Smart Street Light System for a Smart City using IoT (LoRa) (Suresh Babu, 2023).

The project comprises the installation of a network of IoT-enabled sensors and LoRa communication modules-equipped smart street lights. These sensors may gather data in real-time, such as ambient light levels, traffic patterns, and weather conditions, and send it to a central control system using LoRa wireless communication technology. Depending on the data gathered, the central control system may automatically monitor and manage the street lights, maximizing their functioning and reducing energy waste. It is driven by sophisticated analytics and machine learning techniques.

The smart street light system provides urban areas with a number of advantages. First, by dynamically altering the brightness of the street lights based on real-time data, it may dramatically cut energy consumption, resulting in significant energy savings and a smaller carbon footprint. By automatically recognising aberrant activity, such as accidents or vandalism, and sending out alerts or taking other appropriate action, it can also increase the city's safety and security.

Thirdly, it can raise the general standard of living for residents by fostering a more cosy and secure environment through enhanced illumination. In addition, the system can reduce the need for human inspections and repairs by offering remote monitoring and diagnostics capabilities.

The project is in accordance with the idea of a "smart city," where cutting-edge technology are used to improve urban surroundings that are more sustainable, effective, and livable. It shows how IoT and LoRa connectivity may transform outdated infrastructure into intelligent, interconnected systems, paving the path for the eventual rollout of smart cities.

A wireless communication technology called LoRa (Long Range) is very well suited for use in smart city applications. LoRa offers low-power, long-distance communication between sensors and other devices, which makes it perfect for use in applications for smart streets to make a smart city. Another benefit of LoRa technology is that it can pass through walls and other obstructions, which is helpful in urban settings where buildings and other structures might hamper wireless communication. It effectively low the cost of maintenance and man power.

Aside from energy savings and increased safety, smart street lighting provides additional benefits such as lower maintenance costs and better monitoring of system performance. Smart street lights may be remotely monitored and controlled utilising advanced communication technologies, allowing communities to swiftly identify and address any issues that develop.

Smart street technology is characterised by the use of sensors, cameras, poles, electric tools, and other apparatus to collect real-time data on traffic patterns, air quality, temperature, and other environmental aspects. Utilising this information can improve air quality, reduce congestion, and improve traffic flow.

Smart street technology can also assist in monitoring the condition of infrastructure, such as bridges, buildings, and roadways, in order to detect any flaws before they become serious safety hazards.

By integrating LoRa technology into smart street applications, cities may gather real-time data on traffic patterns, air quality, temperature, and other environmental factors. Utilising this information can enhance air quality, lessen congestion, and improve traffic flow. Additionally, LoRa sensors can be used to keep tabs on the condition of infrastructure like roads, bridges, and buildings, enabling potential problems to be found before they become serious safety concerns.

Overall, smart street lighting is a significant tool for developing more sustainable and efficient communities. Cities may increase the efficiency of their lighting systems, cut energy consumption and costs, and improve community safety and livability by using the power of sensors, modern communication systems, and data analysis.

People must move around occasionally to go to work, school, or to take care of other everyday necessities. This makes travel a necessary element of human existence. Every time, valuable time and energy are spent illuminating roadways; this is impossible without light. In order to assist both motorists and pedestrians on the road, street lights are erected on roads. With the addition of intelligence and control, smart lighting can help a city cut its biggest energy expense, its street lights. Smart lighting offers remote lighting control that can more effectively change how long the lights are on for to reduce energy expenses without compromising public safety. Any public street light system that adapts to the demands of pedestrians, vehicles, and other road users is referred to as an intelligent street light. It is also known as adaptive street lighting since it dims when there is no need for it or when movement is detected. By including actuators, sensors, and cameras in the design, street lights can be made intelligent or smart. This enables automatic motion detection, picture taking or comparison, and triggers as necessary. Nowadays, networks enable communication between various street lights. The concept of a smart-street light system has inspired initiatives from a number of prestigious businesses. The public's need for efficiency has increased as a result of Light Emitting Diode (LED)'s status as the future of illumination. Because of their superior efficiency and longer life span, LEDs have advanced in technology to become one of the best solutions for indoor lighting (Al-Hinai & Al-Shehri, 2020). However, for other illumination needs, other technologies with high intensity discharge lamps and electrodes fluorescent are still used due to their robustness, efficiency, and cost. The main goal of this research is to create a street light that is automated and controlled to meet the needs of automobiles, pedestrians, and drivers.

REVIEW OF LITERATURE

Define the Problem

The issue for the "Smart Street Light" project is the inefficiency and lack of intelligence in standard street lighting systems, which results in wasted energy, increased operational expenses, and poor lighting conditions. Furthermore, standard street lighting systems are incapable of adapting to changing environmental circumstances such as weather, ambient light levels, and pedestrian/vehicular traffic patterns (Camponogara et al., 2013). This can lead to wasteful energy consumption and reduced pedestrian and motorist safety. The majority of street lights run on set schedules or with manual controls, resulting in wasteful energy use during low-traffic periods or insufficient lighting during peak hours. Furthermore,

Figure 1. Sensors connection schematic

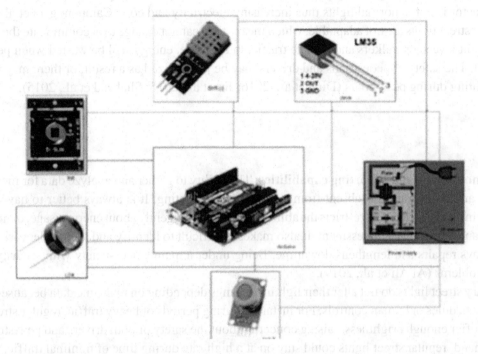

street light maintenance and repair are frequently reactive and time-consuming, resulting in delays in fixing broken lights and increased operational costs (Cheng et al., 2013; Ding et al., 2016).

However, despite the efforts made to improve the condition, problems still need to be resolved. This article will identify and discuss the issues with the Smart Street lights that hinder its effectiveness and performance (Shahzad et al., 2015).

ISSUE 1

Inefficient energy consumption: Standard Street lights operate on set schedules or with manual controls, resulting in inefficient energy consumption and thus it need of more man power. They may remain on during periods of low traffic or when there is adequate natural light, squandering energy and raising operational costs. No matter whether there is enough natural light or foot or vehicle traffic, they come on at a specified time and stay on for a set period of time. Because of this, they may waste energy by remaining on when not necessary, resulting in higher operating expenses and more cost wastage (Khandelwal & Katiyar, 2021).

ISSUE 2

Lack of adaptability: Ordinary Street lights are unable to change their behavior in response to alterations in the weather, ambient light levels, and patterns of foot and vehicle traffic. Because of this, there may be insufficient lighting during peak hours or reduced safety for both pedestrians and drivers. The adaptive factor is not in normal lights thus increasing electricity and cost (Camponogara et al., 2013).

Normal street lights are not adaptable, which means they cannot change to accommodate the weather, ambient light levels, or walkers and vehicle traffic, in that case, energy will be wasted when people are not around. The safety of pedestrians and drivers may be jeopardized as a result, or there may be insufficient lighting during peak hours (Ding et al., 2016; Jin et al., 2015; Shahzad et al., 2015).

ISSUE 3

Limited monitoring and reporting capabilities: The ability to gather and analyze data for monitoring, reporting, and optimization is absent from standard street lighting. It is always better to have security especially in public areas. This restricts the ability to decide intelligently about energy usage, maintenance planning, and performance assessment. It also makes it difficult to identify and fix problems right away, which delays repairs and lengthens downtime. Being under a maintained society with security help to sort out problems (Al-Ali et al., 2019).

Ordinary street lights do not alter their lighting settings depending on real-time data because they run on preset schedules or human controls. For instance, during periods of heavy traffic, regular street lights might not offer enough brightness, raising concerns about the safety of both drivers and pedestrians. On the other hand, regular street lights could stay on at a high rate during time of minimal traffic, which is unneeded and inefficient (Pinto et al., 2014).

LITERATURE SEARCHING

- M. R. Hossain, M. A. Matin, and M. M. Hassan's "A Review of Smart Street Lighting Systems in Smart Cities". The idea of smart street lighting systems in smart cities is covered in this article, along with a thorough analysis of the various technologies including IoT and LoRa—used in these systems.
- The "IoT-Based Smart Street Lighting System for Smart Cities" by S. Balamurugan and S. Sowmiya. This study provides a LoRa-based Internet of Things-based smart street lighting system for smart cities. The system enables remote monitoring and control of street lighting over a low-power, long-range wireless network.
- "Smart Street Lighting System Using LoRa Technology for Energy Conservation in Smart Cities" by T. Q. Vinh and P. T. Thuy. In order to save energy in smart cities, this article suggests a system of LoRa-enabled smart street lighting. The technology uses sensors to determine whether there are any automobiles or pedestrians present, and then modifies the illumination intensity as necessary.
- "Design and Implementation of a Smart Street Light System for Smart Cities using IoT" by S. Rajesh and K. S. Kavitha. The design and installation of a smart street light system utilising IoT and LoRa communication technology are presented in this study. To cut maintenance costs and optimise energy use, the system has clever algorithms.
- "Smart City Lighting: A Review of the Implementation and Applications of IoT-Based Systems" by L. M. Castro-Sitiriche, F. J. González-Castaño, and A. I. Marqués-García. This paper provides a comprehensive review of the implementation and applications of IoT-based smart city lighting

systems, including those that use LoRa technology. The paper discusses the benefits of these systems, such as improved energy efficiency and enhanced safety.

SEARCH STRATEGY

We employed a combination of terms linked to "Smart Street light system" including "Smart Street light", "traffic", "IOT"," Lora", "smartlights", "sensors", to carry out our literature research. To find appropriate pieces that were referenced by the publications and papers in our original search results, we also used reference tracking.

Smart street light systems for smart cities that use Internet of Things (IoT) technology have gotten a lot of interest in recent years because of their potential for reducing energy consumption while boosting the performance of street lighting systems. We look at some of the existing research on smart street light systems for smart cities that use Long Range (LoRa) IoT technologies in this literature study.

SUMMARY

A vital part of a smart city that enhances energy efficiency, sustainability, and offers a variety of community advantages is the smart street light system. An advanced structure called a smart street light system for smart cities employs sensors and Internet of Things (IoT) technologies to enhance the functionality and efficiency of street lighting. By automating street lights and enabling real-time monitoring, remote management, and control, this system enables them to react to shifting environmental circumstances while using less energy.

The Internet of Things (IoT) network is connected to street lights, which are fitted with sensors, as part of the smart city concept. These intelligent street lights are intended to provide greater lighting and increase public safety while lowering maintenance costs and improving energy efficiency.

The Smart Street Light idea intends to improve the operation of conventional street lights by incorporating IoT technology into them, allowing them to run more effectively and offer the community with improved lighting and safety (Suresh Babu, 2023).

In order to have smart cities, it is essential to employ LoRa technology in smart street lighting systems. This technology increases energy efficiency, lowers costs, improves public safety, and gives city planners valuable data.

Smart street lights are connected using LoRa, an IoT technology that offers long-range, low-power wireless connectivity. Smart street lights may connect with each other and the central control system via LoRa, making it possible to monitor and manage illumination levels, energy consumption, and other variables in real-time.

Additional features like parking sensors, security cameras, and environmental sensors can be added to smart street lights, giving city planners useful information and enhancing the city's overall livability. The incorporation of LoRa technology also enables remote management and monitoring, which eliminates the need for manual maintenance and promotes resource utilisation that is more effective.

Overall summary, the application of LoRa technology in smart street lighting systems is an essential component in the creation of smart cities, increasing public safety, lowering expenses, and improving energy efficiency. It also gives city planners useful information.

Figure 2. Basic component of smart lighting

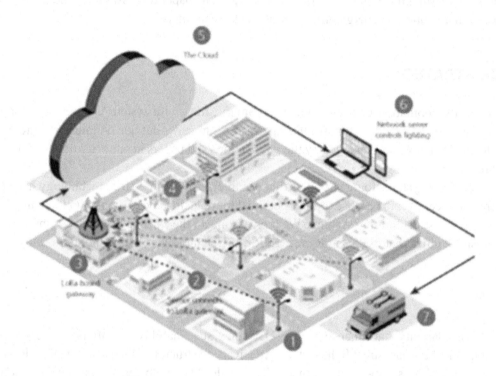

DEFINING THE ARGUMENT

Energy Efficiency: By employing sensors to determine when lighting is required and altering light levels accordingly, smart street light systems can considerably cut energy use. This may lead to significant energy savings and a reduction in the production of greenhouse gases. This technology is especially designed such that more and more electrical energy can be saved.

Cost savings: Smart Street light systems can assist in lowering maintenance and repair expenses. City administrators can swiftly find and fix problems with the lighting system by utilizing sensors and remote monitoring, which eliminates the need for manual inspections and maintenance. Due to the energy saving, the maintenance cost will be reduced.

Enhanced Safety: Smart Street Light Systems can enhance safety by supplying greater lighting in locations that most require it, such as bike lanes and pedestrian walkways. As a result, there may be fewer collisions and better visibility for both automobiles and people. Any kind of problem can be identified and provide safety to the people.

Better Quality of Life: By delivering appropriate lighting conditions that improve the appearance of the city at night, smart street light systems can contribute to the creation of a more pleasant and enjoyable environment for residents and visitors.

Data Insights: Smart Street light systems can give city managers useful data insights about usage patterns, energy use, and maintenance requirements. These data can aid in decision-making, lighting system optimization, and the discovery of additional cost- and efficiency-saving options.

Future-proofing: Putting in place a smart street lighting system is an investment in the city's future. The system is easily upgradeable so that it can benefit from new capabilities and perform better as technology develops and new features become available.

DETAILED ARGUMENT

Devices are used by smart street light systems to determine when lighting is required and to modify light levels accordingly. For instance, the system can enhance brightness when activity is detected and reduce the lights in regions with less vehicular or pedestrian traffic. By eliminating the needless consumption of energy during times of low activity, this can lead to significant energy savings.

City administrators can remotely monitor and control smart street light systems to switch off or change the amount of lights in particular areas as needed. Because manual inspections and repairs can be expensive and time-consuming, this lessens the need for them.

LED lighting technology, which is more energy-efficient than conventional lighting sources like high-pressure neon lamps, is frequently used in Smart Street Light Systems. Because they use up to 80% less energy and last longer, LED lights require fewer replacements altogether.

Real-time energy monitoring is a feature that smart street light systems can offer. This feature enables city managers to monitor energy use and spot areas for development. By doing this, the lighting system can be improved while using less energy.

Integration with Renewable Energy Sources: Smart Street Light Systems may operate off the grid and reduce energy use and carbon emissions even more by integrating with renewable energy sources like solar panels (Suresh Babu et al., 2023b).

Regular maintenance and repairs are necessary for conventional streetlights, which can be costly and time-consuming. However, because smart streetlights have real-time problem and failure detection, maintenance crews are able to take immediate corrective action. By extending the useful lives of streetlights and lowering maintenance expenses, this can lessen the frequency of replacement.

Enhanced safety is one of the most significant benefits of smart technologies, and this is particularly true for smart streetlight. Better roadway and sidewalk lighting from smart streetlights can improve visibility for motorcycle riders, pedestrians and cars. This can lower the number of collisions and make it safer for citizens to travel around the city after dark.

Real-time fault and failure detection is made possible by smart streetlights, allowing maintenance crews to react quickly to problems. By doing this, the chance of accidents brought on by broken lamps can be diminished.

To make cities more dynamic and interesting, smart lighting can alter colour and brightness levels. This can increase cities' allure and draw more tourists and travellers.

Smart streetlights may come with sensors that may identify emergencies like fires and accidents. They can automatically notify emergency services, speeding up response times and increasing the likelihood of a good outcome.

Streetlights that are "smart" can have cameras and other sensors to look for suspicious activities. They can automatically notify law enforcement, improving the likelihood of capturing offenders and lowering crime rates.

Sensors that can identify pedestrians can be added to smart lamps. The danger of accidents can be decreased by adjusting their brightness levels to make sure that pedestrians are visible to motorists and bikers.

By only lighting up areas that need to be lit, smart streetlights can be configured to reduce light pollution. This might lessen the negative effects of artificial illumination on wildlife while also enhancing the standard of living for locals living in light pollution-affected areas.

Intelligent streetlights can considerably lower energy use, resulting in cost savings that can be used towards things like public services, healthcare, and education that can raise quality of life.

Smart street light systems can help to create a more comfortable and delightful environment for inhabitants and visitors by providing the right lighting conditions that enhance the city's image at night.

Devices that track and provide immediate information on traffic patterns, including volume, speed, and direction, can be added to smart street lights. Using this information, traffic flow can be enhanced, which means shorter travel times and less congestion. It can also be used to pinpoint locations that can benefit from new infrastructure or road improvements.

Intelligent street lighting can be set up to notify the authorities of any unexpected behaviour, such as accidents or criminal activities. Additionally, they can be used to keep an eye on public areas and provide information on the flow of vehicles and pedestrians, enhancing public safety.

Devices that track environmental elements including noise levels, air quality, and other environmental conditions can be added to smart street lights. This information can be used to pinpoint places with particularly high pollution levels and put emission reduction plans into action.

Parking space availability can be tracked and provided in real-time by smart street lighting. This can ease traffic congestion and enhance both residents' and visitors' parking experiences generally.

By guaranteeing that infrastructure is planned with the long term in mind, future-proofing can encourage sustainability. Municipalities may cut waste and encourage resource efficiency by creating flexible, adaptable infrastructure.

Smarter lighting infrastructure may be made resilient so that it can endure unforeseen events like natural disasters with the help of future-proofing. In times of disaster, this can serve to reduce disturbance and advance public safety.

DRAFTING

System Architecture Design

The system architecture design is the first phase in developing a smart street light system for a smart city using LoRa technology and the Internet of Things. The system's elements, their roles, and how they interact are all described. Both software and hardware components, such as tools for data processing, analytics, and visualisation, should be used in this design. Hardware components include sensors, microcontrollers, and communication modules.

Sensor Selection

When designing the Smart Street Light System, it is essential to choose the right sensors. Different environmental factors including temperature, humidity, light intensity, and motion should be able to be measured by the sensors. The system requirements and the environment in which it will be deployed should be taken into consideration when choosing a sensor.

Power Management

For the smart street light system to function properly, power management is essential. The power management design should be able to control the power requirements of the system's components, including the sensors, microcontrollers, and communication modules.

Design of Communication Protocols

Effective communication between the various Smart Street Light System components depends on the design of the communication protocols. The system architecture and the communication needs of the various components should serve as the foundation for the communication protocol design.

Data Processing and Analytics

Without data processing and analytics, the Smart Street Light System's architecture is incomplete. The system ought to have the ability to process the data gathered by the sensors and provide the municipal officials with useful data. When building the data processing and analytics process, the requirements for data storage, processing, and visualisation should be taken into consideration.

Security

Security must come first in the design of any IOT system, including the Smart Street Light System. The design should include security components like encryption, authentication, and authentication to safeguard the data and system components from unauthorised access.

COMMUNICATION WITH FINDINGS

In a smart city, communication between devices is crucial for efficient and effective functioning. Device to device communication is essential for a smart city's smooth operation. An vital part of the infrastructure of a smart city, smart street lighting can communicate with other equipment to improve their operation.

Smart lighting fixtures can communicate via a variety of wired or wireless protocols, including Wi-Fi, Bluetooth, ZigBee, and LoRaWAN. The street lights can communicate with other gadgets like sensors, cameras, and other street lights thanks to these protocols.

For determining the presence of humans or automobiles, for instance, smart street lights can connect with sensors and change the lighting. In addition, they may interface with cameras to take and send real-time pictures of weather, traffic, and security-related issues to the city's central monitoring system (Suresh Babu et al., 2023a).

LoRaWAN is a long-range, lightweight wireless network that allows smart street lights to connect with other gadgets like sensors, cameras, and other street lights. Each smart street light serves as a gateway for the LoRaWAN protocol's star network topology, allowing additional devices within its range to connect to the network.

Using LoRaWAN, smart street lights may broadcast information to a central management system, allowing for real-time monitoring and administration of the city's lighting infrastructure. This data can include lighting levels, energy usage, and temperature. LoRaWAN may also be used to transfer data from other gadgets like traffic sensors, parking sensors, and environmental sensors, giving a comprehensive picture of the city's infrastructure.

Furthermore, in order to share crucial information and insights for improved decision-making and optimised city operations, smart street lights can also interface with other smart city systems, such as traffic, garbage, and emergency services.

In general, communication in smart street lighting is crucial for developing an urban environment that is more effective, sustainable, and secure. It makes it possible to collect and analyse data more effectively, which results in more informed decision-making, better resource management, and improved citizen services.

Overall, the use of LoRaWAN for communication in smart street lighting makes it possible to create a more sustainable, connected, and efficient city infrastructure, which has advantages like decreased energy use, increased public safety, and improved citizen services.

REQUIREMENTS ANALYSIS

Requirement analysis is an important process in software development that involves identifying, analyzing, and documenting the needs and constraints of stakeholders for a given system. Here are some requirements for a Smart Street Light System for Smart City using IoT (LoRa):

A.   FUNCTIONAL REQUIREMENTS:

Automatic On/Off:
Based on predetermined parameters like the time of day or the presence of pedestrians and cars, the system need to be able to automatically turn on and off the street lights.
Remote Control:
The system should enable administrators to remotely control the street lights, including turning them on/off, adjusting brightness levels, and scheduling maintenance.
Real-time Monitoring:
Real-time monitoring of street light performance, including energy use, bulb health, and failure rates, should be offered via the system.
Energy Efficiency:
By using motion sensors to only activate lights when necessary and lowering lights during times of low traffic, the system should be created to save energy and prevent light pollution.
Fault Detection:
The system should be able to ect faults in the street lights and notify administrators of the problem.

B.   NON-FUNCTIONAL REQUIREMENTS:

Scalability:

The system should be scalable to accommodate a large number of street lights and data volume.

Reliability:

The system should be reliable and available 24/7.

Security:

The system should be designed with robust security features to prevent unauthorized access and data breaches.

Compatibility:

The system should be compatible with different types of street lights, sensors, and communication protocols.

User Interface:

The user interface should be intuitive and user-friendly, enabling administrators to easily manage the system.

C. PERFORMANCE REQUIREMENTS:

Response Time:

The system should respond quickly to user requests and provide real-time monitoring of street lights.

Throughput:

The system should be able to handle a large volume of data from multiple sources simultaneously.

Latency:

The system should have low latency to ensure that street lights respond quickly to changing conditions.

Availability:

The system should be available 24/7 with minimal downtime.

SYSTEM SPECIFICATION

The system requirements for a Smart Street Light System for Smart City using IoT (LoRa) would depend on several factors such as the scale of the implementation, the number of devices to be deployed, the expected traffic volume, and the features required. However, here are some general requirements that may be necessary:

HARDWARE:

- LoRa gateway: This is used to connect the street lights to the internet.
- LoRa nodes: These are attached to the street lights to monitor and control them.
- Sensors: The sensors can be used to detect motion, light levels, temperature, and other environmental factors.
- Microcontrollers: These are used to process data and communicate with the LoRa gateway.

SOFTWARE:

- Firmware: This is the software that runs on the microcontrollers and enables them to communicate with the gateway and sensors.

- Backend system: This is the system that receives data from the sensors and manages the street lights.
- Frontend system: This is the user interface that allows administrators to view and control the street lights.

CONNECTIVITY:

- LoRaWAN network: This is the network used to connect the street lights to the internet.
- Cellular network: This can be used as a backup in case the LoRaWAN network is unavailable.

POWER:

- Power source: The street lights may need to be powered using mains electricity or solar power.
- Battery backup: A backup power source can be used in case of power outages.

SECURITY:

- Data encryption: Data transmitted over the network should be encrypted to prevent unauthorized access.
- Authentication: Only authorized users should be able to access the system.
- Firewall: A firewall can be used to prevent unauthorized access to the system.

It's important to note that these requirements are not exhaustive, and the specific requirements for a Smart Street Light System for Smart City using IoT (LoRa) may vary based on the specific implementation.

Figure 3. System architecture

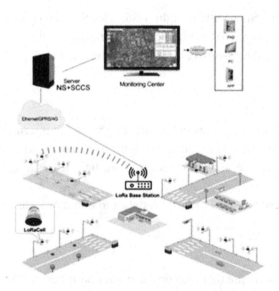

SYSTEM ARCHITECTURE

Figure 4. Visual model

PROPOSED SYSTEM

Street light fixtures:

LED street light fixtures with wireless communication capability and sensors for motion detection and ambient light sensing.

Centralized control system:

A central control system that can manage and oversee the operation of all the city's street lights is known as a centralised control system. The lights would be controlled by this system, which would also control brightness levels and look for errors and malfunctions.

Wireless communication network:

A wireless communication network that enables communication between the street lights and the central control system. This network would make use of Zigbee, LoRa, or NB-IoT technologies.

Cloud-based data analytics platform:

Platform for collecting and analyzing data from streetlights in the cloud: A platform for collecting and analyzing data from streetlights in the cloud to learn more about how well they work and how much energy they use. In order to enhance the performance of the street lights, this platform might potentially employ machine learning approaches.

Mobile application:

A mobile app that enables city administrators to keep tabs on the performance of the street lights and get instant notifications for problems.

Renewable energy sources:

Combination of energy from renewable sources, such as solar and wind power, to lessen dependency on the grid and supply backup power during blackouts.

Figure 5. Proposed system

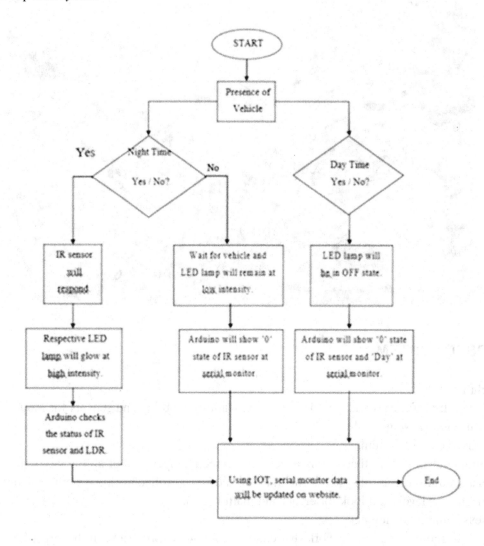

IMPLEMENTATION

Modules

Light Control Module:

   This module is responsible for controlling the street lights. It can receive commands from the central control system to turn the lights on or off, adjust their brightness, and set the schedules for when they should be turned on or off.

Sensor Module:

This module includes various sensors such as light, temperature, humidity, motion, and sound sensors. These sensors can be used to detect the presence of people, vehicles, or animals, and adjust the brightness of the lights accordingly.

LoRa Gateway:

LoRa is a low-power, long-range wireless communication technology that can be used to connect the different modules in the Smart Street Light System. The LoRa gateway serves as a bridge between the sensors and the central control system.

Central Control System:

This module is responsible for managing the Smart Street Light System. It can receive data from the sensors, send commands to the light control module, and analyze the data to optimize the performance of the system.

Power Management Module:

This module is responsible for managing the power supply to the street lights and other modules in the system. It can monitor the power usage of the system and optimize it to reduce energy consumption.

Data Storage and Analytics Module:

This module can be used to store the data generated by the sensors and analyze it to gain insights into the usage patterns of the street lights. This data can be used to optimize the performance of the system and reduce energy consumption.

FUTURE WORK

By using motion sensors to only activate lights when necessary and lowering lights during times of low traffic, the system should be created to save energy and prevent light pollution.

Integrate renewable energy sources: The current street lighting system's dependency on grid power is one of its major drawbacks. The system can be made more sustainable and effective by including renewable energy sources like solar, wind, or kinetic energy.

Implement predictive maintenance: Using predictive preventative maintenance methods is a way to keep maintenance costs to a minimum and ensure that the smart street light system operates at peak efficiency. The system can identify any problems before they arise using IoT sensors, enabling prompt maintenance and repairs.

Add environmental sensors: The smart street light system can benefit from the addition of environmental sensors to track changes in air quality, humidity, and temperature. The lighting system can be modified using this knowledge, which will also help the city's environment.

Create a smartphone application: By creating a smartphone application, users will be able to report any malfunctioning street lighting. Users of the programme can regulate the lights according to their preferences and receive real-time updates on the system's status.

Integrating smart parking systems: Integrating smart parking systems into a smart street lighting system can help to ease traffic congestion and boost parking effectiveness. The system may direct cars to the closest available parking spot by giving them real-time information about parking spots, which reduce time and traffic congestion.

Enhanced connectivity and communication: Using advanced communication technologies like 5G or other high-speed wireless networks, can make it possible for the street lights and the central control system to communicate more quickly and reliably. This may enable more brief reaction times, improved coordination, and enhanced system performance.

Integration with smart city applications: By integrating the smart street light system with other smart city applications, such smart parking, trash management, or public safety, it is possible to achieve synergies that improve city administration effectiveness. For instance, the system can make illumination adjustments depending on real-time information about events, emergencies, or public gatherings using data from other smart city applications.

User involvement and citizen involvement:

Its effectiveness can be increased and a sense of community ownership can be fostered by including citizens in the management and maintenance of the smart street light system. Citizens may be able to provide feedback, report issues, and participate in processes that define how the street lighting system is to be administered through the development of user-friendly interfaces, mobile applications, and engagement platforms.

Future development and improvement of the Smart Street Light System for Smart City technologies is very possible. By researching these choices, we may create an urban environment that is more effective, safe, and sustainable.

CONCLUSION

In conclusion, the Smart Street Light System for Smart City is a promising technology that has the potential to revolutionise urban lighting by offering solutions that are cost-effective, energy-efficient, and sustainable. This technology has the potential to make cities smarter and more sustainable through the integration of Internet of Things (IoT) technologies like LoRa.

Multiple benefits come with a smart street light system for a smart city, such as decreased energy use, lower operating costs, improved safety and security, better traffic management, and higher levels of citizen involvement. The system can optimize lighting operations, remotely monitor and operate street lights, forecast maintenance needs, and interface with other smart city applications by utilizing cutting-edge technology like AI, machine learning, data analytics, and connectivity.

The initial adoption costs, infrastructure needs, data privacy and security, connectivity, and public acceptance are some of the difficulties that must be overcome. Collaboration between stakeholders, such as local governments, technology providers, people, and other relevant parties, will be necessary to overcome these issues.

Thus, A technology that has the potential to revolutionize metropolitan areas' lighting systems is the Smart Street Light System for Smart City using IoT. More advantages, including remote monitoring and control, energy economy, better maintenance, and increased safety, can result from the integration of IoT technology with street lighting systems.

The solution can improve system performance insights while dynamically adjusting lighting intensity and consuming less energy. Additionally, the system can communicate over great distances thanks to the usage of LoRa technology, which makes it perfect for large-scale city deployments.

This technology has a huge potential for advancement and innovation, including the incorporation of environmental sensors, AI and machine learning algorithms, and preventative maintenance strategies. Cities that use this technology will become smarter, more sustainable, and more effective.

To conclude, the use of IoT (LoRa) technology to construct a smart street light system for a smart city has several advantages. The project optimises energy consumption, lowers maintenance costs, increases safety, and enhances overall quality of life for citizens by utilising modern sensors, LoRa connectivity, and intelligent algorithms.

The system allows for remote street light monitoring and control, enabling effective energy management, automatic defect identification, and real-time data analysis for improved decision-making. The system's reliance on LoRa technology also guarantees long-range and low-power communication, making it appropriate for widespread smart city deployments.

The study shows how IoT and LoRa may be used to build sustainable and effective urban environments. The installation of IoT (LoRa)-based smart street light systems is one way that smart cities are continuing to develop.

In conclusion, the LoRa-based Smart Street Light System for Smart Cities has enormous potential to alter urban lighting and advance the creation of smarter, more sustainable, and healthier cities. This technology has the potential to help cities all across the world move towards a more promising and environmentally friendly future with sustained study, innovation, and cooperation.

REFERENCES

Al-Ali, A. R., Hussain, M., & Hossain, M. A. (2019). Smart street lighting system: A platform for smart city applications. *Journal of Sensors*, *2019*, 1–12.

Al-Hinai, K., & Al-Shehri, R. (2020). Smart street lighting system using IoT for smart cities. *Journal of Communication*, *15*(10), 968–974.

Al-Sammarraie, A., & Hussain, M. (2019). Smart street lighting for smart cities: A review. *Renewable & Sustainable Energy Reviews*, *103*, 207–214.

Camponogara, D., Ferreira, G. F., Campos, A., & Costa, M. A. D. (2013, November/December). Offline LED Driver for Street Lighting With an Optimized Cascade structure. *IEEE Transactions on Industry Applications*, *40*(6), No-6. doi:10.1109/TIA.2013.2263631

Cheng, C., Cheng, H.-l., & Chung, T.-Y. (2013). A Novel Single-Stage High-Power-Factor LED Street-Lighting Driver with Coupled Inductors. *IEEE Transactions on Industry Applications*. Advance online publication. doi:0.1109/TIA.2014.2304585

Ding, Q., Bo, S., & Zhang, X. (2016). A Traffic light aware Routing Protocol based on Street Connectivity for Urban Vehicular Ad hoc Networks. *IEEE Communications Letters*, *20*(8), 1635–1638. Advance online publication. doi:10.1109/LCOMM.2016.2574708

Jin, H., Jin, S., Chen, L., Cen, S., & Yuan, K. (2015, December). Research on The Lighting Performance of Led Street Lights With Different Color Temperatures. *IEEE Photonics Journal*, *7*(6), 1–9. doi:10.1109/JPHOT.2015.2497578

Khandelwal, R., & Katiyar, V. (2021). Smart street lighting system using IoT for smart cities: A review. *Journal of Ambient Intelligence and Humanized Computing*, *12*(1), 21–38.

Lee, H.-C., & Huang, H.-B. (2014). *A Low-Cost and Noninvasive System for The Measurement and Detection of Faulty Streetlights. IEEE Transaction on Instrumentation and Measurement.*

Mohammadi, A., Yousefi, M., Rostami, A., & Yaghmaee, M. H. (2019). A review of smart street lighting system based on IoT for smart city. *IEEE Access : Practical Innovations, Open Solutions, 7*, 62255–62270.

Pinto, M. F., Soares, G. M., Mendonica, T. R. F., Almeeida, P. S., & Braga, H. A. C. (2014). *Smart Modules for Lighting System Applications and Power Quality Measurements.* IEEE. doi:10.1109/IN-DUSCON.2014.7059448

Shahzad, G., Yang, H., Waheed, A., & Lee, C. (2015). *Energy Efficient Intelligent Street Lighting System Using Traffic Adaptive Control. IEEE Sensors Journal.* doi:10.1109/JSEN.2016.25.57345

Suresh Babu, C. V. (2023). *IoT and its Applications.* Anniyappa Publication.

Suresh Babu, C. V., & .... (2023a). IoT-Based Smart Accident Detection and Alert System. In P. Swarnalatha & S. Prabu (Eds.), *Handbook of Research on Deep Learning Techniques for Cloud-Based Industrial IoT* (pp. 322–337). IGI Global., doi:10.4018/978-1-6684-8098-4.ch019

Suresh Babu, C. V., Ganesh, B. S., Kishoor, T., & Khang, A. (2023b). Automatic Irrigation System Using Solar Tracking Device. In A. Khang (Ed.), *Handbook of Research on AI-Equipped IoT Applications in High-Tech Agriculture* (pp. 239–256). IGI Global., doi:10.4018/978-1-6684-9231-4.ch013

Chapter 7
Overcoming MSME Challenges With Blockchain

Mohammad Izzuddin Mohammed Jamil
https://orcid.org/0000-0002-2967-7870
Universiti Brunei Darussalam, Brunei

ABSTRACT

Emerging technologies are distinct in that they stimulate the creation of automated and intelligent businesses at a quick pace. Business processes are being reimagined and reinvented by these companies. When blockchain was initially introduced to the world in 2008, it was touted as the next great digital revolution. This chapter seeks to offer an overview of blockchain technology by defining it and explaining how it works. However, because blockchain technology is still in its infancy, nothing is known about how this new technology may be used to practical applications. As a result, the chapter highlights its distinct characteristics that set it apart from other technologies. Despite government intervention and an environment that promotes entrepreneurship, MSMEs, which have long been the backbone of any economy, continue to face the same difficulties that small businesses face. This chapter demonstrates how blockchain may assist in resolving these challenges in the hopes of spurring greater research and development in the field of blockchain, particularly in the context of MSMEs.

INTRODUCTION

When the prototype known as the Internet was finished in 1983, it was the first time the world had ever seen the concept of free knowledge being exchanged between everyone across the world, regardless of origin or background, on a scale previously considered impossible. This was amplified when computer scientist Tim Berners-Lee coined the term "World Wide Web" in 1989, giving the Internet a more familiar tone (Tim Berners-Lee Respini, 2018). The Internet has essentially permitted technical comforts that give numerous new chances for everyone, owing to the availability of useful information, throughout this digital era paradigm. Individuals may use this knowledge to tackle a variety of problems ranging from basic social and health concerns like obesity, smoking, and hunger to business difficulties and economic issues including business applications, poverty, and injustice (Lanham, 2006). While the Internet isn't

DOI: 10.4018/978-1-6684-9151-5.ch007

flawless and won't be able to entirely address these difficulties, it has shown to be capable of mitigating negative issues or at the very least reducing the negative repercussions of these issues.

That is especially true for would-be and aspiring entrepreneurs who are prepared to take risks by starting their own firm from the ground up (Millman, Li, Matlay & Wong, 2010). Small businesses now have quick access to any new product ideas, advancements, and technical breakthroughs, as well as a vast quantity of information that may help them better their goods and compete with larger companies, thanks to the Internet. Despite its tremendous advantages, the Internet is not without its drawbacks. The availability of information also means that the corporate environment is more competitive and dynamic than it has ever been, necessitating continual innovation and change in order for organizations to adapt. As a result, in order to survive today's fierce competition and stay ahead of the pack, one must make use of developing technology (Day, Schoemaker & Gunther, 2000). Emerging technologies are viewed as the next step for organizations everywhere since they are frequently considered disruptive technologies, to the point where they may establish a whole new niche market through a process known as cybermediation. According to the book Fundamentals of Businesses (Barney & Hesterly, 2010), in order to get a competitive edge over competitors, one must differentiate oneself in terms of products or services in order to generate value for customers. The use of emerging technologies is one way to help realize and achieve potential competitive advantage, though the nature of emerging technologies means that their practical developments and applications are still unrealized and in their infancy, and thus they have only recently gained prominence and become a topic of discussion (Adner & Levinthal, 2002). This infancy, on the other hand, has an evident value, as it demonstrates that most firms are still unable to or unwilling to use such technology, thus allowing early movers in any field to gain a competitive advantage. Educational technology, information technology, nanotechnology, biotechnology, cognitive science, psychotechnology, robotics, and artificial intelligence are all examples of developing technologies.

Emerging technologies, of course, provide the foundation for firms that want to stay one step ahead of their competition in any field. Businesses, on the other hand, are frequently bemused and charmed by the technological wizardry and unknown complexity of developing technologies as a result of fast technological progress. Due to the huge number of dangers, even experienced investors would not go into the growth of technology. However, blockchain technology is one of the most important new technologies that may be used to great success by organizations and is now trending in both academic research and practical implementations (Underwood, 2016). Indeed, for some bigger businesses, it is already one of the most significant new technologies that they have integrated as part of their business process in today's day (Risius & Spohrer, 2017).

As of today, Blockchain technology has gotten a lot of press in the business sector (Avital, Beck, King, Rossi, & Teigland, 2016), with firms, banks, and customers all arguing for a push toward a trust-free economic transaction (Glaser, 2017, January). This sort of transaction does not need mutual trust or even a direct relationship between the participants. Furthermore, it does away with the need for a third party to act as a mediator. The major disadvantage of having a third party is that the mediators have the authority to define and impose their own terms and conditions, which must be agreed upon by the first and second parties. This is only one illustration of what Blockchain technology can do.

Aside from automation, machine learning, artificial intelligence, augmented reality, and the internet of things, blockchain technologies are regarded as one of the most disruptive technologies, particularly in countries that are flourishing for industry 4.0. While the concept itself is inspiring to the point of being overhyped, blockchain has thus far failed to live up to expectations (Avital, Beck, King, Rossi, & Teigland, 2016). The major difficulty is that, despite high expectations from economic agents like as governments, blockchain knowledge and comprehension are still in their infancy (Mougayar, 2016). Above all, the topic of how Blockchain technology may benefit companies is still being debated by theorists and practitioners alike (Mougayar, 2016), and the problem of how it can have social implications is also being debated. When technology is utilized incorrectly, it can have both positive and negative consequences if it is not carefully handled.

Traditional physical forms of currency, such as cash in the form of banknotes and coins, are frequently affected by inflation, which is a general increase in the price level. Inflation has the effect of eroding the value of savings, which have been amassed after years of hard work. Traditional currency also suffers from the fact that it is held solely by a few wealthy individuals (Oishi, Kesebir & Diener, 2011). The global rise in income inequality implies that conventional money has so far failed to effectively equalize income distribution (Oishi, Kesebir, & Diener, 2011). Blockchain has the potential to level the playing field by making its technology available to the general public.

MSMEs are the most significant of the numerous forms of business organizations that exist in society. MSMEs contribute to a country's economic growth and the achievement of various socio-economic goals, such as increasing employment, providing training to the populace to improve skills, increasing the number of outputs (goods and services) produced, fostering international trade via export and import, and promoting value through the creation of new products and services. MSMEs, on the other hand, confront several challenges, particularly those that are just getting started. For example, one of the most common issues is a lack of capital to launch their businesses.

As a result, the goal of this article is to give academics and scholars an outline of the idea of blockchain technology, as well as to illustrate how Blockchain technology may help MSMEs solve their common difficulties. While blockchain technology has been present for over two decades, there have been very few academic studies on it, particularly in the context of MSME. This is due to the fact that blockchain technology has only grown in relevance and become more well-known since the news of Bitcoin went throughout the world (Wang, Lin & Luo, 2019). Researchers and academics may find researching the properties of Blockchain an avenue for future researches relevant in different sectors, as Blockchain and Bitcoin studies are still in their infancy.

This paper may indirectly stimulate the use of blockchain technology and improve acceptance rates, particularly among MSMEs, but it ultimately serves as a guide for MSMEs, as blockchain technology is frequently complex and lacks a single clear path for MSMEs to follow. MSMEs from all around the world may analyze the benefits of adopting new technology, and then decide for themselves if the benefits exceed the dangers. When used correctly, blockchain may be used as a bridge to obtain a competitive edge over competitors. A structured outline is produced with the displaying of each heading with its own content. Before getting into the core substance of the article, the definitions will act as an appetizer to assist readers gain a fundamental concept of blockchain and MSMEs.

BACKGROUND

Following the creation of cryptocurrencies, notably bitcoin in 2008, the concept of blockchain found its way into literary and practical forums (Buterin, 2014). Early talks have centered on how businesses would be able to make use of such cutting-edge technology. Researchers have enquired about how blockchain might be used to and adopted by the masses at the organizational, industrial, national, and governmental levels. Many authors, unsurprisingly, are focused on bitcoin's applicability. According to

Yli-Huumo, Ko, Choi, Park, and Smolander (2016), less than 20% of the 41 research articles gathered and analyzed have incorporated blockchain into other applications such as licensing and smart contracts, while the remaining 80% have adapted blockchain to bitcoin. While the majority of these are good ideas that blockchain would assist increase process efficiency, there are some who argue that it will come at a cost and with its own set of problems to solve. Blockchain is still in its infancy, with concerns such as scalability (Peck, 2017), security and privacy breaches (Peck, 2017), restricted transaction volumes, high computing costs, and high energy usage that organizations considering it must balance (Mathews, Robles, & Bowe, 2017). Another barrier to Blockchain adoption is a lack of digital literacy (Jamil, M. I. M., & Almunawar, M. N). For instance, in the United States, a developed economy, the rate of digital literacy is low, with just 40% of individuals classified as digitally literate (Feldman, 2018).

However, since then, Blockchain technology has progressed beyond Bitcoin's use and into a number of other practical applications and sectors. Financial services, healthcare, the chemical and energy industries, transportation and communication, and the coffee industry are just a few examples. It's worth noting that the financial business is the one that gets the most attention from academics (Mori, 2016; Pollari, 2016). This is because the financial industry is one of the most prominent adopters of blockchain technology, with FinTech companies and organizations vying to disrupt the market by providing cutting-edge financial services (Pollari, 2016). Traditional problems faced by businesses in the finance industry include process inefficiencies and inadequate cost structures. The difficulty of tracing the original owners of an item in a financial market where ownership is continuously changing has spurred the need for Blockchain (Nofer, Gomber, Hinz, & Schiereck, 2017). The high expense of employing an intermediary is further complicating the process of authenticating assets, and the 2008 financial crisis (Campello, Graham, & Harvey, 2010) has accentuated the necessity to demonstrate original owners of an asset. However, according to Beck, Avital, Rossi, and Thatcher (2017), there exist hurdles to blockchain adoption in the financial industry, with 20% of the constraints attributable to technology and the remaining 80% owing to present business structures and practices.

While the demand for blockchain implementation might smoothly blend in and solve evident concerns, questions must be posed about how safe these are for users, particularly in public and social settings. Should the use of blockchain technology be left in the hands of private companies, or should it remain under the authority of the state? The risks offered by blockchain include the possibility of funds being lost when left in the hands of private organizations, as well as the necessity for new laws to keep up with technological advancements (Sapczyski, 2019; lnes, Ubacht & Janssen, 2017).

The immaturity of Blockchain technology necessitates a proof of concept, in which the viability of ideas and concepts is thoroughly researched and studied in order to demonstrate its practical potential through demonstrations (lnes, Ubacht, & Janssen, 2017). Its youth also implies that the themes are all over the place, rather than being organized into a single step or process that explains each concept or dimension consistently. It's worth noting that there aren't many empirical studies, case studies, or instances in the subject of blockchain. This is unsurprising, given many aspects of blockchain remain unexplored by researchers, despite the fact that many publications have addressed the basics. As a result, blockchain isn't installed merely for the purpose of it; it's implemented because there are problems that need to be solved, and blockchain happens to be the solution.

Empirical experiments (Sikorski, Haughton, & Kraft, 2017) have been undertaken in the chemical and energy industries, where Blockchain has been used to ease machine-to-machine interactions between industrial facilities that are exchanging electricity with one another. This leads to the creation of a market electricity framework, the goal of which is to offer a proof-of-concept (Chitchyan, & Murkin, 2018) for the possible application of Blockchain technology in the chemical sector to increase efficiency.

Another proof-of-concept for Blockchain technology is in the setting of coffee shops (Beck, Stenum Czepluch, Lollike, & Malone, 2016; Thiruchelvam, Mughisha, Shahpasand, & Bamiah, 2018), where these businesses use old analogue payment methods such as prepaid punch cards. Coffee shops operate on the basis of trust, therefore the presence of a middleman is required; otherwise, transactions between businesses and consumers would be impossible. Incorporating blockchain technology into the structure of payment processes and solutions will eliminate the need for any intermediary. Despite the various benefits given by blockchain, scalability problems, prices, and authenticity remain the most pressing concerns in its deployment. Mermon (2018) stated that the two most important challenges in the implementation of blockchain on small-scale projects are scalability and security, and he proposed solutions for secure implementations in the form of consensus mechanisms.

Health Information Technology (HIT) has so far failed to live up to its hype and promises of revolutionizing the healthcare business in terms of information processing efficiency. The lack of information, as well as the volume of erroneous information, has shown to be a barrier to quicker information transmission (Wong, Yee & Nohr, 2018). This is mostly owing to the fact that information is sensitive, as well as a lack of confidence among people in the chain of command, as well as the possibility of human judgment and error while sending such data. In order to increase efficiency, a shift in mentality from an information-based model to a healthcare model based on value and trust is required (lnes, Ubacht, & Janssen, 2017; lnes, Ubacht, & Janssen, 2017). This is accomplished through the use of blockchain, which removes the issue of trust from the equation and uses blockchain's "smart contract" function to automate the process and eliminate human mistake and judgment. lnes, Ubacht, and Janssen (2017) stated from a similar point of view, but in a different context, that mindsets must shift from technology-driven to need-driven governance (akin to value) in order for administrative processes to benefit from technology.

Some writers (Yuan, & Wang, November 2016; Balasubramaniam, Gul, Menon, & Paul, 2020) have used their imagination to solve the practical question of whether blockchain can be incorporated into intelligent transportation systems (ITS). Because of the potential security afforded by blockchain, a framework has been developed that shows a link between blockchain-based intelligent transportation systems and parallel transportation management systems (PtMS). The disadvantages of more centralised (and more bureaucratic) transportation networks can be addressed by blokchain's decentralized character.

The Internet of Things (IoT) is another new technology that is up there with Blockchain technology in terms of being disruptive and giving any organization a competitive edge (Biswas & Muthukkumarasamy, 2016, December). Other new technologies are unavoidably incorporated within the scope of the transition to smart cities. Particularly, it has been suggested that communication may be fully based on Blockchain (Biswas & Muthukkumarasamy, 2016, December; Huh, Cho, & Kim, 2017, February). However, compared to other endpoint devices such as smartphones, tablets, or computers, these IoT devices have limited compute, storage, and network capacity, and it is at this centralized point where they are most vulnerable to attacks (Khan, & Salah, 2018; Huh, Cho, & Kim, 2017, February) and are prone to hacking.

Scholars have not done much conceptual and empirical study on blockchain in the context of Micro, Small, and Medium-sized Enterprises (MSMEs). One of the early conversations, however, is about how blockchain might be utilized as a platform to help MSMEs gain access to capital. When it comes to external sources of funding, such as banks and financial institutions, MSMEs, unlike major businesses, face an uphill battle at first. This is because, owing to their limited assets as collateral, there is no known method of repaying their obligations in the case of failure or bankruptcy, therefore banks and financial institutions are hesitant to lend large sums of money. However, Wang (2020, April) and Wang, Lin, and Luo (2019) suggest that a new credit evaluation system based on blockchain is required to alleviate this problem and provide MSMEs with near-zero collateral. MSMEs with low-risk, high-quality goods can use information dissemination to demonstrate their reliability and risk class, boosting their chances of getting a bank loan even without collateral (Wang, Lin, & Luo 2019).

Due to significant hazards concerns about Intellectual Property (IP), it's no wonder that MSMEs perceive open-innovation as a risk that's frequently not worth the time and effort (de la Rosa, Gibovic, Torres, Maicher, Miralles El-Fakdi & Bikfalvi, 2016, December). The smart contract structure of blockchain mitigates this issue by requiring users to sign contracts that provide for timestamping of any changes in IP as well as remedial processes in the event of any unauthorised usage of IP. As a result, blockchain enables greater IP protection, resulting in better open-innovation management for MSMEs.

The Initial Coin Offering (ICO) has gradually been superseded by a new breakthrough in equity called Security Token Offering (STO) in the realm of stock investments and crowdfunding campaigns (Mazzorana-Kremer, 2019). STOs make use of blockchain technology, resulting in fewer intermediaries and reduced transaction costs. Furthermore, STOs are seen as a more liquid alternative to ICOs, and their rising popularity further emphasizes their suitability for MSMEs.

Ilbiz & Durst, on the other hand, have made one of the most significant breakthroughs in the world of blockchain, especially applied to MSME level (2019). Despite the buzz and excitement around the adoption of blockchain as an innovative solution to many business-related challenges, Ilbiz & Durst (2019) suggest that it may not be feasible for MSMEs. The argument here is that in order for MSME to fully realize the benefits of blockchain, they must follow a personalized strategy or framework, without which MSMEs will likely lose time and money in the process of implementing blockchain.

Another significant area of business that requires blockchain adoption is in the context of MSMEs' operations and supply chain management (Wong, Leong, Hew, Tan & Ooi, 2020). In particular, a survey of the adoption rate of blockchain among MSMEs for supply chain in Klang Valley, Malaysia, was conducted, with data from 194 MSMEs collected. Cost, competitive pressure, complexity, and relative advantage are found to have a strong link with Malaysian SMEs' desire to use BOSCM. Market dynamics, regulatory backing, and senior management support, on the other hand, were unimportant.

MAIN CONTENT AND DISCUSSIONS

The article begins with a definition of blockchain technology in order to provide a better grasp of the issue at hand. There is also a quick description of the Cryptocurrency application. The characteristics that distinguish blockchain as a cutting-edge and developing technology would be included. In addition, while the definition of MSMEs varies by area, it would be included. The aspects of blockchain that are most beneficial and relevant to MSMEs will be discussed, as well as how these features may assist MSMEs overcome common issues.

Definition

Before diving into any type of business application, it's important to understand the fundamentals of any developing technology, such as the definition and idea of blockchain technology. Organizations can keep and record transactions between two parties on a blockchain, which is a constantly changing collection of data. To put it another way, it is a series of blocks that hold and store data. If the information inside the block is altered by modifications or tampering, a new block is generated to reflect the new net sets of data that have been created together with the changed data set. It's a public location where buyers and sellers may keep transactions easily and permanently, and it's a great example of a business application.

The paper states that Blockchain is a distributed ledger that is totally accessible to anybody, similar to a technological demonstration. What's fascinating about Blockchain is that it has the feature that once data is stored in a blockchain, changing it becomes extremely difficult. Before tampering, each block includes data, the block's hash, and the hash of the preceding block. The data that is kept inside a block depends on the kind of blockchain, and it may be customized to any data structure. One of the most prominent blockchains in the world, the Bitcoin blockchain, for example, records information about a transaction involving bitcoin cryptocurrency, such as the sender, recipient, and quantity of coins. A hash is assigned to each block in a blockchain, and the hash is used to identify a block and distinguish it from others. A hash is constantly unique, and anytime tampering is found in a block, a new hash is created, essentially establishing a chain of blocks. Hashes are crucial for blockchains because they are a mathematical technique that only permits one-way functions that are nearly impossible to invert, making them helpful for identifying block changes.

Cryptocurrency Application

The usage of the Bitcoin cryptocurrency as the primary currency distinguishes this new technology. Bitcoin is a type of digital money that may be used to make payments (Wang, Lin & Luo, 2019). In layman's terms, it's simply currency, but it's held in a digital format and asset, and it may be used instead of banknotes and coins. Bitcoin transactions are saved and kept in a set of records known as blocks for safekeeping and tampering. These records, or blocks, contain Bitcoin transactions, which are then recorded on a blockchain. Due to the fact that bitcoin money is validated in the first place, blockchain transactions do not require the services of middlemen, unlike cash transactions. Disintermediation is the process of eliminating middlemen such as commercial banks, credit cards, and internet payment systems like PayPal. Organizations all around the world would regard such a proposition as advantageous since it saves them the costs of hiring intermediaries.

Business Application

Micro, Small, and Medium-sized Enterprises (MSMEs) are one of the numerous sorts of commercial organizations that must effectively use and take use of such technologies (Mazzorana-Kremer, 2019). The question lately hasn't been whether emerging technologies are useful for practical applications and real-world scenarios, but rather how can MSMEs everywhere, particularly in emerging or developing economies, successfully use those technologies to overcome the common challenges that MSMEs face and transform themselves into growth engines. Lack of finance owing to banks' unwillingness to lend, difficulty to develop and scale operations, data fabrication or fraud, lack of technological knowhow and abilities, and lack of brand awareness are examples of such problems. These obstacles are enough to stifle and halt the growth of MSMEs, causing many to collapse within their first few years of operation. Carrigan (2020) found that over 21.5 percent of MSMEs fail in the first year of operation, over 30 percent in the second year, over 50 percent in the fifth year, and a staggering 70 percent in the tenth year.

Paffenholz (1998) and Woywode (1998) found that around half of MSMEs survive for more than five years. According to some writers, just approximately half of MSMEs are still in business after only the first three years of operation (Watson, 2003). MSMEs are the lifeblood of every economy, particularly those in emerging or developing markets, as they generate revenue, employment, and economic growth.

Micro, Small, and Medium-sized Enterprises (MSMEs) are defined differently in different countries, therefore there is no uniform definition of MSMEs. MSMEs, on the other hand, are defined by figures that fall below a given threshold, such as the number of workers, sales turnover, and fixed capital. MSMEs, according to the European Commission (2019), are businesses with less than 250 workers and annual revenues of less than 50 million euros. MSMEs, on the other hand, are defined as businesses with less than 300 workers and annual revenues of less than $15 million, according to the World Bank Group (2011). Small and medium-sized companies (SMEs) are classified as businesses with 10 to 250 workers in most countries, according to the World Trade Organization (2019). Businesses with less than 10 employees are referred to as micro-businesses. Micro-enterprises are not included in the definition of SMEs, according to the United Nations Development Programme (1999). For example, SMEs are defined as companies with five to 200 workers that operate in the formal sector owing to their registration as a firm. These are distinct from microenterprises, which employ a tiny number of people (approximately one to five), have even more severe financial and resource restrictions, and are considered part of the informal sector.

Features of Blockchain

This section examines the characteristics that distinguish Blockchain from other types of money as well as other upcoming technologies. The unique characteristics of blockchain will be examined, and then examples of how these features may be used to address significant issues faced by MSMEs would be presented.

Openness

Openness is defined by two characteristics: first, the blockchain's code is open source (Schmeiss, Hoelzle, Tech, 2019). To put it another way, anyone may access the network (Mendes, Rodrigues, Fonseca, Lopes, Garca-Alonso & Berrocal, September 2018). Users with access to the Internet can test the source code to ensure that any transaction is legitimate.

Second, it is permissionless, which implies that anybody may download it and join the omnichannel network (Deuber, Magri & Thyagarajan, 2019, May). A permissionless blockchain network, according to proponents, requires no access control or selective limitation of access for any users. In other words, when apps are added or information in a block or node changes, no approvals or permissions are necessary. Blockchain is on a list of vital technologies for businesses because of its transparency and ease. Because it is more user-friendly and does not require physical access to see data, blockchain is better to previous techniques.

It should be emphasized, however, that the degree of openness of blockchain is determined by the blockchain's domain. Anyone who wants to engage in a public domain can do so, and any node can join the network for free. However, this might result in crowded networks, slowing transaction speed and capacity while also consuming a lot of energy, thus raising expenses. Private domains, on the other hand, are stringent in that they no longer allow anybody to engage without the creators' consent. Private domains are often reserved for close-knit communities or groups with limited membership. While private domains do not have the same limitations as public domains, the lack of access to the general public is regarded as counterintuitive to the original goal of blockchain.

Smart Contracts: Trust and Transparency

The blockchain concept was created with the premise that trust must be established between each transaction. In the actual world, this would necessitate the involvement of a third party who is regarded as trustworthy and has a lengthy track record of reliability. However, Blockchain provides a superior option that eliminates the need to find a trustworthy third party. The smart contract is a feature of the blockchain technology (Karamitsos, Papadaki & Al Barghuthi, 2018). Consider the following scenario: two parties meet and agree on the terms and conditions of a contract. All ledger entries are available in real time, ensuring complete transparency throughout the process. Furthermore, the contract is very secure, as blockchain guarantees that the contract's requirements are satisfied before moving on to the next phase. Furthermore, there is no need for a middleman because acceptance to the terms and conditions is automatic. Because all procedures are automated, multiple approvals are not required, resulting in a more transparent, efficient, and time-saving manner of contract creation.

The nature of Smart Contracts eliminates the need for a third party, and the automated process provided by Smart Contracts speeds up operations and eliminates human mistakes (Macrinici, Cartofeanu, & Gao, 2018). Both parties may access the shared ledger of previous transactions, and the openness allows for greater confidence. In the business world, Blockchain technology may be used to build a permanent, public, and transparent ledger system for tracking sales, purchases, assets, workers, customers, and suppliers.

Proof-of-Work, Tracking Data, and Security

To define proof-of-work, it is a situation in which one party, the prover, is needed to obtain agreement from the other, the verifier, that a specific amount of computing effort has been done for a specific reason (Vukoli, 2015, October). After then, the verifier may validate the spending with little or no work on their side. Proof-of-strength work's rests in its ability to thwart any type of denial-of-service attack, as well as frauds.

However, the different time-stamping techniques that allow it to capture any changes made in a timestamp are the core purpose of the proof-of-work features. The notion of unmodified data recording enables a more accurate tracking of every transaction back to its source. Proof-of-work guarantees security, which prevents fraud, and therefore promotes confidence, thanks to its verification capability and tracking procedure. This security assures that none of the parties engaged in a transaction may lie about it. The more extensions a Blockchain has, the more difficult it is to manipulate data, enhancing the level of security. Rather than overwriting previous blocks, blockchains are generally designed to add and extend new blocks onto existing blocks.

Decentralisation

Blockchain data is frequently stored over a peer-to-peer (P2P) network, implying that it is not managed, organized, or kept centrally (Glaser, 2017, January). Decentralization has a variety of distinct characteristics. To begin with, blockchain's decentralised nature implies that every user (or node) in the network can be trusted because each node has access to the blockchain system, providing for information transparency. This eliminates the time-consuming requirement of obtaining authorization from the centralised node. In a centralised network, there is always one administrator who is in control of all the nodes, and if any changes are made, a copy is kept in that official node. As a result, this official node is subject to hacker and scammer attacks, and the entire information structure is at risk of being lost.

This takes us to the second, and perhaps most crucial, benefit of having a decentralized system: the lack of weak places that computer crackers may attack in a centralised system (Hardwick, Gioulis, Akram & Markantonakis, 2018, July). Blockchain reduces a variety of dangers associated with data being stored centrally by storing data and information throughout its peer-to-peer network, and in the case of an attack, information is not at risk of being destroyed because data quality is maintained across all nodes.

While decentralisation may cause verification challenges, such as how to know when modifications to the blockchain are done, there are a variety of ways to get around these issues. When a transaction is conducted between peers, it is validated by nodes existing in the network, since decentralised ledger technology maintains data in an immutable way. When peers validate a transaction, they must ensure that the data is accurate.

Challenges Faced by MSMEs

Difficulty of Funding

When it comes to MSME finance, blockchain technology has the ability to entirely "reinvent the wheel." The tough task of obtaining financial capital or finance for their businesses is one of the most prevalent problems that MSMEs encounter, regardless of whether they are based in developing or developed countries. Due to MSMEs' lack of security as collateral, banks are typically hesitant to lend any exorbent or lump sum amount of money. Thus, a credit rating system based on Blockchain that can represent the credit worthiness of MSMSs may be created to solve this problem (Wang, 2020, April). The assessment system would include intelligent characteristics under a distributed Blockchain technology, such as the capacity to give credit records with immutable timestamps and records that can be tracked back to their source. As a result, MSMEs will be able to display their transaction history in order to demonstrate their trustworthiness (Ilbiz & Durst, 2019). On the other side, this new approach helps banks to differentiate between good and bad businesses, and the transparency of blockchain allows banks to quickly decide which businesses to fund.

By automating what was formerly a laborious process, blockchain resurrects the potential of peer-to-peer lending practices that have evolved outside of the traditional banking system. MSME can choose to finance through an external source such as an Initial Coin Offering (ICO) or other similar crowdfunding initiatives if they do not want to go via the bank. However, in the equity markets, an updated version of ICO called as Security Token Offering (STO) (Mazzorana-Kremer, 2019) that utilizes the Blockchain technology has since emerged. STO enables MSMEs to raise funds through equity instead of relying on a third party. The blockchain characteristics also enable for the automated handling of commissions, overhead paperwork, brokerage fees, and share exchanges, reducing red tape and bureaucracy and saving time. The main problem with this crowdfunding or investment method is that it is unregulated, and in many countries, any type of ICO is unregulated, and they are frequently the subject of fraud prosecutions, particularly when investors are involved.

Cost Reduction and Supply Chain

MSMEs must, at the very least, seek to survive in order to continue their company activities in the foreseeable future, or face operational discontinuity. Other goals include developing and growing the company, and in order to attain these goals, expenses must be cut throughout the board. MSMEs have traditionally placed cost-cutting or cost-reduction at the top of their priority list of long-term goals. This means lowering operational and transaction costs as much as possible in order to compete effectively with other businesses or even larger companies, and Blockchain technology can help them do so (Garca-Bauelos, Ponomarev, Dumas, & Weber, September 2017). There are typically intermediates in a normal business channel or chain, such as agents, factors, brokers, banks, and others, who play a role in confirming and controlling a transaction between two parties. However, the adoption of Blockchain eliminates the necessity for MSMEs to outsource these services, as well as the requirement for third-party intervention, resulting in cost savings.

An ordinary route of distribution in the sphere of commerce comprises of producers who make the commodities. Wholesalers, on the other hand, buy in bulk to take advantage of purchasing economies, then sell those items in modest quantities to retailers while maintaining a diverse product range (Saberi, Kouhizadeh, Sarkis & Shen, 2019). Finally, merchants sell the items to the final purchasers, the customers. The cost of products is gradually marked-up at every transaction, as a result of the length of a normal supply chain, with the responsibility of paying the greatest expenses falling on the end customers. MSMEs have gone via a distribution route like this in this regard. MSMEs, on the other hand, may use blockchain to create a channel between two parties with no middleman, assuring no markups and the lowest possible pricing. Furthermore, MSME may track their items using the hashes in blockchains. For example, because the quantity of food produced by farmers to the end client is easily measurable via blockchain, it may assist SMEs in tracking food delivery supply chains effectively along the distribution channel.

Competing at International Level

In today's world, the subject no only focuses around MSMEs' regional competitive strategies, but now includes strategies for competing worldwide. Internationalisation is the process through which MSMEs join the international market or markets outside of their home countries (Matlay, Ruzzier, Hisrich & Antoncic, 2006). However, with internationalisation comes the possibility of having to compete with companies whose goods are founded on unethical and unjust business methods. When you add in the dramatic effect of globalization, which has effectively turned the entire globe into one giant extended market, competition on the global arena is fierce, and counterfeit and phony items are the standard.

As a result, Blockchain provides the ideal option for MSMEs to successfully combat these harmful goods and compete successfully on the global arena (Ganne, 2018). As products flow through the blockchain ledger, they can be readily traced back to their source. The smart contract feature of blockchain also allows MSMEs to do deal with untrustworthy and unknown overseas parties without relying on third parties to facilitate the transaction. It provides a platform where trust isn't a consideration and trade may be done with people who don't have a track record. Smart contracts allow SMEs to specify arbitrary criteria for executing business operations, and these contracts execute value transactions autonomously as long as peers meet the preset conditions. The smart contract will then execute the contract on behalf of the trade parties autonomously. Smart contracts might be a good way to offer and improve business prospects for risk-averse MSMEs that want to access foreign markets but are afraid to deliver their products to untrustworthy consumers.

Secure and Faster Payments

While MSMEs are satisfied to rely on traditional payment methods, Blockchain provides a new way to make safe payments (Miller, Bentov, Kumaresan & McCorry, 2017). Because Blockchain is a distributed ledger technology that does not require the intervention of a third party, it allows small businesses to conduct secure and safer transactions. MSMEs may utilize tools and software to pay suppliers or remote staff in a way that is faster, more secure, and less expensive than traditional ways, using the Bitcoin cryptocurrency as an example. Furthermore, you may transfer and receive money at low rates all around the world with total transparency and security. This is generally done using public blockchains, which have scalability concerns. However, there have been advancements in this field. Additionally, other systems, like as Ripple, are not public blockchains yet benefit from extremely fast transaction rates.

Blockchain also addresses the issue of late payments and lengthy payment processes. This technology works as a secure link between the recipient and the sender, allowing for a speedier and more trustworthy payment procedure. Blockchain is particularly beneficial for MSMEs that want to make payments from other nations or continents where money transfers might take a lengthy time. MSMEs need to gain a head start with quicker payment systems compared to their peers in the same sector for certain MSMEs, especially in locations where rivals are typically a hotspot, or industries that are deemed ideal competition.

Hacking

MSMEs find it difficult to make a large initial investment in a sophisticated security system due to a lack of capital funding and financing capability, making them vulnerable to attacks from outside sources such as distributed denial-of-service (DDOS) or scams that frequently target websites and online services. While this does not affect MSMEs that do not have an online presence, MSMEs have a lower degree of security than their bigger counterparts, making them a target for hackers and scammers. The decentralised nature of blockchain, on the other hand, protects MSMEs against cyber-attacks (Park & Park, 2017). Rather than concentrating data and rights on a single area to which administrators have complete access, data and privileges are shared equally across all nodes or users. This implies that if an attack were to occur, only one node would be affected, and data may still be preserved.

E-commerce is all the rage in today's commercial world, particularly in a goalball setting that has recently completed COVID-19. However, it also implies that the internet environment is vulnerable to identity theft, frauds, and fraud, and that blockchain can provide the required online security.

Cloud Data Storage

Distributed cloud storage solutions are cloud data storage systems that use blockchain technology as its foundation (Ilbiz & Durst, 2019). The difference between a traditional cloud storage provider and a blockchain-based cloud solution is that the former simply leases out storage spaces in its data center, the quantity of which is determined by the fee paid to the provider. However, the latter type of cloud storage includes a peer-to-peer (P2P) network or system, which connects a group of computer systems in a network over the Internet.

The additional money that can be earned when the MSME decides to rent out its underutilized hard drive to customers or workers is one of the advantages of this solution over traditional ones. The second benefit is the security provided by blockchain characteristics, which means there is no point of vulnerability for hackers to attack, as there is in the case of centralization (Do & Ng, 2017, June). Because of the P2P nature of the cloud solution, files may be exchanged with relative confidence and security without compromising data quality, resulting in increased efficiency without the need to obtain permissions.

Finally, due to the dispersion of data over the network, the download and upload speeds are above average, further boosting efficiency (Li, Song, Mei, Li, Cheng & Sun, 2018). This is especially crucial during seasons with variable demand, and it is always in MSMEs' long-term interests to develop and scale their operations, which is referred to as growth. MSMEs' growth is described as an increase in sales turnover over time, as well as an increase in the number of employees, however there are additional growth indicators and measures, such as increased profit, assets, and equity. However, the most commonly utilized growth metrics are sales turnover and employment. This is critical for MSMEs seeking for a rapid transaction to grow their operations, despite the fact that latency is frequently a concern with quick transactions; for example, during a congested network, an application confirmation of a transaction may take a long time.

Attracting and Retaining Customer

Start-ups are MSMEs that are relatively new to the market and have just recently began operating. They recently decided to exit their pre-startup period, in which they used their funds to kickstart their business operations. Unlike major businesses, these start-ups are relatively unknown to the general public and consumers, and they do not have a large number of assets. As a result, start-ups lack a brand name, and buyers have yet to get acquainted with them. Due to friction systems, high prices, time delays, low client retention, and redemption rates, traditional consumer loyalty programs are not realizing their full potential.

To get over this problem, MSMEs may utilize blockchain as a customer retention or loyalty program, offering tokens to consumers for every transaction in a frictionless blockchain network (Harvey, Moorman, & Toledo, 2018). Because the tokens are connected to the blockchain network, they may be accessed at any time via a web browser or a customer's smartphone. Every every transaction ever performed between the MSME and consumers is recorded in an immutable and time-stamped distributed database entry on the blockchain. Each transaction and its record can be tracked simply, but they are also immutable, prohibiting fraud, manipulation, and duplicate spending. Customers, on the other hand, may utilize the omnichannel capacity to transfer, sell, or swap their tokens for other loyalty tokens on open marketplaces. Customers would be encouraged to return and conduct business with that MSME as a result of this retention and incentive program. The retention program's lucrative aspect will also entice new consumers to purchase items from the MSME.

Errors and Online Identification

Blockchain technology, as a decentralized ledger, records data in an immutable manner. An immutable ledger, in layman's terms, means that the system is closed to errors caused by human error (Páez, Pérez, Ramrez, Montes, & Bouvarel, 2020). As a result, when a transaction is made between peers, it is validated by the network's nodes. When peers validate a transaction, they must ensure that the data is accurate. This is also very beneficial for MSMEs that want to avoid staff forgeries or company fraud.

The subject of online identity verification is one area where blockchain may make a significant difference. Because of the digital era, a rising number of MSMEs are prioritizing having an online presence, resulting in increased need for online security (Páez, Pérez, Ramrez, Montes, & Bouvarel, 2020). With the implementation of a peer-to-peer network that allows for a decentralized identity, the danger of identity theft and fraud might be removed thanks to blockchain. As a result, blockchain enables a new and more effective method of identifying a person without the need for a third party. The benefits include increased verification dependability, which aids MSMEs in speeding up business processes and increasing organizational efficiency.

FRAMEWORK OF CHALLENGES AND SOLUTION APPROACHES

From the aforementioned features of blockchain that are highly beneficial and conducive towards solving or at least mitigating the issues typically faced by MSMEs, a Framework of Challenges and Solution Approaches is devised in Figure 1 to showcase the important summary.

Figure 1. Framework of challenges and solution approaches to overcoming MSME challenges with blockchain

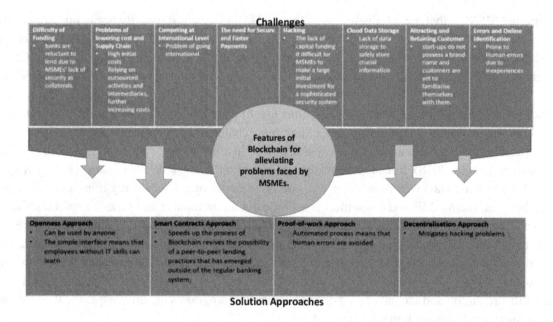

FUTURE RESEARCH DIRECTIONS

It should go without saying that additional study into blockchain in the context of MSMEs is required in a number of areas. However, rather than a broad introduction of blockchain as in this chapter, it would be preferable to go into more particular specifics. Blockchain implementation in supply chains, blockchain acceptance rates in different areas, and even blockchain use in businesses such as insurance, restaurants, manufacturing, and tourism are examples of such features. The lack of empirical research merely indicates that further study is required. There has been an overemphasis on the good aspects of Blockchain, necessitating a more critical examination of its limits.

CONCLUSION

To summarize, Blockchain is a significant new technology by its very nature. Due to a lack of knowledge and awareness about this new technology, an overview of what blockchain is and how it works in technical terms is required. The characteristics that separate Blockchain from other technologies are what make it unique, providing any company that successfully implements blockchain with an extraordinary competitive edge as well as several commercial options to stay ahead of the competition.

As illustrated in this article, Blockchain may be used to tackle a number of organizational issues. Micro, Small, and Medium-sized Enterprises (MSMEs) are probably the most important of the many types of organizations because of their involvement in the creation of jobs, the development of new goods, the promotion of competition, and the generation of income for governments. While this paper advocates for the use of Blockchain technology to address the various challenges and issues faced by average MSMEs, it should be noted that Blockchain has its own limitations, and caution should be exercised in ensuring that the initial investment in blockchain implementation is carefully and methodologically planned.

REFERENCES

Adner, R., & Levinthal, D. A. (2002). The emergence of emerging technologies. *California Management Review*, *45*(1), 50–66. doi:10.2307/41166153

Avital, M., Beck, R., King, J., Rossi, M., & Teigland, R. (2016). *Jumping on the Blockchain Bandwagon: Lessons of the Past and Outlook to the Future*. Academic Press.

Balasubramaniam, A., Gul, M. J. J., Menon, V. G., & Paul, A. (2020). Blockchain For Intelligent Transport System. *IETE Technical Review*, 1–12.

Barney, J. B., & Hesterly, W. S. (2010). *Strategic management and competitive advantage: Concepts*. Prentice Hall.

Beck, R., Avital, M., Rossi, M., & Thatcher, J. B. (2017). *Blockchain technology in business and information systems research*. Academic Press.

Beck, R., Stenum Czepluch, J., Lollike, N., & Malone, S. (2016). *Blockchain–The gateway to trust-free cryptographic transactions*. Academic Press.

Bharti, A. K. (2019, November). A Study of Emerging Areas in Adoption of Blockchain Technology and it's Prospective Challenges in India. In *2019 Women Institute of Technology Conference on Electrical and Computer Engineering (WITCON ECE)* (pp. 146-153). IEEE.

Biswas, K., & Muthukkumarasamy, V. (2016, December). Securing smart cities using blockchain technology. In *2016 IEEE 18th international conference on high performance computing and communications; IEEE 14th international conference on smart city; IEEE 2nd international conference on data science and systems (HPCC/SmartCity/DSS)* (pp. 1392-1393). IEEE. 10.1109/HPCC-SmartCity-DSS.2016.0198

Buterin, V. (2014). Ethereum white paper: A next generation smart contract & decentralized application platform. *First Version, 53.*

Campello, M., Graham, J. R., & Harvey, C. R. (2010). The real effects of financial constraints: Evidence from a financial crisis. *Journal of Financial Economics, 97*(3), 470–487. doi:10.1016/j.jfineco.2010.02.009

Chitchyan, R., & Murkin, J. (2018). Review of blockchain technology and its expectations: Case of the energy sector. arXiv preprint arXiv:1803.03567.

Day, G. S., Shoemaker, P. J., & Gunther, R. (2000). *Wharton on management of emerging technology.* John Wiley & Sons.

de la Rosa, J. L., Gibovic, D., Torres, V., Maicher, L., Miralles, F., El-Fakdi, A., & Bikfalvi, A. (2016, December). On intellectual property in online open innovation for SME by means of blockchain and smart contracts. *3rd Annual World Open Innovation Conf. WOIC.*

Deuber, D., Magri, B., & Thyagarajan, S. A. K. (2019, May). Redactable blockchain in the permissionless setting. In *2019 IEEE Symposium on Security and Privacy (SP)* (pp. 124-138). IEEE. 10.1109/SP.2019.00039

Do, H. G., & Ng, W. K. (2017, June). Blockchain-based system for secure data storage with private keyword search. In *2017 IEEE World Congress on Services (SERVICES)* (pp. 90-93). IEEE. 10.1109/SERVICES.2017.23

European Commission. (2019). *The new SME definition: user guide and model declaration.* Retrieved from: https://ec.europa.eu/growth/smes/business-friendly-environment/sme-definition/

Feldman, S. (2018). *A visual representation of America's digital literacy.* Retrieved from: https://www.weforum.org/agenda/2019/10/americans-get-a-failing-grade-for-digital-literacy#:~:text=A%20new%20report%20by%20Pew,tech%20policies%20and%20data%20privacy

Ganne, E. (2018). *Can Blockchain revolutionize international trade?* World Trade Organization.

García-Bañuelos, L., Ponomarev, A., Dumas, M., & Weber, I. (2017, September). Optimized execution of business processes on blockchain. In *International Conference on Business Process Management* (pp. 130-146). Springer. 10.1007/978-3-319-65000-5_8

Glaser, F. (2017, January). Pervasive decentralisation of digital infrastructures: a framework for blockchain enabled system and use case analysis. *Proceedings of the 50th Hawaii international conference on system sciences.* 10.24251/HICSS.2017.186

Hardwick, F. S., Gioulis, A., Akram, R. N., & Markantonakis, K. (2018, July). E-voting with blockchain: An e-voting protocol with decentralisation and voter privacy. In *2018 IEEE International Conference on Internet of Things (iThings) and IEEE Green Computing and Communications (GreenCom) and IEEE Cyber, Physical and Social Computing (CPSCom) and IEEE Smart Data (SmartData)* (pp. 1561-1567). IEEE. 10.1109/Cybermatics_2018.2018.00262

Harvey, C. R., Moorman, C., & Toledo, M. (2018). How blockchain can help marketers build better relationships with their customers. *Harv. Bus. Rev.* Available online at: https://hbr. org/2018/10/how-blockchain-can-helpmarketers-build-better-relationships-with-their-customers

Huh, S., Cho, S., & Kim, S. (2017, February). Managing IoT devices using blockchain platform. In *2017 19th international conference on advanced communication technology (ICACT)* (pp. 464-467). IEEE. 10.23919/ICACT.2017.7890132

Ilbiz, E., & Durst, S. (2019). The Appropriation of Blockchain for Small and Medium-sized Enterprises. *Journal of Innovation Management*, 7(1), 26–45. doi:10.24840/2183-0606_007.001_0004

Jamil, M. I. M., & Almunawar, M. N. Importance of Digital Literacy and Hindrance Brought About by Digital Divide. In *Encyclopedia of Information Science and Technology* (5th ed., pp. 1683–1698). IGI Global.

Karamitsos, I., Papadaki, M., & Al Barghuthi, N. B. (2018). Design of the blockchain smart contract: A use case for real estate. *Journal of Information Security*, 9(3), 177–190. doi:10.4236/jis.2018.93013

Khan, M. A., & Salah, K. (2018). IoT security: Review, blockchain solutions, and open challenges. *Future Generation Computer Systems*, 82, 395–411. doi:10.1016/j.future.2017.11.022

Lanham, R. A. (2006). *The economics of attention: Style and substance in the age of information.* University of Chicago Press.

Li, R., Song, T., Mei, B., Li, H., Cheng, X., & Sun, L. (2018). Blockchain for large-scale internet of things data storage and protection. *IEEE Transactions on Services Computing*, 12(5), 762–771. doi:10.1109/TSC.2018.2853167

Macrinici, D., Cartofeanu, C., & Gao, S. (2018). Smart contract applications within blockchain technology: A systematic mapping study. *Telematics and Informatics*, 35(8), 2337–2354. doi:10.1016/j.tele.2018.10.004

Mathews, M., Robles, D., & Bowe, B. (2017). *BIM+ blockchain: A solution to the trust problem in collaboration?* Academic Press.

Matlay, H., Ruzzier, M., Hisrich, R. D., & Antoncic, B. (2006). SME internationalization research: Past, present, and future. *Journal of Small Business and Enterprise Development*, 13(4), 476–497. doi:10.1108/14626000610705705

Mazzorana-Kremer, F. (2019). Blockchain-Based Equity and STOs: Towards a Liquid Market for SME Financing? *Theoretical Economics Letters*, 9(5), 1534–1552. doi:10.4236/tel.2019.95099

Memon, M., Hussain, S. S., Bajwa, U. A., & Ikhlas, A. (2018, August). Blockchain Beyond Bitcoin: Blockchain Technology Challenges and Real-World Applications. In *2018 International Conference on Computing, Electronics & Communications Engineering (iCCECE)* (pp. 29-34). IEEE. 10.1109/iCCECOME.2018.8658518

Mendes, D., Rodrigues, I., Fonseca, C., Lopes, M., García-Alonso, J. M., & Berrocal, J. (2018, September). Anonymized distributed PHR using blockchain for openness and non-repudiation guarantee. In *International Conference on Theory and Practice of Digital Libraries* (pp. 381-385). Springer. 10.1007/978-3-030-00066-0_45

Millman, C., Li, Z., Matlay, H., & Wong, W. C. (2010). Entrepreneurship education and students' internet entrepreneurship intentions. *Journal of Small Business and Enterprise Development*, *17*(4), 569–590. doi:10.1108/14626001011088732

Mori, T. (2016). Financial technology: Blockchain and securities settlement. *Journal of Securities Operations & Custody*, *8*(3), 208–227.

Mougayar, W. (2016). *The business blockchain: promise, practice, and application of the next Internet technology*. John Wiley & Sons.

Nofer, M., Gomber, P., Hinz, O., & Schiereck, D. (2017). Blockchain. *Business & Information Systems Engineering*, *59*(3), 183–187. doi:10.100712599-017-0467-3

Oishi, S., Kesebir, S., & Diener, E. (2011). Income inequality and happiness. *Psychological Science*, *22*(9), 1095–1100. doi:10.1177/0956797611417262 PMID:21841151

Ølnes, S., Ubacht, J., & Janssen, M. (2017). *Blockchain in government: Benefits and implications of distributed ledger technology for information sharing*. Academic Press.

Páez, R., Pérez, M., Ramírez, G., Montes, J., & Bouvarel, L. (2020). An Architecture for Biometric Electronic Identification Document System Based on Blockchain. *Future Internet*, *12*(1), 10. doi:10.3390/fi12010010

Park, J. H., & Park, J. H. (2017). Blockchain security in cloud computing: Use cases, challenges, and solutions. *Symmetry*, *9*(8), 164. doi:10.3390ym9080164

Peck, M. E. (2017). Blockchain world-Do you need a blockchain? This chart will tell you if the technology can solve your problem. *IEEE Spectrum*, *54*(10), 38–60. doi:10.1109/MSPEC.2017.8048838

Pollari, I. (2016). The rise of Fintech opportunities and challenges. *Jassa*, (3), 15.

Respini, E. (Ed.). (2018). *Art in the Age of the Internet: 1989 to Today*. Yale University Press.

Saberi, S., Kouhizadeh, M., Sarkis, J., & Shen, L. (2019). Blockchain technology and its relationships to sustainable supply chain management. *International Journal of Production Research*, *57*(7), 2117–2135. doi:10.1080/00207543.2018.1533261

Schmeiss, J., Hoelzle, K., & Tech, R. P. (2019). Designing governance mechanisms in platform ecosystems: Addressing the paradox of openness through blockchain technology. *California Management Review*, *62*(1), 121–143. doi:10.1177/0008125619883618

Sikorski, J. J., Haughton, J., & Kraft, M. (2017). Blockchain technology in the chemical industry: Machine-to-machine electricity market. *Applied Energy, 195*, 234–246. doi:10.1016/j.apenergy.2017.03.039

Słapczyński, T. (2019). Blockchain technology and cryptocurrencies-legal and tax aspects. *Zeszyty Naukowe Wyższej Szkoły Finansów i Prawa w Bielsku-Białej, 23*(1), 31–36.

Thiruchelvam, V., Mughisha, A. S., Shahpasand, M., & Bamiah, M. (2018). Blockchain-based technology in the coffee supply chain trade: Case of burundi coffee. *Journal of Telecommunication, Electronic and Computer Engineering, 10*(3-2), 121-125.

Underwood, S. (2016). *Blockchain beyond bitcoin*. Academic Press.

United Nation Development Programme. (1999). *Small and Medium Enterprise Development*. Retrieved from: http://web.undp.org/evaluation/documents/Essentials-on-SME.pdf

Vukolić, M. (2015, October). The quest for scalable blockchain fabric: Proof-of-work vs. BFT replication. In *International workshop on open problems in network security* (pp. 112-125). Springer.

Wang, R., Lin, Z., & Luo, H. (2019). Blockchain, bank credit and SME financing. *Quality & Quantity, 53*(3), 1127–1140. doi:10.100711135-018-0806-6

Wang, W. (2020, April). A SME Credit Evaluation System Based on Blockchain. In *2020 International Conference on E-Commerce and Internet Technology (ECIT)* (pp. 248-251). IEEE. 10.1109/ECIT50008.2020.00064

Wong, L. W., Leong, L. Y., Hew, J. J., Tan, G. W. H., & Ooi, K. B. (2020). Time to seize the digital evolution: Adoption of blockchain in operations and supply chain management among Malaysian SMEs. *International Journal of Information Management, 52*, 101997. doi:10.1016/j.ijinfomgt.2019.08.005

Wong, M. C., Yee, K. C., & Nohr, C. (2018). Socio-technical consideration for blockchain technology in healthcare. *Studies in Health Technology and Informatics, 247*, 636–640. PMID:29678038

World Bank Group. (2011). *Small and Medium Enterprises A Cross-Country Analysis with a New Data Set*. Retrieved from: https://documents1.worldbank.org/curated/en/967301468339577330/pdf/WPS5538.pdf

World Trade Organisation. (2019). *Micro, small and medium-sized enterprises*. Retrieved from: https://www.wto.org/english/thewto_e/minist_e/mc11_e/briefing_notes_e/bfmsmes_e.htm#:~:text=In%20most%20countries%2C%20small%20and,referred%20to%20as%20micro%20firms.&text=In%20recent%20years%2C%20the%20interest,the%20WTO%20framework%20has%20increased

Yli-Huumo, J., Ko, D., Choi, S., Park, S., & Smolander, K. (2016). Where is current research on blockchain technology?—A systematic review. *PLoS One, 11*(10), e0163477. doi:10.1371/journal.pone.0163477 PMID:27695049

Yuan, Y., & Wang, F. Y. (2016, November). Towards blockchain-based intelligent transportation systems. In *2016 IEEE 19th International Conference on Intelligent Transportation Systems (ITSC)* (pp. 2663-2668). IEEE. 10.1109/ITSC.2016.7795984

ADDITIONAL READING

Drescher, D. (2017). *Blockchain basics* (Vol. 276). Apress. doi:10.1007/978-1-4842-2604-9

Nofer, M., Gomber, P., Hinz, O., & Schiereck, D. (2017). Blockchain. *Business & Information Systems Engineering*, *59*(3), 183–187. doi:10.100712599-017-0467-3

Swan, M. (2015). *Blockchain: Blueprint for a new economy*. O'Reilly Media, Inc.

KEY TERMS AND DEFINITIONS

Blockchain: A chain of blocks represents a database that is shared across a network of computers. It is extremely difficult to alter a record after it has been put to the chain.

Emerging Technology: A branch of technology with yet-to-be-realized practical applications They differ from other types of technology in that they are capable of upsetting the status quo.

Micro, Small, and Medium-Sized Enterprises: Numbers below a specific threshold characterize businesses, notably the number of employees and sales turnover. MSMEs, for example, are defined as businesses with less than 250 workers and annual revenues of less than 50 million euros, according to the European Commission (2019).

Peer-to-Peer: Network: A network that lets a group of nodes, such as computer systems, to join without the need for an administrator, assuring data quality and privilege equality.

Proof-of-Work: A consensus method for confirming transactions that is also responsible for the production of new blocks whenever a blockchain is updated.

Smart Contract: An agreement with sophisticated protocols that enables process automation and eliminates the need for middlemen or third parties.

Chapter 8
Human–Computer Interaction for Knowledge Discovery for Management

Faiq Mahmood

Government College University, Faisalabad, Pakistan

Khairia Mehmood

Government Collage University, Faisalabad, Pakistan

Wasim Bari

https://orcid.org/0000-0003-2329-3857

Government College University, Faisalabad, Pakistan

Mohsin Bashir

Government College University, Faisalabad, Pakistan

ABSTRACT

The rising volume of data in our networked world is a huge problem that necessitates practical and user-friendly solutions. Computational approaches may be useful, but we must recognize that problem-solving knowledge is stored in the human mind, not in robots. A strategic goal for finding answers to data-intensive problems might be to combine two domains that provide optimal preconditions: human-computer interaction (HCI) and knowledge discovery (KDD). HCI is concerned with human vision, cognition, intelligence, decision-making, and interactive visualization approaches; hence, it focuses mostly on supervised methods. KDD is primarily concerned with intelligent machines and data mining, namely the creation of scalable algorithms for discovering previously undiscovered associations in data, and hence focuses on automatic computational approaches. A proverb illustrates this perfectly: "Computers are incredibly fast, accurate, but stupid. Humans are incredibly slow, inaccurate, but brilliant."

DOI: 10.4018/978-1-6684-9151-5.ch008

INTRODUCTION

The relevance of data-intensive sciences is growing as a result of the exponential development in data quantity and complexity, rising processing power, and the availability of new computer technologies (Kousez et al. 2009). The enormous, complicated, and sometimes illogically or completely unstructured data is one of the major problems of the networked 21st century (Holzinger et al. 2013). New, effective, and user-friendly data processing technologies are needed to handle the data's growing volume. Traditional techniques for data interpretation frequently fall short of end users' rising expectations. It's interesting that several sophisticated computational tools have recently been created by independent groups with various philosophies: Researchers in data mining and machine learning frequently have faith in the ability of their statistical techniques to find important patterns, often automatically and without human intervention. However, as end user comprehension and control are reduced, the risks of modelling artefacts increase (Shneiderman et al., 2001, 2002).

As computer systems (Von-Neuman machines) lack the "plastic" components that make up the nervous system that are fundamental to human thinking, they run the danger of producing outcomes that are subpar. Peter Naur asserts that a unique, non-digital method is necessary to comprehend human thought, citing Synapse-State theory as one example (Naur et al. 2008).

As Herbert Simon recognized 40 years ago, an abundance of data leads to a poverty of concentration, and it is required to distribute that attention effectively among the overwhelming variety of information that may absorb it. Moreover, this data avalanche has been expedited by mobile, ubiquitous computers, ubiquitous sensors, and cheap cost storage. In order to deal with this predicament and the expanding data deluge, it is important to strive towards ensuring efficient human control over powerful machine intelligence through the integration of methods involving machine learning and visual analytics. To aid human comprehension and decision-making, cutting-edge computational and user-centered approaches must be used.

A creative energies of techniques, methodologies, and strategies from two fields—HCI, with its significance to intelligence, and KDD, with its focus on cognitive computing—provides the ideal framework for addressing these challenges. KDD aims to support human intellect with machine intelligence by uncovering novel, hitherto undiscovered insights within the sea of data. The main contribution of HCI-KDD is to enable end users to discover and recognize previously unknown and possibly relevant and useful information, in accordance with the principle that "science is to test hypotheses, engineering is to put these notions into business" (Holzinger et al. 2011). It is the process of identifying new, trustworthy, and maybe useful data patterns with the goal of understanding these patterns for decision-making.

This chapter provides a thorough overview and synopsis of the key fundamental subjects, such as Human Computer Interaction (HCI) and Knowledge Discovery (KDD). The interaction of HCI with other areas is then discussed, followed by a review of the KDD process and all of its stages, including Data Selection, Cleansing, etc., with a focus on the Data Mining stage. The peculiarity of the HCI-KDD combination is then briefly explained. It also offers potential paths for more research in its conclusion. The major benefit of this chapter is that it might serve as an excellent introduction for people who are new to the subject.

HUMAN-COMPUTER INTERACTION

Meaning and Definition

Communication, cognitive psychology, cognitive science, sociology, computer programming, industrial engineering, and many other disciplines are combined in the multidisciplinary field of HCI. First, HCI researchers focused on making personal computers more accessible. Nevertheless, as new technologies spread, such as the Internet and cellphones, computer use started to move away from desktop platforms and towards mobile ones. Moreover, HCI has steadily added additional topics.

It no longer makes sense to regard HCI as a specialty of computer science; HCI has grown to be broader, larger and much more diverse than computer science itself. HCI expanded from desktop office applications to include games, learning and education, commerce, health and medical applications, emergency planning and response, and system to support collaboration and community. It expanded from early graphical user interface to include myriad interaction techniques and devices, multi-modal interactions, tool support for model-based user interface specification, and a host of emerging ubiquitous, handheld and context-aware interactions. – John M. Carroll, author and a founder of the field of human-computer interaction

HCI History

With a history spanning more than 40 years, HCI is a discipline that is constantly expanding. Prior to the 1960s, programmers were the main users of computers, and one of their main objectives was to research the features of the user interface that improved operational efficiency. Although new fields including computer engineering, computer animation, machine intelligence, and information systems contributed to HCI research, the mid-1960s through the 1970s were defined by a concentration on human-computer interaction. The field of human-computer interaction (HCI) has its roots in engineering, especially in the study of computer programming and the efficient use of computers to accomplish users' goals. This, however, did not fully express what usability meant. Usability research should focus on how well a user or organization can use a machine, as suggested by Bevan (2001) in his article "International Principles for HCI and Usability" (Bevan et al. 2001). Usability research should also consider how a machine was developed, its user interface and interactions, and how well it can be used by users.

The HCI area was initially both broad and dispersed due to the lack of a precise definition of usability. User interface and end-user application difficulties have become more complex with the introduction of personal computers. Also, the growth of cognitive science—a discipline that unites psychology, languages, philosophy, and anthropology—made it feasible to analyze human thought and role in the process of engineering and computer science. For instance, at the Palo Alto Research Center (PARC), founded by Xerox, discussions of how research study could be implemented to human interaction with machines had already started in the early 1970s. The center attempted to use standard psychological concepts to enhance the operation of the system (Card et al., 1983).

Carroll (2003) referred to the 1980s as "the golden age" of HCI since interaction theory began to gain traction and HCI officially established itself as a field (Carroll et al., 2003). HCI is one of the nine primary disciplines of computer science, according to the Association for Computing Machinery (ACM), the most well-known professional computing association in the world for academics and professionals (Denning et al., 1989). In 1980, ACM also established the "Human Aspects of Computing" department. HCI researchers concentrated on enhancing the machines' capabilities to accomplish ergonomic objectives and to maximize usability (Rogers et al., 2012). The GOMS (Goals, Operators, Methods, and Selection rules) paradigm, which examines fundamental human activities during HCI to cut down on pointless system interactions and enhance interface design, is a cornerstone of this strategy. But the connection between the machine and the human was only one of "using and being used," with users acting as operators and programmers and computers acting as instruments for human activity.

As HCI research advanced, designers and engineers began to understand the importance of computers as active agents that are able to learn and solve issues in addition to processing information. To explain the communication techniques people employed to seek different goals via computers, interactional theories and models also started to develop. By equating the human and machine worlds, designers in the HCI sector have begun to employ metaphors (such as desktop, card stack, and typewriter) as designing tools to help people better grasp computer-based technology. To better comprehend human users, HCI researchers have begun to apply social scientific research techniques (such as surveys, interviews, experiments, and ethnography). However, HCI study in the 1980s was still viewed as the study of usability, focusing on ergonomic objectives like time studies (for example, the Hick-Hyman law and Fitts's law, which explained the amount of time needed for a person to perform specific actions under various conditions), error recognition (for example, the Keyboard shortcut Level Model, which is a form of GOMS framework that enables for error estimation), system prognosis, and retrieval (Carroll et al., 2003).

HCI research flourished in the 1990s because of the quick advancement of personal computer technology and the introduction of portable and ubiquitous gadgets. People's daily life had progressively included computing and the Internet. In the same period, the multidisciplinary expansion and popularity of the human sciences served as another source of inspiration for the development of HCI. For instance, Suchman (1987) used discourse analysis from the field of interpersonal communication to research HCI and viewed human-computer interaction as a type of conversation. Suchman created ideas that might offer direction for certain circumstances and issues pertaining to human-computer interaction by utilizing techniques from cognitive science such as field research and ethnography (Suchman et al., 1987).

Since 2000, the focus of HCI research has shifted from only performing conventional user testing to a new paradigm of researching "user experience," or how people feel while interacting with computer-based devices and include people in the design process. The use of effective interpersonal principles (such as politeness and gender impact) in interactive systems has become essential with a deeper understanding of the role that people play in the connection between user and machine. The study of HCI can also assist us in overcoming typical human limitations (such as limited experience, motivation, and physical incapacity) to aid the fulfilment of instrumental goals, according to communication academics.

HCI Research Projects

Two viewpoints dominate research in the field—computer science/engineering and social science/ humanities—creating a "essential conflict" that supports the field's life (Carroll et al., 2006). From the standpoint of computer science and engineering, HCI focuses on interfaces and network design to enhance usability. Software is developed by designers and engineers to produce graphical user interfaces and user-friendly systems (such as interactive Web features, context-aware systems, information visualization, etc.)

that simplify communication between people and computers. HCI studies the cognitive and behavioral processes that users utilize while interacting with machines or other people using these innovations, as well as the social systems that are created around these interactions, from a social-scientific/humanistic perspective. Designers frequently utilize the concept of interpersonal interaction to influence the layout of computers and associated media interfaces in order to promote natural and fluid interactions between people and computers.

Importance of HCI

HCI is required for creating user-friendly interfaces that people with different capabilities and levels of expertise can readily utilise. Most significantly, human-computer interaction may be advantageous for groups who lack formal training and knowledge about interacting with certain computing systems.

Effective HCI designs save users from having to consider the complexities and subtleties of using the computer system. User-friendly interfaces provide efficient, efficient, and natural user interactions.

1- Application in Daily lives

Contemporary technology has influenced our everyday activities and infiltrated our daily life. To benefit from HCI technology, it is not necessary to own or utilize a computer or smartphone. Whether a person uses an Automated teller machine, a food vending machine or a snack machine, they almost always interact with HCI. This is because the creation of these technologies' intuitive and efficient user interfaces relies so heavily on HCI.

2-Industrial use

In sectors whose everyday operations rely on computer technology, HCI is generally viewed as a critical business-driving element. Well-designed systems ensure that employees are comfortable using them for daily duties. Even for staff with little expertise, HCI systems are easy to use.

HCI must be thoroughly understood while developing backup systems, like the ones employed in power plants or in air traffic control (ATC). In these cases, the aim of HCI is to guarantee that any non-expert person can utilize the system and handle protection situations if necessary.

3-Crucial for software progress

HCI is a crucial component of businesses that create software for end users. These organizations create digital products using HCI concepts in order to make them usable. Following HCI principles is crucial since the product's usability determines whether or not it will be purchased since the end-user will ultimately utilize it.

In short, the field of human computer interaction, which is involved with the design, assessment, and deployment of interaction digital systems for human use, is vital in today's society. Several facets of our everyday life, like the use of cell phones, social networking sites, online shopping, and numerous other digital services, demonstrate the significance of HCI. By offering user-friendly designs, it improves the user experience and raises users' interest in technology. Moreover, by automating repetitive operations, it boosts productivity and fosters a sense of availability among regular users via improving communication. Perhaps it may be claimed that it has improved people's quality of life and has become a necessary discipline in the modern world.

KNOWLEDGE DISCOVERY

The development of tools and systems that can produce and gather enormous volumes of data is a result of the need for information. The game of information acquisition is played by many domains, particularly those involving decision-making. Finance, banking, retail trade, manufacture, surveillance and diagnostics, health care, marketing, and data collecting in science are a few examples. Terabyte-sized datasets, often known as data warehouses, may now be produced because to improvements in storage space and digital data collection tools like scanners. By the end of the century, for instance, NASA's Earth Observation System is anticipated to return data at rates from several terabytes per hour (Way, 1991). Thousands of transactions from routine everyday activities, including checkout-register sales at supermarkets or department stores, are captured by modern scanning technology.

The expansion in the quantity of materials made available via the web presents another difficulty for searching and indexing inside a "database" that is always evolving and expanding. The amount and complexity of the recorded information base limits our capacity to sift through the data and transform it into relevant information. By fact, the sheer volume of data often renders human interpretation impossible, making the effort put into gathering the data pointless. There are now a number of effective methods being utilized to help sift out useful information. Knowledge Discovery in Databases describes how these different technologies are used to retrieve information (KDD).

In 1989, the phrase "knowledge discovery in databases," or KDD, was created to emphasize the application at high level of specific Data Mining (DM) techniques to the general process of determining information in given information (Fayyad et al., 1996). Fayyad views DM as a component of the KDD process' stages. The DM phase primarily involves the methods used to extract and count patterns from data. These days, the two names are frequently used interchangeably.

"KDD's primary goal is to gather information (or information) from databases that include lower-level data (Fayyad et al, 1995). There are numerous official definitions of KDD, but they all agree that the goal is to gather data by identifying patterns in it. Let's look at the definition offered by Smyth, Piatetsky-Shapiro, and Fayyad "Finding legitimate, new, potentially helpful, and ultimately intelligible patterns in data is a difficult process known as knowledge discovery in databases (Fayyad et al, 1995). The objective is to separate out from unprocessed data anything that might not be immediately apparent but is useful or illuminating upon discovery. Data mining techniques are used to pull out knowledge from raw data. Data mining is just one phase of a multidimensional process that falls under the larger umbrella of KDD.

KNOWLEDGE DISCOVERY IN DATABASE

Databases that employ knowledge discovery are able to utilise the enormous amounts of information that are being generated every day. As data warehouses grow in size, it becomes more difficult for humans to see patterns in the data, therefore KDD harnesses the computing power to help. Novel analytical and pattern-extraction techniques are being created and tailored for KDD. Whatever approach is employed based on the intended results and the domain. Throughout the KDD process, the correctness of the captured data cannot be ignored. Knowledge of a certain domain helps with the subjective evaluation of KDD outcomes.

The data mining stage of KDD has received a lot of attention, but previous stages, such data cleansing, are just as important for the quality of the outcomes. The advantages of using finding driven methods of data mining to draw out useful data from huge, complicated datasets are endless. Effective applications are emerging in fields and businesses where data retrieval is advancing faster than human capacity for content analysis. Users need to be aware of any potential ethical dilemmas while utilizing sensitive data.

It is significant to emphasize that KDD cannot be carried out in a human-free environment. Understanding the area that the data is to be taken is necessary for choosing a data collection and subset. For instance, a database could contain client addresses that are irrelevant for identifying trends in the procurement of food goods at a supermarket. During the data mining stage of KDD, the search space is decreased by removing unrelated data components from the dataset. The random sample and makeup are decided upon at this point if the data can be studied using a sample of the data.

PROCESS OF KNOWLEDGE DISCOVERY

1-Cleaning

Databases are infamous for being "noisy" or having incomplete or erroneous data. Data is cleaned up at the preprocessing step. In doing so, it may be necessary to remove "outliers" where appropriate, decide how to handle missing data fields, account for time series data, and do any necessary standardization of data (Fayyad et al., 1996).

2- Transformation

In the transformation phase, efforts are made to keep the data's validity while limiting or reducing the amount of data items that are reviewed. This step involves organizing data, altering its type (for example, from nominal to numeric), and defining new or "derived" properties.

3-Mining

Now, one or more data mining techniques, such as categorization, regression, or clustering, are applied to the data. Many iterative implementations of specific techniques of data mining are frequently used in the KDD component that incorporates data mining. " For instance, a circulation supervisor might need to first use grouping to segment the subscriber database before using rule induction to automatically generate a categorization for each desired cluster in order to create an accurate, symbolic categorization model for predicting whether journal subscribers will renew their memberships (Simoudis et al., 1996).

4-Presentation

The analysis and recording of the findings from the earlier processes constitute the last step. At this point, actions might include going back to a prior phase in the KDD process to further hone the information collected or converting the knowledge into a user-friendly format. Visualizing the retrieved patterns is a frequent interpretative method. Critical analysis of the findings is necessary, and any discrepancies with previously held beliefs or information should be cleared up. For data mining to be successful, it is essential to comprehend and commit to each stage.

DATA MINING MODELS

Many of the several model functions used by KDD are, Map or categorize data into one of a number of preset classifications (Hand et al., 1981). A bank may create groups based on debt-to-income ratios, for instance. The classification algorithm identifies which of the two classifications an applicant belongs to and then uses the information to produce a loan decision.

1-Regression

A learning function known as regression "projects a data item to a genuine prediction variable" (Hand et al., 1981). Regression analysis involves comparing a specific example of an electricity bill to a predefined norm for the same time frame and looking for departures from the norm.

2-Clustering

Maps a data item into one of many categorical classes (or clusters), where the classifications, unlike in classification, must be derived from the data. By identifying organic groupings of data objects using resemblance measurements or probability density models, clusters are formed (Fayyad et al, 1996). Grouping patients according to the symptoms they are displaying is an illustration of this strategy. None of the cluster's need be exclusive of one another.

3-Summarization

Creating a brief summary of the data. The average and standard deviation of individual data items within the sample are frequent examples of these strategies.

4-Dependency modeling

Creating a model that illustrates the relationship between the variables. An illustration might be a model that demonstrates how strongly the ambient temperature and electrical use are associated.

APPLICATIONS OF KDD

Numerous knowledge discovery techniques have been put into practice effectively. "SKICAT is a system that automatically recognizes, and categories images of sky objects obtained from a significant astronomical sky survey. SKICAT can categorize dim sky objects more precisely than astronomers can (Fayyad et al, 1995). Falcon informs banks of potential fraudulent credit card transactions, while the FAIS system utilized by the criminal justice system finds financial transactions that may suggest money laundering. KDD is being used to identify suspicious activity on two fronts (Simoudis et al., 1996). To learn more about consumer behavior, Market Basket Analysis (MBA) has combined discovery driven data mining approaches. In fields like Biological Sciences, Global Climate Change Modeling, and others where the amount of data is greater than our capacity to interpret it, more applications are being deployed.

PRIVACY CONCERNS AND KNOWLEDGE DISCOVERY

Sensitive data is being gathered and kept in these enormous data warehouses, while this practice is not exclusive to knowledge discovery. There have been questions regarding whether data need to be shielded against KDD-style access. The moral and ethical problems with privacy invasion are inextricably linked to pattern recognition. Protection measures are being proposed to stop technological abuse.

KNOWLEDGE DISCOVERY COMPUTING FOR MANAGEMENT

Large amounts of data have been gathered in many different domains, including everyday life, industry, and the environment, thanks to the confluence of technology that makes it possible for disparate technologies to work together as a whole. Knowledge discovery technology has become increasingly popular in order to examine such enormous amounts of data. Bigdata knowledge may be used in a variety of industries as a tool to help human decision-making. Knowledge may take many different forms, including relationships, groups, categories, and rules for data variables. Knowledge is employed in modern management to make effective decisions. Also, managers use knowledge discovery computers to look for more detailed information. Information management technology is used in people's daily lives in the areas of healthcare, interactive systems, recommendations, artificial intelligence systems, and behavioral guidelines. Knowledge-based management is used in several sectors to manage customers, the lifetime of machines, and the production of new products. Knowledge-based management is used in the environment for risk management, traffic data, virus information, and weather forecasting. As a result, the management method of acquiring and utilizing knowledge has been studied and used in many different contexts. In light of this, study has been done on the development and implementation of new knowledge in the fields of government, business, and academia. Timeseries data keep producing new data as time passes. Knowledge Discovery Computing must be developed in order to identify knowledge alterations and expansions in the context of changing and expanding knowledge. Knowledge discovery computing is required to enable efficient information search and management since knowledge also comes in a variety of forms depending on user needs.

RESEARCH CONCLUSIONS OF THE KNOWLEDGE DISCOVERY FOR MANAGEMENT

Researchers and practitioners are invited to present and discuss research findings and knowledge discovery technology for management solutions in the special issue, which will be published in March 2020. By the collaboration of international research and development teams, a variety of studies and solutions have been developed to uncover new information and apply it to management. Through exchanging knowledge, it is feasible to generate fresh added value and begin a discussion about the use of knowledge discovery computers in management to enhance human life quality.

CNN (Convolutional Neural Network) was suggested as the knowledge-based clustering model in Chung and Jung's research (Chung et al., 2020). By utilizing ontology-based context knowledge, it is possible to go beyond the limitations of traditional knowledge-based healthcare. The suggested method uses CNN deep learning to produce inferred knowledge that can be used to obtain a great deal of excellent data and expand knowledge in order to analyze knowledge-based statistics and time - series analysis and activate the optimized healthcare service governance for users whose circumstances have changed.

By combining defect detection capabilities in an interactive system, Lee et al., 2020, introduced the memory attentiveness and coding temporal utterances approach for managing the enhanced knowledge. The suggested approach aims to enhance the human-machine interaction prevalent in both academic and industrial settings. The approach integrates information by employing LSTM (Long Short Term Memory) based on End-to-End interactive analysis function to produce knowledge and solve the problem that requires massive text data and labels. The base of knowledge is generated using the word2vec and encoding results. User conversations are saved to memory, and the knowledge base is used to choose the best response.

In order for knowledge-based information systems of ICT enterprises, Park et al., 2020 investigated the availability and authenticity process in the plan measurement method. In the mechanism, the replies of ICT specialists are analyzed using the AHP (Analytic Hierarchy Process) technique, and the dynamic structure of the accessibility mechanism is looked for using the event sequence diagram (CLD) for dynamic simulation methodology. The evolving system may control the change in status of elements in the stock flow diagram and integrate causal links in the cognition map. The knowledge produced via the application of AHP assessment and CLD is employed in a variety of simulations to assist the decision-making process for information non-disclosure or the policy implementation point.

In their study, Lee and Cho investigated the use of knowledge discovery computing to support computational thinking. It develops information based on the comprehension of software education to enable students on how to effectively express and manage knowledge using computers, similar to computational thinking. The linkage of the problem needing computational thinking is examined using students' comprehension focused on Sequence, Automation, Abstraction, and Algorithm. Regression models, factor analysis, and modelling results for academic outcomes are used to derive knowledge based on computational thinking. In order to give the right information to learners, decision-making tools such as coefficient of correlation and clustering findings are employed (Lee et al., 2020).

The knowledge-based multimodal decision-making approach for the management of individual users' nutrition was established in the study by Kim and Chung [5]. It deduces users' individual health state and suggests healthy food items based on dietary nutrition ontology. In order to produce and enhance knowledge about food items whose nutrition structures are comparable to those of users' chosen food products, the technique also uses users' dietary habits and dietary nutrition similarity. It suggests the nutrients that are necessary for certain users based on the deduced outcomes of ontologies and user choice (Kim et al., 2020).

HCI AND KDD

The age of big data is here. Terabyte and petabyte-sized volumes of intricate digital data are increasingly frequent. They are changing our society and the way that science, the government, and businesses carry out their research and development. Big data analytics may profit from collaboration across both fields (HCI and KDD), and their junction is where the answer resides. Even though both disciplines have been working on ways to extract usable information from data for a long time, there has historically been minimal interaction between them. Whereas HCI focuses on human-centered interaction and visualization, data mining emphasizes scalable, automated solutions.

Hence, an innovative and promising strategy is to integrate the best of both worlds, HCI-KDD, with the primary objective of complementing human intellect with machine intelligence, in order to uncover fresh, unrecognized data insights (Holzinger et al., 2012). Now, one would object: Why would we require a pairing of two areas, each of which is sufficiently huge on its own? One explanation is that the mixture facilitates the supply of reciprocal advantages for both discipline and permits problem-solving when it is impossible to do so from a single disciplinary perspective. The same is true for cross-disciplinary and inter-disciplinary viewpoints: while tie approaches (Holzinger et al., 2011) are essentially research outside the bounds of their component disciplines, inter-disciplinary approaches are a "mix of disciplines" without joint relations or incorporation from other relevant disciplines (Holzinger et al., 2010). The implementation of shared frameworks, which bring together concepts, theories, and perspectives from those disciplines, allows team members from different disciplines to work together on a common problem (Mobjörk et al., 2010) (Wickson et al., 2006) (Lawrence et al., 2004). As a result, trans-disciplinary approaches are known towards an advantageous fusion of fields of study, including trying to reach a business impact. Such cross-disciplinary research is conducted with the stated goal of resolving multifaceted, complicated issues, particularly those (like those connected to sustainability) where there is a nexus between natural and artificial systems (Wickson et al., 2006). This brings up the adage from the abstract's conclusion that computers are "very fast, extremely accurate, and dumb." Humans are immensely imprecise, sluggish, and smart. They have incredible power when combined. This adage is precisely addressed by a strategic, synergistic, and subsequent integration of elements from HCI and KDD.

CONCLUSION

The field of human-computer interaction (HCI) focuses on issues related to human vision, cognition, intelligence, and sense-making, as well as, most importantly, the interaction between people and machines. Several facets of our everyday life, like the use of cell phones, social networking sites, online shopping, and numerous other digital services, demonstrate the significance of HCI. By offering user-friendly designs, it improves the user experience and raises users' interest in technology.

Knowledge Discovery from Data (KDD) is a branch of artificial intelligence that primarily focuses on the creation of algorithms for robotic data mining. Databases that employ knowledge discovery are able to utilize the enormous amounts of information that are being generated every day. As data warehouses grow in size, it becomes more difficult for humans to see patterns in the data, therefore KDD harnesses the computing power to help. Novel analytical and pattern-extraction techniques are being created and tailored for KDD.

Large areas of the deep, undiscovered, and complementary subfields exist in both disciplines. In the nexus of HCI and KDD, there is both a significant challenge and a potential answer to many present issues in the data-intensive sciences. Hence, a revolutionary strategy to improve human intelligence through computational intelligence is to integrate HCI & KDD. HCI-primary KDD's contribution is to make it possible for end users to locate and identify previously undiscovered knowledge that may be valuable and employable. It is the process of locating fresh, reliable, and possibly practical data patterns with the intention of comprehending such data patterns.

The domain expert has explicit domain expertise, and by allowing him to engage with data sets, he may be able to recognize, extract, and comprehend relevant information to learn new, previously undiscovered information and acquire new insight into his sets of data.

REFERENCES

Bevan, N. (2001). International standards for HCI and usability. *International Journal of Human-Computer Studies*, *55*(4), 533–552. doi:10.1006/ijhc.2001.0483

Card, S. K., Moran, T. P., & Newell, A. (1983). *The psychology of human computer interaction*. Erlbaum.

Carroll, J. M. (Ed.). (2003). *HCI models, theories, and frameworks: Toward a multidisciplinary science*. Morgan Kaufmann.

Carroll, J. M. (2014). Soft versus hard: The essential tension. In Human-Computer Interaction and Management Information Systems: Applications. Advances in Management Information Systems (pp. 440-448). Routledge.

Chung, K., & Jung, H. (2020). Knowledge based dynamic cluster model for healthcare management using convolutional neural networks. *Information Technology and Management*, *21*(1), 41–50. doi:10.100710799-019-00304-1

Denning, P. J., Comer, D. E., Gries, D., Mulder, M. C., Tucker, A. B., Turner, A. J., & Young, P. R. (1989). Computing as a discipline. *Communications of the ACM*, *32*(1), 9–23. doi:10.1145/63238.63239

Fayyad, U., Piatetsky-Shapiro, G., & Smyth, P. (1996a). From data mining to knowledge discovery in databases. *AI Magazine*, *17*(3), 37–37.

Fayyad, U., Piatetsky-Shapiro, G., & Smyth, P. (1996b). The KDD process for extracting useful knowledge from volumes of data. *Communications of the ACM*, *39*(11), 27–34. doi:10.1145/240455.240464

Fayyad, U., & Simoudis, E. (1995). Knowledge Discovery and Data Mining Tutorial MA1. *Fourteenth International Joint Conference on Artificial Intelligence (IJCAI-95)*. www-aig.jpl.nasa.gov/public/kdd95/tutorials/IJCAI95- tutorial.html

Hand, D. J. (1981). *Discrimination and Classification*. John Wiley and Sons.

Holzinger, A. (2011). *Successful management of research & development*. BoD–Books on Demand.

Holzinger, A. (2012). On knowledge discovery and interactive intelligent visualization of biomedical data. In *Proceedings of the Int. Conf. on Data Technologies and Applications DATA* (pp. 5-16). Academic Press.

Holzinger, A., Stocker, C., Ofner, B., Prohaska, G., Brabenetz, A., & Hofmann-Wellenhof, R. (2013). Combining HCI, natural language processing, and knowledge discovery-potential of IBM content analytics as an assistive technology in the biomedical field. *Computer, 42*(1), 26–34.

Kim, J. C., & Chung, K. (2020). Knowledge-based hybrid decision model using neural network for nutrition management. *Information Technology and Management, 21*(1), 29–39. doi:10.100710799-019-00300-5

Kouzes, R. T., Anderson, G. A., Elbert, S. T., Gorton, I., & Gracio, D. K. (2009). The changing paradigm of data-intensive computing. *Computer, 42*(1), 26–34. doi:10.1109/MC.2009.26

Lawrence, R. J. (2004). Housing and health: From interdisciplinary principles to transdisciplinary research and practice. *Futures, 36*(4), 487–502. doi:10.1016/j.futures.2003.10.001

Lee, S., Lee, D., Hooshyar, D., Jo, J., & Lim, H. (2020). Integrating breakdown detection into dialogue systems to improve knowledge management: Encoding temporal utterances with memory attention. *Information Technology and Management, 21*(1), 51–59. doi:10.100710799-019-00308-x

Lee, Y., & Cho, J. (2020). Knowledge representation for computational thinking using knowledge discovery computing. *Information Technology and Management, 21*(1), 15–28. doi:10.100710799-019-00299-9

Mobjörk, M. (2010). Consulting versus participatory transdisciplinarity: A refined classification of transdisciplinary research. *Futures, 42*(8), 866–873. doi:10.1016/j.futures.2010.03.003

Naur, P. (2007). Computing versus human thinking. *Communications of the ACM, 50*(1), 85–94. doi:10.1145/1188913.1188922

Naur, P. (2008). *The neural embodiment of mental life by the synapse-state theory.* Naur. Com Publishing.

Park, S. T., Jung, J. R., & Chang, L. (2020). A study on policy measure for knowledge-based management in ICT companies: Focused on appropriability mechanisms. *Information Technology and Management, 21*(1), 1–13. doi:10.100710799-019-00298-w

Rogers, Y. (2012). HCI theory: Classical, modern, and contemporary. *Synthesis Lectures on Human-Centered Informatics, 5*(2), 1–129. doi:10.2200/S00418ED1V01Y201205HCI014

Shneiderman, B. (2001, December). Inventing discovery tools: Combining information visualization with data mining. In *Discovery Science: 4th International Conference, DS 2001 Washington, DC, USA, November 25–28, 2001 Proceedings* (pp. 17-28). Springer Berlin Heidelberg.

Shneiderman, B. (2002a). Creativity support tools. *Communications of the ACM, 45*(10), 116–120. doi:10.1145/570907.570945

Shneiderman, B. (2002b). Inventing discovery tools: Combining information visualization with data mining. *Information Visualization, 1*(1), 5–12. doi:10.1057/palgrave.ivs.9500006

Simoudis, E. (1996). Reality check for data mining. *IEEE Intelligent Systems, 11*(05), 26–33.

Suchman, L. A. (1987). *Plans and situated actions: The problem of human-machine communication.* Cambridge University Press.

Wickson, F., Carew, A. L., & Russell, A. W. (2006). Transdisciplinary research: Characteristics, quandaries and quality. *Futures, 38*(9), 1046–1059. doi:10.1016/j.futures.2006.02.011

Chapter 9
Use and Applications of Blockchain Technology in Human Resource Management Functions

Vandana Madaan
Maharishi Markandeswar (Deemed), India

Ram Singh
ⓘ https://orcid.org/0000-0002-6565-3091
Maharishi Markandeswar (Deemed), India

Anil Dhawan
Mukand Lal National College, India

ABSTRACT

Organizations from different sectors are using blockchain technology, but still it is only 0.5% of the world population that is using blockchain technology in 2019, but there is a steady increase in its demand, and it is anticipated that this demand will increase to 80% of the population using it. HR is becoming an inevitable strategic function of the organizations, and blockchain is helping the organizations to overhaul the HR functioning. HR managers are using blockchain in various processes such as recruitment and selection, validation, mapping skills, processing payroll, security of data, and prevention of frauds. This chapter attempts to identify the characteristics and uses of blockchain technology and scope of its application in human resource management. The study would be conducted by reviewing the extant literature from various secondary sources of data collection. The study will assist in providing an insight about implementation of blockchain in HRM and also facilitate in organizational decision making about the implementation of technology.

DOI: 10.4018/978-1-6684-9151-5.ch009

INTRODUCTION

In the last 10 years, internet has become a need of the hour and has been an integral part of our life (Melcherts, 2017). Like other technologies, creators did not consider that one technology can affect other technologies. Blockchain and artificial intelligence (AI), among other innovative technologies have profound impact on business functions (Michailidis, 2021). Blockchain is not confined to cryptocurrencies but is much more. It is being implemented from banking to supply chain to healthcare and even to HR functions (Constantinide, 2020). Block Chain technology is a new born technology on the way of evolution, creating an era which aims at developing each and every section in the organization. Block chain technology, gain importance because of Bitcoin or cryptocurrencies technology but it actually assures security, confidentiality and transparency that every organization needs (Nakamoto, 2019). Block Chain is perceived as a revolution in technology offering profound impact on a large scale in different sectors like healthcare, supply chain, finance, voting systems, real-estate management, e-governance, education and allied (Salah, Ahmed, Dahshan, 2020).

Blockchain can serve as possible solution for almost all the functions of the organizations from manufacturing, production, to supply chain (Hughes et al., 2019). Although human resource management (HRM) has evolved, with almost all possible functions being digitized (Mishra and Akman, 2010), less attention has been paid to the perspective that how HRM of the organizations can be revamped for better with blockchain. Fifty eight percent human resource (HR) professionals have detected fake credentials on resume of candidates, as per CareerBuilder. People hoax their skills, responsibilities, employment dates, job titles, academic degrees, companies worked for, accolades/awards received (Bhaduri, 2018; Sakran, 2019). Blockchain can help in verification of all these details in real time, thus protecting interests of organization in long run. Blockchain will overhaul the functioning of HRM in organizations. Blockchain will enable employees to share sensitive information with their employers. Information such as qualifications, accomplishments, references and skills could be digitally verified and hence giving assurance to the employers. The technology will enable recruitment, verification, smart contract, secure transactions, attendance, compliance, auditing, fraud prevention and data protection (Spence, 2018). There are certain startups operative which use blockchain to deliver HR Solutions such as pay roll, people operation and awards, applicant data transparency and freelancer ecosystem (Mire, 2018). However, blockchain as an integrative technology in HRM is still not seen in organizations.

LITERATURE REVIEW

Blockchain is the mainstay for the digital currency Bitcoin and other cryptocurrencies making the financial transactions benign without a bank or other financial intermediaries. Blockchain includes a historical record of data, also called a s blocks. With onset of every transaction a new block is created and is then connected chronologically in a series with the next block through irreversible nodes, representing like a block chain. It is a logbook of digital transactions connected in sequence one after another. Blockchain is a buzzword drawing attention of industry, academia and practitioners. It is a shared, decentralized, distributed ledger and tamper- resilient system facilitating recording of transactions and keeping track of assets in a business (PwC 2017a; Gupta, 2017; Hsiao et al., 2018). The list of records is growing, that is secured, linked and identified. This is done by a cryptographic hash called as block which is time stamped. These blocks are inter connected through nodes arranged in chronological order containing the hash to the previous block in order to create a block chain (Crosby et al., 2016). The security and integrity feature of block chain technology has drawn the attention of leaders across the industries as the technology has the potential of disrupting and improving the efficiencies and communication in the organizations and even outside as it helps to connect all involved parties on one platform (Dunham, 2017; Schatsky and Muraskin, 2015).

BLOCKCHAIN CLASSIFICATIONS

Block chain networks can be classified into three categories based on the control mechanism as reading a block chain, submitting transactions and participating in the process. The three categories are: Public, Private and Hybrid. Public blockchain requires no permission and anyone with internet access can use it as it is shared publicly and all transactions are in public such as Bitcoin. On the other hand, in private blockchain sharing is done with selected participants on permission. In Hybrid blockchain, processes are used in combination of public and private blockchains, where some processes are permission based while some are publicly shared.

HUMAN RESOURCE MANAGEMENT AND BLOCKCHAIN TECHNOLOGY

The future of human resource management is dependent of technology and so the need and integration of technology in human resource practices is highlighted in recent years (Stone et al., 2015). Use of technology in talent management in the form of talent analytics has helped the organizations in creating a high performing pool of talent which contributes to improved performance of organization (Sivathanu and Pillai, 2019). There is a clear indication that there is leverage in using technology but that too effectively. The use and application of technology and software in Human Resource Departments is not a new development (Shrivastava and Shaw, 2003; Hendrickson, 2003). The technological applications are generally for internal purposes like talent acquisition, development and retention but there is a debate that whether this digital transformation at workplace has the capability to support HR managers in strategically taking decisions (Marler and Parry, 2016; Sivathanu and Pillai, 2019). The use of technology, tools and software in HR significantly helps in reducing the administrative work, enabling the HR leaders to contribute strategically to the organizational development and growth (Marler and Parry, 2016). Henceforward, HR function needs to integrate and transform by adopting novel tools and technology of the digital age platforms to be a strategic driver of the organization because of increasing role of technology in HRM. On the contrary, other researchers are of the viewpoint that there is a possibility that owing to increase in role of blockchain technology in HR, the role of HR leaders become less attractive and might reduce the importance of HR in organizations (Strohmeier and Parry, 2014).

RESEARCH METHODOLOGY AND OBJECTIVES

The present chapter has two fold objectives:

- To identify the characteristics and uses of Block chain technology

- To understand the scope of the application of blockchain technology in human resource management.

The extant literature has been surveyed using google scholar, research gate, EBSCO, books, magazines, blogs, social media, and journals. Based on literature survey, relevant articles related to block chain technology; its use and applications in various industries, role of block chain technology in HRM were identified for research work.

BLOCKCHAIN CHARACTERISTICS AND ADVANTAGES

Characteristics of Blockchain can be classified as functional characteristics and emergent characteristics. Functional characteristics are those which are mandatory for functioning, without which the system may not exist or function properly. Functional Characteristics of Blockchain are Decentralized network, Distributed Ledger, Consensus, Immutable (Finality) and Security. Emergent characteristics are derived are emerged as a result of functional characteristics. In the case of Blockchain, the emergent characteristics are Disintermediation, Life long validity, Transparency, Encryption, real time updates and smart contracts.

Figure 1. Characteristics of blockchain technology
Source: Authors compilation

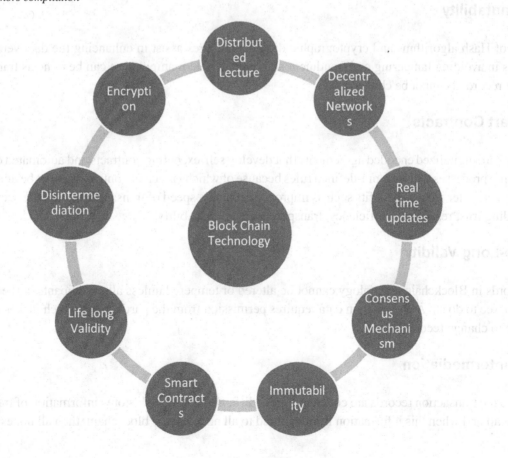

Distributed Ledger

anyone rather it is stored as distributed copies amongst multiple computers. Thus the data is available on numerous computers at a time, enabling all users to share records.

Decentralized Networks

Blockchain is decentralized in its nature and so potentially can change the organizational dynamics by changing the span of control and creating boundary less structures.

Real-Time Updates

Since the block chain has the provision for preserving the old transactions forever, adds the new transactions to the chain on a permanent basis so that anyone can view the same on distributed ledger.

Consensus Mechanism

It promotes shared leadership as the consensus mechanism aids to evade fraudulent activities as participants can validate transactions individualistically.

Immutability

Use of Hash algorithms and cryptographic digital signatures assist in enhancing the data veracity and helps in avoiding tampering and fraudulent activities as data manipulation can be done as transactions once recorded cannot be changed.

Smart Contracts

These are digitalized encoded agreements that develop self-executing contracts and automated decision-making processes that have pre-defined rules because of which breach of contracts cannot be done. Smart Contracts offer various benefits such as improved accuracy, speed of transactions, safety & security and building trust resulting in efficiency, transparency and traceability.

Life-Long Validity

Records in Blockchain technology cannot be altered or tempered unless all participants in the chain do not agree to do so. Any change in data requires permission from the participants which makes it impossible to change records falsely.

Disintermediation

Since the transaction records are coded in blocks differently and block stores information of transaction in detail and when this information is transmitted to all nodes in the blockchain, then all nodes are notified collectively. The validity of the transaction is done using two keys that is, public key or private key and thus intermediaries are removed.

Encryption

It uses a hash function, a type of cryptography that converts data into a hexadecimal code and it cannot be reversed to improve the original input and thus helps in preserving data integrity.

APPLICATIONS OF BLOCKCHAIN IN HUMAN RESOURCES

In order to leverage benefits Organization goals and objectives must be aligned with HR Priorities and the HR function has to focus more on strategic activities by rethinking, integrating, transforming and enabling itself. Although all functional areas of HR are now being digitized but still less consideration has been given to overhaul HR functions with the deployment of block chain technology.

In the recent years, blockchain has helped in digital revolution of HR processes enhancing the productivity by automating greater processes resulting in overall increase in efficiency and effectiveness of various HR processes. This has contributed to a range of benefits such trust, reduction in cost, automation, increased speed of processing, rationalized processes and disintermediation. Smart contracts-based automation aids in improving the operational efficiency. Blockchain technology can be used in various HR processes such as recruitment and selection, validation, mapping skills, compensation system or payroll, compliance, benefits and reward administration, performance management, data security and prevention frauds. This will enable the HR departments to execute processes effectively and efficiently. Digital transformation at work enabled by blockchain will help HR managers in strategic decision making as it significantly reduces administrative work and increases productivity. Blockchain deployment in various HR processes is explained below:

1. **Validation:** Application of blockchain technology in HR enables effective validation of the talent acquisition processes. Earlier Hr managers had to spend a large portion of their time in reviewing resumes or CVs of potential candidates, verifying documentation and credentials, background checks for the recruitment and selection process. It use to take lot of time and resources in Hr function as it is a time consuming and a complex process having profound impact in the long run. But deployment of block chain helps in complete revival of the verification and validation process of credentials in comparison to the traditional methods of validation which resulted in time and cost overruns (CareerBuilder, 2017). The distributed ledger characteristic of block chain technology supports skill validation, trainings, certificates and last employment history as a single source of truth and results in eliminating the intermediaries, vendors and recruiting agencies. Blockchain helps in automation and improving the speed of verification process of candidates and so aids in supporting the issues of speed, effort, cost, precision and transparency during the process of hiring as the candidates in the quest of job manipulate the data or do falsification of information to increase their chances of selection. 58 percent of the HR managers have identified forged credentials as people swindle their skills, roles and responsibilities, job titles, academic accolades, academic qualifications, last employer and many more. Use of block chain can support HR managers in real time verification of all details and contributing in safeguarding the interests of the organization in long run as the

process of recruitment and selection can be developed effective and streamlined to the extent possible (PwC, 2017b). Blockchain helps HR professionals through its secured data-sharing feature to successfully verify the probable employee's credentials in the recruitment and selection process. The application of blockchain in the recruitment and selection provides a check of the potential candidates to avert false information (i.e., unsuitable references or manipulated performance evaluations) on their resumes. Blockchain averts applicants from exaggerations or underreporting as all information of the applicant is recorded permanently and verified by participants with knowledge of that individual in the hiring process. As all pertinent information is tested using blockchain and changes to the information are approximately impossible to make, thus making the recruitment process see-through and decisions trustworthy. With increased levels of transparency, it also alleviates the concern that other candidates might be getting ahead of them by applying to the same job with fraudulent resumes and qualifications. Blockchain technology enables HR managers to effortlessly verify potential recruits and their backgrounds by making the process of application transparent. The correct information and high level of transparency offered by blockchain can create a bigger level of trust in organizational decision-making. Without blockchain technology, the prospect for the presence of deceitful information in the application process is larger in absence of full-proof authentication of the information. Although blockchain cannot guarantee all imprecisions or trappings of CVs will be detected, but it can effectively reduce the number of such incidents. Blockchain technology guarantees that this evolutionary combination will evolve the process of Recruitment & Selection in a way that it would be easy and would make it more applied. As this technology will be implemented into the process of Recruitment & Selection, it can inspect and regulate the Credential Verification, historical background, and data security (Salah et al., 2020). Verification of the job history that is being shared by the job applicants is a support of the recruitment and its process that costs time, money and accuracy (Sarda et al., 2018). So today it is known that blockchain can help to improve various facets of the processes being used in recruitment and selection that includes, verification, avoidance of frauds and can even boost the confidence of recruiters. Also, CV and data verification could help recruiters to select the best candidates faster, minimizing the time that is needed (Salah et al., 2020).

2. **Skill Mapping:** Skill mapping is not a one- time exercise but a never- ending activity that has been the integral job of most of the HR professionals in organizations. Charting and aligning the right person in the right job at right time is the most challenging task in today's situation due to different skills that the individual possesses. Hence, there is a requirement to select the right person that fits with the team and organization culture to make it easier to encourage, train, develop, and manage performance of employee and eventually retaining the talent. Once the intense effort of recruitment is concluded by HR professionals, now they wish to make all necessary efforts to encourage and retain those employees who are hired by the organizations. Higher employee retention rates garner huge benefits to the organizations as they help in saving huge costs of turnover in terms of time, effort and resources, i.e. including the cost of recruiting, selecting, motivating and retaining the human resources (HireRight,2018). Blockchain implementation will enable the employees to share their qualifications, achievements, skills, references, and other subtle information with their employers so that the same can be verified digitally and thus gives assurance to the employers. HR managers can also authenticate essential employee information (i.e. previous performance valuations at parent companies or subsidiaries, skills shown based on previous assignment and antiquity of task completion, etc.) before adding any individual to a project team. Blockchain technology

allows HR managers to recognize their employees' skills and strengths and access their learning records. Application of analytics and artificial intelligence (AI) to the data can enable HR managers to match individuals to various roles and profiles in the organizations much more accurately and effectively (Scott, 2016).

3. **Training Support:** Blockchain technology implementation helps in creation of verifiable and in HR creates a verifiable and correct history of training records and initiatives. Whenever an employee learns any new skill or completes a training program, it is made visible in the blockchain to all participants. Often employees acquire skills and qualifications from various training institutions that are beyond the domain of organization. However, the process of authenticating, confirming, and accounting these autonomous and focused external credentials in the organization's skills repository can often be limited. But the implementation of Blockchain technology in HR processes would enable the employers to track, combine, and appraise all the external credentials and qualifications on to an employee's record on permanent basis.

4. **Payroll System:** One of the most time-consuming tasks in organizations is processing payroll as it includes management of various operational tasks and ensuring the regulatory compliance. All this process in payroll operations takes a significant amount of time and effort, that's why most of the large scale organizations outsource their payroll processing activities, such as time-keeping sheets, administration of payroll data, medical &health benefits and other allied activities of payroll. Although outsourcing the payroll activities brings forth many advantages to the organizations but the biggest concern is how to maintain the confidentiality and security of data (Burke, 2017). One of the most shared illustrations of deployment of blockchain technology in HR processes is streamlining the payroll system. The HR department can use the blockchain to keep track of time and attendance, payment options, protection from frauds, and administration benefits at much lesser costs, at a faster speed, and without the requirement of third parties and intermediaries. Handling payroll processing of Expatriate compensation that requires cross-border payments and tax compliance which is a complex, expensive and ineffective process that comprises accounting for numerous local tax codes, processing complex sets of forms, adjusting the exchange rate instability, and completing the validations across several financial intermediaries. Blockchain Technology has enabled enables global organizations to effectively manage these cross-border payments of their employees in foreign jurisdictions at a much lower cost to employers in the long run while providing benefits to the employees in terms of more real-time payments with lesser deductions. Greater security and quicker settlement features of blockchain will massively help in overseas payroll processing.

5. **Contingent Workforce Payment:** The increasing drift towards employing contingent workforce has become a global phenomenon. Although, the contingent workforce bids bigger flexibility, managing their details, skills, timesheets, but vendor settlement remains the biggest challenge for the HR departments. Blockchain has its application in this area too as its secured distributed ledger features enables HR managers to validate information related to the contingent workforce transaction on a real-time basis and process the payment instantaneously. Blockchain using the identity verification process can identify the bank accounts, taxation information and process the contingent workforce payments after following the contingent workers' timesheets, work, and supplier invoice reconciliation. It can remove numerous manual processes of authentication, validation, and authorization, and can automatically activate payments through smart contracts, possibly based on a specific event. The smart contract feature of blockchain act as a assurance that whenever the assigned work or task is accomplished, the payment will be made to the respective employee or contractor properly

and in a timely manner. Blockchain-supported smart contracts enable automation to replace many of the manual tasks and time delays in payments processing of the contingent workforce.

6. **Compensation, Benefits, and Rewards Administration:** Blockchain-enabled smart contracts can be used in various HR processes such as distributing employee compensation, benefits, and rewards as they can automatically release the amount once employee meets certain pre-defined rules or conditions. Blockchain-enabled smart contracts are agreements between two or more contracting parties which can be automatically enforced without any intermediaries or human setting operations. The HR department can specify conditions and criteria for instant distribution of payment in the form of a smart contract as it helps HR in the instant distribution of compensation, benefits, and rewards without delay or fraud. The use of pre-defined conditions for release of payment will prevent the possibility of delay, or arbitrariness after those conditions are met. The clear pre-determination of conditions will enhance objectivity; lessen ambiguity or discrimination, and arbitrary denials of compensation, benefits and rewards as both parties abide by their duty to perform their promissory obligations. Employees and organizations would both benefit from having a predetermined objective criterion for compensation, benefits, and rewards. Thus, blockchain facilitates the HR department to automate most of the interaction between HR, the finance department, other departments, and the employee through smart contracts for transparent and automated data-driven decision-making. It also adds significantly to HR going paperless, and that significantly cuts the overhead cost and enhances speed as well as effectiveness.

7. **Performance Management:** Performance management plays a crucial role in an individual's success as it is connected to an individual's compensation, recognition, and career path. Blockchain technology implementation in HR simplifies effective performance management by verifying the work history of potential recruits before employment, and verification of past assignments as well as performance evaluations. Thus, it lessens manual efforts, documentation, and personal bias and brings in more objectivity and transparency in performance evaluation (Sekhar, 2017). When employees move from one organization to another, their performance is not consistently recorded. Blockchain leads to all-inclusive and transparent performance management based on more unvarying and agreed-upon practices for evaluation. It also enables employees to keep a record of their performance as they move across the organizations. On blockchain implementation in HR, when an individual is assigned a project in the organization, the immediate supervisor can create a block for performance evaluation that can be validated by all the stakeholders (client, team lead, and peers) as they provide feedback on work performance during the project. As employees move internally across various departments in the organization, blockchain-enabled role-based access to hiring project managers helps them in making the right and fast decisions while selecting project team members within the organization. Blockchain technology would make the performance evaluation and management process in the organizations automated, reliable, and streamlined (Buckingham and Goodall, 2015).

8. **Data Security:** HR professionals are required to maintain high volumes of data, including pay, bank details, medical records, employee performance, disciplinary records, expense reimbursement, and personally identifiable information (PII) which are usually held on centralized servers. This huge amount of sensitive data that is handled by the HR departments makes them vulnerable of being exploited by cyber-attackers and hackers. Hence, creating the necessity to develop some safeguards in place so as to prevent the data from such cyber-attacks and fraud and finally maintain security of data. Blockchain Technology can actually address this risk of data integrity as the

data transmitted in the blockchain network is fully distributed and encrypted, thereby assisting in avoiding deceitful activities and supporting data privacy. Implementing blockchain in HR can help cross thwart both internal as well as external frauds and hacks of sensitive employee data records (Michailidis, 2021).

CHALLENGES IN APPLICATION OF BLOCKCHAIN IN HRM

Blockchain networks are associated with a few challenges. Firstly, it requires huge storage as during the validation process, the whole blockchain is involved. Secondly, since the block size is fixed, only a few transactions can be performed per second who in turn results in delay in transactions thereby increasing the cost per transaction. Thirdly, on the other hand, if the size of block is increased, it causes added delay in block circulation. Fourth, it is even possible to create fake blocks by network nodes and can even generate reverse confirmed transactions. Fifth, it is possible to generate blocks rapidly but requires increased power consumption and these results in that the valid blocks are not able to get their share of resources in block chain networks. Another significant challenge of blockchain networks is the energy consumption. These transactions consume huge amount of energy. It is estimated that each Bitcoin transaction consumes 80,000 times more energy as compared to a credit card transaction (Sial, 2019)

FUTURE SCOPE OF THE STUDY

Acquisition of eminence swiftly, block chain technology is reckoned amongst the hot trends that businesses must keep an eye on to stay ahead. This new trend is bringing substantial advancements and new opportunities in every industry. The Present chapter has studied the application of Blockchain technology in human resource management and in future the same can be discovered in finance, in cloud storage, cyber security, digital advertising and many more. There shouldn't be any unwillingness in accepting that block chain technology will attract and benefit numerous possible businesses and organizations.

CONCLUSION

There is a need to efficiently leverage the blockchain positioning in HR as it meaningfully helps in enhancing the performance of various HR processes. Blockchain enables HR managers to focus more on strategic HR tasks thereby reducing time, cost, and lot of administrative work, that helps in increasing the overall efficiency and effectiveness of HR processes. Blockchain deployment facilitates HR Professionals to effectively manage some of the fundamental HR processes so as to spend time on other strategic activities that require human intervention. Blockchain system helps in overhauling the functioning of HR in organizations with automation of processes enabled by the smart contract-based system. The growing status of blockchain, the prioritization, and selection of a particular HR process and resistance to change prevent organizations from adopting blockchain in the HR domain. Lack of understanding of blockchain technology mechanism along with its functionality by HR professionals and the unavailability of skilled resources to develop and manage blockchain solutions in HR are also some of the challenges. Another challenge is the immutability of smart contracts as they may result in undesired outcomes (lack of accountability) in unpredicted scenarios (i.e., scenarios that were not accounted for in the computer codes). The smart contract cannot be easily changed as blockchain transactions and "blocks" are irreversible. However, this can be resolved by an effective ex-post grievance redressal system or dispute resolution mechanism. The major drivers of successful blockchain application in HR are the top management support, the technological readiness of the organization, and the motivation and training of HR professionals for blockchain adoption.

REFERENCES

Bhaduri, A. (2018). *People@work*. Retrieved from Hindu Business Line, available at: https:// www. thehindubusinessline.com/specials/people-at-work/adopting-blockchain-tech-in-hr/ article22881175.ece#

Buckingham, M., & Goodall, A. (2015). Reinventing performance management. *Harvard Business Review*, *93*(4), 40–50.

Burke, I. (2017). *It's not all paperwork: How does HR really spend their time?* Available at: www.business. com/articles/its-not-all-paperwork-how-does-hr-really-spend-their-time/

CareerBuilder. (2017). *75% Of HR managers have caught a lie on a resume*. Available at: https://press. careerbuilder.com/2017-09-14-75-of-HR-Managers-Have-Caught-a-Lie-on-a-Resume-According-to-aNew-CareerBuilder-Survey

Crosby, M., Pattanayak, P., Verma, S., & Kalyanaraman, V. (2016). Blockchain technology: Beyond bitcoin. *Applied Innovation*, *2*(6-10), 71.

Dunham, S. (2017). *Blockchain's potential impact on HR and payroll*. Available at: www.symmetry. com/ payroll-tax-insights/blockchains-potential-impact-on-hr-and-payroll

Hendrickson, A. R. (2003). Human resource information systems: Backbone technology of contemporary human resources. *Journal of Labor Research*, *24*(3), 381–394. doi:10.100712122-003-1002-5

HireRight. (2018). *2018 Employment screening benchmark report*. Available at: www.hireright.com/ resources/view/2018-employment-screening-benchmark-report

Hsiao, J. H., Tso, R., Chen, C. M., & Wu, M. E. (2018). Decentralized E-voting systems based on the blockchain technology. In Advances in Computer Science and Ubiquitous Computing: CSA-CUTE 17 (pp. 305-309). Springer Singapore. doi:10.1007/978-981-10-7605-3_50

Hughes, L., Dwivedi, Y. K., Misra, S. K., Rana, N. P., Raghavan, V., & Akella, V. (2019). Blockchain research, practice and policy: Applications, benefits, limitations, emerging research themes and research agenda. *International Journal of Information Management*, *49*, 114–129. doi:10.1016/j.ijinfomgt.2019.02.005

Madhani, P. M. (2022). Blockchain Applications in HR: Key Advantages. *HRM Review*, *18*(1), 17–26.

Marler, J. H., & Parry, E. (2016). Human resource management, strategic involvement and e-HRM technology. *International Journal of Human Resource Management*, *27*(19), 2233–2253. doi:10.1080/09585192.2015.1091980

Melcherts, H.E. (2017). The Internet of Everything and Beyond: The Interplay between Things and Humans. *Human Bond Communication: The Holy Grail of Holistic Communication and Immersive Experience*, 173-185.

Michailidis, M. P. (2018). Hie Challenges of AI and Blockchain on HR Recruiting Practices. *The Cyprus Review*, *30*(2).

Mire, S. (2018), Retrieved from Disruptor Daily: available at: https://www.disruptordaily.com/blockchain-market-map-human-resources

Mishra, A., & Akman, I. (2010). Information technology in human resource management: An empirical assessment. *Public Personnel Management*, *39*(3), 271–290. doi:10.1177/009102601003900306

Nakamoto, S. (2019). *Bitcoin: A peer-to-peer electronic cash system*. Manubot.

PwC. (2017a). *How blockchain technology could impact HR and the world of work*. Available at: www.pwc.ch/en/insights/hr/how-blockchain-can-impact-hr-and-the-world-of-work.html

PwC. (2017b). *The talent challenge: harnessing the power of human skills in the machine age*. Available at: www.pwc.com/gx/en/ceo-survey/2017/deep-dives/ceo-survey-global-talent.pdf

Salah, D., Ahmed, M. H., & ElDahshan, K. (2020). Blockchain Applications in Human Resources Management: Opportunities and Challenges. In *Proceedings of the Evaluation and Assessment in Software Engineering* (pp. 383-389). 10.1145/3383219.3383274

Sarda, P., Chowdhury, M. J. M., Colman, A., Kabir, M. A., & Han, J. (2018, August). Blockchain for fraud prevention: a work-history fraud prevention system. In *2018 17th IEEE international conference on trust, security and privacy in computing and communications/12th IEEE international conference on big data science and engineering (TrustCom/BigDataSE)* (pp. 1858-1863). IEEE. 10.1109/TrustCom/BigDataSE.2018.00281

Schatsky, D., & Muraskin, C. (2015). Beyond bitcoin: Blockchain is coming to disrupt your industry. *Deloitte Insight, 7.*

Scott, R. (2016). *How blockchain, chatbots and PDRs will disrupt HR technology*. Available at: www.insidehr.com.au/how-blockchain-chatbots-and-pdrs-will-disrupt-hr-technology/

Sekhar, C. (2017). *Enhance employee performance management experience with blockchain*. LinkedIn. Available at: www.linkedin.com/pulse/enhance-employee-performance-managementexperience-blockchain-aknr

Shrivastava, S., & Shaw, J. B. (2003). Liberating HR through technology. *Human Resource Management, 42*(3), 201-222.

Sial, M. F. K. (2019). Blockchain Technology–Prospects, Challenges and Opportunities. *IEEE Blockchain, Technical Briefs*. Available at https://blockchain.ieee.org/technicalbriefs/june-2019/blockchain-technology-prospects-challenges-and-opportunities

Sivathanu, B., & Pillai, R. (2020). Technology and talent analytics for talent management–a game changer for organizational performance. *The International Journal of Organizational Analysis*, *28*(2), 457–473. doi:10.1108/IJOA-01-2019-1634

Spence, A. (2018). *Blockchain and Chief Human Resource Officer*. Blockchain Research Institute.

Stone, D. L., Deadrick, D. L., Lukaszewski, K. M., & Johnson, R. (2015). The influence of technology on the future of human resource management. *Human Resource Management Review*, *25*(2), 216–231. doi:10.1016/j.hrmr.2015.01.002

Strohmeier, D. E. P. A. P. S. (2014). HRM in the digital age–digital changes and challenges of the HR profession. *Employee Relations*, *36*(4). Advance online publication. doi:10.1108/ER-03-2014-0032

Zalan, T. (2018). Born global on blockchain. *Review of International Business and Strategy*, *28*(1), 19–34. doi:10.1108/RIBS-08-2017-0069

Chapter 10
Intelligent Data Encryption Classifying Complex Security Breaches Using Machine Learning Technique

Somendra Tripathi
Faculty of Engineering and Technology, Rama University, India

Hari Om Sharan
Rama University, India

C. S. Raghuvanshi
Rama University, India

ABSTRACT

Attacks targeting cybersecurity are getting more widespread and complex over time. Additional innovation and rapid application development methodology within combative tactics have been required due to the increasing complexity and technological sophistication that have been developing. While still extensively used and encouraged, previous approaches to penetration detection and packet inspection are not sufficient for meeting the preferences of changing security threats. Machine learning is being touted as a supplementary justification for keyloggers, trojan horses, and other cyberattacks as computational capabilities and affordability keep on increasing. The total amount of information gathered by electronic objects has drastically increased in recent years as a consequence of the fast and easy efficiency innovations in some of those peripherals and their use in a range of applications.

INTRODUCTION

Whereas cybercrime is on the steady increase, cybersecurity is always developing. Even though they are appearing progressively often and widely enough, advanced and powerful atrocities are now viewed as a series of standards (Vemuri et al., 2005). This ongoing change allows for significant entrepreneurship in cybersecurity protection.

DOI: 10.4018/978-1-6684-9151-5.ch010

There are currently strategies in physical locations, and a proportion of these tools and methodologies are still commonly utilized. The architectures for recognizing and preventing security vulnerabilities (IDS/IPS) keep a watchful eye out for malware attacks or circumvention of restrictions. The effective implementation of biometrics IDS in identifying malware that matches these characteristics depends on its reliance on existing malware (Bita Darvish Rouhani, 2018). On the contrary extreme, behaviour in the future, IDS learns what is conventional for a system and notifies on every trigger something which differs significantly from this too. Notwithstanding overall performance, both forms do have those upsides and downsides (Kumari et al., 2019). Cryptography solutions are absolutely worthless versus zero-day attacks or fresh malware since they rely on signatures of established threats.

Cybersecurity is the categorization of laws, strategies, resources, and mechanisms that form an alliance to vindicate the utilization, confidentiality, and truthfulness of software applications, communications, equipment, and records from imposition (Jindal et al., 2019). There were also countermeasures against cyberattacks in the proposal: communication, hosting, and different and multiple. There are numerous technologies that continue to function in seclusion to detect and prevent bombings and spot privacy breaches, notably firewalls, antivirus software, intrusion detection and prevention systems (IDPSs), and intrusion protection systems (IPSs) (Sangani, 2017).

Because they rely on a higher end of the scale that is challenging to create considering the variety of infrastructure and applications, classical behaviour in the past solutions may be inadequate for anomaly detection. Another choice is full data packet analysis, but this is tedious and time-consuming and reflects sensitive user data.

Nevertheless, a lot of conquerors keep on going to hold an opportunity because when attackers are only required to comprehend one weakness in the applications that demand safeguarding (Yin et al., 2017). The threat landscape started growing in tandem with the number of systems connected through the internet, which has raised the great opportunity of an act of violence. Additionally, cybercriminals are beginning to grow more knowledgeable, helping create malware that completely eliminates multifactor authentication and minimal flaws that allow them to survive for prolonged amounts of time (Mayhew et al., 2015), with uncertainty created. Methodologies that have never been attempted before or are frequently versions of known vulnerabilities are known as negligible achievements.

Commoditization of hacking techniques, which greatly facilitates sharing of information without making informed choices of exactly how to construct vulnerabilities, exacerbates the problem (Universe, 2014). Defensive players can and should look out for information security from individuals or groups inside of an establishment that victimize their maximum permissible direct exposure in addition to combating against inner and outer missile strikes.

Machine learning (ML) has attracted a lot of attention across a variety of applications and academic disciplines, notably in cybercrime. Machine learning techniques may be used to assess and categories undesirable actors from a vast amount of available data as hardware and processing power become more widely available (Alperin-Sheriff & Peikert, 2014). Numerous machine learning algorithms and techniques fall within the supervised and unsupervised learning categories. In the context of Classification, where input corresponds to an output, or Regression, where input corresponds to a continuous output, supervised learning algorithms are used. Clustering is primarily used for unsupervised learning, which has been used for exploratory analysis and dimension reduction (Armknecht et al., 2013).

LITERATURE REVIEW

By providing a thorough examination of machine learning and deep learning methodology and techniques for electronic communications integrity in wireless services, these similar transactions artificial intelligence with electronic information security (Armknecht et al., 2015).

The following is a summary of the study's significant contribution:

- We offer a thorough analysis of the various deep learning and machine learning models applied to mobile network electronic information security. Many machine learning and deep learning approaches are briefly explained.
- We provide a brief overview of cyberattacks and an application-focused study of their databases.
- For prospective researchers and enthusiasts to examine, we highlight the present open difficulties and potential future research areas in the areas of mobile networks, electronic data security, and cyber dangers.

The entirety of our information is connected to a vast global network that links numerous devices. Electronic devices' capabilities are likewise expanding every day, which encourages more information to be produced and shared (Altman et al., 1986). Similar to how the frequency of security breaches has increased as mobile network topologies become more complicated and varied.

Traditional data analytics methods might not be able to handle the Big Data (BD) generated by various devices due to its enormous volume (Aono et al., 2016). Yet, this exponential growth in data presents novel opportunities for many types of attackers to launch attacks by availing use of shortcomings in data analytics (such as SQL injection, OS fingerprinting, malicious code execution, etc.). In this research, we evaluated machine learning (ML) and deep learning (DL)-based models and strategies that are capable of identifying and mitigating both known and undiscovered assaults. Our research was motivated by the aforementioned debate (NetGroup, n.d.).

In attempting to detect and mitigate attacks, Machine Learning (ML) and Deep Learning (DL) based strategies have the capacity to learn from traffic patterns while employing training and testing datasets over a wide range of network domains (Tavallaee et al., 2009). We also suggested a Secure Data Analytics (SDA) architecture based on DL and ML to characterize normal or attack input data. A danger framework is established by abstracting a complete taxonomy of SDA. This threat model utilizes different criteria, including efficiency, latency, accuracy, dependability, and attacks introduced by the attackers, to actually fix different research hardship in SDA (Apiletti et al., 2009).

Cyberattacks have nearly doubled as more organizations adopt approaches to digital transformation. According to the Online Fraud Research Center, 2021 has been a record-breaking year in the United States, with the number of data breaches at the end of the third quarter surpassing all of 2022 by 32% (Han et al., 2002). AI and machine learning can guard against these advanced threats, which cybercriminals employ in order closed down networking. Undoubtedly, these technologies are rapidly advancing to become standard tools for cybersecurity experts in their continuous constant battle against dubious actors.

Here are following ways that AI and machine learning in cybersecurity might assist as enterprises plan their usage of these technologies (Brahmi et al., 2012):

- **Finding Irregularities**

AI and machine learning are used to uncover abnormalities that might be signs of an attack by using behavioral analysis and constantly changing parameters.

- **Future Data Breaches Forecasting**

Future data breaches may be predicted using AI and machine learning, which allows for the processing of vast volumes of data of various forms.

- **Improving The Detection and Reaction Times**

AI and machine learning are far faster at identifying dangers than humans because they can quickly examine large volumes of data. Also, they may quickly improve reaction times by applying fixes and removing threats (Zadeh, 1965). Today's cyberattacks may swiftly enter an organization's infrastructure; thus, success depends on having sharpener detection and reaction times.

- **Reducing It Expenses**

AI and machine learning reduce the effort required to detect and respond to cyber threats, making them cost-effective technologies. The average cost reduction is 12%, with some organizations lowering their costs more than 15%, according to the Capgemini report (Kuok et al., 1998).

- **Improving The Efficiency of Cyber Analysts**

Cyber analysts' responsibilities are enhanced by machine learning and artificial intelligence when they don't have to spend as much time mechanically sorting through information archives. These techniques can immediately contact cyber analysts of an aggression while establishing the attack's characteristic, better encouraging managers to determine the best course of action (Agrawal et al., 1993). Cybersecurity prognosticators are capable of handling a variety of multifaceted menaces with less manual processes if people 's actions are endlessly and thoroughly examined.

- **Enhancing Your Security Posture Generally**

Because when statistics is submitted and those same technological innovations gain insight into past patterns, computer security improves stronger over time as they get better at spotting suspicious activities. Moreover, they safeguard an organization's infrastructure at both the macro and micro levels by creating more powerful barriers than are possible with manual techniques (Bivens et al., 2002).

- **Data Accommodation**

Data accommodation is the first and most important stage in putting the Machine Learning model into action. To train the model, data is gathered and cleaned in this stage. Datasets in their raw form are meaningless and contain no information. It may occasionally contain inaccurate values that compromise the model's accuracy. Datasets may have missing values, which should be identified and addressed before the model is trained (Lippmann & Cunningham, 2000).

Furthermore, datasets should be gathered from reliable sources; otherwise, the model's performance may suffer (Morel, 2011).

Data is categorized into two categories:

Ø **Qualitative Data**: Data which is defined in measurable terms like numbers, values, and quantity
Ø **Quantitative Data**: Data which cannot be measured in numeric terms rather it can only be described

MALICIOUS HACKS VS MACHINE LEARNING

At all since, there were 21.65 billion spyware threats in 2022 alone. That quantity makes it impossible for people to manage. Surprisingly, machine learning is stepping in to make up for the shortcomings.

Machine learning, a component of artificial intelligence, produces techniques employing verifiable events and scientific techniques to predict a computer's activity (Internet Security Scanner (ISS), n.d.). After and then, the computer can modify its behavior's and even carry out tasks for which it wasn't intentionally designed.

Microsoft's Windows Defender, a programme that uses many layers of machine learning to identify and block threats, thwarted the attempt. The crypto-miners were stopped nearly immediately after they began digging. There are additional instances where Microsoft's software prevented similar assaults from happening.

Figure 1. Cyber security threats

How It's Using Machine Learning

Microsoft leverages Windows Defender Advanced Threat Prevention (ATP), its proprietary cybersecurity framework, for proactive defensive, breach detection, automated investigation, and response. Windows

Windows 10 devices come with Defender ATP, which uses cloud AI, several levels of machine learning, and automated upgrades to detect threats.

Is Machine Learning Enough to Stop Cybercrime?

Some tasks that machine learning excels at include swiftly scanning enormous volumes of data and conducting statistical analysis on it. Because cybersecurity systems produce enormous amounts of data, it is not surprising that the technology is so helpful (Hornik et al., 1989).

According to Raffael Marty, chief research and intelligence officer of cybersecurity company Forcepoint, "We have more and more data available, and the data is typically telling a story. "You should be able to identify the deviations from the norm if you know how to examine the data."

Those variations occasionally indicate dangers. The application of machine learning is expanding across many industries as a result of that crucial function. It is used for jobs that call for voice and picture recognition. Even the best Go player in the world has lost to it in a game of his own. Although cybersecurity has improved, Marty argues that people are still essential.

"AI will spread throughout the security industry. It's maturing," observed George Kurtz, the founder and CEO of CrowdStrike, in late 2022 (Rosenblatt, 1958). "AI is not a company; it is a feature. It will contribute to the solution of a certain issue. Yet not all issues can be resolved by AI.

MACHINE LEARNING METHODS

Extreme Learning Machine

A learning technique called the Extreme Learning Machine (ELM) makes use of feedforward neural networks with one or more layers of hidden nodes. The method tunes these hidden nodes at random and calculates analytically the associated output weights. The developers claim that their learning method for feedforward neural networks may train 2,000 times quicker than traditional learning algorithms and can deliver high generalization performance (Huang, Zhu, and Siew 2019).

Figure 2. Simplified illustration of ELM algorithm

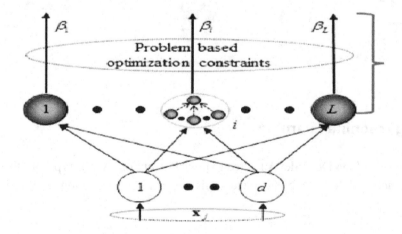

Random Forest

Combining multiple classification trees to carried out classification and regression tasks, Random Forest (RF) is a supervised machine learning technique (Ho 1995). Given that it uses the idea of numerous trees voting with a majority, the Variational Forest method is regarded as an ensemble machine learning algorithm. The output of the process, which is a class prediction, is derived from the sum of all the classes predicted by each individual tree. Recent research has examined how well Random Forest can defend against security assaults, especially injection attacks, spam filtering, malware detection, and more (Kapoor, Gupta, and Kumar 2018 and Khorshidpour, Hashemi, and Hamzeh 2015) (Cannady, 1998).

Figure 3. Simplified illustration of the random forest algorithm

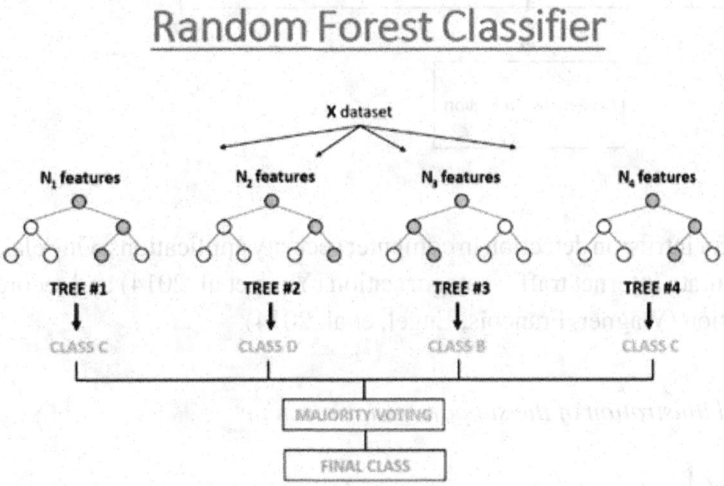

Gradient Boosting

Gradient boosting is a machine learning approach for classification and regression problems that generates a prediction model in the form of a group of weak prediction models, often decision trees (Wikipedia 2019b). It combines the components of an additive model, a weak learner, and a loss function. Weak learners are added to the model to reduce the loss function (Jolliffe, 2002).

The fundamental idea behind gradient boosting is to repeatedly use residual patterns to improve models that have poor predictions (Grover 2017). The modelling of residuals will terminate when it reaches a point when there is no longer any discernible pattern in the residuals (otherwise it might lead to overfitting). To do this mathematically, the loss function must be minimized until the test loss achieves its minimum.

Support Vector Machine

A supervised learning model called the Support Vector Machine (SVM) is utilized for regression and classification analysis (Wikipedia 2019d). Due to its great accuracy and low computational cost, it is highly favored (Lu & Traore, 2004).

Figure 4. Simplified illustration of the gradient boosting algorithm

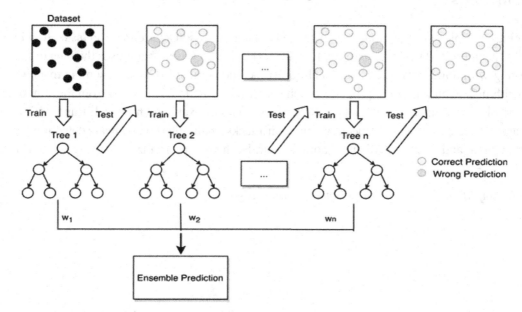

SVM is utilized for intrusion detection in computer security applications. One class SVM was utilized, for instance, for accurate Internet traffic categorization (Yuan et al. 2014) and records analysis based on a novel kernel function (Wagner, Francois, Engel, et al. 2014).

Figure 5. Simplified illustration of the support vector machine

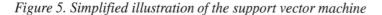
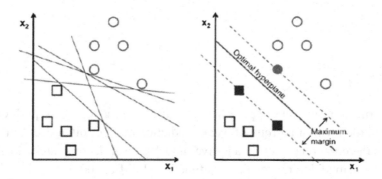

Logistic Regression

Binary classification is done using the supervised learning model of logistic regression. The phrase itself is a Statistics borrowing. The method's foundation is based on logistic functions, a sigmoid curve applicable to many domains, including neural networks. The likelihood of categorization issues with two alternative outcomes is modelled using logistic regression. To determine if network traffic is malicious or not, logistic regression can be employed.

Figure 6. Simplified illustration of the logistic regression

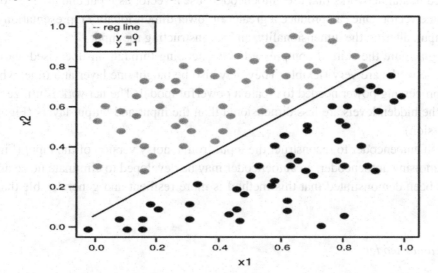

MAIN ISSUE WITH NETWORK SECURITY DATA

Really a small fraction of the communication is malevolent, and the majority of it is unimportant. This makes it challenging for the model to understand what is dangerous. Also, because the network's topology affects how the model learns, there is a large danger of imbalanced datasets during the training phase, whereas a network-independent approach is desired.

Besides that, traffic analysis engages with a network that has a dynamic structure: links between servers may form and disappear in response to new requests and new users joining the network, and communications are time-dependent. Hence, discovering new, unidentified botnets is a significant issue for network security.

DEEP LEARNING METHODS USED IN CYBER SECURITY

Deep Learning methodology provided for each technique are following:

1.   Deep Belief Networks:

Deep Convolutional Neural Models were first introduced in a landmark study by Hinton (DCNs). These DCNs belong to a group that consists of several layers of hidden units connected only between the layers and not between the units within each layer. DCNs are trained without supervision. Usually, to rebuild the input, they are trained by changing the weights of each hidden layer separately (Quinlan, 1986).

2.   Deep Autoencoders:

Unsupervised neural networks that use autoencoders use a vector as input and attempt to match the output to the same vector. One can produce a greater or lower dimensionality representation of the data by taking the input, altering the dimensionality, and reconstructing the input.

Because they acquire the skill of compressed data encoding through unsupervised learning, these kinds of neural networks are very flexible. They may also be taught one layer at a time, which lowers the amount of processing power needed to create a powerful model. The network is utilized to encode the data when the hidden levels are less dimensional than the input and output layers (Figure 7). (i.e., feature compression)

By training an autoencoder to reconstruct the input from a noisy version of the input (Figure 7), referred to as a denoising autoencoder, an autoencoder may be developed to eliminate noise and be more resilient. It has been demonstrated that this method is more resilient and generalizable than standard autoencoders.

Figure 7. Deep autoencoder

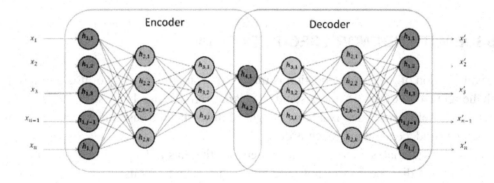

Figure 8. Denoising autoencoder

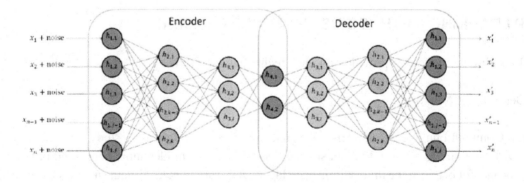

3.   Restricted Boltzmann Machines:

The fundamental units of DBNs are restricted Boltzmann machines (RBMs), which are two-layer, bipartite, undirected graphical models (data can flow in both directions rather than just one). RBMs are unsupervised and may be trained one layer at a time, just as autoencoders. Input layer is the top layer, while concealed layer is the bottom layer (Figure 8).

Figure 9. Restricted Boltzmann machine

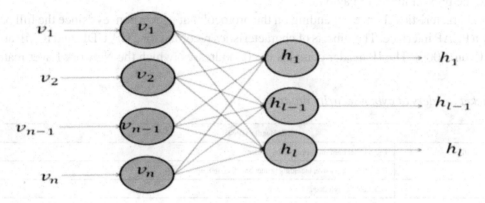

CYBER-SECURITY DATA SETS FOR MACHINE LEARNING AND DATA MINING

The information is essential for both ML and DM methods.

Understanding the data these approaches employ is essential in order to comprehend how various authors have implemented various ML and DM algorithms. This is because these techniques learn from the data that is already accessible. The many forms of data used by the ML and DM approaches—packet capture (PCAP) (Zhengbing et al., 2008), NetFlow, and other network data—are described in depth in this section. As a result, Part IV, which elaborates on the techniques, merely mentions if a method uses pcap, NetFlow, or other network data and skips any detailed descriptions of the data. The low-level specifics of the data sets are covered in the next subsections, they are following:

- **Packet-Level Data**

The Internet Engineering Task Force (IETF) has 152 IPs listed, including frequently used protocols such User Datagram Protocol (UDP), Internet Control Message Protocol (ICMP) (Baralis et al., 2008), Transmission Control Protocol (TCP), Internet Gateway Management Protocol (IGMP), etc. The Internet's packet network traffic is created by user applications that follow these protocols. An application programming interface (API) known as pcap can be used to record the network packets that are sent and received at the computer's physical interface (such as its Ethernet port). The front-end packet capture software libraries for several network tools, such as protocol analyzers, packet sniffers, network monitors, network IDSs, and traffic generators, are Libpcap and WinPCap (the Unix and Windows versions, respectively). Tcpdump, Wireshark, Snort, and Nmap are a few well-known applications that consume PCAP data.

An Ethernet frame is made up of the Ethernet header (the Media Access Control [MAC] address) and up to 1500 bytes (the Maximum Transmission Unit [MTU]) of payload at the network physical layer.

The IP packet is contained in this payload and is made up of the IP (or transport layer) header and the IP payload. Data or other encapsulated higher-level protocols, such as Network File System (NFS), Server Message Block (SMB), Hypertext Transfer Protocol (HTTP), BitTorrent, Post Office Protocol (POP) Version 3, Network Basic Input/Output System (NetBIOS), telnet, and Trivial File Transfer Protocol (TFTP), may be present in the IP payload.

The data characteristics change depending on the protocol that packet conveys since the full packet is recorded by a PCAP interface. The subsets of characteristics recorded for TCP, UDP, and ICMP are listed in Table I (Lyon, 2009). The IP header contains the IP addresses, which the Network Layer manages.

Table 1. Packet headers of cyber-security datasets

IP Header (IPv4)	
Internet Header Length	The number of 32-bit words in the header
Total Length	The entire packet size, including header and data, in bytes
Time to Live	This field limits a datagram's lifetime
Protocol	The protocol used in the data portion of the IP datagram
Source address	This field in the IPv4 address of the sender of the datagram
Destination address	This field in the IPv4 address of the receiver of the datagram
TCP Packet	
Source port	Identifies the sending ports
Destination port	Identifies the receiving ports
Sequence number	Initial or accumulated sequence number
Data offset	Specifies the size of the TCP header in 32-bit words
Flag (control bits)	NS, CWR, ECE, URG ACK, PSH, SYN, FIN

- **NetFlow Data:** Cisco first debuted NetFlow as a router capability. It is possible for the router or switch to gather IP network traffic as it enters and leaves the interface. A network flow, according to Cisco's NetFlow version 5, is a collection of unidirectional packets that all have the same seven packet attributes: ingress interface, source IP address, destination IP address, IP protocol, source port, destination port, and IP type of service. A NetFlow Exporter, a NetFlow Collector, and an Analysis Console make up the logical NetFlow architecture. Today, NetFlow is available in ten different versions. Versions 1 through 8 are comparable; however, beginning with version 9, etFlow differs significantly. For versions 1 to 8, the feature set in Table II (Lippmann et al., 2000)

Table 2. Netflow packet header of cyber security datasets

Net Flow Data: Simple Network Management Protocol (SNMP)	
Ingress Interface	Router Information
IP Protocol	IP protocol number
Source port	UDP or TCP port
Destination port	UDP or TCP port
IP type of service	Priority level of the flow

- **Public Data Sets:** Experiments and publications often use and mention the Defense Advanced Research Projects Agency (DARPA) 1998 and DARPA 1999 data sets. The Cyber Systems and Technologies Group of the Massachusetts Institute of Technology Lincoln Laboratory (MIT/LL) produced the DARPA 1998 set. Based on TCP/IP network data, Solaris Basic Security Module log data, and Solaris file system dumps for user and root, a simulation network was constructed and data were assembled. In reality, the constructed data set was made up of information about the operating system (OS) and the network. The first 7 weeks of the data collection were designated as the training set, while the final 2 weeks were designated as the testing set. In the weeks leading up to the training and testing, attack scenarios were organized.

Tavallaee et al. conducted a thorough analysis of the KDD 2011 data set, which contains around 4 million records of normal and attack traffic. They discovered several significant drawbacks. There were a few inherent issues that were identified, including the need to synthesize network and attack data (after sampling the actual traffic) due to privacy concerns, an undetermined number of packets being dropped due to traffic overflow, and ambiguous attack definitions. Moreover, Tavallaee et al. conducted their own categorization trials and statistical analyses.

REFERENCES

Agrawal, R., Imielinski, T., & Swami, A. (1993). Mining association rules between sets of items in large databases. *Proc. Int. Conf. Manage. Data Assoc. Comput. Mach. (ACM)*, 207–216. 10.1145/170035.170072

Alperin-Sheriff, & Peikert. (2014). Faster bootstrapping with polynomial error. In *Advances in Cryptology - CRYPTO 2014* (pp. 297–314). Springer.

Altman, R., Asch, E., Bloch, D., Bole, G., Borenstein, D., Brandt, K., Christy, W., Cooke, T. D., Greenwald, R., Hochberg, M., Rothschild, B., Segal, M., Sokoloff, L., & Wolfe, F. (1986, August). Development of criteria for the classification and reporting of osteoarthritis: Classification of osteoarthritis of the knee. *Arthritis and Rheumatism*, 29(8), 1039–1049. doi:10.1002/art.1780290816 PMID:3741515

Aono, Y., Hayashi, T., & Phong, L. T. (2016). Scalable and secure logistic regression via homomorphic encryption. In *Proceedings of the 6th ACM Conference on Data and Application Security and Privacy (CODASPY'16)*. ACM. 10.1145/2857705.2857731

Apiletti, D., Baralis, E., Cerquitelli, T., & D'Elia, V. (2009, April). Characterizing network traffic by means of the NetMine framework. *Computer Networks*, 53(6), 774–789. doi:10.1016/j.comnet.2008.12.011

Armknecht, F., Boyd, C., Carr, C., Gøsteen, K., Jáschke, A., Reuter, C. A., & Strand, M. (2015). *A Guide to Fully Homomorphic Encryption*. Technical Report 1192.

Armknecht, F., Katzenbeisser, S., & Peter, A. (2013, May). Group homomorphic encryption: Characterizations, impossibility results, and applications. *Designs, Codes and Cryptography*, 67(2), 209–232. doi:10.100710623-011-9601-2

Arnes, A., Valeur, F., Vigna, G., & Kemmerer, R. A. (2006). Using Hidden markov models to evaluate the risks of intrusions: System architecture and model validation. *Lecture Notes in Computer Science*, *4219*, 145–164. doi:10.1007/11856214_8

Baralis, E., Cerquitelli, T., & D'Elia, V. (2008). *Generalized Itemset Discovery by Means of Opportunistic Aggregation*. Tech. Rep., Politecnico di Torino. https://dbdmg.polito.it/twiki/ bin/view/Public/ NetworkTrafficAnalysis

Bilge, L., Sen, S., Balzarotti, D., Kirda, E., & Kruegel, C. (2014, April). 2014 Exposure: A passive DNS analysis service to detect and report malicious domains. *ACM Transactions on Information and System Security*, *16*(4), 1–28. doi:10.1145/2584679

Bita Darvish Rouhani, M. (2018). Deepsecure: Scalable provably-secure deep learning. DAC, 2:1–2:6.

Bivens, A., Palagiri, C., Smith, R., Szymanski, B., & Embrechts, M. (2002). Network-based intrusion detection using neural networks. *Intell. Eng. Syst. Artif. Neural Netw.*, *12*(1), 579–584.

Brahmi, H., Imen, B., & Sadok, B. (2012). *OMC-IDS: At the cross-roads of OLAP mining and intrusion detection. In Advances in Knowledge Discovery and Data Mining*. Springer.

Cannady, J. (1998). Artificial neural networks for misuse detection. *Proc. 1998 Nat. Inf. Syst. Secur. Conf.*, 443–456.

Google. (n.d.-a). https://www.google.com/search?q=Simplified+illustration+of+the+Random+Forest +Algorithm+figure&sxsrf=APwXEde_MKabNtJy0lGGIsvwE4L3tfyEYA:1680239486778&source= lnms&tbm=isch&sa=X&ved=2ahUKEwjfvPzts4X-

Google. (n.d.-b). https://www.google.com/search?q=Simplified+illustration+of+the+Gradient+Boosting+Algorithm+figure&tbm=isch&ved=2ahUKEwi787Pvs4X-AhUmBbcAHSP1CGYQ2-

Han, H., Lu, X., & Ren, L. (2002). Using data mining to discover signatures in network-based intrusion detection. *Proc. IEEE Comput. Graph. Appl.*, 212–217.

Hornik, K., Stinchcombe, M., & White, H. (1989). Multilayer feedforward networks are universal approximators. *Neural Networks*, *2*(5), 359–366. doi:10.1016/0893-6080(89)90020-8

Internet Security Scanner (ISS). (n.d.). IBM. Available: http://www.iss.net

Jindal, A., Marnerides, A. K., Scott, A., & Hutchison, D. (2019). Identifying security challenges in renewable energy systems: A wind turbine case study. *Proceedings of the Tenth ACM International Conference on Future Energy Systems, e-Energy '19*, 370–372. 10.1145/3307772.3330154

Jolliffe, T. (2002). *Principal Component Analysis* (2nd ed.). Springer.

Kumari, A., Tanwar, S., Tyagi, S., Kumar, N., Parizi, R. M., & Choo, K.-K. R. (2019). Fog data analytics: A taxonomy and process model. *Journal of Network and Computer Applications*, *128*, 90–104. doi:10.1016/j.jnca.2018.12.013

Kuok, C. M., Fu, A., & Wong, M. H. (1998). Mining fuzzy association rules in databases. *SIGMOD Record*, *27*(1), 41–46. doi:10.1145/273244.273257

Lippmann, R., Haines, J., Fried, D., Korba, J., & Das, K. (2000). The 1999 DARPA offline intrusion detection evaluation. *Computer Networks, 34*(4), 579–595. doi:10.1016/S1389-1286(00)00139-0

Lippmann, R. P., & Cunningham, R. K. (2000). Improving intrusion detection performance using keyword selection and neural networks. *Computer Networks, 34*(4), 597–603. doi:10.1016/S1389-1286(00)00140-7

Lu, W., & Traore, I. (2004). Detecting new forms of network intrusion using genetic programming. *Computational Intelligence, 20*(3), 470–489. doi:10.1111/j.0824-7935.2004.00247.x

Lyon, G. F. (2009). *Nmap Network Scanning: The Official Nmap Project Guide to Network Discovery and Security Scanning*. Insecure.

Mayhew, M., Atighetchi, M., Adler, A., & Greenstadt, R. (2015). Use of machine learning in big data analytics for insider threat detection. MILCOM 2015 - 2015 IEEE Military Communications Conference, 915–922. doi:10.1109/MILCOM.2015.7357562

Morel, B. (2011). Artificial intelligence and the future of cybersecurity. *Proc. 4th ACM Workshop Secur. Artif. Intell.*, 93–98. 10.1145/2046684.2046699

Mukkamala, A., Sung, A., & Abraham, A. (2005). *Cyber security challenges: Designing efficient intrusion detection systems and antivirus tools.* In V. R. Vemuri (Ed.), *Enhancing Computer Security with Smart Technology* (pp. 125–163). Auerbach.

NetGroup. (n.d.). *Politecnico di Torino, Analyzer 3.0.* Available: http://analyzer.polito.it

NSKT Global. (n.d.). https://www.nsktglobal.com/what-are-the-biggest-cybersecurity-threats-in-2021-

Quinlan, R. (1986). Induction of decision trees. *Machine Learning, 1*(1), 81–106. doi:10.1007/BF00116251

Rosenblatt, F. (1958). The perceptron: A probabilistic model for information storage and organization in the brain. *Psychological Review, 65*(6), 386–408. doi:10.1037/h0042519 PMID:13602029

Sangani. (2017). *Global data to increase 10x by 2025: Data age 2025.* Academic Press.

Tavallaee, M., Bagheri, E., Lu, W., & Ghorbani, A. (2009). A detailed analysis of the KDD Cup 1999 data set. *Proc. 2nd IEEE Symp. Comput. Intell. Secur. Defense Appl.*, 1–6.

Universe. (2014). *The digital universe of opportunities: Rich data and the increasing value of the internet of things.* Academic Press.

Wikipedia. (2019). *Type of Service.* https://en.wikipedia.org/wiki/Type_of_service

Yin, C., Zhu, Y., Fei, J., & He, X. (2017). A deep learning approach for intrusion detection using recurrent neural networks. *IEEE Access : Practical Innovations, Open Solutions, 5*, 21954–21961. doi:10.1109/ACCESS.2017.2762418

Zadeh, L. (1965). Fuzzy sets. *Information and Control, 8*(3), 338–35. doi:10.1016/S0019-9958(65)90241-X

Zhengbing, H., Zhitang, L., & Junqi, W. (2008). A novel network intrusion detection system (NIDS) based on signatures search of data mining. *Proc. 1st Int. Conf. Forensic Appl. Techn. Telecommun. Inf. Multimedia Workshop (e-Forensics '08)*, 10–16.

Chapter 11
Machine Learning Methods and IoT for Smart Parking Models and Approaches

Veerendra Singh

(iD) https://orcid.org/0009-0009-4024-0168

Faculty of Engineering and Technology, Rama University, India

Rajendra Kumar

Faculty of Engineering and Technology, Rama University, India

ABSTRACT

Smart parking models and approaches aim to optimize the use of parking spaces, reduce traffic conges-tion, and provide a more efficient parking experience. There are various models, and approaches are used like sensor-based parking, IoT-based parking, mobile-based parking, automatic parking systems, and shared parking. Overall, these models and approaches aim to optimize parking usage, reduce traffic congestion, and improve the overall parking experience for users. By leveraging new technologies and innovative approaches, smart parking solutions can help make urban areas more efficient and sustainable.

1. INTRODUCTION

Smart parking is a technology-driven approach that utilizes various methods such as Internet of Things (IoT), Machine learning (ML), and Artificial Intelligence (AI) to improve management and utilization of parking spaces. The primary goal of this system is to minimize traffic congestion, enhance the parking experience for drivers, and optimize the usage of available parking spaces.

Smart parking systems work by leveraging various sensors, cameras, and other IoT devices to moni-tor the availability of parking spaces in actual time. This information is then relayed to a central system, which uses ML algorithms to analyze the data and predict future availability of parking spaces (Mane, Deoghare, Nagmote, Musle, & Sarwade, 2015).

DOI: 10.4018/978-1-6684-9151-5.ch011

Smart parking systems offer numerous benefits such as reducing traffic congestion, minimizing emissions, improving traffic flow, and enhancing the overall parking experience for drivers. This system is helpful for the drivers who spend quiet time for searching parking, which can significantly reduce fuel consumption and emissions.

Overall, smart parking systems are an innovative solution to the growing problem of parking space management in urban areas. They provide a cost-effective and efficient way to manage parking spaces, and with the help of advanced ML and IoT technologies, they can be continuously optimized to meet the changing needs of drivers and cities.

A smart parking system could consist of various components (Renuka & Dhanalakshmi, 2015), such as:

- Sensors: These could be embedded in the ground or on walls, and would detect the presence of vehicles in parking spaces. They could use different technologies, such as ultrasonic or infrared sensors.
- Network: The sensors would be connected to a network, which could be a wireless mesh network or a wired connection. The network could also connect to a central server, which would receive data from the sensors and process it.
- Mobile app or web portal: Users could access the smart parking system through a mobile app or web portal. They could see the availability of parking spaces in real-time and reserve a spot.
- Payment gateway: The smart parking system could integrate with a payment gateway, allowing users to pay for parking through the app or web portal.
- LED displays: LED displays could be installed at the entrance and inside the parking lot, showing the availability of parking spaces and guiding drivers to available spots.
- Cameras: Cameras could be installed at the entrance and exit of the parking lot, providing additional security and helping to identify vehicles.

Figure 1. Artificial intelligence

1.1 Artificial Intelligence

AI stands for 'Artificial Intelligence' which is the area of computer science and engineering. It focuses on creating such machines which can perform tasks in such a way that require human intelligence to complete. AI systems use algorithms and statistical models to process data and make predictions based on that data. There are various types of AI systems, likewise machine learning, deep learning, and natural language processing, each with their specific applications and capabilities. AI is used in various industries, including healthcare, finance, education, and entertainment, to automate processes, improve decision-making, and create new products and services.

1.2 Machine Learning

Machine learning is a part of artificial intelligence that emphasizes on permitting machines to improve their performance on a specific task over time from data. In machine learning, algorithms are trained on a large dataset of examples, which are used to identify patterns and make predictions or decisions on new data. This process involves selecting appropriate features or variables, creating a model that maps these inputs to outputs, and optimizing the model's parameters to minimize errors or maximize performance.

There are various types of machine learning algorithms such as supervised learning, unsupervised learning, semi-supervised learning, and reinforcement learning. In supervised learning, the algorithm is based on trained labeled data, where each example is paired with a corresponding label or target variable. In unsupervised learning, the algorithm is based to identify patterns in unlabeled data, without any explicit guidance. In semi-supervised learning, the algorithm is based on the combination of labeled and unlabeled data. In reinforcement learning, the algorithm is based on actions in an environment to maximize a reward signal (Renuka & Dhanalakshmi, 2015).

Machine learning has numerous applications in various areas, such as image and speech recognition, natural language processing, predictive analytics, and robotics. However, machine learning also increases concerns about bias, and ethical issues, which require careful consideration and mitigation.

1.3 IoT

IoT stands for the Internet of Things. It refers to those types of machines which are fitted with sensors, software, and connectivity such as, vehicles, buildings and other objects, allowing them to collect and exchange data over the internet. The IoT allows for real-time monitoring, control, and automation of various processes, and can be used in various industries such as healthcare, manufacturing, transportation, and agriculture, among others.

The devices in an IoT system can range from simple sensors to complex systems, and they can communicate with each other and with other devices, such as smart phones or computers, using a variety of communication protocols. The data collected from these devices can be analyzed to derive insights and improve the efficiency and effectiveness of various processes.

The IoT is expected to have a significant impact on many aspects of daily life, from smart homes and connected cars to smart cities and industrial automation. However, there are also concerns about security and privacy in IoT systems, as well as the potential for job displacement as automation increases.

Smart parking systems use IoT and machine learning to optimize parking space utilization and improve the parking experience for users. Machine learning algorithms can be used to predict parking demand and recommend available parking spots, while IoT sensors can be used to detect and communicate parking occupancy.

There are several machine learning methods (Pham, Tsai, & Nguyen, 2015) that can be used in smart parking systems:

ϖ Regression models: Regression models can be used to predict parking demand based on historical data. This information can be used to optimize parking space allocation and pricing.

ϖ Clustering: Clustering can be used to group parking spaces based on their occupancy patterns. This information can be used to parking space allocation and improve parking management.

ϖ Decision trees: Decision trees can be used to make decisions about parking space allocation and pricing based on multiple factors, such as location, time of day, and parking demand.

ϖ Neural networks: Neural networks can be used to predict parking demand based on multiple factors, such as weather, events, and traffic.

IoT sensors can be used to detect parking occupancy and communicate this information to users. There are several types of IoT sensors that can be used in smart parking systems:

¬ Ultrasonic sensors: Ultrasonic sensors can be used to identify the presence of a vehicle in a parking place.

¬ Magnetic sensors: Magnetic sensors can be used to identify the presence of a vehicle in a parking.

¬ Infrared sensors: Infrared sensors can be used to identify the presence of a vehicle in a parking.

¬ Camera-based sensors: Camera-based sensors can be used to identify the presence of a vehicle in a parking and provide visual confirmation of parking violations.

Overall, combining machine learning methods and IoT sensors can lead to more efficient and effective smart parking systems, which can save time and reduce traffic congestion for drivers.

2. SMART PARKING OPERATION

Smart parking systems use a combination of technologies, such as sensors, cameras, and wireless networks, to detect the availability of parking spaces and communicate that information to drivers. Here's how they typically work:

- Sensors: Smart parking systems use sensors, such as ultrasonic or magnetic sensors, to detect the presence of a vehicle in a parking space. The sensors can detect in such a way that parking space is occupied or vacant.

- Data transmission: The sensors send this data to a central server or cloud-based system through wireless networks such as Wi-Fi or cellular networks.

- Data analysis: The server or cloud-based system analyzes the data from the sensors and generates real-time information about the availability of parking spaces.

- Communication: The system communicates this information to drivers through various means, such as mobile apps, electronic signage, or in-vehicle navigation systems.
- Payment processing: In some smart parking systems, drivers can use the mobile app to pay for parking, which is then automatically charged to their account.

By providing real-time information on parking space availability and making it easier for drivers to find out the parking space and pay for that, smart parking systems can help reduce congestion and improve the overall parking experience (Computing, 2016). They can also help cities and businesses optimize their parking resources and reduce the environmental impact of vehicles circling for parking.

2.1 Sensors in Smart Parking

There are different types of sensors that can be used in smart parking systems (Andriana, 2012). Here are some examples:

¬ Ultrasonic Sensors: Ultrasonic sensors are mostly used in smart parking systems. They work by creating sound waves and measuring the time it takes for the waves to come back from objects in their path. This allows them to identify the presence and proximity of vehicles.

¬ Infrared Sensors: Infrared sensors use infrared radiation to identify the presence of vehicles. They work by emitting a beam of infrared light and measuring the amount of light that is reflected back to the sensor.

¬ Magnetic Sensors: Magnetic sensors use the earth's magnetic field to identify the presence of vehicles. They work by measuring the variations in the magnetic field caused by the vehicle presence in parking.

¬ Camera-Based Sensors: Camera-based sensors use computer vision algorithms to identify the presence of vehicles. They work by analyzing images captured by cameras mounted on poles or other structures.

¬ Inductive Loop Sensors: Inductive loop sensors use a wire loop buried beneath the surface of the parking lot to identify the presence of vehicles. They work by measuring the variations in the magnetic field caused by the vehicle presence in parking above the loop.

2.2 Data Transmission in Smart Parking System

In a smart parking system, data transmission involves sending information about parking availability, location, and occupancy from the parking sensors to a central database or server, where it can be processed and analyzed. Here are the basic steps involved in data transmission in a smart parking system (Rahul Patil, 2014):

¬ Sensor Data Acquisition: Parking sensors collect data about parking availability and occupancy. This data can include information such as the presence or absence of a vehicle, the size of the vehicle, and the duration of the parking session.

¬ Data Processing: The data collected by the parking sensors is processed to extract the relevant information and prepare it for transmission. This can involve filtering, formatting, and compressing the data.

¬ Data Transmission: Once the data has been processed, it is transmitted over a wireless or wired network to a central database or server. The method of transmission can vary depending on the type of sensor used, the distance between the sensors and the server, and the network infrastructure available.

¬ Data Storage: The data is stored in a central database or server, where it can be accessed and analyzed by the smart parking system's software. This data is used to give real-time information about parking availability, optimize parking resources, and improve overall parking management.

Overall, the data transmission process in a smart parking system is critical to its effectiveness and efficiency, as it enables real-time monitoring and management of parking resources.

2.3 Data Analysis in Smart Parking

In this system, data analysis involves using advanced analytical techniques to extract insights and patterns from the data collected by parking sensors. Here are some examples of how data analysis takes place in a smart parking system:

¬ Occupancy Analysis: By analyzing the occupancy data collected by parking sensors, smart parking systems can determine which parking spaces are most frequently used, which are least used and how long vehicles typically park in a given location. This information can be used to optimize parking resources and identify areas of high demand.

¬ Predictive Analytics: By analyzing historical data on parking patterns, smart parking systems can predict future demand for parking in a particular area. This information can be used to proactively manage parking resources and avoid congestion and overutilization of parking spaces.

¬ Real-Time Monitoring: By analyzing real-time data from parking sensors, smart parking systems can provide real-time updates on parking availability and direct drivers to available parking spaces (Pham, Tsai, & Nguyen, 2015). This can help reduce traffic congestion and improve the overall parking experience.

¬ Revenue Optimization: By analyzing parking usage patterns and occupancy rates, smart parking systems can optimize pricing strategies to maximize revenue. For example, parking rates can be adjusted based on demand and occupancy levels, or dynamic pricing strategies can be implemented based on real-time data.

Overall, data analysis is a crucial component of smart parking systems, as it enables real-time monitoring and management of parking resources, improves the parking experience for drivers, and optimizes revenue for parking operators.

2.4 Communication in Smart Parking

Communication is a critical component of a smart parking system. Effective communication allows parking sensors, servers, and other system components to exchange data and information in real-time (Pham, Tsai, & Nguyen, 2015). Here are some examples of communication methods used in smart parking systems:

¬ Wireless Communication: Many smart parking systems use wireless communication system such as Wi-Fi, Bluetooth, or cellular networks to connect parking sensors to a central server or database. Wireless communication enables real-time monitoring of parking occupancy and availability, and allows drivers to access parking information on their mobile devices.

¬ Wired Communication: Some smart parking systems use wired communication protocols such as Ethernet or fiber-optic cables to connect parking sensors to a central server or database. Wired communication can provide faster and more reliable data transmission, but may be more expensive to install and maintain.

¬ Cloud-Based Communication: Many smart parking systems use cloud-based communication platforms to store and analyze data collected by parking sensors. Cloud-based communication can provide real-time updates on parking availability and occupancy, and allows parking operators to access parking data from anywhere with an internet connection.

¬ Human-to-Machine Communication: Smart parking systems may also include human-to-machine communication methods such as touchscreens, kiosks, or mobile apps. These communication methods allow drivers to access real-time parking information, reserve parking spaces, and pay for parking using their mobile devices.

Overall, effective communication is critical for the successful operation of a smart parking system. By enabling real-time monitoring and management of parking resources, communication can improve the parking experience for drivers and optimize revenue for parking operators.

2.5 Payment Processing in Smart Parking

Payment processing is an essential component of a smart parking system. It allows drivers to pay for parking using different payment methods, including credit cards, mobile payments, and other digital payment platforms. Here are some examples of payment processing methods used in smart parking systems (El-seoud et al., 2016):

¬ Payment Kiosks: Payment kiosks are typically located near parking lots or garages and allow drivers to pay for parking using cash, credit cards, or other payment methods. Payment kiosks may also allow drivers to purchase parking passes or pre-pay for parking sessions.

¬ Mobile Payment Apps: Many smart parking systems offer mobile payment apps that allow drivers to pay for parking using their mobile devices. Mobile payment apps typically accept credit cards, mobile payment platforms like Apple Pay or Google Wallet, or other digital payment methods.

¬ In-Vehicle Payment Systems: Some smart parking systems allow drivers to pay for parking using in-vehicle payment systems that are integrated into the car's infotainment system. These systems can be convenient for drivers, but may require additional hardware or software integration.

¬ Automatic Payment Processing: Some smart parking systems use automatic payment processing methods, such as automatic toll systems or license plate recognition technology, to charge drivers for parking. Automatic payment processing can be convenient for drivers, but may require additional infrastructure and technology.

Overall, payment processing is a critical component of a smart parking system, as it allows drivers to pay for parking quickly and conveniently using a variety of payment methods. By enabling seamless payment processing, smart parking systems can improve the parking experience for drivers and optimize revenue for parking operators.

3. SMART PARKING MODELS

There are several smart parking models that have been developed and implemented in various cities around the world. Here are three common smart parking models (El-seoud et al., 2016):

¬ On-street Parking Model: This model focuses on optimizing the use of on-street parking spaces in urban areas. It typically involves the use of sensors or cameras to monitor parking spaces and provide real-time information about available spots to users. The model can also include dynamic pricing to adjust the cost of parking based on demand.

¬ Off-street Parking Model: This model focuses on optimizing the use of off-street parking facilities, such as parking garages or lots. It typically involves the use of sensors or cameras to monitor parking spaces and provide real-time information about available spots to users. The model can also include dynamic pricing to adjust the cost of parking based on demand.

¬ Mixed-Use Parking Model: This model combines on-street and off-street parking to provide a comprehensive parking solution in urban areas. It typically involves the use of sensors or cameras to monitor parking spaces in both on-street and off-street locations and provide real-time information about available spots to users. The model can also include dynamic pricing to adjust the cost of parking based on demand.

Overall, the choice of a smart parking model depends on the specific needs and constraints of a given application. On-street parking models are ideal for dense urban areas with limited parking options, while off-street parking models are better suited for areas with larger parking facilities. Mixed-use parking models offer a comprehensive parking solution that can address the needs of both types of areas.

3.1 On-Street Parking Model

The on-street parking model is designed to optimize the use of on-street parking spaces in urban areas. It typically involves the use of sensors or cameras to monitor parking spaces and provide real-time information about available spots to users. Here are some key features of the on-street parking model:

¬ Real-time Availability: The on-street parking model provides users with real-time information about available parking spots in their vicinity. This can be done through mobile apps or digital signage, allowing users to quickly find and reserve a spot.

¬ Dynamic Pricing: The on-street parking model can include dynamic pricing to adjust the cost of parking based on demand. This can help to incentivize users to park in less crowded areas and promote more efficient use of parking spaces.

¬ Enforcement: The on-street parking model typically includes enforcement measures to ensure that parking regulations are followed. This can include parking meters or digital payment systems that require users to pay for their parking time.

¬ Analytics: The on-street parking model can also provide analytics to parking operators and city planners, allowing them to analyze parking usage patterns and optimize parking operations. This can help to improve traffic flow, minimize congestion, and increase revenue.

Overall, the on-street parking model can help to optimize the use of limited parking spaces in urban areas, reduce traffic congestion, and provide a more convenient and efficient parking solution for users. However, it requires careful planning, implementation, and enforcement to ensure its effectiveness.

3.2 Off-Street Parking Model

The off-street parking model is designed to optimize the use of off-street parking facilities, such as parking garages or lots. It typically involves the use of sensors or cameras to monitor parking spaces and provide real-time information about available spots to users. Here are some key features of the off-street parking model:

¬ Real-time Availability: The off-street parking model provides users with real-time information about available parking spots in the parking facility. This can be done through mobile apps or digital signage, allowing users to quickly find and reserve a spot.
¬ Dynamic Pricing: The off-street parking model can include dynamic pricing to adjust the cost of parking based on demand. This can help to incentivize users to park in less crowded areas and promote more efficient use of parking spaces.
¬ Navigation: The off-street parking model can provide users with navigation assistance to help them find the most convenient parking spot in the facility. This can be done through digital signage or mobile apps.
¬ Security: The off-street parking model typically includes security measures to ensure the safety of the parking facility and its users. This can include surveillance cameras, access control systems, and regular patrols.
¬ Analytics: The off-street parking model can also provide analytics to parking operators and city planners, allowing them to analyze parking usage patterns and optimize parking operations. This can help to improve traffic flow, minimize congestion, and increase revenue.

Overall, the off-street parking model can help to optimize the use of larger parking facilities, reduce traffic congestion, and provide a more secure and convenient parking solution for users. However, it also requires careful planning, implementation, and enforcement to ensure its effectiveness.

3.3 Mixed-Use Parking Model

A mixed-use parking model refers to a parking structure or facility that is designed to serve multiple purposes beyond just parking vehicles. The idea is to make the best use of the available space by incorporating other uses such as retail, residential, office, or recreational facilities into the parking structure.

The mixed-use parking model is becoming increasingly popular in urban areas where there is a high demand for parking spaces but limited land availability. By combining parking with other uses, developers can maximize land use, generate additional revenue, and create a more vibrant and active urban environment.

There are several benefits to this approach, including:

¬ Reduced parking demand: Incorporating other uses into a parking structure can help reduce the overall parking demand in the area by providing alternative modes of transportation, such as walking or cycling, and reducing the need for single-occupancy vehicles.

¬ Increased revenue: By incorporating other uses, developers can generate additional revenue streams beyond parking fees. This can include rental income from residential or commercial tenants, as well as revenue from retail sales.

¬ Improved urban design: Mixed-use parking structures can be designed to blend in with their surroundings and add to the overall urban fabric of the area. They can also help to activate streetscapes by providing pedestrian-friendly retail spaces or public spaces.

Overall, the mixed-use parking model is an innovative approach to urban design that maximizes land use and generates additional revenue streams while providing much-needed parking spaces for urban residents and visitors.

4. SMART PARKING APPROACHES

There are several approaches to smart parking, each with its unique advantages and disadvantages. Here are three common smart parking approaches (Yasin & Khamas, 2012):

¬ Sensor-based Approach: This approach involves the use of sensors placed on parking spaces to identify the presence of vehicles. The sensors send data to a central server, which can provide real-time information about available parking spots to users. This approach is highly accurate and reliable, but it can be expensive to install and maintain the sensors.

¬ Camera-based Approach: This approach involves the use of cameras to monitor parking spaces and identify the presence of vehicles. The cameras send data to a central server, which can provide real-time information about available parking spots to users. This approach is less expensive than the sensor-based approach, but it may be less accurate and reliable, especially in low-light conditions.

¬ Mobile App-based Approach: This approach involves the use of a mobile app that users can use to find available parking spots. The app relies on user input, such as the location of parked vehicles or the availability of parking spots, to provide real-time information about available parking spots to other users. This approach is less expensive than the sensor-based or camera-based approach, but it may be less accurate and reliable, especially if users do not provide accurate information.

Overall, the choice of a smart parking approach depends on the specific needs and constraints of a given application. Sensor-based approaches are highly accurate but expensive, while mobile app-based approaches are less expensive but rely on user input. Camera-based approaches offer a middle ground between cost and accuracy.

5. HOW DOES IOT WORK IN SMART PARKING?

IoT (Internet of Things) plays a key role in the functioning of a smart parking system. Here's how IoT works in a smart parking system (Pham, Tsai, & Nguyen, 2015):

¬ Parking Sensors: IoT-enabled parking sensors are used to identify the presence of vehicles in parking spaces. These sensors use a variety of technologies, such as ultrasonic, infrared, or magnetic sensors, to detect the presence of a vehicle and transmit this data wirelessly to a central server or database.
¬ Communication Networks: IoT-enabled smart parking systems use wireless communication networks, such as Wi-Fi, Bluetooth, or cellular networks, to transmit data between parking sensors, servers, and other system components. These allow parking operators to monitor parking occupancy and availability in real-time and provide this information to drivers via mobile apps or other communication methods.
¬ Cloud-Based Data Storage and Analysis: IoT-enabled smart parking systems typically use cloud-based platforms to store and analyze parking data. This allows parking operators to access real-time parking information from anywhere with an internet connection and use data analytics to optimize parking operations and revenue.
¬ Mobile Apps and Other Interfaces: IoT-enabled smart parking systems also include mobile apps or other interfaces that allow drivers to access real-time parking information, reserve parking spaces, and pay for parking using their mobile devices.

Overall, IoT plays a critical role in the functioning of a smart parking system by enabling real-time monitoring of parking occupancy and availability, and allowing parking operators to optimize parking operations and revenue. By leveraging IoT technology, smart parking systems can provide a convenient, efficient, and secure parking experience for drivers.

5.1 IoT-Based Sensors in Smart Parking

IoT (Internet of Things) based sensors are a key component of a smart parking system, as they allow parking operators to monitor parking occupancy and availability in real-time. Here are some details about IoT-based sensors used in smart parking (Pham, Tsai, & Nguyen, 2015):

¬ Types of IoT Sensors: There are several types of IoT sensors used in smart parking systems, including ultrasonic, infrared, and magnetic sensors. These sensors use IoT technology to wirelessly transmit data about parking occupancy and availability to a central server or database.
¬ Installation: IoT-based sensors are typically installed in individual parking spaces or in the ground near parking spaces. They are designed to be low-power and long-lasting, using batteries or other power sources that can last for several years without needing to be replaced.
¬ Data Collection and Analysis: IoT-based sensors collect data on parking occupancy and availability, which is transmitted wirelessly to the central server or database. This data is analyzed using data analytics tools to optimize parking operations and revenue.
¬ Benefits of IoT Sensors: IoT-based sensors offer several benefits for parking operators and drivers. For parking operators, IoT sensors can help optimize parking operations and revenue by providing

real-time parking data and analytics. For drivers, IoT sensors can help reduce the time and frustration of finding a parking spot, improving the overall parking experience.

Overall, IoT-based sensors are a critical component of a smart parking system, allowing parking operators to monitor parking occupancy and availability in real-time, optimize parking operations and revenue, and provide a convenient and efficient parking experience for drivers. By leveraging IoT technology, smart parking systems can offer a range of benefits for both parking operators and drivers.

5.2 IoT-Based Communication Networks in Smart Parking

IoT (Internet of Things) based communication networks are an essential part of a smart parking system, as they enable the transmission of data between sensors, servers, and other components of the system. Here are some details about IoT-based communication networks used in smart parking (Pham, Tsai, & Nguyen, 2015):

¬ IoT Sensors: Smart parking systems use IoT sensors to detect the presence of vehicles in parking spaces. These sensors transmit data wirelessly to a central server or database, providing real-time information about parking occupancy and availability.
¬ IoT Networks: IoT-based communication networks, such as LoRaWAN, Zigbee, or NB-IoT, are used to transmit data between parking sensors, servers, and other components of the smart parking system. These networks are designed to handle large volumes of data and are optimized for low-power consumption, allowing sensors to operate for extended periods without requiring battery replacements.
¬ Cloud-Based Data Storage and Analysis: Smart parking systems typically use cloud-based platforms to store and analyze parking data collected by IoT sensors. This allows parking operators to access real-time parking information from anywhere with an internet connection and use data analytics to optimize parking operations and revenue.
¬ Mobile Apps and Other Interfaces: IoT-based communication networks enable the use of mobile apps and other interfaces that allow drivers to access real-time parking information, reserve parking spaces, and pay for parking using their mobile devices.

Overall, IoT-based communication networks are a critical component of a smart parking system, enabling the transmission of parking data in real-time, facilitating the use of mobile apps and other interfaces, and optimizing parking operations and revenue. By leveraging IoT technology, smart parking systems can provide a convenient, efficient, and secure parking experience for drivers.

5.3 Cloud-Based Data Storage and Analysis by IoT

Cloud-based data storage and analysis are essential components of a smart parking system that leverages IoT (Internet of Things) technology. Here are some details about cloud-based data storage and analysis in smart parking (Pham, Tsai, & Nguyen, 2015):

¬ Data Collection: IoT-based sensors collect data on parking occupancy and availability, which is transmitted wirelessly to a central server or database. This data includes information such as the number of available parking spaces, the location of parked vehicles, and the duration of parking sessions.

¬ Cloud-Based Data Storage: Cloud-based platforms, such as Amazon Web Services (AWS) or Microsoft Azure, are used to store parking data collected by IoT sensors. These platforms provide scalable, secure, and reliable storage that can handle large volumes of data.

¬ Data Analytics: Cloud-based data analytics tools are used to analyze parking data collected by IoT sensors. These tools can provide real-time insights into parking occupancy and availability, helping parking operators optimize parking operations and revenue.

¬ Mobile Apps and Other Interfaces: Cloud-based data storage and analysis enable the use of mobile apps and other interfaces that allow drivers to access real-time parking information, reserve parking spaces, and pay for parking using their mobile devices.

¬ Benefits of Cloud-Based Data Storage and Analysis: By leveraging cloud-based data storage and analysis, smart parking systems can provide a range of benefits for parking operators and drivers. Parking operators can use real-time parking data and analytics to optimize parking operations and revenue, while drivers can enjoy a more convenient and efficient parking experience.

Overall, cloud-based data storage and analysis are critical components of a smart parking system that leverages IoT technology. By using cloud-based platforms and data analytics tools, smart parking systems can provide real-time parking data and insights, optimize parking operations and revenue, and provide a convenient and efficient parking experience for drivers.

5.4 Mobile Apps and Other Interfaces Based on IoT

Mobile apps and other interfaces based on IoT (Internet of Things) technology are important components of a smart parking system, as they provide drivers with real-time information about parking availability and enable them to reserve parking spaces and pay for parking using their mobile devices. Here are some details about mobile apps and other interfaces based on IoT in smart parking (Mane, Deoghare, Nagmote, Musle, & Sarwade, 2015):

¬ Real-Time Parking Information: Mobile apps and other interfaces based on IoT provide drivers with real-time information about parking availability, location, and pricing. This information is collected by IoT-based sensors and transmitted wirelessly to the mobile app or other interface, where it is displayed to drivers in real-time.

¬ Reservation and Payment: Mobile apps and other interfaces based on IoT allow drivers to reserve parking spaces and pay for parking using their mobile devices. This eliminates the need for drivers to use cash or credit cards at parking meters or pay stations, making the parking experience more convenient and efficient.

¬ Navigation and Directions: Mobile apps and other interfaces based on IoT provide drivers with navigation and directions to available parking spaces, helping them find parking quickly and easily.

¬ Personalization: Mobile apps and other interfaces based on IoT can be personalized to provide customized parking information and recommendations based on a driver's location, preferences, and past parking history.

¬ Integration with Other Services: Mobile apps and other interfaces based on IoT can be integrated with other services, such as ride-sharing apps or public transportation systems, to provide a seamless and integrated transportation experience.

Overall, mobile apps and other interfaces based on IoT are essential components of a smart parking system, as they provide drivers with real-time parking information, enable them to reserve parking spaces and pay for parking using their mobile devices, and provide a more convenient and efficient parking experience. By leveraging IoT technology, smart parking systems can offer a range of benefits for drivers and parking operators alike.

6. IMPORTANCE OF IOT BASED SMART PARKING

IoT-based smart parking is an innovative solution that can make parking more efficient, convenient, and safer for drivers. It involves the use of sensors and connected devices to gather data about parking spaces in real-time and provide users with accurate information about available parking spots. Here are some of the benefits and importance of IoT-based smart parking (Mane, Deoghare, Nagmote, Musle, & Sarwade, 2015):

¬ Improved Parking Efficiency: IoT-based smart parking helps to optimize parking spaces by enabling users to find available parking spots quickly and easily. This reduces the time spent driving around in search of parking spaces, thereby reducing traffic congestion, fuel consumption, and air pollution.

¬ Increased Revenue: IoT-based smart parking enables parking operators to increase their revenue by optimizing the use of parking spaces. By accurately tracking parking occupancy and usage patterns, operators can charge more for high-demand parking spots and offer discounts for underutilized ones.

¬ Enhanced User Experience: With IoT-based smart parking, users can easily locate available parking spots using mobile apps, sensors, and other connected devices. This enhances the user experience by reducing the frustration and stress associated with finding parking spots in crowded areas.

¬ Improved Safety: IoT-based smart parking can improve safety by reducing the number of accidents caused by drivers searching for parking spots. The use of sensors and cameras can also enhance security by monitoring parking spaces and detecting any suspicious activity.

¬ Cost Savings: IoT-based smart parking can help reduce operating costs for parking operators by optimizing the use of parking spaces, reducing maintenance costs, and improving efficiency.

Overall, IoT-based smart parking is an innovative solution that can help to transform the parking industry by improving efficiency, reducing traffic congestion, enhancing the user experience, and increasing revenue for parking operators.

7. ROLE OF IOT-BASED SMART PARKING FOR SOCIETY

IoT-based smart parking has the potential to make a significant positive impact on society. Here are some of the key roles that smart parking can play in society (Adam et al., 2015):

¬ Reducing Traffic Congestion: By optimizing parking spaces and providing drivers with real-time information about available parking spots, smart parking can help to reduce traffic congestion in urban areas. This can improve traffic flow and reduce the time and fuel spent on searching for parking spots.

¬ Promoting Sustainable Transportation: Smart parking systems can encourage the use of sustainable modes of transportation, such as public transit, biking, or walking. By providing users with information about the availability of parking spots near transit stops or bike-sharing stations, smart parking can help to reduce the use of personal cars and promote sustainable transportation.

¬ Improving Air Quality: Smart parking can help to reduce the emissions from vehicles caused by traffic congestion and the time spent searching for parking spots. This can lead to improved air quality in urban areas, which can have significant health benefits for the population.

¬ Enhancing Safety: Smart parking systems can help to enhance safety by reducing the number of accidents caused by drivers searching for parking spots. The use of sensors and cameras can also improve security by monitoring parking spaces and detecting any suspicious activity.

¬ Boosting Economic Development: Smart parking can contribute to economic development by improving the efficiency of parking operations and increasing revenue for parking operators. This can also attract more visitors to business districts or tourist attractions by providing a convenient and efficient parking solution.

Overall, IoT-based smart parking has the potential to contribute to a more sustainable, efficient, and safe society by reducing traffic congestion, promoting sustainable transportation, improving air quality, enhancing safety, and boosting economic development.

8. FUTURE ASPECTS OF SMART PARKING

The future of smart parking looks promising, as technology continues to evolve and improve. Here are some potential future aspects of smart parking (Adam et al., 2018).

¬ Integration with Autonomous Vehicles: As autonomous vehicles become more common, smart parking systems will need to integrate with these vehicles to provide a seamless parking experience. This could include automatically reserving and paying for parking spaces, as well as guiding the vehicle to the spot.

¬ Predictive Analytics: Smart parking systems could use predictive analytics to forecast parking demand and adjust pricing accordingly. This could help to optimize the use of parking spaces and increase revenue for parking operators.

¬ Multi-Modal Integration: Smart parking systems could integrate with other modes of transportation, such as bike-sharing or public transit, to provide users with a complete transportation solution. This could include providing parking spots for bikes or integrating parking payments with transit fares.

¬ Environmental Sustainability: Smart parking systems could incorporate environmental sustainability features, such as electric vehicle charging stations or solar-powered sensors. This could help to reduce the carbon footprint of parking operations and promote sustainable transportation.

¬ Personalization: Smart parking systems could use data analytics to personalize the parking experience for individual users. This could include providing preferred parking spots or tailored pricing based on usage patterns.

Overall, the future of smart parking is likely to be characterized by greater integration with other modes of transportation, increased use of data analytics, and a focus on sustainability and personalization.

9. LIMITATIONS OF SMART PARKING SYSTEM

While smart parking systems offer numerous benefits, there are also some limitations that should be considered, such as (Adam et al., 2018):

¬ Cost: The installation and maintenance of smart parking systems can be expensive, which may deter some organizations from implementing them. This can be especially true for smaller parking facilities that may not have the financial resources to invest in advanced technology.

¬ Dependence on technology: Smart parking systems rely heavily on technology, which can be prone to malfunctions and failures. A technical glitch could cause the system to malfunction, leading to delays or inconvenience for users.

¬ Limited user adoption: Some users may be hesitant to adopt smart parking systems due to concerns about data privacy or a lack of familiarity with the technology. This can limit the effectiveness of the system, especially if users prefer to use traditional parking methods.

¬ Accuracy issues: While smart parking systems are designed to be highly accurate, there may be occasional errors in the data collection or analysis, leading to incorrect or inconsistent parking guidance. This can be frustrating for users and may decrease confidence in the system.

¬ Limitations in certain environments: Smart parking systems may not be suitable for all types of parking environments. For example, in areas with heavy snowfall, the sensors or cameras may become obscured, making it difficult to accurately track parking spaces.

In summary, while smart parking systems have many benefits, they also have limitations that should be taken into consideration when evaluating their effectiveness and suitability for a particular parking environment.

10. REMEDIES FOR SMART PARKING SYSTEM

To address some of the limitations of smart parking systems, there are several remedies that can be considered, including (Subramaniam, 2018).

1- Cost reduction: One way to reduce the cost of implementing smart parking systems is to use off-the-shelf hardware and software solutions that can be easily integrated with existing parking infrastructure. This can help to reduce the need for expensive custom development and installation.

2- User education: Educating users on the benefits and ease of use of smart parking systems can help to increase adoption rates. Providing clear and concise instructions and making the system as user-friendly as possible can also help to alleviate concerns about data privacy and technology.

3- Backup systems: To address potential technical glitches or system failures, it is important to have backup systems in place. This could include manual override systems or redundant data storage and processing systems that can take over in case of a failure.

4- Improved accuracy: To address accuracy issues, smart parking systems can be designed with redundant sensors or cameras to provide multiple data points for analysis. The system can also be periodically calibrated and tested to ensure accuracy.

5- Flexibility in design: To address limitations in certain environments, smart parking systems can be designed to be flexible and adaptable to different parking environments. For example, in areas with heavy snowfall, sensors can be designed to be easily removed and replaced during snow removal operations.

Overall, addressing the limitations of smart parking systems requires a multi-faceted approach that includes cost reduction, user education, backup systems, improved accuracy, and flexibility in design. By taking these steps, the effectiveness and adoption rates of smart parking systems can be improved.

11. FUTURE WORK IN SMART PARKING SYSTEM

The future of smart parking systems is likely to focus on improving efficiency, sustainability, and user experience. Here are some potential areas of future work (Hazrin et al., 2008; Murad et al., 2016):

¬ Integration with smart cities: Smart parking systems can be integrated with other smart city infrastructure, such as traffic management systems, to optimize traffic flow and reduce congestion. This can be done by dynamically adjusting parking pricing, providing real-time parking guidance, and incentivizing users to use alternative modes of transportation.
¬ Sustainability: The future of smart parking systems is likely to focus on sustainability by using renewable energy sources such as solar power to power the sensors and other components. Smart parking systems can also be designed to reduce emissions by encouraging the use of electric vehicles and providing charging infrastructure.
¬ Autonomous vehicles: As the adoption of autonomous vehicles increases, smart parking systems can be designed to support these vehicles by providing designated parking areas and charging infrastructure. This can help to increase the efficiency of the parking process and reduce the time required for users to park their vehicles.
¬ Enhanced user experience: Future smart parking systems are likely to focus on enhancing the user experience by providing real-time parking availability information, integrating with navigation and payment systems, and using advanced analytics to provide personalized parking recommendations based on user preferences and behavior.
¬ Security and privacy: Future smart parking systems are also likely to focus on improving security and privacy by using advanced encryption and authentication methods to protect user data and prevent unauthorized access to the system.

Overall, the future of smart parking systems is likely to be characterized by greater integration with other smart city infrastructure, a focus on sustainability, support for autonomous vehicles, enhanced user experience, and improved security and privacy.

CONCLUSION

In conclusion, smart parking systems are becoming increasingly important in urban areas due to their ability to reduce traffic congestion, improve traffic flow, increase revenue for parking lot operators, and provide a more convenient and sustainable parking experience for drivers. With real-time monitoring, mobile apps, automated payment, data analytics, and integration with other smart city systems, smart parking systems offer a more advanced and efficient approach to managing parking resources in urban areas, ultimately making urban areas more livable and accessible for everyone. As cities continue to grow and become more congested, smart parking systems will play an increasingly important role in reducing traffic and improving overall mobility, making urban areas more sustainable and livable for generations to come.

REFERENCES

Adam, Najib, Yasin, Hasliza, Rahim, Soh, & Abdulmalek. (2018). A compact dual-band rectenna for ambient RF energy harvesting. *Microwave and Optical Technology Letters, 60*(11), 2740-2748.

Adam, I., Malek, M.F., Yasin, M.N., & Rahim, H.A. (2015). *RF Energy Harvesting With Efficient Matching Technique For Low Power Level Application*. Academic Press.

Andriana. (2012). Sensor Comparation for Smart Parking System. Academic Press.

Computing, M. (2016). *Smart Car Parking Using Arduino*. Academic Press.

El-seoud, S. A., El-sofany, H., & Taj-eddine, I. (2016). Towards the Development of Smart Parking System using Arduino and Web Technologies. Academic Press.

Hazrin, N., Mohamad, H., Badiozaman, M. H., & Daud, H. (2008). *Smart Parking Reservation System using Short Message Services (SMS)*. https://www.trakaid.com/how-does-smart-parking-generate-new-revenue-streams/

Mane, P., Deoghare, R., Nagmote, S., Musle, S., & Sarwade, S. (2015). Android based Smart Parking System. Academic Press.

MuradS. A. Z.MohyarS. N.HarunA.YasinM. N. M.IshakI. S.SapawiR. (2016). Low noise figure 2.4 GHz down conversion CMOS mixer for wireless sensor network application. 2016 IEEE Student Conference on Research and Development (SCOReD), 1-4. doi:10.1109/SCORED.2016.7810032

Pham, T. N. A. M., Tsai, M., & Nguyen, D. U. C. B. (2015). *A Cloud-Based Smart-Parking System Based on Internet-of-Things Technologies*. doi:10.1109/ACCESS.2015.2477299

Rahul Patil, M. S. (2014). Smart parking system based on reservation (Vol. 2). Academic Press.

Renuka, R., & Dhanalakshmi, S. (2015). *Android Based Smart Parking System Using Slot Allocation & Reservations*. Academic Press.

Subramaniam. (2018). A Stacked Planar Antenna with Switchable Small Grid Pixel Structure for Directive High Beam Steering Broadside Radiation. *International Journal of Engineering & Technology, 7*(2.5), 122-127.

Yasin, M. N. M., & Khamas, S. K. (2012, April). Measurements and Analysis of a Probe-Fed Circularly Polarized Loop Antenna Printed on a Layered Dielectric Sphere. *IEEE Transactions on Antennas and Propagation, 60*(4), 2096–2100. doi:10.1109/TAP.2012.2186259

Chapter 12
Blockchain Methods and Data-Driven Decision Making With Autonomous Transportation

Kawsalya Maharajan
Hindusthan College of Arts and Sciences, India

A. V. Senthil Kumar
https://orcid.org/0000-0002-8587-7017
Hindusthan College of Arts and Sciences, India

Ibrahiem M. M. El Emary
King Abdulaziz University, Saudi Arabia

Priyanka Sharma
https://orcid.org/0000-0002-9503-1170
Swami Keshvanand Institute of Technology, Management, and Gramothan, Jaipur, India

Rohaya Latip
Universiti Putra Malaysia, Malaysia

Namita Mishra
https://orcid.org/0000-0002-3353-0564
I.T.S. School of Management, India

Amit Dutta
All India Council for Technical Education, India

L. Manjunatha Rao
National Assessment and Accreditation Council, India

Meenakshi Sharma
https://orcid.org/0000-0002-6958-8741
University of Petroleum and Energy Studies, India

ABSTRACT

Blockchain encourages artificial intelligence towards intelligence while also increasing its autonomy and credibility. In this chapter, the authors examine the relationship between blockchain technology and artificial intelligence from a more thorough and three-dimensional standpoint. One of the greatest problems with blockchain implementations in IoV is that they cannot meet the computational and energy needs of conventional blockchain systems since IoV nodes are limited in their ability to use resources. A marketplace that enables stakeholders (CSPs, asset suppliers, service providers, regulators, etc.) to interact and exchange value with confidence based on smart provenance and governance may be developed using blockchain and distributed ledger technologies (DLT). These innovations offer a decentralised audit architecture that is safe. Such transactions (who uses what) can be kept on a distributed ledger marketplace in an immutable setting. A decentralised consensus process that does not need mining or incentivization in a permissionless architecture ensures data integrity.

DOI: 10.4018/978-1-6684-9151-5.ch012

THE ROLE OF BLOCKCHAIN TECHNOLOGY IN AUTONOMOUS VEHICLES

Automobile manufacturers are continuously searching for new and improved technology to enhance the performance of their vehicles and the driving experience. The typical car is getting closer to being fully driverless, connected, and electric or hybrid. Blockchain technology is proving to be a workable answer for this, since there is a rising requirement for technology capable of processing the enormous amount of data generated with the highest level of security.

Another significant area where blockchain technology can be useful is in the sharing and management of data. While autonomous cars produce a tonne of data about traffic, vehicle usage, driving habits, and other topics, this data needs to be stored, shared, and examined without jeopardising security. Data management is made faster and more safe by the distributed ledger and cryptography of the blockchain technology. Self-driving cars can evaluate and judge traffic in real-time, prevent accidents, find the best routes, and shorten travel times thanks to this effective data management using blockchain.

SIGNIFICANT IMPORTANCE

Connected mobility is yet another significant application of blockchain technology. Vehicles and other supporting infrastructure in the city and on the roads can communicate with one other quickly and effectively thanks to blockchain technology. In addition to enabling peer-to-peer transactions with a high level of security, it may build a trusted network. According to the Frost & Sullivan analysis, 10% to 15% of connected vehicle transactions will probably be made via blockchain by 2025. Blockchain can unite manufacturers under a single drive and test database that keeps data on simulations, tests, and flaws, enhancing the security of autonomous and networked automobiles.

Smart contracts, which use blockchain technology, can make several parts of driving easier, including paying for tolls, repairs, and insurance. In Automated payments using smart contracts on a blockchain network enable security and transparency while reducing paperwork and saving time. Moreover, faster and more secure authentication of drivers and passengers using blockchain technology is possible.

BLOCKCHAIN TECHNOLOGY IN TERMS OF APPLICABILITY IN TRANSPORT SYSTEMS

Blockchain Technology

Bitcoin's underlying technology, blockchain, has recently drawn a lot of attention. Blockchain functions as an unchangeable ledger that enables decentralised transaction processing. Several industries, including financial services, reputation management, and the Internet of Things (IoT), are seeing the emergence of blockchain-based applications. Blockchain technology still faces several obstacles, including scalability and security issues, which must be resolved. This essay provides a thorough introduction to blockchain technology. First, we give a brief introduction to blockchain architecture before contrasting some common consensus techniques applied across various blockchains. Also briefly addressed are technical difficulties and recent advancements. We also outline potential blockchain trends in the future.

Internet of Vehicles

The Internet of Vehicles (IoV) is a network of automobiles that are fitted with sensors, software, and the intermediary technologies to connect and exchange data over the Internet in accordance with predetermined standards. The Internet of Vehicles (IoV) originated from Vehicular Ad Hoc Networks (also known as "VANET," a type of mobile ad hoc network used for communication between automobiles and roadside systems) and is anticipated to eventually develop into a "Internet of Autonomous Vehicles." IoV is anticipated to be one of the Future Mobility's ACES (autonomous, connected, electric, and shared) enablers. As a product category, road cars rely on a wide range of technological fields, including real-time analytics, inexpensive sensors, and embedded systems. The IoV ecosystem depends on contemporary infrastructure and architectures that share the computational load among numerous processing units in a network in order for these to work together harmoniously. In the consumer sector, discussions about smart cities and driverless cars are the ones where IoV technology is most frequently mentioned. Many of these architectures rely on open-source software and systems to run, such as Subaru, whose infotainment systems are able to gauge a driver's alertness and sound a warning to pull over for a break.

LITERATURE SURVEY

In Ackom et al. (2020), traditional power users have evolved into prosumers—people who produce and consume electricity and can engage in flexible peer-to-peer transactions—thanks to the rapid growth of distributed energy. A distributed ledger technology suited for peer-to-peer transactions is called blockchain. Nevertheless, the single-chain blockchain is unable to enable decentralised power transactions and network security checks at the same time. With the restructuring of the transaction chain and power chain, a double-chain blockchain and the associated transaction model are therefore presented. To enhance prosumer revenues, peer-to-peer autonomous decision-making transactions are accomplished through the transaction chain. Through the power chain with limitations, the security check and modified transaction scheme are accomplished. Peer-to-peer transactions based on the Ethereum blockchain development platform are confirmed in the IEEE 14-node distribution network. The findings indicate that the double-chain blockchain is more efficient at handling transactions than the single-chain blockchain. The suggested solution can support prosumers' autonomous and secure transactions.

In Pashkevich et al. (2020), the essay discusses the major trends in the intellectualization of mobility and transportation systems. It is thought about if blockchain technology could be applied to transportation networks. The article suggests leveraging Blockchain technology to improve cybersecurity by developing a secure and reliable mechanism for transmitting parameters of each vehicle's present state using the signals of nearby vehicles. Using a Blockchain system built on the Exonum platform, the authors have created a tracking system for vehicle actions. The article presents the system's mathematical underpinnings. Elliptic Curve Digital Signature Algorithm is used for data entry and to check that they agree to the transaction (ECDSA).The difficulty of the article's mentioned private key search task has an impact on ECDSA security. The automotive sector needs the support of blockchain technology to advancement in many sectors like Blockchain security in the context of managing driver data, identity authorisation, electronic transactions, etc., sounds too good to be true. Peer-to-peer (P2P) payments for autonomous vehicles, vehicle sovereignty, networked mobility, and a wide range of other applications will all become possible thanks to the use of blockchain in the automotive industry. This mainly has to do with how big systems, like the transportation system, are managed. Simple guidelines and advice should always be followed to avoid catastrophic consequences like traffic jams and accidents. As a result, the proposed system can aid in decision-making with autonomous vehicles and in the investigation of both criminal and traffic offences.

In Pedrosa et al. (2020), making decisions based on data is gradually becoming a crucial aspect of marketing across all business sectors, and it is receiving unheard-of attention in terms of regulations and financial backing. In order to better comprehend data-driven decision-making processes, this article will concentrate on a broad overview of their uses in marketing and associated research. As a result, we hope to develop a viewpoint on the strategic planning and administration of data-based marketing that will supplement what is now known. In order to make informed judgements, marketers that adopt the "data-driven" perspective gain access to a methodology that gives them greater and better control over data as well as a deeper understanding of the organization's data and strategic models.

In Kamble et al. (2021), the automobile sector could be completely transformed by autonomous vehicles, which are attracting a lot of interest from both academics and business. However, the system is vulnerable to aspects of autonomous vehicle systems involving the linking of separate components. Traditional security techniques may not be able to resolve these problems. A potent instrument that can help increase the trust and dependability in such systems is blockchain technology. This study offers a survey on how blockchain might enhance the security as well as other features of AV systems, with a particular focus on the two most important blockchain ecosystems at the time of writing: Ethereum and Bitcoin. According to the results of our poll, blockchain technology can help with a variety of AV-related use cases, including offering shared storage, boosting security, enhancing associated sectors, and optimising vehicular functionality. This article makes recommendations for improvements in the field of autonomous vehicles (AV), which can be made by integrating blockchain technology with ITS or specific vehicle components.

In Chinnasamy and Kavitha (2021), making decisions is a crucial aspect of daily living. The ability to go in the right path is referred to as decision. AI-based data-driven decision-making is currently helping millions of individuals. Data Driven Decision Making provides advice on how to use data-driven decision-making strategies, which improves resource management, to cope with a wide range of technical processes in managing IoT system resources. The most important of the proposals is the one this essay concentrates on: Data collected from the actual world can be sensed, analysed, communicated with, and stored by IoT devices. They may converse with one another as well. Because to the limited capabilities of IoT devices and the ubiquity of many of the apps being created with the technology, there are a number of issues with the IoT ecosystem. Because to the limited capabilities of IoT devices and the ubiquity of many of the apps being created with the technology, there are a number of issues with the IoT ecosystem. The main focus of this paper is on using data to support decision-making in efficient resource management in an IoT scenario with limited resources. It also includes important approaches, methods, and steps. The conceptual Data Driven Machine Learning model, or intelligent decision-making model based on Internet of Things (IoT) data-driven technology, is the focus of this paper's framework proposal. It provides important insights and ideas on the various challenges and potential future research directions in this work.

In Benkhelifa and Al-Ruithe (2017), the system with in public organisations, data governance has grown to be an important strategy for decision-making. Decision-makers are so concerned about the loss of data governance since it hinders their ability to carry out business plans in many nations and has an impact on both operational and strategic choices. Now, public sector organisations have begun to use cloud computing as they attempt to shift their data into the cloud environment. Data governance, in general, and for cloud computing, specifically, is still being researched, and requires more attention from researchers, according to the literature, which also demonstrates that data governance is one of the primary concerns of decision makers who are considering adopting cloud computing. In contrast, this article aims to create a conceptual framework for cloud data governance-driven decision making in the public sector because there isn't currently one.

In Zhang et al. (2019), according to conventional wisdom, a decision problem is tackled by finding the best answer to an analytical programming decision model, a process known as model-driven decision-making. The decision-quality making's and dependability are determined by the model's fidelity, but because many real-world decision issues are inherently complicated, it is difficult or impossible to derive a model using the first principle. Both scholars and practitioners stress the significance of making judgements that are supported by data linked to decision tasks, also known as data-driven decision-making, in order to face the obstacles that are present in the big data era (D 3 M).By utilising data science, it is possible to extract underlying rules or knowledge from data and use it directly to provide decision-making solutions, in addition to allowing decision models to be anticipated in the presence of ambiguity or unknown dynamics. This position paper breaks down the fundamental ideas and widely used methods of data-driven decision-making into two primary categories: programmable data-driven decision-making (P-D 3 M) and nonprogrammable data-driven decision-making (NP-D 3 M). This study establishes a D 3 M technical framework, major techniques, and approaches for both types of D 3 M and also suggests prospective ways and procedures for using data to enhance decision-making.Additionally, it offers concrete instances of D 3 M's application in real-world settings and suggests five areas for additional D 3 M research. This work, in our opinion, will immediately assist researchers and professionals in their comprehension of the foundations of D 3 M and the advancements in technical procedures.

Blockchain Technology on the Way of Autonomous Vehicles Development has been added to the proposed system (Andreoni et al., 2003).

Li et al. (2009) gives a quick overview of the major studies, approaches, models, and developments in fuzzy and linguistic decision-making that have emerged during the past 50 years. In complicated real-world decision-making situations, humans tend to be ambiguous, imprecise, and/or utilise natural language to evaluate decision alternatives, criteria, etc. Fuzzy and linguistic decision-making approaches enable us to address these situations. This article has three objectives. Initially, a survey of the primary paradigms of fuzzy set theory and computing with words-based representation of decision information is provided, each with varying degrees of expressive richness and complexity. Then, three fundamental frameworks for decision-making are looked at: multicriteria decision making, group consensus-driven decision making, and multiperson multicriteria decision making. Third, the essay covers recent developments in complex decision-making frameworks that rely on the "wisdom of the crowd" to make judgements. The difficulties these frameworks face are addressed, and suggestions for crucial future research directions in the area are made.

METHODOLOGY

Blockchains can provide a trustworthy and neutral records storage platform for a massive software device that uses blockchain as a issue. Trust and neutrality come from the subsequent residences, which might be on account of the particular layout of the ledger structure, the network, consensus protocol, and cryptographic mechanisms it uses:

- Transparency – statistics stored on a blockchain are on hand to all participants within the blockchain community. Thus, the information on a public blockchain is seen toall of us on the internet.
- Immutability – due to the allotted consensus technique, as soon as data are appended to the blockchain, they cannot be changed or deleted. But, immutability would possibly be probabilistic for blockchains the use of sure consensus protocols. All of the transactions inside the blockchain community are saved as immutable data. These immutable facts become a public audit path for regulatory purposes.
- Consistency – disbursed consensus and immutability ensure all devoted information are visible to all destiny records manipulations setting up a unmarried fact throughout the blockchain community.
- Equal rights – because of disintermediation, every player of the network has the same rights to control and get entry to the blockchain. With exclusive consensus protocols, those rights can be weighted by using the computation strength or stake owned via the player.
- Availability – each participate within the blockchain network can also host a full duplicate of the blockchain information. Subsequently, from the machine angle, the statistics are available so long as a minimum one node is in the blockchain network.

Figure 1. Blockchain processing structure

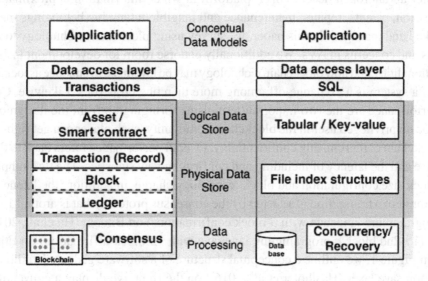

From the software architecture angle, each design shipping structures have developed from being a status symbol to being a necessity inside the present day and age. We cannot imagine a world with out the means of delivery that we have at our disposal these days. With the development of associated technologies, we see a shift to the use of electric powered vehicles and independent automobiles, which might be expected to lessen the stern operating requirements (e.g. personal driving license), energy usage, and environmental effect. self-sustaining vehicles (AVs) are supposed to no longer only and strength-aware, but additionally offer at ease user experience, motive an boom in patron financial savings and additionally lessen the variety of traffic deaths. With decreased non-public possession of vehicles, the price of the carrier provided via the AV will now not be based totally at the emblem, but the quality of carrier and revel in furnished. However, there are positive issues that need to be addressed earlier than AVs can come to be ubiquitous. AVs depend upon accept as true with in the sharing and communication of statistics, be it within components of a single vehicular unit, or multiple motors interacting with every different in a Vehicular advert-hoc network (VANET). AVs use a mess of technologies to make this verbal exchange viable. The nation statistics includes combos of place and time references of objects for unique and non-stop function monitoring, with relation to different gadgets or vehicles across the AV. The running of the AV occurs in tiers - sight (sensors), verbal exchange (vehicle-to-the entirety (V2X) technology), and movement (actuators). Deliver an overview of that technology. V2V specializes in wireless communiqué of applicable statistics among automobiles to provide an extra green driving experience, like higher protection.

Vehicular utilization of multimedia offerings using V2I uses cellular community infrastructures. Smart Transportation systems are better managed with the aid of car-to-roadside or V2R connectivity, using real-time updates on avenue statuses. the 2 major responsibilities of AVs include notion and prediction. The shared statistics and information, the indicators from LiDAR, GPS, and so on. Are vulnerable to a couple of security threats and assaults. Other than the statistics security problems, there arises the priority of legal responsibility control in case of accidents caused by AVs. Block chain is maximum recognized for being extraordinarily relaxed for storing information, in the feel that enhancing previously entered statistics is not possible without affecting every other blocks (within the blockchain). Blockchain technology can offer an unbroken decentralized platform in which information approximately insurance, proof of possession, patents, repairs, maintenance and tangible/intangible belongings may be securely recorded, tracked and managed. In this paper, we survey using blockchain technology to assist address these problems and concerns in AVs. We additionally endorse room for development inside the current vehicular functionalities, and how blockchain technology may be leveraged to enhance associated industries.

Decision of a system is a exchange-off among more than one properties. Likewise, Confidentiality and overall performance are the two important criticisms springing up from the design of blockchain. As there may be no privileged user in the blockchain community, each player can get right of entry to all records on blockchain compromising confidentiality. Overall performance refers back to the transaction processing price and the latency of including and confirming new statistics. The throughput is confined through the block size configuration and block technology charge. in addition, the latency between the submit and commit of a transaction is affected by the consensus protocol, that is around 1 hour (10-minute block c programming language with 6-block confirmations) on Bitcoin (Hu et al., 2016) and round three-minutes (15-2nd block c programming language with 12-block affirmation) on Ethereum (Patel et al., 2020). In Figure 1, we outline a conceptual structure of a software gadget, detailing a blockchain as its information save layer (Haslhofer et al., 2016). on the right, we display a conventional database to focus on our interpretation on how a block chain statistics save may be defined from the traditional view of a database-sponsored utility architecture. Broadly, 3 one-of-a-kind types of programs utilize blockchain technology at its center, particularly, foreign money (e.g., bit coin and micropayments), contracts (e.g., escrow and computerized insurance method based totally on agreed phrases), and asset control (e.g., land registry and digital coupons). Similar to in a conventional database-sponsored application, the conceptual information version underpinning a block chain-primarily based utility wishes to be mapped to the logical and physical degrees of the records store to persist. within the following, we gift our view of a blockchain statistics keep as four layers, particularly logical facts keep, bodily information shop, statistics get admission to, and records processing layer. it's far mentioned that even as the layers are stacked inside the order visible in Figure 1, we present the layers in a special order for the sake of simplifying the dialogue.

A. LOGICAL DATA LAYER

From a database developer's perspective, this level concretizes a conceptual model of the information to a materialized shape together with relational tables in order that the utility can interact with the data shop (e.g., issuing queries to a database). it's far a well-defined vicinity of programming in the traditional database programs, and maximum programming constructs aid this layer in a standardized way (e.g., square over relational tables with JDBC in Java). Here, we observe how this concept applies to the block chain surroundings. The difficulty of accessing the records keep via queries is mentioned separately. This phase makes a specialty of what we consider the "logical models" of block chain-based packages. Mostly, constructs are seen to the database developer at this layer; belongings and smart contracts.

1) Assets

Property encompasses both digital assets like crypto currency and digitalized traditional belongings including stocks or titles, of which blockchains music the ownership. They may be additionally referred to as states in lots of structures, as the number one idea of an asset is to track any piece of facts beyond ownership (e.g., attributes and recognition of a physical object). Blockchains represent assets in approaches:

- UTXO (Unspent Transaction Output) is an asset represented as an output of a transaction and sure to an account. An UTXO can be spent as soon as an enter in a new transaction. The stability of an account is calculated because the sum of all UTXOs (i.e., transactions with unspent outputs) related to the account. Bit coin,
- R3 Corda1and QTUM2 use a UTXO-based totally model.
- Account-stability version keeps a separate access forthe asset stability of each account. The balances of all accounts are traced as the worldwide country of a blockchain community.

Ethereal
Hyperledger3
ESO4
NEO5
Ripple6
and Stellar7 are based totally on this version.

The UTXO version allows parallel transactions and higher privacy as they may be stateless. but, they may be fragmented, which increases computational, garage, and programming complexity. Alternatively, the account-stability model affords an abstract view of an account, bulk transactions, in addition to decreased computational, garage, and programming complexity as they may be tasteful. As is probably anticipated, the tastefulnessof this model limits concurrent transactions and privateers.

2) Smart Contracts another primary construct at this deposit is a clever settlement. A smart agreement is a fixed of executable commands that are activated in response to a message. Whilst executing, those instructions may additionally trade the belongings and generate new messages. In first-technology blockchains, like Bit coin, a simplified shape of smart contracts may be embedded into a transaction as an executable script. In 2nd-technology blockchains, like Ethereal, clever contracts facilitate storing and manipulating records at the blockchain. Compared to saved strategies in databases, smart contracts ensure

that facts they embed can most effective be manipulated by way of calling the accredited capabilities. Therefore, clever contracts may be considered as "data with rules". Remarks: An account (Aka. deal with) is a completely unique reference (i.e., key) to an asset or a smart settlement, e.g., owner of an UTXO in Bitcoin or balance of an Ethereal account. Therefore, in blockchain, the logical records save layer can be abstracted as a key-cost keep that continues tune of money owed and their property or smart contracts.

Figure 2. Autonomous vehicle account creation

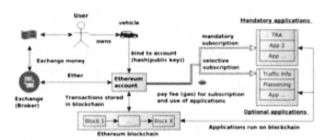

This is much like how a NoSQL database shops its records at this stage. Depending on the blockchain platform, the key's an account and the cost can be of some thing from a simple records structure, object, to a JSON/XML report representing an asset or a smart settlement. Consequently, we are able to country that block chains have a schema less key-fee or file keep at its logical layer. Even as key-value or report shops have emerged because the favored statistics shop for distinctly-scalable programs, a few degree of explicit modeling at this degree is wanted to manage the facts in lots of applications efficaciously. In fact, the dearth of appropriate gear to version facts with rules were identified as an opening in growing and engineering block chain-based totally applications (F. Reid, M. Harrigan,2013). To this point, traditional modeling languages had been used to model blockchain-based packages. For example, UML elegance diagrams are followed to version smart contracts because the settlement languages have a tendency to observe the object-oriented paradigm, e.g., Solidity in Ethereal and JavaScript in Hyperledger (Asch & Guetzkow, 1951).

Collection diagrams are used to model the gadget behavior, wherein clever contracts are explicitly modeled as roles. In terms of extending the prevailing modeling languages for block chain, a version-pushed engineering device Lorikeet extends BPMN (commercial enterprise system model and Notation) to model clever contracts as a statistics store, as well as the enterprise method itself as a set of clever contracts. Even though those early works are precious beginning points, it's miles essential to increase these works to seize particular elements of blockchains (Barcelo & Capraro, 2015).

A 'Vehicular ad-hoc network (VANET)' is a group of stationary and transferring automobiles related thru a wi-fi network. An 'smart transport gadget (ITS)' is an infrastructure wherein automobiles are related with each other the usage of smart devices. The term 'linked self-sufficient automobiles (CAVs)' refers to a set of self reliant cars which can connect with the internet and provide improved records sharing within the form of chance data, sensory and localization information and environmental perception. the 2 lessons of attacks are physical get entry to and far off get entry to assaults. Physical get right of entry to assaults encompass invasive assaults like code change, code injection, packet sniffing, packet fuzzing and in-automobile spoofing. Remote get entry to attacks encompass outside signal spoofing and jamming. they have proposed a blockchain-primarily based solution in which each IoT device (sensor/ actuator) and the automobile is registered to the community earlier than they begin acquiring any of the services. Initially, the vehicular number alongside IoT device statistics will be saved on the blockchain. In view of the high amount of computation power and time in an effort to be wished for the massive amount of statistics generated further, they endorse that handiest the IoT devices shop applicable facts to the blockchain, which can also then be analyzed. Any alteration on facts can then easily be detected as it will adjust preceding records as nicely. To start with, there is no stable mechanism to maintain a music of compromised sensors which are a vital part of the environment of CAVs. moreover, in a scenario in which CAVs are used for a cab-reserving carrier, technical professionals might also hack into the gadget and trade essential records like injuries the auto has been associated with, for personal profits. Facts falsification assault is a number one security problem wherein cars in a community depend upon records received from other motors. the standard encryption schemes like AES will no longer be possible for CVs since they produce a massive amount of records as referred to via Jolfaei and Kant (2019). Key control could end up an problem for each tool and that they cause a potential weakness within the system The normal blockchain networks have many drawbacks. a few limitations consist of dealing via crypto-currencies (in place of believe messages/events) and better latency (decreased with the aid of the usage of 2-stages inside the proposed network). The proposed network could use 2-levels and the first stage will include approved nodes (located in exceptional areas). If an RSU node wants to turn out to be a player of the community, it need to first get demonstrated through the accepted nodes. the second one level consists of registered RSU nodes. The vehicles register with its close by RSU, after which the RSU verifies the identity of the vehicle and shops it on the blockchain. The RSU additionally receives facts generated with the aid of the motors, like traffic congestion, coincidence-associated information, etc. This statistics is distributed to the neighboring roadside nodes for it to be established within the blockchain community of RSUs. There exists no significant authority in this complete system, as a consequence enabling decentralization.

The complexity of supported facts sorts and the extent of their manipulation are restrained by using the design of the clever contract language. As an instance, tokens are belongings which are embedded inside a smart settlement. In Ethereal and Hyper ledger, a consumer-described schema can also be enforced. Whilst a JSON object or CSV document introduced as an asset could be emulated as a set of tables inside a clever contract to conquer schema less nature of blockchains, it's far critical that clever contracts aren't over-engineered such that their price-efficiency and protection are misplaced.

B. Bodily Statistics LAYER

A conventional view of a physical facts store might involve knowledge exclusive index systems (e.g., B-tree and Hash table) that are highly optimized for searching and retrieving information objects. on this section, we have a look at in what bodily bureaucracy the blockchain information are represented and their implications on reading and writing. As proven in Figure 1, we see the records at this degree in 3 levels, namely transactions, blocks, and the ledger. A selected set of valid transactions form a block, at the same time as a set of blocks that fulfill the consensus protocol is protected in the ledger. The term transaction in blockchain can imply various things depending on the context. It can refer to the operation that manipulates the data stored on a block chain, as well as the statistics shape that stores the parameters utilized by the operation. to differentiate the 2 usages, here we use the term transaction report to mean the records structure. We reserve the time period transaction itself for wherein we discuss data access and processing operations.

1) Transaction Data

A transaction record holds each the parameters and consequences of "blockchain records operations" accomplished on the assets and clever contracts (i.e., the logical constructs from the previous layer). Common operations are creating new debts, exchanging property, or creating/executing smart contracts. An essential feature of a transaction document is, as soon as chosen to be covered in a block, the document is permanently stored inside the block reaching immutability. Most blockchains also consistently save the failed transactions. This is because of blockchain's roots to the monetary area, in which every information document in blockchain is a monetary transaction requiring utmost transparency. Because the block chain transaction data are immutable, the best manner to correct any errors is to issue a reverse transaction. each transaction report has a precise identifier and stored as a key-fee pair within a block.

2) Block

Every block includes a list of transaction facts (may be empty if blocks are built periodically). Therefore, the precise content material and structure of a block are stricken by that of transaction facts it contains and implementation of the blockchain. For example, the transaction records in a Bitcoin or Hyperledger block are dependent in a Merkle tree, while a Trie is used in an Ethereum block (Patel et al., 2020). Furthermore, a block can preserve different data systems, including the worldwide kingdom. For example, an Ethereum block continues song of all account balance pairs of property and smart contracts the usage of some other attempts. In Hyperledger, a key-fee shop (e.g., LevelDB or CouchDB) is used to maintain song of the worldwide kingdom. The block size is a configurable parameter and is concern to a exchange-off among velocity of block records replication, interblock generation time, and transaction throughput (Foley et al., 2019). The block length can be laid out in several approaches. as an example, Bitcoin specifies a restrict on information (in MB) while Ethereum specifies a restriction on computation (as fuel restrict) in step with block.

3) Ledger

Blockchain is a unmarried worldwide list (chain) of blocks, in which each block is "chained" lower back to the preceding block through the inclusion of the hash of a representation of the previous block's information. Bitcoin, Ethereum, and Hyperledger are widespread examples of one of this chain of blocks. alternatively,

Hashgraph8 ="hide">uses="tipsBox"> a Directed Acyclic Graph (DAG) of blocks.

The ledger of IOTA9is a DAG of person transactionsrather than blocks.

Remarks: The bodily styles of blockchain statistics is interconnected in the 3 degrees explained above. As mentioned, the ="hide">internal="tipsBox"> enterprise and data systems of those tiers depend upon the implementation of a specific block chain platform. No matter the differences in block implementations, facts storage fashions in blockchains are as a substitute restricted and optimized for garage, rather than for searching and indexing, not like the traditional counterparts. that is because the records storage is carried out to assure the particular houses of blockchain, lessen information storage and transmission charges, and to help monetary transactions. maximum blockchain ledgers inclusive of Bitcoin and Ethereum are fully replicated wherein property, transactions, clever contracts, and blocks are duplicated on every node within the blockchain network. While Hyperledger replicates handiest to all of the nodes in a channel, that's a logical subset of nodes in the blockchain community that is allowed to get admission to each deferent facts. Such excessive-stage of replication complements immutability as any trade to facts on a small fraction of nodes cannot have an effect on the statistics on other nodes without going through the consensus procedure. However, contrary to distributed databases, such replication does now not growth transaction throughput nor reduce latency. This is because of the consensus manner that tries to decorate the consistency of information by means of ideally electing one node because the miner to construct the following block, and then replicating it to all other nodes. Rather, blockchains which includes R3 Corda and BigchainDB10 shard the ledger (saved as a database) throughout a hard and fast of nodes to offer higher throughput and latency characteristics. A comparable impact is predicted in Ethereal 2.0 when it implements shading.

Figure 3. The layer access connection over driven data

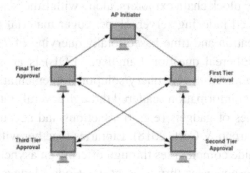

C. INFORMATION ACCESS LAYER

On this section, we look at the API-level get entry to the information save. As depicted in Figure 1, between the utility and the records store, the conventional records get admission to mechanism generally wraps round square (established query Language) statements to problem information examine/write operations, and the practice of dealing with the CRUD (Create, read, replace, and Delete) operators is properly installed.

1) Create and Update

Inside the CRUD-centric view of statistics access, transactions assist simplest the create and replace operators. As an instance, a transaction can change the ownership of a name or debit cryptocurrency from one account and credit to any other. A transaction may also be used to set up and initiate the execution of a smart settlement. Some blockchains in addition distinguish transactions used to control money owed and belongings from clever contracts, e.g., Ethereum refers to them as transactions and messages.

2) Delete

Not one of the blockchain answers explicitly aid the delete operator to ensure immutability. But, a transaction may want to be used to set an asset to a null value or trade a state to an unusable nation. Further, property created or embedded in a clever contract may be distorted by calling the proper smart agreement feature through a transaction. Whilst ="hide">this could="tips Box">emulate the behavior of a delete operator, all modifications are recorded on the blockchain.three) examine compared to databases, analyzing block chain statistics isn't straightforward. For example, as block chain transactions use a receipt-based transient synchronous communication, they do now not directly return consequences or indicate whether the transaction is performed. While smart settlement facts may be queried inside a clever agreement characteristic, such capabilities additionally do now not return a result because of the identical cause. Further, we cannot problem examine requests to a blockchain. Rather, we should passively get entry to 7339ff1fc90882f8f31ca1efdd2ac191 statistics elements (property, accounts,

Transactions, smart contracts, and blocks) the use of particular identifiers (IDs). A device used for such querying is called the block chain explorer. A block chain explorer connects to one or more nodes that save recently generated blocks or complete ledger through an software called the block chain purchaser. Block chain purchaser sequentially is going through the ledger, beginning from the maximum current block, looking for the given asset, account, transaction, or clever agreement identification. Consequently, specific querying is needed even to test whether a transaction is popular, rejected, protected, or confirmed.

Comments: presenting extra green records access to the utility layer is a crucial element of blockchain-based totally systems, and there are on-going efforts in this region. For instance, to guide quicker and more complicated queries, many block chain explorers, along with Etherscan11, reproduction the block chain information to a centralized indexing server. Hyperledger material keeps a motive-constructed index to provide a fast identification and time-based totally querying of 7339ff1fc90882f8f31ca1efd-d2ac191 information factors. Ethereal question Language (EQL) is an square-like query language which ambitions to provide a preferred-motive query/solution implementation for blockchain statistics. It permits queries to quick extract information scattered through several statistics within the blockchain using collections of blocks, types of gadgets (e.g., transactions and accounts) and a binary seek tree as its middle language ideas (Barnett & Cerf, 2018). Libraries together with Ethereal web312 and Hyperledger material-network13 hide complexities through offering an asynchronous API to both trouble transactions and query their consequences thru a client. R3 Coda's ledger statistics are maintained in a relational database to allow each examine and write queries using sq. BigchainDB is an opportunity layout in which a NoSQL query language is used to both study and write blockchain statistics some other problem with modern-day IoT networks is that of scalability. as the variety of gadgets linked via an IoT network grows, current centralized systems to authenticate, authorize and connect distinctive nodes in a community will become a bottleneck. This would necessitate massive investments into servers that could deal with a massive quantity of statistics change, and the complete network can move down if the server becomes unavailable. In public blockchains inclusive of Bitcoin, very time and computationally extensive mining-based consensus mechanisms are regularly used to set up believe among absolutely nameless parties. Accordingly huge transaction times result which ends up now not most effective in bad performance but additionally poor scalability. This ends in the advent of side chains so as to offload the transaction processing from the principle chain. In cases of business to commercial enterprise (B2B) and business to customer (B2C) interactions, the use of private and permissioned blockchain is favored. Non-public blockchains have a discounted quantity of nodes, which ends up in a much faster consensus mechanism and in well known improves scalability and performance. There are actually new blockchains coming up, termed as blockchain three.0, which are based totally at the standards of DLT. These blockchains improve scalability and performance by means of the usage of DAG (Directed Acyclic Graph) and novel validation and vote casting mechanism (Bjørnskov, 2012). Some other mechanism proposed with the aid of Lyubomir Stoykov et al. (n.d.) is the VIBES architecture. VIBES uses configurable enter parameters like network-information and variety of miners, to offer a flexible solution. The simulator affords information about through put and cost-in line with-transaction. To bypass a majority of the heavy computations for big scale applications, the paper indicates enhancing scalability through fast-forward computing. This enables whole simulations earlier than time. Nodes try to estimate computational prices and ask for permission to rapid ahead. After inexperienced-lights the operation, the orchestrator declares the operation complete and skips forward.

2.7 Use of Blockchain to Ensure Security

An important worry inside self sufficient automobiles is the high dependence on IoT devices. Those IoT devices are frequently vulnerable to distributed Denial of carrier (DDoS) assaults. Blockchain technology can prove to be extremely beneficial in this element. Be in decentralized, blockchain gets rid of unmarried point of failure based totally attacks, and also provides a medium for auditable and traceable adjustments. Further, blockchains offer assist with authentication and identity of gadgets over a distributed database.

2. Eight Troubles and Upgrades Related to AVs

With the expectation of AVs becoming a norm, the wide variety of AVs on the street will move on growing. As self-riding cars are geared up with greater sensors and network connectivity than non-self sufficient ones, the wide variety of security vulnerabilities and Hence, assault surface of an AV is absolutely extended. Adversaries today are becoming increasingly more skillful. Those capabilities coupled with possible low-value offensive devices can permit them to interrupt into vehicle security systems without difficulty and inside the worst case allow unauthorized complete manager of the vehicle or statistics tampering. In addition, with autonomy, comes lack of duty. When autonomous automobiles are concerned in injuries (collisions between themselves, or collisions with conventional cars, pedestrians or other items), how ought to such activities be recorded for forensic purposes to decide liability? In addition, how may want to such recorded occasions be proven, relied on, and now not tampered? Such problems grow to be essential whilst there exist incentives for distinct events worried to tamper with the recorded occasions to avoid punitive penalties.

The anticipated functionalities of independent automobiles could be stronger because of the integration of car sensors and blockchain. The revolution of autonomous motors together with the resource of blockchain era ought to affect carefully related industries too.as an example, using blockchain in these AVs could negate the need of center events, be it brokers in fleet control structures or journey sharing organizations like Uberthree.1 Decentralized storage and safety mechanism. On surveying, we observed that blockchain can serve as shared garage to facilitate twist of fate control and additionally can be used to address protection assaults on AVs. Underneath is the special précis of the 2 cases. Twist of fate Reporting and Verification.

Cognizance on event recording mainly for accident forensics. They advocate evidence of occasion as a consensus mechanism, a recording and broadcasting mechanism for the occasions that manifest. The collections of statistics are universal as new nodes to the blockchain depending at the credit rating of the verifier and player nodes(motors). The credit rating is a degree of the way 'relied on' a car is. This consists of being a witness or a verifier to a coincidence. Because there's no tangible award provided via the evidence of event protocol, credit score ratings are an attempt at incentivisation. Higher credit score rankings may also mirror as lower coverage charges at the vehicle. In addition, they adumbrate the protocols essential for implementing the device. Inspiration for a reward based smart card information-sharing framework is proposed through Singh (2017) for intelligent vehicle verbal exchange using blockchain. The concept is summary and introduces a block chain network model for communiqué over a VCC (Vehicular Cloud communiqué) for reporting protection-vital incidents and (the opportunity or occurrences of) risks to drivers. It makes use of proof of riding because the consensus mechanism wherein the incentivisation is provided by crypto tokens in the form of IVTP (smart automobile agree with points).

RESULT AND DISCUSSION

The accepted consensus mechanisms for blockchain - evidence of work, Stake, and Authority - are criticized in a few studies papers for their inability to preserve the decentralization of manage in the blockchain, sooner or later ensuing inside the awareness of energy inside the areas with higher computational strength and sources, respectively. However, proposed alternatives to those, as stated in the papers, lack problems. For shared data of AV lifecycle and logs for vehicle sharing, each player at the chain should be capable of verify the on-chain statistics with the aid of the virtue of its lifestyles alone. Since the verification outcomes from the consensus mechanism, which operates simplest at the on-chain facts, it follows that the records source must additionally be on-chain.

Those statistics resources ought to be intrinsic to the blockchain for verification to appear as part of the working. except it is made feasible to embed a few form of metadata within the AV data that make its source on-chain, the verification stays external in all structures presently proposed, rendering the consensus mechanism of little use by way of itself. Looking at the capability of blockchains as an atmosphere, we opine that during such use cases it remains underutilised. An increase inside the range of motors (nodes) will add to this statistics, reducing the efficiency of the gadget. A probable answer might be to shop handiest the bare minimum facts at the blockchain and keep the relaxation of the records on a shared report device like IPFS. Feasibility of Computation. Blockchain consensus mechanism calls for a massive quantity of computational energy. Those computations might not be viable on AV swhich would possibly in flip bring about low throughput of the gadget, through inflicting an boom in latency. Exploring the present day proposals and analyzed opportunities, improvements in the AV zone with blockchain or DLTs might improve the revel in around presenting coverage, with extended offerings round presenting a clean driving record, or for car lending or sharing. DLTs will facilitate mainstream adoption of vehicle sharing by using scheduling and matching rides with out the need for a intermediary. Distributed ledger technology can allow records on car availability to be made publicly available so that users and vehicle proprietors can in shape trips without difficulty.

Figure 4. The data-driven decision with slot analysis

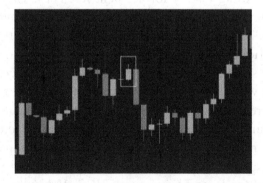

Blockchain could also resource in powerful deliver chain control inside the freight tindustry. However, clearly the usage of block chain technology does no longer ensure the powerful shipping and transport of products. Tampering with RFID tags connected to items and instances of smuggling can lead to incorrect facts saved on the block chain, which voids the use of blockchain within the first area. With vehicles turning into driverless, the difficulty of charge may be tackled by using offering a fee approach this is intrinsic or facilitated with the aid of the blockchain infrastructure itself. This will mean that payments for parking and toll, price may be performed using cryptocurrencies. However, the use of crypto currencies will be adverse in case of a fifty one% miner assault. However, this sort of attack requires huge computation on famous blockchain systems like Bitcoin and Ethereum. Inside the case of smaller blockchains, it isn't hard to amass the computational strength for those attacks, and such an assault may want to very a lot be feasible. Therefore, self sufficient cars must be very cautious before deciding on their preferred blockchain for payments. In addition, the volatility of crypto currencies is a massive drawback for the adoption of blockchain-based payments specifically if its miles to be integrated as a long time answer with independent automobiles.

This volatility is an outcome of kingdom-precise economic policies and standards, and no longer an innate assets of cryptocurrencies itself. An optimistic approach would possibly expect that this stability increases; an overly constructive method may say that fiat currencies shall be measured in phrases of crypto currencies in the destiny (communicate of the prevailing scenario). a sensible approach is to gauge. This paper makes a specialty of effective graph representation of blockchain transactions and visualizing anomaly transaction graphs. The paper proposed 3 algorithms to extract facts from the blockchain community and to generate 3 distinctive kind of graphs particularly transaction graph, deal with graph and cash drift graph.

From the constructed graphs, we proven that the cope with graph and the transaction graph of the Bitcoin and the money float transaction graph of the Ethereum are greater appropriate to visualize the patterns related with the anomalous transactions. Effectiveness of the algorithms had been tested by way of using the real Bitcoin core facts and XBlock (Etherium Public API) datasets. The graph styles visualize through Neo4j and proven how those patterns replicate the anomaly transactions. eventually, lots of this work can be seen as records extraction and characteristic engineering for a graph based dataset of blockchain transactions. this type of dataset will be treasured in different tasks including system-getting to know-based totally analytics, which is our on the spot future paintings It isn't feasible to deal with all protection assaults referred to in segment 3A, however blockchain-primarily based solutions can be applied to prevent positive safety assaults. The issues of code change and code injection can be decreased with the aid of incorporation of a permissioned blockchain. This can prevent the unauthorized get right of entry to to the AVs and consequently reduce the opportunity of such attacks. Outside alerts like GPS and LiDAR alerts, can be validated by the usage of blockchain to prevent external signal spoofing assaults. Blockchain, with its key traits of decentralization, immutability and transparency, has genuine capability of being adopted in AVs because of its ability to seamlessly tackle many issues that AVs are predicted to have. on this paper, we have supplied a complete literature evaluate on the contemporary use cases of blockchain era in autonomous motors. We first furnished a top level view of self reliant cars accompanied by an review of blockchain architecture. We then investigated the cutting-edge use instances by means of partitioning them into 3 vast organizations on the premise of usage of blockchain in autonomous automobiles - as a decentralized storage and protection mechanism, for improving AV Functionalities, and for optimizing associated Industries. Sooner or later, we supplied a short evaluation of those use instances, discussing their relevance and troubles. As a destiny scope, Bitcoin's Lightning network (LN) can be implemented for fee channels or for number one fee rail coordination for freight chain sports.

CONCLUSION

They block chain are seeing the boom of blockchain applications attaining a ways past the preliminary craze of Bitcoin. A consequence of the fast adoption of the era is that, in lots of instances, a blockchain is regularly used as an architectural factor in a big-scale distributed software system to shop information, which not most effective range broadly in both format and content, but also express a number of complex utility area necessities. Therefore, carefully analyzing blockchains to understand and assess its capabilities and troubles as a records keep is a well timed and relevant subject matter to the instructional and industry groups who're seeking to use the era. To finish, we would love to focus on some of the primary Admittedly, there are other subjects that have not been discussed in depth however really worth further studies together with the green integration and indexing schemes designed for multiple blockchain information stores which can be heterogeneous, or greater distinct examination of clever contract generation and appropriate use of it in managing records. We plan to explore a few of these issues within the destiny. For example, our instantaneous destiny paintings consist of looking into architectural patterns and template designs to integrate more than one blockchain records stores. First, having a clear information of a blockchain as a facts save, and be able to realize and compare the traits of blockchains as regards to the conventional statistics shops will help software developers layout and put into effect a blockchain-based utility more correctly. Our contributions in this regard are three folds:

(i) We supplied a fresh view of a blockchain as a statistics save, conceptualizing its logical and physical layer capabilities in comparison to the conventional statistics shops,

(ii) We analyses the diverse records placement alternatives, emphasizing the effect of each layout option on an overall gadget,

(iii) We showed the crucial tasks and tools concerned in administering/operating a blockchain as a facts keep. Second, if one appears beyond digital currencies, current statistics management problems for blockchains pose both risks and opportunities. We particularly recognized two categories for discussions; information analytics and information governance. Much of the focus on blockchain technology has often been on methodologies to develop new applications. Methods and tools for analysing blockchain statistics at scale, and the use of blockchains to allow new kinds of records analytics are emerging subjects. facts governance is some other region of importance that warrants greater hobbies from the research and enterprise communities.

FUTURE ENHANCEMENT

Cars won't simply be used for getting around anymore, and blockchain platforms will play a big part in the upcoming technological revolution. Even if integrating new technologies is never easy, it is obvious that blockchain will transform the mobility industry and bring to light previously unimaginable possibilities. Blockchain has the potential to transform the way data is handled in the cars of the future, whether it's safeguarding financial information or increasing shared ownership security. Blockchain offers a clear and impenetrable method of exchanging data, which in the near future will be of the utmost importance to automakers, notwithstanding any potential doubts along the way.

REFERENCES

Ackom, Yang, Zhao, Xiang, & Yang. (n.d.). A Double-chain Blockchain with Economic Attributes and Network Constraints of Prosumer Transactions. *IEEE Transactions on Industrial Informatics.*

Andreoni, J., Harbaugh, W., & Vesterlund, L. (2003). The carrot or the stick: Rewards, punishments, and cooperation. *The American Economic Review*, *93*(3), 893–902. doi:10.1257/000282803322157142

Ariely, D. (2008). *Predictably Irrational*. Harper Collins.

Asch, S. E., & Guetzkow, H. (1951). Effects of group pressure upon the modification and distortion of judgments. In Documents of Gestalt Psychology. Carnegie Press.

Barcelo, H., & Capraro, V. (2015). Group size effect on cooperation in one-shot social dilemmas. *Scientific Reports*, *5*(1), 7937. doi:10.1038rep07937 PMID:25605124

Barnett, S. B., & Cerf, M. (2018). Trust the Polls? Neural and recall responses provide alternative predictors of political outcomes. *Advances in Consumer Research. Association for Consumer Research (U. S.)*, *46*, 374–377.

Benkhelifa & Al-Ruithea. (2017). A conceptual framework for cloud data governance-driven decision making. *International Conference on the Frontiers and Advances in Data Science (FADS).*

Bjørnskov, C. (2012). How does social trust affect economic growth? *Southern Economic Journal*, *78*(4), 1346–1368. doi:10.4284/0038-4038-78.4.1346

Chinnasamy, A., & Kavitha, D. (2021). Ai Integration in Data Driven Decision Making for Resource Management in Internet of Things(Iot): A Survey. *10th International Conference on Internet of Everything, Microwave Engineering, Communication and Networks (IEMECON).*

Foley, S., Karlsen, J. R., & Putnin¸s, T. J. (2019). Sex, drugs, and bitcoin: How much illegal activity is financed through cryptocurrencies? *Review of Financial Studies*, *32*(5), 1798–1853. doi:10.1093/rfs/hhz015

Haslhofer, Karl, & Filtz. (2016). O bitcoin where art thou? insight into large-scale transaction graphs. *SEMANTiCS.*

Hu, T., Liu, X., Chen, T., Zhang, X., Huang, X., Niu, W., Lu, J., Zhou, K., & Liu, Y. (2021). Transaction-based classification and detection approach for ethereum smart contract. *Information Processing & Management*, *58*(2), 102462.

Kamble, N., & Gala, R. (2021). Using blockchain in autonomous vehicles. In Artificial intelligence and blockchain for future cybersecurity applications (pp. 285-305). Academic Press.

Pashkevich, A., & Makarovab, I. (2020). Blockchain Technology on the Way of Autonomous Vehicles Development. *Transportation Research Procedia*, *44*, 168–175. doi:10.1016/j.trpro.2020.02.024

Patel, V., Pan, L., & Rajasegarar, S. (2020). Graph deep learning based anomaly detection in ethereum blockchain network. In *International Conference on Network and System Security*. Springer.

Pedrosa, I., Bernardino, J., & Borges, M. (2021). Data-driven decision making strategies applied to marketing. *16th Iberian Conference on Information Systems and Technologies (CISTI).*

Reid, F., & Harrigan, M. (2013). *An analysis of anonymity in the bitcoin system. In Security and privacy in social networks*. Springer.

Zhang, Lu, Han, & Yan. (2019). Data-Driven Decision-Making (D3M): Framework, Methodology, and Directions. *IEEE Transactions on Emerging Topics in Computational Intelligence, 3*(4).

Chapter 13
Plant Disease Classification Using Deep Learning Techniques

Hari Kishan Kondaveeti

https://orcid.org/0000-0002-3379-720X

VIT-AP University, India

Chinna Gopi Simhadri

https://orcid.org/0000-0002-8311-7495

VIT-AP University, India

Sudha Ellison Mathe

https://orcid.org/0000-0003-2806-5407

VIT-AP University, India

Sunny Dayal Vanambathina

VIT-AP University, India

ABSTRACT

Artificial intelligence (AI) has been a growing field in recent years, with the development of deep learning (DL) techniques providing new opportunities for plant disease classification. Convolutional neural networks (CNNs) and other advanced techniques such as transfer learning, deep ensemble learning, and others have been used to classify plant diseases with high accuracy. However, these techniques are not only complex but also challenging to implement, making it important to provide a comprehensive understanding of their use in plant disease classification. This chapter aims to explore the use of deep learning techniques for plant disease classification. It will provide an overview of the various DL techniques and their applications in the classification of plant diseases. It will also provide a comprehensive understanding of transfer learning, deep ensemble learning, and other advanced methods in plant disease classification. Additionally, the chapter will provide case studies to illustrate the practical applications of DL techniques in plant disease classification.

DOI: 10.4018/978-1-6684-9151-5.ch013

INTRODUCTION

Every year, the population of the Earth grows by approximately 1.6%, leading to a heightened demand for plant-based products Ensuring crops are protected from diseases is important in meeting this increasing demand for food, not just in terms of quantity but also quality (Strange, R. N et al., 2005). The impact of plant diseases on the global economy is significant, costing around US$220 billion annually. The agricultural sector, which is crucial to India's economic development, drives the nation's economy in a significant way. With a contribution of 15.87% to the country's Gross Domestic Product (GDP), agriculture has significant weight in shaping the overall economic development of India. Additionally, this sector employs a large portion of the nation's /workforce, with an estimated 54.15% of the population being engaged in agriculture-related activities. In India, the loss of more than 35% of crop productivity due to pests and diseases, as reported by the Indian Council of Agricultural Research, puts food security at risk in light of the increasing number of pests and diseases (Uthayakumar et al., 2017).

Plants can be plagued by diseases resulting from various agents such as fungi, bacteria, viruses, pests, and others. These diseases can exhibit symptoms like leaf spots, blights, root rot, fruit rot, fruit spots, wilting, dieback and decline. This significantly impacts food security by reducing crop yields, leading to food scarcity and even starvation in certain regions. Plant diseases have risen, severely impacting agriculture and food security. Early identification of these diseases is essential for controlling their spread and treating affected plants. It is also a key factor in making informed decisions in agriculture production. Plant diseases usually exhibit distinctive marks or lesions on leaves, flowers, or fruits, and each disease has its own specific pattern for diagnosis. Leaves are the primary focus for detecting plant diseases, as most symptoms show up there.

The traditional method involves physically examining the leaves and crowns of plants for signs of disease. This can be a time-consuming and specialized process, particularly because different types of crops can exhibit different symptoms. The machine learning method, on the other hand, involves using algorithms to classify diseases based on pre-processed images of the plants.

Implementing machine learning involves a sequence of actions that segregate the infected areas via image preprocessing, extracting meaningful features from these images, and applying classification techniques like support vector machines, K-nearest neighbor, or random forest to classify the diseases founded on these features. Image characteristics, such as leaf texture, type, and color, are the frequently utilized features. (Lu, J et al., 2021).

The exposure of several AI techniques has resulted in the recognition of several methods for early disease detection. Among these AI techniques, Deep Learning (DL) technologies are advantageous due to their ability to extract and recognize features using a CNN model, thereby enabling automatic detection of plant leaf diseases. Deep learning has various applications in agriculture, including: Crop classification and yield prediction, Pest and disease detection, Soil moisture and nutrient mapping and Weather forecasting. This chapter will explore the classification of plants using Transfer Learning, Deep ensemble learning and some advanced techniques.

BACKGROUND

Deep Learning

Deep learning is a branch of ML that specifically utilizes artificial neural networks to improve the learning process. In contrast to ML, which uses simpler algorithms, DL aims to replicate human thinking through these neural networks. With advancements in Big Data analytics, these networks can now be more complex, allowing computers to rapidly recognize patterns and respond to complex situations. This has led to successful applications of deep learning in image classification, language translation, and speech recognition, and the ability to solve pattern recognition problems without human assistance.

In deep learning, artificial neural networks are constructed with layers of interconnected nodes that are designed to mimic the neural organization of the human brain. Interconnecting the nodes within and across layers determines the network's depth. While human neurons receive multiple signals from other neurons, in artificial neural networks, nodes communicate with weighted values, and the most heavily weighted node has the greatest impact on the next layer. The final layer processes the weighted inputs to generate an output. Although advanced hardware is used in deep learning, training a neural network can still take several weeks, due to the large volume of data and complex mathematical calculations involved.

The three most popular deep learning architectures are

- Convolutional Neural Networks (CNNs)
- Recurrent Neural Networks (RNNs)
- Generative Adversarial Networks (GANs)

Convolutional Neural Networks

A CNN is an artificial neural network that utilizes deep learning techniques to analyze data organized in a grid-like layout, such as an image. CNNs are widely used in computer vision applications such as image categorization, object identification, and image synthesis. The network has numerous layers, including convolutional, activation, and pooling, which combine to extract significant features from images and produce accurate predictions. CNNs are used in the image, voice, and natural language processing due to their high performance.

A CNN typically consists of several layers to be used in a plant leaf disease:

- *Convolutional layer:* This layer performs convolutional operations on the input image to extract local features related to plant diseases.
- *Pooling layer:* To reduce the size of the output feature maps and prevent overfitting, a pooling layer could be added after each convolutional layer.
- *Activation layer:* An activation function such as ReLU could be applied after each convolutional layer to introduce non-linearity in the network.
- *Batch normalization layer:* To improve the stability and performance of the network, batch normalization could be added after each activation layer.

- *Dropout layer:* To further prevent overfitting, a dropout layer could be added after the last batch normalization layer.
- *Flattening layer:* To convert the output feature maps into a one-dimensional vector, a flattening layer could be added before the fully connected layers.
- *Fully connected layer:* The flattened output could then be fed into one or more fully connected layers to perform a dot product between the input and weights and produce the final output.
- *Output layer:* The final fully connected layer can predict the probabilities of the input image belonging to different disease classes based on the loss function used to train the network. The layer can then produce these probabilities as its output.

The trend of utilizing various technologies to enhance crop production has increased significantly in recent times. Accurately diagnosing plant diseases is a crucial factor for achieving higher crop yields, and techniques such as image processing, machine learning, and deep learning can assist in identifying these diseases. Out of all these techniques, deep learning has shown greater effectiveness, particularly through the use of CNNs, in detecting plant diseases compared to other methods. These networks have the capability to identify important features from images and categorize them accordingly.

The convolutional layers in a CNNs analyze the visual pattern of input images and determine if a certain disease is present. With proper training on extensive datasets featuring both healthy and diseased plant images, CNNs can effectively identify various types of plant diseases. Classifying plant diseases using Convolutional Neural Networks involves Data collection, Preprocessing, Network architecture, Training, Validation, Testing and Deployment. A CNN identifies leaf diseases in images by learning to recognize specific patterns and features through multiple processing layers. The Architecture of CNN can shown in Figure 1.

Figure 1. Architecture of convolutional neural network

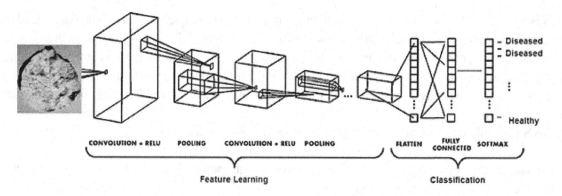

The main advantages of CNNs are ability to identify local patterns, handling high-dimensional data, Translation invariance, parameter sharing and transfer learning.

Recurrent Neural Networks

Recurrent Neural Networks are a type of neural network intended to handle sequential data, such as speech, language, and time-series data. Unlike conventional neural networks that process inputs as stand-alone instances, RNNs have a memory mechanism that allows them to utilize information from previous steps in the sequence to inform their predictions. The network processes the input sequence one step at a time and updates a hidden state that summarizes information from previous steps. This hidden state, along with the current input, is then used as input for the next step and the process repeats until the end of the sequence. The final hidden state is used to generate a prediction or output. RNNs are widely used in tasks like speech recognition, language translation, and video classification.

Lee et al. (Lee, et al., 2020) proposes a new technique using a RNN to identify infected regions and extract disease classification features. The RNN-based approach is more robust and generalizable than traditional CNN methods, accurately locating infectious diseases in plants. In another work (Sreedevi et al., 2022), the authors proposed an approach which utilizes deep learning and artificial intelligence-assisted techniques for tomato leaf disease classification. It includes pre-processing, spot segmentation, deep feature extraction, optimal feature selection, and disease classification using Modified Recurrent Neural Network. The method demonstrates improved classification efficiency with high accuracy, specificity, and sensitivity values.

Recurrent Neural Networks to identify leaf diseases is based on their processing of sequential data such as time-series information about plant growth and the progression of symptoms, or images capturing different views or stages of the disease. The network updates its hidden state, which summarizes past information, with each input in the sequence, using it to make predictions for the current step. The final hidden state then provides a prediction about the disease present in the image. By training the network on a dataset of time-series data on plant growth and disease progression, it can learn the correlation between the growth of the plant and the symptoms of the disease, allowing it to make predictions on new plants based on their growth patterns. The main advantages of RNNs are to handle sequential data, memory of past inputs, handling variable-length sequences and real-time processing.

Generative Adversarial Networks

GANs are a deep learning model that produces new data samples that are similar to a training set. They are comprised of two neural networks, a generator and a discriminator, working in opposition. The generator creates new data while the discriminator assesses whether it is authentic or not. The two networks are trained together through an adversarial process, with the generator trying to produce convincing fake data, and the discriminator trying to accurately identify it as fake (Radford, A et al., 2015). The training continues until the generator produces data that is close enough to the real data. GANs have many applications including image synthesis, style transfer and semi-supervised learning. The main advantage of Generative Adversarial Networks is their ability to generate new data that resembles the distribution of real-world data. This makes them useful for various applications such as Image synthesis, Data augmentation, Anomaly detection and Semi-supervised learning.

GANs are not usually applied to directly diagnose plant leaf illnesses. Rather, they are frequently utilized for creation purposes like creating novel images, sounds, or other data. Nevertheless, GANs can potentially be employed as a means for data expansion by producing fresh synthetic data that can be utilized to teach other AI models for leaf disease identification. For instance, a GAN could be trained on a dataset that contains both healthy and sick plant leaf images to produce new synthetic images showcasing varying forms of healthy and diseased leaves. These fake images can then be utilized to expand the original dataset and enhance the accuracy of AI models that diagnose plant leaf illnesses. However, this technique remains a subject of ongoing research and further investigation is necessary to validate the usefulness of GANs in this field.

Plant disease recognition is traditionally done visually, which is biased and time-consuming. ML methods built on plant leaf images have been proposed, but limited training data can cause overfitting. A new method, combining GAN and label smoothing regularization (LSR), improved accuracy by 24.4% (Bi et al., 2020). DATFGAN is a generative adversarial network that enhances the quality of agricultural disease images, which are often unclear and lead to poor identification. It uses dual-attention and topology-fusion techniques to turn images into clear, high-resolution ones, while reducing the number of parameters. DATFGAN outperforms other methods in visual and identification tasks, demonstrating its practical usefulness (Dia, Q et al., 2020).

Transfer Learning

Transfer learning is a technique in machine learning where a model trained on one task is used as a starting point for a related task. This allows the model to use its prior knowledge and experience to improve its performance on the new task, rather than starting from scratch. The goal of transfer learning is to reduce the amount of training data and computation required for a new task, and to improve generalization performance.

Plant leaf disease detection is a challenging computer vision task that involves recognizing patterns of disease symptoms on plant leaves. Due to the variability of the symptoms and the complexity of the leaf structures, building an accurate machine learning model for this task can be difficult.

One approach to tackle this challenge is to use transfer learning. In transfer learning, a pre-trained CNN is used as a starting point and fine-tuned on a smaller dataset of labeled plant leaf images. The pre-trained CNN has already learned general image features, such as edges, shapes, and textures, from a large-scale image classification task, such as ImageNet. By fine-tuning the CNN on the plant leaf images, the network can learn to recognize patterns associated with different types of plant leaf diseases.

Here's a step-by-step process for using transfer learning for plant leaf disease detection:

- *Choose a pre-trained CNN:* The first step is to select a pre-trained CNN that is well-suited for the task of plant leaf disease detection. Some popular choices include VGG, Inception, and ResNet, which have been used in various studies for plant leaf disease detection. The choice of the pre-trained CNN may depend on factors such as the size of the dataset and the specific plant diseases of interest.
- *Prepare the dataset:* The next step is to prepare the dataset of plant leaf images. The dataset should include images of both healthy and diseased leaves, as well as labels indicating the type of disease present in each image. The dataset may need to be augmented to increase the variability of the images, such as by rotating, flipping, or scaling the images.
- *Fine-tune the CNN:* The pre-trained CNN is then fine-tuned on the dataset of plant leaf images. The early layers of the CNN, which have learned general image features, are usually kept fixed, while the latter layers are retrained on the new task of disease detection. During fine-tuning, the parameters of the CNN are updated using backpropagation with a smaller learning rate to adjust to the new task.
- *Evaluate the model:* Once the model has been fine-tuned, assessing its performance on a distinct test dataset is necessary. One can utilize metrics like accuracy, precision, and recall to evaluate the

model's effectiveness. The model may need to be further optimized, such as by adjusting hyper-parameters or adding regularization techniques, to improve its performance.

• *Deploy the model:* Once the model has been trained and evaluated, it can be deployed for use in plant disease detection applications. The model can be used to classify new plant leaf images as healthy or diseased, or to identify the specific type of disease present in the image.

The Architecture of plant leaf disease classification using transfer learning can be shown in Figure 2.

Figure 2. The architecture of transfer learning

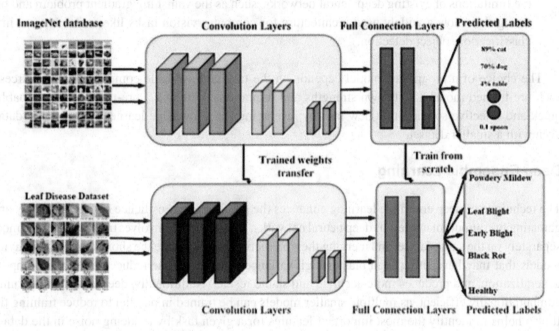

In transfer learning, a pre-trained model can be fine-tuned for a specific task by updating the parameters of the model with task-specific data. This is typically done by:

• Freezing the pre-trained layers and training a classifier or task-specific layer on top of the frozen layers with the task-specific data.
• Fine-tuning the entire model by training all the layers with the task-specific data. This is usually done when the task-specific dataset is larger and more diverse compared to the pre-training dataset.

Pre-Trained Models

Pre-trained models are deep learning algorithms trained on a massive dataset for a particular task and then made available for other related tasks. They are a starting point for transfer learning, where the pre-learned weights can be fine-tuned for a new but related task.

There are several pre-trained models widely used for various computer vision tasks, which include the following:

- *VGG16:* Simonyan et al. (Simonyan et al., 2014) proposed a family of VGG models with varying depths and configurations for image classification tasks.
- *ResNet:* He et al. (He et al., 2016) introduced a novel architecture for deep neural networks that enabled training of much deeper models than previously possible.
- *InceptionNet:* Szegedy et al. (Szegedy et al., 2014) ntroduced the Inception module for InceptionNet architecture and achieved state-of-the-art results on the ILSVRC dataset.
- *MobileNet:* Howard et al. (Howard et al., 2017) proposed a family of mobile-friendly neural network architectures optimized for mobile devices with limited computational resources.
- *DenseNet:* Huang et al. (Huang, G. et al., 2017) introduced this architecture to address some of the limitations of existing deep neural networks, such as the vanishing gradient problem and overfitting. It is now a widely used architecture for computer vision tasks like segmentation, image classification, object detection.

The choice of a pre-trained model depends on the task and available computational resources, as each pre-trained model has its own strengths and limitations. Utilizing a pre-trained model enables a quick and effective solution to a new task by leveraging the knowledge learned from a large dataset, even with a smaller dataset.

Deep Ensemble Learning

The technique of deep ensemble learning enhances the precision and resilience of predictions by amalgamating the outputs of numerous deep neural networks. This approach involves training multiple models separately on the same dataset and merging their predictions to overcome the shortcomings of individual models that may have either high bias or high variance. This technique reduces overfitting, improves generalization, and produces more accurate and stable results. Additionally, deep ensemble learning is computationally efficient, as multiple smaller models can be trained in parallel to reduce training time. It also helps to identify the most important features for a given task by reducing noise in the data and highlighting the critical features. Deep ensemble learning is extensively used in many fields such as image classification, speech recognition, natural language processing, and reinforcement learning, making it a valuable tool in the deep learning toolbox. Block diagram of ensemble learning as shown in Figure 3.

Figure 3. Ensemble learning

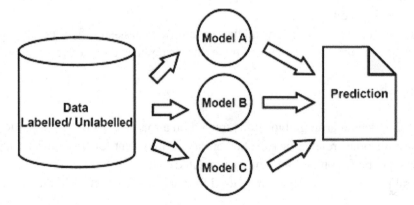

The key to deep ensemble learning is to train multiple models independently and combine their predictions to produce a more accurate and robust result. The diversity of the individual models is what makes the ensemble more powerful, and each model can capture different patterns in the data.

Leaf disease classification using deep ensemble learning works as follows:

- *Dataset Preparation:* Collect and prepare a dataset of leaf images, labeled with their corresponding disease types.
- *Model Training:* Train multiple deep learning models, such as convolutional neural networks, on the training set. Each model can have different architectures, hyperparameters, or data augmentation techniques.
- *Model Evaluation:* Evaluate the models on the validation set to take the top-performing models for the ensemble. The evaluation metrics can include accuracy, precision, recall, F1-score, or confusion matrix.
- *Prediction Combination:* Combine the predictions of the selected models using averaging, weighted averaging, or other ensemble methods. The combined predictions should be more accurate and robust than the predictions of individual models.
- *Model Testing:* Test the ensemble model on the testing set to measure its performance on unseen data. The testing metrics can include accuracy, sensitivity, specificity, or ROC-AUC.
- *Model Refinement:* If the performance of the ensemble model is not satisfactory, refine the models or ensemble method by adjusting the hyperparameters, adding or removing models, or using different ensemble methods.

Ensembling techniques possess unique strengths and weaknesses, and selecting a particular technique depends on the task requirements and data characteristics. Generally, combining the predictions of multiple models through ensembling techniques can boost the accuracy and resilience of machine learning models.

There are several types of ensembling techniques, including:

- Bagging (Bootstrapped Aggregation): This technique reduces the variance and improves the accuracy of machine learning models by training multiple models on different subsets of the training data. By aggregating the predictions of the models, Bagging produces a final prediction that is more robust and less prone to overfitting.
- Boosting: This technique trains multiple models sequentially, where each model concentrates on the samples that the earlier models misclassified. The final prediction is obtained by integrating the weighted predictions of the individual models.
- Stacking: This technique trains multiple base models on the same data and then trains a meta-model on the predictions of the base models. The final prediction is obtained from the meta-model.
- Blending: This technique is similar to stacking, but instead of training a meta-model, the predictions of the base models are combined using a weighted average.
- Random Forest: This technique is an extension of bagging that uses decision trees as base models. The final prediction is obtained by averaging the predictions of the individual trees.
- Gradient Boosting Machine (GBM): This technique is an extension of boosting that uses decision trees as base models. The final prediction is obtained by combining the weighted predictions of the individual trees.

- Adaboost: This is a popular boosting algorithm that adaptively adjusts the weights of the samples to focus on the samples that are misclassified by the previous models.

Deep ensemble learning can improve the accuracy and efficiency of various tasks related to leaf disease, such as detection, classification, localization, monitoring, and management. It achieves this by combining the predictions of multiple deep learning models, each trained to identify different aspects of the leaf disease. By doing so, it can overcome the limitations of individual models, such as overfitting or bias, and improve the generalization and interpretability of the classification task. Deep ensemble learning can accurately detect the presence of a disease in a leaf, classify different disease classes, localize the disease to specific regions of interest within the leaf image, monitor the progression or regression of a disease over time, and optimize disease management by combining the predictions of multiple models with other data sources such as weather, soil, or cultural practices. However, this technique requires careful preparation, training, and evaluation to ensure optimal performance and avoid overfitting or underfitting.

ADVANCED TECHNIQUES

Plant disease detection has evolved with non-invasive methods gaining popularity in recent decades, primarily due to the limitations of traditional and laboratory-based techniques. While the traditional method of visual inspection by an agronomist is less accurate, costly, and labor-intensive, many rural producers lack access to this method. Moreover, laboratory-based tests have complex methods and time requirements, making them less preferable for plant disease detection. In traditional methods for identifying crop diseases, experts visually inspect crops and diagnose diseases based on their experience and knowledge. However, this technique can be inefficient, error-prone, and limited in scope. Therefore, researchers are exploring ways to develop an automated mechanism that can quickly and accurately detect and diagnose crop diseases.

One technique that has grown admiration in recent years is the use of various image processing techniques, where different types of imaging systems, such as visible light, spectral, thermal, fluorescence imaging, etc., are used to capture information from crops. The images captured by these imaging systems are then processed using a variety of image processing techniques, such as filtering, segmentation, feature extraction, etc. The processed images are then used to train and test ML algorithms, which can automatically determine crop diseases found on the patterns and features present in the images. Classical machine learning algorithms used in automated systems faced limitations due to small datasets and hand-crafted feature extraction methods. The size of the datasets was not sufficient for the algorithms to learn from, and the feature extraction process was limited in scope as it relied on domain experts to manually select and engineer features. Consequently, these systems had limited performance and could only identify a narrow range of crops and diseases.

With advancements in computer vision and Graphics Processing Unit (GPU) technology, deep learning has emerged as a promising tool to enhance automated techniques for identifying crop diseases (Bhagwat et al., 2021). DL models can automatically learn and extract features from images, without the need for hand-crafted feature extraction methods. This makes them more versatile and capable of capturing complex patterns that may not be apparent to human experts.

Moreover, deep learning models can achieve higher performance than classical machine learning algorithms, especially when large amounts of data are available. They can also be trained on diverse datasets to identify a wider range of crops and diseases. Additionally, the use of GPUs has enabled real-time disease identification, allowing immediate intervention to avoid the extent of crop diseases.

In recent years, researchers have been developing deep learning architectures tailored for crop disease identification. These models often use CNNs to learn features from crop images and classify them according to the presence or absence of disease. By improving the accuracy and speed of automated techniques, these developments have the potential to revolutionize crop disease management and reduce crop loss.

AUTOENCODERS

Autoencoder is a neural network based unsupervised learning algorithm used for tasks like dimensionality reduction, feature extraction, and data reconstruction. Additionally, it can produce new data by sampling from the learned internal representation (Bisong, E et al., 2019). Early detection of plant diseases is crucial for maintaining the quantity and quality of agricultural produce. However, current methods for detecting plant diseases are often expensive and time-consuming, which can be particularly challenging for smallholder farmers. Recent advances in AI research have made it possible to develop automatic plant disease detection systems. However, many of these systems rely on shallow machine learning architectures that require well-designed feature extractors to transform raw data into discriminative forms. The performance of these machine learning methods is heavily influenced by the quality of the extracted features.

Autoencoders (AEs) are a class of neural network models that can learn to reproduce input data as output. Variants of AEs have been developed to improve their performance, including the Variational Autoencoder (VAE) and Denoising Autoencoder (DAE). The VAE and AE differ in how they represent latent attributes: the VAE uses probability distributions, whereas the AE uses a function (Zilvan et al., 2019). The DAE and AE differ in that the DAE adds noise to the input before encoding it.

In plant leaf disease analysis, Autoencoders can be utilized as a means of feature extraction. This involves collecting a dataset containing both healthy and diseased leaves, preprocessing the images and training the autoencoder on healthy leaf images. Afterward, the encoder part is used to extract features from both healthy and diseased leaf images, which are then used as input to a supervised classifier such as a neural network or a support vector machine to predict whether a new leaf image is healthy or diseased.

REINFORCEMENT LEARNING

Machine learning refers to the field of computer programming that involves the creation of programs capable of completing tasks and improving themselves using data or experience. Within ML, there are three distinct subfields: unsupervised learning, supervised learning, and reinforcement learning. Unsupervised learning involves the creation of a data representation, often through clustering tasks. Supervised learning involves training a model to categorize new data using labeled examples through tasks such as classification and regression, while reinforcement learning aims to control a dynamic system. ML model performance is evaluated by assessing its ability to execute a task on new data, but overfitting can occur when a model performs well on training data but not on unseen data.

Reinforcement Learning (RL) refers to a sequential decision-making problem in which an agent interacts with an uncertain and dynamic environment to maximize a utility function that measures its performance. The agent learns a policy that maps observations to actions by exploring the environment and receiving feedback in the form of rewards. RL algorithms can be categorized as model-based or model-free based on whether the agent learns a model of the environment's dynamics. RL is widely applicable to fields such as robotics, gaming, and recommendation systems (Gautron et al., 2022). A key challenge in RL is the exploration-exploitation tradeoff, in which the agent must explore the environment to gather information while simultaneously exploiting its knowledge to maximize its reward. RL researchers have developed several techniques to address this challenge.

Deep Reinforcement Learning (DRL) is an advanced AI technique that has been successfully applied in agriculture. It uses a trial-and-error approach to learn how to make decisions that maximize a reward function. DRL can optimize various tasks in agriculture, such as crop management, pest control, and irrigation scheduling. DRL can learn the optimal irrigation strategy for a crop by considering environmental conditions and growth stages (Bu et al., 2019). By adjusting the irrigation schedule and amount of water applied based on factors such as soil moisture, temperature, and humidity, DRL can help reduce water waste, increase crop yields, and lower costs associated with water and energy usage.

GENERATIVE ADVERSARIAL NETWORKS

Generative Adversarial Networks (GANs) are a machine learning model that consists of two interconnected networks: a generator and a discriminator. The generator is trained to create new data that resembles the training data, while the discriminator is trained to distinguish between the real data and the generated data. During training, the generator produces new data and the discriminator classifies it as real or fake. The generator is updated to produce data that is increasingly difficult for the discriminator to distinguish from the real data. This process continues until the generator can create new data that is indistinguishable from the real data.

GANs have been used in several applications related to plant disease classification. One of the primary advantages of using GANs in this context is that they can generate synthetic images that can augment the available dataset, thereby improving the performance of the classification models. GANs have been used to generate synthetic images of plant leaves with different levels of disease symptoms, which were then combined with real images to train a classification model. The resulting model was shown to outperform a similar model that was trained solely on real images.

In another application, GANs were used to create a dataset of synthetic images of plant leaves with different disease symptoms. These synthetic images were then used to train a deep CNN for disease classification, which achieved higher accuracy than a similar CNN trained on real images alone.

GANs have also been used in combination with transfer learning to classify plant diseases using limited data. In this approach, a pre-trained CNN is used as the discriminator in a GAN framework, and the generator is trained to generate synthetic images that can improve the performance of the CNN in classifying plant diseases.

Liu et al. (Liu et al., 2020) proposed Leaf GAN model represents a promising solution for the data augmentation of grape leaf disease images, and has the potential to increase the accuracy of disease identification models, ultimately contributing to the control of grape leaf diseases and ensuring the healthy development of the grape industry. Abbas et al. (Abbas A. et al., 2021) proposed a method that generates synthetic images using C-GAN, which is then used to train a DenseNet121 model on both synthetic and real images for the classification of ten categories of tomato leaf diseases. The proposed method achieves high accuracy and shows superiority over existing methodologies, and has significant potential impact in the agriculture sector. However, other performance metrics, data quality and size, and generalizability to new, unseen data should also be taken into consideration when evaluating the model. Overall, the use of GANs to generate synthetic data sets for plant health monitoring and control is a promising area for further research and development.

SENSORS FOR IMAGING SYSTEM

The use of imaging sensors and techniques is becoming increasingly popular in the field of plant disease identification and management. The several imaging techniques mentioned have different advantages and can provide different types of information about the plants and their health.

- *Thermal imaging:* measures the temperature of leaves and can detect changes in temperature that may indicate stress or disease.
- *Multispectral imaging*: captures images at different wavelengths of light and can provide information about plant pigments and other indicators of health.
- *Fluorescence imaging*: detects fluorescence emissions from plant tissues and can provide information about photosynthetic efficiency and other parameters related to plant health.
- *Hyperspectral imaging*: captures images at many narrow spectral bands, providing detailed spectral information that can be used for identification of specific diseases.
- *Visible imaging*: captures images in the visible spectrum of light and can provide high-resolution images for visual inspection and analysis.
- *3D imaging*: creates a three-dimensional model of the plant, which can be useful for identifying disease patterns and other structural abnormalities.
- *Magnetic resonance imaging (MRI):* a non-invasive imaging strategy that can produce detailed information about the internal structures of plants and can be used to study the effects of diseases on plant tissues.

CASE STUDIES OF PLANT DISEASE CLASSIFICATION

The reliability of leaf bioassays for predicting disease resistance on fruit: a case study on grapevine resistance to downy and powdery mildew.

The study discovered several important results. Firstly, grapevine leaf bioassays can effectively predict disease resistance in fruit in the field. Secondly, specific grapevine genotypes that carry certain genes are highly effective at preventing downy and powdery mildew. Additionally, the study found that disease severity is higher in fruit bunches compared to leaves and that the level of disease varies among grapevine genotypes. Moreover, the study showed that early bioassays on grapevine leaves are an effective method to ensure disease resistance of grapevine genotypes in the field. Lastly, the study demonstrates that a Bayesian decision theory framework can be used to predict the accuracy of selecting grapevine genotypes based on an OIV-452 threshold in leaf bioassays (Calonnec et al., 2012).

Comparative study on the performance of deep learning implementation in the edge computing: Case study on the plant leaf disease identification.

This study explores the effectiveness of four pre-trained CNN deep learning models, as an edge solution for detecting plant diseases using the PlantVillage dataset. The study addresses the issue of unbalanced class distribution by applying image transformation techniques and down sampling. The initial results show that DenseNet121 exhibits the highest accuracy of 96.4% among the models tested, making it the model of choice for further evaluation. The study assesses the consistency of the model across a range of hardware and software configurations by testing it on various endpoint devices and programming environments. The outcomes demonstrate that the model can maintain high recall values, precision, and F1 scores when deployed as an edge solution (VPU). This finding suggests that the model has the potential to be implemented as an embedded application for detecting plant diseases (Wei et al., 2022).

DEVELOPMENT OF AN EMPIRICAL TOMATO CROP DISEASE MODEL: A CASE STUDY ON GRAY LEAF SPOT

Developing a disease model to predict the incidence and risk of tomato gray leaf spots is a contribution of this study. The model comprises three sub-models: a leaf wetness model, a disease occurrence-warning model, and a disease incidence model. The study analyzes plant disease epidemiology to select appropriate methods for model calibration and performance evaluation. The performance of the model was evaluated using several indicators, including the area under the receiver operating characteristic curve, root mean square error, and mean absolute error. The Logistic equation provided the best fit for the model. The developed model helps tomato growers make informed decisions and avoid significant economic losses due to the disease. The study contributes to the management of tomato gray leaf spot and can be potentially applied to other countries facing similar issues (Wang et al., 2019).

A SYSTEMATIC LITERATURE REVIEW OF MACHINE LEARNING TECHNIQUES DEPLOYED IN AGRICULTURE: A CASE STUDY OF BANANA CROP

The study looked at analysis papers that used ML techniques in agriculture, especially in producing banana plants and bananas. It identified a need for more datasets to improve disease identification and compared popular ML techniques to determine their effectiveness in identifying issues such as disease classification, chilling injuries, ripeness, and moisture content in banana crops. The study aimed to bridge research gaps and enhance the early identification of diseases in crops to ultimately improve agricultural productivity, which is crucial given the global economy heavily relies on agricultural productivity (Sahu,P. et al., 2022).

IMAGE PROCESSING SYSTEM BASED IDENTIFICATION AND CLASSIFICATION OF LEAF DISEASE: A CASE STUDY ON PADDY LEAF

The cultivation of paddy in the southern regions of India is a vital part of the country's infrastructure, and diseases such as bacterial leaf blight, brown spot, and leaf smut significantly affect the productivity of the crop. To address this problem, a proposed methodology for identifying and classifying various paddy leaf diseases has been developed. The methodology involves pre-processing of images, segmentation, feature extraction, and classification using the k-nearest neighbors' algorithm.

The methodology uses image processing techniques to identify and classify paddy leaf diseases, which is a novel application in the field of agriculture. The approach is comprehensive and has achieved an accuracy of 89.47%, which is impressive (N, M., & Gowda, K. J., 2020). However, the longer training time required for the framework is a limitation that needs to be addressed in the future.

The proposed work is not limited to the detection and classification of paddy leaf diseases. It can be extended to other crops such as wheat, sugar cane, corn, and maize, which is a significant advantage. Additionally, the proposed methodology can be used to suggest suitable soil for better yield, which highlights the potential of the approach in addressing broader challenges in the agriculture sector.

CONCLUSION AND FUTURE RESEARCH DIRECTIONS

The field of Artificial Intelligence has been rapidly growing in recent years, with advancements in deep learning techniques providing new opportunities for plant disease classification. However, these techniques can be complex and challenging to implement, making it essential to provide a comprehensive understanding of their use in plant disease classification. This book chapter aims to explore deep learning techniques for plant disease classification, with several objectives in mind.

This book chapter covers various topics, including an overview of deep learning techniques, transfer learning, deep ensemble learning, and other techniques for plant disease classification. It also covers case studies on plant disease classification using deep learning. This book chapter provides valuable insights and recommendations for researchers, practitioners, and students who are interested in applying deep learning techniques to plant disease classification. It highlights the potential of deep learning in developing more accurate and efficient plant disease classification systems and provides recommendations for future research in this area.

Deep learning has shown tremendous promise in the field of plant disease classification and has the potential to greatly improve crop yield and reduce economic losses due to plant diseases. Here are some future directions for deep learning in this field:

- *Incorporating multi-modal data:* While most current plant disease classification models rely solely on visual information, there is an increasing amount of data available from other modalities such as hyperspectral imaging, infrared imaging, and chemical analysis. Integrating these different modalities into deep learning models could potentially improve the accuracy of plant disease classification.

- *Transfer learning:* Transfer learning involves taking a pre-trained model and fine-tuning it for a new task. Applying transfer learning to plant disease classification could allow for more efficient use of data and improve the accuracy of models, especially in cases where data is limited.

- *Explainable AI:* As the use of deep learning models becomes more widespread in agriculture, it will be important to have models that can provide transparent explanations for their decisions. Developing explainable deep learning models for plant disease classification could help farmers better understand the risks and benefits of different treatments and management practices.

- *Incorporating temporal information:* Plant diseases evolve over time, so incorporating temporal information into deep learning models could improve their accuracy. This could be done by using time-series data or by incorporating information about the progression of the disease into the model.
- *Addressing class imbalance*: Plant diseases are often rare, meaning that datasets for plant disease classification are often highly imbalanced. Addressing class imbalance through techniques such as oversampling, undersampling, or generating synthetic data could help improve the accuracy of deep learning models.
- *Edge computing*: In many cases, the infrastructure for data processing and analysis is limited in rural areas where agriculture is the primary industry. Developing deep learning models that can run efficiently on low-power devices could enable farmers to use these models for disease classification directly on the farm, without requiring a network connection.

CHALLENGES

Plant disease classification using deep learning faces several challenges, including:

- *Limited availability of large and diverse datasets:* Deep learning models require large and diverse datasets for effective training. However, creating such datasets for plant diseases can be challenging, especially for rare or newly emerging diseases. This can result in models that are not robust enough to handle variations in disease symptoms.
- *Difficulty in capturing subtle differences:* Some plant diseases can have subtle differences in their symptoms that may be difficult to capture accurately with computer vision techniques. This can result in misclassification of diseases or false positives.
- *Variability in environmental conditions:* Environmental situations, such as light, humidity, and temperature, can affect the appearance of plant diseases, leading to variations in symptoms. This can make it difficult to accurately classify diseases, especially if the training data is not diverse enough to capture these variations.
- *Lack of interpretability*: DL models can be difficult to interpret, which can make it challenging to know why a model is making a particular classification decision. This can make it difficult for plant pathologists to validate the accuracy of the model's classifications.
- *Limited transferability*: Deep learning models trained on one dataset may not derive well to other datasets or different plant species. This can limit the practical application of these models in real-world scenarios.
- *Cost and complexity*: Developing and deploying deep learning models can be expensive and complex, requiring specialized hardware and expertise. This can limit their adoption, especially in resource-constrained settings.
- *Ethical considerations*: The use of deep learning models in plant disease classification raises ethical concerns around data privacy, algorithmic bias, and the potential displacement of human expertise in the field of plant pathology. These concerns need to be carefully addressed to ensure that the use of DL is both effective and ethical.

These challenges need to be carefully addressed to ensure that the use of DL is both effective and ethical in the field of plant pathology.

REFERENCES

Abbas, A., Jain, S., Gour, M., & Vankudothu, S. (2021). Tomato plant disease detection using transfer learning with C-GAN synthetic images. *Computers and Electronics in Agriculture, 187,* 106279. doi:10.1016/j.compag.2021.106279

Bhagwat, R., & Dandawate, Y. H. (2021). A Review on Advances in Automated Plant Disease Detection. *International Journal of Engineering and Technology Innovation, 11*(4), 251–264. doi:10.46604/ijeti.2021.8244

Bi, L., & Hu, G. (2020). Improving image-based plant disease classification with generative adversarial network under limited training set. *Frontiers in Plant Science, 11,* 583438. doi:10.3389/fpls.2020.583438 PMID:33343595

Bisong, E., & Bisong, E. (2019). Autoencoders. *Building Machine Learning and Deep Learning Models on Google Cloud Platform: A Comprehensive Guide for Beginners,* 475-482.

Bu, F., & Wang, X. (2019). A smart agriculture IoT system based on deep reinforcement learning. *Future Generation Computer Systems, 99,* 500–507. doi:10.1016/j.future.2019.04.041

Calonnec, A., Wiedemann-Merdinoglu, S., Delière, L., Cartolaro, P., Schneider, C., & Delmotte, F. (2012). The reliability of leaf bioassays for predicting disease resistance on fruit: A case study on grapevine resistance to downy and powdery mildew. *Plant Pathology, 62*(3), 533–544. doi:10.1111/j.1365-3059.2012.02667.x

Dai, Q., Cheng, X., Qiao, Y., & Zhang, Y. (2020). Crop leaf disease image super-resolution and identification with dual attention and topology fusion generative adversarial network. *IEEE Access : Practical Innovations, Open Solutions, 8,* 55724–55735. doi:10.1109/ACCESS.2020.2982055

Gautron, R., Maillard, O. A., Preux, P., Corbeels, M., & Sabbadin, R. (2022). Reinforcement learning for crop management support: Review, prospects and challenges. *Computers and Electronics in Agriculture, 200,* 107182. doi:10.1016/j.compag.2022.107182

He, K., Zhang, X., Ren, S., & Sun, J. (2016). Deep residual learning for image recognition. In *Proceedings of the IEEE conference on computer vision and pattern recognition* (pp. 770-778). IEEE.

Howard, A. G., Zhu, M., Chen, B., Kalenichenko, D., Wang, W., Weyand, T., & Adam, H. (2017). *Mobilenets: Efficient convolutional neural networks for mobile vision applications.* arXiv preprint arXiv:1704.04861.

Lee, S. H., Goëau, H., Bonnet, P., & Joly, A. (2020). Attention-based recurrent neural network for plant disease classification. *Frontiers in Plant Science, 11,* 601250. doi:10.3389/fpls.2020.601250 PMID:33381135

Liu, B., Tan, C., Li, S., He, J., & Wang, H. (2020). A data augmentation method based on generative adversarial networks for grape leaf disease identification. *IEEE Access : Practical Innovations, Open Solutions, 8*, 102188–102198. doi:10.1109/ACCESS.2020.2998839

Lu, J., Tan, L., & Jiang, H. (2021). Review on Convolutional Neural Network (CNN) Applied to Plant Leaf Disease Classification. *Agriculture, 11*(8), 707. doi:10.3390/agriculture11080707

N, M., & Gowda, K. J. (2020). Image Processing System based Identification and Classification of Leaf Disease: A Case Study on Paddy Leaf. *2020 International Conference on Electronics and Sustainable Communication Systems (ICESC)*. doi:10.1109/ICESC48915.2020.9155607

Radford, A., Metz, L., & Chintala, S. (2015). *Unsupervised representation learning with deep convolutional generative adversarial networks.* arXiv preprint arXiv:1511.06434.

Sahu, P., Singh, A. P., Chug, A., & Singh, D. (2022). A Systematic Literature Review of Machine Learning Techniques Deployed in Agriculture: A Case Study of Banana Crop. *IEEE Access : Practical Innovations, Open Solutions, 10*, 87333–87360. doi:10.1109/ACCESS.2022.3199926

Simonyan, K., & Zisserman, A. (2014). *Very deep convolutional networks for large-scale image recognition.* arXiv preprint arXiv:1409.1556.

Sreedevi, A., & Manike, C. (2022). A smart solution for tomato leaf disease classification by modified recurrent neural network with severity computation. *Cybernetics and Systems*, 1–41. doi:10.1080/01969722.2022.2122004

Szegedy, C., Liu, W., Jia, Y., Sermanet, P., Reed, S., Anguelov, D., ... Rabinovich, A. (2015). Going deeper with convolutions. In *Proceedings of the IEEE conference on computer vision and pattern recognition* (pp. 1-9). IEEE.

Uthayakumar, J., Vengattaraman, T., & Amudhavel, J. (2017). A simple lossless compression algorithm in wireless sensor networks: An application of wind plant data. *The IIOAB Journal, 8*(2), 281–288.

Wang, H., Sanchez-Molina, J. A., Li, M., & Berenguel, M. (2019). Development of an empirical tomato crop disease model: A case study on gray leaf spot. *European Journal of Plant Pathology, 156*(2), 477–490. doi:10.100710658-019-01897-7

Wei, S. J., Al Riza, D. F., & Nugroho, H. (2022). Comparative study on the performance of deep learning implementation in the edge computing: Case study on the plant leaf disease identification. *Journal of Agriculture and Food Research, 10*, 100389. doi:10.1016/j.jafr.2022.100389

Zilvan, V., Ramdan, A., Suryawati, E., Kusumo, R. B. S., Krisnandi, D., & Pardede, H. F. (2019). Denoising Convolutional Variational Autoencoders-Based Feature Learning for Automatic Detection of Plant Diseases. *2019 3rd International Conference on Informatics and Computational Sciences (ICICoS)*. 10.1109/ICICoS48119.2019.8982494

ADDITIONAL READING

Abhilasha, V., Rathore, V. S., & Chaplot, N. (2021). Analysis of Diseases in Plant's Leaves Using Deep Learning Techniques. *Information and Communication Technology for Competitive Strategies (ICTCS 2020)*, 973–983. doi:10.1007/978-981-16-0882-7_88

Ambeth Kumar, V., Malathi, S., Balas, V. E., Favorskaya, M., & Perumal, T. (Eds.). (2021). *Smart Intelligent Computing and Communication Technology*. Advances in Parallel Computing. doi:10.3233/APC38

Boulent, J., Foucher, S., Théau, J., & St-Charles, P. L. (2019). Convolutional Neural Networks for the Automatic Identification of Plant Diseases. *Frontiers in Plant Science*, *10*, 941. Advance online publication. doi:10.3389/fpls.2019.00941 PMID:31396250

Chawade, A., Van Ham, J., Blomquist, H., Bagge, O., Alexandersson, E., & Ortiz, R. (2019). High-Throughput Field-Phenotyping Tools for Plant Breeding and Precision Agriculture. *Agronomy (Basel)*, *9*(5), 258. doi:10.3390/agronomy9050258

De Castro, A. I., Shi, Y., Maja, J. M., & Peña, J. M. (2021). UAVs for Vegetation Monitoring: Overview and Recent Scientific Contributions. *Remote Sensing (Basel)*, *13*(11), 2139. doi:10.3390/rs13112139

Haider, K., Prasandeep, Ahmed, M., Pal, A., Rawat, S. S., Gupta, V., Shaw, R. N., & Ghosh, A. (2023). A Comprehensive Study of Plant Disease Detection Using Deep Learning Methods. *Communications in Computer and Information Science*, *1749*, 441–458. doi:10.1007/978-3-031-25088-0_40

Huang, G., Liu, Z., Van Der Maaten, L., & Weinberger, K. Q. (2017). Densely connected convolutional networks. In *Proceedings of the IEEE conference on computer vision and pattern recognition* (pp. 4700-4708). IEEE.

Liakos, K., Busato, P., Moshou, D., Pearson, S., & Bochtis, D. (2018). Machine Learning in Agriculture: A Review. *Sensors (Basel)*, *18*(8), 2674. doi:10.339018082674 PMID:30110960

Liu, J., & Wang, X. (2021). Plant diseases and pests detection based on deep learning: A review. *Plant Methods*, *17*(1), 22. Advance online publication. doi:10.118613007-021-00722-9 PMID:33627131

Messina, G., & Modica, G. (2020). Applications of UAV Thermal Imagery in Precision Agriculture: State of the Art and Future Research Outlook. *Remote Sensing (Basel)*, *12*(9), 1491. doi:10.3390/rs12091491

Rangarajan Aravind, K., Maheswari, P., Raja, P., & Szczepański, C. (2020). Crop disease classification using deep learning approach: an overview and a case study. *Deep Learning for Data Analytics*, 173–195. doi:10.1016/B978-0-12-819764-6.00010-7

Ronzhin, A., Berns, K., & Kostyaev, A. (2021). Agriculture Digitalization and Organic Production. In *Proceedings of the First International Conference, ADOP 2021*. Springer Publishing.

Saleem, P., & Arif, M. (2019). Plant Disease Detection and Classification by Deep Learning. *Plants*, *8*(11), 468. doi:10.3390/plants8110468 PMID:31683734

Strange, R. N., & Scott, P. R. (2005). Plant disease: A threat to global food security. *Annual Review of Phytopathology*, *43*(1), 83–116. doi:10.1146/annurev.phyto.43.113004.133839 PMID:16078878

Usharani, B. (2022). House Plant Leaf Disease Detection and Classification Using Machine Learning. *Advances in Systems Analysis, Software Engineering, and High Performance Computing*, 17–26. doi:10.4018/978-1-7998-8161-2.ch002

Zhang, N., Yang, G., Pan, Y., Yang, X., Chen, L., & Zhao, C. (2020). A Review of Advanced Technologies and Development for Hyperspectral-Based Plant Disease Detection in the Past Three Decades. *Remote Sensing (Basel)*, *12*(19), 3188. doi:10.3390/rs12193188

KEY TERMS AND DEFINITIONS

Artificial Intelligence (AI): It is a field of computer science that focuses on developing intelligent machines that can perform tasks that typically require human intelligence, such as learning, problem-solving, perception, and decision-making.

Augmentation: It is a technique to artificially increase the size of a training dataset by creating modified copies of the original data. This is often done by applying various transformations, such as rotations, flips, and color changes, to the original data.

Classification: An algorithm is trained to predict a category or class for new input data based on patterns it learned from labeled examples. The algorithm tries to categorize new data into pre-defined groups or classes.

Computer vision: It is a field of artificial intelligence that focuses on enabling machines to interpret and understand visual data from the world. It involves developing algorithms and techniques to enable machines to see, perceive, and recognize objects, patterns, and features in images and videos.

Convolutional Neural Network (CNN): It is a type of deep neural network that is commonly used in computer vision tasks such as image recognition and classification. It uses convolutional layers to automatically learn and extract features from images.

Deep Learning (DL): DL is a subset of machine learning that uses artificial neural networks to model and solve complex problems by learning from large amounts of data.

Edge Computing: Edge computing is a distributed computing paradigm that brings computation and data storage closer to the location where it is needed.

Feature Extraction: It is the process of automatically extracting or selecting a subset of relevant features or patterns from raw data, such as images or signals, to facilitate further analysis or classification. Its goal is to reduce the dimensionality of the data while preserving the most important information for downstream tasks.

Generative Adversarial Network (GAN): GAN is used in unsupervised machine learning to generate new data samples that are similar to a given dataset. It consists of two parts: a generator network that creates new samples, and a discriminator network that evaluates the authenticity of the generated samples.

Image Processing: Image processing is a field of study that involves the analysis, manipulation, and enhancement of digital images using mathematical algorithms and computational techniques.

Machine Learning (ML): ML is a subset of AI that involves training algorithms to make predictions or decisions based on input data, rather than being explicitly programmed to perform a specific task.

Neural Network: It is a type of machine learning algorithm modeled after the structure and function of the human brain, consisting of interconnected nodes that work together to process input data and produce output predictions.

Object Detection: It is a computer vision technique that involves automatically identifying and localizing objects within an image or video frame.

Optimization: Refers to the process of finding the best possible features for a given problem or objective, subject to constraints and limitations.

Overfitting: Overfitting refers to a situation where a machine learning model is excessively complex and performs well on training data, but poorly on new, unseen data.

Supervised Learning: It is a type of machine learning in which an algorithm learns from labeled data to make predictions or decisions about new, unseen data. The goal is to learn a mapping function from the input data to the output data.

Transfer Learning: It refers to the process of leveraging knowledge from one task to another related task, allowing a model to learn more efficiently and effectively with less training data. It involves using a pre-trained model as a starting point and adapting it to a new problem domain.

Unsupervised Learning: An algorithm learns from unlabeled data to discover hidden patterns or relationships without being given specific output labels or feedback. The goal is to find structure or patterns in the input data.

Chapter 14
Investments in IS/IT Projects:
The Healthcare Sector

Jorge Vareda Gomes
https://orcid.org/0000-0003-0656-9284
Universidade Lusófona, Portugal

Mario Romão
https://orcid.org/0000-0003-4564-1883
ISEG, Universidade de Lisboa, Portugal

ABSTRACT

The main objective of investments in information systems and technology is to increase operational efficiency, reduce costs, and improve the quality levels provided by organizations. In the last decades, IS/IT has positioned itself as a strategic tool that, through innovative combinations, has allowed the flexibility that organizations need to respond to current challenges. The health sector has sought to improve its effectiveness and efficiency through the adoption of IS/IT solutions to enhance quality of services, i.e., patient safety, organizational efficiency, and end-user satisfaction. Hospitals are complex organizations, and this complexity increases the opportunity for unavoidable human error. A poorly integrated system can decrease operational efficiency and reduce the quality of health services. The issue remains controversial. This study aims to review the literature on the topic and explore the trends and challenges that arise today. The study concludes that emerging technologies can offer opportunities for all organizations that effectively know how to better exploit them.

INTRODUCTION

The main objective of investments in information systems and technology (IS/IT) is to increase operational efficiency, reduce costs and improve the quality levels provided by organizations. The creation of organizational value through investments in IS/IT remains one of the main topics for researchers (Dehning et al., 2004; Roztocki & Weistroffer, 2008). Some early studies (Dos Santos et al., 1993; Hitt & Brinjolfsson, 1996; Im et al., 2001; Rai et al., 1997; West & Courtney, 1993) doubt the economic

DOI: 10.4018/978-1-6684-9151-5.ch014

value of IS/IT, although, the vast majority of authors finds empirical evidence and theoretical arguments in favor of operational and strategic relevance of IS/IT (Aral et al., 2007; Beccalli, 2007; Dedrick et al., 2003; Dehning et al., 2003; Han et al., 2011; Kim et al., 2009; Kohli & Grover, 2008; Lee et al., 2011; Lin et al., 2006; Mahmood & Mann, 2005; Neirotti & Paolucci, 2007; Peslak, 2003; Ramírez et al., 2010; Santhanam & Hartono, 2003; Swierczek & Shrestha, 2003; Zhang, 2005).

Despite the great euphoria around these systems, organizations are increasingly pressured to justify the large investments in IS/IT assets (Gomes et al., 2013). The decision-making process on investments in IS/IT is not always as objective and transparent as it is said, there are significant flaws that compromise the achievement of objectives and their related benefits (Berghout et al., 2005).

Organizations only seek benefits and value in monetary terms and forget about the intangible impacts that these investments have on organizations. It is very common for organizations to focus on the technical aspects, "how does it work?", rather than reflecting on the social aspects, "how is it adopted and what impacts does it have? or even from a business perspective," is delivering value?" (Gomes & Romão, 2017).

The healthcare industry represents a very specific context, where complexity and dynamism dominate, making it particularly different from other industries, and it too has been impacted by the rapid and growing emergence of IS/IT implementations (Chau & Hu, 2002; Westbrook et al., 2004). IS/IT investments in the health sector have been referred as a key instrument that facilitates the communication, processing and transmission of information by electronic means, with the aim of improving the quality of processes related to the provision of health care (Bukachi & Pakenham-Walsh, 2007; Drury, 2005; Häyrinen et al., 2008). The difficulties encountered in the implementation of IS/IT solutions and the evaluation of the respective benefits have been recognized as a problem (Lueg & Lu, 2012, 2013). Improving the performance and the return on investments in IS/IT has been the focus of research in recent decades. Supported by the theory of competitive strategy, several authors argue that IS/IT can be very profitable if they are not easily replicated or can differentiate the product (Mithas et al., 2012). Investments in IS/IT are now disseminated globally, adopted and used in many sectors, including the healthcare. Although, the promotion of population health has been the classic objective of public health practices and policies (Dawson & Verweij, 2007), in recent decades, new goals in terms of autonomy and equality have been introduced (Munthe, 2008). According to the World Health Organization, the use of IS/IT in health is not just technology but is a means to achieve a series of desired results throughout the world health system (WHO, 2005). As stated by the European Community, the objective of IS/IT for health is significantly improving the quality, access and effectiveness of health care for all citizens (EC, 2006). This movement towards computer information systems began in the 1970s with the aim of allowing access to the Electronic Health Record (EHR) (Shortliffe & Barnett, 2014). Results of EHR implementation showed a significant improvement in the quality of care, cost-effectiveness, customer orientation and timely access to accurate information (Gagnon et al., 2014). Despite the potential benefits of CSR, its implementation remains a difficult and complex task whose success and productivity depend on a wide range of factors (Yusof et al., 2008; Terry et al., 2008).

METHODOLOGY

This study aims to review the literature on the topic of IS/IT projects in the health area, using articles published in health management journals. Two steps were carried out to achieve this objective. Firstly, the selection of academic documentation and, secondly, the content analysis. The first step was carried out by collecting manuscripts based on a review of relevant literature, using the main databases, namely, ProQuest, Sciencedirect/Elsevier, Ebscohost, Emerald, Jstore, Medline/Pubmed, Taylor

& Francis Online, Sagepub, and Wiley, using the keywords: IS/IT in Health, Success of IS/IT in Health, Health IS/IT Projects Health IS/IT Investments and Health IS/IT Implementations.

The second phase selected the documents that meet the objectives of the study.

BACKGROUND

IS/IT in Healthcare

The investments in IS/IT have the potential to dramatically change the way individuals, professionals or even society perceive the healthcare sector, and also provide great opportunities to support healthcare professionals, and to improve effectiveness and efficiency in this field. The focus of investments in ICT projects lies mainly in improvements on the organizational performance and business efficiency, in other words, improving processes and changing the ways the work is performed (Ammenwerth, 2004; Ward & Daniel, 2012; WHO, 2011, 2015). The use of IS/IT by citizens and their families in the search for health information is increasing (Andreassen et al., 2007). Since the 1990s, the health sector has sought to improve its effectiveness and efficiency by adopting IS/IT to increase service quality levels, namely, patient safety, organizational efficiency and patient satisfaction (Bates & Gawande, 2002; Pan et al., 2005; Raghupathi & Tan, 1999). Health IS/IT implementations represent the integrated effort to collect, process, report and use health information and knowledge to influence the formulation of policies, action programs and research and further states that they are essential for the effective functioning of health systems. health worldwide (WHO, 2006). The broader meaning of these systems refers to any system that captures, stores, manages or transmits information related to the health of individuals or the activities of organizations working in the health sector (Bukachi & Pakenham-Walsh, 2007; Mäenpää et al., 2009; Low & Chen, 2012). The use of IS/IT in healthcare provides important support for specialized services, and increases efficiency, quality, safety and also reduces medical errors (Low & Chen, 2012). Hospitals are complex organizations and this complexity widens the opportunity for unavoidable human error (Weick & Sutcliffe, 2001). A poorly integrated IS/IT can increase the frequency of medical errors, decrease operational efficiency and reduce the quality of health services (Themistocleous et al., 2009). Despite the remarkable progress, failures have still been reported in the integration of technically sound systems in service processes (Lorenzi & Riley, 2003).

We live times when healthcare providers generate amounts of personal data about patients and the main obstacle to managing this growing volume of information is the difficulty, or inability, of sharing information between systems and organizations (Grimson et al., 2000). The greatest evolution in the role of information in the health system, namely in the doctor-patient relationship, is related to the huge flow of medical information or health information present on the internet (Katz & Rice, 2002; Netlleton et al., 2011; Murray et al., 2003). In this new reality, patients began to play a more active role in their own health (Collste, 2002). The medical information available for the clinical decision-making process has increased significantly, however, accessibility of health data is still difficult, resulting in poor decisions and sometimes medical errors (Tierney, 2001).

IS/IT tools were developed to increase the accessibility and management of medical information with the aim of supporting medical decisions, increasing coordination between different health care providers and promoting the use of guidelines, improving overall quality care (Demiris & Kneale, 2015). However, in addition to providing new capabilities, new technologies also provide technical, social, organizational, economic, cultural, and political dimensions of work (Anderson & Aydin, 1994). IS/IT processes have the potential to significantly reduce the rate of these medical errors by providing relevant, real-time information to everyone who needs it (Bates et al., 2001; Chaudhry et al., 2006). An important challenge for the future is to seek a real clinical integration of systems. Integration between providers and hospitals has historically been a goal continually pursued, but rarely achieved. It will become crucial that the design of future applications be more easily integrated into existing systems through an open communication interface (Geissbuhler et al., 2001).

There is a growing consensus that organizational factors are much more critical for successful IS/IT implementation than technical considerations (Gomes & Romão, 2016; Markus, 2000). The necessary change is much easier if all stakeholders are committed, and the sooner that commitment is achieved, the smoother the path to a successful outcome (Bradley, 2006). The use of IS/IT is recognized as an important factor in promoting clinical practices and supportive care (Anderson, 1997; Kumar & Preetha, 2012) and is generally widespread in any country as a key instrument in the provision of health care and public health (Drury, 2005; Lymberis & Dittmar, 2007). Nowadays, IS/IT systems are the "heart" of health organizations, they perform and support all major systems, namely:

1. Patient centralized system - manages comprehensive patient care information such as medical records and appointment scheduling (Cliff, 2012; Krist & Woolf, 2011; Snyder et al., 2011).
2. Administrative support - recording key business processes and routine transactions of organizations, such as patient admission, discharge and transfer, or account processing (Jiang et al., 2000; Peabody et al., 2004).
3. Clinical system - Specific data collection for patient care, research, management, planning and maintenance of data repositories (Ammenwerth & de Keizer, 2005; Gardner & Shabot, 2001).
4. Specific systems (cardiology, radiology, laboratory...) - support the acquisition and analysis of specific functions of the different departments (Paré & Sicotte, 2001).
5. Telemedicine - provides and supports health services over distances via electronic communications and IT (Gawande & Bates, 2000).
6. Clinical decision support systems - specifically designed to aid clinical decision making (Kaushal, et al., 2003).
7. Hospital's information system - integrated hospital information processing systems. Support health activities operational, tactical and strategic levels (Ammenwerth & de Keizer, 2005; Van der Meijden et al., 2003).
8. Cloud computing services, as software as a service application - exploited by scientists and medical communities for their potential in advance and accelerate research and reduce costs (Sultan & Sultan, 2012).

The globally accepted assumption is that IS/IT can and does have a positive effect on health, although the evidence supporting its practical use is low (Wootton, 2009). In fact, many decisions about the implementation of IS/IT in health are made with little or no information about the impact and consequences of its use (Kazanjian & Green, 2002).

IS/IT Project Failures

We have seen a growing increase in investments in IS/IT in the health area and this phenomenon has expanded dramatically in recent decades. The overall investments for each large hospital are huge, however, the overall benefits and costs of hospital information systems have rarely been evaluated (Byrne et al., 2010). When the systems are evaluated, the vast majority do not reach the pre-defined objectives (Heeks, 2002) and there are also some doubts that they improve the productivity of health professionals (Smith et al., 2009). Numerous failures in the computerization of the health sector have been reported (Brailer & Terasawa, 2003; Barrett et al., 2003; Dick et al., 1997; Godard, 2000; Poon et al., 2004; Southon et al., 1999; Yasnoff et al., 2004) demonstrating a lack of planning and poor decisions, sometimes taken under political pressure. The final result brought enormous expenditure of financial resources and the loss of confidence in IS/IT by users and managers. Investments in healthcare IS/IT are financially relevant and continue to grow around the world. While the potential and benefits of using technological innovation in healthcare are great, the risks are also substantial. Therefore, it seems sensible that organizations should pay more attention to adopting formal project appraisals and benefit management methodologies to ensure that the expected benefits of investments are eventually realized (Dibb, 2001; Ward at el., 1996; Heeks & Davies, 1999).

The results of the implementation of IS/IT projects in the health area revealed a waste of financial resources in the acquisition of large systems, which proved to be totally ineffective. Studies have identified high failure rates in IS/IT projects in several sectors, especially in hospitals (Heeks & Davies, 1999; Kaplan & Harris-Salamone, 2009; Sumner, 1999; Wears & Berg, 2005).

Heeks (2008) states that 35% of IS/IT projects are total failures and 50% are partial failures, with only 15% being considered successful. Similarly, Kaplan and Harris-Salamone (2009) confirmed a higher value of 30% for failure rates of large health information technology projects.

Why Do IS/IT Systems Implementations Fail in Healthcare Organizations?

Health projects are a complex undertaking, which largely depends on the quality of existing information (Bose, 2003). Organizations need to have three types of skills to produce successful projects (Lorenzi & Riley, 2003):

1. Technical skills - which include a wide range of skills, such as technical knowledge, experience and skills
2. Project management skills - which include the knowledge, techniques and skills needed to successfully manage IS/IT projects
3. People and Organizational Skills - which includes the wide range of skills needed to effectively interact with all IS/IT stakeholders.

Several reasons are pointed out for the failures of projects in the health industry, namely:

1. Lack of management commitment (Bukachi & Pakenham-Walsh, 2007)
2. Difficulties in engaging health professionals and lack of focus on end users (Elder & Clarke, 2007)
3. Incorrect specification requirements (Lucas, 2008; Gauld, 2007)
4. Inadequate change process (Yeo, 2002)

5. Little knowledge of the complexity of health systems (Al-Ahmad et al., 2009)
6. Lack of investment in human resources (Elder & Clarke, 2007; Bukachi & Pakenham-Walsh, 2007).

In various aspects, IS/IT implementations in healthcare are different from other projects from other industries. The key main differences were related to the environment, the diversity of systems and the devices that need to work, together with the challenge of integration and interoperability which is required to meet the expectations of different stakeholder groups regarding that which constitutes project success (Abouzhara, 2011).

The Success of IS/IT Healthcare Projects

IS/IT implementations are part of the continuous improvement cycle of healthcare quality and are based on several key success factors: Reliable information, engagement of all stakeholders in all phases of work improvement and an adequate infrastructure involving multidisciplinary teams (Brandrud et al., 2011). The success in the strategic use of IS/IT projects in the health area depends on the integration of all systems, such as patient records, clinical decision support, transaction processing, digital images, and information reporting (Jensen, 2013). When several information systems are interoperable on a standardized platform, all stakeholders can streamline the implementation process and improve the quality of the system (Grossmann et al., 2014).

The success of the IS/IT project also refers to user satisfaction, usage, perceived useful ness and system quality (Sabherwal et al., 2006). Seven different stages were proposed in the development of health information system (Haux, 2006):

1. Shift from paper-based systems to computer-based processing and storage.
2. Shift from local to global information system architectures.
3. Health information system used by professionals and patients/consumers.
4. Data used for patient care, healthcare planning and clinical research.
5. Shift of focus from technical health IS problems to change management and strategic information management.
6. Shift from alpha-numerical data to clinical images and data on a molecular level.
7. Steady increase in new technologies for continuous monitoring of health status.

Critical Success Factors (CSFs)

The difficulty of implementing IS/IT projects in health, as well as evaluating their performance, have been the subject of several studies in recent decades (Lueg & Lu, 2012; Santos et., 2014; Kaplan & Harris -Salamone, 2009). Most of this research focuses on identifying critical success factors (CSFs) or best practices that allow organizations to successfully complete their projects (Santos et al., 2014; Hung et al., 2014; Ghazvini & Shukur, 2013). Although, CSFs have been criticized as offering over-simplified solutions that are difficult to realize in practice, since many contextual circumstances also influence the outcome (Berg, 2001; Wagner et al., 2006).

A comprehensive literature review on large scale IS/IT projects executed in ten different countries identified eighteen CSFs for organizations IS/IT systems implementations (Koumaditis et al., 2013). Five of them are common to those identified in health, namely:

1. Top management support
2. Information systems adjustments
3. Business process adjustments
4. Organizational resistance
5. Capacity of key team members.

Must has been written regarding the development of IS/IT initiatives in healthcare sector. The publications emphasized two main aspects; the slowness of adoption of these initiatives and the resistance to change (Lorenzi & Riley, 2003; Sharma & Yetton, 2003; Leonard, 2000, 2004).

These authors highlighted a set of reasons why physicians failed on IS/IT acceptance, namely:

1. On an adequate base support
2. Absence of user-friendly interfaces
3. Difficulties on the information collection process
4. In adequate training plan
5. Lack of leadership in IS/IT that was respected by physicians
6. Organization control default over the clinical practices.

IS/IT interventions are perceived as interfering with the role of traditional medicine. Resistance is greatest when IS/IT interventions do not add additional value to practical medical practices (Leonard & Winkelman, 2002). There are also reports of innovative approaches to improving IS/IT in healthcare adoption (Burke, 2002; Cranfield et al., 2015; Cresswell et al., 2013).

The research effort focused mainly on identifying elements that effectively ensure IS/IT implementations, mainly on:

1. Identifying insufficiencies and difficulties of information that are exclusively of health
2. Identifying areas where IS/IT implementations can make the most difference
3. Build systems that support shared goals
4. Design and develop scalable tools, provider-patient interfaces and Internet forms
5. Invest in existing resources.

Success is something that can be judged on several dimensions such as effectiveness, efficiency, organizational attitudes and commitment, employee and patient satisfaction.

Leonard (2004) identifies a set of CSFs for the adoption of new technologies, such as:

1. Resistance to change
2. Industry experience in the use of technology
3. Training before and during the transition
4. Buy-in or contribution from stakeholder groups
5. Level of effective reporting on outcome measures during and after implementation
6. Level of effectiveness in dealing with implementation.

According to Medlin et al. (2006) successful IS/IT implementations in the healthcare are mainly due to:

1. Strong leadership
2. Affective management
3. Realistic funding
4. Constant improvement of the strategy
5. Processes incorporating new research results and technical innovation.

However, Robinson (2007) highlighted factors such as:

1. Adequate leadership.
2. Good communication
3. Detailed implementation roadmap
4. Establishment of measurable goals
5. Specific attention to the preparation of human resources in terms of motivation and training.

Furthermore, Tempfer and Nowak (2011) identified other factors, namely:

1. Adequate funding
2. Partnerships
3. Advanced project logistics
4. Small-scale projects
5. Adequate internal and external communication

The work of Reyes-Alcázar et al. (2012) noted that the CSFs that need to be considered for the healthcare sector are the following:

1. A patient-centered approach: end-user needs and expectations (Mead & Bower, 2000)
2. Leadership: the importance of improving the quality of health care (West et al., 2004)
3. Teamwork: a multidisciplinary process focused on a healthcare team that shares common goals (Mickan, 2005)
4. Autonomy and responsibility: greater autonomy among health professionals (Harrison & Dowswell, 2002)
5. An integrated view of health care; the quality of patient care as perceived by end users is a key element (Torres-Olivera, 2003)
6. Professional competences: the promotion of competences stimulates professional development (Reyes-Alcázar et al., 2012)
7. Focus on results: o measurement and evaluation of clinical performance, hospital management and end-user satisfaction
8. Internal and external audits: cycle of continuous quality improvement (Patton, 2008; Hyrkäs & Lehti, 2003; Le Brasseur et al., 2002).

FUTURE TRENDS

The introduction of IS/IT can radically affect healthcare organizations and healthcare delivery (Ammenwerth et al., 2004). Despite the growing role and importance of IS/IT in healthcare, understanding why, how and when technology enables productivity improvement is in its early stages, most often resulting in a delay in productivity growth (Jorgenson & Stiroh, 2000).

Health processes depend on the quality of data/information and knowledge. In this context, management information plays a crucial role. Numerous studies have demonstrated the positive effects of the use of IS/IT in health care (Lenz & Reichert, 2007). The support of these systems is an important asset for specialized services, which increases the quality and safety of patient care, minimizing the probability of medical errors (Low & Chen, 2012). Supported by IS/IT, the complex medical decision-making process can be significantly improved in several ways (Lenz & Reichert, 2007), such as:

1. Contributing to improve data quality, such as timeliness or completeness (Van Walraven, et al., 2004)
2. Contribute to better monitoring a patient's current status (Bates et al., 2001)
3. Detect mismatches between existing guidelines and the actual patient care process (Shiffman, 2004)
4. Generate reminders to ensure planned actions are not forgotten
5. Helping to calculate drug dosage from previously entered data (Ambrisko & Nemeth, 2004)
6. Calculation of disease probabilities (Hejlesen, 2005).

The benefits that a good IS/IT system can bring to health organizations are mainly:

1. Better citizen access to health systems;
2. Reduce the risk of errors due to lack of data/information;
3. Reduce the time needed to provide clinical reports;
4. Reduce costs by avoiding repetitive efforts and unnecessary resources.

The challenges to be faced to successfully implement of these solutions are several, namely:

1. Interoperability
2. Timeliness, integrity, availability and confidentiality of data/information
3. Software alignment with sound application architecture principles and content management frameworks
4. Establishment of rules that allow the user to give informed consent to access to their data by professionals
5. Ensuring how to overcome the enormous difficulties of a change management process.

An important challenge for the future is to seek a real clinical integration of systems. Clinical integration between providers and hospitals has historically been a goal, still continuously pursued but rarely achieved. It will be crucial that the design of future applications be more easily integrated into existing systems, some of them legacy systems, through open communication interfaces that meet known standards. Healthcare IS/IT projects can lead the industry towards an interconnected healthcare platform, providing an optimized technology infrastructure that combines traditional, cloud-based technologies and hybrid computing models, bringing together the disparate parts of the healthcare ecosystem, thus enabling better care, workforce mobility and security-enhanced data delivery models.

CONCLUSION

Rapid developments in the healthcare sector are mainly driven by demographic changes, which include an increasing aging population, chronic diseases, cultural changes, advances in science and technology, widespread access to digital networks and awareness of the need to improve quality and safety. in the provision of health services. Today's technology plays a significant role in enabling the rapid storage, retrieval and sharing of patient records and other important information. At the same time, patients expect their confidential personal information to be handled appropriately to ensure accuracy and confidentiality.

Healthcare organizations are increasingly challenged on how to ensure a fair return on IS/IT investments. IS/IT has been referred to as key instruments to respond to these new trends, both in terms of access to health information and in terms of efficiency in the provision of health care. It also can improve the efficiency of services, through better management of resources, allowing great savings. A patient-centered information system can track individual health issues and treatment over time, giving insights into the individual's optimal diagnosis and treatment, as well as how to improve service delivery.

The main objective of IS/IT is to manage information from all health-related activities, including planning, monitoring, coordination and decision-making. Real-time access, exchange and receipt of clinical data provided by the system has improved clinical documentation, reduced duplication of services and better supported decision making. IS/ITs are designed to support clinicians in accessing and working with a variety of patient information and promoting the sharing of quality healthcare information. Adequate training is one of the main determinants for the successful adoption of IS/IT by health professionals and has a great influence on the good integration of technologies in clinical practice. Authors identify organizational culture as exerting a positive influence on the development of superior project management practices. As mentioned before, investments in IS/IT in the health area bring many benefits to the day-to-day of organizations.

IS/IT implementations have shown that technology changes roles, strategies, and paths to success, highlighting that recognition of these new trends recommends examining new technologies to avoid security threats and redesigning them to avoid unwanted accidents. The study of the success or failure of these initiatives has become of vital importance for the performance of these organizations.

REFERENCES

Abouzhara, M. (2011). Causes of failure in Healthcare IT projects. *Proceedings of the 3th International Conference on Advance Management Science, IPEDR, 19, IACSIT*. Available at: http://ipedr.com/vol19/9- ICAMS2011-A00018.pdf

Al-Ahmad, A., Al-Fagih, K., Khanfar, K., Alsamara, K., Abuleil, S., & Abu-Salem, H. (2009). A taxonomy of an IT project failure: Root causes. *International Management Review, 5*(1), 93–104.

Ambrisko, T., & Nemeth, T. (2004). A computer program for calculating of doses and prices of injectable medications based on body weight or body surface area. *Canadian Journal of Veterinary Research, 68*, 62–65. PMID:14979437

Ammenwerth, E., Brender, J., Nykänen, P., Prokosch, H. U., Rigby, M., & Talmon, J. (2004). Visionand strategies to improve evaluation of health information systems: Reflections and lessons based onthe HIS-EVAL workshop in Innsbruck. *International Journal of Medical Informatics, 73*(6), 479–491. doi:10.1016/j.ijmedinf.2004.04.004 PMID:15171977

Ammenwerth, E., & de Keizer, N. (2005). An inventory of evaluation studies of information technology in healthcare: Trends in evaluation research 1982–2002. *Methods of Information in Medicine, 44*, 44–56. doi:10.1055-0038-1633922 PMID:15778794

Anderson, J. G. (1997). Clearing the way for physicians' use of clinical information systems. *Communications of the ACM, 40*(8), 83–90. doi:10.1145/257874.257895

Anderson, J. G., & Aydin, C. E. (1994). Overview: Theoretical perspectives and methodologies for the evaluation of health care information systems. In J. G. Anderson, C. E. Aydin, & S. J. Jay (Eds.), *Evaluating health care information systems: Methods and applications* (pp. 5–29). Sage Publications, Inc.

Andreassen, H. K., Bujnowska-Fedak, M. M., Chronaki, C. E., Duritru, R. C., Pudele, I., Santana, S., & Wynn, R. (2007). European citizens' use of E-health services: A study of seven countries. *BMC Public Health, 7*(53), 1–7. doi:10.1186/1471-2458-7-53 PMID:17425798

AralS.BrynjolfssonE.Van AlstyneM. (2007) Information, Technology and Information Worker Productivity Task Level Evidence. *Information System Research.* Available at: SSRN: https://ssrn.com/abstract=942310

Barrett, M. J., Holmes, B. J., & McAulay, S. E. (2003). *Electronic Medical Records: A Buyer's Guide for Small Physician Practices.* California HealthCare Foundation.

Bates, D., Cohen, M., Leape, L., Overhage, J., Shabot, M., & Sheridan, T. (2001). Reducing the frequency of errors in medicine using information technology. *Journal of the American Medical Informatics Association : JAMIA, 8*(4), 299–308. doi:10.1136/jamia.2001.0080299 PMID:11418536

Bates, D., & Gawande, A. A. (2002). Error in medicine: What have we learned? *Annals of Internal Medicine, 132*(9), 763–767. doi:10.7326/0003-4819-132-9-200005020-00025 PMID:10787381

Beccalli, E. (2007). Does IT investment improve bank performance? Evidence from Europe. *Journal of Banking & Finance, 31*(7), 2205–2230. doi:10.1016/j.jbankfin.2006.10.022

Berg, M. (2001). Implementing information systems in health care organisations: Myths and challenges. *International Journal of Medical Informatics, 64*(2-3), 143–156. doi:10.1016/S1386-5056(01)00200-3 PMID:11734382

Berghout, E., Nijland, M., & Grant, K. (2005). Seven ways to get your favoured IT project accepted-politics in IT evaluation. *The Electronic Journal of Information System Evaluation, 8*(1), 31–40.

Bose, R. (2003). Knowledge management-enabled health care management: Capabilities, infrastructure, and decision-making. *Expert Systems with Applications, 24*(1), 59–71. doi:10.1016/S0957-4174(02)00083-0

Bradley, G. (2006). *Benefit Realization Management: A Practical Guide for Achieving Benefits through Change.* Gower Publishing.

Brailer, D. J., & Terasawa, E. L. (2003). *Use and Adoption of Computer-Based Patient Records.* California HealthCare Foundation.

Brandrud, A. S., Schreiner, A., Hjortdahl, P., Helljesen, G. S., Nyen, B., & Nelson, E. C. (2011). Three Success Factors for Continual Improvement in Healthcare: An Analysis of the Reports of Improvement Team Members. *BMJ Quality & Safety, 20*(3), 251–259. doi:10.1136/bmjqs.2009.038604 PMID:21209149

Bukachi, F., & Pakenham-Walsh, N. (2007). Information technology for health in developing countries. *Chest, 132*(5), 1624–1630. doi:10.1378/chest.07-1760 PMID:17998362

Burke, D., Wang, B., Wan, T., & Diana, N. (2002). Exploring Hospitals' Adoption of Information Technology. *Journal of Medical Systems, 26*(4), 349–355. doi:10.1023/A:1015872805768 PMID:12118818

Byrne, C. M., Mercincavage, L. M., Pan, E. C., Vincent, A. G., Johnston, D. S., & Middleton, B. (2010). The value from investments in health information technology at the U.S. Department of Veterans Affairs. *Health Affairs, 29*(4), 629–638. doi:10.1377/hlthaff.2010.0119 PMID:20368592

Chau, P. Y., & Hu, P. (2002). Investigating healthcare professionals' decisions to accept telemedicine technology: An empirical test of competing theories. *Information & Management, 39*(4), 297–311. doi:10.1016/S0378-7206(01)00098-2

Chaudhry, B., Wang, J., Wu, S., Maglione, M., Mojica, W., Roth, E., Shekelle, P. G., & … . (2006). Systematic Review: Impact of Health Information Technology on Quality, Efficiency, and Costs of Medical Care. *Annals of Internal Medicine, 144*(10), 742–752. doi:10.7326/0003-4819-144-10-200605160-00125 PMID:16702590

Cliff, B. (2012). Using Technology to Enhance Patient-Centered Care. *Journal of Healthcare Management, 57*(September/October). PMID:23087992

Collste, G. (2002). The Internet doctor and medical ethics Ethical implications of the introduction of the Internet into medical encounters. *Medicine, Health Care, and Philosophy, 5*(2), 121–125. doi:10.1023/A:1016083021422 PMID:12168987

Cranfield, S., Hendy, J., Reeves, B., Hutchings, A., Collin, S., & Fulop, N. (2015). Investigating healthcare IT innovations: A "conceptual blending" approach. *Journal of Health Organization and Management, 29*(7), 1131–1148. doi:10.1108/JHOM-08-2015-0121 PMID:26556172

Cresswell, K., Bates, D., & Sheikh, A. (2013). Ten key considerations for the successful implementation and adoption of large-scale health information technology. *Journal of the American Medical Informatics Association : JAMIA, 20*(e1), e9–e13. doi:10.1136/amiajnl-2013-001684 PMID:23599226

Dawson, A., & Verweij, M. (Eds.). (2007). *Ethics, Prevention, and Public Health.* Oxford University Press.

Dedrick, J., Gurbaxani, V., & Kraemer, K. L. (2003). Information technology and economic performance: A critical review of the empirical evidence. *ACM Computing Surveys, 35*(1), 1–28. doi:10.1145/641865.641866

Dehning, B., Richardson, V. J., Urbaczewski, A., & Wells, J. D. (2004). Re-examining the Value Relevance of Ecommerce Initiatives. *Journal of Management Information Systems, 21*(1), 57–84. doi:10.1080/07421222.2004.11045788

Dehning, B., Richardson, V. J., & Zmud, R. W. (2003). The Value Relevance of Announcements of Transformational Information Technology Investments. *Management Information Systems Quarterly*, *27*(4), 637–656. doi:10.2307/30036551

Demiris, G., & Kneale, L. (2015). Informatics Systems and Tools to Facilitate Patient-centered Care Coordination. *IMIA Yearbook of Medical Informatics*, *10*(1), 15–21. PMID:26293847

Dibb, S. (2001). Customer Relationship Management and Barriers to the One Segment. *Journal of Financial Services Marketing*, *6*(1), 10–23. doi:10.1057/palgrave.fsm.4770037

Dick, R. S., Steen, E. B., & Detmer, D. E. (Eds.). (1997). *The Computer-Based Patient Record: An Essential Technology for Health Care* (revised edition). Committee on Improving the Patient Record, National Academy of Sciences.

Dos Santos, B. L., Peffers, K. G., & Mauer, D. C. (1993). The Impact of Information Technology Investment Announcements on the Market Value of the Firm. *Information Systems Research*, *4*(1), 1–23. doi:10.1287/isre.4.1.1

Drury, P. (2005). The eHealth agenda for developing countries. *World Hospitals and Health Services*, *41*, 38–40. PMID:16512063

EC. (2006). *ICT for Health and i2010: Transforming the European healthcare landscape -Towards a strategy for ICT for Health*. Information Society & Media Directorate General, European Commission. Available at: https://ec.europa.eu/digital-single-market/en/news/ict-health-and-i2010-transforming-european-healthcare-landscape

Elder, L., & Clarke, M. (2007). Past, present and future: Experiences and lessons from telehealth projects. *Open Medicine : a Peer-Reviewed, Independent, Open-Access Journal*, *1*(3), 166–170. PMID:21673948

Gagnon, M. P., Ghandour, E. K., Talla, P. K., Simonyan, D., Godin, G., Labrecque, M., & Rousseau, M. (2014). Electronic health record acceptance by physicians: Testing an integrated theoretical model. *Journal of Biomedical Informatics*, *48*, 17–27. doi:10.1016/j.jbi.2013.10.010 PMID:24184678

Gardner, R. M., & Shabot, M. M. (2001). Patient-monitoring Systems. In Biomedical Informatics: Computer Applications in Health care and Biomedicine. New York: Springer Science+Business Media, LLC.

Gauld, R. (2007). Public sector information systems project failures: Lessons from a New Zealand hospital organization. *Government Information Quarterly*, *24*(1), 102–114. doi:10.1016/j.giq.2006.02.010

Gawande, A., & Bates, D. (2000). The use of information technology in improving medical performance. Part II. Physician-support tools. *Medscape General Medicine*, *2*, E13. PMID:11104459

Geissbuhler, A., Lovis, C., Lamb, A., & Spahni, S. (2001). Experience with an XML/HTTP-based federative approach to develop a hospital-wide clinical information system. *Studies in Health Technology and Informatics*, *84*(1), 735–739. PMID:11604834

Ghazvini, A., & Shukur, Z. (2013). Security challenges and success factors of electronic healthcare system. *Procedia Technology*, *11*, 212–219. doi:10.1016/j.protcy.2013.12.183

Goddard, B. L. (2000). Termination of a contract to implement an enterprise electronic medical record system. *Journal of the American Medical Informatics Association : JAMIA, 7*(6), 564–568. doi:10.1136/jamia.2000.0070564 PMID:11062230

Gomes, J., & Romão, M. (2016). Improving the success of IS/IT projects in Healthcare: Benefits and Project Management approaches. In Advances in Intelligent Systems and Computing (vol. 444, pp. 547-556). New Advances in Information Systems and Technologies, Springer International Publishing AG, Part of Springer Science+Business Media.

Gomes, J., & Romão, M. (2017). Aligning Information Systems and Technology with Benefit Management and Balanced Scorecard. In S. De Haes & W. Van Grembergen (Eds.), *Strategic IT Governance and Alignment in Business Settings* (pp. 112–131). IGI Global., doi:10.4018/978-1-5225-0861-8.ch005

Gomes, J., Romão, M., & Caldeira, M. (2013). The Benefits Management and Balanced Scorecard Strategy Map: How They Match. *International Journal of IT/Business Alignment and Governance, 4*(1), 44–54. doi:10.4018/jitbag.2013010104

Grimson, J., Grimson, W., & Hasselbring, W. (2000). The system integration challenge in health care. *Communications of the ACM, 43*(6), 49–55. doi:10.1145/336460.336474

Grossmann, C., Powers, B., & McGinnis, J. M. (2011). *Digital Infrastructure for The Learning Health System: The Foundation for Continuous Improvement in Health and Health Care.* Institute of Medicine, The National Academies Press.

Han, K., Chang, Y. B., & Hahn, J. (2011). Information Technology Spillover and Productivity: The Role of Information Technology Intensity and Competition. *Journal of Management Information Systems, 28*(1), 115–145. doi:10.2753/MIS0742-1222280105

Harrison, S., & Dowswell, G. (2002). Autonomy and bureaucratic accountability in primary care: What English general practitioners say. *Sociology of Health & Illness, 24*(2), 208–226. doi:10.1111/1467-9566.00291

Haux, R. (2006). Health information systems – past, present, future. *International Journal of Medical Informatics, 75*(3-4), 268–281. doi:10.1016/j.ijmedinf.2005.08.002 PMID:16169771

Häyrinen, K., Saranto, K., & Nykänen, P. (2008). Definition, Structure, Content, Use and Impacts of Electronic Health Records: A Review of the Research Literature. *International Journal of Medical Informatics, 77*(5), 291–304. doi:10.1016/j.ijmedinf.2007.09.001 PMID:17951106

Heeks, R. B. (2002). Information Systems and Developing Countries: Failure, Success, and Local Improvisations. *The Information Society, 18*(2), 101–112. doi:10.1080/01972240290075039

Heeks, R. B. (2008). *Success and failure rates of e-Government in developing/transitional countries: Overview.* Building Digital Opportunities Programme, Information Exchange, University of Manchester's Institute for Development Policy and Management.

Heeks, R. B., & Davies, A. (1999). Different approaches to information age. In R. B. Heeks (Ed.), *Reinventing Government in the Information Age.* Routledge.

Hejlesen, O., Olesen, K., Dessau, R., Beltoft, I., & Trangeled, M. (2005). Decision support for diagnosis of lyme disease. *Studies in Health Technology and Informatics, 116*, 205–210. PMID:16160260

Hitt, L. M., & Brinjolfsson, E. (1996). Productivity, business profitability, and consumer surplus: Three different measures of information technology value. *Management Information Systems Quarterly, 20*(2), 121–142. doi:10.2307/249475

Hung, S. Y., Chen, C., & Wang, K. H. (2014). Critical success factors for the implementation of integrated healthcare information systems projects: An organizational fit perspective. *Communications of the Association for Information Systems, 34*(1), 775–796. doi:10.17705/1CAIS.03439

Hyrkäs, K., & Lehti, K. (2003). Continuous quality improvement through team supervision supported by continuous self-monitoring of work and systematic patient feedback. *Journal of Nursing Management, 11*(3), 208–226. doi:10.1046/j.1365-2834.2003.00369.x PMID:12694365

Im, K. S., Dow, K. E., & Grover, V. (2001). A reexamination of IT investment and the market value of the firm - An event study methodology. *Information Systems Research, 12*(1), 103–117. doi:10.1287/isre.12.1.103.9718

Jensen, T. B. (2013). Design Principles for Achieving Integrated Healthcare Information Systems. *Health Informatics Journal, 19*(1), 29–45. doi:10.1177/1460458212448890 PMID:23486824

Jiang, J., Muhanna, W., & Klenin, G. (2000). User resistance and strategies for promoting acceptance across system types. *Information & Management, 37*(1), 25–36. doi:10.1016/S0378-7206(99)00032-4

Jorgenson, D., & Stiroh, K. (2000). Raising the speed limit: US economic growth in the information age. In *Economic growth in the information age*. MIT Press. https://www.brookings.edu/bpea-articles/raising-the-speed-limit-u-s-economic-growth-in-the-information-age/

Kaplan, B., & Harris-Salamone, K. (2009). Health IT success and failure: Recommendations from literature and an AMIA workshop. *Journal of the American Medical Informatics Association : JAMIA, 16*(3), 291–299. doi:10.1197/jamia.M2997 PMID:19261935

Katz, J. E., & Rice, R. E. (2002). *Social Consequences of Internet Use: access, involvement, and interaction*. MIT Press. doi:10.7551/mitpress/6292.001.0001

Kaushal, R., Shojania, K., & Bates, D. (2003). Effects of Computerized Physician Order Entry and Clinical Decision Support Systems on Medication Safety. A Systematic Review. *Archives of Internal Medicine, 163*(12), 1409–1416. doi:10.1001/archinte.163.12.1409 PMID:12824090

Kazanjian, A., & Green, C. (2002). Beyond effectiveness: The evaluation of information systems using a comprehensive health technology assessment framework. *Computers in Biology and Medicine, 32*(3), 165–177. doi:10.1016/S0010-4825(02)00013-6 PMID:11922933

Kim, J. K., Xiang, J. Y., & Lee, S. (2009). The impact of IT investment on firm performance in China: An empirical investigation of the Chinese electronics industry. *Technological Forecasting and Social Change, 76*(5), 678–687. doi:10.1016/j.techfore.2008.03.008

Kohli, R., & Grover, V. (2008). Business value of IT: An essay on expanding research directions to keep up with the times. *Journal of the Association for Information Systems, 9*(1), 23–39. doi:10.17705/1jais.00147

Koumaditis, K., Themistocleous, M., & Rupino da Cunha, P. (2013). SOA implementation critical success factors in healthcare. *Journal of Enterprise Information Management, 26*(4), 343–362. doi:10.1108/JEIM-06-2012-0036

Krist, A. H., & Woolf, S. H. (2011). A Vision for Patient-Centered Health Information Systems. *Journal of the American Medical Association, 305*(3), 300–301. doi:10.1001/jama.2010.2011 PMID:21245186

Kumar, S., & Preetha, G. S. (2012). Health Promotion: An Effective Tool for Global Health. *Indian Journal of Community Medicine, 37*(1), 5–12. doi:10.4103/0970-0218.94009 PMID:22529532

Le Brasseur, R., Whissell, R., & Ojha, A. (2002). Organizational learning, transformational leardship, and implementation of continuous quality improvement in Canadian Hospitals. *Australian Journal of Management, 27*(2), 141–162. doi:10.1177/031289620202700203

Lee, S., Xiang, J. Y., & Kim, J. K. (2011). Information Technology and Productivity: Empirical Evidence from the Chinese Electronics Industry. *Information & Management, 48*(2/3), 79–87. doi:10.1016/j.im.2011.01.003

Lenz, R., & Reichert, M. (2007). IT support for healthcare processes: Premises, challenges, perspectives. *Data & Knowledge Engineering, 61*(1), 39–58. doi:10.1016/j.datak.2006.04.007

Leonard, K. J. (2000). Information Systems for Healthcare: Why we haven't had more success: The Top 15 Reasons. *Healthcare Management Forum, 13*(3), 45–51. doi:10.1016/S0840-4704(10)60776-4 PMID:15892319

Leonard, K. J. (2004). Critical Success Factors Relating to Healthcare's Adoption of New Technology: A Guide to Increasing the Likelihood of Successful Implementation. *ElectronicHealthcare, 2*(4), 72–81.

Leonard, K. J., & Winkelman, W. (2002). Developing Electronic Patient Records: Employing Interactive Methods to Ensure Patient Involvement. *Proceedings of the Proceedings of the 28th Meeting of the European Working Group on Operational Research Applied to Health Services (ORAHS)*, 241-255.

Lin, W. T., & Shao, B. B. (2006). Assessing the input effect on productive efficiency in production systems the value of information technology capital. *International Journal of Production Research, 44*(9), 1799–1819. doi:10.1080/00207540500353889

Lorenzi, N. M., & Riley, R. (2003). Organizational issues = change. *International Journal of Medical Informatics, 69*(2-3), 97–203. doi:10.1016/S1386-5056(02)00105-3 PMID:12810124

Low, C., & Chen, Y. (2012). Criteria for the evaluation of a cloud- based hospital information system outsourcing provider. *Journal of Medical Systems, 36*(6), 3543–3553. doi:10.100710916-012-9829-z PMID:22366976

Lucas, H. (2008). Information and communications technology for future health systems in developing countries. *Social Medicine (Social Medicine Publication Group), 66*(10), 2122–2132. doi:10.1016/j.socscimed.2008.01.033 PMID:18343005

Lueg, R., & Lu, S. (2012). Improving efficiency in budgeting: An interventionist approach to spreadsheet accuracy testing. *Problems and Perspectives in Management, 10*, 32–41.

Lueg, R., & Lu, S. (2013). How to improve efficiency in budgeting: The case of business intelligence in SMEs. *European Journal of Management, 13*(2), 109–120. doi:10.18374/EJM-13-2.13

Lymberis, A., & Dittmar, A. (2007). Advanced Wearable Health Systems and Applications: Research and Development Efforts in the European Union. *IEEE Engineering in Medicine and Biology Magazine, 26*(3), 29–33. doi:10.1109/MEMB.2007.364926 PMID:17549917

Mäenpää, T., Suominen, T., Asikainen, P., Maass, M., & Rostila, I. (2009). The outcomes of regional healthcare information systems in health care: A review of the research literature. *International Journal of Medical Informatics, 78*(11), 757–771. doi:10.1016/j.ijmedinf.2009.07.001 PMID:19656719

Mahmood, M. A., & Mann, G. J. (2005). Information technology investments and organizational productivity and performance: An empirical investigation. *Journal of Organizational Computing and Electronic Commerce, 15*(3), 185–202. doi:10.120715327744joce1503_1

Markus, M. L., Axline, S., Petrie, D., & Tanis, C. (2000). Learning from adopters' experiences with ERP: Problems encountered, and success achieved. *Journal of Information Technology, 14*(4), 245–265. doi:10.1080/02683960010008944

Mead, N., & Bower, P. (2000). Patient-centeredness: A conceptual framework and review of empirical literature. *Social Science & Medicine, 51*(7), 1087–1110. doi:10.1016/S0277-9536(00)00098-8 PMID:11005395

Medlin, C., Chowdhury, M., Jamison, D., & Measham, A. (2006). Improving the Health of Populations: Lessons of Experience. In *Disease Control Priorities in Developing Countries* (2nd ed.). World Bank.

Mickan, S. (2005). Evaluating the effectiveness of health care teams. *Australian Health Review, 29*(2), 211–217. doi:10.1071/AH050211 PMID:15865572

Mithas, S., Tafti, A., Bardhan, T., & Goh, J. M. (2012). Information Technology and Firm Profitability: Mechanisms and Empirical Evidence. *Management Information Systems Quarterly, 36*(1), 205–224. doi:10.2307/41410414

Munthe, C. (2008). The Goals of Public Health: An Integrated, Multidimensional Model. *Public Health Ethics, 1*(1), 39–52. doi:10.1093/phe/phn006

Murray, E., Lo, B., Pollack, L., Donelan, K., Catania, J., Lee, K., Turner, R., & ... . (2003). The Impact of Health Information on the Internet on Health Care and the Physician-Patient Relationship: National U.S. Survey among 1.050 U.S. Physicians. *Journal of Medical Internet Research, 5*(3), e17. doi:10.2196/jmir.5.3.e17 PMID:14517108

Neirotti, P., & Paolucci, E. (2007). Assessing the strategic value of Information Technology: An analysis on the insurance sector. *Information & Management, 44*(6), 568–582. doi:10.1016/j.im.2007.05.005

Netlleton, S., Burrows, R., O' Malley, L., & Watt, I. (2011). Health e-types? *Information Communication and Society, 7*(4), 531–553. doi:10.1080/1369118042000305638

Pan, E., Johnston, D., Walker, J., Adler-Milstein, J., Bates, D. W., & Middleton, B. (2005). *The Value of Healthcare Information Exchange and Interoperability*. Health Information Management and Systems Society.

Paré, G., & Sicotte, G. (2001). Information technology sophistication in health care: An instrument validation study among Canadian hospitals. *International Journal of Medical Informatics, 63*(3), 205–223. doi:10.1016/S1386-5056(01)00178-2 PMID:11502433

Patton, M. Q. (2008). *Utilization-Focused Evaluation* (4th ed.). Sage Publications.

Peabody, J. W., Luck, J., Jain, S., Bertenthal, D., & Glassman, P. (2004). Assessing the Accuracy of Administrative Data in Health Information Systems. *Medical Care, 42*, 1066-1072. https://www.jstor.org/stable/4640857

Peslak, A. R. (2003). A firm level study of information technology productivity using financial and market-based measures. *Journal of Computer Information Systems, 43*(4), 72–80.

Poon, E. G., Blumenthal, T., Jaggi, M., Honour, M. N., Bates, D. W., & Kaushal, R. (2004). Overcoming barriers to adopting and implementing computerized physician order entry in US hospitals. *Health Affairs, 23*(4), 184–190. doi:10.1377/hlthaff.23.4.184 PMID:15318579

Raghupathi, W., & Tan, J. (1999). Strategic use of information technology in healthcare: A state-of-the-art. *Topics in Health Information Management, 1*(1), 1–15. PMID:10539419

Rai, A., Patnayakuni, R., & Patnayakuni, N. (1997). Technology investment and business performance. *Communications of the ACM, 40*(7), 89–97. doi:10.1145/256175.256191

Ramírez, R., Melville, N., & Lawler, E. (2010). Information technology infrastructure, organizational process redesign, and business value: An empirical analysis. *Decision Support Systems, 49*(4), 417–429. doi:10.1016/j.dss.2010.05.003

Reyes-Alcázar, V., Torres-Olivera, A., Núñes-García, D., & Almuedo-Paz, A. (2012). Critical Success Factors for Quality Assurance in Healthcare Organisations. In M. Savsar (Ed.), *Quality Assurance Management*. Academic Press. doi:10.5772/33081

Robinson, C. (2007). Clinician adoption of healthcare information technology. *Canadian Nursing Informatics, 2*(1), 4–21.

Roztocki, N., & Weistroffer, H. R. (2008). Event Studies in Information Systems Research: A Review. *Proceedings of the Americas Conference on Information Systems*. Available at: http://aisel. aisnet.org/amcis2008/248

Sabherwal, R., Jeyaraj, A., & Chowa, C. (2006). Information System Success: Individual and Organizational Determinants. *Management Science, 52*(12), 1849–1864. doi:10.1287/mnsc.1060.0583

Santhanam, R., & Hartono, E. (2003). Issues in linking information technology capability to firm performance. *Management Information Systems Quarterly, 27*(1), 125–153. doi:10.2307/30036521

Santos, C., Santos, V., Tavares, A., & Varajão, J. (2014). Project Management Success in Health – The need of additional research in public health projects. *Procedia Technology, 16*, 1080–1085. doi:10.1016/j.protcy.2014.10.122

Sharma, R., & Yetton, P. (2003). The contingent effects of management support and task interdependence on successful information systems implementation. *Management Information Systems Quarterly, 27*(4), 533–556. doi:10.2307/30036548

Shiffman, R., Michel, G., Essaihi, A., & Thornquist, E. (2004). Bridging the guideline implementation gap: A systematic, document-centered approach to guideline implementation. *Journal of the American Medical Informatics Association : JAMIA, 11*(5), 418–426. doi:10.1197/jamia.M1444 PMID:15187061

Shortliffe, E. H., & Barnett, G. O. (2014). Biomedical data: their acquisition, storage and use. In *Biomedical informatics* (pp. 39–66). Springer. doi:10.1007/978-1-4471-4474-8_2

Smith, P. C., Mossialos, E., Papanicolas, I., & Leatherman, S. (2009). *Performance measurement for health system improvement: experiences, challenges and prospects.* Cambridge University Press.

Snyder, C. F., Wu, A. W., Miller, R. S., Jensen, R. E., Bantug, E. T., & Wolff, A. C. (2011). The role of informatics in promoting patient-centered care. *Cancer Journal (Sudbury, Mass.), 17*(4), 211–218. doi:10.1097/PPO.0b013e318225ff89 PMID:21799327

Southon, F., Sauer, C., & Dampney, C. (1999). Lessons from a failed information systems initiative: Issues for complex organisations. *International Journal of Medical Informatics, 55*(1), 33–46. doi:10.1016/S1386-5056(99)00018-0 PMID:10471239

Sultan, N., & Sultan, Z. (2012). The application of utility ICT in healthcare management and life science research: a new market for a disruptive innovation? In *Proceedings of EURAM 2012 Conference - Social Innovation for Competitiveness, Organizational Performance and Human Excellence, June 6-8.* Rotterdam School of Management.

Sumner, M. (1999). Critical Success Factors in Enterprise Wide Information Management Systems Projects. *Proceedings of Americas Conference on Information Systems.* 10.1145/299513.299722

Swierczek, F. W., & Shrestha, P. K. (2003). Information technology and productivity: A comparison of Japanese and Asia-Pacific banks. *The Journal of High Technology Management Research, 14*(2), 269–288. doi:10.1016/S1047-8310(03)00025-7

Tempfer, C., & Nowak, P. (2011). Consumer participation and organizational development in health care: A systematic review. *Wiener Klinische Wochenschrift, 123*(13–14), 408–414. doi:10.100700508-011-0008-x PMID:21739200

Terry, A. L., Thorpe, C. F., Giles, G., Brown, J. B., Harris, S. B., Reid, G. J., Stewart, M., & ... . (2008). Implementing electronic health records: Key factors in primary care. *Canadian Family Physician Medecin de Famille Canadien, 54*(5), 730–736. PMID:18474707

Themistocleous, M., Mantzana, V., & Morabito, V. (2009). Achieving Knowledge Management Integration through EAI: A Case Study from Healthcare Sector. *International Journal of Technology Management, 47*(1-3), 114–126. doi:10.1504/IJTM.2009.024117

Tierney, W. (2001). Improving clinical decisions and outcomes with information: A review. *International Journal of Medical Informatics, 62*(1), 1–9. doi:10.1016/S1386-5056(01)00127-7 PMID:11340002

Torres-Olivera, A. (2003). La gestión por procesos asistenciales integrales: Una estrategia necesaria. *Atencion Primaria, 31*(9), 561–563. doi:10.1016/S0212-6567(03)79216-6 PMID:12783744

Van der Meijden, M., Tange, H., Troost, J., & Hasman, A. (2003). Determinants of success of inpatient clinical information systems: A literature review. *Journal of the American Medical Informatics Association : JAMIA, 10*(3), 235–243. doi:10.1197/jamia.M1094 PMID:12626373

Van Walraven, C., Mamdani, M., Fang, J., & Austin, P. (2004). Continuity of care and patient outcomes after hospital discharge. *Journal of General Internal Medicine, 19*(6), 624–631. doi:10.1111/j.1525-1497.2004.30082.x PMID:15209600

Wagner, E., Scott, S., & Galliers, R. (2006). The creation of 'best practice' software: Myth, reality and ethics. *Information and Organization, 16*(3), 251–275. doi:10.1016/j.infoandorg.2006.04.001

Ward, J., & Daniel, E. (2012). *Benefits Management: How to increase the Business Value of Your IT Projects* (2nd ed.). John Wiley and Sons., doi:10.1002/9781119208242

Ward, J., Taylor, P., & Bond, P. (1996). Evaluation and realization of IS/IT benefits: An empirical study of current practice. *European Journal of Information Systems, 4*(4), 214–225. doi:10.1057/ejis.1996.3

Wears, R. L., & Berg, M. (2005). Computer technology and clinical works: Still waiting for Godot. *Journal of the American Medical Association, 293*(10), 1261–1263. doi:10.1001/jama.293.10.1261 PMID:15755949

Weick, K. E., & Sutcliffe, K. M. (2001). *Managing the unexpected: Assuring high performance in an age of complexity*. Jossey-Bass.

West, B., Lyon, M., McBain, M., & Gass, J. (2004). Evaluation of a clinical leadership initiative. *Nursing Standard, 19*(5), 33–41. doi:10.7748/ns.19.5.33.s61 PMID:15524254

West, L. A., & Courtney, J. F. (1993). The Information Problems in Organisations - A Research Model for the Value of Information and Information Systems. *Decision Sciences, 24*(2), 229–251. doi:10.1111/j.1540-5915.1993.tb00473.x

Westbrook, J., Braithwaite, J., Iedema, R., & Coiera, E. (2004). Evaluating the impact of information communication technologies on complex organizational systems: A multi-disciplinary multi-method framework. *Studies in Health Technology and Informatics, 107*, 1323–1327. PMID:15361029

WHO. (2005). *Connecting for Health: Global Vision, Local Insight*. Report for the World Summit on the Information Society. Geneva, Switzerland: World Health Organization. https://www.who.int/ehealth/resources/wsis_report/en/

WHO. (2006). *Building foundations for eHealth: Progress of Member States*. Geneva, Switzerland: World Health Organization. https://www.who.int/goe/publications/build_foundations/en/

WHO. (2011). *Global Health and Ageing*. National Institutes of Health publication n°.11.7737/oct.2011. National Institute on Aging, World Health Organization. https://www.who.int/ageing/publications/global_health.pdf, 19/07/2017.

WHO. (2015). *World report on ageing and health*. Geneva, Switzerland: World Health Organization. Available at: http://apps.who.int/iris/bitstream/10665/186463/1/9789240694811_eng.pdf?ua=1, 19/07/2017.

Wootton, R. (2009). The future use of telehealth in the developing world. In *Telehealth in the Developing World*. Royal Society of Medicine Press.

Yasnoff, W. A., Humpheys, B. L., Overhage, J. M., Detmer, D. E., Brennan, P. F., Morris, R. W., & Fanning, J. P. (2004). A consensus action agenda for achieving the national health information infrastructure. *Journal of the American Medical Informatics Association : JAMIA, 11*(49), 332–338. doi:10.1197/jamia.M1616 PMID:15187075

Yeo, K. T. (2002). Critical failure factors in information system projects. *International Journal of Project Management, 20*(3), 241–246. doi:10.1016/S0263-7863(01)00075-8

Yusof, M. M., Kuljis, J., Papazafeiropoulou, A., & Stergioulas, L. K. (2008). An evaluation framework for health information systems: Human, organization and technology-fit factors (HOT-fit). *International Journal of Medical Informatics, 77*(6), 386–398. doi:10.1016/j.ijmedinf.2007.08.011 PMID:17964851

Zhang, M. J. (2005). Information systems, strategic flexibility and firm performance: An empirical investigation. *Journal of Engineering and Technology Management, 22*(3), 163–184. doi:10.1016/j.jengtecman.2005.06.003

ADDITIONAL READING

Agarwal, N., & Rathod, U. (2006). Defining success for software projects: An exploratory revelation. *International Journal of Project Management, 24*(4), 358–370. doi:10.1016/j.ijproman.2005.11.009

Ammenwerth, E., & de Keizer, N. (2005). An inventory of evaluation studies of information technology in healthcare: Trends in evaluation research 1982–2002. *Methods of Information in Medicine, 44*, 44–56. doi:10.1055-0038-1633922 PMID:15778794

Berghout, E., Nijland, M., & Grant, K. (2005). Seven ways to get your favoured IT project accepted politics in IT evaluation. *The Electronic Journal of Information System Evaluation, 8*(1), 31–40.

Bose, R. (2003). Knowledge management-enabled health care management: Capabilities, infrastructure, and decision-making. *Expert Systems with Applications, 24*(1), 59–71. doi:10.1016/S0957-4174(02)00083-0

Bukachi, F., & Pakenham-Walsh, N. (2007). Information technology for health in developing countries. *Chest, 132*(5), 1624–1630. doi:10.1378/chest.07-1760 PMID:17998362

Cliff, B. (2012, September/October). Using Technology to Enhance Patient-Centered Care. *Journal of Healthcare Management, 57*(5), 301–303. doi:10.1097/00115514-201209000-00003 PMID:23087992

Dick, R. S., Steen, E. B., & Detmer, D. E. (Eds.). (1997). *The Computer-Based Patient Record: An Essential Technology for Health Care* (revised edition). Committee on Improving the Patient Record, National Academy of Sciences.

Eysenbach, G. (2001). What is e-health? *Journal of Medical Internet Research*, *3*(2), e20. doi:10.2196/jmir.3.2.e20 PMID:11720962

Glaser, J. (2005). More on management's role in IT project failure. *Healthcare Financial Management*, *59*(1), 82–84. PMID:15689017

Heeks, R. B. (2006). Health Information Systems: Failure, success and improvisation. *International Journal of Medical Informatics*, *75*(2), 125–137. doi:10.1016/j.ijmedinf.2005.07.024 PMID:16112893

Jensen, T. B. (2013). Design Principles for Achieving Integrated Healthcare Information Systems. *Health Informatics Journal*, *19*(1), 29–45. doi:10.1177/1460458212448890 PMID:23486824

Kaplan, B., & Harris-Salamone, K. D. (2009). Health IT success and failure: Recommendations from literature and an AMIA workshop. *Journal of the American Medical Informatics Association : JAMIA*, *16*(3), 291–299. doi:10.1197/jamia.M2997 PMID:19261935

Kumar, S., & Preetha, G.S. (2012). Health Promotion: An Effective Tool for Global Health. *Indian Journal of Community Medicine*, *37*(1), 5–12.

Lenz, R., & Reichert, M. (2007). IT support for healthcare processes: Premises, challenges, perspectives. *Data & Knowledge Engineering*, *61*(1), 39–58. doi:10.1016/j.datak.2006.04.007

Lewis, D., Hodge, N., Gamage, D., & Whittaker, M. (2011). Understanding the role of technology in health information systems. *Pacific Health Dialog*, *18*(1), 144–154. PMID:23240349

Mickan, S. M. (2005). Evaluating the effectiveness of health care teams. *Australian Health Review*, *29*(2), 211–217. doi:10.1071/AH050211 PMID:15865572

Munthe, C. (2008). The Goals of Public Health: An Integrated, Multidimensional Model. *Public Health Ethics*, *1*(1), 39–52. doi:10.1093/phe/phn006

Rahimi, B., & Vimarlund, V. (2007). Methods to evaluate health information systems in health care settings: A literature review. *Journal of Medical Systems*, *35*(5), 397–432. doi:10.100710916-007-9082-z PMID:17918694

Robinson, C. (2007). Clinician adoption of healthcare information technology. *Canadian Nursing Informatics*, *2*(1), 4–21.

KEY TERMS AND DEFINITIONS

IS/IT for Healthcare: Refers to any tool or framework that enhances the communication, processing or transmission of information by electronic means for improving human health (Bukachi and Pakenham-Walsh, 2007).

Project Management: Is the process within organization where temporary endeavours are undertaken for beneficial change and added value (Nokes, 2007), requiring a multi-dimensional set of skills and a professional practice of managerial knowledge (Hodgson, 2002; Kerzner, 2013).

Project Success: Is measured by its efficiency in the short term and its effectiveness in achieving the expected results in the medium and the long term (Jugdev et al., 2001; Müller & Jugdev, 2012).

Chapter 15
A Comparative Study of Different Digitalization Indexes

Olena Korzhyk
Universidade Autónoma de Lisboa, Portugal

Jorge Vareda Gomes
iD https://orcid.org/0000-0003-0656-9284
Universidade Lusófona, Lisboa, Portugal

Gonçalo João
CICEE, Universidade Autónoma de Lisboa, Portugal

ABSTRACT

Digitalization is nowadays one of the fastest developing processes. The adoption of digital technologies can provide innumerous opportunities for the organizations to evolve and gain competitive advantage by leveraging technologies to respond to dynamic expectations and demands. Information about the country's digitalization level is essential to decision makers in both public and private organizations. It can present insights into which areas need the most investment, and furthermore to gain feedback on the outcomes of these investments. To assess the evolution of this process in different countries, various indexes were proposed and employed by different corporations. Indexes are analyzed thoroughly by their structure, coverage, weights, methodology, and ranking. The result of the practical work is an equivalence table which shows the percentage of their similarity. Additionally, a new digitalization index is proposed, based on the result of the previous comparison, which can be applied to analyze both public and private sector of the country's digitalization level.

INTRODUCTION

Digitalization is becoming an inevitable part of the growth of entrepreneurship in the modern world (Satalkina & Steiner, 2020; Ungureanu, 2021). Digitalization assessment is not yet used in all countries and prevents them from leading in innovation, multi-channel service delivery and advancement

DOI: 10.4018/978-1-6684-9151-5.ch015

in e-commerce and the digital economy (Shin, Ho & Pak, 2020). Although digital technologies still do not have a recognized model for evaluating economic effects, growth and development (Stremousova & Buchinskaia, 2019), many studies have been carried out about the impact of the digital transition on specific sectors and processes of the economy (Tarasova, Averina & Pecherskaya, 2020). This work focuses on the nature of digitalization and the type of assessments that are carried out on digitalization processes. For this, it is important to define the digitalization, compare digitalization rates and find the most ideal among the suggested variants (Kotarba, 2017). Four digital indexes were chosen, considering their importance and nature. DESI (European Union) and the ICT Development Index (International Telecommunications Union) which belong to the public sector and the DiGiX (BBVA) and CISCO Digital Readiness (CISCO) to the private sector. Digital indices vary geographically and are compared by territory (Konovalova, Kuzmina & Zhironkin, 2020). The assessment of digitalization in different regions can vary dramatically due to political situations, ideologies, cultures and levels of development (Petrenko et al., 2017). As digitalization is a recent process (Lederer, Knapp & Schott, 2017), the research is based on the latest data and definitions. This work can be applied to all demographic groups and communities. The most specific aspect is to develop an ideal digital assessment of the country, company and location. This is done through the verification of equivalence between the most used digital indexes and the conclusion of the most important aspects for this process (Kotarba, 2017).

BACKGROUND

Digitization, Digitalization, Digital Transformation, and the Digital Economy

Digitization, digitalization, and, later, digital transformation are drivers of change in the corporate world, as they establish new internet-based technologies with implications for society (Unruh & Kiron, 2017).

Digitization (i.e., the process of converting analog data into digital datasets) is the framework for digitalization, which is defined as the exploitation of digital opportunities. Digital transformation is then defined as the process that is used to restructure economies, organizations and society (Annarelli et al., 2021); Brennen & Kreiss, 2016; Unruh & Kiron, 2017). Digitization and digitalization are often used interchangeably, but there are important conceptual differences. Digitization is the technical process of converting analogue signals to digital signals (Tilson, Lyytinen, & Sørensen, 2010). Digitalization is the sociotechnical process of leveraging digitized products or systems to develop new organizational procedures, business models, or commercial offerings (Brynjolfsson & McAfee, 2014). While digitization describes a technology or system of technologies in terms of what it is and its capabilities, digitalization accounts for why that technology is relevant to a specific process or organization (Saarikko et al., 2020).

For Petrenko (2017), digitalization is the transition from the analog form of transferring information to the digital form, with the assumption of not only digitizing, but also creating a new innovative product with new consumer properties and functionality. The process of digitalization leads to digital transformation that is defined as a process of restructuring economies, institutions, and society (Annarelli et al., 2021). Unruh and Kiron (2017) define digital transformation as the restructuring at the level of economic systems, institutions and society that takes place through digital diffusion. In recent decades, global companies have not only faced technological changes that have major impacts on business, greater flexibility, responsiveness and individualization of products, but they have also presented enormous challenges, namely, in rapid technological change, increasing complexity and changing customer preferences and legal requirements (Sidorenko & Khisamova, 2020). This new situation has transformed an increasingly challenging corporate context (Lerch & Gotsch, 2015). Informational progress in everyday life, with the rapid development of information technologies and the internet of things, has already reached all sectors of the economy and we are rapidly moving towards the digital economy (UNCTAD, 2019). Digital transformation belongs to "Industry 4.0" in the sphere of manufacturing and service development, designed to create "intelligent manufacturing" and integrate it into all aspects of human life, customizing it to the tasks of everyone (Bataev & Aleksandrova, 2020). To achieve the benefits associated with a successful adoption of digital transformation, companies need to take the initiative and develop specific capabilities at various organizational and operational levels of their business model (Eller et al., 2020). The digital transformation increases the profitability of the company by simplifying processes and interactions within the company. The technologies linked to the digital transformation such as big data, artificial intelligence, cloud computing, social networks and the internet of things, offer new uses based on innovation and focused on the needs of the consumer (Mahraz et al., 2019). The term "digital economy" is increasingly heard by politicians, businessmen and the media. It is the physical transformation of information, with the help of digital devices, to create a new form of communication, in addition to processing the enormous amount of information that can be provided from anywhere in the world (Nemoto & López González, 2021). The digital economy describes an economic system where the use of information and communication technology is widespread, and which includes: (Nemoto & López González, 2021):

- Basic infrastructure (high-speed Internet access, computing power, security services),
- E-business (business models with high use of ICT for front and back-office functions),
- E-Commerce (use of ICT in business-to-business (B2B), business-to-consumer (B2C) and consumer-to-consumer (C2C) transactions).

The digital economy is growing rapidly (Lederer, Knapp & Schott, 2017). Daily, issues related to the digitalization of the economy are discussed by national governments, international organizations, large corporations, small and medium-sized enterprises (UNCTAD, 2019). The size of the digital economy is estimated to range from 4.5% to 15.5% of the world's GDP (UNCTAD, 2019). Investors are actively funding technology companies such as Apple, Amazon, Google, Facebook and Microsoft that represent 21% of all publicly traded US companies (Galloway, 2020). The main role in this process is played by the application of production digitization, implementation of technologies related to Industry 4.0 with big data analysis, using artificial intelligence and industrial internet of things (UNCTAD, 2019). Expectations regarding the economic effectiveness of implementing these technologies are optimistic (Gronum, Steen & Verreynne, 2016). According to researchers, investment in the internet of things in 20 countries (US, Switzerland, Finland, Sweden, Norway, Netherlands, Denmark, UK, Japan, Germany, Australia, Republic of Korea, Canada, China, France, Spain, Brazil, Italy, India and Russia) will provide additional GDP growth of $10.6 trillion (Purdy & Davarzani, 2015). According to World Economic Forum (2016), every US dollar devoted to investment in digital technology over the past 30 years has increased GDP by US$20. And every dollar devoted to non-digital investment has increased GDP by just US$3 (Xu & Cooper, 2017). It is expected that by 2025, 24.3% of the world GDP will receive digital technologies such as artificial intelligence and cloud computing (Kumar, 2019). The characteristic feature of the digital economy is its connection with the on-demand economy, which foresees not the sale of goods and services, but their access now or when necessary. On the supply side, new technologies are emerging in all industries. For example, big data usage technology identifies the needs and products desired by users. Also, 3D printing technology helps to achieve custom production and design. The boundary between supply and demand has become increasingly blurred. For industry leaders, it is necessary to provide information that they have a supervisory board and executive with digital expertise. Must be multigenerational, diverse, and experienced enough to advise on rapidly changing business and technology topics such as cybersecurity. Digital transformation must be conducted at the CEO and board level of the organization. From a business perspective, the organization must ensure that it is working with industry clusters, has a business strategy consistent with its role in the industry and the implementation of digitization will be rewarded by superior performance. From a talent and leadership perspective, industry leaders must address both technical and creative digital skills in talent strategy, recruit the best talent, and have an action plan to assess employee effectiveness (Laurens, 2019). For governments and policy makers the tasks may wary. They must accomplish the government operations and mission. Government operations mean that the customer service model is user friendly, using open standards and easily accessible in line with industry digital best practices, Also, there should exist the platform for rapid multi-stakeholder interaction and corporate consultation; clarity on the implication of the global security, privacy and cross border data flows in the industry, timeline to coordinate and resolve challenges with industry stakeholders (World Economic Forum, 2016). Government mission is in understanding the implications for the industry when addressing the societal opportunities, implementing flexible policy frameworks to realize benefits in the short and medium term. Policy makers should consider for policies that are currently subject to legal challenge and increase the relevance of regulations and policy frameworks to foster innovation while protecting customer interests (World Economic Forum, 2016). For consumer industry there is a huge open market for digital transformation. There are four digital transformation themes – consumer data flow and value capture, experience economy, omni-channel retail and digital operating model (Rachinger et al., 2019).

Similarities and Differences Between Indexes and ID Rating

The main indicators measuring the level of the digital economy are analyzed here. It is shown that each of the indices has different methodological approaches to determining the level of digitization and contains several factors (Table 1).

Table 1. Indexes of digital development (Kononova,2015)

Initials	Name of Index	Source	1st Publication	Countries Covered	Partial Indicators
DESI	Digital Economy and Society Index	European Union	2014	28	33
CISCO	Digital Readiness Index	CISCO Company	2016	141	30
DIGIX	The Digitization Index	BBVA	2015	100	22
IDI	Information and Computer Technology Development Index	International Trade Union	2006	180	13

The most developed countries also have the highest levels of digitization of their own economies, with ample access to high-quality internet, a high level of scientific and technological capacity development and a wide access to information (Kononova, 2015).

METHODOLOGY

Case Study

The methodology used in this research, which consists of the use of one or more qualitative methods of collecting information. The sources of information are predominantly organizational sources, such as conference materials, reports and strategy documents, government sources, like publications, national statistics and reports, as well as printed or online articles. The main methodological comparison tools are clear explanations about the structure of digitization indexes and their respective sub-indicators. Sub-indicators may vary in names, but data used for assessment may be the same or very similar.

Digital Economy and Society Index (DESI)

The Digital Economy and Society Index (DESI) is a composite index prepared annually by the European Commission since 2015 that seeks to assess the digital competitiveness of Member States, following its evolution over time (European Commission, 2020). The index measures the digital maturity of the 28 EU economies through a set of quantitative indicators that make up the final score.

DESI 2020 considers 37 indicators and is divided into the following dimensions: (1) Connectivity; (2) Human Capital; (3) Use of Internet Services; (4) Integration of Digital Technology; and (5) Digital Public Services. The progress of the country is defined by the sum of all these parameters (Table 2).

Methodology of evaluation (European Commission, 2020) uses 3 level structure of evaluation, dimension, sub-dimension, and indicator (Appendix 1). The indicators descriptions, breakdown, units of measurement, sources of information and also the weighting of indicators (Appendix 1). In the Figure 1 is presented the ranking of EU countries with the DESI index, with reference to the average value of the index (European Commission, 2020).

Digitalization Index (DiGiX)

The DiGiX Digitalization index was created by BBVA company (Banco Bilbao Vizcaya Argentina) and it is considered as one of the largest financial institutions of the world (Cámara, 2020). DiGiX index evaluates the behaviour of institutions and agents and factors that help the community to use the information and communication technology to increase the competitiveness (Cámara & Tuesta, 2017).

DiGiX aims to capture the digitization status over the world in order to compare digitization degrees across countries and identify areas requiring action. Collaboration of governments, financial institutions, and regulatory bodies will be necessary to enhance digitization to serve society (Cámara, 2020).

DIGIX analyses 100 countries through six main components (Table 3): affordability, adoption of users and enterprises, costs, regulations, infrastructure and contents (Kravchenko et al., 2019). Each dimension is in turn divided into several individual indicators. Each dimension summarizes information of several individual indicators (from 1 up to 6). The indicators included in the index are grouped in six dimensions

Table 2. Digital economy and society index (DESI) (European Commission, 2020a)

Dimension	Explanation
Connectivity	Connectivity is the dimension, which revels the level of fixed broadband coverage, what is the percentage of households which use broadbands, DSL, cable, MiMAx and FTTP. Next is the mobile broadband, described in number of people who use mobile data per 100 people. Also, the internet connection is about speed, which is enough when it is more than 30 Mbps. The last sub-factor of connectivity is affordability, comparison of fixed price of broadband between 12 and 30 Mbps.
Human capital	Human capital is the degree to which citizens of the European union can use the Internet and other tools and services. Use of internet parameter indicates the productivity of people in the time of using the digital providers.
Digital public service	Digital public service is a branch of so-called eGovernment. It is about the modernization of the public administration for better serving of citizens. Connectivity factor is about the broad infrastructure and the quality of it.
Use of Internet	Use of Internet value is the content, communication and transactions. People search different content in digital tools, like news, music, video, games. Lately the communication is getting the higher rank, and e-communication consists of social networking, mailing and video calls. The transactions online are shopping or banking. Digital skills can be basic, advanced or developing. Basic skills element in the table shows the amount of Internet users who access at least once a week and people who are using editing, mailing or installing. Advanced and developing skills already have higher level, and people who use Internet or tools already not only for personal use on everyday basis, but they make certain contribution into development of digitalization or use the means of it for educative purposes in other spheres of science. Such people are Information and Communication Technology specialists (ICT specialist hereinafter) like ICT professionals, technicians, service managers. Also, to the advance users are connected people with degree of science, technology, mathematics, engineering.
Integration of Digital Technology	Integration of Digital Technology value includes business digitalization and ecommerce. Electronic formation sharing is the first characteristic of the business digitalization. It is number of businesses who used software's for resource planning or sharing the information between the functional departments like accounting, production, marketing and planning. Second characteristic is the Radio Frequency Identification (RFID) ratio which is the extend of technologies for delivery or identification of goods. Next goes the social media, when businesses use more than social media, for example networks, websites, blogs, and many others. The business should create own profile or account and fulfil the legislative requirements for advertisement. Invoices which are not made manually by the company, but digitally in standard forms and they are being automatically processed.

Figure 1. Ranking of countries DESI index
Source: European Commission (2020).

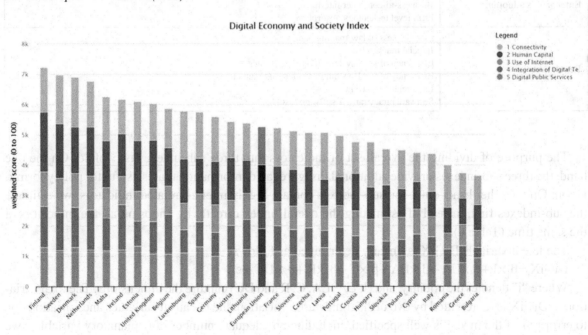

that represent three broad pillars: supply conditions (infrastructure and costs), demand conditions (user, government and enterprise adoption), and institutional environment (regulation). DIGIX differs from other indexes in the literature due to the lack of human capital indicators. A more restricted definition was chosen and only variables directly related to digitization are considered. DIGIX assumes that behind a set of correlated variables, there is an underlying latent structure that can be identified through a latent variable, as in the case of digitization. Weighting indicators or sub-indexes is critical to maximizing the information from a data set included in an index. A good composite index should contain important information from all indicators but should not be heavily biased towards one or more of these indicators. The two-stage principal components methodology was applied to estimate the degree of digitization as an indexing strategy. The dataset contains causal variables that summarize the information for digitization and each causal variable relates to different dimensions that define digitization.

Table 3. DIGIX index components (adapted from Cámara & Tuesta, 2017)

Components	Indicators
Affordability	Fixed broadband internet tariffs Internet & telephony competition
Infrastructure	3G or more mobile network coverage International internet bandwidth (in bits/s per internet user and in Mbit/s) Secure internet services
Contents	Government Online Service Index
User's adoption	Active mobile-broadband subscriptions Fixed (wired)-broadband subscriptions Use of virtual social networks Households with internet Individual using internet
Enterprise's adoption	Business-to-business internet use Business-to-consumer internet use Firm-level technology absorption
Regulation	Effectiveness of law-making bodies Judicial independence Efficiency of legal system in setting disputes Efficiency of legal system in challenging regulations Laws relating to ICTs Software piracy rate, % software installed

The purpose of dividing the overall set of indicators into three sub-indexes is twofold. On the one hand, the three sub-indexes provide additional disaggregated information that is useful for policy formulation. On the other hand, since the sub-indexes contain highly inter correlated indicators, we estimate the sub-indexes first, instead of estimating the overall index directly by choosing all the indicators at the same time (Table 4).

The latent variable DiGiX is linearly determined as follows:

$$DiGiX_i = \beta_1 \times I_i + \beta_2 \times UA_i + \beta_3 \times EA_i + \beta_4 \times C_i + \beta_5 \times R_i + \beta_6 \times DC_i + \varepsilon_i$$

Where "i" denotes the country, and (I, UA, EA, C, R and DC) capture the dimensions. The total variation in DiGiX is represented by two orthogonal parts: variation due to causal variables and variation due to error (ε_i). If the model is well specified, including an adequate number of explanatory variables, we

Table 4. DiGiX variance by indicator (Cámara & Tuesta, 2017)

% Explained Variance	First Component
Infrastructure (I)	47%
Costs (C)	58%
Regulation (R)	80%
User´s adoption (UA)	80%
Enterprise's adoption (EA)	90%
Digital Content (DC)	100%
BBVA-DIGIX	64%

can reasonably assume that the total variation in DiGiX can be largely explained by the variation in the causal variables. The relative weights (importance) of each dimension, β_j, in the DiGiX are computed as:

$$\beta_j = \frac{\sum_{j=1} \lambda j \Phi jk}{\sum_{j=1} \lambda j}$$

Where λ_j represents the variance of the jth principal component (weights), for our index, the first component and k the number of variables in the overall index or in each dimension. The Appendix 2 presents the weights by indicator and by dimension. The application of a min-max transformation preserves the order of, and the relative distance between, the scores. Each score in the DiGiX is between 0 and 1, with higher values representing better performance.

$$Z_{ij} = \frac{xij - \min\left(xj\right)}{\max\left(xj\right) - \min\left(xj\right)}$$

The Figure 2 presented the countries according with the DiGiX index.

ICT Development Index (IDI)

The ICT Development Index (IDI) is a composite index that has been reported, since 2009, by the International Telecommunication Union (ITU, 2018). The index is intended to measure the progress of each country towards the information society, respectively it is as a tool able to describe the current state of development of the ICT sector (Preda et al., 2019). IDI framework includes 3 dimensions which represent the combination of factors needed for each country in the transformation process: the availability of ICT structure and access, the level of ICT usage, and the capability to use ICTs effectively.

The IDI has 3 sub-indexes and 11 indicators. The "ICT access" sub-index includes 5 infrastructure and access indicators, the "ICT use" sub-index comprises 3 intensity and usage indicators, and the "ICT skills" sub-index includes 3 proxy indicators showing relevant skills for ICTs. Each IDI sub-index is

Figure 2. DIGIX comparison among countries
Source: Cámara and Tuesta (2017)

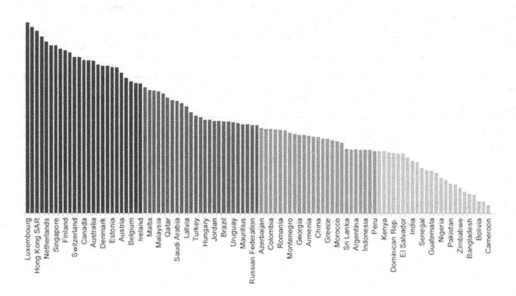

calculated as a simple average of its indicators (ITU, 2017). The list and description of the ICT indicators is as follows:

ICT Access

International Internet bandwidth (bit/s) per internet user

It is the total used Internet bandwidth capacity, calculated in megabits, taking to consideration average of incoming and outgoing internet traffic (Preda et al., 2019).

Percentage of household with computer

Computers are desktop, tablet, laptops and other similar. Telephone devices as smartphones and mobile phones, smart TVs are not included. Computer of the household is not necessary belongs to the owner but is considered as an asset of the household.

Percentage of households with Internet access

This index includes the availability of Internet for all members of the households at any time.

1. Population covered by at least 3G mobile networks
2. Fixed-broadband subscriptions by speed tiers, equal to or above 10 Mbit/s (Preda et al., 2019)

ICT Use

Percentage of individuals using the Internet

Individuals who used Internet in the last three months by any device. This is still not very developed indicator, as data is taken from the national statistic offices and some developing countries do not conduct this statistic.

Active mobile-broadband subscriptions per 100 inhabitants

It is a sum of dedicated (USB modems or dongles) and standard (with access to Internet via HTTP) mobile subscriptions, used on computer or handset devices.

1. Mobile-broadband Internet traffic (per mobile-broadband subscription)
2. Fixed-broadband Internet traffic (per fixed-broadband subscription)
3. Mobile phone ownership (Preda et al., 2019)

ICT Skills

Mean years of schooling

Secondary gross enrolment ratio

This ratio is explaining the enrolment to certain education level, regardless of the age. It is calculated as a percentage of school-age population to the actual level of education.

Tertiary gross enrolment (Preda et al., 2019).

There are five steps in methodology of ICT index calculation: imputation of missing data, normalization of data, weighting and aggregation, calculating the IDI and sensitivity analysis. There are various techniques to calculate the missing data. Mostly it is used the hot-deck imputation to impute the missing data. The similar characteristics for the hot-deck imputation are Gross National Income per capita and the geographic location (ITU, 2018). Normalization of data is needed because the unit of measurement should be the same for all sub-indexes, otherwise it will not be possible to align the data. Normalization procedure can allow to check the countered progress over the time. The distance to the reference measure is a chosen method of normalization (ITU, 2019). Reference measure is a goalpost, or the perfect

measure. To set up the correct evaluation, it is necessary to have the table of weights of indicators (Appendix 2). Sensitivity analysis was carried out to investigate the robustness of the Index results in terms of the relative position in the overall ranking, using different combinations of methods and techniques to compute the Index (Figure 3).

Figure 3. The EU 28 countries ranked by their ICT development index 2017
Source: ITU (2017)

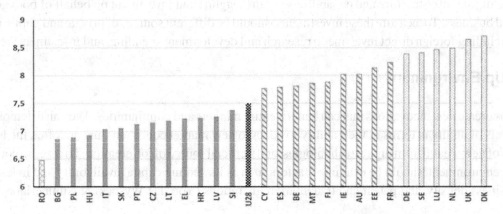

CISCO Global Digital Readiness Index

CISCO provides recent reports and profound studies of digitalization as the main profit for this company is consulting and cybersecurity, as well as selling the hardware. The information is taken from the CISCO Global Digital Readiness Index 2019 Report (CISCO, 2020). The document consists of:

Basic Needs

The true value of technology and infrastructure is delivered through a population's ability to take advantage of it. Without a population's basic needs met, communities are not able to reap the benefits of technology. To measure a population's basic needs, the assessed data are relating to life expectancy, the mortality rate of children under five years of age, and access to basic services such as electricity and safe drinking water (Yoo, De Wysocki & Cumberland, 2018).

Human Capital

The ability to utilize and create advanced digital services is determined in part by the digital skills level within the workforce. There are examined four factors to determine the presence of an appropriately skilled labour force that is available to support digital innovation: the total labour force participation rate, adult literacy rate, and the country's education quality and average years of schooling.

Ease of Doing Business

Human capital skills can only contribute to the economy if people are gainfully employed, so having a thriving business ecosystem is another key determinant of a country's digital readiness. This was measured by examining the ease of doing business within each country, including factors such as: local rule of law, the Ease of Doing Business Index, the Logistics Performance Index (LPI) infrastructure rating, and the time it takes businesses to obtain access to electricity.

Business and Government Investment

Building digital infrastructure and capabilities requires significant investment on behalf of both government and business. To measure these investments, should be different sources of private and public investment, including foreign direct investment, research and development spending, and investment freedom.

Start-Up Environment

Start-ups create new innovations that can benefit entire markets and communities. They also demonstrate high levels of agility in terms of their ability to adapt to new market conditions and are often the leading creators of new wealth from digital technologies, and a crucial source of job creation. To assess a country's start-up environment, should be examined factors such as its venture capital availability and investment, new business density, and patent and trademark registrations (Yoo, De Wysocki & Cumberland, 2018)

Technology Adoption

In the technology adoption indicator, it is evaluated the demand for digital products and services. The sub-indicators are mobile device penetration, internet usage and cloud services, such as cloud service spent and IT forecast data.

Technology Infrastructure

Technology infrastructure means the infrastructure available to enable the digital activities and conceited consumers. It is measured by the level of mobile and fixed broadband subscriptions, secure internet servers and networking services (Yoo, De Wysocki & Cumberland, 2018).

In the methodology of the CISCO company report it is mentioned that they use the company use the holistic method using the sub-indicators, apply to the 141 countries, and have a rating scale of 0 to 25. The datapoints for the Cisco Digital Readiness Index are reputable sources, such as United Nations, World Economic Forum, World Bank, Heritage Foundation, International Monetary Fund, Centre for American Entrepreneurship, International Labour Organization, World Health Organization and World Justice Project (CISCO, 2020). In the Appendix 3 is shown the metrics and sources for evaluating each component of the CISCO index and the sub-indicators and indicators percentages of Cisco Digital Readiness Index. This information is going to be used to find out the equivalences of indexes in the following chapter. Below is introduced the top five and bottom five results of Cisco Digital Readiness index (Figure 4).

Figure 4. Top 5 of Cisco digital readiness index
Source: Adapted from CISCO (2020)

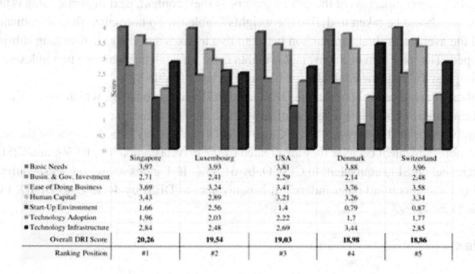

	Singapore	Luxembourg	USA	Denmark	Switzerland
■ Basic Needs	3,97	3,93	3,81	3,88	3,96
■ Busin. & Gov. Investment	2,71	2,41	2,29	2,14	2,48
■ Ease of Doing Business	3,69	3,24	3,41	3,76	3,58
■ Human Capital	3,43	2,89	3,21	3,26	3,34
■ Start-Up Environment	1,66	2,56	1,4	0,79	0,87
■ Technology Adoption	1,96	2,03	2,22	1,7	1,77
■ Technology Infrastructure	2,84	2,48	2,69	3,44	2,85
Overall DRI Score	20,26	19,54	19,03	18,98	18,86
Ranking Position	#1	#2	#3	#4	#5

Singapore is known as the country with the highest quality of life and in the CISCO analysis it is taking the first place by the level of basic needs, ease of doing business and human capital. Slightly below Singapore, Luxembourg. USA, Denmark and Switzerland show with the win formula of high results in ease of doing business, basic needs, human capital and technology infrastructure.

DISCUSSION

Each index consists of indicators and contains on each indicator there is one or more sub indicators. To make the comparison as accurate as possible, the sub-indicators of the proposed four indexes were compared and considered each ones' percentage weights. This information was taken from the tables of weights from de previous chapter. These values are needed not only to understand more precisely the equivalence between indexes, but also for defining key sub-indicators, which have higher value to consider.

Sub-Indicators Equivalence

Some of indexes have a lot of matching sub-indicators by their content. By the comparison (Table 5) we can define that the most common evaluators, such as: mobile broadband coverage with at least 3G connection, fixed and mobile broadband subscriptions, internet user skills, level of business digitalization in the technology adoption, cloud database, and logistics, e-commerce availability, e-government and research and development spending.

The sub-indicators differ, in the first place, because of the difference in definition of the organizations that created them. Indexes of public organizations such as DESI and ICT development differ in the assessment of society's advanced skills, online banking, mobile and fixed internet traffic. Private indexes such as DiGiX and CISCO differ in the assessment of indicators such as use of social media, judicial independence, efficiency of the legal system in resolving challenging disputes and regulations, patents and trademark registrations, and secure Internet servers. After comparing the sub-indicators by content, the next step will be to define the weights. Although the sub-indicators are matched by their content, they have different weights for the index itself.

After making the comparison of the sub-indicators by their content, next important step is to find out the equivalence should be taken to define the weights (Table 6). To normalize the sub-indicators were considered the average. A dual comparison between two indexes and their all-matching sub-indicators was developed. The total sum of the average weights is the equivalence between two indexes.

Following matrix of all the equivalences between indexes (Table 7)

The highest equivalence is between the DESI and DIGIX index, 69.85%, which means that the indicators of these indexes not only are very similar by the context and data.

High equivalence is also between DIGIX and CISCO indexes, 66.19%. It might be the reason that indexes are more equivalent because they are created by the private companies, BBVA and CISCO. With a little difference, DESI is equivalent to CISCO, by 61.85%. ICT index shows the least equivalence by the matching indicators to all other indexes. It is equivalent to DESI by 44.13%, to DIGIX by 43.85% and to CISCO by 41.99%.

New Index

After analysing the equivalences between the most used digitalization evaluation indexes, it can be concluded which factors have been the most valuable in the index calculation.

The indicators and sub-indicators weights are based on the average weight of similar matching indicators from the compared indexes. The proposed index has the following indicators:

- Connection - this indicator is displaying network coverage, broadband, and speeds.

Table 5. Equivalence of indicators

Sub-Indicator	DESI	%	DIGIX	%	ICT	%	CISCO	%
A	Broadband price	6,25	Fixed broadband tariffs	4,5				
B	Mobile broadband	6,25	3G or more Mobile network coverage	6	Population covered by at least 3G mobile networks	8		
C	Internet use	5	Individuals using the Internet	3,8	Percentage of individuals using the Internet	8	Internet usage	4
D	Internet user skills	12,5			Percentage of individuals using the Internet Secondary gross enrolment ratio Tertiary gross enrolment	6,67 6,67 6,67	Average years of schooling The education quality	5,34 5,34
E	Advanced skills and development (ICT graduate specialists)	12,5						
F	Activities online	5	Use of virtual social networks	3,8				
G	Transaction (banking shopping)	5	Business to Consumer use	6,33				
H	Business digitalization	10	Firm level technology adaptation	6,33				
I	eCommerce	10	Business to Business Consumer use	6,33			Investment Freedom Venture capital availability	4 4
J	eGovernment	15	Government online service Index Effectiveness of law-making bodies	20			Research and development spending Private and Public investment	4 4
K	Fixed broadband take-up	6,25	Fixed (wired) broadband subscription	3,8	Fixed broadband subscriptions by speed	8	Level of fixed broadband subscriptions	4
L			Internet and telephony competition	4,5	Fixed broadband subscriptions by speed	8	Mobile device penetration	4
M			Households with Internet	3,8	Percentage of households with Internet	8	Household internet access	4

continued on following page

Table 5. Continued

Sub-Indicator	DESI	%	DIGIX	%	ICT	%	CISCO	%
N			Judicial independence	3				
O			Efficiency of legal system in settling the disputes and regulations	6				
P			Laws regarding ICT	3			Local rule of law	4
Q			International Internet bandwidth	6	International Internet bandwidth	8		
R			Software privacy rate and percentage of software installed	3			Patent and trademark registrations	4
S			Secure Internet servers	6			Secure Internet servers	4
T	Mobile broadband	6,25	Active mobile broadband subscriptions	3,8	Active mobile broadband Subscriptions per 100 inhabitants	8	Level of mobile subscriptions	4
U					Mobile and fixed internet traffic	16		
V					Percentage of household with computer	8		
W							Life expectancy	5,33
X							Mortality rate	5,33
Y							Access to basic services	5,33
Z							The total labour participation rate	5,33

- Government regulation – includes the government online and privacy and ICT goals.
- Business integration – e-commerce and possibility to conduct the business easily.
- Users' analysis – price per broadband, content of use, fixed price per broadband and content of use.

The weight of sub-indicators is calculated as the average from the equivalent indexes and by settling priorities

CONCLUSIONS, LIMITATIONS, AND FUTURE RESEARCH

The last few decades have seen rapid changes in technology and the growing proliferation of digitized devices and services. The pace of change is likely to accelerate with the development of artificial intel-

Table 6. Index equivalence

DESI (W1) to DiGiX (W2) Equivalence			
Matching Sub-Indicator	Weight W1 (%)	Weight W2 (%)	Average = (W1+W2)/2 (%)
A	6,25	4,5	5,38
B	6,25	6	6,13
C	5	3,8	4,40
F	5	3,8	4,40
G	5	3,8	4,40
H	10	6,33	8,17
I	10	6,33	8,17
J	15	20	17,5
K	6,25	3,8	5,03
T	6,25	3,8	5,03
The DESI index is equivalent to the DiGiX in			**69,85%**
DESI (W1) to ICT (W3) equivalence			
Matching sub- indicator	Weight W1 (%)	Weight W3 (%)	Average = (W1+W3)/2 (%)
A	6,25	8	7,13
A	6,25	8	7,13
B	6,25	8	7,13
C	5	8	6,50
D	12,5	20	16,25
K	6,25	8	7,13
T	6,25	8	7,13
The DESI index is equivalent to the ICT in			**44,13%**
DESI (W1) to CISCO (W4) equivalence			
Matching sub- indicator	Weight W1 (%)	Weight W4 (%)	Average = (W1+W4)/2 (%)
C	5	4	4,5
D	12,5	10,67	11,59
H	10	20	15
I	10	8	9
J	15	8	11,5
K	6,25	4	5,13
T	6,25	4	5,13
The DESI index is equivalent to the CISCO in			**61,85%**

continued on following page

Table 6. Continued

DiGiX (W2) to ICT (W3) equivalence			
Matching sub- indicator	Weight W1 (%)	Weight W4 (%)	Average = (W1+W4)/2 (%)
B	6	8	7
C	3,8	8	5,9
K	3,8	8	5,9
L	4,5	8	6,25
M	3,8	8	11,5
Q	6	8	5,9
T	3,8	8	5,9
The DIGIX index is equivalent to the ICT in			43,85%
DiGiX (W2) to CISCO (W4) equivalence			
Matching sub- indicator	Weight W2 (%)	Weight W4 (%)	Average = (W2+W4)/2 (%)
C	3,8	4	3,9
H	6,33	20	13,17
I	6,33	8	7,16
J	20	8	14
K	3,8	4	3,9
L	4,5	4	4,25
M	3,8	4	3,9
P	3	4	3,5
R	3	4	2,5
S	6	4	5
T	3,8	4	3,9
The DIGIX index is equivalent to the CISCO in			66,19%
ICT (W3) to CISCO (W4) equivalence			
Matching sub- indicator	Weight W3 (%)	Weight W4 (%)	Average = (W3+W4)/2 (%)
C	8	4	6
D	13,3	10,67	11,99
K	8	4	6
L	8	4	6
M	8	4	6
T	8	4	6
The ICT index is equivalent to the CISCO in			41,99%

ligence, robotics, biotechnology and nanotechnology. Digitalization is directly connected to the digital economy. Digital economy is supported by the dissemination of information and communication technologies to all industry sectors with a focus on increasing productivity. The digital transformation of the economy is changing the conventional patterns of business structure, the way consumers obtain services, information and goods, and also how countries need to adapt to these new regulatory challenges.

Table 7. Results of overall index equivalence

	DIGIX	ICT	CISCO	DESI
DIGIX		43,85%	66,19%	69,85%
ICT	43,85%		41,99%	44,13%
CISCO	66,19%	41,99%		61,85%
DESI	69,85%	44,13%	61,85%	

Table 8. Proposed Index sub-indicators and weights

Indicator	Sub-Indicator	Weight (%)
Connection	3G or more mobile network coverage	7
	Fixed broadband	6
	Active mobile broadband subscriptions	6
	Maximum speed coverage	7
Government regulation	Government online	15
	Laws regarding ICT	3
	Privacy rate	3
Business integration	E-commerce	10
	Ease of doing business	15
Users' analysis	Internet usage	5
	Content of use	10
	Fixed price per broadband	5
	Cloud service availability	8

Digitization is closely associated with the adoption of digital technologies and the increase in their use. According to DESI the level of digital performance of EU countries increased to 52.45% in 2019 compared to 44.35% and 39.05% in 2016 and 2014, respectively (see https://digital-agenda-data.me/).

To measure the country digitalization level, it is useful to have an index of evaluation. Nowadays, there is no standardized methods to make this analysis, so the most acknowledged indexes of digital evaluation have been here investigated: DESI, DIGIX, ICT Development Index and CISCO Networking Index.

From the results of the comparison of indexes, it is concluded that there are equivalences. The equivalences are not very strong and these discrepancies in evaluation might be caused by different approaches from public and private companies. The index created included four indicators: Connection, government regulation, business integration and user analysis. The connection indicator includes 3G or more mobile network coverage, fixed broadband, mobile broadband and maximum speed sub-indicators. Government regulation contains such sub-indicators: online government, ICT related laws and privacy tax. Business integration is e-commerce and ease of doing business. The user analysis indicator includes internet usage, usage content, fixed price for broadband and cloud service availability.

As a contribution, the study proposed an approach for measuring digitization, which is based on measurable data and can be applied to carry out the digital assessment of any country. Using the proposed index, we can analyse, explain and predict the level of digitization and gaps to be improved. The main limitation is that the index has not been tested for reliability, which is also a challenge for future research.

Conflict of Interest

The authors declare that they have no conflict of interest.

REFERENCES

Annarelli, A., Battistella, C., Nonino, F., Parida, V., & Pessot, E. (2021). Literature Review on Digitalization Capabilities: Co-citation Analysis of Antecedents, Conceptualization and Consequences. *Technological Forecasting and Social Change, 166*, 120635. doi:10.1016/j.techfore.2021.120635

Bataev, A., & Aleksandrova, A. (2020). Digitalization of the World Economy: Performance Evaluation of Introducing Cyber-Physical Systems. *9th International Conference on Industrial Technology and Management (ICITM)*, 265-269. 10.1109/ICITM48982.2020.9080378

Brennen, J. S., & Kreiss, D. (2016). Digitalization. In K. B. Jensen, E. W. Rothenbuhler, J. D. Pooley, & R. T. Craig (Eds.), *The International Encyclopedia of Communication Theory and Philosophy* (pp. 556–566). Wiley-Blackwell. doi:10.1002/9781118766804.wbiect111

Brynjolfsson, E., & McAfee, A. (2014). *The second machine age: Work, progress, and prosperity in a time of brilliant technologies*. WW Norton & Company.

Cámara, N. (2020). *Global DiGiX 2020 Update: A Multidimensional Index of Digitization*. BBVA Research. Retrieved from https://www.bbvaresearch.com/en/publicaciones/digix-2020-update-a-multi-dimensional-index-of-digitization/

Cámara, N., & Tuesta, D. (2017) *DiGiX: The Digitization Index*. Working paper n°17, BBVA Research, Madrid, Spain. Retrieved from https://www.bbvaresearch.com/en/publicaciones/digix-the-digitization-index/

CISCO. (2020). *Cisco Global Digital Readiness 2019*. White paper. Retrieved from https://www.cisco.com/c/dam/en_us/about/csr/reports/global-digital-readiness-index.pdf

Eller, R., Alford, P., Kallmuenzer, A., & Peters, M. (2020). Antecedents, consequences, and challenges of small and medium-sized enterprise digitalization. *Journal of Business Research, 112*, 119–127. doi:10.1016/j.jbusres.2020.03.004

European Commission. (2020a). *Digital Economy and Society Index (DESI) 2020: Thematic chapters*. Retrieved from https://digital-strategy.ec.europa.eu/en/policies/desi

European Commission. (2020b). *Broadband Coverage in Europe 2019: Mapping progress towards the coverage objectives of the Digital Agenda*. Retrieved from https://op.europa.eu/en/publication-detail/-/publication/077cc151-f0b3-11ea-991b-01aa75ed71a1

European Commission. (2020c). *Digital Economy and Society Index (DESI) 2020: Methodological note*. Retrieved from https://digital-strategy.ec.europa.eu/en/policies/desi

Galloway, S. (2020). *Post Corona: From Crisis to Opportunity, Portfolio.* Portfolio.

Gronum, S., Steen, J., & Verreynne, M.-L. (2016). Business Model Design and Innovation: Unlocking The Performance Benefits of Innovation. *Australian Journal of Management, 41*(3), 585–605. doi:10.1177/0312896215587315

ITU. (2017). *Measuring the Information Society Report, 1.* Geneva, Switzerland: ITU Publications. Retrieved from https://www.itu.int/en/ITU-D/Statistics/Pages/publications/mis2017.aspx

ITU. (2018). *Measuring the Information Society Report.* Executive Summary. Geneva, Switzerland: ITU Publications. Retrieved from https://www.itu.int/pub/D-IND-ICTOI-2018

ITU. (2019). *The ICT Development Index (IDI) Methodology, indicators and definitions.* Retrieved from https://www.itu.int/en/ITU-/Statistics/Documents/statistics/ITU_ICT%20Development%20Index.pdf

Kononova, K. (2015). Some aspects of ICT Measurement: Comparative Analysis of E-indexes. *Proceedings of the 7th International Conference in Information and Communication Technologies in Agriculture, Food and Environment (HAICTA 2015).*

Konovalova, M. E., Kuzmina, O. Y., & Zhironkin, S. A. (2020). Digital Technologies as a Factor of Expanding the Investment Opportunities of Business Entities. In S. Ashmarina, M. Vochozka, & V. Mantulenko (Eds.), *Digital Age: Chances, Challenges and Future, ISCDTE 2019. Lecture Notes in Networks and Systems, 84.* Springer. doi:10.1007/978-3-030-27015-5_23

Kotarba, M. (2017). Measuring digitalization: Key metrics. *Foundations of Management, 9*(1), 123–138. doi:10.1515/fman-2017-0010

Kravchenko, O., Leshchenko, M., Marushchak, D., Vdovychenko, Y., & Boguslavska, S. (2019). Digitalization as a global trend and growth factor of the modern economy. *SHS Web of Conferences, 65,* 434–443. 10.1051hsconf/20196507004

Kumar, V. (2019). What Industry 4.0 Means for the Global Economy. *Industry Wired.* Retrieved from https://industrywired.com/what-industry-4-0-means-for-the-global-economy/

Laurens, R. (2019). *Get Fit for Digital Business: A Six-Step Workout Plan to Get Your Organisation in Great Shape to Thrive in a Connected Commercial World* (1st ed.). Routledge. doi:10.4324/9780429462146

Lederer, M., Knapp, J., & Schott, P. (2017). The digital future has many names - How business process management drives the digital transformation. *6th International Conference on Industrial Technology and Management, ICITM 2017,* 22–26. 10.1109/ICITM.2017.7917889

Lerch, C., & Gotsch, M. (2015). Digitalized Product-Service Systems in Manufacturing Firms. *Research Technology Management, 58*(5), 45–52. doi:10.5437/08956308X5805357

Mahraz, M., Benabbou, L., & Berrado, A. (2019) A Systematic literature review of Digital Transformation. *Proceedings of the International Conference on Industrial Engineering and Operations Management.*

Nemoto, T., & González, J. L. (2021). Digital trade inventory: Rules, standards and principles. OECD Trade Policy Papers, No. 251, OECD Publishing. doi:10.1787/18166873

Petrenko, S. A., Makoveichuk, K. A., Chetyrbok, P. V., & Petrenko, A. S. (2017). About readiness for digital economy. *2017 IEEE II International Conference on Control in Technical Systems (CTS)*, 96-99, 10.1109/CTSYS.2017.8109498

Preda, A. M., Crişan, D. A., Stanica, J. L., & Samuel, A. N. A. (2019). Innovation and ICT Development: An Analysis for the EU-28 Member States. *Journal of Information Systems & Operations Management*, *13*(2), 154–163.

Purdy, M., & Davarzani, L. (2015). *The Growth Game-Changer: How the Industrial Internet of Things can drive progress and prosperity*. Accenture Strategy. Retrieved from https://fliphtml5.com/wful/iehy/basic

Rachinger, M., Rauter, R., Müller, C., Vorraber, W., & Schirgi, E. (2019). Digitalization and its influence on business model innovation. *Journal of Manufacturing Technology Management*, *30*(8), 1143–1160. doi:10.1108/JMTM-01-2018-0020

Saarikko, T., Westergren, U., & Blomquist, T. (2020). Digital transformation: Five recommendations for the digitally conscious firm. *Business Horizons*, *63*(6), 825-839. . doi:10.1016/j.bushor.2020.07.005

Satalkina, L., & Steiner, G. (2020). Digital Entrepreneurship and its Role in Innovation Systems: A Systematic Literature Review as a Basis for Future Research Avenues for Sustainable Transitions. *Sustainability (Basel)*, *12*(7), 2764. doi:10.3390u12072764

Shin, S. C., Ho, J. W., & Pak, V. Y. (2020). Digital Transformation through e-Government Innovation in Uzbekistan. *International Conference on Advanced Communication Technology, ICACT*. 10.23919/ICACT48636.2020.9061507

Sidorenko, E. L., & Khisamova, Z. I. (2020). The Readiness of the Economy for Digitalization: Basic Methodological Approaches. In Digital Age: Chances, Challenges and Future. ISCDTE 2019. Lecture Notes in Networks and Systems, 84. Springer. doi:10.1007/978-3-030-27015-5_37

Stavytskyy, A., Kharlamova, G., & Stoica, E. (2019). The Analysis of the Digital Economy and Society Index in the EU. *Baltic Journal of European Studies*, *9*(3), 245–261. doi:10.1515/bjes-2019-0032

Stremousova, E., & Buchinskaia, O. (2019). Some Approaches to Evaluation Macroeconomic Efficiency of Digitalisation. *Business. Management in Education*, *17*(2), 232–247. doi:10.3846/bme.2019.11326

Tarasova, T. M., Averina, L. V., & Pecherskaya, E. P. (2020). Digitalization of the Public Sector of the Regional Economy. In Digital Age: Chances, Challenges and Future, ISCDTE 2019. Lecture Notes in Networks and Systems, 84. Springer. doi:10.1007/978-3-030-27015-5_32

Tilson, D., Lyytinen, K., & Sørensen, C. (2010). Research commentary - digital infrastructures: The missing IS research agenda. *Information Systems Research*, *21*(4), 748–759. doi:10.1287/isre.1100.0318

UNCTAD. (2019). *Value Creation and Capture: Implications for Developing Countries*. Digital Economy Report 2019. New York: United Nations Publications. Retrieved from https://unctad.org/webflyer/digital-economy-report-2019

Ungureanu, A. (2021). The Digitalization Impact on the Entrepreneurial Leadership in the 21st Century. *International Journal of Social Relevance & Concern*, *9*(1), 25–32. doi:10.26821/IJSRC.9.1.2021.9109

Unruh, G., & Kiron, D. (2017). Digital transformation on purpose. *MIT Sloan Management Review*. Retrieved from https://sloanreview.mit.edu/article/digital-transformation-on-purpose/

World Economic Forum. (2016). *Digital Transformation of Industries: Demystifying Digital and Securing $100 Trillion for Society and Industry by 2025*. Geneva, Switzerland: World Economic Forum. Retrieved from https://reports.weforum.org/digital-transformation/wp-content/blogs.dir/94/mp/files/pages/files/wef1601-digitaltransformation-1401.pdf

Yoo, T., De Wysocki, M., & Cumberland, A. (2018). *Country Digital Readiness: Research to Determine a Country's Digital Readiness and Key Interventions*. Research: Modelling an Inclusive Digital Future, CISCO. Retrieved from https://www.cisco.com/c/dam/assets/csr/pdf/Country-Digital-Readiness-White-Paper-US.pdf

ADDITIONAL READING

ITU. (2020). *Handbook for the collection of administrative data on telecommunications/ICT*, 2020 edition. Geneva, Switzerland: ITU Publications. Retrieved from https://www.itu.int/en/ITU-D/Statistics/Pages/publications/handbook.aspx

Linde, L., Sjödin, D., Parida, V., & Gebauer, H. (2021). Evaluation of Digital Business Model Opportunities. *Research Technology Management*, *64*(1), 43–53. doi:10.1080/08956308.2021.1842664

OECD. (2020). *OECD Digital Economy Outlook 2020*. OECD Publishing. doi:10.1787/bb167041-

World Economic Forum. (2016). *Digital Transformation of Industries: Demystifying Digital and Securing $100 Trillion for Society and Industry by 2025*. Geneva, Switzerland: World Economic Forum. Retrieved from https://www.weforum.org/reports/digital-transformation-of-industries/

KEY TERMS AND DEFINITIONS

Cisco Digital Readiness Index: Was developed to holistically measure a country's level of digital readiness.

Digital Economy: Describes an economic system where the use of information and communication technology is widespread.

Digital Economy and Society Index: (DESI): Is a composite index prepared annually by the European Commission since 2015 that seeks to assess the digital competitiveness of Member States, following its evolution over time.

Digital Transformation: Is the process that is used to restructure economies, organizations and society.

Digitalization: Is the sociotechnical process of leveraging digitized products or systems to develop new organizational.

Digitization: Is the technical process of converting analogue signals to digital signals.

DiGiX Digitalization Index: Was created by BBVA company (Banco Bilbao Vizcaya Argentina) and it is considered as one of the largest financial institutions of the world.

ICT Development Index (IDI): Is a composite index that has been reported, since 2009, by the International Telecommunication Union.

APPENDIX 1: DESI INDEX

Table 9. The structure of DESI index (adapted from European Commission, 2015)

Dimension	Sub Dimension	Indicator
Connectivity	Fixed broadband take-up Fixed broadband coverage Mobile broadband Broadband price index	Overall fixed broadband take-up At least 1000 Mbps fixed broadband take-up Fast broadband (NGA) coverage Fixed Very High-Capacity Network (VHCN) coverage 4G coverage Mobile broadband take-up 5G readiness Broadband price index
Human capital	Internet user skills Advanced skills and development	Basic digital skills At least basic software skills ICT specialists and graduates Female ICT specialists
Digital public service	E-Government	E-government users Pre-filled forms Online service completion Digital public services for businesses Open data
Use of Internet services	Internet use Activities online Transactions	People who never used Internet Internet users News, music, videos and games Video calls Social networks Doing an online course Banking Shopping Selling online
Integration of Digital Technology	Business digitalization E-Commerce	Electronic information sharing Social media Big data Cloud SME's selling online e-Commerce turnover Selling online cross-border

Table 10. DESI connectivity dimension (adapted from European Commission, 2020b)

Indicator	Description	Breakdown	Unit	Source
1a1 - Overall fixed broadband take-up	% of households subscribing to fixed broadband	All households	% of households	Eurostat – Community survey on ICT usage in Households and by Individuals
1a2 – At least 100 Mbps fixed broadband take-up	% of households subscribing to fixed broadband of at least 100 Mbps, calculated as overall fixed broadband take-up (source: Eurostat) multiplied with the percentage of fixed broadband lines of at least 100 Mbps	All fixed broadband subscriptions	% of households	European Commission, through the COCOM and Eurostat - Community survey on ICT usage in Households and by Individuals
1b1 – Fast broadband (NGA) coverage	% of households covered by fixed broadband of at least 30 Mbps download. The technologies considered are FTTH, FTTB, Cable Docsis 3.0 and VDSL	All fixed broadband subscriptions	% of households	Broadband coverage in Europe studies for the European Commission
1b2 – Fixed Very High-Capacity Network (VHCN) coverage	% of households covered by any fixed VHCN. The technologies considered are FTTH and FTTB for 2015-2018 and FTTH, FTTB and Cable Docsis 3.1 for 2019	All fixed broadband subscriptions	% of households	Broadband coverage in Europe studies for the European Commission by IHS Markit, Omdia and Point Topic
1c1 – 4G coverage	% of populated areas with coverage by 4G - measured as the average coverage of telecom operators in each country	All fixed broadband subscriptions	% of households	% of populated areas with coverage by 4G - measured as the average coverage of telecom operators in each country
1c2 – Mobile broadband take-up	Number of mobile data subscriptions per 100 people	All subscriptions	Subscribers per 100 people	European Commission services, through the Communications Committee (COCOM)
1c3 – 5G readiness	The amount of spectrum assigned and ready for 5G use by the end of 2020 within the so-called 5G pioneer bands. These bands are 700 MHz (703-733 MHz and 758- 788 MHz), 3.6 GHz (3400-3800 MHz) and 26 GHz (1000 MHz within 24250-27500 MHz). All three spectrum bands have an equal weight	5G pioneer bands	% of harmonised spectrum	European Commission services, through the Communications Committee (COCOM)
1d1 – Broadband price index	The broadband price index measures the prices of representative baskets of fixed, mobile and converged broadband offers	All fixed, mobile and converged Broadband offers	Score (0-100)	Broadband retail prices study, annual studies for the European Commission

Source: Eurostat (https://ec.europa.eu/eurostat/cache/metadata/en/isoc_i_esms.htm)

Table 11. DESI human capital dimension (adapted from European Commission, 2020c)

Indicator	Description	Breakdown	Unit	Source
2a1 – At least basic digital skills	Individuals with 'basic' or 'above basic' digital skills in each of the following four dimensions: information, communication, problem solving and software for content creation (as measured by the number of activities carried out during the previous 3 months).	All individuals (aged 16-74)	% of individuals	Eurostat - Community survey on ICT usage in Households and by Individuals
2a2 – Above basic digital skills	Individuals with 'above basic' digital skills in each of the following four dimensions: information, communication, problem solving and software for content creation (as measured by the number of activities carried out during the previous 3 months).	All individuals (aged 16-74)	% of individuals	Eurostat - Community survey on ICT usage in Households and by Individuals
2a3 – At least basic software skills	Individuals who, in addition to having used basic software features such as word processing, have used advanced spreadsheet functions, created a presentation or document integrating text, pictures and tables or charts, or written code in a programming language.	All individuals (aged 16-74)	% of individuals	Eurostat - Community survey on ICT usage in Households and by Individuals
2b1 – ICT specialists	Employed ICT specialists. Broad definition based on the ISCO-08 classification and including jobs like ICT service managers, ICT professionals, ICT technicians, ICT installers and servicers.	Individuals In employment aged 15-74	% of individuals in employment aged 15-74	Eurostat – Labour force survey
2b2 – Female ICT specialists	Employed ICT specialists. Broad definition based on the ISCO-08 classification and including jobs like ICT service managers, ICT professionals, ICT technicians, ICT installers and servicers.	Females in employment aged 15-74	% of females in employment aged 15-74	Eurostat - Labour force survey
2b3 – ICT graduates	Individuals with a degree in ICT	Graduates	% of graduates	Eurostat (table educ_uoegrad03, using selection ISCED11=ED5)

Source: Eurostat (https://ec.europa.eu/eurostat/cache/metadata/en/isoc_i_esms.htm)

Table 12. DESI use of internet dimension (adapted from European Commission, 2020c)

Indicator	Description	Breakdown	Unit	Source
3a1 – People who never used the internet	Individuals who never used the internet	All individuals (aged 16-74)	% of individuals	Eurostat - Community survey on ICT usage in Households and by Individuals (I_IUX)
3a2 – Internet users	Individuals who used the internet at least once a week	All individuals (aged 16-74)	% of individuals	Eurostat - Community survey on ICT usage in Households and by Individuals (I_IUSE)
3b1 – News	Individuals who used the internet to read online news sites, newspapers or news magazines	All individuals (aged 16-74)	% of individuals who used internet in the last 3 months	Eurostat - Community survey on ICT usage in Households and by Individuals (I_IUNW1
3b2 – Music, videos and games	Individuals who used the internet to play or download games, images, films or music	All individuals (aged 16-74)	% of individuals who used internet in the last 3 months	Eurostat - Community survey on ICT usage in Households and by Individuals
3b3 – Video on demand	Individuals who used the internet to use video on demand services and servicers.	All individuals (aged 16-74)	% of individuals who used internet in the last 3 months	Eurostat - Community survey on ICT usage in Households and by Individuals
3b4 – Video calls	Individuals who used the internet to make telephone or video calls (e.g. Skype)	All individuals (aged 16-74)	% of individuals who used internet in the last 3 months	Eurostat - Community survey on ICT usage in Households and by Individuals (I_IUPH1)
3b5 – Social networks	Individuals who used the internet to participate in social networks (create user profile, post messages or other contributions)	All individuals (aged 16-74)	% of individuals who used internet in the last 3 months	Eurostat - Community survey on ICT usage in Households and by Individuals (I_IUSNET)
3b6 – Doing an online course	Individuals who used the internet to do an online course (on any subject)	All individuals (aged 16-74)	% of individuals who used internet in the last 3 months	Eurostat - Community survey on ICT usage in Households and by Individuals (I_IUOLC)
3c1 – Banking	Individuals who used the internet to use online banking	All individuals (aged 16-74)	% of individuals who used internet in the last 3 months	Eurostat - Community survey on ICT usage in Households and by Individuals (I_IUBK)
3c2 – Shopping	Individuals who ordered goods or services online	All individuals (aged 16-74)	% of internet users (last year)	Eurostat - Community survey on ICT usage in Households and by Individuals (I_BLT12)
3c3 – Selling online	Individuals who sold goods or services online	All individuals (aged 16-74)	% of individuals who used internet in the last 3 months	Eurostat - Community survey on ICT usage in Households and by Individuals (I_IUSELL)

Source: Eurostat (https://ec.europa.eu/eurostat/cache/metadata/en/isoc_i_esms.htm)

Table 13. DESI integration of digital technology (adapted from European Commission, 2020c)

Indicator	Description	Breakdown	Unit	Source
4a1 – Electronic information sharing	Businesses who have in use an ERP (enterprise resource planning) software package to share information between different functional areas (e.g., accounting, planning, production, marketing)	All enterprises (no financial sector, 10+ employees)	% of enterprises	Eurostat - Community survey on ICT usage and eCommerce in Enterprises (E_ERP1)
4a2 – Social media	Integration of digital technology dimension is as well based on Eurostat statistics. Businesses using two or more of the following social media: social networks, enterprise's blog or microblog, multimedia content sharing websites, wiki-based knowledge sharing tools. Using social media means that the enterprise has a user profile, an account or a user license depending on the requirements and the type of the social media	All individuals (aged 16-74)	% of enterprises	Eurostat - Community survey on ICT usage and eCommerce in Enterprises (E_SM1_GE2))
4a3 – Big data	Enterprises analysing big data from any data source	All individuals (aged 16-74)	% of enterprises	Eurostat - Community survey on ICT usage and eCommerce in Enterprises (E_BD)
4a4 – Cloud	Businesses purchasing at least one of the following cloud computing services: hosting of the enterprise's database, accounting software applications, CRM software, computing power	All individuals (aged 16-74)	% of individuals who used internet in the last 3 months	Eurostat - Community survey on ICT usage and eCommerce in Enterprises
4b1 – SMEs Selling online	SMEs selling online (at least 1% of turnover)	SMEs (no financial sector, 10-249 employees)	% of SMEs	Eurostat - Community survey on ICT usage and eCommerce in Enterprises (E_ESELL)
4b2 – e-Commerce turnover	SMEs total turnover from e-commerce	SMEs (no financial sector, 10-249 employees)	% of turnover	Eurostat - Community survey on ICT usage and eCommerce in Enterprises (E_ETURN)
4b3 – Selling online crossborder	SMEs that carried out electronic sales to other EU countries	SMEs (no financial sector, 10-249 employees)	% of SMEs	Eurostat - Community survey on ICT usage and eCommerce in Enterprises (E_AESEU)

Source: Eurostat (https://ec.europa.eu/eurostat/cache/metadata/en/isoc_i_esms. htm)

Table 14. DESI - Digital public services dimension (adapted from European Commission, 2020c)

Indicator	Description	Breakdown	Unit	Source
5a1 – eGovernment users	Individuals who sent filled forms to public authorities over the internet in the previous 12 months	All individuals (aged 16-74)	% of internet users who, during the previous year, needed to send filled forms to the public administration.	Eurostat – Community survey on ICT usage in Households and by Individuals (IGOV12RT)
5a2 – Prefilled forms	Amount of data that is pre-filled in public service online forms	Services assessed in the e- government benchmark	Score (0 to 100)	E-government benchmark
5a3 – Online service completion	The share of administrative steps that can be done online for major life events (birth of a child, new residence, etc.)	Services assessed in the e- government benchmark	Score (0 to100)	E-government benchmark
5a4 – Digital public services for businesses	The indicator broadly reflects the share of public services needed for starting a business and conducting regular business operations that are available online for domestic as well as foreign users. Services provided through a portal receive a higher score, services which provide only information (but must be completed offline) receive a more limited score.	Services assessed in the e- government benchmark	Score (0 to 100)	E-government benchmark
5a5 – Open data	This composite indicator measures to what extent countries have an open data policy in place (including the transposition of the revised PSI Directive), the estimated political, social, and economic impact of open data and the characteristics (functionalities, data availability and usage) of the national data portal.	Aggregate score	% of maximum score	European data portal

Source: Eurostat (https://ec.europa.eu/eurostat/cache/metadata/en/isoc_i_esms.htm)

Table 15. Weighting of indicators DESI index (adapted from Stavytskyy, 2019)

Indicator	Sub-indicators	Weighting %	Total Weighting %
Connectivity	Fixed broadband take-up Fixed broadband coverage Mobile broadband Broadband price index	6,25 6,25 6,25 6,25	25
Human Capital	Internet user skills Advanced skills and development	12,5 12,5	25
Use of Internet Services	Internet use 5 Activities online 5 15 Transaction 5	5 5 5	15
Integration of digital Technology	Business digitalization E-Commerce	10 10	20
Digital Public Services	E-Government	15	15

APPENDIX 2: ICT DEVELOPMENT

Table 16. ICT development index: Table of weights (adapted from ITU, 2011)

Indicator	Sub-Indicators	Weighting %	Total Weighting %
ICT Acess	International Internet bandwidth per internet user Percentage of household with computer Percentage of households with Internet access Population covered by at least 3G mobile networks Fixed-broadband subscriptions by speed tiers	8 8 8 8 8	40
ICT use	Percentage of individuals using the Internet Active mobile-broadband subscriptions per 100 inhabitants Mobile-broadband Internet traffic Fixed-broadband Internet traffic Mobile phone ownership	8 8 8 8 8	40
ICT Skills	Mean years of schooling Secondary gross enrolment ratio Tertiary gross enrolment	6,7 6,7 6,7	20

APPENDIX 3

Table 17. Metrics and sources of CISCO index (adapted from Cisco Systems, 2018) and table of weights of CISCO index (adapted from Yoo et al., 2018)

Digital Readiness Components (Indicator)	Definition	Metric (Sub-Indicators)	Sub-Indicators Value %	Total Value %
Basic Needs	Basic human needs for a population to thrive	Life Expectancy https://population.un.org/wpp/Download/Standard/Mortality/ Mortality Rate (Under Age 5) https://www.unicef.org/media/79371/file/UN-IGME-child-mortal ity-report-2020.pdf.pdf Access to basic services https://www.unwater.org/who-and-unicef-launch-updated-estima tes-for-water-sanitation-and-hygiene/ https://www.who.int/news/item/18-06-2019-1-in-3-people-globa lly-do-not-have-access-to-safe-drinking-water-unicef-who	5.33 5.33 5.33	16
Business and Government Investment	Private and public investment in innovation and technology	Foreign Direct Investment https://www.imf.org/external/pubs/ft/fandd/basics/20_direct-invest.htm Research and Development Expenditure http://uis.unesco.org/apps/visualisations/research-and-devel opment-spending/ Investment Freedom (Heritage Foundation) https://www.heritage.org/index/investment-freedom	4 4 4	12
Ease of Doing Business	Basic infrastructure/ policies needed to support business continuity	Ease of Doing Business Index https://www.doingbusiness.org/en/rankings Rule of Law World https://worldjusticeproject.org/our-work/research-and-data/w jp-rule-law-index-2020 Logistics Performance Index https://lpi.worldbank.org/ (LPI) – Infrastructure Rating https://lpi.worldbank.org/international/global?order=Infrast ructure	4 4 4 4	16
Human Capital	Skilled labour force available to support digital innovation (build and maintain)	Labour Force Participation Rate https://data.worldbank.org/indicator/SL.TLF.CACT.ZS Adult Literacy Rate http://uis.unesco.org/en/topic/literacy Education Index (Years of School) https://hdr.undp.org/en/content/human-development-index-hdi Harmonized Test Score (World Bank) https://govdata360.worldbank.org/indicators/hc58163b0	4 4 4 4	16
Start-up Environment	Environment which fosters innovation within a community	New Business Density https://data.worldbank.org/indicator/IC.BUS.NDNS.ZS Patents Granted and Trademarks Registered https://www.wipo.int/ipstats/en/statistics/glossary.html Venture Capital Investment and Availability https://tcdata360.worldbank.org/indicators/h8a7ea3d1	4 4 4	12
Technology Adoption	Demand for digital products / services	Mobile Cellular Penetration https://www.itu.int/en/ITU-D/Statistics/Pages/stat/default.a spx Internet Usage https://www.itu.int/en/ITU-D/Statistics/Pages/stat/default.a spx Cloud Services (Spend, IT Forecast Data) (Gartner) https://www.gartner.com/en/newsroom/press-releases/2020-11-1 7-gartner-forecasts-worldwide-public-cloud-end-user-spending -to-grow-18-percent-in-2021	4 4 4	12
Technology Infrastructure	The infrastructure available to enable digital activities and Connected consumers (IoT, Cloud)	Mobile Broadband Subscriptions https://www.itu.int/en/ITU-D/Statistics/Pages/stat/default.a spx Fixed Broadband Subscriptions https://www.itu.int/en/ITU-D/Statistics/Pages/stat/default.a spx Secure Internet Servers https://www.netcraft.com/ Household Internet Access https://www.itu.int/en/ITU-D/Statistics/Pages/stat/default.a spx	4 4 4 4	16

Chapter 16
Using Blockchain to Ensure Supply Chain Traceability

Pedro Azevedo
tb.lx, Portugal

Jorge Vareda Gomes
https://orcid.org/0000-0003-0656-9284
Universidade Lusófona, Portugal

Mario Romão
https://orcid.org/0000-0003-4564-1883
ISEG, Universidade de Lisboa, Portugal

ABSTRACT

Supply chains can span a huge number of countries, cross many borders, and require interoperation of a multitude of organizations. This vastness impacts business competitiveness since it adds complexity and can difficult securing traceability, chain of custody, and transparency. The authors propose that assuring chain of custody and traceability via blockchain allows organizations to demonstrate product provenance, integrity, and compliance. This work proposes that to effect true traceability the more complete approach is to connect both the supply chain actors (SCAs) and products identifications using digital certificates. A blockchain is used to manage the traceability of products and validation of the identities. Importing, verifying, and storing the certificates uses an off-chain data storage solution for products certificates. To create, validate the certificates, and setup the chain of trust, a public key infrastructure (PKI) was designed as part of the proposal. The results were architectural artifacts, including an Ethereum smart contract and a PKI-based certificate authentication system.

1 INTRODUCTION

Blockchain (BC) is a recent technology that was first introduced with the Bitcoin cryptocurrency (Houben & Snyers 2018). However, BC technological capabilities are not only applicable to cryptocurrency and so it has been proposed to be used in other applications. According to Guo & Yu (2022) BC proposes to add several features to any application, namely: decentralization, autonomy, integrity, immutability,

DOI: 10.4018/978-1-6684-9151-5.ch016

verification, fault-tolerance, anonymity, auditability, and transparency. Blockchain is proposed to be a viable method of tracking assets while guaranteeing security and data integrity (Meidute-Kavaliauskiene, et al., 2021). The benefits of blockchain-based tracing include the security of information sharing, real-time collection of product data, transparency, and visibility in the supply chain, as well as quality control throughout the entire lifecycle (Agrawal et., 2021). According to several authors most of these features seem to make a perfect fit to supply chains since they support the key basic objectives: quality, speed, dependability, cost and flexibility (Casey et al. 2017; Dinh et al., 2017; Kaur & Parashar, 2022).

1.1 Problem Relevance

For supply chain a recent duo of aspects: traceability and provenance have gained more importance. The focus on these aspects aims to allow the industries and customers dependent on supply chain to become assured of the products and processes sustainability (Kshetri 2018; Pal & Kant, 2019). While it is common nowadays for logistics operators to accurately track packages at the transportation stages, that type of granularity is either lost or many times not possible at all stages of the supply chains since they have become much more international, complex and interorganizational spanning (Kim et al. 2018).

From literature it is clear that the loss of traceability and provenance information the main factor that affects existing sustainability and compliance certification efforts making it crucial and the focus of research in the context of supply chains (Garcia-Torres et al., 2019). The traceability aspect additionally will also permit the optimization of supply chains which has always been one of the most preeminent topics for businesses as it highly influences a firm's success (Kros et al. 2019). This traceability optimization aspect of the supply chain is then the main driving reason that has led some companies to make trials for Supply Chains using BC for traceability (Berg & Myllymaa, 2021; Wang et al. 2019). Examples are; Maersk – tracking global shipping, Alibaba – reduce food fraud, Lockheed Martin – improve cybersecurity, Everledger – implement diamonds and wine certificates, Walmart – monitor pork produce in China, Modum – safe drug delivery, Intel – track seafood supply chain, Bext360 – bring transparency into the coffee bean supply chain (Kshetri 2017).

1.2 Summary of the Solution

This article proposes that to effect true and complete traceability the solution is to connect both the Supply Chain Actors (SCAs) and products identifications and provenance certificates. With the proposed approach the chosen BC and the designed Smart Contracts will be used to manage the traceability and validation of the identities while the storage, importing, exporting and verification of production and provenance certificates uses another existing architecture solution off-chain: WalliD[1] (Tavares et al. 2018). To create, validate the certificates and setup the chain of trust, an appropriate PKI (Public Key Infrastructure) with the corresponding CAs (Certificate Authorities) was designed as part of the proposal. To instantiate the problem and apply the solution a real food supply chain example was chosen. The chosen example uses the widely adopted and EU commission sponsored label and quality certificate system: Protected Designation of Origin (PDO). The main advantage of this proposed solution with an aggregated BC and Certificate architecture is that all SCAs (including producers, logistics operators, sellers and the end consumers/buyers) can use the system to view and self-verify the validity of both the traceability and the provenance claims.

In summary this work aims to provide a concrete answer to the supply chain traceability problem for the use case of supply chain certifiable actors, producers, products and consumers. The answer is a complete traceability system that provides both SCAs and the customers the highest level of traceability by assuring provenance, chain of custody and traceability verifiability and visibility to the SCAs and customers. The solution proposal consists of a set of artifacts (architecture diagrams and workflows, Ethereum SC and a PKI infrastructure) that followed the Design Science Research (DSR) methodology. Along the following points, we present a literature review covering various topics related to the scope of our study, like the chosen Blockchain and its impact on supply chains and their actors, the limitations and challenges of supply chains by using BC, the concepts of traceability, provenance, chain of custody, the supply chain agents and the requirements involved on their involvement. Then the research methodology based in the Design Science approach is introduced, and the proof-of-concept results are then analysed and discussed. The proof of concepts includes an architecture and a Use Case functionality for the Protected Designation of Origin for alimentary products (beef). Finally, the conclusions and future work are presented.

2 LITERATURE REVIEW

2.1 Blockchain Contributes to Supply Chain Management

According to Weber et al (2016) Blockchain can be used as a technology that supports the collaborative process required by a Supply Chain and is proposed as an alternative to having a centralized trusted party. Since then the industry has been alerted to the potential benefits of the use of BC to SC and according to Chang et al. (2020) BC adoption in Supply Chain Management (SCM) is expected to boom over the next 5 years and is one of the BC applications with more growth potential where the market is estimated to grow at a compound annual growth rate of 87%.

2.1.1 Blockchain Aspects Benefiting Supply Chains

The mostly stated contributions of blockchain to Supply Chain Management are the traceability and transparency aspects (Moosavi, 2021). Already several use cases have been studied and designed by Francisco and Swanson (2018) to illustrate how blockchain could improve traceability, efficiency, and decrease waste in a food supply chain. Blockchain could also help achieve robust cybersecurity and increase trust as demonstrated by Kshetri, 2018 and Ying et al., 2018. There are several BC features that can offer advantages or trade-offs in SCM (Litke et al. 2019): Firstly, scalability may be improved since all actors participate in a common ledger without a single point of interaction. There also may also be a performance increase measurable in a reduced time for assurance of transaction verification compared to centralized and escrow services (e.g., bank payment liquidity or manual verification of a bill of lading) made possible due to automatic execution of contracts. Additionally, the consensus mechanism provides trust to all actors in the chain and offers privacy since although the transactions are verified, the actor's identity might be kept private via the BC specific addressing scheme. Furthermore, the SCM location dependency becomes more flexible by effectively allowing to make transactions autonomous from country regulations and laws. There is also the expectation of reduced cost by allowing faster payments while SCs (Smart Contracts) allow for faster dispute resolution. There are three generic benefits of BC to SC in 3 main topics (Somapa et al., 2018; Wang et al (2019): improvement of SC visibility, ensuring secure information sharing and trust and increased operational effectiveness.

2.1.2 Blockchain Benefits to Supply Chain Actors

Perboli et al (2018) used a lean approach to design and evaluate real world use cases that combine BC and SC. In their analysis there are specific benefits to each actor in the supply chain: producer, transporter, distributer, warehouse, final user/customer. For the producer, the value propositions of BC are the improvement of production planning and certification via Enterprise Resource Planning (ERP) integration, introduction of Stock Keeping Unit (SKU) certificates into BC and the reduction of the bullwhip effect since improving supply chain visibility allows for increased production requirements accuracy. For the distributor, the visibility of the whole supply chain allows for better inventory update and the reduction of counterfeit, theft, wrong delivery, product recalls, paperwork and the increase in ease of compliance. For the transporter/carrier, the benefits are the forecast improvement and the time slot reservation by using more real time information on the actual state of the product location and of the processing phase. For the final user, the benefits depend on the segment: Business-to-Business or Business-to-Consumer. Regarding the first, it will benefit more of easier stock management and expiration/recall management while the later will benefit more in better brand value management by providing the consumer better health protection and guarantees with more transparent sustainability or compliance claims.

2.1.3 Blockchain Adoption Path in Supply Chains

Dobrovnik et al. (2018) propose an adoption path for BC in supply chains and logistics. They propose that companies should focus first on single use cases to minimize risks of adoption and to start with proof on concepts that require little coordination with third parties and that allow for IT skills to be developed and learn the technology nuances. Specifically, they mention the use case of reconciling multiple companies' internal databases since it is a contained problem that brings major benefits. The second proposed adoption approach it to tackle the transactions across boundaries as, in example, reducing the paperwork by migrating the bills of lading (responsibility ownership documents used in shipping industry) into BC. Thirdly they recommend focusing on replacing functionalities that do not require that end users significantly change their behaviour. As an example, replacing paper certificates in the diamond industry. Finally, the introduction of new business models or new logics of value creation over BC, as for example using new SCs to act to prioritize specific air corridors.

2.1.4 Problems and Challenges of SC Over BC

A particularly challenging aspect for supply chains over BC has been reported by Weber et al. (2016) and is the latency and latency variance of transaction completion. In a public Ethereum platform the average latency for a modelled supply chain scenario was measured to about 23s. This problem has been reported to be mitigated in a private customized BC with average latency around 2.8 seconds. Another answer to the low performance problem of BC is claimed by Xu et al (2019). Their study focused on providing traceability assurance via improving certificate traceability systems. These systems receive the certificates issued by inspection authorities, that verify the quality and originality of the products, and store and expose them to other interested parties for accountability purposes. The authors proposed and implemented a proof of concept that moved the centralized certificate traceability system to a decentralized system over BC to avoid the risk of tampering by unreliable employees or firms. Their answer to the lower performance problem however is that it is acceptable in that use case since the number of certified suppliers and products is low. Another problem that affects the effectiveness of supply chains over BC is that the number of stakeholders in global supply chains tend to undermine any traditional type or mechanism for enforcing security. Xu et al. (2018) in their work proposed to enhance the security of said supply chains via the binding of the physical and cyber worlds using digital certificates for both employees, devices and products that are responsible to enter and check the product data in the supply chain.

2.2 SCM Traceability Conceptual Framework

The main problem in SCM when adopting BC is to ensure complete traceability. Many different aspects that provide complete traceability have already been mentioned and it is then important to provide clear definitions and context to their use and relationship to supply chains to have a conceptual framework on how to build a SC with more complete traceability. As mentioned by Keogh (2018), GS1 supply chain industry expert with 35 years of experience in the SC field the concepts of Provenance, Traceability and Chain of Custody (CoC) are often misused but their understanding and differentiation provides a stepwise conceptual framework on how to understand and approach the traceability network.

2.2.1 Provenance

Even before BC was developed it had already been identified that provenance management was a cross-cutting "hard" problem in science, industry and society. In Cheney et al (2009) provenance was defined as the metadata about the origin, context and history of change of origin in associated objects and processes. To assure provenance, there must be some metadata that identifies the item and its geographic characteristic and some functionality that transmits that information along the supply chain. At the time of the rise of the web and search engines it seemed that it was possible to make the claim that all metadata could be indexed, and provenance could be assured. However, several problems with the reality of provenance in SCM were pointed out: provenance was incomplete, unreliable, insecure, heterogeneous, difficult to integrate and non-portable across systems. At the time no real complete solution for provenance assurance was possible although the combination of sematic web and detailed causal graphs was suggested as a path forward. To make evident the difference of applying BC to the provenance problem, Montecchi et al (2019) applied a slogan "It's real, trust me" when proposing a framework that provides traceability, certifiability, trackability, verifiability and most importantly the increase of provenance knowledge. This increase in provenance knowledge comes from providing provenance assurances, namely: origin tracing, authenticity certification, custody tracking and integrity verification. These will in turn benefit firms by reducing business risks (real or perceived) which can be further categorized in physical, performance, social, psychological and financial risks.

2.2.2 Chain of Custody

According to GS1 (2017), chain of custody or cumulative tracking in the context of a supply chain is a time-ordered registry of the sequence of parties who take physical custody of an object or collection of objects as it moves through a supply chain network. Chain of custody historically comes from the legal requirement perspective to provide proof of the tracking process. In highly regulated sectors (such as food, arms and drugs) chain of custody is critical and serves as the basis of both provenance and traceability assurance. According to ISEAL Alliance[2] (2016) the key propositions of a chain of custody system are to: identify the origin of a product (final or intermediate), ensure a custodial sequence along the supply chain, ensure that a certified product matches the certification characteristics, link, monitor and protect a claim at a certain stage of the chain with a claim at another point of the chain and finally to improve transparency. ISEAL Alliance (2016) proposes several custody models where the choice of the model depends on the claims the system or the actors wish to make. The models (in decreasing order of connectivity with a certain provenance claim) are identity preservation, segregation, mass balance overview and certificate trading.

2.2.3 Traceability

Has been defined in many different standards (EU Regulation (EC) No 178/2002[3], ISO 9000:2015[4], FAO CODEX Alimentarius CXG 60-2006[5]) and it can be summarized by: "the origin of materials and parts, the processing history, and the distribution and location of the product after delivery". Traceability comes from a business requirement perspective of tracking the movement of products and when origin information is preserved it is said to include provenance information. According to the most recent GS1 Global Traceability Standard, V2.0[6] these traceability concepts (Provenance, Traceability and CoC) when implemented correctly can be used to provide different levels of traceability functionality in supply chains. According to Sermpinis and Sermpinis (2018) there are two types of traceability: forward traceability the ability to find the locality at any point of the supply chain and backward traceability which is the ability to find the origin of any product given certain search criteria. Providing traceability is important for the food industry as is recommended[7] by the European Parliament in GMOs and GM free products. To provide traceability using BC in supply chains a possible approach is to tokenize the goods and use Smart Contracts (SCs) to model their transformation (Westerkamp et al. 2019). The BC in SCM traceability model has also been considered for risk management when supporting a Hazard Analysis and Critical Control Points System (HACCP) (Rahmadika et al 2018). BC enabled traceability using SCs is also well adapted to the post supply chain and has been proposed in a Product Ownership Management System (POMS) that detects counterfeits via combining the Radio Frequency Identification (RFID) product tags with a Ethereum BC system (Toyoda et al 2017).

2.3 Standards for Traceability Data

The already mentioned GS1 V2.0 standard proposes to make the bridge between physical products and their digital counterparts. According to GS1, traceability data that can be collected can be defined to answer the following five questions at each point of any business process role. "Who" – is typically identified by a Global Location Number (GLN) code (constituted by Company Prefix, Location Reference and Check Digit). "What" – can be a combination of identifiers based on Global Trade Identification Number (GTIN) with increased traceability granularity: class-level (GTIN), lot-level (GTIN + batch/lot ID - Identification) or instance level (GTIN + serial ID). When in transport process the GTIN may be coupled with the Serial Shipping Container Code (SSCC) – this is a pallet IDs that is created in during packing (by the shipping party) and loses the context and value after receipt by (the receiving party). "Where" – is typically identified by a GLN but can be extended by a GLN extension component to identify internal locations within a site, the Serial GLN (SGLN). "When" can be answered via a time stamp which should include date and time (including time zone and Coordinated Universal Time (UTC) time offset). Finally, "Why" should state the role of the party in the chain with typical roles being: harvesting, manufacturing, shipping, transporting, receiving and selling. Some additional information might be added if shipping is required: Global Shipment Identification Number (GSIN) or Global Identification Number for Consignment (GINC) when a bill of lading requires that the logistic unit has common delivery or shipping.

3 RESEARCH METHODOLOGY

The DSR methodology was defined by Hevner et al. (2004) as proactive problem-solving paradigm with the objective to create, apply and evaluate useful artifacts that have as objective to forward the human business and social capabilities in the context of information and management systems. The DSR requires that the result of applying the methodology are artifacts and these can be defined either as constructs, models, methods or instantiations. To carried out the DSR, Hevner et al. (2004) established a set of 7 rules or guidelines: (1) problem relevance, (2) research rigor, (3) design as a research problem, (4) design as an artifact, (5) design evaluation, (6) research contributions and (7) communication of the research (Hevner & Chatterjee, 2010). In this study the process of investigation was literature review, definition of problems and requirements, definition of architecture and functionality, interview with use case SCAs, production of artifacts, application of use case and finally an interactive review of artifacts. The produced artifacts were a solution architecture, the Smart Contracts, plus the PKI and digital certification scheme required to support the solution.

3.1 Research Objective

This research proposal intends to address the traceability problem by formulating a solution that leverages existing BC functionalities and certificate validation and storage architectures and allows SCAs to gain confidence and verifiable knowledge on a product's traceability in a decentralized manner. To provide context and guide the analysis and design of the solution an alimentary traceability case study has been selected and studied. The research problem then can be formulated as follows: "How to implement a supply chain traceability system using a certificate validation architecture using blockchain?"

3.2 Research Problem and Questions

The research problem can be summarized as: "How to implement complete traceability and provenance in Supply Chains using Blockchain?"

The research problem was partitioned into more specific research questions in order to facilitate research and design of a solution:

- Question 1 - What are the relevant attributes and functionalities (requirements) that must be considered to implement complete traceability in Supply Chain?
- Question 2 - What would be a feasible and applicable solution architecture using available technologies to implement a certified traceability supply chain system?

- Question 3 - What are the required components and their functionality to implement the solution architecture?
- Question 4 - What is the required business logic to effectively manage the products ID and data transversally in the SC system?
- Question 5 - How to validate the product's ID, relevant data and certificates of provenance?
- Question 6 - How can the end user validate the provenance and traceability at the post supply chain?
- Question 7 - How can this system apply to an exemplary supply chain that requires traceability and provenance assurance?

3.3 Stakeholder Definition

To understand the stakeholders needs in the supply chain traceability problem it is important to understand their identity and context in the supply chain. In Fig. 1 the relevant stakeholders / agents are mapped according to their use and impact on the supply chain: Supply Chain Actors, SC Certifiers, post SC Actors.

Figure 1. Supply chain organization

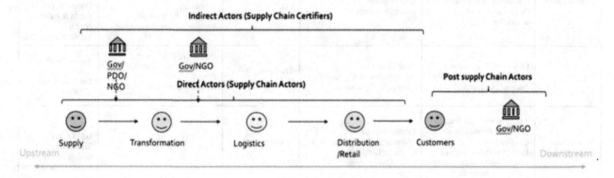

The actual supply chain users can be grouped as direct actors where they are involved in the same business use case and are directly responsible in the normal managing of the supply chain (Suppliers, Transformation, Logistics, Distribution/Retail). For the purposes of traceability each SCA has different problems requirements and thus will have different role in managing the SC Products (see Table 1 for a description of the SCA attributes pertaining to traceability). The users/buyers of the products after the retail/seller are considered to belong to the Post Supply Chain. These are either end-user consumers or organizations related to consumer interests (Consumers, Consumer groups/Environmental groups - review and influences public opinion on product attributes and impacts, Governmental agencies - verifies product safety and regulations). There are also groups or organizations that influence the working of the supply chain (require that processes or documentation follow guidelines) but that do not participate directly in the supply chain operation. In what influences the traceability problem and the certificates it is possible to group the supply chain certifiers according to the type of certificate:

- Government: certifies products that are in accordance with governmental regulations.

- PDO: certifies products in accordance with PDO regulations.
- NGO: certifies products in accordance with Non-Governmental Organization regulations.

3.4 Stakeholder Requirements

To understand which functionalities are required for SCAs it is important to define their reported weaknesses and limitations. This was performed in the previously presented review of literature. From that review we derived the following list of SCA requirements for the products and the certificate handling.

Table 1. Supply chain actors' problems and requirements

Actor	Weakness/Limitation	Consequent Problems	Aspect to Improve	Requirements	Authors
Supply	Ability to prove globally the origin, authenticity and quality of the products and producers	Counterfeiting Loss of brand equity	Provenance	Register valid SC Actor Register products with information and proof of origin	Lu & Xu (2018) Montecchi, et al. (2019)
Transformation	Difficulty to monitor the quality and origin of supplies. Limitations in monitoring the product to the final destination.	Contamination Loss of quality Loss of brand equity	Traceability CoC	Register valid SC Actor Transform products while maintaining certificate traceability Register valid SC Actor Register transfer of ownership	Aung & Chang (2013) Golan et al. (2004) GS1 Standards Document (2012) Sahoo & Halder (2020) Verzijl et al. (2015)
Logistics	Lack of visibility and trust of the transfers of ownership (internal or external).	Delays and theft No attribution of responsibility Interoperability costs	Traceability CoC	Register valid SC Actor Register transfer of ownership Provide visibility to certified product inventory, location, owner	Agrawal et al. (2020) Sahoo & Halder (2020)
Distribution/ Retail	Ability to verify the inventory, origin and authenticity of certified products. Lack of visibility and trust of the transfers of ownership (internal or external).	Counterfeiting Misrepresentation of quantities Customer Legal action Loss of brand image	Traceability CoC		Agrawal et al. (2020) GS1 Global Traceability Standard (2017) Sahoo & Halder (2020)
Final customer	No independent confirmation of the quality, origin and sustainability of products	Health and monetary impacts Distrust in business Concern for environment and sustainability	Provenance Traceability Chain of custody	Provide visibility to supply chain trace and certificates.	Cartier et al (2018) Keogh (2018)

3.5 Analysis of Requirements

Based on the review of literature the main SCM problems related to traceability that were found are: access control, impersonation, counterfeiting, theft and wrongful delivery, certifying uniqueness of products, visibility, managing product recalls and brand value. According to the review of literature to solve these problems it is crucial to improve the 3 aspects of the defined traceability conceptual framework: provenance (metadata about the origin and associated objects, processes and users), traceability (ability to trace the history, application or location of an object) and the chain of custody (time-ordered sequence of parties with physical custody of an object). The state-of-the-art literature review of SCM over BC provided indications on the required functionalities that are needed to implement more complete traceability namely: (1) Manage the SCA access authorization via a certification mechanism. (2)

Bind the physical and digital worlds by restricting access to supply chain product data only to certified actors and devices. (3) Use of a lightweight tokenization of products for representation of the products. (4) Allow the import of certificates and verify the true identity of both SCAs and products using said certificates. (5) Allow for certification data to be univocally linked with the SCAs and product tokens. (6) Allow processing and transfer of ownership procedures while maintaining the identity chain of custody and respective certificate linkages. (7) Reduce supply chain perceived risks in the post supply chain by allowing the customers to view certification information.

So, the central capability to verify a digital identity and ensure that only that participant, device or product can use that identity is an essential functionality that is required in supply chains that implement traceability. This functionality has 3 parts: (1) being able to verify the digital signature, (2) being able to verify the certificate of a CA has the correct attributes and finally (3) that the participant is the correct owner of the certificate. This traceability functionality was translated into a requirement to setup a PKI involving the SCAs, the product Certificate Authorities (CAs) and that extends to the certified products. According to the literature review it was also possible to summarize the required attributes for a SCM with more complete traceability with verifiable: "user identity" (SCA ID and certificate), "product identity" (Product ID and certificate), "transfer of custody" (two-sided verification of SCA and product IDs), "uniqueness" (ledger of unique product IDs, "location of products" (geographic reference), and "timestamp of operations". From the required functionality and attributes, it was possible to select a supporting applicable technology and derive the corresponding improvement of the traceability aspect (Table 2).

Table 2. Applicable technology and the corresponding improvement of the traceability aspect

ID	Requirement	Applicable Technology – Proposed Solution	Problem That It Solves	Supported Concept/ Added Value
1	SCA registration validation and access control	Public Key Infrastructure (PKI) and SCs – uses certificate to establish and maintain assurance of the identity.	Access control- only allowed SC actors can interact with SCM. Requires registration/verification of the certificates	Support Traceability
2	SCA sign on operations	Ethereum BC and SC logic– associate EBC addresses to validated identities. Any EBC has to interact by using a signed transaction.	Impersonation - The validated participants are required to sign all operations and make proof of their identity	Support Traceability
3	Register products certificates	SC logic and PKI – associate product identifiers with their certificates	Counterfeiting - only original products information is introduced into the SCM	Assure Provenance
4	Correct transfer of ownership	SC logic - provides 2-sided transfer of ownership.	Theft and wrongful delivery – register of each transfer of ownership is registered	Implement Chain of custody
5	Verify ownership and product certificate validity	SC logic and PKI - to verify the current ownership of a product and if the certificate is valid or has been revoked.	Product ownership and certificate validation - requires a check of ownership and if the certificate is valid.	Implement Traceability and assure provenance
6	Transform products	SC logic - use of SC functions to tracks the transformation of certified products	Certificate and inventory management – requires that transformed products maintain the certification source.	Support traceability, provenance
7	Product certificate retrieval.	JavaScript, SC logic and PKI- use of SCs and an external URL for certificate visibility.	Standards, health, compliance, brand value - requires controlled access to the chain of product certificates.	Implement Provenance visibility

4 RESULTS

4.1 Solution Design

Following the literature survey research results, in order to design a solution to provide a supply chain system with complete traceability we must focus on providing solutions to the problems raised by the main three concepts:

- Provenance – provide metadata about the origin, context and history of change of products and producers
- Traceability – provide record of the trace history, application and location of a produce in the SC
- Chain of custody – provide time-ordered sequence of events the parties create when they take physical custody of an object or collection of objects as it moves through a supply chain network.

In table 3 we described the identification of the problems of each concept as it related to SCAs and Products. Following the DSR, the use cases and the architecture are the design artifacts that provide the solutions for the research problems.

Table 3. Mapping between problems, solutions, and artifacts

Concept	Problems	Solutions	Use Cases to Implement
Provenance	Proof of SCA Identity	Identity validation and storage	A - Register SCA
	Proof of product authenticity with origin attributes	Certified Product registry	B - Register Product C/D - Get/Set Product Attributes and Certificates H – Import ID and Certificate
	Provide visibility to supply chain trace and certificates	Provide visibility to specific product certificate and trace data	I/J –Retrieve/Validate ID and Certificates K – View Product Certificate
Traceability	Register changes to the product data (location, owner)	Changes to product are registered via traceable transactions	C - Get/Set Product Attributes F/G - Ownership Transfer to/Receive from
	Transform products while maintaining certificate traceability	Provide access control to view / modify product data	E. Transform Product
	Provide visibility to supply chain trace and certificates	Provide visibility to specific product certificate and trace data	I/J –Retrieve/Validate ID and Certificates K – View Product Certificate
Chain of Custody	Register and view the transfer of ownership (among SCAs)	Provide distributed mechanism for change of custody	F/G - Ownership Transfer to/Receive from
	Provide visibility to supply chain trace and certificates	Provide visibility to specific product certificate and trace data	I/J –Retrieve/Validate ID and Certificates K – View Product Certificate

4.2 Proposed Functionality

According to Weber et al. (2016) BC can be used as the collaborative process execution machine. This is performed in 3 steps. Firstly, translating the process specifications/requirements into Smart Contracts.

Secondly using the BC computational infrastructure to organize the collaborative processes. Thirdly using the BC triggers to connect physical and digital world. This proposal adds to that proposal the use digital cryptographic certificates to establish both: SCA and product identity and authenticity inside/post a distributed and untrusted supply chain. The digital representation of supply chain products is supported by a lightweight tokenization of the products and their associated processes in a SC. In this proposal the certificates are only linked to the tokens and to have a minimum increase of BC storage and avoid the cost for the importing and validation of the certificates in the SCM. To implement the previously defined requirements a set of SCM traceability functions/use cases were defined to be implemented in the Ethereum SC (with the Smart Contract business logic). The SCAs can operate the SCM by calling the SC functions[8] (Fig. 2). Architecture workflows for referenced use cases A to G are described in AN-NEX 1, use cases H and I are described in ANNEX 2.

Figure 2. Proposed functionality

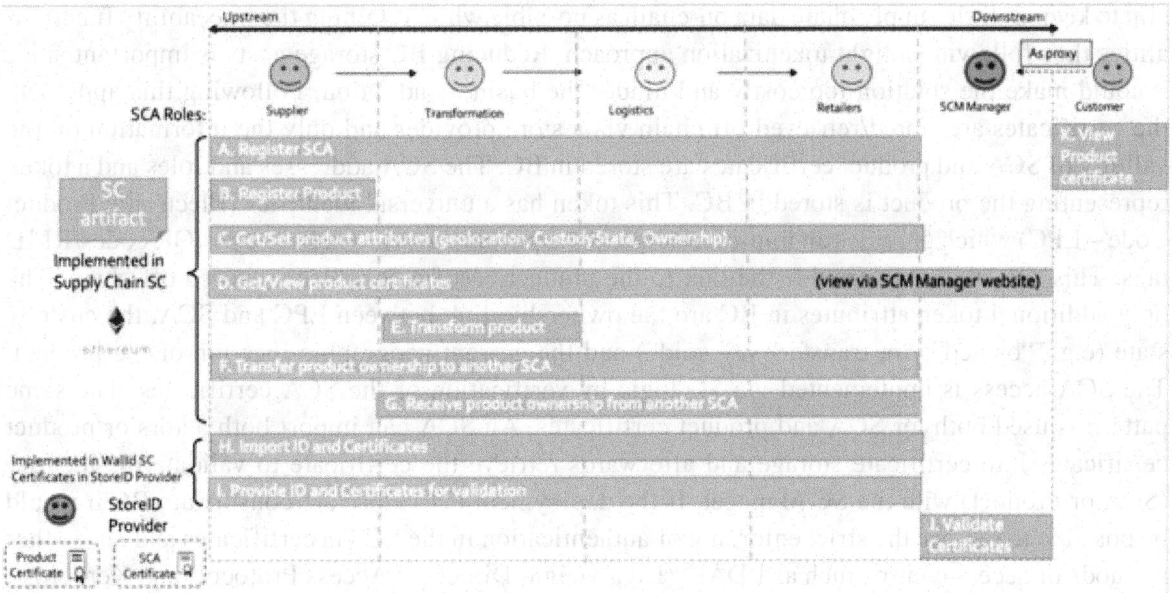

4.3 Design Aspects

Due to BC's unique capabilities and features several design aspects and trade-offs must be considered when designing a SCM over BC. The decision to use private/consortium vs. public BC systems will depend on the selected industry use case, its requirement for global public access and will have impacts on the decentralization, the scalability and latency/latency variance of transactions. A public BC like Ethereum is globally accessible, fully decentralized and has higher availability due to the number of nodes. One trade-off of a public BC is that its transactions are expected to have higher latency and latency variance so the scalability aspect is not under control of the participating organizations and the BC code will generally follow a standard that is defined by a distributed improvement proposal scheme. As an example, an operation over Ethereum public BC is expected to take tens of seconds or more, varying much on the load on the system and so the latency is not under control of the SCM participants. This latency and latency variance problem can be mitigated to a few seconds per transaction if a private or consortium BC is used. However, a trade-off of that approach would be to lose some of the global access and availability features. In what regards scalability a private or consortium BC can scale its throughput without having to increase the number of nodes since it is possible for example to specifically configure consensus mechanisms that allow for faster transaction validation. For the use case in analysis in this article and for the proposal both public or private BC networks are possible to be used and there is no dependency to any BC public/private flavor. Another design aspect to consider is how to store some or all the SCM data: on-chain or off-chain. When user data is stored on-chain (as a variable in a SC) it is more costly (at least 2x more but can vary depending on the BC) but is potentially more performant since the data is retrieved from BC immediately. If data is stored off-chain the SC can interact with it but is less performant since it requires querying the off-chain system so we should expect a more complex implementation and possibly the addition of latency to the solution. The proposal in this article is to aim to keep as little supply chain data on-chain as possible while retaining the traceability functionalities thus following a light tokenization approach. Reducing BC storage costs is important since it could make the solution too costly and hinder the business adoption. Following this approach, the certificates are stored/retrieved off chain via a store provider and only the information on the validity of SCA and product certificates are stored in BC. The SCA addresses and roles and a token representing the product is stored in BC. This token has a universal identifier (Electronic Product Code – EPC) which provides an immediate link to the physical world via Bar codes/QR codes/RFID tags. This EPC will also provide the link to the product certificate which is stored off-chain. The only additional token attributes in BC are the ownership link between EPC and SCA, the custody state (e.g., "owned", "in transfer" or" sold") and the current geographic location of the product. The SCA access is implemented via SC logic by verification of the SCA certificates. The same pattern is used both for SCA and product certificates. An SCA can import both actors or product certificates into certificate storage and afterwards retrieve the certificate to validate the identity (SCA or Product) with the SC Manager. If the deployment is to a private/consortium BC it would be possible to remove the strict enforcing of authentication in the SC via certificates and have other methods of access control such as LDAP[9] (Lightweight Directory Access Protocol) and Kerberos[10] to improve performance and prevent attacks on the BC consensus. It could be argued that private BCs provide better security from the start since only allowed users can use the BC. However, one of the main security risks to any BC is the protection of the private keys and the integrity of the SC code, which is non-dependent on network infrastructure control but on good security practices and hardened and well-maintained SC code. As a preliminary step and to interact with the SCM, a SCA must first create a BC account. A BC account is considered to be the public and private keypair that are connected to the user address and the funds (both stored in the network). To manage the account more easily an interface/wrapper is used, and this is what is generically called a BC Wallet. Interworking with BC with the user wallet can be performed in several ways. For this solution proposal we selected Metamask[11] since it allows to streamline the end-user experience by having an interaction with a responsive website while also allowing the use of both hardware wallets (e.g., Ledger[12] with Metamask) and online wallets (e.g., MyEtherWallet (MEW)[13] with Metamask).

4.4 Proposed Architecture

The proposed architecture uses a Ethereum BC SC to implement the already presented use cases. As mentioned, the SCAs interact with the BC using their wallets via Metamask with calls to the SC code using a JavaScript based interface (Web3 API[14]) (Figure 3).

Figure 3. Proposed architecture

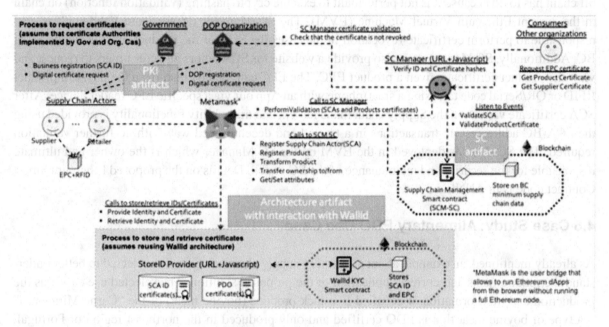

The state of the supply chain, all its actors and products are tokenized in Ethereum via the Smart Contract. This proposal uses digital certificates for user and product authentication and so it requires that recognized organizations implement a PKI (to generate digital certificates and provide the chain of trust). In the case of public market products governments and certification organizations are among the best candidates for establishing a PKI for businesses operating on global supply chains. It is possible to have the PKI implemented directly by consortium organizations when the use cases are restricted to specific businesses or industry sectors. This proposal requires that only validated SCAs (the ones which can provide an ID and certificate that match and verifies) can register products into the SC system. The SCA and products certificates are digital certificates that attest of the business identity (e.g., when registering with national government agency) or attest that the product has unique distinguishing and certified characteristics (such as in the case of PDO (Protected Designation of Origin) where the products and processes are verified and certified by a selected PDO regulator organization. The importing and retrieval aspects of the SCA and product certificates is performed with the reuse of the Know Your Customer (KYC) solution from WalliD adapted for identities such as organizations and products. Details on the Certificate Import and Validation functionality using WalliD KYC (off-chain solution) are described in ANNEX 2.

In this proposal the products in the supply chain are referenced by an industry referencing standard, the EPC – Electronic Product Code which is a unique identifier commonly used in supply chains as described in the case of livestock supply chain by Hartley et al. (2014). The supply chain can operate with products without certification (since it is optional to provide them) but the main business value of this proposal should be for products that require authenticity validation. The validation of certificate hashes for both SCA identity and products is performed off-chain by the Supply Chain Manager entity (that includes the role of "Certificate Validator"). Another deciding factor to have certificate validation off chain has to do because it is not performant to execute crypto hashing (validation function) on chain in the current Ethereum Virtual Machine (EVM). The SC Manager ("Certificate Validator") is also responsible to perform certificate revocation in the cases the SCA or the product must leave the SCM BC. Additionally, SC Manager can also provide a website for SCA actors and consumers to request and view the product certificate given a product EPC. The EPC can then be read from the physical product RFID or QR/Serial code tag using a smartphone with an App our via a specific EPC reader device. After SCA certificate validation the Supply chain management and traceability functionality is provided using the SCA BC addresses via transactions in a trusted and decentralized way with no further validation required. The SCM-SC is deployed in the EVM by the SC Manager which is the owner and ultimate responsible for the security and maintenance of the SC code[15]. Details on the proposed Ethereum Smart Contract code is in ANNEX 3

4.5 Case Study: Alimentary PDO Use Case

As already mentioned, an example about alimentary supply chain use case was selected to better understand the requirements and correct application of the proposed solution. The selected use case was the production and transformation of certified livestock produce (bovine meat) of the "Carne Mirandesa" – a type of bovine meat that is PDO certified and only produced in the northeast region of Portugal. This PDO is already currently certified using a combination of paper certificates and products tags or stickers that are shipped with the product. From an interview with a producer and retailer 3 document samples were collected: the certificate that links the Government ID of the animal (SNIRA[16] ID) with the PDO ID and certificate of the brand "Mirandesa" (Geneology ID), the transformation identifier that is shipped with the bovine meat that shows the reference to the animal (SNIRA ID) and the sale point invoice that attests to the purchase of the carcass and served meals with the reference to the batch attested by the a governmental agency (SNIRA ID). The unique identifier that is used across the supply chain is the Electronic Product Code (EPC) that is linked with both the SNIRA ID and the Genealogy ID (EPC-SNIRA ID-Genealogy ID). The product certificate to be generated has then to hold these 3 fields in the X509[17] certificate request as mandatory fields to be certified together with the public key hash of the producer (supplier actor in the SCM). In summary each product will be issued a X509 certificate by the producer. This particular CA chain of trust requires three SCA certificates: one for the root CA (the Government CA), another for the intermediate CA (the PDO association CA) and finally one for the SCA producer. The summaries of the use case data and PKI certificate setup are presented in ANNEX 4 and ANNEX 5. To streamline the production of X509 certificates the request for product certificates can be automated by an application at the producer side that requires that the producer inputs the triad of X509 attributes that need to be certified (EPC, SNIRA-ID, PDO-ID) and then issues the certificate request and at the CA's side a backend IT system that issues the X509 certificate after the verification processes have been validated. It should also be noted that as a product is processed in the supply chain its EPC code may change from animal EPC (type SGTIN) to carcass EPC (type SSCC) and carton tag EPC (type SGTIN). However even in this case the proposed solution SmartContract code is capable of maintaining reference to the original certified EPC and its owner SCA and support complete certificate traceability. This EPC code change is also described by GS1 in Hartley et al. (2014) where a livestock traceability proof of concept (PoC) was implemented. In that PoC the EPC codes are read from RFID tags but in that case, they were inserted into a centralized SCM application to provide the required traceability metadata while in this proposal the EPC is stored in BC. As in the PoC in this proposal the EPCs can suffer change due to processing the meat thus the requirement for the previously presented "transform product" function in the SCM SmartContract to keep the EPC and certificate link[18].

5. CONCLUSIONS AND FUTURE WORK

As presented before, we posited and fully described a complex research problem. This complexity stems from two factors, the relative novelty of the technology and the combination of several existing solutions (Ethereum Smart Contracts, Digital Certificates, PKI and WallId certificate storage). This combination allows to propose a solution application for a supply chain when it is imperative to assure the traceability and the authenticity of the products sold over that value chain.

5.1 Research Contribution and Solution Benefits

The research contribution of this work is a solution that aims to answer the research problem of providing complete traceability for a supply chain using blockchain. The main benefit of the solution is that it allows for a group of independent participants to implement a decentralized supply chain system with a complete traceability model for certified products. Another benefit is that via the PKI allow for SCAs themselves to import certificates and customers to view them thus providing trust among participants and the end customers. The proposed architecture simplifies the storage of the certificates by reusing a KYC system (used in banking and credential verification) to both store and validate these certificates. If any certificate fails validation or is revoked (e.g., expiration) it can be added to a CRL (Certificate Revocation List) by the CA (as is usual in PKIs) and the SC Manager simply sets an invalid certificate flag in the SC. If a SCA own certificate is revoked it no longer has access to the chain of trust until it provides a valid certificate. If the product certificate is revoked the product token can still be managed in the SCM but the certificates will be shown as expired or invalid to SCAs and customers (allowing the supply chain to operate while the certificate issue is being resolved). During operation, the SCAs have access via the Blockchain to the ownership status, the operations timestamps, the full chain of certificates and the transfer locations (if added) which can be further processed by SCAs own internal Supply Chain Management systems to interoperate with other IT systems (analytics) and optimize the supply chain.

5.2 Limitations

The main drawbacks of the solution are its dependency on a PKI (for SCAs and products), a centralized and hierarchical trust model and the dependency on a central entity (Supply Chain Manager) for certificate validation. Regarding the dependency on PKI the minimum requirements are its setup by a national or regional or any trusted authority in a privately owned supply chain and that the SCAs must subscribe to an authentication scheme for their identities and products. Regarding the SC Manager this actor is required to deploy the proposed SmartContract into the Ethereum BC and to be the entity responsible to be the "certificate validator". A possible alternative to the use of a centralized PKI (and possibly to replace also the SC Manager) would to use a decentralized approach as has been recently proposed with Self-Sovereign Identities (SSI) and the usage of Decentralized Identifiers (DIDs) as defined by W3C. Instead of digital certificates some previous solutions propose the import of scanned paper certificates. This is the case of "origin Chain" implementation, but this seems a stegap approach since such verification is more complex to implement and may require manual intervention to fix misreading or damage to the paper certificates. A more technology-oriented approach would be the use of IoT devices and RFID tags with digital certificates where all authentication and verification is automated with higher granularity and the added security of a physical security token. An alternative for the SCAs certification-based authorization is to replace it with a simpler although less decentralized and autonomous authentication system (e.g., LDAP) but this has the drawback of increased complexity and complexifying the security and management aspects in cases of global SCMs. If only a sectorial industry approach is required and the global decentralization and autonomy is not necessary and it would be more advantageous to operate over a consortium BC, with the benefits of lower latencies/latency variances and centralized SCM control.

5.3 Future Work

There remain open points that are left for possible future work and development of a Proof of Concept (PoC). The first open point is that the SC lacks the functionality for all SCAs to add product certificates (currently only suppliers) in the case of transformation of products. Additionally, it is still undefined when to delete product references after the products go to the post supply chain. Some attention should be given also to the issue of certificate validation outside of the BC. One of the possible criticisms of the proposed solution is that of not achieving complete decentralization since due to the centralized PKI and proposing a certificate validation mechanism to be implemented off chain. As previously mentioned it would be very interesting to explore the adoption of SSI and DIDs as a non-centralized approach to the identity and certificate validation problems. For future work, besides the open issues it is left the development and implementation of a PoC that would allow the deployment of a fully-working/testable SCM with this architecture. Also, for future work would be the design of an incentive scheme that would allow for the implementation of the "Certificate Validator" function. This functionality should be possible to implement by third parties in the public Ethereum BC. A future PoC would also require the implementation of a test framework (in JavaScript) to interact with the SC via the Web3 API and the companion browser or possibly IoT software add-ons to facilitate user interaction with the SCM. In addition to real use case validation of the proposal a PoC would allow to measure operating and information storage costs plus the operational feasibility and business competitivity (in terms of required IT infrastructure).

CONFLICT OF INTEREST

The authors declare that they have no conflict of interest.

REFERENCES

Agrawal, T. K., Kumar, V., Pal, R., Wang, L., & Chen, Y. (2021). Blockchain-based framework for supply chain traceability: A case example of textile and clothing industry. *Computers & Industrial Engineering*, *154*, 107130. doi:10.1016/j.cie.2021.107130

Antonopoulos, A. M., & Wood, G. (2018). *Mastering Ethereum: Building Smart Contracts and DApps*. O'Reilly Media, Inc.

Aung, M. M., & Change, S. S. (2014). Traceability in a food supply chain: Safety and quality perspectives. *Food Control*, *39*, 172–184. doi:10.1016/j.foodcont.2013.11.007

Bartoletti, M., & Pompianu, L. An empirical analysis of smart contracts: platforms, applications, and design patterns. In *International Conference on Financial Cryptography and Data Security* (pp. 494-509). Springer.

Berg, J., & Myllymaa, L. (n.d.). *Impact of blockchain on sustainable supply chain practices* [Master Thesis]. Jönköping International Business School, University of Jönköping, Sweden.

Cartier, L. E., Ali, S. H., & Krzemnicki, M. S. (2018). Blockchain, Chain of Custody and Trace Elements: An Overview of Tracking and Traceability Opportunities in the Gem Industry. *The Journal of Geology*, *36*(3), 212–227. doi:10.15506/JoG.2018.36.3.212

Casey, M., & Wong, P. (2017). Global supply chains are about to get better, thanks to blockchain. *Harvard Business Review*, *13*, 1–6.

Chang, Y., Iakovou, E., & Shi, W. (2020). Blockchain in Global Supply Chains and Cross Border Trade: A Critical Synthesis of the State-of-the-Art. *International Journal of Production Research*, *58*(7), 2082–2099. doi:10.1080/00207543.2019.1651946

Cheney, J., Chong, S., Foster, N., Seltzer, M., & Vansummeren, S. (2009). *Provenance: A future history. In Proceedings of the 24th ACM SIGPLAN conference on Object oriented programming systems languages and applications*. ACM. http://nrs.harvard.edu/urn-3:HUL.InstRepos:5346327

Dinh, T., Liu, R., Zhang, M., Chen, G., Ooi, B., & Wang, Ji. (2017). *Untangling Blockchain: A Data Processing View of Blockchain Systems*. arXiv:1708.05665v1 [cs.DB].

Dobrovnik, M., Herold, D., Fürst, E., & Kummer, S. (2018). Blockchain for and in Logistics: What to Adopt and Where to Start. *Logistics*, *2*(18), 18. Advance online publication. doi:10.3390/logistics2030018

GS1 Global Traceability Standard. (2017). *GS1's framework for the design of interoperable traceability systems for supply chains*. https://www.gs1.org/sites/default/files/docs/traceability/GS1_Global_Traceability_Standard_i2.pdf

GS1 Global Traceability Standard. (2012). *Business Process and System Requirements for Full Supply Chain Traceability*. https://www.gs1.org/docs/traceability/Global_Traceability_Standard.pdf

Garcia-Torres, S., Albareda, L., Rey-Garcia, M., & Seuring, S. (2018). Traceability for sustainability – literature review and conceptual framework. *Supply Chain Management*. Advance online publication. doi:10.1108/SCM-04-2018-0152

Guo, H., & Yu, X. (2022). A survey on blockchain technology and its security. Blockchain. *Research and Applications*, *3*, 100067.

Hartley, G., & Sundermann, E. (2014). The Efficacy of Using the EPC global Network for Livestock Traceability: A Proof of Concept. GS1.

Hevner, A., & Chatterjee, S. (2010). Design Science Research in Information Systems. In *Design Research in Information Systems. Integrated Series in Information Systems, 22*. Springer. doi:10.1007/978-1-4419-5653-8_2

Houben, R., & Snyers, A. (2018). *Cryptocurrencies and blockchain: Legal context and implications for financial crime, money laundering and tax evasion.* Policy Department for Economic, Scientific and Quality of Life Policies. Directorate-General for Internal Policies.

ISEAL Alliance. (2016). *Chain of custody models and definitions.* https://www.isealalliance.org/sites/default/files/resource/2017-11/ISEAL_Chain_of_Custody_Models_Guidance_September_2016.pdf

Kaur, P., & Parashar, A. (2022). A Systematic Literature Review of Blockchain Technology for Smart Villages. *Archives of Computational Methods in Engineering*, *29*(4), 2417–2468. doi:10.100711831-021-09659-7 PMID:34720578

Keogh, J. G. (2018). *Blockchain, Provenance, Traceability & Chain of Custody.* https://bit.ly/2LaJ6x7

Kim, H. M., & Laskowski, M. (2018). Toward an ontology-driven blockchain design for supply-chain provenance. *International Journal of Intelligent Systems in Accounting Finance & Management*, *25*(1), 18–27. doi:10.1002/isaf.1424

Kros, J., Liao, Y., Kirchoff, J., & Zemanek, J. Jr. (2019, January-June). Traceability in the Supply Chain. *International Journal of Applied Logistics*, *9*(1), 1–22. doi:10.4018/IJAL.2019010101

Kshetri, N. (2018). Blockchain's roles in meeting key supply chain management objectives. *International Journal of Information Management*, *39*, 80–89. doi:10.1016/j.ijinfomgt.2017.12.005

Litke, A., Anagnostopoulos, D., & Varvarigou, T. (2019). Blockchains for Supply Chain Management: Architectural Elements and Challenges Towards a Global Scale Deployment. *Logistics*, *3*(5), 5. Advance online publication. doi:10.3390/logistics3010005

Lu, Q., & Xu, X. (2017). *Adaptable Blockchain-Based Systems: A Case Study for Product Traceability.* IEEE Software, November/December.

Martin, R. C. (2017). *Clean architecture: A Craftsman's Guide to Software Structure and Design.* Pearson Education.

Meidute-Kavaliauskiene, I., Yıldız, B., Çigdem, S., & Cincikaite, R. (2021). An Integrated Impact of Blockchain on Supply Chain Applications. *Logistics*, *5*(33), 33. Advance online publication. doi:10.3390/logistics5020033

Montecchi, M., Plangger, K., & Etter, M. (2019). It's real, trust me! Establishing supply chain provenance using blockchain. *Business Horizons*, *62*(3), 283–293. doi:10.1016/j.bushor.2019.01.008

Moosavi, J., Naeni, L. M., Fathollahi-Fard, A. M., & Fiore, U. (2021). Moosavi1, J., Naeni1, L., Fathollahi-Fard, A., & Fiore, U.: Blockchain in supply chain management: a review, bibliometric, and network analysis. *Environmental Science and Pollution Research International*. Advance online publication. doi:10.100711356-021-13094-3

Pal, A., & Kant, K. (2019). Using Blockchain for Provenance and Traceability in Internet of Things-Integrated Food Logistics. *Computer*, *52*(12), 94–98. doi:10.1109/MC.2019.2942111

PDO. (n.d.). *Protected Designation of Origin*. European Commission Geographical indications and quality schemes. https://agriculture.ec.europa.eu/farming/geographical-indications-and-quality-schemes/geographical-indications-and-quality-schemes-explained_en#pdo

Perboli, G., Musso, S., & Rosano, M. (2018). Blockchain in logistics and supply chain: A lean approach for designing real-world use cases. *IEEE Access : Practical Innovations, Open Solutions*, *6*, 62018–62028. doi:10.1109/ACCESS.2018.2875782

Rahmadika, S., Kweka, B. J., Latt, C. N. Z., & Rhee, K. H. (2018). A Preliminary Approach of Blockchain Technology in Supply Chain System. In *2018 IEEE International Conference on Data Mining Workshops (ICDMW)* (pp. 156-160), IEEE. 10.1109/ICDMW.2018.00029

Sahoo, S., & Halder, R. (2021). Traceability and ownership claimof data on big data marketplace using blockchain technology. *Journal of Information and Telecommunication*, *5*(1), 35–61. doi:10.1080/24751839.2020.1819634

Sermpinis, T., & Sermpinis, C. (2018). *Traceability Decentralization in Supply Chain Management Using Blockchain Technologies*. arXiv preprint arXiv:1810.09203.

Somapa, S., Cools, M., & Dullaert, W. (n.d.). Characterizing supply chain visibility - a literature review. *International Journal of Logistics Management*. https://doi.org/ doi:10.1108/IJLM-06-2016-0150

Tavares, M., Guerreiro, A., Coutinho, C., Veiga, F., & Campos, A. (2018). WalliD: Secure your ID in an Ethereum Wallet. In *2018 International Conference on Intelligent Systems (IS)* (pp. 714-721). IEEE. 10.1109/IS.2018.8710547

Toyoda, K., Mathiopoulos, P. T., Sasase, I., & Ohtsuki, T. (2017). A novel blockchain-based product ownership management system (POMS) for anti-counterfeits in the post supply chain. *IEEE Access : Practical Innovations, Open Solutions*, *5*, 17465–17477. doi:10.1109/ACCESS.2017.2720760

W3C. (n.d.). *Decentralized Identifiers (DIDs) v1.0 Core architecture, data model, and representations*. https://www.w3.org/TR/did-core/

Wang, Y., Singgih, M., Wang, J., & Rit, M. (2019). Making sense of blockchain technology: How will it transform supply chains? *International Journal of Production Economics*, *211*, 221–236. doi:10.1016/j.ijpe.2019.02.002

Weber, I., Xu, X., Riveret, R., Governatori, G., Ponomarev, A., & Mendling, J. (2016). Untrusted Business Process Monitoring and Execution Using Blockchain. In M. La Rosa, P. Loos, & O. Pastor (Eds.), Lecture Notes in Computer Science: Vol. 9850. *Business Process Management. BPM 2016*. Springer. doi:10.1007/978-3-319-45348-4_19

Westerkamp, M., Victor, F., & Kupper, A. (2019). Tracing manufacturing processes using blockchain-based token compositions. *Digital Communications and Networks*, 6(2), 167–176. doi:10.1016/j.dcan.2019.01.007

Xu, L., Chen, L., Gao, Z., Chang, Y., Iakovou, E., & Shi, W. (2018). Binding the Physical and Cyber Worlds: A Blockchain Approach for Cargo Supply Chain Security Enhancement. In *2018 IEEE International Symposium on Technologies for Homeland Security* (pp. 1-5). IEEE. 10.1109/THS.2018.8574184

Xu, X., Lu, Q., Liu, Y., Zhu, L., Yao, H., & Vasilakos, A. V. (2019). Designing blockchain based applications a case study for imported product traceability. *Future Generation Computer Systems*, 92, 399–406. doi:10.1016/j.future.2018.10.010

Ying, W., Jia, S., & Du, W. (2018). Digital enablement of blockchain: Evidence from HNA group. *International Journal of Information Management*, 39, 1–4. doi:10.1016/j.ijinfomgt.2017.10.004

ENDNOTES

[1]   WalliD product: https://wallid.io/

[2]   ISEAL Alliance - global membership association for credible sustainability standards

[3]   EU Regulation (EC) No 178/2002 at: https://bit.ly/35il6Ra

[4]   ISO 9000:2015 at: https://www.iso.org/standard/45481.html

[5]   FAO CODEX Alimentarius CXG 60-2006 at: https://bit.ly/2meiPUS

[6]   Latest GS1 standard at: https://www.gs1.org/standards/traceability/traceability/2-0

[7]   EU traceability recommendations at: https://ec.europa.eu/food/plant/gmo/traceability_labelling_en

[8]   Details on the Proposed SCM Functions are available in https://github.com/Supply-Chain-Traceability/SolutionProposal

[9]   An application protocol for accessing and maintaining distributed directory information services.

[10]   A computer-network authentication protocol that uses tickets to allow nodes to prove their identity.

[11]   Metamask documentation. Retrieved from https://bit.ly/2ATNqeE

[12]   Ledger is one example of a hardware Ethereum wallet: https://www.ledger.com/

[13]   MyEtherWallet is one example of a software Ethereum wallet: https://www.myetherwallet.com/

[14]   Web3 API is Ethereum Javascript API that allows to interact with an Ethereum node: https://web3js.readthedocs.io/en/v1.2.4/

[15]   A more detailed description of the architecture use cases is available in https://github.com/Supply-Chain-Traceability/SolutionProposal

[16]   SNIRA (Sistema Nacional de Informação e Registo Animal) is the national Portuguese Government livestock registry: https://www.ifap.pt/snira

[17]   X.509 is a cryptographic standard defined by ITU-T standardization body that defines the format of public key certificates (used in https and electronic signatures): https://tools.ietf.org/html/rfc5280

[18]   For details on use case samples, EPC details, the PKI certificate request and revocation see https://github.com/Supply-Chain-Traceability/SolutionProposal

Chapter 17
Identification of the Problem and Research Methodology

Pradeep Kumar

https://orcid.org/0000-0002-0206-9808
Teerthanker Mahaveer University, India

Rajeev Kumar

https://orcid.org/0000-0002-4141-1282
G.L. Bajaj Institute of Technology and Management, India

Kumar Balwant Singh
L.S. College, Muzaffarpur, India

Madhurendra Kumar
Centre for Development of Advanced Computing, India

ABSTRACT

Internet and applications have become an essential part of life nowadays. We are now at the stage where we can think about future smart cities as we are having various driving forces in the form of web-based applications. The main phenomena behind data-computing can be considered as for keeping data persistent, secure, available, and relevant for the information in real time. In the chapter, the authors proposed blockchain representation-based application process that is a low cost and efficient application for true sense ubiquitous usage that is also the demand of current time. The implemented application is providing a huge data security scenario for a web application system, and it is dealing with the efficient information processing towards storage, processing, and access of the information in a real time. In this chapter, the authors provided various schemes for high availability of on-demand data with proper asymmetric algorithms techniques.

DOI: 10.4018/978-1-6684-9151-5.ch017

1 INTRODUCTION

Even quicker than many had anticipated decades ago, technology advancement is advancing. The massive research effort being made by the scientific community, which aspires to improve human life by creating a vision of a smarter world, is what's causing technology to advance at such a rapid pace. The development and implementation of smart city prototypes, which include smart houses, factories, autos, transit, and various smart human gadgets, has been heavily supported by academic research and industry adoption. The success of this futuristic human society was made possible by many fundamental technologies. The Internet of Things (IoT), Software-Defined Networking (SDN), Artificial Intelligence (AI), Cloud, Fog, and Edge Computing, interruption systems, blockchain, cryptocurrencies and cybersecurity, cryptography methods are a few examples, although they are not the only ones. Furthermore, blockchain was able to improve these technologies by adding new features that are essential for the total automation needed in smart environments.

In addition to IoT, SDN offers intelligent control and administration of the underlying network through dynamic and programmable control. IoT networks are ideally suited for SDN because of how quickly the number of devices, where they are located, and how much data they send change. Furthermore, SDN enables the incorporation of AI and machine learning into the decision-making procedures for load balancing, computational offloading, traffic control, and data flow in the network. IoT is seen as a key component in allowing smart city innovation and, consequently, SDN. However, it calls for laborious computations and storage needs, which are incompatible with low-power and IoT devices with scarce resources. Cloud, fog, and edge computing technologies were mainly developed to assist in providing storage and computing resources as compensated services to manage such networks.

As a commercial service, cloud computing offers theoretically limitless computational and storage capacity. They are typically found in large data centers that are positioned in remote areas. The enormous volume of traffic that IoT devices generate can overwhelm the core network due to the distance. The service response time (delay) for IoT devices is also impacted by this distance, especially when they require feedback on their requests. A delay of just a few milliseconds could have disastrous consequences in time-sensitive Internet of Things applications like self-driving automobiles. Fog and Edge Computing technologies, for example, provide solutions to these problems by bringing such resources closer to the IoT infrastructure. They reduce latency and save network bandwidth by preprocessing and analyzing IoT data earlier before sending it to the cloud for more intensive processing and long-term storage.

The futuristic notion of "trustless" smart cities we previously discussed requires one missing technological link for all those technologies. A third-party trusted party is typically required to establish trust among the IoT devices performing the transactions in order to facilitate communication among numerous IoT devices, which are typically produced or owned by various enterprises. In this situation, blockchain can fill the gap and offer a decentralized way to establish this trust mechanism. IoT devices can also be used as a method to manage the trading of digital assets, carry out monetary transactions between them, and keep a permanent record of the transactions carried out by IoT devices. In reality, blockchains are capable of much more than that. They can assist mitigate some of the current disadvantages of SDN, Cloud, Fog, and Edge solutions for IoT applications and progress the growth of the IoT sector in Figure 1.

In this chapter we will be exploring the identified gap with respect to the problem statement is as a broad view, the various constituting components towards the formation of the system, their interactions, and measures. Several blockchain phases like Supply Chain, Finance, Customer Experience, Emerging Areas, Focus on Digital Payments, and Digital Identities are also being discussed how they solve the

Figure 1. Blockchain, SDN, AI, cloud, fog, and edge computing technology integration

recurrent industry problems. Later in this chapter, the other requirements of hardware and software will also be explored, finally, the proposed solution and the implementation's theoretical aspects will be discussed as a path of the research formation and flow.

2 PROBLEM IDENTIFICATION

Recently, both the business world and the academic community have given cryptocurrencies a lot of attention. The capital market for Bitcoin, sometimes referred to as the first cryptocurrency, reached $10 billion in 2016. (coindesk, 2016). The foundational component of Bitcoin is the blockchain. In 2008, a proposal for blockchain technology was made, and it was put into use in 2009. (Nakamoto, 2008). All committed transactions are kept on a blockchain, also referred to as a public ledger, which keeps them in a series of blocks. As fresh blocks are added to the chain, it keeps expanding. The decentralization, persistency, anonymity, and auditability of blockchain technology are significant features. By merging a variety of fundamental technologies, such as cryptographic hashing and asymmetric cryptography-based digital signatures, blockchain may function in a decentralized setting, and a distributed consensus mechanism. A transaction can happen decentralized thanks to blockchain technology. Blockchain can therefore dramatically lower costs and increase productivity.

Despite the fact that it has a lot of potential for developing new internet services, the blockchain technology is now plagued by a number of technical issues. To begin with, scalability is a serious issue. An average of one Bitcoin block is created every 10 minutes, and it can only be 1 MB in size. As a result, the Bitcoin network can only processing 7 transactions per second, so high-frequency trading is not possible. However, larger blocks require more storage space, and therefore propagate around the network more slowly. Users will thus to keep up with a strong blockchain. Centralization will result from this over time. As a result, it is now difficult to balance security and block size. Second, it has been shown that egotistical mining techniques can produce more income than is reasonable (Eyal and Sirer, 2014). To generate more money in the future, miners conceal their extracted blocks. Because of the possibility of frequent branching, blockchain development is hampered. Therefore, in order to resolve this issue, some remedies must be proposed. Additionally, it has been shown that even when individuals just use their private key and public key to complete transactions, privacy leakage in blockchain can still happen (Biryukov et al., 2014). It's even possible to find the user's actual IP address. There are certain major issues with the current consensus methods, such as proof of work (PoW) and proof of stake (PoS). PoS consensus could lead to the phenomenon that the affluent get richer, whilst PoW wastes too much electricity. In order to advance blockchain technology, these issues must be resolved.

The biggest finding of this study till now after the above-said chapters and detailed literature review is the dependency of such systems on the blockchain used behind. The detailed exploration, identification, methodology, and dependencies of different participated components need to be investigated. Hence, in the next section, we have explored the same.

2.1 Applications, Challenges, and Solutions in Blockchain

Blockchain technology is viewed as having the ability to digitally modify and disrupt a number of industry areas, including finance, supply chain, healthcare, marketing, and entertainment. But because of its widespread use, difficulties and impediments can be seen. The journal of future internet's special issues on "Blockchain: Applications, Challenges, and Solutions" examines in the applications of this popular research area, its difficulties, and the benefits it offers various business sectors. Two groups can be made from this chapter: (1) the evaluation of applications, and (2) technical answers to technological problems.

The first collection contains evaluations of blockchain applications across several industries. A PRISMA-based systematic review is used by Rocha et al. to examine blockchain applications in the farming sector. They discovered Blockchain applications for support in the fields of finance, energy, logistics, the environment, agriculture, livestock, and industry in 71 publications. As the majority of the prototypes are still in the development or laboratory stages, they draw the conclusion that there has been little research done on using blockchain in the farming sector. Nevertheless, as the apps develop, they might eventually encourage more reliable and flexible information at a lower cost. Antal et al article provides a summary of blockchain applications, problems, solutions, and use for developing decentralized apps. The technical options were systematically categorized using an application framework for blockchain with three tiers. The document offers a step-by-step manual for decentralizing the conception and execution of conventional systems. The Machine-to-Everything (M2X) economy concept is presented by Leiding et al. and is built on a distributed, open, and decentralized smart-contract architecture. Value exchange, collaboration, and business implementations are all made feasible by M2X, which promotes the associated multi-stakeholder ecosystem. Kapassa and Themistocleous investigate blockchain software programmed in the area of Demand-Response Management (DRM) for the Internet of Vehicles (IoV) using a Systematic Literature Review (SLR) technique. They are left with DRM in the IoV that is based on blockchain research problems.

The second group of papers discusses technological answers to the problems that blockchain technology is currently facing. Sun et al. off-chain method relieves blockchain nodes' storage burden while maintaining the accuracy data from off-chain sources. The issue is fixed by utilising Hyperledger Fabric (HLF). According to the authors' experimental findings, their approach performs significantly better than the original HLF. Akbar et al. to give the miner or validator a fair mining return, we describe a hybrid method that combines Proof-of-Stake (PoS) and Proof-of-Work (PoW) techniques. Based on the results of the experiments, the suggested technique can decrease the chance of intrusions executing double mining. Xu et al. EconLedgers is a consensus mechanism based on small-scale Internet of Video Things (IoVT) edge networks can use Electrical Network Frequency (ENF), which offers safe and portable distributed ledgers. A novel Proof-of-ENF (PoENF) method serves as the foundation for the suggested consensus mechanism. A proof-of-concept prototype has been created and put through testing in a real-world IoVT network setting. The prototype's testing results support the viability of EconLedger's concept to provide a mostly decentralized and trust-free security infrastructure for IoVT edge networks. Finally, Yiu uses a series of security analyses in comparison to existing supply chain industry solutions with centralized architectures to identify creating blockchain-based decentralized ecosystems for product tractability and anti-counterfeiting: important decentralization domains, fundamental system requirements, and workable techniques.

This chapter explores the use of blockchain technology, its difficulties, and potential solutions. We now discover some fundamental issues that exist in the actual world and how this ground-breaking technology can be utilized to address them.

2.1.1 Cross-Border Payments

The Problem: To put it mildly, the situation with regard to overseas payments made through banking sectors is disorganized. It involves several steps and a lot of middlemen. Each stage of the procedure requires a large investment of time and resources, in addition to taking a lot of time. The average transaction cost for payments made globally is really roughly 7%, according to the World Bank. How much is that?

By eliminating all middlemen and laborious procedures, blockchain contributes to the process's streamlining by reducing the weight of unneeded delays. The payment is nearly immediately delivered to the recipient when a transaction is logged because to its smart and secure distributed ledger. Compared to the approach now in use, it also offers superior accountability and security because the transaction cannot be modified or reversed. According to Deloitte, blockchain transactions save the parties involved between 40% and 80% on remittance expenses when compared to traditional methods. Furthermore, rather of having to wait days, in around 4 to 6 seconds, the entire transaction is processed and completed. Blockchain is undoubtedly a better solution for international financial transactions when you take into account the benefits of improved security and transparency.

Several finance businesses are currently adopting blockchain to address this issue. Famous people in the industry include:

Circle: Users can securely transfer money (in a variety of supported currencies) to over 29 different countries.

Ripple: It makes it possible for banks, payment processors, and exchanges of digital assets to send and receive money quickly and cheaply over the world.

WeTrade: Through the use of a new digital platform called We Trade, banks and companies may collaborate to provide safe, open, and opportunity-rich transactions throughout all of Europe.

2.1.2 Supply Chain Management

The Problem: Supply chain management refers to the organization and implementation of all interconnected phases leading up to the release of the finished product. It frequently entails a network of people or organizations that start with raw material providers, directs movement through product producers before dropping to distributors. A well-optimized supply chain ensures maximum productivity while reducing fraud and overhead costs. Putting this into effect in the real world is a very difficult undertaking, as you might anticipate. Some operations have already been automated using AI and machine learning, but blockchain has the ability to completely transform this industry.

Several examples of businesses utilizing blockchain to manage their supply chains effectively are:

Origin-trail: They provide a mechanism for exchanging data that connected supply chains can utilize.

Open-port: The direct connection between shippers and carriers enabled by a blockchain platform lowers costs and improves supply chain management.

Walmart: One of the largest retailers, Walmart, is using blockchain to enhance its supply chain.

2.1.3 Traditional Contracts and Agreements: Accountability Issues

The Problem: Fundamentally, the reason we get into contracts and agreements is because the parties to the transaction don't trust one another. We must adhere to a legal procedure that involves several steps, additional parties, and a tone of paperwork in order to create contracts. Middlemen spend a lot of time and money as a result. Think back to the previous time you prepared a contract and the cost of hiring an attorney to create all the required legal papers, as well as the amount of time You invested time getting to and from downtown to gather each signature. Even while we consider these disadvantages to be standard when forming contracts and agreements, utilizing blockchain technology, especially smart contracts, can prevent all of these. Consequently, blockchain has successfully addressed this issue in the real world.

Blockchains, however, make it possible for something called Smart Contracts, a clever solution and potential substitute for conventional contracts and agreements. The natural next query is, "What is a smart contract?" A blockchain may store a little bit of code known as a smart contract. These are configured to perform specified activities, ideally executing a transaction as soon as the requirements stated in the lines of code are satisfied. Due to the fact that smart contracts are kept on the blockchain, they cannot be altered or interfered with. Additionally, because everything is open to the public and accessible, everything is transparent.

Numerous entrepreneurs and businesses have already switched to using smart contracts in place of conventional agreements. Here are some noteworthy mentions:

Tradelanse: By making agreements and conventional contracts easier, it aids in the digitisation of the supply chain.

Tradeix: Blockchain is being used by Tradeix to rewrite working capital financing and trading. They benefit banks, value-added suppliers, alternative funders, and so on!

2.1.4 Theft of Identity

The Problem: In the end, all that constitutes your identity is a set of assertions about your personal identity. You must provide your home-based address, passport number, driver's license number, social security number, and other information. Governments use and store all of these data points in centralized databases. One of these documents could be stolen by a malicious person who then uses security weaknesses to steal your identity. They are now able to utilize your identity for financial gain or to establish credit in your name. This is a really significant issue! In fact, many thieves conceal their crimes by using stolen identities obtained from the deceased. Therefore, this is a problem that exists in the actual world that blockchain has resolved.

Identity management-related blockchain firms have proliferated in droves. Here are a few illustrations:

Validate ID: The business offers complete electronic signature services as well as digital identification solutions using Blockchain technology. Their goal is to deliver straightforward, affordable services with first-rate security.

NewBanking: Users of NewBanking can disclose their identities online without having to worry about their private information being compromised or lost.

Sovrin: The first self-sovereign identification (SSI) network is provided by Sovrin.

Uport: Uport enables the company to create a reliable environment and give its partners and clients a secure means to transact.

2.1.5 Health Care Organizations' Management and Protection of Patient Data

The Problem: Currently, patient data is recorded and managed by centralised systems in healthcare institutions. These could be less reliable and contain misleading information. There have been numerous instances of hospital data breaches where patient information, including credit card details and genomic testing records, was compromised, was taken. In actuality, data breaches between 2009 and 2017 affected nearly 176 million patient records. Additionally, the way that patient data is now shared between hospitals is a complete mess. Changes in hospitals are regularly made by patients. Periodically, they are admitted to hospitals across networks owing to crises. They are currently required to generate a new medical record, due to the current system's inability to quickly and easily exchange patient records from their primary care provider, which results in a loss of time and money.

All hospitals will be able to access a decentralized, transparent, and public patient data record thanks to the use of blockchain technology. The entire issue of inter-hospital communication is also handled because there is no way to alter the data. Security follows next. Blockchain technology can help you protect your sensitive data while yet remaining open and transparent by masking your identity using secure codes. The information won't be available until you give a private key, if and when that's ever required.

Blockchain technology is widely used in the health industry by businesses to better manage and secure patient data. Here are some household names:

BurstIQ: The business offers Blockchain technologies to assist healthcare organizations in securely and efficiently managing enormous amounts of patient data.

MedicalChain: It aids in preserving the accuracy of medical records. The patient's name is kept secret and hidden from prying eyes, even if doctors, hospitals, and laboratories may request patient information.

2.1.6 Online Piracy and Digital Copyright

The Problem: Do you realize that copyright infringement causes the US film and television business industry to lose roughly $71 billion annually? Media piracy and illicit distribution are ongoing legal battles that major media companies like Sony and others are actively engaged in. But why are these sectors of the economy hurting so much? The media industries may shock you to learn that, the economic models and practices utilized in the past, particularly in the music industry, were appropriate when physical copies were the norm. The system struggles with the digital world. The streaming market is currently dominated by a small number of elite players who have embraced the digitization trend.

Sony is one of the most well-known companies in the sector that is aggressively promoting the idea of using blockchain for DRM.

2.1.7 Public Sectors and Governmental Systems

The Problem: In most local governments and public sectors around the world, all of the operations are carried out using antiquated systems and methods, which are expensive, time-consuming, and conducive to corruption. Insecure data regarding governments, for instance, may be highly risky due to internal data breaches. Then there are methods that need a lot of manpower but also add to the expense and take a lot of time. A centrally organized organization also leaves possibilities for extensive internal corruption and abuse. Increased mistrust between the populace and the government can emerge from this, which often leads to greater issues for the state.

Dubai will be among the first cities in the world to implement a blockchain policy. This will make it possible for their government to support blockchain-based transactions wherever possible.

2.1.8 Fundraising and Crowdsourcing

The Problem: Crowdfunding is becoming more and more popular because it makes it simple for businesses and startups to get the money they need in an easy, plain, and affordable way. Furthermore, it has been and continues to be the primary means of raising money for charitable organizations. However, despite this, there are a number of issues with crowdfunding platforms, starting with investor exploitation, security worries, and even unlawful activities. Due to all of this, investors become afraid and leave crowdfunding platforms. As a result, the way things are now conducted is causing problems for both the organizations and the investors.

Until recently, literally hundreds of businesses raised money via securities. Petro has amassed more over $5 billion in its campaign, making it by far the most successful of the group.

2.1.9 Real Estate

The Problem: Real estate market conditions right now are a complicated muddle. It is insufficient to just have the cash to buy the land, for instance, if you want to buy a new house. A lot of paperwork, background checks, and middlemen will be used in this drawn-out procedure, which will take a long time to complete. This will obviously cost more money and take up a lot more of your time, but it will also be stressful. Finally, there is the concern over seller fraud, which refers to the act of selling a property that was never actually theirs.

Using a blockchain, you can digitally store your real estate and other property assets. Consequently, it is immutable, meaning that it cannot be altered. A record of every successful transaction is also kept for future reference. All of these factors make it hard for someone to steal and sell another person's property. Similar to that, once you acquire ownership of a property, it is recorded forever on the blockchain and cannot be altered or denied. Additionally, by automating the majority of the time-consuming formalities and streamlining the entire process, you may take advantage of blockchain's decentralized nature in combination with smart contracts.

Many businesses and startups are currently using blockchain to transform the real estate industry. Several instances include:

Propy: They were among the first businesses to employ smart contracts when purchasing and selling real estate. A $60,000 apartment in Ukraine was the first transaction carried out utilizing their technique.

PropertyClub: It is a firm with headquarters in New York that provides a blockchain-based marketplace where users can use smart contracts to purchase, trade, and invest in real estate holdings.

2.1.10 Sports and ESports

The Problem: The sports and ESports sectors use a traditional method of producing income. This calls for creating marketing campaigns to sell event tickets and subscriptions to networks that show live sports, among other things. Despite not being optimized; the model is still usable. For instance, it doesn't offer viewers incentives for participating, which can boost interest in sports and ESports. Furthermore, a small amount of crowdfunding, which is unusual in this industry but has a lot of promise to assist athletes get paid for their performance. Blockchain technology can be simply used to overcome all of these problems.

SportyCo: The business provides cryptocurrency financial support for athletes.

PlayerTokens: To encourage fan participation, the business assists in tokenizing players.

This concludes our brief discussion of some current concerns in various business sectors and how blockchain technology might assist in resolving these issues. In order to prepare the path for the future, several mentions are also included in this list of existing businesses and new businesses using the technology.

2.2 Benefits of Blockchain Technology

Blockchain performance can entice investors with the promise of a significant reward. It is critical to confirm that the prerequisites are met before integrating this technology into a business solution. There should be a standard resting mechanism to evaluate the merits and downsides of blockchain-based solutions. This procedure can be divided into two parts: phase of testing and standardization. The developers' claims regarding their blockchain solutions are verified in the first round using a set of predetermined standards. In the testing phase, the effectiveness of the blockchain-based solution will be evaluated. For instance, the proprietor of an online retailer is concerned with the effectiveness of the blockchain-based solution. Although, it is important to assess the platform's throughput, capacity, and latency using standardized techniques.

Businesses can create digital archives of their findings using blockchain technology, and after registering the proof-of-concepts and designs for new ideas, they can issue a certificate. Any IP asset's legality, existence, and ownership may be proven with this certificate. Utilizing the unique cryptography layer, all notarized information, including trade secrets and copyright claims, may be kept confidential and secure.

Public blockchain, private blockchain, and consortium blockchain are the three broad categories currently used to describe blockchain systems (Buterin, 2015). We contrast these three blockchain types from various angles. Table 3.1 presents the comparison. Public blockchain can draw a lot of users because it is accessible to everyone. Furthermore, communities are quite active. Public blockchains are being developed daily. The consortium blockchain has a wide range of possible business applications. At the moment, Blockchain frameworks are being created by Hyperledger for commercial consortiums (Hyperledger, 2015). Furthermore, Ethereum provides many tools for developing consortium blockchains. Many companies continue to employ private blockchain for its auditability and effectiveness.

2.3 Blockchain to Solve the Recurrent Industry Problems

Blockchain, in contrast to conventional systems, enables direct peer-to-peer transfers of digital resources. Blockchain technology was initially a system designed to support the popular cryptocurrency Bitcoin. Satoshi Nakamoto first proposed Bitcoin in 2008, and it was released in 2009. Since then, the capital market has grown significantly, reaching $10 billion in 2016. A blockchain is essentially a collection of blocks that records all committed transactions in a public ledger. The chain continues to grow as more blocks are added. The blockchain uses a number of important technologies, including as distributed consensus techniques, cryptographic hashes, and digital signatures, to operate in a decentralized con-

Table 1. Difference between consortium blockchain, private blockchain, and public blockchain

Properties	Public Blockchain	Consortium Blockchain	Private Blockchain
A decision reached by consensus	Every miner	Chosen group of nodes	One organization
Read authorization	Public	Possibly open to the public or not	Either open to the public or closed
Immutability	Incredibly difficult to alter	Perhaps altered	Perhaps altered
Efficiency	Low	High	High
Centralized	No	Partial	Yes
Consensus process	Permission less	Permissioned	Permissioned
Nature	Decentralized and Open	Restricted and Controlled	Restricted and Controlled
Participants	Anonymous and tenacious	Trusted and Recognized	Trusted and Recognized
Consensus Procedures	Pow, PoS, DPoS	BFT	BFT, RAFT
Read or Write Permission	Permission-less	Permissioned	Permissioned
Immutability	Infeasible to temper	Could be tempered	Tempered and under control
Scalability	High	Low	High
Frequency of transaction approvals	Long (10 minutes or more)	Short	Short
Consumption of energy	High	Low	Low
Transparency	Low	High	High
Observation	Dispersive in terms of disintermediation	Reduced data duplication and quicker transaction times make it cost-effective.	Reduced data duplication and quicker transaction times make it cost-effective.
Example	Ethereum, Bitcoin, Litecoin, Factom, Block stream, and Dash	Ripple, R3, Hyperledger	Multichain, Block stack, Bankchain

text. Due to the decentralized nature of all transactions, there is no requirement for any middlemen to validate or verify any of them. Decentralization, transparency, immutability, and auditability are some of the important traits of chains.

In the whole process blockchain, solves various industry problems through the quality based algorithms. Therefore, some initiatives must be made to overcome these blockchain-related problems. These figure 3.2 involve as the following: -

i. Blockchain in Education

Every educational institution is required to maintain records of student test scores, teacher demographic data, and certifications and diplomas granted to students. It need the participation of many stakeholders to monitor all of these elements. Blockchain is recognized as the best solution for reliably and adaptable record-keeping. In many nations, improving the teaching and learning processes presents numerous difficulties. By maintaining data in an effective and accurate manner, blockchain can aid in managing these difficulties. Furthermore, neither geography nor time can impede learning. In partnership with British Telecommunications, the Knowledge Media Institute of the Open University in the United Kingdom has launched a blockchain-based project called Open Blockchain. When used in educational institutions, blockchain offers several advantages:

Figure 2. Representation of blockchain-based applications

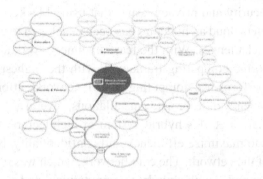

- Information about students and/or departments that is safe and secure.
- You can define access restrictions effectively.
- The consistency of the data is maintained
- All users build trust with one another.
- Prices are decreased
- Identity verification is possible for both students and resource owners.
- It is quick and easy to evaluate student performance.

ii. Finance Management

A smart contract can be used to connect the blockchain to a system for managing student loans. The student's achievement, income, and other factors all factor into the payback process. Processing and approval take more time in a traditional loan management system. Social Finance (SoFi), a blockchain-based system for managing student loans, has been created to reduce the amount of time needed. It cuts down on documentation overhead, middleman fees, and processing time. The Secure Bitcoin and Ethereum were employed by Automated Lending Technology (ALT) Lending Company, a personal loan management firm. The operating principles of blockchain technologies and its two varieties, public and private, were explored by Morkunas et al. They gave examples of how the nine elements of a recognized business model framework are impacted by blockchain. They gathered data on this process from South Africa, North America, Europe, and other nations that use blockchain technology. They listed a number of challenges, including high expenses brought on by the need for specialised developers and difficult integration. To solve the issues in the business sector and enhance supply chain resilience, blockchain architecture and potential solutions have been offered in a period of increased risks and uncertainties. In this proposed design, the following five elements were covered: source of data, action, production of blocks, consensus, link, and interface. It was assessed how blockchain-based risk management differed from traditional risk management.

The lifecycle management of financial products via a blockchain-based trading platform was presented in the architecture. In this architecture, there were two financial institutions with each having three departments, all of which were connected to a P2P network, and these institutions handled the product management. The envisioned network of businesses encompassed fundamental processes as well as the development, modification, and processing of products. The universities were permitted to build and alter the product once they had each issued a certificate. The other departments were in charge of transaction execution and verification.

iii. Blockchain Privacy and Security

In this, we go over the security and privacy issues that using blockchain technology raises. Based on this technology, a distributed cloud architecture has been developed to enhance privacy and security concerns, two contemporary challenges. With the least amount of work and security, this architecture enables on-demand access to the computing framework with the highest concentration. It has a few parameters that make high-performance computing on IoT networks affordable. After examining the difficulties, viability, and efficiency of IoT-related installations, several academics examined blockchain as a security component. Sharma et al.'s hybrid system of architecture for a smart city included an Argon2-based PoW strategy to maximize efficiency and confidentiality. Networks at the core and the edge were the two sections of the network. The core network, which was in charge of generating blocks and edge nodes, contained the nodes with abundant computational and storage capabilities. The nodes in this network served as a centralized server and had limited storage and processing power. However, the work did not employ a caching approach or an efficient distribution strategy. The use cases for blockchain are thoroughly examined in terms of security and privacy.

iv. Blockchain with IoT

Over the past few years, IoT-based applications have become more and more common in a range of sectors, including smart city, healthcare system, education, government sectors, and social media applications. All users have open access to a large number of datasets in IoT-based networks. Blockchain technology is utilized to ensure the confidentiality and accuracy of these shared data sets. An overview of the integration of blockchain and IoT can be seen in Figure 3.3. The IoT network includes several devices or nodes that are connected by sensors. An enormous amount of data is gathered by a cloud service on the IoT platform. In tiny networks, a gateway connects lots of nodes. In a big network, gateways based on the cluster are also used to connect a lot of nodes. A set of public and private keys are kept on each node. Every node in the network produces a blockchain-based digital profile record using its public key as part of the registration procedure. The private key is used to establish a digital signature when a node receives and the gateway approves a transaction. A protocol for communicating with the blockchain network is synchronized by and maintained by the blockchain by connecting numerous Internet of Things devices. Two protocols were put up by Danzi et al. for the synchronization and management of traffic across blockchain and Internet of Things networks. They evaluated the bandwidth demand and the synchronization time.

Figure 3. Blockchain architecture with IoT

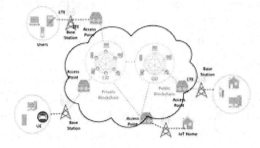

v. Transportation in Blockchain

The expansion and development of technology advancements led to the creation of the intelligent transportation system (ITS). The implementation of a smart framework in transportation can reduce the need for human, monetary, and material resources while also significantly enhancing the automation and traffic management procedures. The smart transportation and logistics framework (BCTLF), which combines blockchain and IoT to supply the logistics for transportation, was suggested by Traditional vehicular communication systems are susceptible to privacy violations, which might jeopardize security messages conveying sensitive data about individuals, such as a vehicle's make, model, and driver's identification, and the location of the vehicle. The usage of a pseudonym to hide this information was a well-known strategy for handling this issue. Numerous papers have demonstrated that the expense of maintaining these pseudonyms may rise and that it will be challenging to distribute certificates. The decentralization and dispersion features of blockchain technology can lessen these restrictions.

vi. Blockchain in Health System

Numerous patient records and other health-related data must be handled by the medical and healthcare industries in a secure manner. Increased focus on patient care quality when such data is accurately recorded. Singh et al. published a paradigm for Electronic Health Records (EHRs) that makes use of smart contracts with a JavaScript foundation. To gather more precise medical data, a different team of researchers put up a smart contract-based system. Figure 3.4 demonstrates how blockchain technology improves the security of patient and health information.

Figure 4. Blockchain in healthcare system

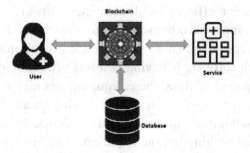

vii. Government Security in Blockchain

Blockchain technology is essential to the growth of social and governmental activities for e-governance. Currently, a centralized database on several duplicate servers is used to preserve information like employee IDs. This centralized system is, however, susceptible to a variety of assaults, such as Distributed Denial of Service (DDoS) and Denial of Service (DoS) attacks. A wide range of services, including voting records, property registrations, patent transfers, criminal records, and permits for driving and other activities, can be provided via blockchain technology. The application of various blockchain-related technologies is a major focus for many researchers. In order to protect the integrity of the ledger, shared and authorized transactions are kept in a distributed system, and each block has a hash value. Blockchain data is present on every node, and the chain as a whole has not changed in a way that may corrupt the blocks. With the help of this technology, at any time, records can be retrieved and submitted for e-governance. The countries known as the Digital 5 (D5)—South Korea, Estonia, the UK, Israel, and New Zealand are also included in Ojo et al. analysis of the implications of the blockchain on these countries. The D5 nations agreed to employ a system of digital governance and have pushed their people to become technologically savvy for usage at home and in the workplace in order to build a strong digital economy. The following are some of these network groups' goals:

- Providing citizens with services based on they require
- Users exchanging standard procedures and equipment
- Permitting rivalry between businesses or other commercial entities on a level playing field
- Providing children with the opportunity to how to code and accomplish next-generation objectives
- Taking the pledge to segment, help and educate one another

The D5 nations have undertaken a variety of activities in several fields to attain the goals and objectives. In the following industries, they've created and digitalized their services:

- South Korea: administration and finances
- Estonia: economy and health
- United Kingdom: finances, social security & welfare, education, and government service
- Israel: financial and economic
- New Zealand: energy and agriculture

2.4 Hardware and Software Aspects

To use the developed application efficiently, all computer software/ applications requires certain hardware components and maybe some other software for the smooth functioning of the application. These pre-requisites are generally known as recommended requirements for any program developed. More specifically, each software is having two sets of requirements; they can be minimum and recommended. After a period of time, these requirements may be changed as the increase in computational power or new recourses are needed by having an advanced version of the application. By having certain technological requirements, these demands increase. In general, hardware and software requirements are nothing but the requirement of any particular device on which our developed software can be executed flawlessly.

Various factors that must be taken into account may cause hardware requirements to alter. Making the right assumptions while choosing the suitable hardware specifications is a crucial topic to cover. While selecting appropriate hardware and software some precautions that must be taken care of are as follows-

- The minimum size or requirement of developed software
- Number of users of the software
- Maximum simultaneous users for particular application
- Complexity of the product
- Search queries count involved
- Database size
- Web server requirements

These are some questions to be answered while selecting appropriate software and hardware. These must be considered first in estimating the requirements for any software product. Table 3.2 Recommended Web Server Hardware Requirements.

Table 2. Recommended web server hardware requirements

Item	Combined Web and Database Server (Minimal)	Combined Web and Database Server (Recommended)	Web Server (Minimal)	Web Server (Recommended)
Processor	2 x 1,6 GHz CPU	4 x 1,6 GHz CPU	1,6 GHz CPU	2 x 1,6 GHz CPU
RAM	3,5 GB RAM	7 GB RAM	1,75 GB RAM	3,5 GB RAM
HDD	For the data on the student portal, it is recommended that there be more than 40 GB of unoccupied space (non-system drive is preferred) As stated in the software requirements for the programme, it is advised that you have at least one 40 GB free space available (system drive)			
Widely used blockchain Development Tools	Remix IDE.	Truffle Framework.	Solc. Source: karl. tech	Solium
	Geth	Embark	Ganache	Ether Scripter
	Blockchain As a Service (BaaS)	Metamask	Mist	Blockchain Testnet

i. Software Requirements

The underlying technology of cryptocurrencies like Ethereum and Bitcoin is well-known. Numerous industries, including healthcare, logistics and supply chains, insurance, financial services, and much more, could be drastically changed by it. Blockchain technology is being used by companies like IBM and Samsung in order to provide businesses and startups with fresh approaches and solutions. Blockchain appears to be developing at the highest rate on the platform, surpassing expertise in Tensor Flow and machine learning. These tools where the developed application web server installed must requires the software requirements as listed in the following: -

ii. Hardware Requirements

Supported Operating Systems

- Windows 11, 10, 8, 7

Supported Databases with developed application

- Including High Availability features (Always On Availability Groups, Windows Server Failover Cluster)

Java Plateform Framework

- Eclipse or more required new version

Supported versions of IIS or IIS Express

- IIS versions 7+
- IIS Express versions 8+ (default, installed for you)

3 RESEARCH FORMATION

The underlying research is being carried out as a sequence of standard research flow. This research is formed as a phased study towards the attainment of the targeted objectives. Starts from the introduction of the underlying research context, statement of the problem & objectives setting to the proposal, results, and discussion. The workflow diagram of the same is given below in figure 3.5, the research formation and workflow.

Figure 5. Research formation diagram

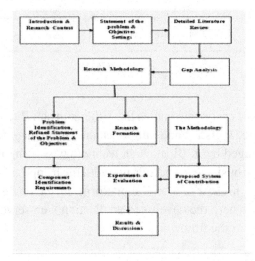

4 RESEARCH METHODOLOGY

The deep-web information can be retrieved one at a time which leads to the insufficient of results as at a time we can query out one database server, so a lot insufficiency of results. Rather than this single-web query interface legacy approach, we can use a more intelligent approach by building an integrated web-query interface for a certain domain that will serve as the sole entry point to query several database servers at once.

Additional fresh approaches to the integration of connected data-based online forms, as forth by many researchers over time. In addition to presenting a novel method for combining web query interfaces into a single integrated web query interface for a certain domain, this thesis study also aims to suggest related data principles. Beginning from the casing of domain-specific web-query-interfaces to the creation of the integrated-web-query-interface, the proposed framework will follow a data-integration-system formation. A domain-independent ontology will be developed as the description of the underlying web-query-interface technology (as linked data resources and to deed semantic-integration among the web-query-interfaces). The proposed system's enactment assessed performance metrics like precision, recall, and security score for different domains as books, movies, students, subjects.

5 CHAPTER SUMMARY

In this chapter we have explored and analyzed in applications, challenges and solutions in blockchain statement of the problem. Further we have refined problem statement in view of findings and summaries of the trending and foundation researches. All the standard phases of the development cycle have also been depicted and discussed in details. Later as per the need of the study and desired system we have explored and studied all the essential components of the system, the requirements like software and hardware also been explored in this chapter too. Later in this chapter the complete research formation has been explored and depicted for the better understanding of the underlying research. Finally, research methodology towards that view of proposed system formation has also been produced. The system will be produced in a layered/phased in applications, challenges and solutions in blockchain development process.

REFERENCES

Akbar, N. A., Muneer, A., ElHakim, N., & Fati, S. M. (2021). Distributed Hybrid Double-Spending Attack Prevention Mechanism for Proof-of-Work and Proof-of-Stake Blockchain Consensuses. *Future Internet*, *13*(11), 285. doi:10.3390/fi13110285

Alketbi, A., Nasir, Q., & Abu Talib, M. (2020, December). Novel blockchain reference model for government services: Dubai government case study. *Int. J. Syst. Assurance Eng. Manage.*, *11*(6), 1170–1191. doi:10.100713198-020-00971-2

Antal, C., Cioara, T., Anghel, I., Antal, M., & Salomie, I. (2021). Distributed Ledger Technology Review and Decentralized Applications Development Guidelines. [CrossRef]. *Future Internet*, *13*(3), 62. doi:10.3390/fi13030062

Asad, M., Kumar, M., Shah, P. K., & Sinha, A. K. (2021, December). Business Growth Forecast using Saket Data Mining Methodology. In *2021 10th International Conference on System Modeling & Advancement in Research Trends (SMART)* (pp. 99-103). IEEE. 10.1109/SMART52563.2021.9676278

Banotra, A., Sharma, J. S., Gupta, S., Gupta, S. K., & Rashid, M. (2021). *Use of blockchain and Internet of Things for securing data in healthcare systems*. In K. J. Giri, S. A. Parah, R. Bashir, & K. Muhammad (Eds.), *Multimedia Security: Algorithm Development, Analysis and Applications, Algorithms for Intelligent Systems* (pp. 255–267). Springer.

Bao, S., Cao, Y., Lei, A., Asuquo, P., Cruickshank, H., Sun, Z., & Huth, M. (2019). Pseudonym management through blockchain: Cost-efcient privacy preservation on intelligent transportation systems. *IEEE Access : Practical Innovations, Open Solutions*, *7*, 80390–80403. doi:10.1109/ACCESS.2019.2921605

Chen, B., Tan, Z., & Fang, W. (2018). Blockchain-based implementation for nancial product management. *Proc. 28th Int. Telecommun. Netw. Appl. Conf. (ITNAC),* 1-3.

Da Silva, R. R. G., de Oliveira, L., & Talamini, E. (2021). Blockchain Applications in Agribusiness: A Systematic Review. *Future Internet, 13*(4), 95. doi:10.3390/fi13040095

Danzi, P., Kalor, A. E., Stefanovic, C., & Popovski, P. (2018). Analysis of the communication traffic for blockchain synchronization of IoT devices. *Proc. IEEE Int. Conf. Commun. (ICC),* 1-7. 10.1109/ICC.2018.8422485

Elisa, N., Yang, L., Chao, F., & Cao, Y. (2018). A framework of blockchainbased secure and privacy-preserving E-government system. *Wireless Networks,* (Dec), 1–11. doi:10.100711276-018-1883-0

Esposito, C., De Santis, A., Tortora, G., Chang, H., & Choo, K. R. (2018, January). Blockchain: A panacea for healthcare cloud-based data security and privacy? *IEEE Cloud Comput., 5*(1), 31–37. doi:10.1109/MCC.2018.011791712

Ghosh, Chatterjee, Shetty, & Datta. (2020). *An sdn-iot-based framework for future smart cities: Addressing perspective.* Academic Press.

Gräther, W., Kolvenbach, S., Ruland, R., Schütte, J., Torres, C., & Wendland, F. (2018). Blockchain for education: Lifelong learning passport. *Proc. 1st ERCIM Blockchain Workshop,* 1-8.

Han, M., Li, Z., He, J., Wu, D., Xie, Y., & Baba, A. (2018). A novel blockchain-based education records verification solution. *Proc. 19th Annu. SIG Conf. Inf. Technol. Educ.,* 178-183. 10.1145/3241815.3241870

Harthy, K. A., Shuhaimi, F. A., & Ismaily, K. K. J. A. (2019). The upcoming blockchain adoption in higher-education: Requirements and process. *Proc. 4th MEC Int. Conf. Big Data Smart City (ICBDSC),* 1-5. 10.1109/ICBDSC.2019.8645599

Hasan, M., Rahman, A., & Islam, M. J. (2020). DistB-CVS: A distributed secure blockchain based online certificate verification system from Bangladesh perspective. *Proc. Technol., 28,* 29. doi:10.1109/ICAICT51780.2020.9333523

Humayun, M., Jhanjhi, N., Hamid, B., & Ahmed, G. (2020, June). Emerging smart logistics and transportation using IoT and blockchain. *IEEE Internet Things Mag., 3*(2), 58–62. doi:10.1109/IOTM.0001.1900097

Jirgensons, M., & Kapenieks, J. (2018, June). Blockchain and the future of digital learning credential assessment and management. *J. Teacher Educ. Sustainability, 20*(1), 145–156.

Kapassa, E., & Themistocleous, M. (2022). Blockchain Technology Applied in IoV Demand Response Management: A Systematic Literature Review. *Future Internet, 14*(5), 136. doi:10.3390/fi14050136

Kumar, P., Kumar, M., Singh, K. B., Tripathi, A. R., & Kumar, A. (2021, December). Blockchain Security Detection Condition Light Module. In *2021 10th International Conference on System Modeling & Advancement in Research Trends (SMART)* (pp. 363-367). IEEE. 10.1109/SMART52563.2021.9676302

Leiding, B., Sharma, P., & Norta, A. (2021). The Machine-to-Everything (M2X) Economy: Business Enactments, Collaborations, and e-Governance. *Future Internet, 13*(12), 319. doi:10.3390/fi13120319

Mikroyannidis, A., Domingue, J., Bachler, M., & Quick, K. (2018). Smart blockchain badges for data science education. *Proc. IEEE Frontiers Educ. Conf. (FIE),* 1-5. 10.1109/FIE.2018.8659012

Min, H. (2019, January). Blockchain technology for enhancing supply chain resilience. *Business Horizons, 62*(1), 35–45. doi:10.1016/j.bushor.2018.08.012

Mohanty, S. N., Ramya, K. C., Rani, S. S., Gupta, D., Shankar, K., Lakshmanaprabu, S. K., & Khanna, A. (2020, January). An efficient lightweight integrated blockchain (ELIB) model for IoT security and privacy. *Future Generation Computer Systems, 102*, 1027–1037. doi:10.1016/j.future.2019.09.050

Morkunas, V. J., Paschen, J., & Boon, E. (2019, May). How blockchain technologies impact your business model. *Business Horizons, 62*(3), 295–306. doi:10.1016/j.bushor.2019.01.009

Mosteanu, N. R. (2020). Digital systems and new challenges of nancial management-FinTech, XBRL, blockchain and cryptocurrencies. *Inf. Secur. Manage., 21*(174), 9.

Navadkar, Nighot, & Wantmure. (2018). Overview of blockchain technology in government/public sectors. *Int. Res. J. Eng. Technol., 5*(6), 2287-2292.

Nguyen, X.-T. (2018, June). Lessons from case study of secured transactions with bitcoin. *SMU Sci. Tech. Law Rev., 21*, 181.

Ølnes, S., Ubacht, J., & Janssen, M. (2017, September). Blockchain in government: Bene ts and implications of distributed ledger technology for information sharing. *Government Information Quarterly, 34*(3), 355–364. doi:10.1016/j.giq.2017.09.007

Rahman, A., Islam, M. J., Sunny, F. A., & Nasir, M. K. (2019). DistBlockSDN: A distributed secure blockchain based SDN-IoT architecture with NFV implementation for smart cities. *Proc. 2nd Int. Conf. Innov. Eng. Technol. (ICIET),* 1-6. 10.1109/ICIET48527.2019.9290627

Ray, P. P., Chowhan, B., Kumar, N., & Almogren, A. (2021, July). BIoTHR: Electronic health record servicing scheme in IoT-blockchain ecosystem. *IEEE Internet of Things Journal, 8*(13), 10857–10872. doi:10.1109/JIOT.2021.3050703

Sankar, L. S., Sindhu, M., & Sethumadhavan, M. (2017). Survey of consensus protocols on blockchain applications. *Proc. 4th Int. Conf. Adv. Com-put. Commun. Syst. (ICACCS),* 1-5. 10.1109/ICACCS.2017.8014672

Saunders, L. (2019). *FinTech and consumer protection: A snapshot.* Nat. Consum. Law Center, Boston, MA, USA, Tech. Rep. 6-7.

Shah, P. K., Pandey, R. P., & Kumar, R. (2016, November). Vector quantization with codebook and index compression. In *2016 International Conference System Modeling & Advancement in Research Trends (SMART)* (pp. 49-52). IEEE.

Sharma, P. K., Chen, M.-Y., & Park, J. H. (2017). A software dened fog node based distributed blockchain cloud architecture for IoT. *IEEE Access : Practical Innovations, Open Solutions, 6*, 115–124. doi:10.1109/ACCESS.2017.2757955

Sharma, P. K., & Park, J. H. (2018, September). Blockchain based hybrid network architecture for the smart city. *Future Generation Computer Systems, 86*, 650–655. doi:10.1016/j.future.2018.04.060

Sun, H., Pi, B., Sun, J., Miyamae, T., & Morinaga, M. (2021). SASLedger: A Secured, Accelerated Scalable Storage Solution for Distributed Ledger Systems. [CrossRef]. *Future Internet, 13*(12), 310. doi:10.3390/fi13120310

Xu, R., Nagothu, D., & Chen, Y. (2021). EconLedger: A Proof-of-ENF Consensus Based Lightweight Distributed Ledger for IoVT Networks. *Future Internet, 13*(10), 248. doi:10.3390/fi13100248

Yiu, N. C. (2021). Toward Blockchain-Enabled Supply Chain Anti-Counterfeiting and Traceability. *Future Internet, 13*, 86. https://101blockchains.com/problems-blockchain-solve/

Zhang, P., White, J., Schmidt, D. C., Lenz, G., & Rosenbloom, S. T. (2018, July). FHIRChain: Applying blockchain to securely and scalably share clinical data. *Computational and Structural Biotechnology Journal, 16*, 267–278. doi:10.1016/j.csbj.2018.07.004 PMID:30108685

Chapter 18
Unveiling the Path to Knowledge Sharing and Innovation in Metaverse Virtual Communities

Mohammad Daradkeh

https://orcid.org/0000-0003-2693-7363

University of Dubai, UAE & Yarmouk University, Jordan

ABSTRACT

Despite the potential benefits of knowledge sharing in these communities, the process of knowledge sharing is complex and unique within the metaverse. Therefore, a comprehensive understanding of the knowledge sharing dynamics in virtual communities within the metaverse domain is crucial. This chapter provides a comprehensive overview of the knowledge sharing landscape in metaverse virtual communities and outlines a roadmap for more efficient knowledge sharing and innovation in these communities. Based on a review of relevant practices and previous research, a knowledge sharing model is formulated to account for the unique impact of the metaverse on these communities. The process of knowledge sharing involves gathering community knowledge, internalizing situational knowledge, and sharing it through broadcasting and diffusion. The chapter offers valuable insights for researchers, practitioners, and policymakers in the field of virtual communities and knowledge sharing and provides a foundation for future research in this area.

INTRODUCTION

The metaverse, with its seamless integration of various technologies such as virtual reality, artificial intelligence, big data, 5G networks, and blockchain, has sparked a new era of imagination and innovation in the future of human society. As virtual communities continue to emerge and grow within this environment, it becomes increasingly important to study and understand the dynamics of knowledge sharing that occur within these communities (Hassani, Huang, & MacFeely, 2022; Huynh-The et al.,

DOI: 10.4018/978-1-6684-9151-5.ch018

2023). Knowledge sharing, as a fundamental aspect of human communication and collaboration, plays a crucial role in the development and growth of virtual communities (Bolger, 2021; Buhalis, O'Connor, & Leung, 2023; Cappannari & Vitillo, 2022). By exploring and understanding the behavior and patterns of knowledge sharing in virtual communities within the metaverse, it becomes possible to identify opportunities for enhancing the efficiency and creativity of these communities. Moreover, with the increasing dependence on virtual communities in various aspects of our lives, it is vital to understand the potential implications and challenges of knowledge sharing within these communities, so that appropriate measures can be taken to mitigate risks and promote positive outcomes. The study of knowledge sharing in virtual communities within the metaverse is therefore a critical aspect of shaping the future of human society in this digital age (Dahan et al., 2022; Dwivedi et al., 2022; Hariharan, Risling, Felic, & Ostertag, 2023).

The purpose of this chapter is to delve into the topic of knowledge sharing in virtual communities within the metaverse and to provide a comprehensive understanding of the behavior and patterns that exist in these communities. This chapter aims to be a valuable resource for scholars, researchers, and practitioners who are interested in exploring and advancing the field of knowledge sharing in virtual communities. The chapter is designed to provide an in-depth examination of the current state of knowledge sharing in virtual communities within the metaverse, including a review of previous research and a thorough analysis of the potential changes in knowledge sharing patterns under the impact of the metaverse.

The main objective of this chapter is to provide a comprehensive roadmap for enhancing knowledge sharing and fostering innovation in virtual communities within the metaverse. To achieve this, the chapter will propose a future-oriented model of knowledge sharing in virtual communities that incorporates the unique characteristics of metaverse environments and existing knowledge sharing patterns in virtual communities. The study draws upon various sources of information and relevant data, including previous research studies, practical examples of virtual communities such as VRChat, Roblox, and Second Life, and the latest developments in technology. The proposed model will serve as a guide for practitioners and researchers in the field to enhance knowledge sharing and innovation in virtual communities, and to promote the development of these communities within the metaverse.

This chapter aims to contribute to the advancement of the field of knowledge sharing in virtual communities by providing valuable insights and references for further research and practical applications. The findings of this research will have the potential to shape the future of virtual communities and drive the development of virtual community forms, thus improving the efficiency and creativity of knowledge sharing in virtual communities. The comprehensive understanding of knowledge sharing behavior and patterns in virtual communities within the metaverse, as well as the roadmap for more efficient knowledge sharing and innovation, will have far-reaching implications for the future of human society in this digital age.

RESEARCH STATUS AND THEORETICAL BASIS

Connotation of Metaverse

Metaverse is a general concept describing future iterations of the Internet, consisting of a continuously shared three-dimensional virtual space connected to a perceptible virtual world (Allam, Bibri, Jones, Chabaud, & Moreno, 2022; Mourtzis, Angelopoulos, & Panopoulos, 2023). The term originated in the science fiction novel "Snow Crash" by N. Stephenson, in which the plot takes place in a virtual space where real humans live with virtual people through VR devices (Inder, 2023; Magalhães et al., 2022). Since the emergence of the metaverse to date, there has not been a unified definition of the metaverse, and different vendors and scholars have their own interpretations of the metaverse. The burgeoning of the metaverse has a significant relationship with Facebook founder M. Zuckerberg's interview at TheVerge, in which he expressed his desire to turn Facebook into a metaverse company (Kraus et al., 2023; Nguyen, 2022). He also believed that the metaverse was the future of the Internet. Since then, many scholars and entrepreneurs have started to explore the concept of metaverse. Yang et al. (2022) argues that the metaverse needs to achieve a high degree of realism, where people's lives in reality can be mapped to the metaverse space. Cappannari and Vitillo (2022) argues that the metaverse is a virtual space parallel to and independent from the real world, a digital virtual world that is increasingly realistic. Duan et al. (2021), the founder of r. Beamable, divided the metaverse according to different levels. Following the advent of the metaverse, many companies have sought to implement the concept, taking Roblox (Allam, Sharifi, Bibri, Jones, & Krogstie, 2022; Mystakidis, 2023), a gaming company listed in the U.S., as an example, which was the first company to build a metaverse ecology. Later, major manufacturers have been investing in building the metaverse.

The metaverse aims to build a sustainable virtual shared space while maintaining the perception and experience of the real world, which requires adhering to the values of co-creation, co-building, sharing, and co-governance, and fully integrating new technologies such as big data, artificial intelligence, virtual reality, 5G, blockchain, and 3D engines (Buhalis, Lin, & Leung, 2022; Chen & Lee, 2021; Njoku, Nwakanma, Amaizu, & Kim, 2023). The technical core of metaverse depends on integration and application, and its underlying technologies are shown in Table 1. Different disciplines have different views on the exploration of metaverse. However, in the field of graphical information, considering only virtualization and digitization is not a prospect for the development of intelligent libraries. The concept of intelligent libraries needs to be gradually realized. Only by continuously introducing the underlying technologies of metaverse and upgrading the intelligent services of libraries can we eventually realize the profound integration of metaverse and libraries.

Table 1. Major underlying technologies of metaverse

Underlying Technologies	Implemented Functions
Artificial intelligence, digital twin	Meta-universe ecology
Blockchain	Access Verification
Artificial Intelligence, Cloud Computing	Underlying algorithms
Expanded reality, robotics, brain-computer interface	Virtual Reality Simulation
5G	Unhindered Networks

Current Status of Related Research

The field of Metaverse and its associated virtual communities has garnered considerable attention from scholars and researchers in recent years. The origins of this concept can be traced back to 2003 when it was initially conceptualized as a network of interconnected virtual spaces where users could engage in various activities such as creation, trading, and more (Dahan et al., 2022; Hariharan et al., 2023; Julian,

Chung, & Wang, 2023). The launch of Second Life, a popular 3D virtual game, further solidified the Metaverse as a mainstream concept and sparked various studies exploring its potential in terms of revenue generation (Mystakidis, 2023), educational models (Park & Kim, 2022), social dynamics (Qamar, Anwar, & Afzal, 2023), ethical considerations (Dai, Wang, & Gao, 2022), and economic implications such as inflation (Buhalis et al., 2023).

Virtual communities, as defined by scholars, refer to groups of individuals who share information voluntarily and consciously through the Internet (Kraus et al., 2023; Ramasundaram, Pandey, Shukla, Alavi, & Wirtz, 2023). These communities are known for their dynamic flow of knowledge from individuals to the group (Salem & Dragomir, 2022). Research on knowledge sharing in virtual communities can be divided into two categories: micro and macro. Micro-level research focuses on the various factors that influence knowledge sharing behavior among individuals in virtual communities, such as motivation for attachment, social support orientation, trust, altruism, and self-efficacy (Şarlıoğlu, Boyacı, & Akca, 2023; Tait & Pierson, 2022; Teubner & Camacho, 2023). On the other hand, macro-level research examines the role of disciplinary level in knowledge exchange effectiveness, highlighting that it can have a significant direct and moderating effect on knowledge exchange (Weking, Desouza, Fielt, & Kowalkiewicz, 2023).

These studies have provided valuable insights into the psychology and sociology of knowledge sharing in virtual communities and have proposed various measures to enhance the process. The results of these studies provide a strong theoretical foundation for further research on knowledge sharing in virtual communities, particularly within the context of the Metaverse.

The field of research on knowledge sharing in virtual communities has been continuously developing, and various studies have explored the impact factors that promote knowledge sharing behaviors among individuals in these communities. These studies have analyzed the psychological and sociological perspectives of virtual community users' willingness to share and proposed measures to enhance the development of knowledge sharing in virtual communities. Moreover, there have been studies that examine the overall picture of knowledge flow in virtual communities, including the construction of a knowledge sharing model based on Social Network Services (SNS) and Yuki's knowledge spiral theory (Ukko, Saunila, Nasiri, Rantala, & Holopainen, 2022), the coupling mechanism of virtual community knowledge sharing based on social system theory (Y. Wang et al., 2022), and the multiple derivation model of knowledge co-creation in virtual network communities (Yang et al., 2022).

These studies emphasize the dynamic learning process of virtual community knowledge sharing, which encompasses not only knowledge transfer but also knowledge selection, absorption, refinement, and sharing (Mystakidis, 2023). They also focus on the complete process of a user's knowledge selection, internalization, innovation within the community, and eventual sharing with other community users.

The current research on the metaverse has laid the foundation for the conceptualization of a knowledge sharing model for virtual communities in the metaverse. This model would integrate big data, blockchain, virtual reality, and other advanced technologies as its backbone, with situational knowledge modules as its flesh and blood, and social forms in the metaverse scenario as its soul. This model has the potential to offer valuable insights and references for further research and practical applications in the field of knowledge sharing in virtual communities in the metaverse.

Reference Theoretical Model

The current research on the metaverse has drawn on multiple theoretical frameworks to analyze the knowledge transformation and sharing dynamics within virtual communities. One such framework is the

SECI (Socialization, Externalization, Combination, and Internalization) model, which was proposed by Nonaka and Takeuchi in 1995 and refined in 2000. It outlines the four forms of mutual transformation between tacit knowledge (unwritten and subjective knowledge) and explicit knowledge (codified and objective knowledge) (Qamar et al., 2023).

The knowledge chain model, as proposed by American scholar Holsapple et al., aims to link organizational knowledge with the core competitiveness of an organization. The model is based on five stages of knowledge dissemination: knowledge acquisition, knowledge selection, knowledge generation, knowledge internalization and knowledge externalization (Y. Wang et al., 2022). Each individual in an organization acts as a node in the knowledge activity and the knowledge chain reflects the interaction between the individual level and the organizational level in the process of knowledge creation (Zhang et al., 2022). The model is used to promote the effective dissemination of knowledge and to ensure that the knowledge generated within an organization is used to drive its competitiveness.

Csikzentmihalyi's immersion theory, on the other hand, focuses on the psychological aspects of immersion experiences. According to the theory, immersion experiences refer to individuals' complete involvement in a particular activity, leading to a state of forgetfulness of their surroundings and a loss of self-awareness or sense of time (Wang, Yu, Bell, & Chu, 2022). The theory consists of three parts: the antecedent variables of immersion experience, immersion experience itself, and the outcomes brought about by immersion experience (Pamucar, Deveci, Gokasar, Tavana, & Köppen, 2022). The concept of immersion experience is not only important in the field of psychology, but also has applications in various other fields, including virtual and augmented reality, human-computer interaction, and game design.

THE "GENETIC MUTATION" OF KNOWLEDGE SHARING FROM VIRTUAL COMMUNITY TO METAVERSE DOMAIN

The metaverse represents a new frontier in the evolution of virtual communities, as they shift from being solely 2D internet-based social platforms to 3D virtual communities that exist in a spatially-rich, immersive environment. This transformation not only affects the form and structure of virtual communities, but also the core elements that make up knowledge sharing. The transformation of knowledge sharing can be explained by looking at the changes in space, resources, behavior, and subjects (Buhalis et al., 2023).

In terms of space, the shift from 2D to 3D means that virtual communities now have a more tangible presence, allowing for a more realistic representation of people and objects. This can lead to a deeper sense of community and collaboration as well as increased opportunities for knowledge sharing, as participants can now interact with each other in a more immersive environment. In terms of resources, the use of cutting-edge technologies such as big data, blockchain, and virtual reality in the metaverse provides a wealth of information and tools that can be leveraged to enhance the knowledge sharing experience (Hariharan et al., 2023).

The transformation of virtual communities in the metaverse also affects behavior, as participants are now able to engage in more natural, intuitive interactions with each other. This can lead to increased collaboration, creativity, and innovation as users can share ideas, work together on projects, and exchange feedback in real-time. Finally, the transformation of virtual communities affects the subjects, or the participants themselves, as they are now able to express themselves in more diverse, multi-faceted ways. This can lead to a greater sense of community and belonging, as well as increased opportunities for personal and professional growth as users learn from each other and exchange new ideas and perspectives (Huynh-The et al., 2023).

Spatialization of Shared Space

The existence of virtual communities is poised for a major transformation as we move into the era of the metaverse. Currently, virtual communities exist primarily in the form of online forums, where users interact with one another through text-based posts and lack a sense of spatial immersion and meaningful interaction. This has resulted in a lack of motivation for users to participate in knowledge sharing, leading to low levels of willingness among virtual community members (Hwang, 2023).

In the metaverse, virtual communities will be transformed into true communities, consisting of multiple private metaverses where each user will have their own "private domain." Within these private domains, community knowledge resources will be displayed as three-dimensional modules that users can access and interact with. In addition to private domains, virtual communities will also have corresponding public spaces or "public domains," which will provide users with a variety of environments for knowledge exchange and interaction, such as academic conferences, virtual classrooms, and other activities (Inder, 2023).

Examples of this form of virtual community can already be seen in platforms such as VRchat, a large-scale online virtual reality game for multiple players, where players exist in a virtual world as virtualized characters and can have their own "homes" and share models they created in a public domain (Jamil, Rahman, & Fawad, 2022). Similar examples include Roblox, where players can not only experience the virtual world, but also create games and build scenes in a scene creation studio, and then share their works with other players to experience (Jeon, 2023). These practices provide a glimpse into the future form of virtual community spaces and the potential they hold for enhancing the knowledge sharing experience.

The future of virtual communities in the metaverse arena will bring about significant changes to the way knowledge is shared and presented. With the advancement of technology, flat and traditional forms of sharing such as text and video will become less relevant in virtual metaverse communities, and the representation of knowledge in three-dimensional form will become the norm.

In a three-dimensional virtual metaverse community, explicit knowledge will be presented in a more immersive and comprehensive manner, providing a deeper understanding and retention of the knowledge by the recipient. This transformation from traditional forms of explicit knowledge to 3D representation enhances the experience of the recipient during the knowledge sharing process. Instead of fragmented pieces of information, explicit knowledge will be organized and integrated into a comprehensive and systematic three-dimensional module (Julian et al., 2023).

In contrast, the traditional externalization of implicit knowledge through language and text in virtual communities often results in a loss of information and a less immersive experience for the recipient. In the metaverse, the implicit knowledge can be reconstructed in situ, creating a virtual space flow that mimics the scenario in which the implicit knowledge was generated. This process not only reduces the loss of information but also allows the recipient to experience the complete process of the implicit knowledge generation, leading to a more precise and immersive absorption of the implicit knowledge. By reconstructing implicit knowledge in the metaverse, the process of externalizing knowledge transforms from language and text to a virtual simulation, which enhances the recipient's understanding and retention of the implicit knowledge (Kraus et al., 2023).

Decentralization of Shared Behaviors

In the past process of knowledge sharing in virtual communities, knowledge sharing and publication were generally carried out by the community platform. In this process, the virtual community played the role of a bridge connecting users to each other, thus creating a one-to-many relationship structure that to some extent impeded direct interaction between users and was inconsistent with the decentralized co-creation and sharing concept in the metaverse (Maddahi & Chen, 2022).

Under the metaverse, the behavior pattern of knowledge sharing will tend to be more decentralized. When users interact with knowledge, they can directly find the metaverse coordinates of the knowledge receivers and enter the other party's "private domain" for knowledge interaction after obtaining the user's authorization through invitation or application. In this face-to-face direct interaction, implicit knowledge can be socialized to implicit knowledge, while the traditional virtual community implicit knowledge socialization process can only be carried out offline. In the metaverse, users can achieve remote on-site interaction through their avatars (Magalhães et al., 2022). This point-to-point knowledge transfer can bypass the virtual community sharing center and achieve point-to-point knowledge sharing. This interweaving of knowledge sharing in the metaverse community's countless nodes will form a complex knowledge interaction network. The traditional virtual community knowledge sharing center's position will also gradually fade in this decentralized network. In this scenario, the virtual community's role is more like a "policeman" to manage the community's knowledge sharing and prevent false information, illegal information, and other content from circulating and spreading in this network. On the other hand, in the metaverse virtual experiment scenario, the nearly accessible knowledge innovation output makes the number of core users who share a large amount of knowledge in the traditional virtual community greatly increase, and the user group that shares knowledge will also show a clear decentralization.

Personalization of the Knowledge Sharing Experience

The metaverse is a three-dimensional virtual world that allows users to immerse themselves in a personalized experience, so the personalization of knowledge sharing experiences in virtual communities is also an inevitable trend. In traditional virtual communities, knowledge resources are shared in a one-size-fits-all format, which can limit the interaction and absorption of knowledge by different users. The knowledge sharing experiences in the metaverse, on the other hand, will be highly personalized. In the metaverse, knowledge resources can be reconstructed into modules and knowledge modules can be designed and customized according to the needs of different users. For example, a user who is interested in a certain field of study can choose to focus on knowledge modules related to that field, while another user who wants to learn more about a particular topic can choose to focus on knowledge modules related to that topic. Additionally, users can also design their own personal learning paths based on their knowledge needs, interests, and learning styles. This personalization of knowledge sharing experiences will not only increase user motivation to participate in knowledge sharing, but also improve their knowledge absorption efficiency (Mourtzis et al., 2023).

Collaboration in the Metaverse

The subjects of virtual community knowledge sharing are composed of the virtual community and community users (Mystakidis, 2023). In past virtual community knowledge sharing, users generally displayed their knowledge through language text or created video footage, among other forms. However, the 3D and situational construction of knowledge content in the metaverse can make it challenging for knowledge contributors of different professional backgrounds to build and share knowledge on their own.

In virtual communities, users with various knowledge backgrounds and abilities exist. When building a knowledge resource, knowledge from multiple professions may need to be invoked. These users can interact directly with each other and, with user permission granted, connect through the "wormholes" in the metaverse, a channel that links private metaverse, to achieve knowledge collaboration and construction. Admittedly, this mode of collaboration is highly dependent on users with virtual resource building skills. This is where the role of the virtual community, as another important entity in knowledge sharing, can be shown. The virtual community can provide technical support for user information resource building and sharing, such as Roblox providing development software for scene building with corresponding development tutorials and classroom teachings (Njoku et al., 2023). This way, users and virtual communities can collaborate and share knowledge, which may become the mainstream of future virtual community knowledge sharing.

The metaverse also offers great potential for collaboration in virtual communities. In traditional virtual communities, collaboration is often limited to simple text-based communication and document sharing, which can limit the effectiveness of collaboration. In the metaverse, however, users can collaborate in a more immersive and interactive environment, allowing for more effective and efficient collaboration. For example, in the metaverse, users can collaborate on projects in virtual workspace, where they can use virtual tools and resources to work together on tasks, such as designing and creating virtual objects, brainstorming ideas, and discussing complex concepts in a visual and interactive way. Collaboration in the metaverse can also take place in virtual classrooms, where users can participate in virtual lectures, discussions, and group projects with other users from all over the world (Qamar et al., 2023).

In conclusion, the metaverse will bring a huge transformation to virtual communities, with changes in the form of shared resources, decentralization of shared behaviors, personalization of the knowledge sharing experience, and collaboration opportunities. With the development of virtual reality technology, it is highly likely that virtual communities in the metaverse will become an important platform for knowledge sharing, co-creation, and collaboration in the future.

CONSTRUCTION OF KNOWLEDGE SHARING MODEL IN METAVERSE COMMUNITY

The construction of a knowledge sharing model in the metaverse community is a crucial aspect in the integration of virtual communities within the metaverse. With advancements in AI, XR, and blockchain technologies, the virtual community is undergoing a transformation in terms of the way knowledge is shared and exchanged. This new operating logic is characterized by a shared spatial dimension, situational sharing of resources, decentralized shared behavior, and coordinated sharing of entities.

The virtual community knowledge sharing model in the metaverse domain is designed to better meet the needs of users by incorporating the latest technological advancements. The AI, XR, and blockchain technologies provide a new framework for knowledge sharing in virtual communities. The new virtual community knowledge sharing model incorporates traditional virtual community knowledge sharing methods with the latest changes in the metaverse, offering a more comprehensive and immersive experience for users.

The new knowledge sharing model includes visualized content selection, immersive learning of the necessary knowledge modules, creation through virtual experimentation, and sharing of innovative knowledge within the community through a knowledge broadcast. This new knowledge sharing model offers a dynamic and collaborative platform for users to share and exchange information, fostering a more diverse and inclusive knowledge network.

Overall, the construction of a knowledge sharing model in the metaverse community is a crucial step in the evolution of virtual communities. With the integration of AI, XR, and blockchain technologies, the new knowledge sharing model offers a more comprehensive and immersive experience for users, allowing for the creation and exchange of new knowledge and ideas. The visualization of this knowledge sharing model is shown in Figure 1.

Figure 1. Knowledge sharing model of virtual communities in the metaverse field

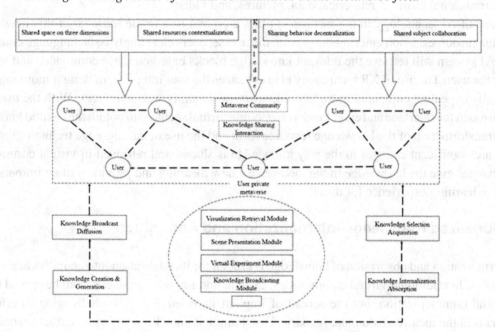

Spatialized Knowledge Selection and Retrieval

In the metaverse community, users first enter their private metaverse to access the community's knowledge resources. Unlike traditional virtual communities that rely on keyword-based retrieval, the metaverse community's knowledge resources are presented in a three-dimensional form, including both explicit knowledge in the form of interactive three-dimensional books and implicit knowledge in the form of virtualized scenarios. This new form of resource sharing is made possible through the integration of AI, XR, and blockchain technologies.

To retrieve knowledge, users can simply use language commands, and AI will retrieve the relevant knowledge blocks and present them in a visual format. The integration of XR technology improves the visibility and interactivity of the user interface, allowing users to access the knowledge they need by touching the interface and entering the corresponding virtual scenario. This new form of knowledge selection and retrieval is more immersive and interactive compared to the traditional virtual community's web interface, and provides a more dynamic and engaging experience for users.

AI technology plays a crucial role in the retrieval of these new forms of knowledge resources. The AI system can retrieve knowledge blocks based on users' language commands, ensuring that users can easily access the knowledge they need. The transformation of knowledge resource form also changes the form of retrieval results, moving away from numerical, pictorial, or video-based formats to virtual scenarios that offer a more immersive and interactive experience for users.

The introduction of the metaverse has revolutionized the way in which knowledge is shared in virtual communities. No longer are traditional methods of keyword-based retrieval sufficient in the face of this new form of sharing knowledge in the metaverse. The knowledge resources available in the metaverse are diverse, encompassing both tangible knowledge in the form of three-dimensional modules, as well as implicit knowledge in the form of virtual scenarios. These new forms of knowledge are a departure from the traditional forms of numerical data, pictures, and videos.

The use of AI technology in the metaverse plays a crucial role in the retrieval of this new form of knowledge resources. Upon entering the private metaverse, users can simply issue language commands, and the AI system will retrieve the relevant knowledge blocks based on these commands and visualize them for the user. The use of XR technology also enhances the user interface, making it more interactive and visually appealing compared to traditional virtual community web interfaces. With the use of XR, users can touch the interface and enter the corresponding virtual scenario to obtain the desired knowledge.

The transformation of the knowledge resource form and the use of cutting-edge technologies like AI and XR are significant changes in the way knowledge is shared and retrieved in virtual communities. These changes give the knowledge in the metaverse a new meaning and provide a more immersive and interactive learning experience for users.

Situationalized Knowledge Internalization and Absorption

The internalization and absorption of knowledge is crucial for its integration into an individual's knowledge system. In traditional virtual communities, explicit and implicit knowledge can be spread through posting and communication, but the spread of implicit knowledge can be challenging to effectively implement. In the metaverse domain, scenario-based implicit knowledge refers to virtual scenarios that generate implicit knowledge through immersive learning experiences.

In these virtual scenarios, learners can acquire relevant skills and knowledge through repeated practice from a first-person perspective. The internalization and absorption of explicit knowledge in the metaverse is facilitated by the transformation of knowledge from explicit to implicit in the virtual environment. For example, a real-time simulation system of a pressurized water reactor nuclear power plant can simulate typical nuclear power plant accidents in real-time, providing implicit knowledge reserves for on-site personnel facing emergency situations (Ramasundaram et al., 2023). Similarly, a high-speed railway operation scheduling and command virtual simulation system trains employees on the implicit knowledge of various scenarios faced during the operation scheduling process (Sabtu, 2023).

In the metaverse, such virtual simulation systems can be constructed as virtual scenario modules, allowing users to access and obtain relevant implicit knowledge by selecting different virtual scenario modules. This approach provides a more immersive and interactive way of learning compared to traditional methods, allowing users to internalize and absorb knowledge more effectively. As a result, the metaverse presents a unique opportunity for the internalization and absorption of knowledge in virtual communities, breaking free from the limitations of traditional virtual communities and offering new possibilities for knowledge sharing and learning.

Creation and Generation of Knowledge Black Boxes

The metaverse virtual community is a place where knowledge is shared and assimilated among its users. The community users integrate the acquired knowledge and, when they encounter areas that can be improved, they can experiment and create in the private domain of the community. The virtual experimental scene of the metaverse serves as a platform for the production of knowledge scenario modules.

In systems science, the term "black box" is used to describe a system whose internal workings are largely unknown. The term is used to illustrate how the system is viewed as a whole module, without considering its internal composition and dynamic mechanisms. In the context of the metaverse, the knowledge scenario module can be considered a "black box" for the user, who only sees the input-output relationships of the system and judges its function and structure accordingly (Şarlıoğlu et al., 2023).

For instance, the implicit knowledge scenario of "fire emergency avoidance" can be divided into different subcategories, such as fire emergency avoidance in different places. In the process of experiencing the knowledge black box, users do not need to understand its internal structure and elements. Instead, they simply need to substitute their avatar into the generation process of tacit knowledge, resulting in the acquisition of the corresponding tacit knowledge. The input of the "knowledge black box" is the user in the form of an avatar, and the output is the physical user with the corresponding tacit knowledge.

Furthermore, users can generate new explicit knowledge through experimental innovation in the virtual experiment scenario. In the decentralized sharing process of the metaverse, the generated knowledge black boxes are recorded in the form of NFT (non-fungible tokens) to ensure authenticity and ownership. This decentralized approach helps to preserve the knowledge and maintain its credibility, allowing users to have a trustworthy source of information (Siyaev & Jo, 2021).

Private Knowledge Broadcasting and Diffusion

In the private domain of users, the knowledge black box generated through the virtual scenario construction of tacit knowledge must be authenticated and published by the group through the knowledge broadcasting module in order to achieve effective knowledge sharing in the community. To achieve this goal in the metaverse domain, blockchain technology is deemed to be the most appropriate means of realizing the broadcasting of knowledge black boxes within the community (Teubner & Camacho, 2023).

With blockchain's distributed storage and recording capabilities, knowledge sharing by a private domain node in the community is recorded and stored by all nodes in the community. The use of NFT technology allows for the traceability of knowledge black boxes when they are shared in the community, and the personal information of users authorized to modify the knowledge black boxes is included in the development history of the knowledge black boxes. Additionally, when community users purchase the right to use a knowledge black box, this transaction is recorded by all user nodes in the community. As a result, knowledge sharing and transactions in the community are overseen and governed by the community through the chain of knowledge black boxes and transaction records.

Moreover, the publication of innovative knowledge must go through a rigorous authentication process to verify its quality. The "public domain" of virtual communities in the metaverse provides a suitable platform for the authentication and sharing of knowledge communities. Through the display of knowledge in the form of black boxes in the public domain, the community's evaluation of a certain knowledge can be obtained. This helps to ensure the credibility and trustworthiness of the knowledge shared in the community.

DEVELOPMENT STRATEGY OF KNOWLEDGE SHARING IN METAVERSE COMMUNITY

The advent of the metaverse has the potential to revolutionize the knowledge sharing model in virtual communities. To effectively implement this model within the metaverse domain, it is crucial to focus on the following four key areas of improvement. These areas are critical for ensuring the development and growth of knowledge sharing in virtual communities within the metaverse field. By addressing these areas, virtual communities in the metaverse will be well-equipped to facilitate seamless and effective knowledge sharing among their users.

Construction of Community Resource Evaluation System Oriented Towards Knowledge Selection and Retrieval

The effective selection and acquisition of knowledge resources is essential to the knowledge sharing process in virtual communities. With numerous resources available in the meta-universe field, it can be challenging for users to identify high-quality resources for their needs. Therefore, the establishment of a community resource evaluation system is vital to ensure users are able to select and acquire the best resources for their learning and knowledge needs.

The most practical way to evaluate community resources is through the experiences of users. When a knowledge module is authenticated and displayed in the public domain of the virtual community, users can be granted access to the module to provide their feedback and ratings. These ratings can then be recorded and visualized to form the initial score of the knowledge module. Over time, as users continue to use and transform the knowledge module, they can provide further ratings which are accumulated to form an overall score of the knowledge module (Weking et al., 2023).

This dynamic evaluation system provides users with valuable information when searching for knowledge resources. They can refer to the scores to determine the quality of the resources, helping them make informed decisions and select the best resources for their needs. The result of this process is a more streamlined and effective knowledge sharing process in the virtual community.

In conclusion, the construction of a community resource evaluation system is essential for the selection and acquisition of high-quality knowledge resources in virtual communities. By leveraging the experiences of users, the dynamic evaluation system will provide valuable information to users, helping them make informed decisions and ultimately facilitating the knowledge sharing process within the virtual community.

Virtual Community Resource Reconstruction Oriented Towards Knowledge Internalization and Absorption

The virtual communities in the metaverse domain require a reconstruction of their knowledge resources to effectively promote knowledge internalization and absorption by its users. This transformation from traditional virtual communities to the metaverse represents the "great migration" of information resources from the two-dimensional world to the three-dimensional world. To realize the goal of knowledge sharing, virtual communities must simulate existing knowledge in a 3D manner and classify it accordingly, allowing users to have a realistic experience of utilizing knowledge in virtual space.

For tacit knowledge, virtual communities can create a virtual scenario that mimics the process of generating the knowledge content, providing users with an immersive experience when acquiring it. This immersive and realistic experience will facilitate efficient internalization and absorption of the knowledge. As for the users themselves, their digital twins, which are not just virtual projections of their entity but also contain various information about it, will be reconstructed in the metaverse domain. The information data stored within the digital twin will become the foundation for personalized knowledge push to the user, thereby promoting efficient knowledge absorption (Xiong & Wang, 2022; Yang et al., 2022).

With the user's digital twin, virtual communities can also reconstruct their form in the metaverse, with the information and data set as the "inside" and the virtual image as the "outside". In this way, virtual communities can facilitate knowledge sharing by providing a personalized and immersive experience for users, promoting internalization and absorption of knowledge.

Community Research-Oriented Space Construction Oriented Towards Knowledge Generation

In the metaverse, the ability to create and generate knowledge is greatly enhanced by the construction of community research-based spaces. These spaces provide a platform for users to engage in knowledge innovation and share their new discoveries and ideas with others.

The virtual experiment spaces within virtual communities can be designed to resemble real-world research institutions, laboratories, and factories. This design provides a familiar and intuitive environment for users to engage in knowledge creation and generation. Alternatively, users can create their own research spaces with customized scenarios, which allows for greater flexibility and creativity in the knowledge creation process (Pamucar et al., 2022).

For example, in the field of automobile design, users can enter a virtual factory and test their designs through physical simulations, such as crash tests and wind tunnel tests. This allows for real-time testing and optimization of car structures under different conditions, leading to the generation of new and valuable knowledge. Additionally, users can also construct scenarios to generate a black box of tacit knowledge, which can be shared and used by others in the virtual community.

Having a community research-based space also encourages knowledge innovation among users. The ability to experiment and test ideas in a virtual environment allows users to take more risks and pursue new and unconventional ideas, leading to a more dynamic and constantly evolving knowledge sharing process.

In summary, the construction of community research-based spaces in virtual communities is crucial for fostering knowledge innovation and encouraging the creation and generation of new knowledge. This, in turn, supports the growth and development of the virtual community as a whole and its knowledge sharing model.

Community Knowledge Personalization Push Oriented Towards Knowledge Broadcasting and Diffusion

The broadcast and diffusion of knowledge within the metaverse community requires personalized pushing to ensure that it reaches its intended audience effectively. The traditional method of sharing knowledge within a community may result in a lack of relevance and purpose, leading to information confusion. To mitigate this, big data technology can be utilized to personalize the push of knowledge.

By collecting information about the users in the virtual community, such as their occupation, gender, and age, user profiles can be created. This information can then be analyzed to determine what kind of knowledge the user may need or be interested in. This will result in precise knowledge being pushed to the user, making the broadcast and diffusion of knowledge within the community more relevant and effective (Nguyen, 2022).

Moreover, big data mining techniques can be employed to classify the users in a community into different demand groups. Based on this information, when a user searches for a particular piece of knowledge, they can be pushed relevant knowledge that has been searched for by other users in the same group. This will enhance the overall knowledge broadcasting and diffusion process within the virtual community.

Research-based spaces within the virtual community also play a crucial role in the diffusion of knowledge. When users conduct knowledge innovation in these spaces, it can lead to an exponential increase in community-wide knowledge innovation. However, if all of this innovative knowledge is pushed indiscriminately to other users in the community, it may lead to confusion. By using big data mining techniques to personalize the push of knowledge, this confusion can be avoided and the knowledge can be broadcast and diffused effectively within the virtual community.

In conclusion, the personalized push of knowledge within the metaverse community is essential to ensure that knowledge is broadcast and diffused effectively. The utilization of big data technology and research-based spaces within the virtual community can enhance the overall process of knowledge broadcasting and diffusion (Jamil et al., 2022; Koo, Kwon, Chung, & Kim, 2022; Maddahi & Chen, 2022).

FUTURE RESEARCH DIRECTIONS

The development of virtual communities in the metaverse domain is still in its early stage, and there is much room for future research. One future direction is to collect more empirical data and test the validity of the knowledge sharing model in virtual communities in the metaverse domain. Another future direction is to explore the potential of blockchain technology in promoting the openness and fairness of knowledge sharing in virtual communities in the metaverse domain. Moreover, the impact of virtual communities in the metaverse domain on human social behavior and social norms also requires further study (Şarlıoğlu et al., 2023; Shen, Tan, Guo, Zhao, & Qin, 2021).

Future research directions can focus on verifying the proposed knowledge sharing model through practical experiments, collecting and analyzing data to validate the proposed model, and exploring the potential risks and challenges of virtual communities in the metaverse and developing corresponding solutions. Additionally, further studies can also be conducted to improve the personalized pushing mechanism, enhance the security and reliability of virtual communities, and optimize the overall user experience in virtual communities (Buhalis et al., 2023; Huynh-The et al., 2023; Mourtzis et al., 2023; Qamar et al., 2023; Sabtu, 2023; Y. Wang et al., 2022; Weking et al., 2023).

CONCLUSION

In conclusion, the reorganization of knowledge flow in virtual communities in the metadata domain brings new changes in the aspects of sharing space, resources, behaviors, and subjects compared to traditional virtual communities. By using the black box theory, a complete knowledge sharing model of metaverse virtual communities was established, which considers the process of knowledge sharing from three-dimensional selection and acquisition to scenario-based knowledge internalization and absorption, to knowledge black box creation and generation, and finally to the whole community through broadcasting and diffusion. The proposed model provides a reference for the development of future knowledge sharing theory and practice in virtual communities.

However, it is important to acknowledge the limitations of this study. Currently, there is limited practical experience in virtual communities in the metaverse domain and a lack of empirical conditions. The knowledge sharing model proposed in this study needs further validation through real-world experiments and data collection.

In addition, the development of virtual communities in the metaverse also brings potential risks and challenges, such as security issues, resource monopoly, digital addiction, and the need for proper facility layout and platform security, as well as clear community rules. These factors must be carefully considered when building virtual communities in the future (Nguyen, 2022; Park & Kim, 2022; Polyviou & Pappas, 2022).

Despite these limitations, the contribution of this study is significant in providing a comprehensive understanding of the knowledge sharing process in virtual communities in the metaverse domain. The proposed model serves as a valuable reference for future research and development in this field.

In the process of building virtual communities in the metaverse domain, it is recommended to pay attention to the following aspects. Firstly, it is necessary to build a secure infrastructure to ensure the safety and stability of virtual communities. Secondly, it is recommended to explore the role of blockchain technology in promoting the openness and fairness of knowledge sharing. Thirdly, it is necessary to pay attention to the impact of virtual communities in the metaverse domain on human social behavior and social norms, and to build corresponding community norms and regulations to guide the healthy development of virtual communities. Finally, it is recommended to continuously collect empirical data and test the validity of the knowledge sharing model in virtual communities in the metaverse domain, so as to provide a solid theoretical foundation for the future development of virtual communities in the metaverse domain.

REFERENCES

Allam, Z., Bibri, S., Jones, D., Chabaud, D., & Moreno, C. (2022). Unpacking the ‘15-Minute City’ via 6G, IoT, and Digital Twins: Towards a New Narrative for Increasing Urban Efficiency, Resilience, and Sustainability. *Sensors (Basel)*, 22(4), 1369. doi:10.339022041369 PMID:35214271

Allam, Z., Sharifi, A., Bibri, S., Jones, D., & Krogstie, J. (2022). The Metaverse as a Virtual Form of Smart Cities: Opportunities and Challenges for Environmental, Economic, and Social Sustainability in Urban Futures. *Smart Cities*, 5(3), 771–801. doi:10.3390martcities5030040

Bolger, R. (2021). Finding Wholes in the Metaverse: Posthuman Mystics as Agents of Evolutionary Contextualization. *Religions*, *12*(9), 768. doi:10.3390/rel12090768

Buhalis, D., Lin, M., & Leung, D. (2022). Metaverse as a driver for customer experience and value co-creation: implications for hospitality and tourism management and marketing. *International Journal of Contemporary Hospitality Management*. doi:10.1108/IJCHM-05-2022-0631

Buhalis, D., O'Connor, P., & Leung, R. (2023). Smart hospitality: From smart cities and smart tourism towards agile business ecosystems in networked destinations. *International Journal of Contemporary Hospitality Management*, *35*(1), 369–393. doi:10.1108/IJCHM-04-2022-0497

Cappannari, L., & Vitillo, A. (2022). XR and Metaverse Software Platforms. In Roadmapping Extended Reality (pp. 135-156). doi:10.1002/9781119865810.ch6

Chen, Q., & Lee, S. (2021). Research Status and Trend of Digital Twin: Visual Knowledge Mapping Analysis. *International Journal of Advanced Smart Convergence*, *10*(4), 84–97. doi:10.7236/IJASC.2021.10.4.84

Dahan, N., Al-Razgan, M., Al-Laith, A., Alsoufi, M., Al-Asaly, M., & Alfakih, T. (2022). Metaverse Framework: A Case Study on E-Learning Environment (ELEM). *Electronics (Basel)*, *11*(10), 1616. doi:10.3390/electronics11101616

Dai, Y., Wang, J., & Gao, S. (2022). Advanced Electronics and Artificial Intelligence: Must-Have Technologies Toward Human Body Digital Twins. *Advanced Intelligent Systems*, *4*(7), 2100263. doi:10.1002/aisy.202100263

Duan, H., Li, J., Fan, S., Lin, Z., Wu, X., & Cai, W. (2021). Metaverse for Social Good: A University Campus Prototype. *Proceedings of the 29th ACM International Conference on Multimedia*. 10.1145/3474085.3479238

Dwivedi, Y., Hughes, L., Baabdullah, A., Ribeiro-Navarrete, S., Giannakis, M., Al-Debei, M., Dennehy, D., Metri, B., Buhalis, D., Cheung, C. M. K., Conboy, K., Doyle, R., Dubey, R., Dutot, V., Felix, R., Goyal, D. P., Gustafsson, A., Hinsch, C., Jebabli, I., ... Wamba, S. (2022). Metaverse beyond the hype: Multidisciplinary perspectives on emerging challenges, opportunities, and agenda for research, practice and policy. *International Journal of Information Management*, *66*, 102542. doi:10.1016/j.ijinfomgt.2022.102542

Hariharan, A., Risling, M., Felic, A., & Ostertag, T. (2023). *Integration of Smart Glasses for Knowledge Transfer in Industrial Remote Maintenance: Learnings from Practice.* Paper presented at the Extended Reality and Metaverse, Cham, Switzerland.

Hassani, H., Huang, X., & MacFeely, S. (2022). Impactful Digital Twin in the Healthcare Revolution. *Big Data and Cognitive Computing*, *6*(3), 83. doi:10.3390/bdcc6030083

Huynh-The, T., Pham, Q., Pham, X., Nguyen, T., Han, Z., & Kim, D. (2023). Artificial intelligence for the metaverse: A survey. *Engineering Applications of Artificial Intelligence*, *117*, 105581. doi:10.1016/j.engappai.2022.105581

Hwang, Y. (2023). When makers meet the metaverse: Effects of creating NFT metaverse exhibition in maker education. *Computers & Education*, *194*, 104693. doi:10.1016/j.compedu.2022.104693

Inder, S. (2023). Entrepreneurial Opportunities in Metaverse. In M. Gupta, P. Jindal, & S. Bansal (Eds.), *Promoting Consumer Engagement Through Emotional Branding and Sensory Marketing* (pp. 52–62). IGI Global.

Jamil, S., Rahman, M., & Fawad, M. (2022). A Comprehensive Survey of Digital Twins and Federated Learning for Industrial Internet of Things (IIoT), Internet of Vehicles (IoV) and Internet of Drones (IoD). *Applied System Innovation, 5*(3), 56. doi:10.3390/asi5030056

Jeon, J. (2023). The impact of XR applications' user experience-based design innovativeness on loyalty. *Cogent Business & Management, 10*(1), 2161761. doi:10.1080/23311975.2022.2161761

Julian, H., Chung, T., & Wang, Y. (2023). Adoption of Metaverse in South East Asia: Vietnam, Indonesia, Malaysia. In P. C. Lai (Ed.), *Strategies and Opportunities for Technology in the Metaverse World* (pp. 196–234). IGI Global. doi:10.4018/978-1-6684-5732-0.ch012

Koo, C., Kwon, J., Chung, N., & Kim, J. (2022). Metaverse tourism: Conceptual framework and research propositions. *Current Issues in Tourism*, 1–7. doi:10.1080/13683500.2022.2122781

Kraus, S., Kumar, S., Lim, W., Kaur, J., Sharma, A., & Schiavone, F. (2023). From moon landing to metaverse: Tracing the evolution of Technological Forecasting and Social Change. *Technological Forecasting and Social Change, 189*, 122381. doi:10.1016/j.techfore.2023.122381

Maddahi, Y., & Chen, S. (2022). Applications of Digital Twins in the Healthcare Industry: Case Review of an IoT-Enabled Remote Technology in Dentistry. *Virtual Worlds, 1*(1), 20–41. doi:10.3390/virtualworlds1010003

Magalhães, L., Magalhães, L., Ramos, J., Moura, L., de Moraes, R., Gonçalves, J., Hisatugu, W. H., Souza, M. T., de Lacalle, L. N. L., & Ferreira, J. (2022). Conceiving a Digital Twin for a Flexible Manufacturing System. *Applied Sciences (Basel, Switzerland), 12*(19), 9864. doi:10.3390/app12199864

Mourtzis, D., Angelopoulos, J., & Panopoulos, N. (2023). Blockchain Integration in the Era of Industrial Metaverse. *Applied Sciences (Basel, Switzerland), 13*(3), 1353. doi:10.3390/app13031353

Mystakidis, S. (2023). Sustainable Engagement in Open and Distance Learning With Play and Games in Virtual Reality: Playful and Gameful Distance Education in VR. In Research Anthology on Virtual Environments and Building the Metaverse (pp. 297-312). IGI Global.

Nguyen, T. (2022). Toward Human Digital Twins for Cybersecurity Simulations on the Metaverse: Ontological and Network Science Approach. *JMIRx Med, 3*(2), e33502. doi:10.2196/33502

Njoku, J., Nwakanma, C., Amaizu, G., & Kim, D. (2023). Prospects and challenges of Metaverse application in data-driven intelligent transportation systems. *IET Intelligent Transport Systems, 17*(1), 1–21. doi:10.1049/itr2.12252

Pamucar, D., Deveci, M., Gokasar, I., Tavana, M., & Köppen, M. (2022). A metaverse assessment model for sustainable transportation using ordinal priority approach and Aczel-Alsina norms. *Technological Forecasting and Social Change, 182*, 121778. doi:10.1016/j.techfore.2022.121778

Park, S., & Kim, Y. (2022). A Metaverse: Taxonomy, Components, Applications, and Open Challenges. *IEEE Access: Practical Innovations, Open Solutions, 10*, 4209–4251. doi:10.1109/ACCESS.2021.3140175

Polyviou, A., & Pappas, I. (2022). *Metaverses and Business Transformation.* Paper presented at the Co-creating for Context in the Transfer and Diffusion of IT, Cham, Switzerland.

Qamar, S., Anwar, Z., & Afzal, M. (2023). A systematic threat analysis and defense strategies for the metaverse and extended reality systems. *Computers & Security, 128*, 103127. doi:10.1016/j.cose.2023.103127

Ramasundaram, A., Pandey, N., Shukla, Y., Alavi, S., & Wirtz, J. (2023). Fluidity and the customer experience in digital platform ecosystems. *International Journal of Information Management, 69*, 102599. doi:10.1016/j.ijinfomgt.2022.102599

Sabtu, M. (2023). Metaverse and Soft Skills Development Through Video Games. In M. Anshari, M. Syafrudin, & G. Alfian (Eds.), *Metaverse Applications for New Business Models and Disruptive Innovation* (pp. 120–132). IGI Global. doi:10.4018/978-1-6684-6097-9.ch008

Salem, T., & Dragomir, M. (2022). Options for and Challenges of Employing Digital Twins in Construction Management. *Applied Sciences (Basel, Switzerland), 12*(6), 2928. doi:10.3390/app12062928

Şarlıoğlu, G., Boyacı, E., & Akca, M. (2023). Information and Communication Technologies in Logistics and Supply Chain Management in Turkey: Human Resource Practices and New Challenges. In N. Sharma & K. Shalender (Eds.), *Managing Technology Integration for Human Resources in Industry 5.0* (pp. 174–197). IGI Global. doi:10.4018/978-1-6684-6745-9.ch011

Shen, B., Tan, W., Guo, J., Zhao, L., & Qin, P. (2021). How to Promote User Purchase in Metaverse? A Systematic Literature Review on Consumer Behavior Research and Virtual Commerce Application Design. *Applied Sciences (Basel, Switzerland), 11*(23), 11087. doi:10.3390/app112311087

Siyaev, A., & Jo, G. (2021). Towards Aircraft Maintenance Metaverse Using Speech Interactions with Virtual Objects in Mixed Reality. *Sensors (Basel), 21*(6), 2066. doi:10.339021062066 PMID:33804253

Tait, E., & Pierson, C. (2022). Artificial Intelligence and Robots in Libraries: Opportunities in LIS Curriculum for Preparing the Librarians of Tomorrow. *Journal of the Australian Library and Information Association, 71*(3), 256–274. doi:10.1080/24750158.2022.2081111

Teubner, T., & Camacho, S. (2023). Facing Reciprocity: How Photos and Avatars Promote Interaction in Micro-communities. *Group Decision and Negotiation.* Advance online publication. doi:10.100710726-023-09814-4

Ukko, J., Saunila, M., Nasiri, M., Rantala, T., & Holopainen, M. (2022). Digital twins' impact on organizational control: Perspectives on formal vs social control. *Information Technology & People, 35*(8), 253–272. doi:10.1108/ITP-09-2020-0608

Wang, M., Yu, H., Bell, Z., & Chu, X. (2022). Constructing an Edu-Metaverse Ecosystem: A New and Innovative Framework. *IEEE Transactions on Learning Technologies*, 1–13. doi:10.1109/TLT.2022.3226345

Wang, Y., Su, Z., Zhang, N., Xing, R., Liu, D., Luan, T., & Shen, X. (2022). A Survey on Metaverse: Fundamentals, Security, and Privacy. *IEEE Communications Surveys and Tutorials*, 1–1. doi:10.1109/COMST.2022.3202047

Weking, J., Desouza, K., Fielt, E., & Kowalkiewicz, M. (2023). Metaverse-enabled entrepreneurship. *Journal of Business Venturing Insights, 19*, e00375. doi:10.1016/j.jbvi.2023.e00375

Xiong, M., & Wang, H. (2022). Digital twin applications in aviation industry: A review. *International Journal of Advanced Manufacturing Technology*, *121*(9), 5677–5692. doi:10.100700170-022-09717-9

Yang, C., Tu, X., Autiosalo, J., Ala-Laurinaho, R., Mattila, J., Salminen, P., & Tammi, K. (2022). Extended Reality Application Framework for a Digital-Twin-Based Smart Crane. *Applied Sciences (Basel, Switzerland)*, *12*(12), 6030. doi:10.3390/app12126030

Zhang, Z., Wen, F., Sun, Z., Guo, X., He, T., & Lee, C. (2022). Artificial Intelligence-Enabled Sensing Technologies in the 5G/Internet of Things Era: From Virtual Reality/Augmented Reality to the Digital Twin. *Advanced Intelligent Systems*, *4*(7), 2100228. doi:10.1002/aisy.202100228

Chapter 19
Machine Learning and IoT for Smart Parking Models and Approaches

R. Abilasha
Hindusthan College of Arts and Sciences, India

A. V. Senthil Kumar
https://orcid.org/0000-0002-8587-7017
Hindusthan College of Arts and Sciences, India

Ibrahiem M. M. El Emary
King Abdulaziz University, Saudi Arabia

Namita Mishra
https://orcid.org/0000-0002-3353-0564
I.T.S. School of Management, India

Veera Talukdar
https://orcid.org/0000-0002-9204-5825
RNB Global University, India

Rohaya Latip
Universiti Putra Malaysia, Malaysia

Ismail Bin Musirin
Universiti Teknologi MARA, Malaysia

Meenakshi Sharma
https://orcid.org/0000-0002-6958-8741
University of Petroleum and Energy Studies, India

ABSTRACT

There is an increase in the number of vehicles in last two decades. So, it becomes important to make effective use of technology to enable free parking in public and private places. In conventional parking systems, drivers face complexity in finding vacant parking slots. It requires more human involvement in the parking zone. To deal with the issue, the authors propose a smart parking system based on IoT and machine learning techniques to manage the real time management of parking and qualms. The proposed solution makes use of smart sensors, cloud computing, cyber physical system. It is victorious in addressing the challenges such as demonstrating status of parking slot in advance to end-user, use of reserved and unreserved parking slots, erroneous parking, real-time analysis of engaged slots, detecting numerous objects in a parking slot such as bike in car slot, error recognition in more mechanism, and traffic management during crest hours. This minimizes the individual interference, saves time, money, and liveliness.

DOI: 10.4018/978-1-6684-9151-5.ch019

INTRODUCTION

Smart Parking in Larger Cities

In large cities around the world, parking is becoming an issue. The busiest cities in Morocco include. Casablanca began to indicate a need for such innovative parking options. Statistics gathered in Morocco by Moroccans. According to the Ministry of Transportation, there were 40.1 million cars in the nation in 2017. Consequently, there will be more Moroccan. From 2014 to 2017, there were 18 percent fewer cars on the road. Three-quarters of the cars on the road in Morocco are concentrated in Casablanca. (Jamie Arjona et al., 2020).

Figure 1 shows the learning algorithm that analyzes and forecasts parking spots in cropped images taken from the image frame. The parking space allotment is below as shown in Figure 1. The benefit of a deep learning trained model and CCTV cameras is realized.

Figure 1. Bounding boxes of parking slot in CCTV analysis

Searching a parking spot causes stress, increases the pollution rate, and contributes to traffic jams during Wastes the driver's precious time during rush hours. The average amount of time drivers waste looking is thought to be 7:08 For spaces in parking. In cities, this accounts for 30% of all traffic (Faraz Malik Awan et al., 2020). IoT solution designs or the leveraging of image processing solutions are the two main advancements in smart parking machine learning and deep learning. We can address various issues within smart using the latter methods. Parking without incurring the high maintenance and expense necessary for sensor and IoT-based solutions (Rohit Polishetty et al., 2016). Real-time vacancy detection will be the topic of this capstone project through CCTV cameras. We can get a photo of the entire parking lot that includes the spaces we are interested in. Right now's endeavor will. also demand the input of each parking spaces bounding boxes. Designing and putting into action a deep is the goal.

Driver Problematic One in Parking

In useful with large parking areas will be known. It lessens the amount of hardware and sensors required by a sensor-based solution. As the number of vehicles grows every day traffic and parking problem also grows day by day. Searching during the day for open slots for those vehicles the difficulty keeps increasing. Drivers have to wait for a long time, in a queue in order to. Again taking up space, they leave their cars in parking lots Time, energy, and effort. Negligence and Lack of parking discipline also contributes to the problems with parking. People typically park in their vehicles can be found almost anywhere on a road, creating significant. Roadblocks or additional space could be present than what is necessary for their vehicle to park. They're not just occupying more space because of parking Taking up space while also blocking room for another vehicle. The remaining portion of the essay is formatted as follows. As follows: Section 2 talks about the various techniques used in nearby Smart Parking Systems On entire planet. The summary of different is in Section 3 used methodologies. Brief information about the methodology is provided in Section 4 and Section 5 ends used in the proposed system that paper.

Integrated Development Environment on Parking

The IDE programming language LCD display will show openings that are available and the cost. It'll have To obtain the RF (radio repeat) Beneficiary Module stimulates thinking about empty space when a car is present when it does, the manager will instruct using an Arduino. Utilizing the RF Transmitter Module, open the door DC. As soon as a signal is received, the motor forces the door to open. Arduino will merely transmit the signal to DC after receiving it from Arduino RF Receiver Module-powered motor. The boss will send. a code is sent via SMS to the customer's phone with an Arduino and a GSM Module. The timer shall be started as soon as the door opened in a short while this. In the event of an opening, code will be saved in the system which will be delivered to the car's license plate. Wireless transmitter module the vehicle exit plate is going to similarly, be called by utilizing an RF Receiver Module. & arduino. The vehicle's license plate will drive away vehicle and eventually leave the companion vehicle. The car's wheels will have a plate that says "leaving." it lands there due to an Arduino-driven force a particular area. The customer should for stopping out and Give the overseer the provided code when they go on leave Entry way.

A SMS will be sent to the customer. To pay for stopping again, communicate in full using arduino following a customer's. The chairman will offer a direction to stop out the portion vehicle. The space will get a boost from the director. The RF path makes information for the LCD visible Transmission Module. The vehicle will come to a stop how it was stopped in comparison whatever the case, one. There is a notable area of the building's elbow room with cost. Incredibly expensive and challenging is the RF module. To come to pass observing and categorizing the current situation the difficulties faced by drivers in major cities. Two significant problems: parking availability traffic jams and shortages. With an increase in Vehicle needs are growing along with the population every day. The same, its lack of availability or improper management, heavy traffic and parking spots in crowded cities obvious. We consider solutions to these problems might try to maximize use or add more parking spaces and take care of the parking space that is available. And obviously the latter is effective for these reasons for effective use of resources available; we must create an intelligent and. a productive manner to prevent time, money, and resource wastage fuel. Parking in particular calls for safe and prudent behavior Important is the parking system. Finding empty or is a problem that people now face parking spaces that are not occupied.

They invest in this almost 6 to 8 minutes. This is the cause of the problem heavy traffic in the big cities. Many options exist for that. Market-available tools and reduction methods finding a free parking spot is stressful advanced learning. One concept for data or image processing that is useful is. In this region various algorithms are used in deep learning. Such as CNN, RCNN, MASKRCNN, YOLO, etc. (Bill Yang Cai et al., 2019). Smart cities require a smart parking system. In order to get rid of the common issues society with the identified approach. The efficient use of smart management enables time and traffic management.

Machine Learning With IoT

There is a overwhelming increase in number of tools in last two decades. So, it enhances main to create direct use of electronics to authorize hassle free parking at public and/or private places. In established parking wholes, chauffeurs face trouble in judgment feasible parking slots. These plans reject the experience of parking the jeeps on roads, occasion administration in peak hours, wrong parking of a bicycle in a parking place. Moreover, the established plans demand more human attack in a parking district. To handle above pronounced issues, skilled is an critical necessity of cultivating Smart Parking Systems. In this script, the authors intend a Smart Parking System established IoT and Machine learning methods to answer the actual time for action or event administration of parking and doubts. The projected resolution exploits smart sensors, cloud calculating and computerized material method. Development of image for bureaucrat and end-consumer is a bigger challenge as it demands to guarantee smooth listening, control and protection of parking plan. Moreover, it needs to authenticate easy arrangement accompanying an end-consumer. The projected scheme is profitable in vigorously forwarding the challenges in the way that displaying rank of parking opening well earlier completely-consumer, use of constrained and outspoken parking slots, wrong parking, illegitimate parking, actual time for action or event reasoning of free and busy slots, detecting diversified objects in a parking place to a degree bike in convertible opening, weakness discovery in individual or more elements and traffic administration all along peak hours. The system minimizes the human mediation and saves period, services and strength.

External Parking Sources

There is an epidemic increase in number of automobiles in past little age. As per report bestowed by Government 210023289 cabs were recorded in India in 2015. There is an average increase in number of instruments is 17.55 allotment. The institutions to a degree schools, Universities and MNCs witness burdensome flow and efflux of instruments during the whole of the epoch. Vehicles' motorists find it troublesome to catch absolute occasion news about an handy parking opening and directing the parking of the instrument as content of parking place is winning shortened and jeep proportion is growing. The insensitive to others parking of cars on roads causes the question of traffic tie-up and contamination. In allied areas and academic joints, occasion administration is necessary. Smart parking maybe visualized as a smooth, more adept resolution. In current age, Indian Government accepted drives to expand smart capitals. Smart parking plan is an main component of smart centers. Thus, it enhances an essential necessity to start a well-trained, smart and mechanical parking structure. The study of information in accompanying field shows that investigators created Smart Parking Systems to simplify hassle free parking to low public. But the existent orders neglect the wrong parking in a parking opening, parking of diversified tools in a sole place in the way that bike in a bus opening (Nimble et al., 2016). These arrangements do not devote effort to something constrained and outspoken parking slots separately. The existent arrangements further lack in providing a Graphical User Interface (GUI) located managerial instrument panel to resolve actual time for action or event issues (Shree, 2017). Moreover, these wholes demand more human attack for smooth occupied. The above pronounced challenges stimulate us to suggest "Machine Learning and IoT located Real Time Parking System". The projected structure form and persuasive use of schemes entrenched accompanying cyberspace and Wi-Fi relatedness, sensors and processors, object discovery and representation refine algorithms. All maneuvers write accompanying each-different over the Internet.

Internet of Things Connectivity

As technology grows, Internet of Things (IoT) and deep learning concepts can be applied to smart city planning. This will enable us to continuously address urban mobility issues and provide an economically, ecologically and socially sustainable infrastructure. Citizen (Giuseppe Amato et al., 2016). Many intelligent systems today assist drivers by reporting traffic jams, road conditions, accidents and alternative routes, mostly in the form of mobile applications. However, with so many vehicles on the road, parking is still a chore. As (Francesco piccialli et al., 2021) shows, drivers waste many liters of gasoline just looking for a parking space. Typically, 30% of his traffic jams are caused by looking for an empty parking space. As shown in (Bandi Sairam et al., 2020), drivers waste an average of 3.5-14 minutes to find a free parking space. It also causes driver frustration, traffic congestion, fuel consumption and air pollution, all of which are challenges for sustainable development. In this particular case, knowing in advance what parking spaces are available can alleviate this problem. Using deep learning techniques and IoT integration, we can remedy this problem by predicting parking lot occupancy and availability with great accuracy.

Parking Prediction

To solve this problem, different techniques have been proposed by different researchers for different types of data collected in the literature. In existing research, researchers mainly used machine learning techniques and time-series models to calculate parking space occupancy and time from data collected by sensors. Due to the continuous increase in sensor data, traditional decision support systems cannot perform deep neural networks to the extent that deep neural networks can estimate arbitrary nonlinear and linear functions using a large number of samples. Relatively speaking, traditional decision support systems require choosing the right function or the right kernel. Deep learning techniques can then be used to predict occupancy, especially for feed forward networks. Nevertheless, simple deep feed-forward networks fail to integrate time-domain information, which is essential for park prediction, especially for persistence problems. A recurrent neural network (RNN) (R.Senthil Kumar & B Surya, 2020) is a type of neural network that exploits the sequential nature of its input. RNNs are commonly applied to many time-critical tasks such as text prediction, POS tagging, and power consumption. All of these problems have time-dependent inputs. In other words, event estimation is based on previous events. Parking lot occupancy and occupancy duration are both time-series problems. The occurrence of each parking event is highly dependent on the time of day, the end time of the last event (Mohammed Farag & H. A.

Elshenbary, 2020), and crowd sensing. Therefore, RNNs can be used to predict parking lot occupancy and time. In this paper, we propose a framework aimed at predicting the parking space availability of parking spaces in a given city. The proposed system uses a deep learning model, Deep Long Short Term Memory (DLSTM) network (Julien Nyambal & Richard Klien., 2021), and also integrates data collected from various sources on IoT. To train the model, we used the Birmingham parking lot dataset as the main dataset. To validate the model, we used different performance evaluation techniques to estimate the availability of parking spaces at specific points in the parking lot. The proposed intelligent parking system saves search time to find a free parking space. Helps reduce energy consumption by reducing the time it takes to find a free parking space.

LITERATURE SURVEY

Opening discovery structures are a fundamental part of PGI plans (Parking Counseling and Facts. The concluding are top-secret established the discovery arrangement or dossier recommendation. The first type is counter-located plans. They depend sensors at the entrance and exit of parking oodles. They only determine facts on the number of spots accessible in a garage. This way that the parking consumers do not catch some further counseling on place the rooms are free. In addition, these methods are not agreeable accompanying on-longitudinal parking scopes, or dwellings parking rooms. The second type is Wi-Fi or connected sensor-located wholes. They support a large size of dependability. They are used in in-entrance to room parking oodles in the way that buying malls. This type is established establishing sensors in each parking scope. The costs of sensors, transceivers, and treat wholes, and the extreme sustenance needs concerning this somewhat opening discovery plan influence allure affordability and scalability. This exceptionally applies to immense out-of-doors parking oodles accompanying many storage building for vehicles to start. Our project falls under the tertiary classification of PGI wholes: camcorder-located opening discovery. The latest is less priceless distinguished to utilizing sensors because CCTV cameras cover diversified parking rooms accompanying individual sole angle in out-of-doors parking oodles. Further, the unchanging cameras are secondhand for two together opening discovery and common freedom and following (Amala Sonny et al., 2020).

Early connected work inside opening discovery designs established camcorder inputs concentrated on concept dispose of, made in the home feature extractions, and preparation of machine intelligence classifiers on these culled lineaments. Funck and others. begun by equating remark concepts accompanying recommendation figures utilizing principal component reasoning as a base for the discovery (Francesco Piccialli et al., 2021). Next everything following fixated on preparation classifiers in the way that Bayesian, SVM, and Chance Jungle classifiers in addition to a large group of concept transform methods to extract figure visage in the way that corners, edges, consistency, banner, and history deduction. The feature distillation methods secondhand were Filter, Globe, Chilly, and so forth (Francesco Piccialli et al., 2021)(Hoang Tran Vu, 2018).

Because these designs were all established manually devised feature origin, the accuracies were not above 90% and were very angry for one change in weather environments. The plans established convolution affecting animate nerve organs networks upgraded these results. Second hand the VGGNet-F pre-prepared act in accordance with ILSVRC-2012. The authors before retrained the last tiers on the Almeida and others. dataset PKLot also to tweak it. In addition, this work investigates the analyses of the choice of the pre-prepared model and the orders secondhand in fine tuning it. The authors secondhand SGD optimizer accompanying 0.01 knowledge rate. The network was prepared for three thousand redundancies accompanying 128 samples per tiny-bunches. Whole further supports a whole design for the use of specific a model in result by cultivating a consumer connect to set the restricting boxes of workplace and monitor authentic-occasion these parking oodles (Hoang Tran Vu, 2018).

Acharya et. al erected upon Valipour and other's work, with remainder of something. The authors secondhand the alike PKLot dataset in addition to a pre-prepared CNN to extract physiognomy. The novelty in this place work display or take public utilizing a prepared SVM as a classifier and grasping the last twofold manufacturing. This paper again does transfer knowledge on place where stocks are bought place the investigators live, and it is hopeful. The CNN-SVM consolidation was entertaining in the sense that it completed the proneness of two together when secondhand individually (Francesco Piccialli et al., 2021).

Nyambal and others. still secondhand calibrated pre-prepared CNN. The offering of their work is providing the process of accumulating a new dataset of storage building for vehicles representations. Accordingly, it helps accept better by virtue of what the dataset PKLot maybe leveraged. The paper further compares the use of three various solvers when preparation the model (R. Senthil Kumar & B. Surya, 2020). Cazamias and others. Processed on workplace opening discovery inside the opportunity of their class project. The authors likewise secondhand the PKLot dataset. They secondhand a CNN accompanying a natural construction distinguished to the pre-prepared CNNs noticed above. Their CNN design had three convolution coatings accompanying 10, 20, and 30 filters, individually. The essence proportion they secondhand was five pixels by five. They likewise secondhand lot normalization tiers following in position or time each convolution tier. They secondhand top-combining tiers to humiliate the range last of the three convolution coatings. Subsequently, they secondhand three completely affiliated tiers to categorize the recommendation. The paper reached0.9997 veracity on the test set. They further prepared and proven the act in accordance with the three various park camcorder feeds of the dataset to judge the inference of their model (Mohamed Farag & H. A. Elshenbary, 2020).

The last paper value mentioning is the paper accompanying and ready the dataset we are utilizing in this place project. Almeida and others. assembled the PKLot dataset and ready it a writing of dossier group forms, pre-dispose of, the counseling on in what way or manner amount to the preparation and experiment sets, plans on evaluations versification, and potential research guidance (Bandi Sairam, 2020).

J Cynthia,CBharathiPriya, Air cooling Gopinath proposed a paper, that helps to lower occasion to settle the staying domains, as a consequence to it lessens fuel consumption. Sensors hopeful sent in the staying district and through the adjustable use, customer books or the staying room and permits connected to the internet section choice further. Established staying the board foundations use sensors and other agreement piece, still doesn't address arrangement for two together open and close parking spot. Affect Located Smart Ride Parking Scheme Robot located use the get dossier about approachable void staying opening. India's capital New Delhi from 2015 origin determining to accumulate all distinct meaningful detail of action about series of spots for motor vehicle parking and staying domains multi lease foundation of line where race ends control. Design of Connected to the internet reserving for staying room Each standard lord commune, Color of blood sensors are shipped and IR sensors would identify the size of staying rooms, Number of free and scheduled rooms are clearly proved in LCD screen, WIFI piece is applyied for agreement 'tween lightweight request. Order staying room Guiding along route, often over water to staying Opening Imagination in Attendant for Partner to Resolve To enable a customer to appropriate the brilliant staying foundation, customer need to enter accompanying customer ID. Page is created taking advantage of PHP and staying data input, Parking ID, Instrument number, leaving ending, charge total, and graphical portrayal of the staying. Movable request allows the customer to find and sustain a storage building for vehicles aware computer network, route from travel stoop to approachable parking gap is also the projected foundation lessens the operator's exercise and occasion to examine parking spot. (Francesco Piccialli et al., 2021)

NazishFatima, PratikshaJagtap, AkshayaNatkar, Snehal Choudhary bestowed a paper,that demonstrates with old rarities that the model helpless on savvy staying foundation applying IoT finds can be accountable for the traffic obstruction andease best approach to receive a parking opening.In accordance with ultimate current report fashioned a piece Worldwide Parking Institute, we erect that many creative parking concepts have existed grown. Inauguration of verdict a parking gap to leave their boat has finish being Disillusioning issue to the chauffeurs uniformly. Sharp Parking Arrangement applying RFID: Smart Parking Arrangement appropriating visual Wi-Fi Sensor System: This foundation promotes RFID to coordinate the bicycle's singular RFID tag accompanying the inducement in the table when it is implicit apiece RFID person who reads in the series of spots for motor vehicle parking entrance. When welcome boat enters at the parking extent, welcome cab's indifferent plate is checked with the number plate filed while engagement a staying gap. When the cab is efficiently abandoned in the room leaving occasion starts. Smart Parking Arrangement taking advantage of IR sensors: This genius presented foundation resorts to critique agent to uncover the chance of staying rooms. Chance of the scope maybe found simply after bus enters the parking part, so if parking spot isn't approachable it needs to thwart from there and it concede possibility cause traffic obstruction. Formerly the instrument is abandoned and following captured off from the parking room, stopping charges are deducted from your Ewallet. The basic meaning is that they can hold their staying scopes before introducing the workplace (Hoang Tran Vu, 2018).

Basavaraju bestowed a paper in what way following was established. Mainly community is enduring to issues on hesitant jeeps in hesitant openings in a city. More commonly than not community set their exact energy in expecting through parking make ups to leave their cars. Ultimate traffic occurs basically in light of jeep prevent in city localities in this manner things are lazing about in ricocheting through hesitant district atypical conspirator to leave their boats. The leasing arrangement is arranged in specific a approach, that it is decent for confirmed parks, open stops furthermore, roadway side hesitant. Cloud master friendship that gives allocated competency to store news about rank of hesitant scopes in a hesitant district thus presents the form of brilliant hesitant whole and it holds few control centers about each hesitant scopes that will be secondhand Guiding along route, often over water construction: banner open mindedness of parking spots to as remark point for the camcorder. The main attendant displays clients and investigates to positive domain of tightest hesitant news about miscellaneous openings in a alone standard master an district and district from current extent. The manager is hold right to making new hesitant domains by bestowing description or news about the hesitant district and additionally figures out by virtue of what to recollect number of staying rooms for a distinguishing hesitant region and a lot further clear the hesitant openings in a staying district. Making Series of spots for motor vehicle parking Steps connected accompanying scene the Parking Scheme: Suitably increase camcorder to aforementioned an range that written description of past events survived it is obviously shows hesitant beginning (R. Senthil Kumar & B. Surya, 2020).

Debaditya Acharya, Weilin Yan and Kourosh Khoshelham Camerabased projected foundations that present the correct field of unoccupied parking spots that is a essentiality for route of vehicles to empty leaving rooms. Counter located frame everything can just present dossier on the categorical number of empty rooms a suggestion of correction directing the chauffeurs to exact region of the parking spots, and specific foundations can't be prescribed to road staying morality and private staying rooms.

Long student essay (Francesco Piccialli et al., 2021) to expand an IoT-located aid. Fundamentally, they likely to design an wise structure namely worthy calling the ownership of storage building for vehicles in an outnumbered group hours of request. To improve the flow of motors in a particular area, a deep knowledge-located method is used to forecast the parking opening ownership so that humble the probing period for parking. The method is an ensemble individual. The projected plan determines superior results that are better that established procedure of the mean and alone predictors that supplies hereditary and strong forecasting. Paper stating beliefs (Hoang Tran Vu, 2018) aims to increase the effectiveness; to acclimate remodel a 3-scope recommendation way for the dislocation of differing instruments of a convolution dimensional device that drives a machine network. To discover the energetic and various feature title, Authors have projected a Siamese design that assists in lowering belongings produced on account of figure accident. The projected network was grown to address the efficient issues in rustic surroundings that assisted to draw facts about room rank of parking oodles.

Authors in (R. Senthil Kumar & B. Surya, 2020) have supported a smart parking request utilizing a deep knowledge foundation. As a resolution method that appropriates the DL and representation prepare ideas to handle the out passing of news process in the determining systems is projected. Bureaucracy favorably recognizes the parking process through gain figures. A deep categorization of smart parking methods located on park ownership discovery is fashioned in (Mohamed Farag & H.A.Elshenbary., 2020). The authors have projected two forms, individual deep education interconnected system- work. It involves 11 tiers and the different depends on the mean. Suitable way, the open ocean knowledge network in addition to ale net has extreme result. It (Debaditya Acharya & Weilin Yan, 2016) includes object discovery in a park. For that originally constitute a dataset of representations and more a dataset of the empty park named the motif of the garage. Before the dataset is prepared utilizing Convolution Interconnected system and allure looks and top-secret by way of a Twofold SVM classifier and proven accompanying the motive of the park and produce the gap in area in the parking district.

In this place, Deep Extreme Education Procedure (DELM) is secondhand as an treasure to process the representation-located dossier and find the expressionless storage building for vehicles. Attending few processes are complicated in the way that Dossier addition, Pre-prepare, Request tier Forecast, and act. In this place paper (Julien Nyambal & Richard Klein, 2021) the dataset of cut representations of the parking spots is calm and before accompanying the use of the convolution interconnected system we find either spot is idle a suggestion of correction by equating the countenances. Present we secondhand few method connected set up to form and store few files in the way that .json, lable.txt, .caffemodel, and redistribute .contract in the consumer arrangement.

Mein (Vijay Pratap Paidi et al., 2020) has told that the warm camcorder maybe used to discover objects in some critical condition and further it is resorted to in cases of freedom reasons to perceive overheated mechanisms. Conforming to this means, it is used to discover bicycles when they are affecting discharging heat at tyres, diesels, or lights. So fundamentally, the frame to frame dataset of the countenances was given to the 5-fold cross-validation process place Deep knowledge detectors like Yolo-v, Yoloconv, GoogleNet, ResNet18, ResNet50 are used to judge the test dataset providing the results of boat discovery and produce the parking opening. (Fazel Mohammadi et al., 2019) Projected Authentic-Period scheme that is Cloud Based. Because it is a method for Smart Metropolises, for understandable reasons, it endure be an Brainy individual. In this place paper, to evolve a secure and trustworthy cloud-located wise automobile parking method, joined on-location dossier is group is adept. It is secondhand accompanying Wi-Fi sensors. It helps in real time and flooding dossier science of logical analysis on dossier that is composed from IoT that is examined to check the chance of parking oodles dynamically.

Real-Opportunity and Correct Parking Calculation, the authors in (Bill Yang Cai et al., 2019) submitted a Program located Deep Education approach. Appropriating the current incidents in deep convolution affecting animate nerve organs networks (DCNNs) and a singular penetrate for car following, they accumulate news across differing picture frames ina very series of television to discard caused crash by discovery losses and occlusions. It helps to design physical-opportunity program plan.

Remarkably, it bear be correct. The developed system is fashioned restrain mind the smart capitals uses and future WWW of Belongings (IoT). The fast average pause per frame meant that in palpable-realm arrangement the order will be doable in monetary agreements. In (Ghulam Ali et al.,2020), Deep Long Consistent inability to remember Network is working devised for Smart Parking Structure established IoT. In this place paper, convertible parking chance prognosis construction is given that is sensor located in addition to RNN. Too long temporary thought model approach is used to expand a foundation drink- porting a deep long temporary thought network that foresees the motor parking district by utilizing diversified sciences like sensor networks, Computer network of Belongings (IoT) and cloud electronics. By observant the adeptness and veracity of the noticed means eventually-intelligent ride parking opening chance we will notice that alternative in forecast is amazingly insufficient

METHODOLOGY

Dataset Plotting Mechanism

The two datasets were intentional, CNRPark and PKLot datasets. PKLot, holds almost 12416 concepts of parking slots got from diversified parking oodles that were top-secret established weather environments of that 5959 countenances are of active workplace and staying 6457 are of empty parking oodles. CNRPark resides of 150000 described patches and it's downloadable but has significantly large size for clothing. Different positions of luminescence from sun or other source environments that contains few impediments by way of impediments (like timbers, non stationed jeeps or lampposts) and few incomplete or stalked trucks are rounded up by it. This permits to coach a classifier that can distinguish.

Machine Learning Based Parking

ML Can be pretended any of AI that has a scheme capacity to find, help a picked task from the possible datasets secondhand as recommendation. A ML located Smart parking scheme computes the parking district of the determined dataset to receive the rank of parking district as active or free. Additionally, by way of Machine Learning approach and Artificial Intelligence closely associated the parking ownership rank of looming days or period flip through be concluded. Information had connection with workplace in the districts are composed and treated in a here and now by sensors for fear that boats can use feasible parking oodles. For this the sensors secondhand are Ultrasonic Proximity detectors and Electromagnetic parking sensors. Examples: Enhanced Data for GSM Evolution (EDGE), Constrained Application Protocol (CoAP), IPv6 over Low Power Wireless Personal Area Networks (6LoWPAN), General Packet Radio Services (GPRS), 3G/4G natural net- everything etc.

The CNN is so devised established three construction blocks. First, are the loop tiers that create feature capacities. The convolution tier can have diversified filters accompanying each refine bearing a various feature picture. The feature maps are shapely together to produce a feature book namely next shipped to the next tier. The second component is administering non-distance to indicate the non-uninterrupted type of original existence. ReLu function is ultimate prevalent incitement function secondhand in CNN. Finally, the feature books are treated by combining coatings. The combining coatings are used to down sample the countenance and weaken range. This admits custody the scalability of the recommendation and geographical invariance and makeup. To reach good inference potential of the model, we need to confirm the model is not over fitting the preparation dataset.

Figure 2 shows the presented system guides the user to find a free parking slot without any effort and keeps the vehicle secure.

Figure 2. The system identifies the maintenance of the smart parking system

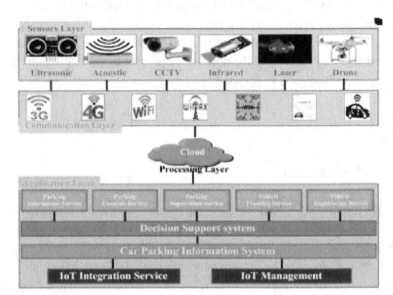

Dropout Regularization

Dropout is a regularization method that helps forestall or lower over fitting. The plan of the failing student tier search out brings to an end the incitement of a portion of neurons in a tier by background their incitement to nothing. The allotment is considered expected 50% or less to not break the knowledge process. These neurons are sampled carelessly at each preparation pass. This forces the model to not depend distinct growth and solve various ways while education weights. The non conformists tiers are considered expected set afterwards the thick coatings and not loop tiers Batch Normalization is a normalization method accomplished on the inputs of each coating alone. The normalization is premeditated for the tiny-clusters alone. This method calculates the mean and difference of each tiny-quantity to make regular it. Then the normalized worth is scaled by a limit Beta and fluctuated by a limit Lambda.

Parking Model Construction

The additional advantage of array normalization in our model construction searches out speed the preparation process because the inputs are normalized. The normalized inputs and outputs admit coatings to discover alone. This method likewise removes the question of the beginning initialization of the interconnected system that influences the conduct each period we start a computer otherwise. Finally, and most basically, cluster normalization can too present image of a regularization player and prevent the over fitting of the model. The regularization effect arises the case that the normalization by tiny parcel adjoins few buzz each occasion to the model's dossier dispersion. Batch normalization is normally linked accompanying failing student coatings because the additional cacophony is narrow.

Iot Based Connectivity

IoT is the trendiest technology right now era IoT uses the network as an agent to establish a connection devices with each other. In these networked devices A unique identifier (UID) is provided to identify them. These devices can include various devices such as computing devices, digital devices and mechanical devices equipment these devices transfer data without human-computer or human-to-human interaction. This technology works together as the first core technologies developers use for intelligent parking systems. in the Internet of Things Internet SPS connects all computer devices and sensors and transmit data without a human intervention Internet connection is required for the destination computing devices and sensors are offered through either wired or wireless connections CNN performs feed forward using neural network neurons. Then go back apart a pass is made to compute the gradient of all neural network parameters to be trained over the applied loss function. The next step is to update the model weights in the direction that minimizes the loss. This update step is decided by the learning rate, which is set as a hyper parameter at the beginning of training. By choosing this course amount affects exercise. A low learning rate can result in the training remaining at a local minimum, while a high one Learning speed can make training chaotic and impossible to find Parking vehicles was very a difficult task these days parking lots, lack of proper information available spaces, look for those spaces, it all adds up until the parking challenge. Find a place our vehicle is not just a waste of time and money and problems, but also causes a lot of damage drivers The problem further extends to traffic congestion, air pollution and environmental damage a proper parking system is urgently needed reduce stand-by parking This article is basically a survey of some proposed parking schemes that have been implemented to overcome parking problems this questionnaire, different methods and the implementations proposed by the authors are discussed, compare them based on these performance, optimization, price and a little more parameters.

Table 1 shows the details of each training experiment separately. It was performed after the model was validated, we ran the following training methodology four times. The authors did the remaining 3 workouts in my workout. Configure each parking camera feed individually.

Training and Testing Models

Almeida et al. Their paper suggests splitting the data into a 50% training subset and a 50% testing subset. The main guideline, according to the same paper, is not to have the same sample of parking lots. Same day for both training, validation and testing subsets. This will skew the results as the model may be skewed. In this case, training and evaluation were performed on the same vehicle that had been parked for extended periods of time during the day. That's all the difference is a subtle one that confuses model training (Bandi Sairam et al., 2020). In our work, we try to follow this rule while leveraging the vast amount of data available.

Table 1. Parking samples with trained and testing phases

Experiment	Number of Training Samples	Number of Iterations per Epoch	Scopped at Epoch	Best Weight at Epoch	Training Time per Epoch
Single parking training on UFPR04	51786	2877	13	5	~488s[slower GPU]
Single parking training on UPFR05	16956	942	12	4	~420s
Single parking training on PUC	43164	2398	13	5	~750s
Multiple parking training	51786	2877	19	11	~860s

Make sure the PK Lot record also has a verification record. Validation set is important for early stopping mechanism, Increases the generalizability of the model. We extracted the file paths of all segmented images and reorganized the data according to the JSON representation shown in table 1. The proposed structure allows you to prioritize class names (that is, occupancy status). Make sure you have a good balance of training/validation/test subsets in terms of class names. The second benefit is retention

Separation of the three parking lot camera feeds abstracts the separation of each camera feed from the others. Finally, and most importantly, I saved the segmented parking lot file paths by date under each parking lot. Lots of camera feeds. This also allowed me to clearly separate training/validation/testing by date. Therefore, we can use Almeida et al. without affecting the ability to segment the dataset two or more pieces. This method is promising because it can be scaled up quickly to apply k-fold cross-validation.

Approach without exceeding the daily rule. For multiple parking training and testing, we split the data set into approximately 50% for training, approximately 10 D44 for validation, and approximately 40% for testing samples. For single parking training and multiple parking tests, split each parking test separately ~70% training, ~10% validating, ~20% testing. Since our goal is individual parking training,

We now use a validation set that aggregates samples to assess and improve generalization ability from three parking lot camera feeds. So I concatenated the validation statements for each parking camera Eat together and use the assembled set to validate your single park training. A detailed summary is provided in Table 2. training, validation, and test sets. We integrated these preprocessing steps into a custom Keras data generator. The latter receives a set of the pass contained in the data generator, split them into batches, read the images in each batch and preprocess them. Make them available in your model for training, validation, or testing. Training method We have initialized all the various data generators required for all training experiments. Then evaluate the model on a subset of 100 samples of the training data,

The model may over fit the data. A model that cannot over fit a small subset of the dataset cannot learn from it larger datasets. After the model was validated, we ran the following training methodology four times. The authors did the remaining 3 workouts in my workout. Configure each parking camera feed individually. Table 1 shows the details of each training experiment separately.

Parking Information System

Parking information system "CPIS" informs the driver of the availability of parking spaces in various parking lots. Parking space availability is a highly time dependent issue. The continuous nature and occupancy period of parking lot occupancy information should be analyzed using time series analysis techniques. In this regard, we applied RNNs to take advantage of the sequential nature of parking lot data. As shown in Figure 3, CPIS relies heavily on the performance of the decision support system to provide accurate information about drive parking space availability. Figure 3 shows that data is collected from different parking lots by different sensors, this data is sent through the communication layer to the processing layer, and the data is stored for processing purposes. From the processing layer, the stored data of different parking lots in response to queries invoked by drivers who want to know the availability of free parking spaces in a particular parking lot or in different parking lots within a particular parking lot. Is captured by the decision support system?. A specific day or period. The acquired data is processed by a deep learning-based decision support system to predict the availability of free parking spaces early. The output of the decision support system is forwarded to CPIS, which informs drivers of parking availability at a specific time on a specific day.

Figure 3 shows that the long-term state C(t) is introduced along with the short-term state h(t). Three gates (input gate, output gate and forget gate) are introduced to control the input flow to the cell. A forget gate combines the current input X(t) with the previous short-term state h(t-1).

Figure 3. Decision support system

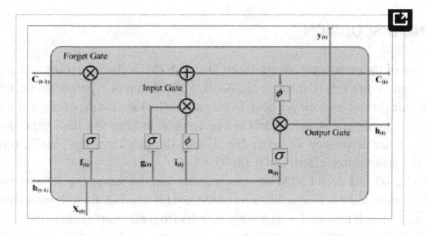

A proposed decision support system for predicting parking space availability uses sensor data as input to predict the availability of parking spaces in different parking lots at a given time. After receiving the data from the sensors, we applied a deep recurrent neural network to predict parking space availability. Of course, RNNs are good at predicting time-dependent events. Parking space availability prediction is a time-dependent problem and can be viewed as a dynamic prediction problem. In this study, DLSTM was applied to predict parking space availability. LSTM is a special type of RNN that can predict long-term dependencies efficiently. The architecture of the LSTM cell is shown in Figure 4.

The computation of f(t) and y(t) is defined as

$$f(t)=\sigma(W_{xf}Tx(t)+W_{hf}Th(t-1)+bf) \quad (1)$$

$$y(t)=\varphi(W_{x}Tx(t)+W_{yy}(t-1)+b) \quad (2)$$

Symbol σ represents the sigmoid function, and φ represents an activation function. The input gate determines the value of the long-term outgoing state C(t) and the output gate O(t) determines the composition of the short-term outgoing state h(t). where f(t) represents a forgetting gate and g(t) is a layer that behaves like a recurrent network. In Figure 4 we can see that the long-term and short-term states and cell outputs are computed by element-wise multiplication denoted by ⊗.

In particular, the current long-term state C(t) is determined by adding the values determined by the forget gate and the input gate denoted by ⊕. The long-term current state C(t) and output y(t) were determined as follows.

c(t)=f(t)⊗C(t)+i(t−1)+i(t)⊗g(t) (3)

DLSTM stacks multiple LSTM layers vertically. The output of each LSTM cell forms the next layer's input sequence and is forwarded to the same layer's connections. Each progressive layer represents the input in a new dimensional space as the input is passed through one of her layers to the other. Therefore, adding layers allows the network to learn new relationships between inputs and outputs in different dimensions. Therefore, in this research, we develop a deep LSTM that predicts the availability of parking lots.

Inputs are passed to the network architecture and each layer produces information according to the given inputs. Therefore, adding more layers increases the chances of finding connections between inputs and outputs to learn well at different levels. Therefore, in this work, we construct a deep LSTM. This is a specific type of neural network that has a hidden state but takes the previous output as input. The output at each layer goes through both his adjacent LSTM cell and the next higher layer.

RESULT AND DISCUSSION

The performance of the proposed network-based Deep LSTM decision support system was evaluated using available sensor data sets (Camero et al., 2018). Three different experiments were performed, one per parking lot, one per day, and one per hour. In the parking lot location experiment, the system predicts empty parking spaces in various parking lots at a given point in time. In a daily experiment, the system predicts parking space occupancy for seven days, Friday through Thursday. Finally, predict his hourly occupancy of the parking space from 08:00. 00-05:

We used 70 for 00 AM deep LSTM network training and the remaining 30% for testing purposes. Then use 20% of the training set for validation and the rest for training. Experiments are run both on the entire dataset and on each parking lot separately. Results from all samples show the overall availability of parking spaces across the city. In contrast, experiments conducted using samples of individual parking spaces show that parking spaces in specific parking lots are available at specific times. In other words, overall results provide an overview of parking space availability, while parking-related results provide information about parking space availability for specific parking spaces. For experimental purposes, we implemented the algorithm using Keras, the most popular deep learning framework. We applied a deep LSTM network to predict parking availability at a specific location, hour, and day of the week.

Parking Intelligent Parking Space Allocation

The results of the entire dataset and individual experiments for 30 parking lots are shown in the table. It shows the performance of the proposed deep LSTM along with performance metrics. RMSE, MAE, MSE, MdAE, MSLE. The overall performance of Deep LSTM is 0.068, 0.0411, 0.0046, 0.028 and 0.002 for RMSE, MAE, MSE, MdAE and MSLE respectively. From these results, we can analyze that the prediction accuracy of the proposed decision support system is 93.2%, 95.9%, 99.6%, 97.2%, and 99.8% respectively in five scales. The values indicate the reliability of the proposed decision support system. In general, all power measurement parameters have a minimum prediction accuracy of 93.2% (RMSE) and a maximum prediction accuracy of 99.8% (MSLE).

Figure 4. Parking slot table space on LSTM

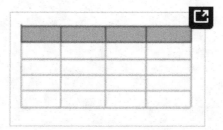

By analyzing the performance of the proposed decision support system for individual parking lots, we find that the mean, maximum, minimum and standard deviation of the RMSE are 0.109, 0.177, 0.048 and 0.028 respectively. Similarly, for MSLE, the mean, maximum, minimum, and standard deviation are 0.006, 0.016, 0.002, and 0.003, respectively. Total results are not considered when calculating the average, maximum, minimum, and standard deviation.

Comparing the five loss functions RMSE, MAE, MSE, MdAE, and MSLE, the experimental results show that MSLE gives the lowest average value compared to the other four loss functions. In addition to MSLE, MSE provides minimum mean compared to other 3 loss functions. On the other hand, RSME shows the highest mean. Among the five loss functions, MSLE and MSE are the best performance evaluation methods.

Figure 5 shows the daily forecast was created so drivers could easily check parking availability on a given day. First, we split the dataset by day and then perform daily predictions by the proposed model. The results produced by Deep LSTM for the daily dataset are shown shows experimental results for parking space availability per day. It shows the performance of the proposed deep LSTM along with performance metrics

In Figure 6, x-axis represents days and y-axis, they extracted the file paths of all segmented images and reorganized the data according to the JSON representation. The proposed structure allows you to prioritize class names (that is, occupancy status). Make sure you have a good balance of training/validation/test subsets in terms of class names.

RMSE, MAE, MSE, MdAE, and MSLE. The daily MSEs for Deep LSTM are 0.0168, 0.0139, 0.0135, 0.0125, 0.0157, 0.0151, and 0.0173 on Monday, Tuesday, Wednesday, Thursday, Friday, Saturday, and Sunday. These values demonstrate the reliability of the proposed decision support system regarding daily parking space availability. Drive helps you schedule rides on specific days of the week. Analyzing the performance of the proposed daytime parking availability decision support system, as shown in Figure, shows that the variation in forecasts is very small over seven days of the week. Results on Saturday and Sunday are less accurate due to unpredictability, but clearly show that the results are more accurate on other days compared to Saturday and Sunday.

The second benefit is retention separation of the three parking lot camera feeds abstracts the separation of each camera feed from the others. Finally, and most importantly, I saved the segmented parking lot file paths by date under each parking lot. Lots of camera feeds. This also allowed me to clearly separate

Figure 5. Training and testing schedule

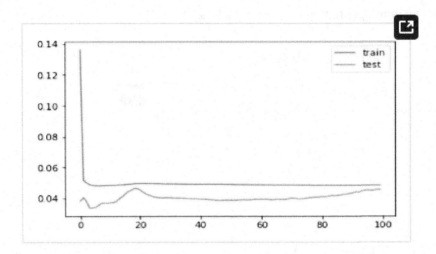

Figure 6. The level of the parking allotment verification according to time

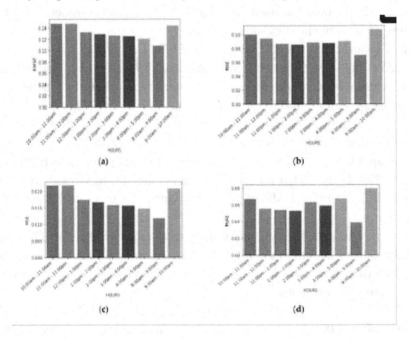

training/validation/testing by date. Therefore, we can use Almeida et al. without affecting the ability to segment the dataset two or more pieces. This method is promising because it can be scaled up quickly to apply k-fold cross-validation.

Approach without exceeding the daily rule. For single parking training and multiple parking tests, split each parking test separately ~70% training, ~10% validating, ~20% testing. Since our goal is to train in individual parking lots. We now use a validation set that aggregates samples to assess and improve generalization ability From three parking lot camera feeds. So I concatenated the validation statements for each parking camera Eat together and use the assembled set to validate your single park training. A detailed summary is provided in Table 1. training, validation, and test sets.

The results presented in (Andebili M.R & Shen H, 2017) cannot be directly compared with the proposed method. Because this method only predicts daily parking space occupancy. Looking at the daily averages of MAE over 7 days, we can observe better performance compared to the work presented in (Andebili M.R & Shen H, 2017). The highest daily MAE is 0.0125 on Thursday and the lowest MAE is 0.0173 on Sunday. It can be observed that the proposed method outperforms existing methods in all daily forecasts. Similarly, the proposed method showed significant performance compared to the results presented in (Stolfi D H et al., 2017), where parking space availability is predicted in terms of parking space availability. The mean absolute error for all parking lots is 0.059. Also, the proposed method is compared with that of (Stolfi D H et al., 2017).

These values demonstrate the reliability of the proposed decision support system with respect to hourly parking space availability. It will help the drivers to schedule their drive on a specific hour of a day. By analyzing the performance of the proposed decision support system on hour-wise parking space availability we can notice that there is a little bit of variation in prediction of parking availability accuracy for no hours of a day as shown in Figure 7. It represents that the performance of proposed decision support system is significant for all hourly slots except three hourly slots from 09: 00 a.m.–10:00 a.m., 10:00 a.m.–11:00 a.m., and 11:00 a.m.–12: 00 p.m., whereas, x-axis represents hours and y-axis represents error rate represents error rate.

Figure 7 shows analyzing the performance of the proposed decision support system on hour-wise parking space availability we can notice that there is a little bit of variation in prediction of parking availability accuracy for no hours of a day.

Figure 7. The performance evaluation of the proposed system

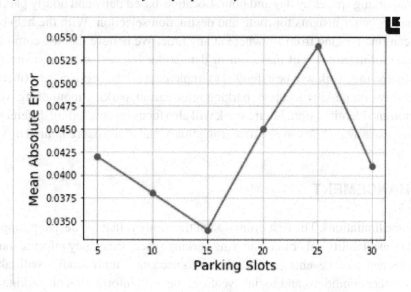

The proposed decision support system was tested on Birmingham parking sensors dataset recorded from April 2016 to December 2016 during 8: 00 a.m. to 4: 30 p.m. During the system verification, the performance of the decision support system was extensively analyzed in three different ways: location-wise, day-wise, and hour-wise. Predict parking space availability by comparing the performance of the proposed technology with existing technology. It turns out that existing techniques focus on the availability of parking spaces at a particular location (Stoli D.H et al., 2017) or on a particular day (Andebili M.R & Shen H, 2017). On the other hand, the proposed method takes into account parking location, day of week and time of day to provide clearer insight into parking space availability. This information helps drivers plan trips to specific locations within the city in relation to the date and time. Helps reduce traffic congestion and fuel consumption by providing location, daily and hourly parking occupancy information. In addition, the proposed IoT-based intelligent parking decision support system and its integration with modern traffic management systems (Carli R et al., 2015) and automatic traffic congestion measurement technology (Ali G et al., 2020) will efficiently reduce traffic congestion and fuel consumption.

CONCLUSION

The development of IoT-based intelligent parking information systems is one of the most requested research challenges for sustainable smart city growth. Help drivers find free parking spaces near their destination (market, office, or home). It also saves time and energy consumption by efficiently and accurately predicting available parking spaces. In this research, we developed an IoT-based smart parking framework. This paper mainly focuses on predicting parking space availability using sensor data. In this context, we have developed a simple and rapid decision support system to support parking information systems regarding the availability of parking spaces during specific hours on weekdays. A decision support system deployed a deep LSTM network to predict parking space availability. The proposed deep LSTM network predicts both global and location-based parking space availability. It also predicts the occupancy rate of parking spaces by day and hour. Location-based daily and hourly parking availability forecasts give drivers better insights for route and destination selection. With the help of the proposed system, drivers can find parking from anywhere at any time. We believe that the combination of cloud technology and sensor networks will make sensor data collection and analysis easier than traditional methods. In the future, this work will be extended to implement all the services described in the adopted smart parking framework: parking location, parking information, parking monitoring, vehicle tracking, vehicle registration and identification. Future work will also focus on developing different techniques for predicting parking space availability in real time using image and video data captured by various sensors.

FUTURE ENHANCEMENT

This study has some limitations. The first limitation of this study is that the decision support system predicts parking space availability only by considering parking space occupancy information. Furthermore, weather conditions and social events are not taken into account. Future studies will take into account information on weather conditions and social events, along with information on parking lot occupancy. Second, the proposed approach was developed considering parking information only. Further studies will examine curb parking availability and traffic congestion information to mitigate the impact of estimation uncertainty.

REFERENCES

Acharya, D. (2016). *Weilin Yan, Real-time image-based parking occu- pancy detection using deep learning*. University of Melbourne.

Al-Jabi & Sammaneh. (2018). *Toward Mobile AR-Based Interactive Smart Parking System*. Academic Press.

Ali, G., Ali, A., Ali, F., Draz, U., Majeed, F., Sana, Y., Ali, T., & Haider, N. (2020). Artificial Neural Network Based Ensemble Approach for Multicultural Facial Expressions Analysis. *IEEE Access : Practical Innovations, Open Solutions, 8,* 134950–134963. doi:10.1109/ACCESS.2020.3009908

Ali, Ali, Irfan, Draz, Sohail, Glowacz, Sulowicz, Mielnik, Faheem, & Martis. (2020). *IoT Based Smart Parking System Using Deep Long Short Memory Network*. Academic Press.

Amato, G. (2016). ISTI-CNR, Car Parking Occupancy Detection Using Smart Camera Networks and Deep Learning. Academic Press.

Amato, Carrara, Falchi, Gennaro, & Vairo. (2020). *A Dataset for Visual Occupancy Detection of Parking Lots*. Academic Press.

Andebili, M. R., & Shen, H. (2017). Traffic and Grid-Based Parking Lot Allocation for PEVs Considering Driver Behavioral Model. *Proceedings of the International Conference on Computing, Networking and Communications (ICNC): Green Computing, Networking, and Communications.*

Awan, Saleem, Minerva, & Cresp. (2020). *A Comparative Analysis of Machine/Deep Learning Models for Parking Space Availability Prediction*. Academic Press.

Bura, H. (2018). An Edge Based Smart Parking Solution Using Camera Networks and Deep Learning. Academic Press.

Cai, Alvarez, Sit, Duarte, & Ratti. (2019). *Deep Learning-Based Video System for Accurate and Real-Time Parking Measurement*. Academic Press.

Camero, N., Toutouh, J., Stolfi, D. H., & Alba, E. (2018). Evolutionary Deep Learning for Car Park Occupancy Prediction in Smart Cities. *Proceedings of the International Conference on Learning and Intelligent Optimization, 386–401.*

Carli, R., Cavone, G., Othman, S. B., & Dotoli, M. (2020). IoT Based Architecture for Model Predictive Control of HVAC Systems in Smart Buildings. *Sensors (Basel), 20*(3), 781. doi:10.339020030781 PMID:32023965

Carli, R., Dotoli, M., Epicoco, N., Angelico, B., & Vinciullo, A. (2015). Automated Evaluation of Urban Traffic CongestionUsing Bus as a Probe. *Proceedings of the IEEE International Conference on Automation Science and Engineering (CASE).* 10.1109/CoASE.2015.7294224

Hasan, Islam, & Alsaawy. (2019). *Smart Parking Model based on Internet of Things (IoT) and TensorFlow*. Academic Press.

Jamie Arjona, M. (2020). Improving Parking Availability Information Using Deep Learning Techniques. *Transportation Research Procedia, 47*, 385–392. doi:10.1016/j.trpro.2020.03.113

Liu, J., Wu, J., & Sun, L. (2020). Control method of urban intelligent parking guidance system based on Internet of Things. *Computer Communications, 153*, 279–285. doi:10.1016/j.comcom.2020.01.063

Mohamed Farag & Elshenbary. (2020). *Deep learning versus traditional methods for parking lots occupancy classification.* Academic Press.

Mohammadi, Nazri, & Saif. (2019). *A Real-Time CloudBased Intelligent Car Parking System for Smart Cities.* Academic Press.

Nebiker, Meyer, Blaser, Ammann, & Rhyner. (2021). *Outdoor Mobile Mapping and AI-Based 3D Object Detection with Low-Cost RGB-D Cameras: The Use Case of On-Street Parking Statistics.* Academic Press.

Nyambal & Klein. (2021). *Automated Parking space detection using CNN, computer Vision and pattern recognition Date.* Academic Press.

Paidi, Fleyeh, & Nyberg. (2020a). *Deep learning-based vehicle occupancy detection in an open parking lot using thermal camera.* Academic Press.

Paidi, Fleyeh, & Nyberg. (2020b). *Dalarna University, Deep learning-based vehicle occupancy detection in an open parking lot using a thermal camera, IET Intelligent Transport System.* Academic Press.

Piccialli, Giampaolo, Prezioso, Crisci, & Cuomo. (2021). *Predictive Analytics for Smart Parking: A Deep Learning Approach in forecasting of IoT Data.* Academic Press.

Polishetty, Roopaei, & Rad. (2016). *A Next-Generation Secure Cloud Based Deep Learning License Plate Recognition for Smart Cities.* Academic Press.

Sairam, B. (2020). *Automated Vehicle Parking Slot Detection System Using Deep Learning.* ICCMC.

Senthil Kumar & Surya. (2020). *Smart Parking Application Using Deep Learning Framework.* Academic Press.

Sonny, A. (2020). *Deep Learning-Based Smart Parking Solution using Channel State Information in LTEbased Cellular Networks.* COMSNETS.

Stolfi, D. H., Alba, E., & Yao, X. (2017). Predicting Car Park Occupancy Rates in Smart Cities. *Proceedings of the International Conference on Smart Cities*, 107–117. 10.1007/978-3-319-59513-9_11

Vu. (2018). *Parking space status interference upon Deep CNN and multitask contrastive network with spatial transform.* IEEE.

Compilation of References

Abbas, A., Jain, S., Gour, M., & Vankudothu, S. (2021). Tomato plant disease detection using transfer learning with C-GAN synthetic images. *Computers and Electronics in Agriculture, 187*, 106279. doi:10.1016/j.compag.2021.106279

Abouzhara, M. (2011). Causes of failure in Healthcare IT projects. *Proceedings of the 3th International Conference on Advance Management Science, IPEDR, 19, IACSIT*. Available at: http://ipedr.com/vol19/9- ICAMS2011-A00018.pdf

Acharya, D. (2016). *Weilin Yan, Real-time image-based parking occu- pancy detection using deep learning*. University of Melbourne.

Ackom, Yang, Zhao, Xiang, & Yang. (n.d.). A Double-chain Blockchain with Economic Attributes and Network Constraints of Prosumer Transactions. *IEEE Transactions on Industrial Informatics*.

Adam, I., Malek, M.F., Yasin, M.N., & Rahim, H.A. (2015). *RF Energy Harvesting With Efficient Matching Technique For Low Power Level Application*. Academic Press.

Adam, Najib, Yasin, Hasliza, Rahim, Soh, & Abdulmalek. (2018). A compact dual-band rectenna for ambient RF energy harvesting. *Microwave and Optical Technology Letters, 60*(11), 2740-2748.

Adner, R., & Levinthal, D. A. (2002). The emergence of emerging technologies. *California Management Review, 45*(1), 50–66. doi:10.2307/41166153

Agrawal, R., Imielinski, T., & Swami, A. (1993). Mining association rules between sets of items in large databases. *Proc. Int. Conf. Manage. Data Assoc. Comput. Mach. (ACM)*, 207–216. 10.1145/170035.170072

Agrawal, T. K., Kumar, V., Pal, R., Wang, L., & Chen, Y. (2021). Blockchain-based framework for supply chain traceability: A case example of textile and clothing industry. *Computers & Industrial Engineering, 154*, 107130. doi:10.1016/j.cie.2021.107130

Ahmed, A. N., Othman, F. B., Afan, H. A., Ibrahim, R. K., Fai, C. M., Hossain, M. S., Ehteram, M., & Elshafie, A. (2019). Machine learning methods for better water quality prediction. *Journal of Hydrology (Amsterdam), 578*, 124084. doi:10.1016/j.jhydrol.2019.124084

Ahmed, R. A., Hemdan, E. E.-D., El-Shafai, W., Ahmed, Z. A., El-Rabaie, E.-S. M., & Abd El-Samie, F. E. (2022). Climate-smart agriculture using intelligent techniques, blockchain and Internet of Things: Concepts, challenges, and opportunities. *Transactions on Emerging Telecommunications Technologies, 33*(11), e4607. doi:10.1002/ett.4607

Akbar, N. A., Muneer, A., ElHakim, N., & Fati, S. M. (2021). Distributed Hybrid Double-Spending Attack Prevention Mechanism for Proof-of-Work and Proof-of-Stake Blockchain Consensuses. *Future Internet, 13*(11), 285. doi:10.3390/fi13110285

Al-Ahmad, A., Al-Fagih, K., Khanfar, K., Alsamara, K., Abuleil, S., & Abu-Salem, H. (2009). A taxonomy of an IT project failure: Root causes. *International Management Review*, *5*(1), 93–104.

Al-Ali, A. R., Hussain, M., & Hossain, M. A. (2019). Smart street lighting system: A platform for smart city applications. *Journal of Sensors*, *2019*, 1–12.

Alessandrino, L., Pavlakis, C., Colombani, N., Mastrocicco, M., & Aschonitis, V. (2023). Effects of graphene on soil water-retention curve, van Genuchten parameters, and soil pore size distribution—A comparison with traditional soil conditioners. *Water (Basel)*, *15*(7), 1297. doi:10.3390/w15071297

Al-Hinai, K., & Al-Shehri, R. (2020). Smart street lighting system using IoT for smart cities. *Journal of Communication*, *15*(10), 968–974.

Ali, Ali, Irfan, Draz, Sohail, Glowacz, Sulowicz, Mielnik, Faheem, & Martis. (2020). *IoT Based Smart Parking System Using Deep Long Short Memory Network*. Academic Press.

Ali, G., Ali, A., Ali, F., Draz, U., Majeed, F., Sana, Y., Ali, T., & Haider, N. (2020). Artificial Neural Network Based Ensemble Approach for Multicultural Facial Expressions Analysis. *IEEE Access : Practical Innovations, Open Solutions*, *8*, 134950–134963. doi:10.1109/ACCESS.2020.3009908

Al-Jabi & Sammaneh. (2018). *Toward Mobile AR-Based Interactive Smart Parking System*. Academic Press.

Alketbi, A., Nasir, Q., & Abu Talib, M. (2020, December). Novel blockchain reference model for government services: Dubai government case study. *Int. J. Syst. Assurance Eng. Manage.*, *11*(6), 1170–1191. doi:10.100713198-020-00971-2

Allam, Z., Bibri, S., Jones, D., Chabaud, D., & Moreno, C. (2022). Unpacking the ‘15-Minute City’ via 6G, IoT, and Digital Twins: Towards a New Narrative for Increasing Urban Efficiency, Resilience, and Sustainability. *Sensors (Basel)*, *22*(4), 1369. doi:10.339022041369 PMID:35214271

Allam, Z., Sharifi, A., Bibri, S., Jones, D., & Krogstie, J. (2022). The Metaverse as a Virtual Form of Smart Cities: Opportunities and Challenges for Environmental, Economic, and Social Sustainability in Urban Futures. *Smart Cities*, *5*(3), 771–801. doi:10.3390martcities5030040

Alperin-Sheriff, & Peikert. (2014). Faster bootstrapping with polynomial error. In *Advances in Cryptology - CRYPTO 2014* (pp. 297–314). Springer.

Alqurashi, F. A., Alsolami, F., Abdel-Khalek, S., Sayed Ali, E., & Saeed, R. A. (2022). Machine learning techniques in internet of UAVs for smart cities applications. *Journal of Intelligent & Fuzzy Systems*, *42*(4), 3203–3226. doi:10.3233/JIFS-211009

Al-Sammarraie, A., & Hussain, M. (2019). Smart street lighting for smart cities: A review. *Renewable & Sustainable Energy Reviews*, *103*, 207–214.

Altawy, R., & Youssef, A. M. (2017). Security, privacy, and safety aspects of civilian drones: A survey. *ACM Transactions on Cyber-Physical Systems*, *1*(2), 1–25. doi:10.1145/3001836

Altman, R., Asch, E., Bloch, D., Bole, G., Borenstein, D., Brandt, K., Christy, W., Cooke, T. D., Greenwald, R., Hochberg, M., Rothschild, B., Segal, M., Sokoloff, L., & Wolfe, F. (1986, August). Development of criteria for the classification and reporting of osteoarthritis: Classification of osteoarthritis of the knee. *Arthritis and Rheumatism*, *29*(8), 1039–1049. doi:10.1002/art.1780290816 PMID:3741515

Amato, Carrara, Falchi, Gennaro, & Vairo. (2020). *A Dataset for Visual Occupancy Detection of Parking Lots*. Academic Press.

Amato, G. (2016). ISTI-CNR, Car Parking Occupancy Detection Using Smart Camera Networks and Deep Learning. Academic Press.

Ambrisko, T., & Nemeth, T. (2004). A computer program for calculating of doses and prices of injectable medications based on body weight or body surface area. *Canadian Journal of Veterinary Research*, *68*, 62–65. PMID:14979437

Ammenwerth, E., Brender, J., Nykänen, P., Prokosch, H. U., Rigby, M., & Talmon, J. (2004). Visionand strategies to improve evaluation of health information systems: Reflections and lessons based onthe HIS-EVAL workshop in Innsbruck. *International Journal of Medical Informatics*, *73*(6), 479–491. doi:10.1016/j.ijmedinf.2004.04.004 PMID:15171977

Ammenwerth, E., & de Keizer, N. (2005). An inventory of evaluation studies of information technology in healthcare: Trends in evaluation research 1982–2002. *Methods of Information in Medicine*, *44*, 44–56. doi:10.1055-0038-1633922 PMID:15778794

Andebili, M. R., & Shen, H. (2017). Traffic and Grid-Based Parking Lot Allocation for PEVs Considering Driver Behavioral Model. *Proceedings of the International Conference on Computing, Networking and Communications (ICNC): Green Computing, Networking, and Communications*.

Anderson, J. G. (1997). Clearing the way for physicians' use of clinical information systems. *Communications of the ACM*, *40*(8), 83–90. doi:10.1145/257874.257895

Anderson, J. G., & Aydin, C. E. (1994). Overview: Theoretical perspectives and methodologies for the evaluation of health care information systems. In J. G. Anderson, C. E. Aydin, & S. J. Jay (Eds.), *Evaluating health care information systems: Methods and applications* (pp. 5–29). Sage Publications, Inc.

Andreassen, H. K., Bujnowska-Fedak, M. M., Chronaki, C. E., Duritru, R. C., Pudele, I., Santana, S., & Wynn, R. (2007). European citizens' use of E-health services: A study of seven countries. *BMC Public Health*, *7*(53), 1–7. doi:10.1186/1471-2458-7-53 PMID:17425798

Andreoni, J., Harbaugh, W., & Vesterlund, L. (2003). The carrot or the stick: Rewards, punishments, and cooperation. *The American Economic Review*, *93*(3), 893–902. doi:10.1257/000282803322157142

Andriana. (2012). Sensor Comparison for Smart Parking System. Academic Press.

Angra, S., & Ahuja, S. (2017). Machine learning and its applications: a review. *Proceedings of the 2017 International Conference On Big Data Analytics and Computational Intelligence, ICBDACI 2017*, 57–60. 10.1109/ICBDACI.2017.8070809

Anita, R., & Sumathi, N. (2019). A study on the measuring the factors of HR analytics on performances management in services sector of selected companies in Chennai. *Journal of Advanced Composition*, *12*(12).

Anitha, C., Komala, C., Vivekanand, C. V., Lalitha, S., & Boopathi, S. (2023). Artificial Intelligence driven security model for Internet of Medical Things (IoMT). *IEEE Explore*, 1–7.

Annarelli, A., Battistella, C., Nonino, F., Parida, V., & Pessot, E. (2021). Literature Review on Digitalization Capabilities: Co-citation Analysis of Antecedents, Conceptualization and Consequences. *Technological Forecasting and Social Change*, *166*, 120635. doi:10.1016/j.techfore.2021.120635

Antal, C., Cioara, T., Anghel, I., Antal, M., & Salomie, I. (2021). Distributed Ledger Technology Review and Decentralized Applications Development Guidelines. [CrossRef]. *Future Internet*, *13*(3), 62. doi:10.3390/fi13030062

Antonopoulos, A. M., & Wood, G. (2018). *Mastering Ethereum: Building Smart Contracts and DApps*. O'Reilly Media, Inc.

Aono, Y., Hayashi, T., & Phong, L. T. (2016). Scalable and secure logistic regression via homomorphic encryption. In *Proceedings of the 6th ACM Conference on Data and Application Security and Privacy (CODASPY'16)*. ACM. 10.1145/2857705.2857731

Apiletti, D., Baralis, E., Cerquitelli, T., & D'Elia, V. (2009, April). Characterizing network traffic by means of the Net-Mine framework. *Computer Networks*, *53*(6), 774–789. doi:10.1016/j.comnet.2008.12.011

AralS.BrynjolfssonE.Van AlstyneM. (2007) Information, Technology and Information Worker Productivity Task Level Evidence. *Information System Research*. Available at: SSRN: https://ssrn.com/abstract=942310

Ariely, D. (2008). *Predictably Irrational*. Harper Collins.

Armknecht, F., Boyd, C., Carr, C., Gøsteen, K., Jáschke, A., Reuter, C. A., & Strand, M. (2015). *A Guide to Fully Homomorphic Encryption*. Technical Report 1192.

Armknecht, F., Katzenbeisser, S., & Peter, A. (2013, May). Group homomorphic encryption: Characterizations, impossibility results, and applications. *Designs, Codes and Cryptography*, *67*(2), 209–232. doi:10.100710623-011-9601-2

Arnes, A., Valeur, F., Vigna, G., & Kemmerer, R. A. (2006). Using Hidden markov models to evaluate the risks of intrusions: System architecture and model validation. *Lecture Notes in Computer Science*, *4219*, 145–164. doi:10.1007/11856214_8

Arora, D., Gautham, S., Gupta, H., & Bhushan, B. (2019). Blockchain-based security solutions to preserve data privacy and integrity. *2019 International Conference on Computing, Communication, and Intelligent Systems (ICCCIS)*, 468–472. 10.1109/ICCCIS48478.2019.8974503

Asad, M., Kumar, M., Shah, P. K., & Sinha, A. K. (2021, December). Business Growth Forecast using Saket Data Mining Methodology. In *2021 10th International Conference on System Modeling & Advancement in Research Trends (SMART)* (pp. 99-103). IEEE. 10.1109/SMART52563.2021.9676278

Asch, S. E., & Guetzkow, H. (1951). Effects of group pressure upon the modification and distortion of judgments. In Documents of Gestalt Psychology. Carnegie Press.

Aung, M. M., & Change, S. S. (2014). Traceability in a food supply chain: Safety and quality perspectives. *Food Control*, *39*, 172–184. doi:10.1016/j.foodcont.2013.11.007

Avital, M., Beck, R., King, J., Rossi, M., & Teigland, R. (2016). *Jumping on the Blockchain Bandwagon: Lessons of the Past and Outlook to the Future*. Academic Press.

Awan, Saleem, Minerva, & Cresp. (2020). *A Comparative Analysis of Machine/Deep Learning Models for Parking Space Availability Prediction*. Academic Press.

Awan, S. H., Ahmed, S., Safwan, N., Najam, Z., Hashim, M. Z., & Safdar, T. (2019). Role of internet of things (IoT) with blockchain technology for the development of smart farming. *Journal of Mechanics of Continua and Mathematical Sciences*, *14*(5), 170–188.

Azadeh, A., Maghsoudi, A., & Sohrabkhani, S. (2009). An integrated artificial neural networks approach for predicting global radiation. *Energy Conversion and Management*, *50*(6), 1497–1505. doi:10.1016/j.enconman.2009.02.019

Babu, A. S., & Supriya, M. (2022). Blockchain Based Precision Agriculture Model Using Machine Learning Algorithms. *2022 International Conference on Breakthrough in Heuristics And Reciprocation of Advanced Technologies (BHARAT)*, 127–132. 10.1109/BHARAT53139.2022.00036

Balasubramaniam, A., Gul, M. J. J., Menon, V. G., & Paul, A. (2020). Blockchain For Intelligent Transport System. *IETE Technical Review*, 1–12.

Banotra, A., Sharma, J. S., Gupta, S., Gupta, S. K., & Rashid, M. (2021). *Use of blockchain and Internet of Things for securing data in healthcare systems.* In K. J. Giri, S. A. Parah, R. Bashir, & K. Muhammad (Eds.), *Multimedia Security: Algorithm Development, Analysis and Applications, Algorithms for Intelligent Systems* (pp. 255–267). Springer.

Bao, S., Cao, Y., Lei, A., Asuquo, P., Cruickshank, H., Sun, Z., & Huth, M. (2019). Pseudonym management through blockchain: Cost-efcient privacy preservation on intelligent transportation systems. *IEEE Access : Practical Innovations, Open Solutions, 7*, 80390–80403. doi:10.1109/ACCESS.2019.2921605

Baralis, E., Cerquitelli, T., & D'Elia, V. (2008). *Generalized Itemset Discovery by Means of Opportunistic Aggregation.* Tech. Rep., Politecnico di Torino. https://dbdmg.polito.it/twiki/ bin/view/Public/NetworkTrafficAnalysis

Barcelo, H., & Capraro, V. (2015). Group size effect on cooperation in one-shot social dilemmas. *Scientific Reports, 5*(1), 7937. doi:10.1038rep07937 PMID:25605124

Barnett, S. B., & Cerf, M. (2018). Trust the Polls? Neural and recall responses provide alternative predictors of political outcomes. *Advances in Consumer Research. Association for Consumer Research (U. S.), 46*, 374–377.

Barney, J. B., & Hesterly, W. S. (2010). *Strategic management and competitive advantage: Concepts.* Prentice Hall.

Barrett, M. J., Holmes, B. J., & McAulay, S. E. (2003). *Electronic Medical Records: A Buyer's Guide for Small Physician Practices.* California HealthCare Foundation.

Bartoletti, M., & Pompianu, L. An empirical analysis of smart contracts: platforms, applications, and design patterns. In *International Conference on Financial Cryptography and Data Security* (pp. 494-509). Springer.

Basheer, I. A., & Hajmeer, M. (2000). Artificial neural networks: Fundamentals, computing, design, and application. *Journal of Microbiological Methods, 43*(1), 3–31. doi:10.1016/S0167-7012(00)00201-3 PMID:11084225

Bataev, A., & Aleksandrova, A. (2020). Digitalization of the World Economy: Performance Evaluation of Introducing Cyber-Physical Systems. *9th International Conference on Industrial Technology and Management (ICITM)*, 265-269. 10.1109/ICITM48982.2020.9080378

Bates, D., Cohen, M., Leape, L., Overhage, J., Shabot, M., & Sheridan, T. (2001). Reducing the frequency of errors in medicine using information technology. *Journal of the American Medical Informatics Association : JAMIA, 8*(4), 299–308. doi:10.1136/jamia.2001.0080299 PMID:11418536

Bates, D., & Gawande, A. A. (2002). Error in medicine: What have we learned? *Annals of Internal Medicine, 132*(9), 763–767. doi:10.7326/0003-4819-132-9-200005020-00025 PMID:10787381

Beccalli, E. (2007). Does IT investment improve bank performance? Evidence from Europe. *Journal of Banking & Finance, 31*(7), 2205–2230. doi:10.1016/j.jbankfin.2006.10.022

Beck, R., Avital, M., Rossi, M., & Thatcher, J. B. (2017). *Blockchain technology in business and information systems research.* Academic Press.

Beck, R., Stenum Czepluch, J., Lollike, N., & Malone, S. (2016). *Blockchain–The gateway to trust-free cryptographic transactions.* Academic Press.

Beer, C., Reichstein, M., Tomelleri, E., Ciais, P., Jung, M., Carvalhais, N., Rödenbeck, C., Arain, M. A., Baldocchi, D., Bonan, G. B., Bondeau, A., Cescatti, A., Lasslop, G., Lindroth, A., Lomas, M., Luyssaert, S., Margolis, H., Oleson, K. W., Roupsard, O., ... Papale, D. (2010). Terrestrial gross carbon dioxide uptake: Global distribution and covariation with climate. *Science, 329*(5993), 834–838. doi:10.1126cience.1184984 PMID:20603496

Benkhelifa & Al-Ruithea. (2017). A conceptual framework for cloud data governance-driven decision making. *International Conference on the Frontiers and Advances in Data Science (FADS)*.

Bentotahewa, V., Hewage, C., & Williams, J. (2021). Solutions to Big Data Privacy and Security Challenges Associated With COVID-19 Surveillance Systems. *Frontiers in Big Data, 4*, 645204. doi:10.3389/fdata.2021.645204 PMID:34977562

Berg, J., & Myllymaa, L. (n.d.). *Impact of blockchain on sustainable supply chain practices* [Master Thesis]. Jönköping International Business School, University of Jönköping, Sweden.

Berghout, E., Nijland, M., & Grant, K. (2005). Seven ways to get your favoured IT project accepted-politics in IT evaluation. *The Electronic Journal of Information System Evaluation, 8*(1), 31–40.

Berg, M. (2001). Implementing information systems in health care organisations: Myths and challenges. *International Journal of Medical Informatics, 64*(2-3), 143–156. doi:10.1016/S1386-5056(01)00200-3 PMID:11734382

Bevan, N. (2001). International standards for HCI and usability. *International Journal of Human-Computer Studies, 55*(4), 533–552. doi:10.1006/ijhc.2001.0483

Bhaduri, A. (2018). *People@work*. Retrieved from Hindu Business Line, available at: https:// www.thehindubusinessline.com/specials/people-at-work/adopting-blockchain-tech-in-hr/ article22881175.ece#

Bhagwat, R., & Dandawate, Y. H. (2021). A Review on Advances in Automated Plant Disease Detection. *International Journal of Engineering and Technology Innovation, 11*(4), 251–264. doi:10.46604/ijeti.2021.8244

Bhandary, M., Parmar, M., & Ambawade, D. (2020). A blockchain solution based on directed acyclic graph for IoT data security using IoTA tangle. *2020 5th International Conference on Communication and Electronics Systems (ICCES)*, 827–832.

Bhargawa, A., & Singh, A. K. (2019). Solar irradiance, climatic indicators and climate change – An empirical analysis. *Advances in Space Research, 64*(1), 271–277. doi:10.1016/j.asr.2019.03.018

Bharti, A. K. (2019, November). A Study of Emerging Areas in Adoption of Blockchain Technology and it's Prospective Challenges in India. In *2019 Women Institute of Technology Conference on Electrical and Computer Engineering (WITCON ECE)* (pp. 146-153). IEEE.

Bi, L., & Hu, G. (2020). Improving image-based plant disease classification with generative adversarial network under limited training set. *Frontiers in Plant Science, 11*, 583438. doi:10.3389/fpls.2020.583438 PMID:33343595

Bilge, L., Sen, S., Balzarotti, D., Kirda, E., & Kruegel, C. (2014, April). 2014 Exposure: A passive DNS analysis service to detect and report malicious domains. *ACM Transactions on Information and System Security, 16*(4), 1–28. doi:10.1145/2584679

Bisong, E., & Bisong, E. (2019). Autoencoders. *Building Machine Learning and Deep Learning Models on Google Cloud Platform: A Comprehensive Guide for Beginners*, 475-482.

Biswas, K., & Muthukkumarasamy, V. (2016, December). Securing smart cities using blockchain technology. In *2016 IEEE 18th international conference on high performance computing and communications; IEEE 14th international conference on smart city; IEEE 2nd international conference on data science and systems (HPCC/SmartCity/DSS)* (pp. 1392-1393). IEEE. 10.1109/HPCC-SmartCity-DSS.2016.0198

Bita Darvish Rouhani, M. (2018). Deepsecure: Scalable provably-secure deep learning. DAC, 2:1–2:6.

Bivens, A., Palagiri, C., Smith, R., Szymanski, B., & Embrechts, M. (2002). Network-based intrusion detection using neural networks. *Intell. Eng. Syst. Artif. Neural Netw., 12*(1), 579–584.

Bjørnskov, C. (2012). How does social trust affect economic growth? *Southern Economic Journal, 78*(4), 1346–1368. doi:10.4284/0038-4038-78.4.1346

Bolger, R. (2021). Finding Wholes in the Metaverse: Posthuman Mystics as Agents of Evolutionary Contextualization. *Religions, 12*(9), 768. doi:10.3390/rel12090768

Boopathi, S. (2023a). Deep Learning Techniques Applied for Automatic Sentence Generation. In Promoting Diversity, Equity, and Inclusion in Language Learning Environments (pp. 255–273). IGI Global. doi:10.4018/978-1-6684-3632-5. ch016

Boopathi, S., Arigela, S. H., Raman, R., Indhumathi, C., Kavitha, V., & Bhatt, B. C. (2022). Prominent Rule Control-based Internet of Things: Poultry Farm Management System. *IEEE Explore*, 1–6.

Boopathi, S., Kumar, P. K. S., Meena, R. S., Sudhakar, M., & Associates. (2023). Sustainable Developments of Modern Soil-Less Agro-Cultivation Systems: Aquaponic Culture. In Human Agro-Energy Optimization for Business and Industry (pp. 69–87). IGI Global.

Boopathi, S. (2023b). Internet of Things-Integrated Remote Patient Monitoring System: Healthcare Application. In *Dynamics of Swarm Intelligence Health Analysis for the Next Generation* (pp. 137–161). IGI Global. doi:10.4018/978-1-6684-6894-4.ch008

Boopathi, S., & Kanike, U. K. (2023). Applications of Artificial Intelligent and Machine Learning Techniques in Image Processing. In *Handbook of Research on Thrust Technologies' Effect on Image Processing* (pp. 151–173). IGI Global. doi:10.4018/978-1-6684-8618-4.ch010

Boopathi, S., Sureshkumar, M., & Sathiskumar, S. (2022). Parametric Optimization of LPG Refrigeration System Using Artificial Bee Colony Algorithm. *International Conference on Recent Advances in Mechanical Engineering Research and Development*, 97–105.

Bose, R. (2003). Knowledge management-enabled health care management: Capabilities, infrastructure, and decision-making. *Expert Systems with Applications, 24*(1), 59–71. doi:10.1016/S0957-4174(02)00083-0

Bradley, G. (2006). *Benefit Realization Management: A Practical Guide for Achieving Benefits through Change*. Gower Publishing.

Brahmi, H., Imen, B., & Sadok, B. (2012). *OMC-IDS: At the cross-roads of OLAP mining and intrusion detection. In Advances in Knowledge Discovery and Data Mining*. Springer.

Brailer, D. J., & Terasawa, E. L. (2003). *Use and Adoption of Computer-Based Patient Records*. California HealthCare Foundation.

Brandrud, A. S., Schreiner, A., Hjortdahl, P., Helljesen, G. S., Nyen, B., & Nelson, E. C. (2011). Three Success Factors for Continual Improvement in Healthcare: An Analysis of the Reports of Improvement Team Members. *BMJ Quality & Safety, 20*(3), 251–259. doi:10.1136/bmjqs.2009.038604 PMID:21209149

Brennen, J. S., & Kreiss, D. (2016). Digitalization. In K. B. Jensen, E. W. Rothenbuhler, J. D. Pooley, & R. T. Craig (Eds.), *The International Encyclopedia of Communication Theory and Philosophy* (pp. 556–566). Wiley-Blackwell. doi:10.1002/9781118766804.wbiect111

Brynjolfsson, E., & McAfee, A. (2014). *The second machine age: Work, progress, and prosperity in a time of brilliant technologies*. WW Norton & Company.

Buckingham, M., & Goodall, A. (2015). Reinventing performance management. *Harvard Business Review, 93*(4), 40–50.

Budyko, M. I. (1969). The effect of solar radiation variations on the climate of the Earth. *Tellus. Series A, Dynamic Meterology and Oceanography, 21*(5), 611–619. doi:10.3402/tellusa.v21i5.10109

Bu, F., & Wang, X. (2019). A smart agriculture IoT system based on deep reinforcement learning. *Future Generation Computer Systems, 99*, 500–507. doi:10.1016/j.future.2019.04.041

Buhalis, D., Lin, M., & Leung, D. (2022). Metaverse as a driver for customer experience and value co-creation: implications for hospitality and tourism management and marketing. *International Journal of Contemporary Hospitality Management.* doi:10.1108/IJCHM-05-2022-0631

Buhalis, D., O'Connor, P., & Leung, R. (2023). Smart hospitality: From smart cities and smart tourism towards agile business ecosystems in networked destinations. *International Journal of Contemporary Hospitality Management, 35*(1), 369–393. doi:10.1108/IJCHM-04-2022-0497

Bui, D. T., Tsangaratos, P., Nguyen, V.-T., Van Liem, N., & Trinh, P. T. (2020). Comparing the prediction performance of a Deep Learning Neural Network model with conventional machine learning models in landslide susceptibility assessment. *Catena, 188*, 104426. doi:10.1016/j.catena.2019.104426

Bukachi, F., & Pakenham-Walsh, N. (2007). Information technology for health in developing countries. *Chest, 132*(5), 1624–1630. doi:10.1378/chest.07-1760 PMID:17998362

Bura, H. (2018). An Edge Based Smart Parking Solution Using Camera Networks and Deep Learning. Academic Press.

Burke, I. (2017). *It's not all paperwork: How does HR really spend their time?* Available at: www.business. com/articles/its-not-all-paperwork-how-does-hr-really-spend-their-time/

Burke, D., Wang, B., Wan, T., & Diana, N. (2002). Exploring Hospitals' Adoption of Information Technology. *Journal of Medical Systems, 26*(4), 349–355. doi:10.1023/A:1015872805768 PMID:12118818

Buterin, V. (2014). Ethereum white paper: A next generation smart contract & decentralized application platform. *First Version, 53.*

Byrne, C. M., Mercincavage, L. M., Pan, E. C., Vincent, A. G., Johnston, D. S., & Middleton, B. (2010). The value from investments in health information technology at the U.S. Department of Veterans Affairs. *Health Affairs, 29*(4), 629–638. doi:10.1377/hlthaff.2010.0119 PMID:20368592

Cai, Alvarez, Sit, Duarte, & Ratti. (2019). *Deep Learning-Based Video System for Accurate and Real-Time Parking Measurement.* Academic Press.

Calonnec, A., Wiedemann-Merdinoglu, S., Delière, L., Cartolaro, P., Schneider, C., & Delmotte, F. (2012). The reliability of leaf bioassays for predicting disease resistance on fruit: A case study on grapevine resistance to downy and powdery mildew. *Plant Pathology, 62*(3), 533–544. doi:10.1111/j.1365-3059.2012.02667.x

Cámara, N., & Tuesta, D. (2017) *DiGiX: The Digitization Index.* Working paper n°17, BBVA Research, Madrid, Spain. Retrieved from https://www.bbvaresearch.com/en/publicaciones/digix-the-digitization-index/

Cámara, N. (2020). *Global DiGiX 2020 Update: A Multidimensional Index of Digitization.* BBVA Research. Retrieved from https://www.bbvaresearch.com/en/publicaciones/digix-2020-update-a-multidimensional-index-of-digitization/

Camero, N., Toutouh, J., Stolfi, D. H., & Alba, E. (2018). Evolutionary Deep Learning for Car Park Occupancy Prediction in Smart Cities. *Proceedings of the International Conference on Learning and Intelligent Optimization, 386*–401.

Campello, M., Graham, J. R., & Harvey, C. R. (2010). The real effects of financial constraints: Evidence from a financial crisis. *Journal of Financial Economics, 97*(3), 470–487. doi:10.1016/j.jfineco.2010.02.009

Camponogara, D., Ferreira, G. F., Campos, A., & Costa, M. A. D. (2013, November/December). Offline LED Driver for Street Lighting With an Optimized Cascade structure. *IEEE Transactions on Industry Applications*, *40*(6), No-6. doi:10.1109/TIA.2013.2263631

Cannady, J. (1998). Artificial neural networks for misuse detection. *Proc. 1998 Nat. Inf. Syst. Secur. Conf.*, 443–456.

Cappannari, L., & Vitillo, A. (2022). XR and Metaverse Software Platforms. In Roadmapping Extended Reality (pp. 135-156). doi:10.1002/9781119865810.ch6

Card, S. K., Moran, T. P., & Newell, A. (1983). *The psychology of human computer interaction*. Erlbaum.

CareerBuilder. (2017). *75% Of HR managers have caught a lie on a resume*. Available at: https://press.careerbuilder.com/2017-09-14-75-of-HR-Managers-Have-Caught-a-Lie-on-a-Resume-According-to-aNew-CareerBuilder-Survey

Carli, R., Cavone, G., Othman, S. B., & Dotoli, M. (2020). IoT Based Architecture for Model Predictive Control of HVAC Systems in Smart Buildings. *Sensors (Basel)*, *20*(3), 781. doi:10.339020030781 PMID:32023965

Carli, R., Dotoli, M., Epicoco, N., Angelico, B., & Vinciullo, A. (2015). Automated Evaluation of Urban Traffic CongestionUsing Bus as a Probe. *Proceedings of the IEEE International Conference on Automation Science and Engineering (CASE)*. 10.1109/CoASE.2015.7294224

Carroll, J. M. (2014). Soft versus hard: The essential tension. In Human-Computer Interaction and Management Information Systems: Applications. Advances in Management Information Systems (pp. 440-448). Routledge.

Carroll, J. M. (Ed.). (2003). *HCI models, theories, and frameworks: Toward a multidisciplinary science*. Morgan Kaufmann.

Cartier, L. E., Ali, S. H., & Krzemnicki, M. S. (2018). Blockchain, Chain of Custody and Trace Elements: An Overview of Tracking and Traceability Opportunities in the Gem Industry. *The Journal of Geology*, *36*(3), 212–227. doi:10.15506/JoG.2018.36.3.212

Casey, M., & Wong, P. (2017). Global supply chains are about to get better, thanks to blockchain. *Harvard Business Review*, *13*, 1–6.

Chang, Y., Iakovou, E., & Shi, W. (2020). Blockchain in Global Supply Chains and Cross Border Trade: A Critical Synthesis of the State-of-the-Art. *International Journal of Production Research*, *58*(7), 2082–2099. doi:10.1080/0020 7543.2019.1651946

Chatrakul Na Ayudhya, U., Prouska, R., & Lewis, S. (2015, July 13). Work-life balance can benefit business during financial crisis and austerity. *Human Resource Management International Digest*, *23*(5), 25–28. doi:10.1108/HRMID-05-2015-0078

Chaudhry, B., Wang, J., Wu, S., Maglione, M., Mojica, W., Roth, E., Shekelle, P. G., & . . . . (2006). Systematic Review: Impact of Health Information Technology on Quality, Efficiency, and Costs of Medical Care. *Annals of Internal Medicine*, *144*(10), 742–752. doi:10.7326/0003-4819-144-10-200605160-00125 PMID:16702590

Chau, P. Y., & Hu, P. (2002). Investigating healthcare professionals' decisions to accept telemedicine technology: An empirical test of competing theories. *Information & Management*, *39*(4), 297–311. doi:10.1016/S0378-7206(01)00098-2

Chen, B., Tan, Z., & Fang, W. (2018). Blockchain-based implementation for nancial product management. *Proc. 28th Int. Telecommun. Netw. Appl. Conf. (ITNAC)*, 1-3.

Cheney, J., Chong, S., Foster, N., Seltzer, M., & Vansummeren, S. (2009). *Provenance: A future history. In Proceedings of the 24th ACM SIGPLAN conference on Object oriented programming systems languages and applications*. ACM. http://nrs.harvard.edu/urn-3:HUL.InstRepos:5346327

Cheng, C., Cheng, H.-l., & Chung, T.-Y. (2013). A Novel Single-Stage High-Power-Factor LED Street-Lighting Driver with Coupled Inductors. *IEEE Transactions on Industry Applications*. Advance online publication. doi:0.1109/TIA.2014.2304585

Chen, J. L., Liu, H. B., Wu, W., & Xie, D. T. (2011). Estimation of monthly solar radiation from measured temperatures using support vector machines – A case study. *Renewable Energy*, *36*(1), 413–420. doi:10.1016/j.renene.2010.06.024

Chen, Q., & Lee, S. (2021). Research Status and Trend of Digital Twin: Visual Knowledge Mapping Analysis. *International Journal of Advanced Smart Convergence*, *10*(4), 84–97. doi:10.7236/IJASC.2021.10.4.84

Chenthara, S., Ahmed, K., Wang, H., Whittaker, F., & Chen, Z. (2020). Healthchain: A novel framework on privacy preservation of electronic health records using blockchain technology. *PLoS One*, *15*(12), e0243043. doi:10.1371/journal.pone.0243043 PMID:33296379

Chen, Y. J., & Wang, L. C. (2019). Privacy protection for internet of drones: A network coding approach. *IEEE Internet of Things Journal*, *6*(2), 1719–1730. doi:10.1109/JIOT.2018.2875065

Chinnasamy, A., & Kavitha, D. (2021). Ai Integration in Data Driven Decision Making for Resource Management in Internet of Things(Iot): A Survey. *10th International Conference on Internet of Everything, Microwave Engineering, Communication and Networks (IEMECON)*.

Chitchyan, R., & Murkin, J. (2018). Review of blockchain technology and its expectations: Case of the energy sector. arXiv preprint arXiv:1803.03567.

Chung, K., & Jung, H. (2020). Knowledge based dynamic cluster model for healthcare management using convolutional neural networks. *Information Technology and Management*, *21*(1), 41–50. doi:10.100710799-019-00304-1

CISCO. (2020). *Cisco Global Digital Readiness 2019*. White paper. Retrieved from https://www.cisco.com/c/dam/en_us/about/csr/reports/global-digital-readiness-index.pdf

Cliff, B. (2012). Using Technology to Enhance Patient-Centered Care. *Journal of Healthcare Management*, *57*(September/October). PMID:23087992

Cline, D. W., Bales, R. C., & Dozier, J. (1998). Estimating the spatial distribution of snow in mountain basins using remote sensing and energy balance modeling. *Water Resources Research*, *34*(5), 1275–1285. doi:10.1029/97WR03755

Collste, G. (2002). The Internet doctor and medical ethics Ethical implications of the introduction of the Internet into medical encounters. *Medicine, Health Care, and Philosophy*, *5*(2), 121–125. doi:10.1023/A:1016083021422 PMID:12168987

Computing, M. (2016). *Smart Car Parking Using Arduino*. Academic Press.

Cooke, F. L., & Saini, D. S. (2010, May). (How) Does the HR strategy support an innovation oriented business strategy? An investigation of institutional context and organizational practices in Indian firms. *Human Resource Management*, *49*(3), 377–400. doi:10.1002/hrm.20356

Corazza, A., Di Martino, S., Ferrucci, F., Gravino, C., Sarro, F., & Mendes, E. (2013). Using tabu search to configure support vector regression for effort estimation. *Empirical Software Engineering*, *18*(3), 506–546. doi:10.100710664-011-9187-3

Cranfield, S., Hendy, J., Reeves, B., Hutchings, A., Collin, S., & Fulop, N. (2015). Investigating healthcare IT innovations: A "conceptual blending" approach. *Journal of Health Organization and Management*, *29*(7), 1131–1148. doi:10.1108/JHOM-08-2015-0121 PMID:26556172

Cresswell, K., Bates, D., & Sheikh, A. (2013). Ten key considerations for the successful implementation and adoption of large-scale health information technology. *Journal of the American Medical Informatics Association : JAMIA, 20*(e1), e9–e13. doi:10.1136/amiajnl-2013-001684 PMID:23599226

Crosby, M., Pattanayak, P., Verma, S., & Kalyanaraman, V. (2016). Blockchain technology: Beyond bitcoin. *Applied Innovation, 2*(6-10), 71.

Da Silva, R. R. G., de Oliveira, L., & Talamini, E. (2021). Blockchain Applications in Agribusiness: A Systematic Review. *Future Internet, 13*(4), 95. doi:10.3390/fi13040095

Dahan, N., Al-Razgan, M., Al-Laith, A., Alsoufi, M., Al-Asaly, M., & Alfakih, T. (2022). Metaverse Framework: A Case Study on E-Learning Environment (ELEM). *Electronics (Basel), 11*(10), 1616. doi:10.3390/electronics11101616

Dai, Q., Cheng, X., Qiao, Y., & Zhang, Y. (2020). Crop leaf disease image super-resolution and identification with dual attention and topology fusion generative adversarial network. *IEEE Access : Practical Innovations, Open Solutions, 8*, 55724–55735. doi:10.1109/ACCESS.2020.2982055

Dai, Y., Wang, J., & Gao, S. (2022). Advanced Electronics and Artificial Intelligence: Must-Have Technologies Toward Human Body Digital Twins. *Advanced Intelligent Systems, 4*(7), 2100263. doi:10.1002/aisy.202100263

Danzi, P., Kalor, A. E., Stefanovic, C., & Popovski, P. (2018). Analysis of the communication traffic for blockchain synchronization of IoT devices. *Proc. IEEE Int. Conf. Commun. (ICC)*, 1-7. 10.1109/ICC.2018.8422485

Dawson, A., & Verweij, M. (Eds.). (2007). *Ethics, Prevention, and Public Health*. Oxford University Press.

Day, G. S., Shoemaker, P. J., & Gunther, R. (2000). *Wharton on management of emerging technology*. John Wiley & Sons.

de la Rosa, J. L., Gibovic, D., Torres, V., Maicher, L., Miralles, F., El-Fakdi, A., & Bikfalvi, A. (2016, December). On intellectual property in online open innovation for SME by means of blockchain and smart contracts. *3rd Annual World Open Innovation Conf. WOIC*.

Dedrick, J., Gurbaxani, V., & Kraemer, K. L. (2003). Information technology and economic performance: A critical review of the empirical evidence. *ACM Computing Surveys, 35*(1), 1–28. doi:10.1145/641865.641866

Dehning, B., Richardson, V. J., Urbaczewski, A., & Wells, J. D. (2004). Re-examining the Value Relevance of Ecommerce Initiatives. *Journal of Management Information Systems, 21*(1), 57–84. doi:10.1080/07421222.2004.11045788

Dehning, B., Richardson, V. J., & Zmud, R. W. (2003). The Value Relevance of Announcements of Transformational Information Technology Investments. *Management Information Systems Quarterly, 27*(4), 637–656. doi:10.2307/30036551

Deloitte. (2016). *Global Human Capital Trends 2016. The new MSME (Micro, Small, and Medium Enterprises) and Startups: Different by design*. Author.

Demattê, J. A. M., Dotto, A. C., Bedin, L. G., Sayão, V. M., & Souza, A. B. (2019). Soil analytical quality control by traditional and spectroscopy techniques: Constructing the future of a hybrid laboratory for low environmental impact. *Geoderma, 337*, 111–121. doi:10.1016/j.geoderma.2018.09.010

Demiris, G., & Kneale, L. (2015). Informatics Systems and Tools to Facilitate Patient-centered Care Coordination. *IMIA Yearbook of Medical Informatics, 10*(1), 15–21. PMID:26293847

Denning, P. J., Comer, D. E., Gries, D., Mulder, M. C., Tucker, A. B., Turner, A. J., & Young, P. R. (1989). Computing as a discipline. *Communications of the ACM, 32*(1), 9–23. doi:10.1145/63238.63239

Deuber, D., Magri, B., & Thyagarajan, S. A. K. (2019, May). Redactable blockchain in the permissionless setting. In *2019 IEEE Symposium on Security and Privacy (SP)* (pp. 124-138). IEEE. 10.1109/SP.2019.00039

Dibb, S. (2001). Customer Relationship Management and Barriers to the One Segment. *Journal of Financial Services Marketing, 6*(1), 10–23. doi:10.1057/palgrave.fsm.4770037

Dick, R. S., Steen, E. B., & Detmer, D. E. (Eds.). (1997). *The Computer-Based Patient Record: An Essential Technology for Health Care* (revised edition). Committee on Improving the Patient Record, National Academy of Sciences.

DiClaudio, M. (2019, April 8). People analytics and the rise of HR: How data, analytics and emerging technology can transform human resources (HR) into a profit center. *Strategic HR Review, 18*(2), 42–46. doi:10.1108/SHR-11-2018-0096

Ding, Q., Bo, S., & Zhang, X. (2016). A Traffic light aware Routing Protocol based on Street Connectivity for Urban Vehicular Ad hoc Networks. *IEEE Communications Letters, 20*(8), 1635–1638. Advance online publication. doi:10.1109/LCOMM.2016.2574708

Dinh, T., Liu, R., Zhang, M., Chen, G., Ooi, B., & Wang, Ji. (2017). *Untangling Blockchain: A Data Processing View of Blockchain Systems.* arXiv:1708.05665v1 [cs.DB].

Dobrovnik, M., Herold, D., Fürst, E., & Kummer, S. (2018). Blockchain for and in Logistics: What to Adopt and Where to Start. *Logistics, 2*(18), 18. Advance online publication. doi:10.3390/logistics2030018

Do, H. G., & Ng, W. K. (2017, June). Blockchain-based system for secure data storage with private keyword search. In *2017 IEEE World Congress on Services (SERVICES)* (pp. 90-93). IEEE. 10.1109/SERVICES.2017.23

Do, H. T., Truong, L. H., Nguyen, M. T., Chien, C. F., Tran, H. T., Hua, H. T., Nguyen, C. V., Nguyen, H. T. T., & Nguyen, N. T. T. (2021). Energy-Efficient Unmanned Aerial Vehicle (UAV) Surveillance Utilizing Artificial Intelligence (AI). *Wireless Communications and Mobile Computing, 2021*, 1–11. doi:10.1155/2021/8615367

Dos Santos, B. L., Peffers, K. G., & Mauer, D. C. (1993). The Impact of Information Technology Investment Announcements on the Market Value of the Firm. *Information Systems Research, 4*(1), 1–23. doi:10.1287/isre.4.1.1

Drury, P. (2005). The eHealth agenda for developing countries. *World Hospitals and Health Services, 41*, 38–40. PMID:16512063

Duan, H., Li, J., Fan, S., Lin, Z., Wu, X., & Cai, W. (2021). Metaverse for Social Good: A University Campus Prototype. *Proceedings of the 29th ACM International Conference on Multimedia.* 10.1145/3474085.3479238

Dunham, S. (2017). *Blockchain's potential impact on HR and payroll.* Available at: www.symmetry.com/ payroll-tax-insights/blockchains-potential-impact-on-hr-and-payroll

Durai, S. K. S., & Shamili, M. D. (2022). Smart farming using machine learning and deep learning techniques. *Decision Analytics Journal, 3*, 100041. doi:10.1016/j.dajour.2022.100041

Du, S., Li, T., Yang, Y., & Horng, S.-J. (2019). Deep air quality forecasting using hybrid deep learning framework. *IEEE Transactions on Knowledge and Data Engineering, 33*(6), 2412–2424. doi:10.1109/TKDE.2019.2954510

Dwivedi, Y., Hughes, L., Baabdullah, A., Ribeiro-Navarrete, S., Giannakis, M., Al-Debei, M., Dennehy, D., Metri, B., Buhalis, D., Cheung, C. M. K., Conboy, K., Doyle, R., Dubey, R., Dutot, V., Felix, R., Goyal, D. P., Gustafsson, A., Hinsch, C., Jebabli, I., ... Wamba, S. (2022). Metaverse beyond the hype: Multidisciplinary perspectives on emerging challenges, opportunities, and agenda for research, practice and policy. *International Journal of Information Management, 66*, 102542. doi:10.1016/j.ijinfomgt.2022.102542

EC. (2006). *ICT for Health and i2010: Transforming the European healthcare landscape -Towards a strategy for ICT for Health.* Information Society & Media Directorate General, European Commission. Available at: https://ec.europa.eu/digital-single-market/en/news/ict-health-and-i2010-transforming-european-healthcare-landscape

Elder, L., & Clarke, M. (2007). Past, present and future: Experiences and lessons from telehealth projects. *Open Medicine : a Peer-Reviewed, Independent, Open-Access Journal, 1*(3), 166–170. PMID:21673948

Elisa, N., Yang, L., Chao, F., & Cao, Y. (2018). A framework of blockchainbased secure and privacy-preserving E-government system. *Wireless Networks*, (Dec), 1–11. doi:10.100711276-018-1883-0

Eller, R., Alford, P., Kallmuenzer, A., & Peters, M. (2020). Antecedents, consequences, and challenges of small and medium-sized enterprise digitalization. *Journal of Business Research, 112*, 119–127. doi:10.1016/j.jbusres.2020.03.004

El-seoud, S. A., El-sofany, H., & Taj-eddine, I. (2016). Towards the Development of Smart Parking System using Arduino and Web Technologies. Academic Press.

Emadi, M., Taghizadeh-Mehrjardi, R., Cherati, A., Danesh, M., Mosavi, A., & Scholten, T. (2020). Predicting and mapping of soil organic carbon using machine learning algorithms in Northern Iran. *Remote Sensing (Basel), 12*(14), 2234. doi:10.3390/rs12142234

Esposito, C., De Santis, A., Tortora, G., Chang, H., & Choo, K. R. (2018, January). Blockchain: A panacea for healthcare cloud-based data security and privacy? *IEEE Cloud Comput., 5*(1), 31–37. doi:10.1109/MCC.2018.011791712

European Commission. (2019). *The new SME definition: user guide and model declaration.* Retrieved from: https://ec.europa.eu/growth/smes/business-friendly-environment/sme-definition/

European Commission. (2020a). *Digital Economy and Society Index (DESI) 2020: Thematic chapters.* Retrieved from https://digital-strategy.ec.europa.eu/en/policies/desi

European Commission. (2020b). *Broadband Coverage in Europe 2019: Mapping progress towards the coverage objectives of the Digital Agenda.* Retrieved from https://op.europa.eu/en/publication-detail/-/publication/077cc151-f0b3-11ea-991b-01aa75ed71a1

European Commission. (2020c). *Digital Economy and Society Index (DESI) 2020: Methodological note.* Retrieved from https://digital-strategy.ec.europa.eu/en/policies/desi

Fairhurst, P. (2014). Big data and HR analytics. *IES Perspectives on HR, 2014*, 7–13.

Fan, J., Wang, X., Wu, L., Zhou, H., Zhang, F., Yu, X., Lu, X., & Xiang, Y. (2018). Comparison of support vector machine and extreme gradient boosting for predicting daily global solar radiation using temperature and precipitation in humid subtropical climates: A case study in China. *Energy Conversion and Management, 164*, 102–111. doi:10.1016/j.enconman.2018.02.087

Fayyad, U., & Simoudis, E. (1995). Knowledge Discovery and Data Mining Tutorial MA1. *Fourteenth International Joint Conference on Artificial Intelligence (IJCAI-95).* www-aig.jpl.nasa.gov/public/kdd95/tutorials/IJCAI95- tutorial.html

Fayyad, U., Piatetsky-Shapiro, G., & Smyth, P. (1996a). From data mining to knowledge discovery in databases. *AI Magazine, 17*(3), 37–37.

Fayyad, U., Piatetsky-Shapiro, G., & Smyth, P. (1996b). The KDD process for extracting useful knowledge from volumes of data. *Communications of the ACM, 39*(11), 27–34. doi:10.1145/240455.240464

Feldman, S. (2018). *A visual representation of America's digital literacy.* Retrieved from: https://www.weforum.org/agenda/2019/10/americans-get-a-failing-grade-for-digital-literacy#:~:text=A%20new%20report%20by%20Pew,tech%20policies%20and%20data%20privacy

Ferrag, M. A., Friha, O., Maglaras, L., Janicke, H., & Shu, L. (2021). Federated Deep Learning for Cyber Security in the Internet of Things: Concepts, Applications, and Experimental Analysis. *IEEE Access : Practical Innovations, Open Solutions, 9*, 138509–138542. doi:10.1109/ACCESS.2021.3118642

Ferrag, M. A., Shu, L., Djallel, H., & Choo, K.-K. R. (2021). Deep learning-based intrusion detection for distributed denial of service attack in agriculture 4.0. *Electronics (Basel), 10*(11), 1257. doi:10.3390/electronics10111257

Finn, R. L., & Wright, D. (2016). Privacy, data protection and ethics for civil drone practice: A survey of industry, regulators and civil society organisations. *Computer Law & Security Report, 32*(4), 577–586. doi:10.1016/j.clsr.2016.05.010

Foley, S., Karlsen, J. R., & Putnin¸s, T. J. (2019). Sex, drugs, and bitcoin: How much illegal activity is financed through cryptocurrencies? *Review of Financial Studies, 32*(5), 1798–1853. doi:10.1093/rfs/hhz015

Gagnon, M. P., Ghandour, E. K., Talla, P. K., Simonyan, D., Godin, G., Labrecque, M., & Rousseau, M. (2014). Electronic health record acceptance by physicians: Testing an integrated theoretical model. *Journal of Biomedical Informatics, 48*, 17–27. doi:10.1016/j.jbi.2013.10.010 PMID:24184678

Galloway, S. (2020). *Post Corona: From Crisis to Opportunity, Portfolio*. Portfolio.

Galvane, Q., Lino, C., Christie, M., Fleureau, J., Servant, F., Tariolle, F. L., & Guillotel, P. (2018). Directing cinematographic drones. *ACM Transactions on Graphics, 37*(3), 1–18. doi:10.1145/3181975

Gangwal, A., Jain, A., & Mohanta, S. (2019). Blood Delivery by Drones: A Case Study on Zipline. *International Journal of Innovative Research in Science, Engineering and Technology, 8*(8), 8760–8766.

Ganne, E. (2018). *Can Blockchain revolutionize international trade?* World Trade Organization.

García-Bañuelos, L., Ponomarev, A., Dumas, M., & Weber, I. (2017, September). Optimized execution of business processes on blockchain. In *International Conference on Business Process Management* (pp. 130-146). Springer. 10.1007/978-3-319-65000-5_8

Garcia-Torres, S., Albareda, L., Rey-Garcia, M., & Seuring, S. (2018). Traceability for sustainability – literature review and conceptual framework. *Supply Chain Management*. Advance online publication. doi:10.1108/SCM-04-2018-0152

Gardner, N., McGranahan, D., & Wolf, W. (2011). *Question for your HR chief: Are we using our people*. Academic Press.

Gardner, R. M., & Shabot, M. M. (2001). Patient-monitoring Systems. In Biomedical Informatics: Computer Applications in Health care and Biomedicine. New York: Springer Science+Business Media, LLC.

Garland, F. C., Garland, C. F., Gorham, E. D., & Young, J. F. (1990). Geographic variation in breast cancer mortality in the United States: A hypothesis involving exposure to solar radiation. *Preventive Medicine, 19*(6), 614–622. doi:10.1016/0091-7435(90)90058-R PMID:2263572

Gauld, R. (2007). Public sector information systems project failures: Lessons from a New Zealand hospital organization. *Government Information Quarterly, 24*(1), 102–114. doi:10.1016/j.giq.2006.02.010

Gautron, R., Maillard, O. A., Preux, P., Corbeels, M., & Sabbadin, R. (2022). Reinforcement learning for crop management support: Review, prospects and challenges. *Computers and Electronics in Agriculture, 200*, 107182. doi:10.1016/j.compag.2022.107182

Gawande, A., & Bates, D. (2000). The use of information technology in improving medical performance. Part II. Physician-support tools. *Medscape General Medicine, 2*, E13. PMID:11104459

Geissbuhler, A., Lovis, C., Lamb, A., & Spahni, S. (2001). Experience with an XML/HTTP-based federative approach to develop a hospital-wide clinical information system. *Studies in Health Technology and Informatics, 84*(1), 735–739. PMID:11604834

Ghazvini, A., & Shukur, Z. (2013). Security challenges and success factors of electronic healthcare system. *Procedia Technology, 11*, 212–219. doi:10.1016/j.protcy.2013.12.183

Ghosh, Chatterjee, Shetty, & Datta. (2020). *An sdn-iot-based framework for future smart cities: Addressing perspective.* Academic Press.

Glaser, F. (2017, January). Pervasive decentralisation of digital infrastructures: a framework for blockchain enabled system and use case analysis. *Proceedings of the 50th Hawaii international conference on system sciences.* 10.24251/HICSS.2017.186

Gnanaprakasam, C., Vankara, J., Sastry, A. S., Prajval, V., Gireesh, N., & Boopathi, S. (2023). Long-Range and Low-Power Automated Soil Irrigation System Using Internet of Things: An Experimental Study. In Contemporary Developments in Agricultural Cyber-Physical Systems (pp. 87–104). IGI Global.

Goddard, B. L. (2000). Termination of a contract to implement an enterprise electronic medical record system. *Journal of the American Medical Informatics Association : JAMIA, 7*(6), 564–568. doi:10.1136/jamia.2000.0070564 PMID:11062230

Gomes, J., & Romão, M. (2016). Improving the success of IS/IT projects in Healthcare: Benefits and Project Management approaches. In Advances in Intelligent Systems and Computing (vol. 444, pp. 547-556). New Advances in Information Systems and Technologies, Springer International Publishing AG, Part of Springer Science+Business Media.

Gomes, J., & Romão, M. (2017). Aligning Information Systems and Technology with Benefit Management and Balanced Scorecard. In S. De Haes & W. Van Grembergen (Eds.), *Strategic IT Governance and Alignment in Business Settings* (pp. 112–131). IGI Global., doi:10.4018/978-1-5225-0861-8.ch005

Gomes, J., Romão, M., & Caldeira, M. (2013). The Benefits Management and Balanced Scorecard Strategy Map: How They Match. *International Journal of IT/Business Alignment and Governance, 4*(1), 44–54. doi:10.4018/jitbag.2013010104

Google. (n.d.-a). https://www.google.com/search?q=Simplified+illustration+of+the+Random+Forest+Algorithm+figure&sxsrf=APwXEde_MKabNtJy0lGGIsvwE4L3tfyEYA:1680239486778&source=lnms&tbm=isch&sa=X&ved=2ahUKEwjfvPzts4X-

Google. (n.d.-b). https://www.google.com/search?q=Simplified+illustration+of+the+Gradient+Boosting+Algorithm+figure&tbm=isch&ved=2ahUKEwi787Pvs4X-AhUmBbcAHSP1CGYQ2-

Grant, W. B., & Tuohimaa, P. (2004). Geographic variation of prostate cancer mortality rates in the United States: Implications for prostate cancer risk related to vitamin D (Beer et al., 2010) (multiple letters). *Int. J. Cancer, 111*, 470–471. doi: .20220 doi:10.1002/ijc

Gräther, W., Kolvenbach, S., Ruland, R., Schütte, J., Torres, C., & Wendland, F. (2018). Blockchain for education: Lifelong learning passport. *Proc. 1st ERCIM Blockchain Workshop, 1*-8.

Griffith, E. F., Schurer, J. M., Mawindo, B., Kwibuka, R., Turibyarive, T., & Amuguni, J. H. (2023). The Use of Drones to Deliver Rift Valley Fever Vaccines in Rwanda: Perceptions and Recommendations. *Vaccines, 11*(3), 605. doi:10.3390/vaccines11030605 PMID:36992189

Grimson, J., Grimson, W., & Hasselbring, W. (2000). The system integration challenge in health care. *Communications of the ACM, 43*(6), 49–55. doi:10.1145/336460.336474

Gronum, S., Steen, J., & Verreynne, M.-L. (2016). Business Model Design and Innovation: Unlocking The Performance Benefits of Innovation. *Australian Journal of Management, 41*(3), 585–605. doi:10.1177/0312896215587315

Grossmann, C., Powers, B., & McGinnis, J. M. (2011). *Digital Infrastructure for The Learning Health System: The Foundation for Continuous Improvement in Health and Health Care*. Institute of Medicine, The National Academies Press.

GS1 Global Traceability Standard. (2012). *Business Process and System Requirements for Full Supply Chain Traceability*. https://www.gs1.org/docs/traceability/Global_Traceability_Standard.pdf

GS1 Global Traceability Standard. (2017). *GS1's framework for the design of interoperable traceability systems for supply chains*. https://www.gs1.org/sites/default/files/docs/traceability/GS1_Global_Traceability_Standard_i2.pdf

Guo, H., & Yu, X. (2022). A survey on blockchain technology and its security. Blockchain. *Research and Applications, 3*, 100067.

Gupta, M. (2020, April 20). HR Analytics: Trend from Data to Predictive Analysis for HR Professionals. *International Journal of Psychosocial Rehabilitation, 24*(5), 2674–2682. doi:10.37200/IJPR/V24I5/PR201969

Haider, M., Ahmed, I., & Rawat, D. B. (2022). Cyber Threats and Cybersecurity Reassessed in UAV-assisted Cyber Physical Systems. *International Conference on Ubiquitous and Future Networks, ICUFN, 2022-July*, 222–227. 10.1109/ICUFN55119.2022.9829584

Halabi, L. M., Mekhilef, S., & Hossain, M. (2018). Performance evaluation of hybrid adaptive neuro-fuzzy inference system models for predicting monthly global solar radiation. *Appl. Energy, 213,* 247–261. doi: .01.035 doi:10.1016/j.apenergy.2018

Han, H., Lu, X., & Ren, L. (2002). Using data mining to discover signatures in network-based intrusion detection. *Proc. IEEE Comput. Graph. Appl.,* 212–217.

Han, M., Li, Z., He, J., Wu, D., Xie, Y., & Baba, A. (2018). A novel blockchain-based education records verification solution. *Proc. 19th Annu. SIG Conf. Inf. Technol. Educ.,* 178-183. 10.1145/3241815.3241870

Hand, D. J. (1981). *Discrimination and Classification*. John Wiley and Sons.

Han, K., Chang, Y. B., & Hahn, J. (2011). Information Technology Spillover and Productivity: The Role of Information Technology Intensity and Competition. *Journal of Management Information Systems, 28*(1), 115–145. doi:10.2753/MIS0742-1222280105

Hanumanthakari, S., Gift, M. M., Kanimozhi, K., Bhavani, M. D., Bamane, K. D., & Boopathi, S. (2023). Biomining Method to Extract Metal Components Using Computer-Printed Circuit Board E-Waste. In *Handbook of Research on Safe Disposal Methods of Municipal Solid Wastes for a Sustainable Environment* (pp. 123–141). IGI Global. doi:10.4018/978-1-6684-8117-2.ch010

Hardwick, F. S., Gioulis, A., Akram, R. N., & Markantonakis, K. (2018, July). E-voting with blockchain: An e-voting protocol with decentralisation and voter privacy. In *2018 IEEE International Conference on Internet of Things (iThings) and IEEE Green Computing and Communications (GreenCom) and IEEE Cyber, Physical and Social Computing (CPSCom) and IEEE Smart Data (SmartData)* (pp. 1561-1567). IEEE. 10.1109/Cybermatics_2018.2018.00262

Hariharan, A., Risling, M., Felic, A., & Ostertag, T. (2023). *Integration of Smart Glasses for Knowledge Transfer in Industrial Remote Maintenance: Learnings from Practice*. Paper presented at the Extended Reality and Metaverse, Cham, Switzerland.

Harrison, S., & Dowswell, G. (2002). Autonomy and bureaucratic accountability in primary care: What English general practitioners say. *Sociology of Health & Illness, 24*(2), 208–226. doi:10.1111/1467-9566.00291

Harthy, K. A., Shuhaimi, F. A., & Ismaily, K. K. J. A. (2019). The upcoming blockchain adoption in higher-education: Requirements and process. *Proc. 4th MEC Int. Conf. Big Data Smart City (ICBDSC)*, 1-5. 10.1109/ICBDSC.2019.8645599

Hartley, G., & Sundermann, E. (2014). The Efficacy of Using the EPC global Network for Livestock Traceability: A Proof of Concept. GS1.

Harvey, C. R., Moorman, C., & Toledo, M. (2018). How blockchain can help marketers build better relationships with their customers. *Harv. Bus. Rev.* Available online at: https://hbr. org/2018/10/how-blockchain-can-helpmarketers-build-better-relationships-with-their-customers

Hasan, Islam, & Alsaawy. (2019). *Smart Parking Model based on Internet of Things (IoT) and TensorFlow*. Academic Press.

Hasan, M., Rahman, A., & Islam, M. J. (2020). DistB-CVS: A distributed secure blockchain based online certificate verification system from Bangladesh perspective. *Proc. Technol.*, *28*, 29. doi:10.1109/ICAICT51780.2020.9333523

Haslhofer, Karl, & Filtz. (2016). O bitcoin where art thou? insight into large-scale transaction graphs. *SEMANTiCS*.

Hassani, H., Huang, X., & MacFeely, S. (2022). Impactful Digital Twin in the Healthcare Revolution. *Big Data and Cognitive Computing*, *6*(3), 83. doi:10.3390/bdcc6030083

Hassija, V., Batra, S., Chamola, V., Anand, T., Goyal, P., Goyal, N., & Guizani, M. (2021). A blockchain and deep neural networks-based secure framework for enhanced crop protection. *Ad Hoc Networks*, *119*, 102537. doi:10.1016/j.adhoc.2021.102537

Haux, R. (2006). Health information systems – past, present, future. *International Journal of Medical Informatics*, *75*(3-4), 268–281. doi:10.1016/j.ijmedinf.2005.08.002 PMID:16169771

Häyrinen, K., Saranto, K., & Nykänen, P. (2008). Definition, Structure, Content, Use and Impacts of Electronic Health Records: A Review of the Research Literature. *International Journal of Medical Informatics*, *77*(5), 291–304. doi:10.1016/j.ijmedinf.2007.09.001 PMID:17951106

Hazrin, N., Mohamad, H., Badiozaman, M. H., & Daud, H. (2008). *Smart Parking Reservation System using Short Message Services (SMS)*. https://www.trakaid.com/how-does-smart-parking-generate-new-revenue-streams/

Heeks, R. B. (2002). Information Systems and Developing Countries: Failure, Success, and Local Improvisations. *The Information Society*, *18*(2), 101–112. doi:10.1080/01972240290075039

Heeks, R. B. (2008). *Success and failure rates of e-Government in developing/transitional countries: Overview*. Building Digital Opportunities Programme, Information Exchange, University of Manchester's Institute for Development Policy and Management.

Heeks, R. B., & Davies, A. (1999). Different approaches to information age. In R. B. Heeks (Ed.), *Reinventing Government in the Information Age*. Routledge.

Hejlesen, O., Olesen, K., Dessau, R., Beltoft, I., & Trangeled, M. (2005). Decision support for diagnosis of lyme disease. *Studies in Health Technology and Informatics*, *116*, 205–210. PMID:16160260

He, K., Zhang, X., Ren, S., & Sun, J. (2016). Deep residual learning for image recognition. In *Proceedings of the IEEE conference on computer vision and pattern recognition* (pp. 770-778). IEEE.

Hema, N., Krishnamoorthy, N., Chavan, S. M., Kumar, N., Sabarimuthu, M., & Boopathi, S. (2023). A Study on an Internet of Things (IoT)-Enabled Smart Solar Grid System. In *Handbook of Research on Deep Learning Techniques for Cloud-Based Industrial IoT* (pp. 290–308). IGI Global. doi:10.4018/978-1-6684-8098-4.ch017

Hendrickson, A. R. (2003). Human resource information systems: Backbone technology of contemporary human resources. *Journal of Labor Research, 24*(3), 381–394. doi:10.100712122-003-1002-5

Hevner, A., & Chatterjee, S. (2010). Design Science Research in Information Systems. In *Design Research in Information Systems. Integrated Series in Information Systems, 22*. Springer. doi:10.1007/978-1-4419-5653-8_2

HireRight. (2018). *2018 Employment screening benchmark report*. Available at: www.hireright.com/resources/view/2018-employment-screening-benchmark-report

Hitt, L. M., & Brinjolfsson, E. (1996). Productivity, business profitability, and consumer surplus: Three different measures of information technology value. *Management Information Systems Quarterly, 20*(2), 121–142. doi:10.2307/249475

Holzinger, A. (2012). On knowledge discovery and interactive intelligent visualization of biomedical data. In *Proceedings of the Int. Conf. on Data Technologies and Applications DATA* (pp. 5-16). Academic Press.

Holzinger, A. (2011). *Successful management of research & development*. BoD–Books on Demand.

Holzinger, A., Stocker, C., Ofner, B., Prohaska, G., Brabenetz, A., & Hofmann-Wellenhof, R. (2013). Combining HCI, natural language processing, and knowledge discovery-potential of IBM content analytics as an assistive technology in the biomedical field. *Computer, 42*(1), 26–34.

Hoogenboom, G. (2000). Contribution of agrometeorology to the simulation of crop production and its applications. *Agricultural and Forest Meteorology, 103*(1-2), 137–157. doi:10.1016/S0168-1923(00)00108-8

Hornik, K., Stinchcombe, M., & White, H. (1989). Multilayer feedforward networks are universal approximators. *Neural Networks, 2*(5), 359–366. doi:10.1016/0893-6080(89)90020-8

Hossain, M. M., Rahman, M. A., Chaki, S., Ahmed, H., Haque, A., Tamanna, I., Lima, S., Ferdous, M. J., & Rahman, M. S. (n.d.). *Smart-Agri: A Smart Agricultural Management with IoT-ML-Blockchain Integrated Framework*. Academic Press.

Houben, R., & Snyers, A. (2018). *Cryptocurrencies and blockchain: Legal context and implications for financial crime, money laundering and tax evasion*. Policy Department for Economic, Scientific and Quality of Life Policies. Directorate-General for Internal Policies.

Howard, A. G., Zhu, M., Chen, B., Kalenichenko, D., Wang, W., Weyand, T., & Adam, H. (2017). *Mobilenets: Efficient convolutional neural networks for mobile vision applications*. arXiv preprint arXiv:1704.04861.

Hr, A. M. M. O. H. P. (2021, January 1). HR Analytics Methodical Measurement Of Hr Processes. *Elementary Education Online, 20*(1). Advance online publication. doi:10.17051/ilkonline.2021.01.713

Hsiao, J. H., Tso, R., Chen, C. M., & Wu, M. E. (2018). Decentralized E-voting systems based on the blockchain technology. In Advances in Computer Science and Ubiquitous Computing: CSA-CUTE 17 (pp. 305-309). Springer Singapore. doi:10.1007/978-981-10-7605-3_50

Huang, G., Huang, G. B., Song, S., & You, K. (2015). Trends in extreme learning machines: A review. *Neural Networks, 61*, 32–48. doi:10.1016/j.neunet.2014.10.001 PMID:25462632

Hughes, L., Dwivedi, Y. K., Misra, S. K., Rana, N. P., Raghavan, V., & Akella, V. (2019). Blockchain research, practice and policy: Applications, benefits, limitations, emerging research themes and research agenda. *International Journal of Information Management, 49*, 114–129. doi:10.1016/j.ijinfomgt.2019.02.005

Huh, S., Cho, S., & Kim, S. (2017, February). Managing IoT devices using blockchain platform. In *2017 19th international conference on advanced communication technology (ICACT)* (pp. 464-467). IEEE. 10.23919/ICACT.2017.7890132

Humayun, M., Jhanjhi, N., Hamid, B., & Ahmed, G. (2020, June). Emerging smart logistics and transportation using IoT and blockchain. *IEEE Internet Things Mag.*, *3*(2), 58–62. doi:10.1109/IOTM.0001.1900097

Hung, S. Y., Chen, C., & Wang, K. H. (2014). Critical success factors for the implementation of integrated healthcare information systems projects: An organizational fit perspective. *Communications of the Association for Information Systems*, *34*(1), 775–796. doi:10.17705/1CAIS.03439

Hu, T., Liu, X., Chen, T., Zhang, X., Huang, X., Niu, W., Lu, J., Zhou, K., & Liu, Y. (2021). Transaction-based classification and detection approach for ethereum smart contract. *Information Processing & Management*, *58*(2), 102462.

Huynh-The, T., Pham, Q., Pham, X., Nguyen, T., Han, Z., & Kim, D. (2023). Artificial intelligence for the metaverse: A survey. *Engineering Applications of Artificial Intelligence*, *117*, 105581. doi:10.1016/j.engappai.2022.105581

Hwang, Y. (2023). When makers meet the metaverse: Effects of creating NFT metaverse exhibition in maker education. *Computers & Education*, *194*, 104693. doi:10.1016/j.compedu.2022.104693

Hyrkäs, K., & Lehti, K. (2003). Continuous quality improvement through team supervision supported by continuous self-monitoring of work and systematic patient feedback. *Journal of Nursing Management*, *11*(3), 208–226. doi:10.1046/j.1365-2834.2003.00369.x PMID:12694365

Ilbiz, E., & Durst, S. (2019). The Appropriation of Blockchain for Small and Medium-sized Enterprises. *Journal of Innovation Management*, *7*(1), 26–45. doi:10.24840/2183-0606_007.001_0004

Im, K. S., Dow, K. E., & Grover, V. (2001). A reexamination of IT investment and the market value of the firm - An event study methodology. *Information Systems Research*, *12*(1), 103–117. doi:10.1287/isre.12.1.103.9718

Inder, S. (2023). Entrepreneurial Opportunities in Metaverse. In M. Gupta, P. Jindal, & S. Bansal (Eds.), *Promoting Consumer Engagement Through Emotional Branding and Sensory Marketing* (pp. 52–62). IGI Global.

Internet Security Scanner (ISS). (n.d.). IBM. Available: http://www.iss.net

ISEAL Alliance. (2016). *Chain of custody models and definitions*. https://www.isealalliance.org/sites/default/files/resource/2017-11/ISEAL_Chain_of_Custody_Models_Guidance_September_2016.pdf

Islam, M. D., Kubo, I., Ohadi, M., & Alili, A. A. (2009). Measurement of solar energy radiation in Abu Dhabi, UAE. *Appl. Energy*, *86*, 511–515. doi: .apenergy.2008.07.012 doi:10.1016/j

ITU. (2017). *Measuring the Information Society Report, 1*. Geneva, Switzerland: ITU Publications. Retrieved from https://www.itu.int/en/ITU-D/Statistics/Pages/publications/mis2017.aspx

ITU. (2018). *Measuring the Information Society Report*. Executive Summary. Geneva, Switzerland: ITU Publications. Retrieved from https://www.itu.int/pub/D-IND-ICTOI-2018

ITU. (2019). *The ICT Development Index (IDI) Methodology, indicators and definitions*. Retrieved from https://www.itu.int/en/ITU-/Statistics/Documents/statistics/ITU_ICT%20Development%20Index.pdf

Jabbar, R., Fetais, N., Krichen, M., & Barkaoui, K. (2020). Blockchain technology for healthcare: Enhancing shared electronic health record interoperability and integrity. *2020 IEEE International Conference on Informatics, IoT, and Enabling Technologies (ICIoT)*, 310–317. 10.1109/ICIoT48696.2020.9089570

Jackson, A., & Culbertson, S. (2013). Bad employees or bad policies: What can organizations do to stop misuse of information technology resources? *The Academy of Management Perspectives*, *27*(1). Advance online publication. doi:10.5465/amp.2013.0026

Jadav, N. K., Rathod, T., Gupta, R., Tanwar, S., Kumar, N., & Alkhayyat, A. (2023). Blockchain and artificial intelligence-empowered smart agriculture framework for maximizing human life expectancy. *Computers & Electrical Engineering*, *105*, 108486. doi:10.1016/j.compeleceng.2022.108486

Jamie Arjona, M. (2020). Improving Parking Availability Information Using Deep Learning Techniques. *Transportation Research Procedia*, *47*, 385–392. doi:10.1016/j.trpro.2020.03.113

Jamil, M. I. M., & Almunawar, M. N. Importance of Digital Literacy and Hindrance Brought About by Digital Divide. In *Encyclopedia of Information Science and Technology* (5th ed., pp. 1683–1698). IGI Global.

Jamil, S., Rahman, M., & Fawad, M. (2022). A Comprehensive Survey of Digital Twins and Federated Learning for Industrial Internet of Things (IIoT), Internet of Vehicles (IoV) and Internet of Drones (IoD). *Applied System Innovation*, *5*(3), 56. doi:10.3390/asi5030056

Janizadeh, S., Avand, M., Jaafari, A., Phong, T. V., Bayat, M., Ahmadisharaf, E., Prakash, I., Pham, B. T., & Lee, S. (2019). Prediction success of machine learning methods for flash flood susceptibility mapping in the Tafresh watershed, Iran. *Sustainability (Basel)*, *11*(19), 5426. doi:10.3390u11195426

Jeevanantham, Y. A., Saravanan, A., Vanitha, V., Boopathi, S., & Kumar, D. P. (2022). Implementation of Internet-of Things (IoT) in Soil Irrigation System. *IEEE Explore*, 1–5.

Jensen, T. B. (2013). Design Principles for Achieving Integrated Healthcare Information Systems. *Health Informatics Journal*, *19*(1), 29–45. doi:10.1177/1460458212448890 PMID:23486824

Jeon, J. (2023). The impact of XR applications' user experience-based design innovativeness on loyalty. *Cogent Business & Management*, *10*(1), 2161761. doi:10.1080/23311975.2022.2161761

Jiang, G., & Wang, W. (2017). Error estimation based on variance analysis of k-fold cross-validation. *Pattern Recognit.*, *69*, 94–106. doi: .2017.03.025 doi:10.1016/j.patcog

Jiang, J., Muhanna, W., & Klenin, G. (2000). User resistance and strategies for promoting acceptance across system types. *Information & Management*, *37*(1), 25–36. doi:10.1016/S0378-7206(99)00032-4

Jiang, Y. (2009). Computation of monthly mean daily global solar radiation in China using artificial neural networks and comparison with other empirical models. *Energy*, *34*(9), 1276–1283. doi:10.1016/j.energy.2009.05.009

Jindal, A., Marnerides, A. K., Scott, A., & Hutchison, D. (2019). Identifying security challenges in renewable energy systems: A wind turbine case study. *Proceedings of the Tenth ACM International Conference on Future Energy Systems, e-Energy '19*, 370–372. 10.1145/3307772.3330154

Jin, H., Jin, S., Chen, L., Cen, S., & Yuan, K. (2015, December). Research on The Lighting Performance of Led Street Lights With Different Color Temperatures. *IEEE Photonics Journal*, *7*(6), 1–9. doi:10.1109/JPHOT.2015.2497578

Jirgensons, M., & Kapenieks, J. (2018, June). Blockchain and the future of digital learning credential assessment and management. *J. Teacher Educ. Sustainability*, *20*(1), 145–156.

Jolliffe, T. (2002). *Principal Component Analysis* (2nd ed.). Springer.

Jorgenson, D., & Stiroh, K. (2000). Raising the speed limit: US economic growth in the information age. In *Economic growth in the information age*. MIT Press. https://www.brookings.edu/bpea-articles/raising-the-speed-limit-u-s-economic-growth-in-the-information-age/

Julian, H., Chung, T., & Wang, Y. (2023). Adoption of Metaverse in South East Asia: Vietnam, Indonesia, Malaysia. In P. C. Lai (Ed.), *Strategies and Opportunities for Technology in the Metaverse World* (pp. 196–234). IGI Global. doi:10.4018/978-1-6684-5732-0.ch012

Kailash & Prathyusha. (2020). HR Analytics Methodical Measurement of HR Processes. *International Journal of Innovative Science and Research Technology, 5*(11).

Kamble, N., & Gala, R. (2021). Using blockchain in autonomous vehicles. In Artificial intelligence and blockchain for future cybersecurity applications (pp. 285-305). Academic Press.

Kapassa, E., & Themistocleous, M. (2022). Blockchain Technology Applied in IoV Demand Response Management: A Systematic Literature Review. *Future Internet, 14*(5), 136. doi:10.3390/fi14050136

Kaplan, B., & Harris-Salamone, K. (2009). Health IT success and failure: Recommendations from literature and an AMIA workshop. *Journal of the American Medical Informatics Association : JAMIA, 16*(3), 291–299. doi:10.1197/jamia.M2997 PMID:19261935

Kapwata, T., & Gebreslasie, M. T. (2016). Random forest variable selection in spatial malaria transmission modelling in Mpumalanga Province,South Africa. *Geospatial Health, 11*(3), 251–262. doi:10.4081/gh.2016.434 PMID:27903050

Karamitsos, I., Papadaki, M., & Al Barghuthi, N. B. (2018). Design of the blockchain smart contract: A use case for real estate. *Journal of Information Security, 9*(3), 177–190. doi:10.4236/jis.2018.93013

Katz, J. E., & Rice, R. E. (2002). *Social Consequences of Internet Use: access, involvement, and interaction.* MIT Press. doi:10.7551/mitpress/6292.001.0001

Kaur, P., & Parashar, A. (2022). A Systematic Literature Review of Blockchain Technology for Smart Villages. *Archives of Computational Methods in Engineering, 29*(4), 2417–2468. doi:10.100711831-021-09659-7 PMID:34720578

Kaushal, R., Shojania, K., & Bates, D. (2003). Effects of Computerized Physician Order Entry and Clinical Decision Support Systems on Medication Safety. A Systematic Review. *Archives of Internal Medicine, 163*(12), 1409–1416. doi:10.1001/archinte.163.12.1409 PMID:12824090

Kazanjian, A., & Green, C. (2002). Beyond effectiveness: The evaluation of information systems using a comprehensive health technology assessment framework. *Computers in Biology and Medicine, 32*(3), 165–177. doi:10.1016/S0010-4825(02)00013-6 PMID:11922933

Keogh, J. G. (2018). *Blockchain, Provenance, Traceability & Chain of Custody.* https://bit.ly/2LaJ6x7

Khan, A. A., Shaikh, Z. A., Belinskaja, L., Baitenova, L., Vlasova, Y., Gerzelieva, Z., Laghari, A. A., Abro, A. A., & Barykin, S. (2022). A blockchain and metaheuristic-enabled distributed architecture for smart agricultural analysis and ledger preservation solution: A collaborative approach. *Applied Sciences (Basel, Switzerland), 12*(3), 1487. doi:10.3390/app12031487

Khandelwal, R., & Katiyar, V. (2021). Smart street lighting system using IoT for smart cities: A review. *Journal of Ambient Intelligence and Humanized Computing, 12*(1), 21–38.

Khan, M. A., & Salah, K. (2018). IoT security: Review, blockchain solutions, and open challenges. *Future Generation Computer Systems, 82*, 395–411. doi:10.1016/j.future.2017.11.022

Kharchenko, V., Illiashenko, O., Fesenko, H., & Babeshko, I. (2022). AI Cybersecurity Assurance for Autonomous Transport Systems: Scenario, Model, and IMECA-Based Analysis. *Communications in Computer and Information Science, 1689 CCIS*, 66–79. doi:10.1007/978-3-031-20215-5_6

Khatibi Bardsiri, V., Jawawi, D. N. A., Hashim, S. Z. M., & Khatibi, E. (2013). A PSO-based model to increase the accuracy of software development effort estimation. *Software Quality Journal, 21*(3), 501–526. doi:10.100711219-012-9183-x

Kim, H. M., & Laskowski, M. (2018). Toward an ontology-driven blockchain design for supply-chain provenance. *International Journal of Intelligent Systems in Accounting Finance & Management, 25*(1), 18–27. doi:10.1002/isaf.1424

Kim, J. C., & Chung, K. (2020). Knowledge-based hybrid decision model using neural network for nutrition management. *Information Technology and Management, 21*(1), 29–39. doi:10.100710799-019-00300-5

Kim, J. K., Xiang, J. Y., & Lee, S. (2009). The impact of IT investment on firm performance in China: An empirical investigation of the Chinese electronics industry. *Technological Forecasting and Social Change, 76*(5), 678–687. doi:10.1016/j.techfore.2008.03.008

King, Z. (2010). *Human Capital Reporting: What information counts in the city.* Academic Press.

Kohli, R., & Grover, V. (2008). Business value of IT: An essay on expanding research directions to keep up with the times. *Journal of the Association for Information Systems, 9*(1), 23–39. doi:10.17705/1jais.00147

Kononova, K. (2015). Some aspects of ICT Measurement: Comparative Analysis of E-indexes. *Proceedings of the 7th International Conference in Information and Communication Technologies in Agriculture, Food and Environment (HAICTA 2015).*

Konovalova, M. E., Kuzmina, O. Y., & Zhironkin, S. A. (2020). Digital Technologies as a Factor of Expanding the Investment Opportunities of Business Entities. In S. Ashmarina, M. Vochozka, & V. Mantulenko (Eds.), *Digital Age: Chances, Challenges and Future, ISCDTE 2019. Lecture Notes in Networks and Systems, 84.* Springer. doi:10.1007/978-3-030-27015-5_23

Koo, C., Kwon, J., Chung, N., & Kim, J. (2022). Metaverse tourism: Conceptual framework and research propositions. *Current Issues in Tourism*, 1–7. doi:10.1080/13683500.2022.2122781

Koshariya, A. K., Kalaiyarasi, D., Jovith, A. A., Sivakami, T., Hasan, D. S., & Boopathi, S. (2023). AI-Enabled IoT and WSN-Integrated Smart Agriculture System. In *Artificial Intelligence Tools and Technologies for Smart Farming and Agriculture Practices* (pp. 200–218). IGI Global. doi:10.4018/978-1-6684-8516-3.ch011

Koshariya, A. K., Khatoon, S., Marathe, A. M., Suba, G. M., Baral, D., & Boopathi, S. (2023). Agricultural Waste Management Systems Using Artificial Intelligence Techniques. In *AI-Enabled Social Robotics in Human Care Services* (pp. 236–258). IGI Global. doi:10.4018/978-1-6684-8171-4.ch009

Kotamena, F., Senjaya, P., Putri, R. S., & Andika, C. B. (2021, March 14). Competence or communication: from HR professionals to employee performance via employee satisfaction. *Jurnal Manajemen Dan Kewirausahaan, 22*(1), 33–44. doi:10.9744/jmk.22.1.33-44

Kotarba, M. (2017). Measuring digitalization: Key metrics. *Foundations of Management, 9*(1), 123–138. doi:10.1515/fman-2017-0010

Koumaditis, K., Themistocleous, M., & Rupino da Cunha, P. (2013). SOA implementation critical success factors in healthcare. *Journal of Enterprise Information Management, 26*(4), 343–362. doi:10.1108/JEIM-06-2012-0036

Kouzes, R. T., Anderson, G. A., Elbert, S. T., Gorton, I., & Gracio, D. K. (2009). The changing paradigm of data-intensive computing. *Computer, 42*(1), 26–34. doi:10.1109/MC.2009.26

KPMG. (2015). *Evidence-based HR. The bridge between your people and delivering business strategy.* Author.

Kraus, S., Kumar, S., Lim, W., Kaur, J., Sharma, A., & Schiavone, F. (2023). From moon landing to metaverse: Tracing the evolution of Technological Forecasting and Social Change. *Technological Forecasting and Social Change, 189,* 122381. doi:10.1016/j.techfore.2023.122381

Kravchenko, O., Leshchenko, M., Marushchak, D., Vdovychenko, Y., & Boguslavska, S. (2019). Digitalization as a global trend and growth factor of the modern economy. *SHS Web of Conferences, 65,* 434–443. 10.1051hsconf/20196507004

Krist, A. H., & Woolf, S. H. (2011). A Vision for Patient-Centered Health Information Systems. *Journal of the American Medical Association, 305*(3), 300–301. doi:10.1001/jama.2010.2011 PMID:21245186

Kros, J., Liao, Y., Kirchoff, J., & Zemanek, J. Jr. (2019, January-June). Traceability in the Supply Chain. *International Journal of Applied Logistics, 9*(1), 1–22. doi:10.4018/IJAL.2019010101

Kshetri, N. (2018). Blockchain's roles in meeting key supply chain management objectives. *International Journal of Information Management, 39,* 80–89. doi:10.1016/j.ijinfomgt.2017.12.005

Kumar, C. R. S., & Mohanty, S. (2021). Current trends in cyber security for drones. *Proceedings - International Carnahan Conference on Security Technology, 2021-October,* 1–5. 10.1109/ICCST49569.2021.9717376

Kumar, P., Kumar, M., Singh, K. B., Tripathi, A. R., & Kumar, A. (2021, December). Blockchain Security Detection Condition Light Module. In *2021 10th International Conference on System Modeling & Advancement in Research Trends (SMART)* (pp. 363-367). IEEE. 10.1109/SMART52563.2021.9676302

Kumar, P., Sampath, B., Kumar, S., Babu, B. H., & Ahalya, N. (2023). Hydroponics, Aeroponics, and Aquaponics Technologies in Modern Agricultural Cultivation. In Trends, Paradigms, and Advances in Mechatronics Engineering (pp. 223–241). IGI Global.

Kumar, V. (2019). What Industry 4.0 Means for the Global Economy. *Industry Wired.* Retrieved from https://industry-wired.com/what-industry-4-0-means-for-the-global-economy/

Kumara, V., Mohanaprakash, T., Fairooz, S., Jamal, K., Babu, T., & Sampath, B. (2023). Experimental Study on a Reliable Smart Hydroponics System. In *Human Agro-Energy Optimization for Business and Industry* (pp. 27–45). IGI Global. doi:10.4018/978-1-6684-4118-3.ch002

Kumari, A., Tanwar, S., Tyagi, S., Kumar, N., Parizi, R. M., & Choo, K.-K. R. (2019). Fog data analytics: A taxonomy and process model. *Journal of Network and Computer Applications, 128,* 90–104. doi:10.1016/j.jnca.2018.12.013

Kumar, R., Kumar, P., Tripathi, R., Gupta, G. P., Gadekallu, T. R., & Srivastava, G. (2021). SP2F: A secured privacy-preserving framework for smart agricultural Unmanned Aerial Vehicles. *Computer Networks, 187,* 107819. doi:10.1016/j.comnet.2021.107819

Kumar, S., & Preetha, G. S. (2012). Health Promotion: An Effective Tool for Global Health. *Indian Journal of Community Medicine, 37*(1), 5–12. doi:10.4103/0970-0218.94009 PMID:22529532

Kuok, C. M., Fu, A., & Wong, M. H. (1998). Mining fuzzy association rules in databases. *SIGMOD Record, 27*(1), 41–46. doi:10.1145/273244.273257

Lal, R. (2020). Soil quality and sustainability. In *Methods for assessment of soil degradation* (pp. 17–30). CRC Press. doi:10.1201/9781003068716-2

Lanham, R. A. (2006). *The economics of attention: Style and substance in the age of information.* University of Chicago Press.

Laurens, R. (2019). *Get Fit for Digital Business: A Six-Step Workout Plan to Get Your Organisation in Great Shape to Thrive in a Connected Commercial World* (1st ed.). Routledge. doi:10.4324/9780429462146

Lawler, E. E., Levenson, A., & Boudreau, J. (2004). *HR Metrics and Analytics Uses and Impacts.* Academic Press.

Lawrence, R. J. (2004). Housing and health: From interdisciplinary principles to transdisciplinary research and practice. *Futures, 36*(4), 487–502. doi:10.1016/j.futures.2003.10.001

Le Brasseur, R., Whissell, R., & Ojha, A. (2002). Organizational learning, transformational leadship, and implementation of continuous quality improvement in Canadian Hospitals. *Australian Journal of Management, 27*(2), 141–162. doi:10.1177/031289620202700203

Lederer, M., Knapp, J., & Schott, P. (2017). The digital future has many names - How business process management drives the digital transformation. *6th International Conference on Industrial Technology and Management, ICITM 2017,* 22–26. 10.1109/ICITM.2017.7917889

Lee, H.-C., & Huang, H.-B. (2014). *A Low-Cost and Noninvasive System for The Measurement and Detection of Faulty Streetlights. IEEE Transaction on Instrumentation and Measurement.*

Lee, S. H., Goëau, H., Bonnet, P., & Joly, A. (2020). Attention-based recurrent neural network for plant disease classification. *Frontiers in Plant Science, 11,* 601250. doi:10.3389/fpls.2020.601250 PMID:33381135

Lee, S., Lee, D., Hooshyar, D., Jo, J., & Lim, H. (2020). Integrating breakdown detection into dialogue systems to improve knowledge management: Encoding temporal utterances with memory attention. *Information Technology and Management, 21*(1), 51–59. doi:10.100710799-019-00308-x

Lee, S., Xiang, J. Y., & Kim, J. K. (2011). Information Technology and Productivity: Empirical Evidence from the Chinese Electronics Industry. *Information & Management, 48*(2/3), 79–87. doi:10.1016/j.im.2011.01.003

Lee, Y., & Cho, J. (2020). Knowledge representation for computational thinking using knowledge discovery computing. *Information Technology and Management, 21*(1), 15–28. doi:10.100710799-019-00299-9

Leiding, B., Sharma, P., & Norta, A. (2021). The Machine-to-Everything (M2X) Economy: Business Enactments, Collaborations, and e-Governance. *Future Internet, 13*(12), 319. doi:10.3390/fi13120319

Lenz, R., & Reichert, M. (2007). IT support for healthcare processes: Premises, challenges, perspectives. *Data & Knowledge Engineering, 61*(1), 39–58. doi:10.1016/j.datak.2006.04.007

Leonard, K. J. (2000). Information Systems for Healthcare: Why we haven't had more success: The Top 15 Reasons. *Healthcare Management Forum, 13*(3), 45–51. doi:10.1016/S0840-4704(10)60776-4 PMID:15892319

Leonard, K. J. (2004). Critical Success Factors Relating to Healthcare's Adoption of New Technology: A Guide to Increasing the Likelihood of Successful Implementation. *ElectronicHealthcare, 2*(4), 72–81.

Leonard, K. J., & Winkelman, W. (2002). Developing Electronic Patient Records: Employing Interactive Methods to Ensure Patient Involvement. *Proceedings of the Proceedings of the 28th Meeting of the European Working Group on Operational Research Applied to Health Services (ORAHS),* 241-255.

Lerch, C., & Gotsch, M. (2015). Digitalized Product-Service Systems in Manufacturing Firms. *Research Technology Management, 58*(5), 45–52. doi:10.5437/08956308X5805357

Levenson, A. (2011). Using targeted analytics to improve talent decisions. *People and Strategy, 34*(2), 34.

Lin, W. T., & Shao, B. B. (2006). Assessing the input effect on productive efficiency in production systems the value of information technology capital. *International Journal of Production Research*, *44*(9), 1799–1819. doi:10.1080/00207540500353889

Lippmann, R. P., & Cunningham, R. K. (2000). Improving intrusion detection performance using keyword selection and neural networks. *Computer Networks*, *34*(4), 597–603. doi:10.1016/S1389-1286(00)00140-7

Lippmann, R., Haines, J., Fried, D., Korba, J., & Das, K. (2000). The 1999 DARPA offline intrusion detection evaluation. *Computer Networks*, *34*(4), 579–595. doi:10.1016/S1389-1286(00)00139-0

Li, R., Song, T., Mei, B., Li, H., Cheng, X., & Sun, L. (2018). Blockchain for large-scale internet of things data storage and protection. *IEEE Transactions on Services Computing*, *12*(5), 762–771. doi:10.1109/TSC.2018.2853167

Litke, A., Anagnostopoulos, D., & Varvarigou, T. (2019). Blockchains for Supply Chain Management: Architectural Elements and Challenges Towards a Global Scale Deployment. *Logistics*, *3*(5), 5. Advance online publication. doi:10.3390/logistics3010005

Liu, B., Tan, C., Li, S., He, J., & Wang, H. (2020). A data augmentation method based on generative adversarial networks for grape leaf disease identification. *IEEE Access : Practical Innovations, Open Solutions*, *8*, 102188–102198. doi:10.1109/ACCESS.2020.2998839

Liu, J., Wu, J., & Sun, L. (2020). Control method of urban intelligent parking guidance system based on Internet of Things. *Computer Communications*, *153*, 279–285. doi:10.1016/j.comcom.2020.01.063

Li, X., Wang, L., & Sung, E. (2008). AdaBoost with SVM-based component classifiers. *Engineering Applications of Artificial Intelligence*, *21*(5), 785–795. doi:10.1016/j.engappai.2007.07.001

Lorenzi, N. M., & Riley, R. (2003). Organizational issues = change. *International Journal of Medical Informatics*, *69*(2-3), 97–203. doi:10.1016/S1386-5056(02)00105-3 PMID:12810124

Low, C., & Chen, Y. (2012). Criteria for the evaluation of a cloud- based hospital information system outsourcing provider. *Journal of Medical Systems*, *36*(6), 3543–3553. doi:10.100710916-012-9829-z PMID:22366976

Lucas, H. (2008). Information and communications technology for future health systems in developing countries. *Social Medicine (Social Medicine Publication Group)*, *66*(10), 2122–2132. doi:10.1016/j.socscimed.2008.01.033 PMID:18343005

Lueg, R., & Lu, S. (2012). Improving efficiency in budgeting: An interventionist approach to spreadsheet accuracy testing. *Problems and Perspectives in Management*, *10*, 32–41.

Lueg, R., & Lu, S. (2013). How to improve efficiency in budgeting: The case of business intelligence in SMEs. *European Journal of Management*, *13*(2), 109–120. doi:10.18374/EJM-13-2.13

Lu, J., Tan, L., & Jiang, H. (2021). Review on Convolutional Neural Network (CNN) Applied to Plant Leaf Disease Classification. *Agriculture*, *11*(8), 707. doi:10.3390/agriculture11080707

Lu, N., Qin, J., Yang, K., & Sun, J. (2011). A simple and efficient algorithm to estimate daily global solar radiation from geostationary satellite data. *Energy*, *36*(5), 3179–3188. doi:10.1016/j.energy.2011.03.007

Lu, Q., & Xu, X. (2017). *Adaptable Blockchain-Based Systems: A Case Study for Product Traceability*. IEEE Software, November/December.

Lu, W., & Traore, I. (2004). Detecting new forms of network intrusion using genetic programming. *Computational Intelligence*, *20*(3), 470–489. doi:10.1111/j.0824-7935.2004.00247.x

Lv, Z., Qiao, L., Hossain, M. S., & Choi, B. J. (2021). Analysis of Using Blockchain to Protect the Privacy of Drone Big Data. *IEEE Network*, *35*(1), 44–49. doi:10.1109/MNET.011.2000154

Lymberis, A., & Dittmar, A. (2007). Advanced Wearable Health Systems and Applications: Research and Development Efforts in the European Union. *IEEE Engineering in Medicine and Biology Magazine*, *26*(3), 29–33. doi:10.1109/MEMB.2007.364926 PMID:17549917

Lyon, G. F. (2009). *Nmap Network Scanning: The Official Nmap Project Guide to Network Discovery and Security Scanning*. Insecure.

Macrinici, D., Cartofeanu, C., & Gao, S. (2018). Smart contract applications within blockchain technology: A systematic mapping study. *Telematics and Informatics*, *35*(8), 2337–2354. doi:10.1016/j.tele.2018.10.004

Maddahi, Y., & Chen, S. (2022). Applications of Digital Twins in the Healthcare Industry: Case Review of an IoT-Enabled Remote Technology in Dentistry. *Virtual Worlds*, *1*(1), 20–41. doi:10.3390/virtualworlds1010003

Madhani, P. M. (2022). Blockchain Applications in HR: Key Advantages. *HRM Review*, *18*(1), 17–26.

Mäenpää, T., Suominen, T., Asikainen, P., Maass, M., & Rostila, I. (2009). The outcomes of regional healthcare information systems in health care: A review of the research literature. *International Journal of Medical Informatics*, *78*(11), 757–771. doi:10.1016/j.ijmedinf.2009.07.001 PMID:19656719

Magalhães, L., Magalhães, L., Ramos, J., Moura, L., de Moraes, R., Gonçalves, J., Hisatugu, W. H., Souza, M. T., de Lacalle, L. N. L., & Ferreira, J. (2022). Conceiving a Digital Twin for a Flexible Manufacturing System. *Applied Sciences (Basel, Switzerland)*, *12*(19), 9864. doi:10.3390/app12199864

Mahmood, M. A., & Mann, G. J. (2005). Information technology investments and organizational productivity and performance: An empirical investigation. *Journal of Organizational Computing and Electronic Commerce*, *15*(3), 185–202. doi:10.120715327744joce1503_1

Mahraz, M., Benabbou, L., & Berrado, A. (2019) A Systematic literature review of Digital Transformation. *Proceedings of the International Conference on Industrial Engineering and Operations Management*.

Makade, R. G., Chakrabarti, S., & Jamil, B. (2019). Prediction of global solar radiation using a single empirical model for diversified locations across India. *Urban Climate*, *29*, 100492. doi:10.1016/j.uclim.2019.100492

Mane, P., Deoghare, R., Nagmote, S., Musle, S., & Sarwade, S. (2015). Android based Smart Parking System. Academic Press.

Markus, M. L., Axline, S., Petrie, D., & Tanis, C. (2000). Learning from adopters' experiences with ERP: Problems encountered, and success achieved. *Journal of Information Technology*, *14*(4), 245–265. doi:10.1080/02683960010008944

Marler, J. H., & Parry, E. (2016). Human resource management, strategic involvement and e-HRM technology. *International Journal of Human Resource Management*, *27*(19), 2233–2253. doi:10.1080/09585192.2015.1091980

Martin, R. C. (2017). *Clean architecture: A Craftsman's Guide to Software Structure and Design*. Pearson Education.

Mateen, F. J., Leung, K. H. B., Vogel, A. C., Cissé, A. F., & Chan, T. C. Y. (2020). A drone delivery network for anti-epileptic drugs: A framework and modelling case study in a low-income country. *Transactions of the Royal Society of Tropical Medicine and Hygiene*, *114*(4), 308–314. doi:10.1093/trstmh/trz131 PMID:31943110

Mathews, M., Robles, D., & Bowe, B. (2017). *BIM+ blockchain: A solution to the trust problem in collaboration?* Academic Press.

Matlay, H., Ruzzier, M., Hisrich, R. D., & Antoncic, B. (2006). SME internationalization research: Past, present, and future. *Journal of Small Business and Enterprise Development*, *13*(4), 476–497. doi:10.1108/14626000610705705

Mayhew, M., Atighetchi, M., Adler, A., & Greenstadt, R. (2015). Use of machine learning in big data analytics for insider threat detection. MILCOM 2015 - 2015 IEEE Military Communications Conference, 915–922. doi:10.1109/MILCOM.2015.7357562

Mazzorana-Kremer, F. (2019). Blockchain-Based Equity and STOs: Towards a Liquid Market for SME Financing? *Theoretical Economics Letters*, *9*(5), 1534–1552. doi:10.4236/tel.2019.95099

McCartney, S., & Fu, N. (2022, January 12). Bridging the gap: Why, how and when HR analytics can impact organizational performance. *Management Decision*, *60*(13), 25–47. doi:10.1108/MD-12-2020-1581

McEnroe, P., Wang, S., & Liyanage, M. (2022). A Survey on the Convergence of Edge Computing and AI for UAVs: Opportunities and Challenges. *IEEE Internet of Things Journal*, *9*(17), 15435–15459. doi:10.1109/JIOT.2022.3176400

Mead, N., & Bower, P. (2000). Patient-centeredness: A conceptual framework and review of empirical literature. *Social Science & Medicine*, *51*(7), 1087–1110. doi:10.1016/S0277-9536(00)00098-8 PMID:11005395

Medlin, C., Chowdhury, M., Jamison, D., & Measham, A. (2006). Improving the Health of Populations: Lessons of Experience. In *Disease Control Priorities in Developing Countries* (2nd ed.). World Bank.

Meenal, R., & Selvakumar, A. I. (2018). Assessment of SVM, empirical and ANN based solar radiation prediction models with most influencing input parameters. *Renewable Energy*, *121*, 324–343. doi:10.1016/j.renene.2017.12.005

Meidute-Kavaliauskiene, I., Yıldız, B., Çigdem, S., & Cincikaite, R. (2021). An Integrated Impact of Blockchain on Supply Chain Applications. *Logistics*, *5*(33), 33. Advance online publication. doi:10.3390/logistics5020033

Melcherts, H.E. (2017). The Internet of Everything and Beyond: The Interplay between Things and Humans. *Human Bond Communication: The Holy Grail of Holistic Communication and Immersive Experience*, 173-185.

Mellit, A. (2008). Artificial Intelligence technique for modelling and forecasting of solar radiation data: A review. *Int. J. Artif. Intell. Soft Comput.*, *1*(1), 52. doi:10.1504/IJAISC.2008.021264

Memon, M., Hussain, S. S., Bajwa, U. A., & Ikhlas, A. (2018, August). Blockchain Beyond Bitcoin: Blockchain Technology Challenges and Real-World Applications. In *2018 International Conference on Computing, Electronics & Communications Engineering (iCCECE)* (pp. 29-34). IEEE. 10.1109/iCCECOME.2018.8658518

Mendes, D., Rodrigues, I., Fonseca, C., Lopes, M., García-Alonso, J. M., & Berrocal, J. (2018, September). Anonymized distributed PHR using blockchain for openness and non-repudiation guarantee. In *International Conference on Theory and Practice of Digital Libraries* (pp. 381-385). Springer. 10.1007/978-3-030-00066-0_45

Michailidis, M. P. (2018). Hie Challenges of AI and Blockchain on HR Recruiting Practices. *The Cyprus Review*, *30*(2).

Mickan, S. (2005). Evaluating the effectiveness of health care teams. *Australian Health Review*, *29*(2), 211–217. doi:10.1071/AH050211 PMID:15865572

Mikroyannidis, A., Domingue, J., Bachler, M., & Quick, K. (2018). Smart blockchain badges for data science education. *Proc. IEEE Frontiers Educ. Conf. (FIE)*, 1-5. 10.1109/FIE.2018.8659012

Millman, C., Li, Z., Matlay, H., & Wong, W. C. (2010). Entrepreneurship education and students' internet entrepreneurship intentions. *Journal of Small Business and Enterprise Development*, *17*(4), 569–590. doi:10.1108/14626001011088732

Min, H. (2019, January). Blockchain technology for enhancing supply chain resilience. *Business Horizons*, *62*(1), 35–45. doi:10.1016/j.bushor.2018.08.012

Mire, S. (2018), Retrieved from Disruptor Daily: available at: https://www.disruptordaily.com/blockchain-market-map-human-resources

Mishra, A., & Akman, I. (2010). Information technology in human resource management: An empirical assessment. *Public Personnel Management*, *39*(3), 271–290. doi:10.1177/009102601003900306

Mithas, S., Tafti, A., Bardhan, T., & Goh, J. M. (2012). Information Technology and Firm Profitability: Mechanisms and Empirical Evidence. *Management Information Systems Quarterly*, *36*(1), 205–224. doi:10.2307/41410414

Mobjörk, M. (2010). Consulting versus participatory transdisciplinarity: A refined classification of transdisciplinary research. *Futures*, *42*(8), 866–873. doi:10.1016/j.futures.2010.03.003

Mohamed Farag & Elshenbary. (2020). *Deep learning versus traditional methods for parking lots occupancy classification*. Academic Press.

Mohammadi, Nazri, & Saif. (2019). *A Real-Time CloudBased Intelligent Car Parking System for Smart Cities*. Academic Press.

Mohammadi, A., Yousefi, M., Rostami, A., & Yaghmaee, M. H. (2019). A review of smart street lighting system based on IoT for smart city. *IEEE Access : Practical Innovations, Open Solutions*, *7*, 62255–62270.

Mohammed, F., Idries, A., Mohamed, N., Al-Jaroodi, J., & Jawhar, I. (2014). UAVs for smart cities: Opportunities and challenges. *2014 International Conference on Unmanned Aircraft Systems, ICUAS 2014 - Conference Proceedings*, 267–273. 10.1109/ICUAS.2014.6842265

Mohanta, B. K., Chedup, S., & Dehury, M. K. (2021). Secure trust model based on blockchain for internet of things enable smart agriculture. *2021 19th OITS International Conference on Information Technology (OCIT)*, 410–415.

Mohanty, S. N., Ramya, K. C., Rani, S. S., Gupta, D., Shankar, K., Lakshmanaprabu, S. K., & Khanna, A. (2020, January). An efficient lightweight integrated blockchain (ELIB) model for IoT security and privacy. *Future Generation Computer Systems*, *102*, 1027–1037. doi:10.1016/j.future.2019.09.050

Montecchi, M., Plangger, K., & Etter, M. (2019). It's real, trust me! Establishing supply chain provenance using blockchain. *Business Horizons*, *62*(3), 283–293. doi:10.1016/j.bushor.2019.01.008

Moosavi, J., Naeni, L. M., Fathollahi-Fard, A. M., & Fiore, U. (2021). Moosavi1, J., Naeni1, L., Fathollahi-Fard, A., & Fiore, U.: Blockchain in supply chain management: a review, bibliometric, and network analysis. *Environmental Science and Pollution Research International*. Advance online publication. doi:10.100711356-021-13094-3

Morel, B. (2011). Artificial intelligence and the future of cybersecurity. *Proc. 4th ACM Workshop Secur. Artif. Intell.*, 93–98. 10.1145/2046684.2046699

Mori, T. (2016). Financial technology: Blockchain and securities settlement. *Journal of Securities Operations & Custody*, *8*(3), 208–227.

Morkunas, V. J., Paschen, J., & Boon, E. (2019, May). How blockchain technologies impact your business model. *Business Horizons*, *62*(3), 295–306. doi:10.1016/j.bushor.2019.01.009

Mosteanu, N. R. (2020). Digital systems and new challenges of nancial management-FinTech, XBRL, blockchain and cryptocurrencies. *Inf. Secur. Manage.*, *21*(174), 9.

Mougayar, W. (2016). *The business blockchain: promise, practice, and application of the next Internet technology*. John Wiley & Sons.

Mourtzis, D., Angelopoulos, J., & Panopoulos, N. (2023). Blockchain Integration in the Era of Industrial Metaverse. *Applied Sciences (Basel, Switzerland)*, *13*(3), 1353. doi:10.3390/app13031353

Mukkamala, A., Sung, A., & Abraham, A. (2005). *Cyber security challenges: Designing efficient intrusion detection systems and antivirus tools*. In V. R. Vemuri (Ed.), *Enhancing Computer Security with Smart Technology* (pp. 125–163). Auerbach.

Munthe, C. (2008). The Goals of Public Health: An Integrated, Multidimensional Model. *Public Health Ethics*, *1*(1), 39–52. doi:10.1093/phe/phn006

Murray, E., Lo, B., Pollack, L., Donelan, K., Catania, J., Lee, K., Turner, R., & ... . (2003). The Impact of Health Information on the Internet on Health Care and the Physician-Patient Relationship: National U.S. Survey among 1.050 U.S. Physicians. *Journal of Medical Internet Research*, *5*(3), e17. doi:10.2196/jmir.5.3.e17 PMID:14517108

Mystakidis, S. (2023). Sustainable Engagement in Open and Distance Learning With Play and Games in Virtual Reality: Playful and Gameful Distance Education in VR. In Research Anthology on Virtual Environments and Building the Metaverse (pp. 297-312). IGI Global.

N, M., & Gowda, K. J. (2020). Image Processing System based Identification and Classification of Leaf Disease: A Case Study on Paddy Leaf. *2020 International Conference on Electronics and Sustainable Communication Systems (ICESC)*. doi:10.1109/ICESC48915.2020.9155607

Nakamoto, S. (2019). *Bitcoin: A peer-to-peer electronic cash system*. Manubot.

Nandutu, I., Atemkeng, M., & Okouma, P. (2023). Integrating AI ethics in wildlife conservation AI systems in South Africa: A review, challenges, and future research agenda. *AI & Society*, *38*(1), 245–257. doi:10.100700146-021-01285-y

Naur, P. (2007). Computing versus human thinking. *Communications of the ACM*, *50*(1), 85–94. doi:10.1145/1188913.1188922

Naur, P. (2008). *The neural embodiment of mental life by the synapse-state theory*. Naur. Com Publishing.

Navadkar, Nighot, & Wantmure. (2018). Overview of blockchain technology in government/public sectors. *Int. Res. J. Eng. Technol.*, *5*(6), 2287-2292.

Nebiker, Meyer, Blaser, Ammann, & Rhyner. (2021). *Outdoor Mobile Mapping and AI-Based 3D Object Detection with Low-Cost RGB-D Cameras: The Use Case of On-Street Parking Statistics*. Academic Press.

Neirotti, P., & Paolucci, E. (2007). Assessing the strategic value of Information Technology: An analysis on the insurance sector. *Information & Management*, *44*(6), 568–582. doi:10.1016/j.im.2007.05.005

Nemoto, T., & González, J. L. (2021). Digital trade inventory: Rules, standards and principles. OECD Trade Policy Papers, No. 251, OECD Publishing. doi:10.1787/18166873

NetGroup. (n.d.). *Politecnico di Torino, Analyzer 3.0*. Available: http://analyzer.polito.it

Netlleton, S., Burrows, R., O' Malley, L., & Watt, I. (2011). Health e-types? *Information Communication and Society*, *7*(4), 531–553. doi:10.1080/1369118042000305638

Nguyen, T. (2022). Toward Human Digital Twins for Cybersecurity Simulations on the Metaverse: Ontological and Network Science Approach. *JMIRx Med*, *3*(2), e33502. doi:10.2196/33502

Nguyen, X.-T. (2018, June). Lessons from case study of secured transactions with bitcoin. *SMU Sci. Tech. Law Rev.*, *21*, 181.

Njoku, J., Nwakanma, C., Amaizu, G., & Kim, D. (2023). Prospects and challenges of Metaverse application in data-driven intelligent transportation systems. *IET Intelligent Transport Systems*, *17*(1), 1–21. doi:10.1049/itr2.12252

Nofer, M., Gomber, P., Hinz, O., & Schiereck, D. (2017). Blockchain. *Business & Information Systems Engineering*, *59*(3), 183–187. doi:10.100712599-017-0467-3

Nolan, S. (2011, February 22). HR analytics. *Strategic HR Review*, *10*(2). Advance online publication. doi:10.1108hr.2011.37210baa.001

Normalini, R., Ramayah, T., & Kurnia, S. (2012, July 20). Antecedents and outcomes of human resource information system (HRIS) use. *International Journal of Productivity and Performance Management*, *61*(6), 603–623. doi:10.1108/17410401211249184

NSKT Global. (n.d.). https://www.nsktglobal.com/what-are-the-biggest-cybersecurity-threats-in-2021-

Nyambal & Klein. (2021). *Automated Parking space detection using CNN, computer Vision and pattern recognition Date*. Academic Press.

Oishi, S., Kesebir, S., & Diener, E. (2011). Income inequality and happiness. *Psychological Science*, *22*(9), 1095–1100. doi:10.1177/0956797611417262 PMID:21841151

Ølnes, S., Ubacht, J., & Janssen, M. (2017). *Blockchain in government: Benefits and implications of distributed ledger technology for information sharing*. Academic Press.

Ølnes, S., Ubacht, J., & Janssen, M. (2017, September). Blockchain in government: Bene ts and implications of distributed ledger technology for information sharing. *Government Information Quarterly*, *34*(3), 355–364. doi:10.1016/j.giq.2017.09.007

Opatha. (2020). HR Analytics: A Literature Review and New Conceptual Model. *International Journal of Scientific and Research Publications*, *10*(6).

Páez, R., Pérez, M., Ramírez, G., Montes, J., & Bouvarel, L. (2020). An Architecture for Biometric Electronic Identification Document System Based on Blockchain. *Future Internet*, *12*(1), 10. doi:10.3390/fi12010010

Paidi, Fleyeh, & Nyberg. (2020a). *Deep learning-based vehicle occupancy detection in an open parking lot using thermal camera*. Academic Press.

Paidi, Fleyeh, & Nyberg. (2020b). *Dalarna University, Deep learning-based vehicle occupancy detection in an open parking lot using a thermal camera, IET Intelligent Transport System*. Academic Press.

Pal, A., & Kant, K. (2019). Using Blockchain for Provenance and Traceability in Internet of Things-Integrated Food Logistics. *Computer*, *52*(12), 94–98. doi:10.1109/MC.2019.2942111

Pamucar, D., Deveci, M., Gokasar, I., Tavana, M., & Köppen, M. (2022). A metaverse assessment model for sustainable transportation using ordinal priority approach and Aczel-Alsina norms. *Technological Forecasting and Social Change*, *182*, 121778. doi:10.1016/j.techfore.2022.121778

Pan, E., Johnston, D., Walker, J., Adler-Milstein, J., Bates, D. W., & Middleton, B. (2005). *The Value of Healthcare Information Exchange and Interoperability*. Health Information Management and Systems Society.

Pang, Z., Niu, F., & O'Neill, Z. (2020). Solar radiation prediction using recurrent neural network and artificial neural network: A case study with comparisons. *Renewable Energy*, *156*, 279–289. doi:10.1016/j.renene.2020.04.042

Paré, G., & Sicotte, G. (2001). Information technology sophistication in health care: An instrument validation study among Canadian hospitals. *International Journal of Medical Informatics*, *63*(3), 205–223. doi:10.1016/S1386-5056(01)00178-2 PMID:11502433

Park, J. H., & Park, J. H. (2017). Blockchain security in cloud computing: Use cases, challenges, and solutions. *Symmetry*, *9*(8), 164. doi:10.3390ym9080164

Park, S. T., Jung, J. R., & Chang, L. (2020). A study on policy measure for knowledge-based management in ICT companies: Focused on appropriability mechanisms. *Information Technology and Management*, *21*(1), 1–13. doi:10.100710799-019-00298-w

Park, S., & Kim, Y. (2022). A Metaverse: Taxonomy, Components, Applications, and Open Challenges. *IEEE Access : Practical Innovations, Open Solutions*, *10*, 4209–4251. doi:10.1109/ACCESS.2021.3140175

Pashkevich, A., & Makarovab, I. (2020). Blockchain Technology on the Way of Autonomous Vehicles Development. *Transportation Research Procedia*, *44*, 168–175. doi:10.1016/j.trpro.2020.02.024

Patel, V., Pan, L., & Rajasegarar, S. (2020). Graph deep learning based anomaly detection in ethereum blockchain network. In *International Conference on Network and System Security*. Springer.

Patton, M. Q. (2008). *Utilization-Focused Evaluation* (4th ed.). Sage Publications.

PDO. (n.d.). *Protected Designation of Origin*. European Commission Geographical indications and quality schemes. https://agriculture.ec.europa.eu/farming/geographical-indications-and-quality-schemes/geographical-indications-and-quality-schemes-explained_en#pdo

Peabody, J. W., Luck, J., Jain, S., Bertenthal, D., & Glassman, P. (2004). Assessing the Accuracy of Administrative Data in Health Information Systems. *Medical Care*, *42*, 1066-1072. https://www.jstor.org/stable/4640857

Peck, M. E. (2017). Blockchain world-Do you need a blockchain? This chart will tell you if the technology can solve your problem. *IEEE Spectrum*, *54*(10), 38–60. doi:10.1109/MSPEC.2017.8048838

Pedrosa, I., Bernardino, J., & Borges, M. (2021). Data-driven decision making strategies applied to marketing. *16th Iberian Conference on Information Systems and Technologies (CISTI)*.

Perboli, G., Musso, S., & Rosano, M. (2018). Blockchain in logistics and supply chain: A lean approach for designing real-world use cases. *IEEE Access : Practical Innovations, Open Solutions*, *6*, 62018–62028. doi:10.1109/ACCESS.2018.2875782

Persson, C., Bacher, P., Shiga, T., & Madsen, H. (2017). Multi-site solar power forecasting using gradient boosted regression trees. *Solar Energy*, *150*, 423–436. doi:10.1016/j.solener.2017.04.066

Peslak, A. R. (2003). A firm level study of information technology productivity using financial and market-based measures. *Journal of Computer Information Systems*, *43*(4), 72–80.

Petrenko, S. A., Makoveichuk, K. A., Chetyrbok, P. V., & Petrenko, A. S. (2017). About readiness for digital economy. *2017 IEEE II International Conference on Control in Technical Systems (CTS)*, 96-99, 10.1109/CTSYS.2017.8109498

Piccialli, Giampaolo, Prezioso, Crisci, & Cuomo. (2021). *Predictive Analytics for Smart Parking: A Deep Learning Approach in forecasting of IoT Data*. Academic Press.

Pinto, M. F., Soares, G. M., Mendonica, T. R. F., Almeeida, P. S., & Braga, H. A. C. (2014). *Smart Modules for Lighting System Applications and Power Quality Measurements*. IEEE. doi:10.1109/INDUSCON.2014.7059448

Polishetty, Roopaei, & Rad. (2016). *A Next-Generation Secure Cloud Based Deep Learning License Plate Recognition for Smart Cities*. Academic Press.

Pollari, I. (2016). The rise of Fintech opportunities and challenges. *Jassa*, (3), 15.

Polyviou, A., & Pappas, I. (2022). *Metaverses and Business Transformation.* Paper presented at the Co-creating for Context in the Transfer and Diffusion of IT, Cham, Switzerland.

Poon, E. G., Blumenthal, T., Jaggi, M., Honour, M. N., Bates, D. W., & Kaushal, R. (2004). Overcoming barriers to adopting and implementing computerized physician order entry in US hospitals. *Health Affairs, 23*(4), 184–190. doi:10.1377/hlthaff.23.4.184 PMID:15318579

Pooyandeh, M., Han, K. J., & Sohn, I. (2022). Cybersecurity in the AI-Based Metaverse: A Survey. *Applied Sciences (Basel, Switzerland), 12*(24), 12993. doi:10.3390/app122412993

Preda, A. M., Crişan, D. A., Stanica, J. L., & Samuel, A. N. A. (2019). Innovation and ICT Development: An Analysis for the EU-28 Member States. *Journal of Information Systems & Operations Management, 13*(2), 154–163.

Purdy, M., & Davarzani, L. (2015). *The Growth Game-Changer: How the Industrial Internet of Things can drive progress and prosperity.* Accenture Strategy. Retrieved from https://fliphtml5.com/wful/iehy/basic

PwC. (2017a). *How blockchain technology could impact HR and the world of work.* Available at: www. pwc.ch/en/insights/hr/how-blockchain-can-impact-hr-and-the-world-of-work.html

PwC. (2017b). *The talent challenge: harnessing the power of human skills in the machine age.* Available at: www.pwc.com/gx/en/ceo-survey/2017/deep-dives/ceo-survey-global-talent.pdf

Qamar, S., Anwar, Z., & Afzal, M. (2023). A systematic threat analysis and defense strategies for the metaverse and extended reality systems. *Computers & Security, 128*, 103127. doi:10.1016/j.cose.2023.103127

Quinlan, R. (1986). Induction of decision trees. *Machine Learning, 1*(1), 81–106. doi:10.1007/BF00116251

Rachinger, M., Rauter, R., Müller, C., Vorraber, W., & Schirgi, E. (2019). Digitalization and its influence on business model innovation. *Journal of Manufacturing Technology Management, 30*(8), 1143–1160. doi:10.1108/JMTM-01-2018-0020

Radford, A., Metz, L., & Chintala, S. (2015). *Unsupervised representation learning with deep convolutional generative adversarial networks.* arXiv preprint arXiv:1511.06434.

Raghupathi, W., & Tan, J. (1999). Strategic use of information technology in healthcare: A state-of-the-art. *Topics in Health Information Management, 1*(1), 1–15. PMID:10539419

Rahmadika, S., Kweka, B. J., Latt, C. N. Z., & Rhee, K. H. (2018). A Preliminary Approach of Blockchain Technology in Supply Chain System. In *2018 IEEE International Conference on Data Mining Workshops (ICDMW)* (pp. 156-160), IEEE. 10.1109/ICDMW.2018.00029

Rahman, A., Islam, M. J., Sunny, F. A., & Nasir, M. K. (2019). DistBlockSDN: A distributed secure blockchain based SDN-IoT architecture with NFV implementation for smart cities. *Proc. 2nd Int. Conf. Innov. Eng. Technol. (ICIET),* 1-6. 10.1109/ICIET48527.2019.9290627

Rai, A., Patnayakuni, R., & Patnayakuni, N. (1997). Technology investment and business performance. *Communications of the ACM, 40*(7), 89–97. doi:10.1145/256175.256191

Ramasundaram, A., Pandey, N., Shukla, Y., Alavi, S., & Wirtz, J. (2023). Fluidity and the customer experience in digital platform ecosystems. *International Journal of Information Management, 69*, 102599. doi:10.1016/j.ijinfomgt.2022.102599

Ramírez, R., Melville, N., & Lawler, E. (2010). Information technology infrastructure, organizational process redesign, and business value: An empirical analysis. *Decision Support Systems, 49*(4), 417–429. doi:10.1016/j.dss.2010.05.003

Ramudu, K., Mohan, V. M., Jyothirmai, D., Prasad, D., Agrawal, R., & Boopathi, S. (2023). Machine Learning and Artificial Intelligence in Disease Prediction: Applications, Challenges, Limitations, Case Studies, and Future Directions. In Contemporary Applications of Data Fusion for Advanced Healthcare Informatics (pp. 297–318). IGI Global.

Rawat, B., Bist, A. S., Apriani, D., Permadi, N. I., & Nabila, E. A. (2022). AI Based Drones for Security Concerns in Smart Cities. [ATM]. *APTISI Transactions on Management, 7*(2), 125–130. doi:10.33050/atm.v7i2.1834

Ray, P. P., Chowhan, B., Kumar, N., & Almogren, A. (2021, July). BIoTHR: Electronic health record servicing scheme in IoT-blockchain ecosystem. *IEEE Internet of Things Journal, 8*(13), 10857–10872. doi:10.1109/JIOT.2021.3050703

Reddy & Keerthi. (2017). HR Analytics - An Effective Evidence Based HRM Tool. *International Journal of Business and Management Invention, 6*(7).

Reid, F., & Harrigan, M. (2013). *An analysis of anonymity in the bitcoin system. In Security and privacy in social networks*. Springer.

Remote Workforce, Virtual Team Tasks, and Employee Engagement Tools in a Real-Time Interoperable Decentralized Metaverse. (2022). *Psychosociological Issues in Human Resource Management, 10*(1), 78. doi:10.22381/pihrm10120226

Respini, E. (Ed.). (2018). *Art in the Age of the Internet: 1989 to Today.* Yale University Press.

Reyes-Alcázar, V., Torres-Olivera, A., Núñes-García, D., & Almuedo-Paz, A. (2012). Critical Success Factors for Quality Assurance in Healthcare Organisations. In M. Savsar (Ed.), *Quality Assurance Management.* Academic Press. doi:10.5772/33081

Robinson, C. (2007). Clinician adoption of healthcare information technology. *Canadian Nursing Informatics, 2*(1), 4–21.

Rogers, Y. (2012). HCI theory: Classical, modern, and contemporary. *Synthesis Lectures on Human-Centered Informatics, 5*(2), 1–129. doi:10.2200/S00418ED1V01Y201205HCI014

Rosenblatt, F. (1958). The perceptron: A probabilistic model for information storage and organization in the brain. *Psychological Review, 65*(6), 386–408. doi:10.1037/h0042519 PMID:13602029

Roztocki, N., & Weistroffer, H. R. (2008). Event Studies in Information Systems Research: A Review. *Proceedings of the Americas Conference on Information Systems.* Available at: http://aisel.aisnet.org/amcis2008/248

Saarikko, T., Westergren, U., & Blomquist, T. (2020). Digital transformation: Five recommendations for the digitally conscious firm. *Business Horizons, 63*(6), 825–839. . doi:10.1016/j.bushor.2020.07.005

Saberi, S., Kouhizadeh, M., Sarkis, J., & Shen, L. (2019). Blockchain technology and its relationships to sustainable supply chain management. *International Journal of Production Research, 57*(7), 2117–2135. doi:10.1080/00207543.2018.1533261

Sabherwal, R., Jeyaraj, A., & Chowa, C. (2006). Information System Success: Individual and Organizational Determinants. *Management Science, 52*(12), 1849–1864. doi:10.1287/mnsc.1060.0583

Sabtu, M. (2023). Metaverse and Soft Skills Development Through Video Games. In M. Anshari, M. Syafrudin, & G. Alfian (Eds.), *Metaverse Applications for New Business Models and Disruptive Innovation* (pp. 120–132). IGI Global. doi:10.4018/978-1-6684-6097-9.ch008

Sahoo, S., & Halder, R. (2021). Traceability and ownership claimof data on big data marketplace using blockchain technology. *Journal of Information and Telecommunication, 5*(1), 35–61. doi:10.1080/24751839.2020.1819634

Sahu, P., Singh, A. P., Chug, A., & Singh, D. (2022). A Systematic Literature Review of Machine Learning Techniques Deployed in Agriculture: A Case Study of Banana Crop. *IEEE Access : Practical Innovations, Open Solutions, 10,* 87333–87360. doi:10.1109/ACCESS.2022.3199926

Said, Khan, & Hameed. (2021). The impact of performance management system on employees' performance. *International Journal of Business and Management Sciences, 2.*

Sairam, B. (2020). *Automated Vehicle Parking Slot Detection System Using Deep Learning.* ICCMC.

Sakthi, U., & DafniRose, J. (2022). Blockchain-enabled smart agricultural knowledge discovery system using edge computing. *Procedia Computer Science, 202,* 73–82. doi:10.1016/j.procs.2022.04.011

Salah, D., Ahmed, M. H., & ElDahshan, K. (2020). Blockchain Applications in Human Resources Management: Opportunities and Challenges. In *Proceedings of the Evaluation and Assessment in Software Engineering* (pp. 383-389). 10.1145/3383219.3383274

Salem, T., & Dragomir, M. (2022). Options for and Challenges of Employing Digital Twins in Construction Management. *Applied Sciences (Basel, Switzerland), 12*(6), 2928. doi:10.3390/app12062928

Sangani. (2017). *Global data to increase 10x by 2025: Data age 2025.* Academic Press.

Sankar, K. M., Booba, B., & Boopathi, S. (2023). Smart Agriculture Irrigation Monitoring System Using Internet of Things. In *Contemporary Developments in Agricultural Cyber-Physical Systems* (pp. 105–121). IGI Global. doi:10.4018/978-1-6684-7879-0.ch006

Sankar, L. S., Sindhu, M., & Sethumadhavan, M. (2017). Survey of consensus protocols on blockchain applications. *Proc. 4th Int. Conf. Adv. Com-put. Commun. Syst. (ICACCS),* 1-5. 10.1109/ICACCS.2017.8014672

Santhanam, R., & Hartono, E. (2003). Issues in linking information technology capability to firm performance. *Management Information Systems Quarterly, 27*(1), 125–153. doi:10.2307/30036521

Santos, C., Santos, V., Tavares, A., & Varajão, J. (2014). Project Management Success in Health – The need of additional research in public health projects. *Procedia Technology, 16,* 1080–1085. doi:10.1016/j.protcy.2014.10.122

Sarda, P., Chowdhury, M. J. M., Colman, A., Kabir, M. A., & Han, J. (2018, August). Blockchain for fraud prevention: a work-history fraud prevention system. In *2018 17th IEEE international conference on trust, security and privacy in computing and communications/12th IEEE international conference on big data science and engineering (TrustCom/BigDataSE)* (pp. 1858-1863). IEEE. 10.1109/TrustCom/BigDataSE.2018.00281

Şarlıoğlu, G., Boyacı, E., & Akca, M. (2023). Information and Communication Technologies in Logistics and Supply Chain Management in Turkey: Human Resource Practices and New Challenges. In N. Sharma & K. Shalender (Eds.), *Managing Technology Integration for Human Resources in Industry 5.0* (pp. 174–197). IGI Global. doi:10.4018/978-1-6684-6745-9.ch011

Satalkina, L., & Steiner, G. (2020). Digital Entrepreneurship and its Role in Innovation Systems: A Systematic Literature Review as a Basis for Future Research Avenues for Sustainable Transitions. *Sustainability (Basel), 12*(7), 2764. doi:10.3390u12072764

Saunders, L. (2019). *FinTech and consumer protection: A snapshot.* Nat. Consum. Law Center, Boston, MA, USA, Tech. Rep. 6-7.

Schatsky, D., & Muraskin, C. (2015). Beyond bitcoin: Blockchain is coming to disrupt your industry. *Deloitte Insight, 7.*

Schmeiss, J., Hoelzle, K., & Tech, R. P. (2019). Designing governance mechanisms in platform ecosystems: Addressing the paradox of openness through blockchain technology. *California Management Review*, *62*(1), 121–143. doi:10.1177/0008125619883618

Schwalje, W. (2012). Rethinking How Establishment Skills Surveys Can More Effectively Identify Workforce Skills Gaps. SSRN *Electronic Journal*. doi:10.2139/ssrn.2017556

Scott, R. (2016). *How blockchain, chatbots and PDRs will disrupt HR technology*. Available at: www. insidehr.com.au/how-blockchain-chatbots-and-pdrs-will-disrupt-hr-technology/

Sekhar, C. (2017). *Enhance employee performance management experience with blockchain*. LinkedIn. Available at: www.linkedin.com/pulse/enhance-employee-performance-managementexperience-blockchain-aknr

Selvakumar, S., Adithe, S., Isaac, J. S., Pradhan, R., Venkatesh, V., & Sampath, B. (2023). A Study of the Printed Circuit Board (PCB) E-Waste Recycling Process. In Sustainable Approaches and Strategies for E-Waste Management and Utilization (pp. 159–184). IGI Global.

Sengeni, D., Padmapriya, G., Imambi, S. S., Suganthi, D., Suri, A., & Boopathi, S. (2023). Biomedical Waste Handling Method Using Artificial Intelligence Techniques. In *Handbook of Research on Safe Disposal Methods of Municipal Solid Wastes for a Sustainable Environment* (pp. 306–323). IGI Global. doi:10.4018/978-1-6684-8117-2.ch022

Senthil Kumar & Surya. (2020). *Smart Parking Application Using Deep Learning Framework*. Academic Press.

Sermpinis, T., & Sermpinis, C. (2018). *Traceability Decentralization in Supply Chain Management Using Blockchain Technologies*. arXiv preprint arXiv:1810.09203.

Sev, J. T. (2017, January 25). Stress Management Strategies: An Approach For Productive Employee Performance In The Nigerian Banking Organizations A Survey Of Commercial Banking Firms In Nigeria. *Archives of Business Research*, *5*(1). Advance online publication. doi:10.14738/abr.51.2526

Shahbazi, Z., & Byun, Y.-C. (2021). Smart manufacturing real-time analysis based on blockchain and machine learning approaches. *Applied Sciences (Basel, Switzerland)*, *11*(8), 3535. doi:10.3390/app11083535

Shah, P. K., Pandey, R. P., & Kumar, R. (2016, November). Vector quantization with codebook and index compression. In *2016 International Conference System Modeling & Advancement in Research Trends (SMART)* (pp. 49-52). IEEE.

Shahzad, G., Yang, H., Waheed, A., & Lee, C. (2015). *Energy Efficient Intelligent Street Lighting System Using Traffic Adaptive Control*. IEEE Sensors Journal. doi:10.1109/JSEN.2016.25.57345

Shamshirband, S., Mohammadi, K., Tong, C. W., Zamani, M., Motamedi, S., & Ch, S. (2016). A hybrid SVM-FFA method for prediction of monthly mean global solar radiation. *Theoretical and Applied Climatology*, *125*(1-2), 53–65. doi:10.100700704-015-1482-2

Sharma, A., & Sharma, T. (2017). HR analytics and performance appraisal system: A conceptual framework for employee performance improvement. *Management Research Review*, *40*(6), 684–697. doi:10.1108/MRR-04-2016-0084

Sharma, P. K., Chen, M.-Y., & Park, J. H. (2017). A software dened fog node based distributed blockchain cloud architecture for IoT. *IEEE Access : Practical Innovations, Open Solutions*, *6*, 115–124. doi:10.1109/ACCESS.2017.2757955

Sharma, P. K., & Park, J. H. (2018, September). Blockchain based hybrid network architecture for the smart city. *Future Generation Computer Systems*, *86*, 650–655. doi:10.1016/j.future.2018.04.060

Sharma, R., & Yetton, P. (2003). The contingent effects of management support and task interdependence on successful information systems implementation. *Management Information Systems Quarterly*, *27*(4), 533–556. doi:10.2307/30036548

Sharma, V., Tripathi, A. K., & Mittal, H. (2022). Technological revolutions in smart farming: Current trends, challenges & future directions. *Computers and Electronics in Agriculture, 201*, 107217. doi:10.1016/j.compag.2022.107217

Shen, B., Tan, W., Guo, J., Zhao, L., & Qin, P. (2021). How to Promote User Purchase in Metaverse? A Systematic Literature Review on Consumer Behavior Research and Virtual Commerce Application Design. *Applied Sciences (Basel, Switzerland), 11*(23), 11087. doi:10.3390/app112311087

Shiffman, R., Michel, G., Essaihi, A., & Thornquist, E. (2004). Bridging the guideline implementation gap: A systematic, document-centered approach to guideline implementation. *Journal of the American Medical Informatics Association : JAMIA, 11*(5), 418–426. doi:10.1197/jamia.M1444 PMID:15187061

Shin, S. C., Ho, J. W., & Pak, V. Y. (2020). Digital Transformation through e-Government Innovation in Uzbekistan. *International Conference on Advanced Communication Technology, ICACT*. 10.23919/ICACT48636.2020.9061507

Shneiderman, B. (2001, December). Inventing discovery tools: Combining information visualization with data mining. In *Discovery Science: 4th International Conference, DS 2001 Washington, DC, USA, November 25–28, 2001 Proceedings* (pp. 17-28). Springer Berlin Heidelberg.

Shneiderman, B. (2002a). Creativity support tools. *Communications of the ACM, 45*(10), 116–120. doi:10.1145/570907.570945

Shneiderman, B. (2002b). Inventing discovery tools: Combining information visualization with data mining. *Information Visualization, 1*(1), 5–12. doi:10.1057/palgrave.ivs.9500006

Shortliffe, E. H., & Barnett, G. O. (2014). Biomedical data: their acquisition, storage and use. In *Biomedical informatics* (pp. 39–66). Springer. doi:10.1007/978-1-4471-4474-8_2

Shrivastava, S., & Shaw, J. B. (2003). Liberating HR through technology. *Human Resource Management, 42*(3), 201-222.

Sial, M. F. K. (2019). Blockchain Technology–Prospects, Challenges and Opportunities. *IEEE Blockchain, Technical Briefs*. Available at https://blockchain.ieee.org/technicalbriefs/june-2019/blockchain-technology-prospects-challenges-and-opportunities

Sidorenko, E. L., & Khisamova, Z. I. (2020). The Readiness of the Economy for Digitalization: Basic Methodological Approaches. In Digital Age: Chances, Challenges and Future. ISCDTE 2019. Lecture Notes in Networks and Systems, 84. Springer. doi:10.1007/978-3-030-27015-5_37

Siingh, D., Singh, R. P., Singh, A. K., Kulkarni, M. N., Gautam, A. S., & Singh, A. K. (2011). Solar activity, lightning and climate. *Surveys in Geophysics, 32*(6), 659–703. doi:10.100710712-011-9127-1

Sikorski, J. J., Haughton, J., & Kraft, M. (2017). Blockchain technology in the chemical industry: Machine-to-machine electricity market. *Applied Energy, 195*, 234–246. doi:10.1016/j.apenergy.2017.03.039

Simonyan, K., & Zisserman, A. (2014). *Very deep convolutional networks for large-scale image recognition.* arXiv preprint arXiv:1409.1556.

Simoudis, E. (1996). Reality check for data mining. *IEEE Intelligent Systems, 11*(05), 26–33.

Singh, A., Gaurav, K., Sonkar, G. K., & Lee, C.-C. (2023). Strategies to measure soil moisture using traditional methods, automated sensors, remote sensing, and machine learning techniques: Review, bibliometric analysis, applications, research findings, and future directions. *IEEE Access : Practical Innovations, Open Solutions, 11*, 13605–13635. doi:10.1109/ACCESS.2023.3243635

Sivathanu, B., & Pillai, R. (2020). Technology and talent analytics for talent management–a game changer for organizational performance. *The International Journal of Organizational Analysis*, *28*(2), 457–473. doi:10.1108/IJOA-01-2019-1634

Siyaev, A., & Jo, G. (2021). Towards Aircraft Maintenance Metaverse Using Speech Interactions with Virtual Objects in Mixed Reality. *Sensors (Basel)*, *21*(6), 2066. doi:10.339021062066 PMID:33804253

Słapczyński, T. (2019). Blockchain technology and cryptocurrencies-legal and tax aspects. *Zeszyty Naukowe Wyższej Szkoły Finansów i Prawa w Bielsku-Białej*, *23*(1), 31–36.

Smith, P. C., Mossialos, E., Papanicolas, I., & Leatherman, S. (2009). *Performance measurement for health system improvement: experiences, challenges and prospects*. Cambridge University Press.

Snell, A. (2007, January 1). Measuring the financial impact of HR: Defining and controlling the areas where HR adds cost and value. *Strategic HR Review*, *6*(2), 28–31. doi:10.1108/14754390780000954

Snyder, C. F., Wu, A. W., Miller, R. S., Jensen, R. E., Bantug, E. T., & Wolff, A. C. (2011). The role of informatics in promoting patient-centered care. *Cancer Journal (Sudbury, Mass.)*, *17*(4), 211–218. doi:10.1097/PPO.0b013e318225ff89 PMID:21799327

Somapa, S., Cools, M., & Dullaert, W. (n.d.). Characterizing supply chain visibility - a literature review. *International Journal of Logistics Management*. https://doi.org/ doi:10.1108/IJLM-06-2016-0150

Sonny, A. (2020). *Deep Learning-Based Smart Parking Solution using Channel State Information in LTEbased Cellular Networks*. COMSNETS.

Southon, F., Sauer, C., & Dampney, C. (1999). Lessons from a failed information systems initiative: Issues for complex organisations. *International Journal of Medical Informatics*, *55*(1), 33–46. doi:10.1016/S1386-5056(99)00018-0 PMID:10471239

Spence, A. (2018). *Blockchain and Chief Human Resource Officer*. Blockchain Research Institute.

Sreedevi, A., & Manike, C. (2022). A smart solution for tomato leaf disease classification by modified recurrent neural network with severity computation. *Cybernetics and Systems*, 1–41. doi:10.1080/01969722.2022.2122004

Stavytskyy, A., Kharlamova, G., & Stoica, E. (2019). The Analysis of the Digital Economy and Society Index in the EU. *Baltic Journal of European Studies*, *9*(3), 245–261. doi:10.1515/bjes-2019-0032

Stolfi, D. H., Alba, E., & Yao, X. (2017). Predicting Car Park Occupancy Rates in Smart Cities. *Proceedings of the International Conference on Smart Cities*, 107–117. 10.1007/978-3-319-59513-9_11

Stone, D. L., Deadrick, D. L., Lukaszewski, K. M., & Johnson, R. (2015). The influence of technology on the future of human resource management. *Human Resource Management Review*, *25*(2), 216–231. doi:10.1016/j.hrmr.2015.01.002

Stremousova, E., & Buchinskaia, O. (2019). Some Approaches to Evaluation Macroeconomic Efficiency of Digitalisation. *Business. Management in Education*, *17*(2), 232–247. doi:10.3846/bme.2019.11326

Strohmeier, D. E. P. A. P. S. (2014). HRM in the digital age–digital changes and challenges of the HR profession. *Employee Relations*, *36*(4). Advance online publication. doi:10.1108/ER-03-2014-0032

Suchman, L. A. (1987). *Plans and situated actions: The problem of human-machine communication*. Cambridge University Press.

Sultan, N., & Sultan, Z. (2012). The application of utility ICT in healthcare management and life science research: a new market for a disruptive innovation? In *Proceedings of EURAM 2012 Conference - Social Innovation for Competitiveness, Organizational Performance and Human Excellence, June 6-8*. Rotterdam School of Management.

Sumathi, M., Rajkamal, M., Raja, S., Venkatachalapathy, M., & Vijayaraj, N. (2022). A crop yield prediction model based on an improved artificial neural network and yield monitoring using a blockchain technique. *International Journal of Wavelets, Multresolution, and Information Processing*, 20(06), 2250030. doi:10.1142/S0219691322500308

Sumner, M. (1999). Critical Success Factors in Enterprise Wide Information Management Systems Projects. *Proceedings of Americas Conference on Information Systems*. 10.1145/299513.299722

Sun, H., Pi, B., Sun, J., Miyamae, T., & Morinaga, M. (2021). SASLedger: A Secured, Accelerated Scalable Storage Solution for Distributed Ledger Systems. [CrossRef]. *Future Internet*, 13(12), 310. doi:10.3390/fi13120310

Suresh Babu, C. V. (2023). *IoT and its Applications*. Anniyappa Publication.

Suresh Babu, C. V., & ... . (2023a). IoT-Based Smart Accident Detection and Alert System. In P. Swarnalatha & S. Prabu (Eds.), *Handbook of Research on Deep Learning Techniques for Cloud-Based Industrial IoT* (pp. 322–337). IGI Global., doi:10.4018/978-1-6684-8098-4.ch019

Suresh Babu, C. V., Ganesh, B. S., Kishoor, T., & Khang, A. (2023b). Automatic Irrigation System Using Solar Tracking Device. In A. Khang (Ed.), *Handbook of Research on AI-Equipped IoT Applications in High-Tech Agriculture* (pp. 239–256). IGI Global., doi:10.4018/978-1-6684-9231-4.ch013

Swierczek, F. W., & Shrestha, P. K. (2003). Information technology and productivity: A comparison of Japanese and Asia-Pacific banks. *The Journal of High Technology Management Research*, 14(2), 269–288. doi:10.1016/S1047-8310(03)00025-7

Syamala, M., Komala, C., Pramila, P., Dash, S., Meenakshi, S., & Boopathi, S. (2023). Machine Learning-Integrated IoT-Based Smart Home Energy Management System. In *Handbook of Research on Deep Learning Techniques for Cloud-Based Industrial IoT* (pp. 219–235). IGI Global. doi:10.4018/978-1-6684-8098-4.ch013

Szegedy, C., Liu, W., Jia, Y., Sermanet, P., Reed, S., Anguelov, D., ... Rabinovich, A. (2015). Going deeper with convolutions. In *Proceedings of the IEEE conference on computer vision and pattern recognition* (pp. 1-9). IEEE.

Tait, E., & Pierson, C. (2022). Artificial Intelligence and Robots in Libraries: Opportunities in LIS Curriculum for Preparing the Librarians of Tomorrow. *Journal of the Australian Library and Information Association*, 71(3), 256–274. doi:10.1080/24750158.2022.2081111

Tarasova, T. M., Averina, L. V., & Pecherskaya, E. P. (2020). Digitalization of the Public Sector of the Regional Economy. In Digital Age: Chances, Challenges and Future, ISCDTE 2019. Lecture Notes in Networks and Systems, 84. Springer. doi:10.1007/978-3-030-27015-5_32

Tavallaee, M., Bagheri, E., Lu, W., & Ghorbani, A. (2009). A detailed analysis of the KDD Cup 1999 data set. *Proc. 2nd IEEE Symp. Comput. Intell. Secur. Defense Appl.*, 1–6.

Tavares, M., Guerreiro, A., Coutinho, C., Veiga, F., & Campos, A. (2018). WalliD: Secure your ID in an Ethereum Wallet. In *2018 International Conference on Intelligent Systems (IS)* (pp. 714-721). IEEE. 10.1109/IS.2018.8710547

Tempfer, C., & Nowak, P. (2011). Consumer participation and organizational development in health care: A systematic review. *Wiener Klinische Wochenschrift*, 123(13–14), 408–414. doi:10.100700508-011-0008-x PMID:21739200

Terry, A. L., Thorpe, C. F., Giles, G., Brown, J. B., Harris, S. B., Reid, G. J., Stewart, M., & ... . (2008). Implementing electronic health records: Key factors in primary care. *Canadian Family Physician Medecin de Famille Canadien*, 54(5), 730–736. PMID:18474707

Teubner, T., & Camacho, S. (2023). Facing Reciprocity: How Photos and Avatars Promote Interaction in Micro-communities. *Group Decision and Negotiation*. Advance online publication. doi:10.100710726-023-09814-4

Themistocleous, M., Mantzana, V., & Morabito, V. (2009). Achieving Knowledge Management Integration through EAI: A Case Study from Healthcare Sector. *International Journal of Technology Management*, *47*(1-3), 114–126. doi:10.1504/IJTM.2009.024117

Thiruchelvam, V., Mughisha, A. S., Shahpasand, M., & Bamiah, M. (2018). Blockchain-based technology in the coffee supply chain trade: Case of burundi coffee. *Journal of Telecommunication, Electronic and Computer Engineering*, *10*(3-2), 121-125.

Tierney, W. (2001). Improving clinical decisions and outcomes with information: A review. *International Journal of Medical Informatics*, *62*(1), 1–9. doi:10.1016/S1386-5056(01)00127-7 PMID:11340002

Tilson, D., Lyytinen, K., & Sørensen, C. (2010). Research commentary - digital infrastructures: The missing IS research agenda. *Information Systems Research*, *21*(4), 748–759. doi:10.1287/isre.1100.0318

Torres-Olivera, A. (2003). La gestión por procesos asistenciales integrales: Una estrategia necesaria. *Atencion Primaria*, *31*(9), 561–563. doi:10.1016/S0212-6567(03)79216-6 PMID:12783744

Toyoda, K., Mathiopoulos, P. T., Sasase, I., & Ohtsuki, T. (2017). A novel blockchain-based product ownership management system (POMS) for anti-counterfeits in the post supply chain. *IEEE Access : Practical Innovations, Open Solutions*, *5*, 17465–17477. doi:10.1109/ACCESS.2017.2720760

Ukko, J., Saunila, M., Nasiri, M., Rantala, T., & Holopainen, M. (2022). Digital twins' impact on organizational control: Perspectives on formal vs social control. *Information Technology & People*, *35*(8), 253–272. doi:10.1108/ITP-09-2020-0608

UNCTAD. (2019). *Value Creation and Capture: Implications for Developing Countries*. Digital Economy Report 2019. New York: United Nations Publications. Retrieved from https://unctad.org/webflyer/digital-economy-report-2019

Underwood, S. (2016). *Blockchain beyond bitcoin*. Academic Press.

Ungureanu, A. (2021). The Digitalization Impact on the Entrepreneurial Leadership in the 21st Century. *International Journal of Social Relevance & Concern*, *9*(1), 25–32. doi:10.26821/IJSRC.9.1.2021.9109

United Nation Development Programme. (1999). *Small and Medium Enterprise Development*. Retrieved from: http://web.undp.org/evaluation/documents/Essentials-on-SME.pdf

Universe. (2014). *The digital universe of opportunities: Rich data and the increasing value of the internet of things*. Academic Press.

Unruh, G., & Kiron, D. (2017). Digital transformation on purpose. *MIT Sloan Management Review*. Retrieved from https://sloanreview.mit.edu/article/digital-transformation-on-purpose/

Uthayakumar, J., Vengattaraman, T., & Amudhavel, J. (2017). A simple lossless compression algorithm in wireless sensor networks: An application of wind plant data. *The IIOAB Journal*, *8*(2), 281–288.

Van der Meijden, M., Tange, H., Troost, J., & Hasman, A. (2003). Determinants of success of inpatient clinical information systems: A literature review. *Journal of the American Medical Informatics Association : JAMIA*, *10*(3), 235–243. doi:10.1197/jamia.M1094 PMID:12626373

van Dooren. (2012). *HR Analytics in practice*. Academic Press.

Van Klompenburg, T., Kassahun, A., & Catal, C. (2020). Crop yield prediction using machine learning: A systematic literature review. *Computers and Electronics in Agriculture*, *177*, 105709. doi:10.1016/j.compag.2020.105709

Van Walraven, C., Mamdani, M., Fang, J., & Austin, P. (2004). Continuity of care and patient outcomes after hospital discharge. *Journal of General Internal Medicine*, *19*(6), 624–631. doi:10.1111/j.1525-1497.2004.30082.x PMID:15209600 van Waveren, S., Rudling, R., Leite, I., Jensfelt, P., & Pek, C. (2023). Increasing Perceived Safety in Motion Planning for Human-Drone Interaction. *Proceedings of the 2023 ACM/IEEE International Conference on Human-Robot Interaction*, 446–455. 10.1145/3568162.3576966

Vanitha, S., Radhika, K., & Boopathi, S. (2023). Artificial Intelligence Techniques in Water Purification and Utilization. In *Human Agro-Energy Optimization for Business and Industry* (pp. 202–218). IGI Global. doi:10.4018/978-1-6684-4118-3.ch010

Vashisth, A., Singh Batth, R., & Ward, R. (2021). Existing Path Planning Techniques in Unmanned Aerial Vehicles (UAVs): A Systematic Review. *Proceedings of 2nd IEEE International Conference on Computational Intelligence and Knowledge Economy, ICCIKE 2021*, 366–372. 10.1109/ICCIKE51210.2021.9410787

Venkateswaran, N., Vidhya, R., Naik, D. A., Raj, T. M., Munjal, N., & Boopathi, S. (2023). Study on Sentence and Question Formation Using Deep Learning Techniques. In *Digital Natives as a Disruptive Force in Asian Businesses and Societies* (pp. 252–273). IGI Global. doi:10.4018/978-1-6684-6782-4.ch015

Voyant, C., Muselli, M., Paoli, C., & Nivet, M. L. (2012). Numerical weather prediction (NWP) and hybrid ARMA/ANN model to predict global radiation. *Energy*, *39*(1), 341–355. doi:10.1016/j.energy.2012.01.006

Vu. (2018). *Parking space status interference upon Deep CNN and multitask contrastive network with spatial transform.* IEEE.

Vukolić, M. (2015, October). The quest for scalable blockchain fabric: Proof-of-work vs. BFT replication. In *International workshop on open problems in network security* (pp. 112-125). Springer.

Vyas, S., Shabaz, M., Pandit, P., Parvathy, L. R., & Ofori, I. (2022). Integration of artificial intelligence and blockchain technology in healthcare and agriculture. *Journal of Food Quality*, *2022*, 2022. doi:10.1155/2022/4228448

W3C. (n.d.). *Decentralized Identifiers (DIDs) v1.0 Core architecture, data model, and representations.* https://www.w3.org/TR/did-core/

Wagner, E., Scott, S., & Galliers, R. (2006). The creation of 'best practice' software: Myth, reality and ethics. *Information and Organization*, *16*(3), 251–275. doi:10.1016/j.infoandorg.2006.04.001

Wang, H., Sanchez-Molina, J. A., Li, M., & Berenguel, M. (2019). Development of an empirical tomato crop disease model: A case study on gray leaf spot. *European Journal of Plant Pathology*, *156*(2), 477–490. doi:10.100710658-019-01897-7

Wang, M., Yu, H., Bell, Z., & Chu, X. (2022). Constructing an Edu-Metaverse Ecosystem: A New and Innovative Framework. *IEEE Transactions on Learning Technologies*, 1–13. doi:10.1109/TLT.2022.3226345

Wang, R., Lin, Z., & Luo, H. (2019). Blockchain, bank credit and SME financing. *Quality & Quantity*, *53*(3), 1127–1140. doi:10.100711135-018-0806-6

Wang, W. (2020, April). A SME Credit Evaluation System Based on Blockchain. In *2020 International Conference on E-Commerce and Internet Technology (ECIT)* (pp. 248-251). IEEE. 10.1109/ECIT50008.2020.00064

Wang, Y., Singgih, M., Wang, J., & Rit, M. (2019). Making sense of blockchain technology: How will it transform supply chains? *International Journal of Production Economics*, *211*, 221–236. doi:10.1016/j.ijpe.2019.02.002

Wang, Y., Su, Z., Zhang, N., Xing, R., Liu, D., Luan, T., & Shen, X. (2022). A Survey on Metaverse: Fundamentals, Security, and Privacy. *IEEE Communications Surveys and Tutorials*, 1–1. doi:10.1109/COMST.2022.3202047

Ward, J., & Daniel, E. (2012). *Benefits Management: How to increase the Business Value of Your IT Projects* (2nd ed.). John Wiley and Sons., doi:10.1002/9781119208242

Ward, J., Taylor, P., & Bond, P. (1996). Evaluation and realization of IS/IT benefits: An empirical study of current practice. *European Journal of Information Systems, 4*(4), 214–225. doi:10.1057/ejis.1996.3

Wears, R. L., & Berg, M. (2005). Computer technology and clinical works: Still waiting for Godot. *Journal of the American Medical Association, 293*(10), 1261–1263. doi:10.1001/jama.293.10.1261 PMID:15755949

Weber, I., Xu, X., Riveret, R., Governatori, G., Ponomarev, A., & Mendling, J. (2016). Untrusted Business Process Monitoring and Execution Using Blockchain. In M. La Rosa, P. Loos, & O. Pastor (Eds.), Lecture Notes in Computer Science: Vol. 9850. *Business Process Management. BPM 2016.* Springer. doi:10.1007/978-3-319-45348-4_19

Weick, K. E., & Sutcliffe, K. M. (2001). *Managing the unexpected: Assuring high performance in an age of complexity.* Jossey-Bass.

Wei, S. J., Al Riza, D. F., & Nugroho, H. (2022). Comparative study on the performance of deep learning implementation in the edge computing: Case study on the plant leaf disease identification. *Journal of Agriculture and Food Research, 10*, 100389. doi:10.1016/j.jafr.2022.100389

Weking, J., Desouza, K., Fielt, E., & Kowalkiewicz, M. (2023). Metaverse-enabled entrepreneurship. *Journal of Business Venturing Insights, 19*, e00375. doi:10.1016/j.jbvi.2023.e00375

West, B., Lyon, M., McBain, M., & Gass, J. (2004). Evaluation of a clinical leadership initiative. *Nursing Standard, 19*(5), 33–41. doi:10.7748/ns.19.5.33.s61 PMID:15524254

Westbrook, J., Braithwaite, J., Iedema, R., & Coiera, E. (2004). Evaluating the impact of information communication technologies on complex organizational systems: A multi-disciplinary multi-method framework. *Studies in Health Technology and Informatics, 107*, 1323–1327. PMID:15361029

Westerkamp, M., Victor, F., & Kupper, A. (2019). Tracing manufacturing processes using blockchain-based token compositions. *Digital Communications and Networks, 6*(2), 167–176. doi:10.1016/j.dcan.2019.01.007

West, L. A., & Courtney, J. F. (1993). The Information Problems in Organisations - A Research Model for the Value of Information and Information Systems. *Decision Sciences, 24*(2), 229–251. doi:10.1111/j.1540-5915.1993.tb00473.x

Wheatley, D. (2016, April 1). Employee satisfaction and use of flexible working arrangements. *Work, Employment and Society, 31*(4), 567–585. doi:10.1177/0950017016631447

WHO. (2005). *Connecting for Health: Global Vision, Local Insight.* Report for the World Summit on the Information Society. Geneva, Switzerland: World Health Organization. https://www.who.int/ehealth/resources/wsis_report/en/

WHO. (2006). *Building foundations for eHealth: Progress of Member States.* Geneva, Switzerland: World Health Organization. https://www.who.int/goe/publications/build_foundations/en/

WHO. (2011). *Global Health and Ageing.* National Institutes of Health publication n°.11.7737/oct.2011. National Institute on Aging, World Health Organization. https://www.who.int/ageing/publications/global_health.pdf, 19/07/2017.

WHO. (2015). *World report on ageing and health.* Geneva, Switzerland: World Health Organization. Available at: http://apps.who.int/iris/bitstream/10665/186463/1/9789240694811_eng.pdf?ua=1, 19/07/2017.

Wickson, F., Carew, A. L., & Russell, A. W. (2006). Transdisciplinary research: Characteristics, quandaries and quality. *Futures, 38*(9), 1046–1059. doi:10.1016/j.futures.2006.02.011

Wikipedia. (2019). *Type of Service.* https://en.wikipedia.org/wiki/Type_of_service

Wild, M. (2009). Global dimming and brightening: A review. *Journal of Geophysical Research, 114*, D00D16. Advance online publication. doi:10.1029/2008JD011470

William, P., Yogeesh, N., Vimala, S., Gite, P., & Associates. (2022). Blockchain technology for data privacy using contract mechanism for 5G networks. *2022 3rd International Conference on Intelligent Engineering and Management (ICIEM)*, 461–465.

Wong, L. W., Leong, L. Y., Hew, J. J., Tan, G. W. H., & Ooi, K. B. (2020). Time to seize the digital evolution: Adoption of blockchain in operations and supply chain management among Malaysian SMEs. *International Journal of Information Management*, *52*, 101997. doi:10.1016/j.ijinfomgt.2019.08.005

Wong, M. C., Yee, K. C., & Nohr, C. (2018). Socio-technical consideration for blockchain technology in healthcare. *Studies in Health Technology and Informatics*, *247*, 636–640. PMID:29678038

Wootton, R. (2009). The future use of telehealth in the developing world. In *Telehealth in the Developing World*. Royal Society of Medicine Press.

World Bank Group. (2011). *Small and Medium Enterprises A Cross-Country Analysis with a New Data Set*. Retrieved from: https://documents1.worldbank.org/curated/en/967301468339577330/pdf/WPS5538.pdf

World Economic Forum. (2016). *Digital Transformation of Industries: Demystifying Digital and Securing $100 Trillion for Society and Industry by 2025*. Geneva, Switzerland: World Economic Forum. Retrieved from https://reports.weforum.org/digital-transformation/wp-content/blogs.dir/94/mp/files/pages/files/wef1601-digitaltransformation-1401.pdf

World Trade Organisation. (2019). *Micro, small and medium-sized enterprises*. Retrieved from: https://www.wto.org/english/thewto_e/minist_e/mc11_e/briefing_notes_e/bfmsmes_e.htm#:~:text=In%20most%20countries%2C%20small%20and,referred%20to%20as%20micro%20firms.&text=In%20recent%20years%2C%20the%20interest,the%20WTO%20framework%20has%20increased

Xiong, M., & Wang, H. (2022). Digital twin applications in aviation industry: A review. *International Journal of Advanced Manufacturing Technology*, *121*(9), 5677–5692. doi:10.100700170-022-09717-9

Xu, L., Chen, L., Gao, Z., Chang, Y., Iakovou, E., & Shi, W. (2018). Binding the Physical and Cyber Worlds: A Blockchain Approach for Cargo Supply Chain Security Enhancement. In *2018 IEEE International Symposium on Technologies for Homeland Security* (pp. 1-5). IEEE. 10.1109/THS.2018.8574184

Xu, R., Nagothu, D., & Chen, Y. (2021). EconLedger: A Proof-of-ENF Consensus Based Lightweight Distributed Ledger for IoVT Networks. *Future Internet*, *13*(10), 248. doi:10.3390/fi13100248

Xu, X., Lu, Q., Liu, Y., Zhu, L., Yao, H., & Vasilakos, A. V. (2019). Designing blockchain based applications a case study for imported product traceability. *Future Generation Computer Systems*, *92*, 399–406. doi:10.1016/j.future.2018.10.010

Yahuza, M., Idris, M. Y. I., Ahmedy, I., Wahab, A. W. A., Nandy, T., Noor, N. M., & Bala, A. (2021). Internet of Drones Security and Privacy Issues: Taxonomy and Open Challenges. *IEEE Access : Practical Innovations, Open Solutions*, *9*, 57243–57270. doi:10.1109/ACCESS.2021.3072030

Yang, C., Tu, X., Autiosalo, J., Ala-Laurinaho, R., Mattila, J., Salminen, P., & Tammi, K. (2022). Extended Reality Application Framework for a Digital-Twin-Based Smart Crane. *Applied Sciences (Basel, Switzerland)*, *12*(12), 6030. doi:10.3390/app12126030

Yang, W., Wang, S., Yin, X., Wang, X., & Hu, J. (2022). A Review on Security Issues and Solutions of the Internet of Drones. *IEEE Open Journal of the Computer Society*, *3*, 96–110. doi:10.1109/OJCS.2022.3183003

Yasnoff, W. A., Humpheys, B. L., Overhage, J. M., Detmer, D. E., Brennan, P. F., Morris, R. W., & Fanning, J. P. (2004). A consensus action agenda for achieving the national health information infrastructure. *Journal of the American Medical Informatics Association : JAMIA*, *11*(49), 332–338. doi:10.1197/jamia.M1616 PMID:15187075

Yeo, K. T. (2002). Critical failure factors in information system projects. *International Journal of Project Management, 20*(3), 241–246. doi:10.1016/S0263-7863(01)00075-8

Yin, C., Zhu, Y., Fei, J., & He, X. (2017). A deep learning approach for intrusion detection using recurrent neural networks. *IEEE Access : Practical Innovations, Open Solutions, 5,* 21954–21961. doi:10.1109/ACCESS.2017.2762418

Ying, W., Jia, S., & Du, W. (2018). Digital enablement of blockchain: Evidence from HNA group. *International Journal of Information Management, 39,* 1–4. doi:10.1016/j.ijinfomgt.2017.10.004

Yiu, N. C. (2021). Toward Blockchain-Enabled Supply Chain Anti-Counterfeiting and Traceability. *Future Internet, 13,* 86. https://101blockchains.com/problems-blockchain-solve/

Yli-Huumo, J., Ko, D., Choi, S., Park, S., & Smolander, K. (2016). Where is current research on blockchain technology?—A systematic review. *PLoS One, 11*(10), e0163477. doi:10.1371/journal.pone.0163477 PMID:27695049

Yoo, T., De Wysocki, M., & Cumberland, A. (2018). *Country Digital Readiness: Research to Determine a Country's Digital Readiness and Key Interventions.* Research: Modelling an Inclusive Digital Future, CISCO. Retrieved from https://www.cisco.com/c/dam/assets/csr/pdf/Country-Digital-Readiness-White-Paper-US.pdf

Yuan, Y., & Wang, F. Y. (2016, November). Towards blockchain-based intelligent transportation systems. In *2016 IEEE 19th International Conference on Intelligent Transportation Systems (ITSC)* (pp. 2663-2668). IEEE. 10.1109/ITSC.2016.7795984

Yu, S., & Carroll, F. (2021). Implications of AI in National Security: Understanding the Security Issues and Ethical Challenges. In *Advanced Sciences and Technologies for Security Applications* (pp. 157–175). Springer. doi:10.1007/978-3-030-88040-8_6

Yusof, M. M., Kuljis, J., Papazafeiropoulou, A., & Stergioulas, L. K. (2008). An evaluation framework for health information systems: Human, organization and technology-fit factors (HOT-fit). *International Journal of Medical Informatics, 77*(6), 386–398. doi:10.1016/j.ijmedinf.2007.08.011 PMID:17964851

Zadeh, L. (1965). Fuzzy sets. *Information and Control, 8*(3), 338–35. doi:10.1016/S0019-9958(65)90241-X

Zalan, T. (2018). Born global on blockchain. *Review of International Business and Strategy, 28*(1), 19–34. doi:10.1108/RIBS-08-2017-0069

Zeng, Z., Wang, Z., Gui, K., Yan, X., Gao, M., & Luo, M. (2020). Daily global solar radiation in China estimated from high-density meteorological observations: A random forest model framework. *Earth Space Sci., 7.* doi:10.1029/2019EA001058

Zhang, Lu, Han, & Yan. (2019). Data-Driven Decision-Making (D3M): Framework, Methodology, and Directions. *IEEE Transactions on Emerging Topics in Computational Intelligence, 3*(4).

Zhang, M. J. (2005). Information systems, strategic flexibility and firm performance: An empirical investigation. *Journal of Engineering and Technology Management, 22*(3), 163–184. doi:10.1016/j.jengtecman.2005.06.003

Zhang, P., White, J., Schmidt, D. C., Lenz, G., & Rosenbloom, S. T. (2018, July). FHIRChain: Applying blockchain to securely and scalably share clinical data. *Computational and Structural Biotechnology Journal, 16,* 267–278. doi:10.1016/j.csbj.2018.07.004 PMID:30108685

Zhang, Z., Wen, F., Sun, Z., Guo, X., He, T., & Lee, C. (2022). Artificial Intelligence-Enabled Sensing Technologies in the 5G/Internet of Things Era: From Virtual Reality/Augmented Reality to the Digital Twin. *Advanced Intelligent Systems, 4*(7), 2100228. doi:10.1002/aisy.202100228

Zhengbing, H., Zhitang, L., & Junqi, W. (2008). A novel network intrusion detection system (NIDS) based on signatures search of data mining. *Proc. 1st Int. Conf. Forensic Appl. Techn. Telecommun. Inf. Multimedia Workshop (e-Forensics '08)*, 10–16.

Zilvan, V., Ramdan, A., Suryawati, E., Kusumo, R. B. S., Krisnandi, D., & Pardede, H. F. (2019). Denoising Convolutional Variational Autoencoders-Based Feature Learning for Automatic Detection of Plant Diseases. *2019 3rd International Conference on Informatics and Computational Sciences (ICICoS)*. 10.1109/ICICoS48119.2019.8982494

About the Contributors

Rajeev Kumar is PostDoc Researcher, IUKL Malaysia and Professor, Moradabad Institute of Technology, Moradabad- (India). He is Visited international countries London, United Kingdom and Mauritius as professional activities. Under his supervision awarded 4 scholar their Ph.D. and 5 Scholar is Ongoing their research work. He is awarded 3 times Best project supervisor award; He is delivered a guest lecture, keynote speaker, chaired a session in many National and International conferences, Faculty Development program and workshop; He is completed one Research Project from DST in Bhimtal; He is organized many IEEE international conferences and workshop. He is authored and coauthored more than 85 papers in refereed international journal (SCI and Non- SCI) and conferences like IEEE, Springer, American Institute of Physics, New York Science international Journal New York City (USA), American Science Journal, BioInfo science Journal, Academic science of international journal (USA), International Journal of researcher, American Journal of Physics (USA) and many international Conferences and National Conferences, like IIT Roorkee (International Conference), etc.

Abu Bakar Abdul Hamid chose academia as his profession in 1992, beginning as a lecturer and later rising to a Professor of Marketing and Supply Chain Management. He holds a BBA and an MBA from Northrop University (USA) and a PhD from the University of Derby, UK. He has demonstrated an excellent record of teaching and supervision for more than 25 years in the academic field, at both undergraduate and postgraduate levels. Above all, his achievement in graduating more than 35 PhD candidates proves his ability, capability, and passion in postgraduate supervisions. He has also produced impactful research and publications which directly strengthen his expertise in his area of interest. In particular, he has published more than 300 articles in competitive international journals, proceedings, books, and book chapters. He also managed to secure several competitive national grants and consultancies for various projects. Such commitment is truly a landmark of an academician. His accolades, academic recognition, and leadership demonstrate his level of professorship. His notable contributions are recognised locally and internationally, as proven by the multiple invitations he has received to be an invited speaker, reviewer, editor in journals, external assessor, and internal or external examiner. With such calibre, he has much to contribute to any academic institution in the world.

Noor Inayah Binti Ya'akub serves as Professor at Faculty of Economics and Management, Faculty of Law and Institute of West Asian Studies, Universiti Kebangsaan Malaysia since 1998 until 2014. She serves as a Director of the Centre for Corporate Planning & Leadership, Deputy Dean for Research Graduate School of Business, and the -rst Head of Quality, Faculty of Law UKM. She serves at Global Wisdom Centre, University Islam Malaysia. She was admitted to the Malaysian Bar as an Advocate &

Solicitor of the High Court of Malaya in 1996 became a quali-ed Shariah lawyer. She practiced law with Messrs. Abraham & Ooi and Co from 1996 to 1998S. She is also a quali-es Syarie lawyer of Negeri Sembilan. She has more than 20 years of experience in teaching Islamic Law, Syariah and Conventional Banking Law, Takaful and Insurance Law, Equity & Trust Law and Business Law and Ethics. She serves as Member of the Board Shariah Committee at CIMB Bank Berhad and Sun Life Malaysia Takaful Berhad. She served as Member of Board Shariah Committee at CIMB Islamic Bank Berhad until March 24, 2017. Currently, she is also a member of the Board of Shariah at Majlis Amanah Raya.

* * *

Hesham Mohammed Ali Abdullah is currently Assistant Professor (Ph.D. in Computer Science), Jouf University, KSA; he acted as assistant professor in Taiz University(Full time) and several private universities(part time) during teaching journey, He obtained Ph.D degree in Computer Science from Bharathiar University, Coimbatore, India in 2018.. he completed his Master of Computer Applications (MCA) degree in 2013 from Bharathiar University, Coimbatore, India. He has received his BSc Degree in July 2006 from The National University, Yemen, His research interests include Cognitive Radio Ad Hoc Network, Wireless Communication, network security, big data, IoT, Machine learning, and Data Visualization. He has publication several papers in national and international journals.

Pedro Azevedo has a degree in Telecomunications Engineering, a master in Management and an MBA. Working in tblx.io part of Daimler Trucks.

C. V. Suresh Babu is a pioneer in content development. A true entrepreneur, he founded Anniyappa Publications, a company that is highly active in publishing books related to Computer Science and Management. Dr. C.V. Suresh Babu has also ventured into SB Institute, a center for knowledge transfer. He holds a Ph.D. in Engineering Education from the National Institute of Technical Teachers Training & Research in Chennai, along with seven master's degrees in various disciplines such as Engineering, Computer Applications, Management, Commerce, Economics, Psychology, Law, and Education. Additionally, he has UGC-NET/SET qualifications in the fields of Computer Science, Management, Commerce, and Education. Currently, Dr. C.V. Suresh Babu is a Professor in the Department of Information Technology at the School of Computing Science, Hindustan Institute of Technology and Science (Hindustan University) in Padur, Chennai, Tamil Nadu, India.

Muhammad Waseem Bari is serving as Assistant Professor at Government College University Faisalabad, Punjab, Pakistan.

Mohsin Bashir is serving as Assistant Professor at Lyallpur Business School, Government College University Faisalabad, Punjab, Pakistan.

Sampath Boopathi is an accomplished individual with a strong academic background and extensive research experience. He completed his undergraduate studies in Mechanical Engineering and pursued his postgraduate studies in the field of Computer-Aided Design. Dr. Boopathi obtained his Ph.D. from Anna University, focusing his research on Manufacturing and optimization. Throughout his career, Dr. Boopathi has made significant contributions to the field of engineering. He has authored and published over 135 research articles in internationally peer-reviewed journals, highlighting his expertise and dedication to advancing knowledge in his area of specialization. His research output demonstrates his commitment to conducting rigorous and impactful research. In addition to his research publications, Dr. Boopathi has also been granted one patent and has three published patents to his name. This indicates his innovative thinking and ability to develop practical solutions to real-world engineering challenges. With 17 years of academic and research experience, Dr. Boopathi has enriched the engineering community through his teaching and mentorship roles. He has served in various engineering colleges in Tamilnadu, India, where he has imparted knowledge, guided students, and contributed to the overall academic development of the institutions. Dr. Sampath Boopathi's diverse background, ranging from mechanical engineering to computer-aided design, along with his specialization in manufacturing and optimization, positions him as a valuable asset in the field of engineering. His research contributions, patents, and extensive teaching experience exemplify his expertise and dedication to advancing engineering knowledge and fostering innovation.

Simhadri Chinna Gopi received his B.Tech degree in Computer Science and Engineering from JNTU Kakinada University, India in 2010. He completed his M.Tech, in Computer Science from the KL University, India in 2012. Currently, he is pursuing Doctor of Philosophy (Ph.D.) in the field of Computer Science and Engineering, VIT-AP University, Andhra Pradesh, India. His research interests include Digital Image Processing, Machine Learning and Deep Learning.

Mohammad Daradkeh is an Associate Professor of Business Analytics and Data Science at the College of Engineering & IT, University of Dubai. Prior to joining the University of Dubai, Dr. Daradkeh worked at Yarmouk University in Jordan and Lincoln University in New Zealand. His research interests are mainly in the areas of Business Intelligence, Data Analytics, and Innovation Management. He has published numerous research papers with reputed publishers such as Elsevier, Springer, Emerald MDPI and IGI. He has presented research papers at various international conferences. He is also a member of the editorial board of several reputed journals.

Anil Dhawan is an Associate Professor with more than 32 years of teaching experience. He has more than 25 publications, 3 books and UGC sponsored research projects to his credit. He is a motivational speaker and coach. Dr. Dhawan is head -department of commerce in Mukand Lal National College, affiliated to Kurukshetra University.

Jorge Gomes is a researcher at ADVANCE, ISEG, School of Economics & Management of the Universidade de Lisboa. He holds a PhD in Management from ISEG and a Masters in Management Sciences from ISCTE-IUL, He also have a post-graduation in Project Management from INDEG/ISCTE, and a degree in Geographic Engineering from the Faculty of Sciences of the Universidade de Lisboa. During the past 30 years, he has worked as an engineer, project manager, quality auditor and consultant. Teaches Management at ULHT, Lisboa. His research interests include Benefits Management, Project Management, Project Success, Maturity Models, IS/IT Investments, IS/IT in Healthcare and IS/IT Management.

Gonçalo João is a researcher at CICEE, UAL, Universidade Autónoma de Lisboa. Holds a PhD in Management from ISEG, Lisbon School of Economics and Management of the University of Lisbon and have a post-graduation in Systems and Information Technology for Organizations also from ISEG. He teaches the course IT Management at UAL, Universidade Autónoma de Lisboa.

Hari Kishan Kondaveeti received his B.Tech degree in Information Technology from Acharya Nagarjuna University, India in 2009. He completed his M.Tech, in Computer Science and Engineering from the JNTUK University, India in 2012 and then joined the Department of CS & SE, AUCE (A), Andhra University, India and got a Doctor of Philosophy (Ph.D.) in the field of Computer Science and Engineering. He worked as Research Associate in a research project funded by Naval Science and Technological Laboratory, India when he was at Andhra University. Currently, he is working as Associate Professor at the School of Computer Science and Engineering, VIT-AP University, Andhra Pradesh, India, and acting as a Deputy Director of Engineering Clinics. He is an IBM Certified Data Science Professional and NASSCOM Associate Analyst certified faculty and handling multiple Data Analytics courses. His research interests include Digital Image Processing, Machine Learning, Data Analytics, Remote Sensing, and IoT. In recent years, he is focusing on collaborating actively with researchers in several other disciplines and trying to develop interdisciplinary projects.

Olena Korzhyk was born in Vyshhorod, Ukraine in 1996. Received a Bachelor's degree in international business and Trade in Andrzej Frycz Modrzewski Krakow University, Poland in 2014 and Master's Degree in Business Management in Universidade Autónoma de Lisboa, Portugal in 2021. Made an Erasmus exchange program in Universidade Lusófona, Lisbon,Portugal in 2016. From 2018 to 2020 worked in financial department for an American manufacturing company of audio equipment and currently working in logistics and supply chain department in multinational telecommunications and information technology company.

A. V. Senthil Kumar is working as a Director & Professor in the Department of Research and PG in Computer Applications, Hindusthan College of Arts and Science, Coimbatore since 05/03/2010. He has to his credit 11 Book Chapters, 265 papers in International and National Journals, 25 papers in International Conferences, 5 papers in National Conferences, and edited Nine books (IGI Global, USA). He is an Editor-in-Chief for various journals. Key Member for India, Machine Intelligence Research Lab (MIR Labs). He is an Editorial Board Member and Reviewer for various International Journals. He is also a Committee member for various International Conferences. He is a Life member of International Association of Engineers (IAENG), Systems Society of India (SSI), member of The Indian Science Congress Association, member of Internet Society (ISOC), International Association of Computer Science and Information Technology (IACSIT), Indian Association for Research in Computing Science (IARCS), and committee member for various International Conferences.

Rajendra Kumar is working as a Professor in Rama University, Kanpur U.P. India in Department of Physics; He received B.Sc. and M.Sc. from Kanpur University with gold medal and Ph. D from CCS University Meerut U.P. with collaboration of NPL India in 2009, qualified CSIR-UGC-NET in 2002. He is teaching last 17 years in UG and PG students. So Many Students are doing doctorial research work under the supervision of him. His research work is in the field of Plasma Polymer thin films, Sensor Technology, solar cell, IOT health care system, Material Physics and Luminescence etc. He is author of more than 25 research papers in national as well as international Journals, and 25 national and international conferences research papers, copyright, and Patents. He is author of international book and book chapter for research which is also in the field of plasma polymerization thin films. He is the member of different Academic and Professional Societies. He is also editors and reviver of various national and international Journals. He is also the chairman of different academic committees in the university.

Rohaya Latip is an Associate Professor at Faculty of Computer Science and Information Technology, University Putra Malaysia. She holds a Ph. D in Distributed Database and Msc. in Distributed System from University Putra Malaysia in 2009 and 2001 respectively. She graduated her Bachelor of Computer Science from University Technology Malaysia, Malaysia in 1999. She was the head of Department of Communication Technology and Network in 2017-2022. She served as an Associate Professor at Najran university, Kingdom of Arab Saudi (2012-2013). She was the Head of HPC section in University Putra Malaysia (2011-2012) and consulted the Campus Grid project and also the Wireless for hostel in Campus UPM project. She was also a Co-researcher at Institute for Mathematic Research (INSPEM) from 2011 to 2019. She is the editorial board of International Journal of Computer Networks and Communications Security (IJCNCS), editorial board of International Journal of Digital Contents and Applications (IJDCA) and editorial board for International Journal of Computer Networks and Applications (IJCNA). Her research interests include Big Data, Cloud and Grid Computing, Network Management, and Distributed Database. For her research work, she won Gold medal at 4th annual International Invention Innovation Competition in Canada, iCAN2018 by Toronto International Society of Innovation & Advanced Skills (TISIAS), two medals at The World Inventor Award Festival (WIAF) 2014 organized by Korea Invention News. She was awarded Gold medal at Malaysia Technology Expo (MTE2014) and Malaysian Innovation Expo (MiExpo2013). She also won Silver medal at National Design, Research and Innovation Expo (PRPI) 2010 and Bronze medal at National Design, Research and Innovation Expo (PRPI) 2007 and 2006 respectively. She has published more than 80 papers in international and national journals, proceedings and posters.

Vandana Madaan is Associate Professor in MM Institute of Management, Maharishi Markandeshwar (Deemed to be University) Mullana Ambala. She is having more than 15 years of experience in academics and having good record in publications.

Faiq Mahmood is serving as Assistant Professor at Government College University Faisalabad, Punjab, Pakistan.

Sudha Ellison Mathe was born in Andhra Pradesh state, India. He received his B.Tech. degree in Electronics and Communications Engineering from Nagarjuna University, Guntur, India, in 2011. He completed his M.E. degree in Embedded Systems from Birla Institute of Technology and Science, Pilani, India, in 2013. He went on to receive his Ph.D degree in the field of VLSI architectures with Cryptographic applications from the National Institute of Technology, Warangal, India, in 2018. Currently, He is working as an Associate Professor for the past 5 years at Vellore Institute of Technology (VIT-AP) University, Amaravati, India. His research areas include VLSI architectures, Post Quantum Cryptography, Finite Field Arithmetic, IoT, FPGA & ASIC design.

Khairia Mehmood is a Ph.D scholar at Government College University Faisalabad, Punjab, Pakistan.

Haji Mohammad Izzuddin Bin Haji Mohammed Jamil is a PhD Candidate in Management at School of Business and Economics, Universiti Brunei Darussalam, conducting research in the field of Entrepreneurship. He received his Bachelor's Degree in Business Administration (Hons) at Coventry University, United Kingdom, and Master's Degree in Management at Universiti Brunei Darussalam. Prior to academia, his industry experiences started when he first became a salesman and distributor, and has since worked in various professions including becoming a Tutor/Teacher, Website and Application Developer, Business Administrative Officer and has experiences starting-up enterprises. His research areas include Entrepreneurship, Growth, and MSMEs. He teaches at Universiti Brunei Darussalam in the field of Management, Accounting and Economics.

Mário José Batista Romão is an Associate Professor of Information Systems at ISEG – University of Lisbon. He is Director of the Masters program in Computer Science and Management. He holds a PhD in Management Sciences by ISCTE-IUL and by Computer Integrated Manufacturing at Cranfiel University (UK). He also holds a MsC in Telecommunications and Computer Science, at IST - Instituto Superior Técnico, University of Lisbon. He is Pos-Graduated in Project Management and holds the international certification Project Management Professional (PMP), by PMI – Project Management International. He has a degree in Electrotecnic Engineer by IST.

Omar S. Saleh earned his B.Sc. in Computer Engineering from the University of Technology-Baghdad in 2006. He received his M.Sc. in Software Engineering from Staffordshire University-APU-Malaysia in 2012. Currently, he has submitted his Ph.D. thesis and is awaiting the final viva. He is presently employed as a lecturer in the Studies, Planning, and Follow-Up Directorate of the Ministry of Higher Education and Scientific Research in Iraq. In his field of expertise, he has authored and co-authored over 30 journal articles, conference publications, and book chapters that delve into the areas of Blockchain, Cloud Computing, Software Architecture, and IoT. Omar is also a reviewer for several indexed journals and has participated in organizing IEEE and other international conferences.

Hari Om Sharan, serving as Dean – Academic Affairs & FET at Rama University Uttar Pradesh, Kanpur (India), is having more than 15 Years of experience in academic as well in research, his research area is AI, Security and HPC. Dr. Sharan received his Ph.D in DNA Computing: A Novel Approach towards the solution of NP-Complete Problems, and his UG (B.Tech) & PG (M.Tech) in Computer Science and Engineering, He has done International certification in Data Science and Artificial Intelligence Machine Learning Deep Learning and its Application. Dr. Sharan also published three (03) books on Mobile Network Technology. Dr. Sharan developed short term course on Artificial Intelligence Machine Learning Deep Learning and its Application, and published 14 patents (National/International) & copyrights mostly in Computer Science and Engineering to serve the nation in the field of research. Dr. Sharan authored and coauthored more than 60 papers in refereed international journal & many international Conferences and National Conferences & serve as editor/Reviewer of different international journals, Springer International Conferences.

Priyanka Sharma is born in Jaipur, Rajasthan, India, in 1991. She Received her B.Tech. degree from Rajasthan Technical University, Kota, Rajasthan India, in 2012 in Information Technology and M.Tech. degree from Rajasthan Technical University, Kota, Rajasthan India, in 2016 in Computer Science. She is working as an Assistant Professor in the department of Computer Science & Engineering,

Swami Keshvanand Institute of Technology, Management & Gramothan, Jaipur, Rajasthan, India. She has guided various M.Tech. and UG scholars. She is member of IEEE, ACM and various professional societies. She has published more than 15 research papers in national and international journals/conferences, book chapters. Also, she has taken part in forums hosted by Infosys, TCS, Oracle, and IBM. Her area of interest is investigating the advancements in machine learning and deep learning applications. She has received accolades on a number of times in a variety of fields, including Designation as an Active Reviewer by some well-known journals. She was also given recognition by Infosys, India, for her remarkable performance in the Campus Link Program.

Rashi Shukla is currently working as an assistant professor in faculty of commerce and management department, Rama University, Kanpur. She has completed his graduation (B.A. in political science) from CSJM University, Kanpur and MBA from KIOT affiliated to Dr A. P.J Abdul Kalam Technical University (Formerly UPTU) Lucknow with specialization in HRM & Marketing. She has also completed Google certification training in digital marketing. She has more than seven years of experience of teaching. She has three research paper publications. She has also presented papers in National and International Seminars. Her interest areas are Human resource management, Organizational behavior, Marketing, HR analytics and General Management. She has also written a book titled, Pharma Marketing Management: Applications Useful for BBA AND MBA as well as for NET Paper II and III/ PSU's (MT)/Other Competitive Exams, with Marketing as a subject.

K. B. Singh, born in 1976, passed B. Sc. Physics (Hons.), M. Sc. Physics with Electronics as special paper, Ph. D. Physics, PGDCA, D. Sc. Physics, being placed in first class with distinction and Gold medalist from B. R. A. Bihar University and indulged in teaching and research. At present he is serving L. S. College, Muzaffarpur as a Assistant Professor. He has attended several national and international conferences. He is associated with Institute of Physics(IOP), London, Indian Science Congress Association(ISCA), Kolkata, Indian Society of Atomic & Molecular Physic (ISAMP), India, Optical Society of America (OSA), Delhi Chapter, Bihar Mathematical Society (BMS), Bihar, Indian Society for technical Education (ISTE), ISMAMS, LASSI, National Academy of Science(NAS), India, Indian Physics Teachers Associations as life member. He has published several research paper, article, and review in journals of national and international repute. He is chief editor of Journal of Physical Sciences, and reviewer of IJSRST, UGC approved journals.

Ram Singh is a New Age Innovative Educationist working as a Professor of Finance & International Business in MM Institute of Management, Maharishi Markandeshwar (Deemed to be University) Mullana-Ambala Haryana. He has earned his PhD in Finance & International Business from HNB Garhwal Central University Srinagar, Garhwal Uttarakhand India. Dr. Singh has a vast teaching and research experience of more than 14 years at the UG, PG, and PhD courses. Currently, 4 students are carrying out their research work under his supervision. Being a researcher and mentor, Dr. Singh holds multifarious positions in the field of academics as, a member of the research council, a member of IQAC, and NBA in the department, member of the Editorial Board of various reputed journals in the domain of Accounting, Finance & General Management, Reviewer in IGI Global, Inderscience Journals, Editor in Wiley, and IGI Global. Besides, Dr. Singh has also been awarded the "Excellent Reviewer Award-2020" by Bilingual Publishing Company Singapore, 'Best Doctoral Thesis Award-2022' by the International Association of Research & Developed Organization India, and 'National Elite Teacher Award-2022' by the International Institute of Organized Research (I2OR) Chennai. Currently, his professional affiliation includes being a member of four National & International academic organizations i.e. Life Member of the Indian Commerce Association (ICA), Life Member in the International Association of Academic plus Corporate Society (IAACS), Life Member in the Indian Academic Researchers Association (IARA), Life Member in the International Institute of Organized Research (I2OR). He also possesses dexterity in research, has published 5 patents, 6 Books, 2 Edited Books, and more than 25 research papers & articles in various National and International Peer-Reviewed, Scopus Journals, 22 Book Chapter in various National & International edited books, and 8 international conference proceedings publication. Dr. Singh has also served as a Resource Person/Session Chair and Co-Chair in 4 National and International Conferences; he has attended various FDPs (Conducted by IIT & NITTTR), QIPs (IITR), workshops, National & International Webinars conducted by renowned institutions.

Sunnydayal Vanambathina has received his B. Tech Degree in Electronics & Communication Engineering from JNTU Hyderabad, India in 2007 and received Master of Technology in Signal Processing from National Institute of Technology Calicut in 2010. He did Ph.D from National Institute of Technology Warangal, India. He visited the University of Seville, Spain under Erasmus Mundus PhD Exchange program during 2013–2014. He did postDoc in University of Crete, Greece. He published several publications and patents. His current areas of research interest are speech enhancement, statistical signal processing, Blind source separation and machine learning techniques.

Index

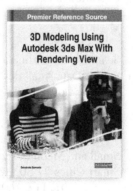

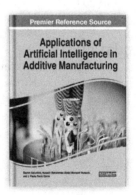

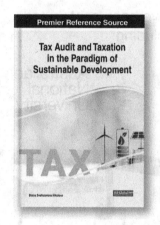

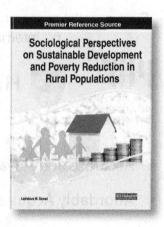

Printed in the United States
by Baker & Taylor Publisher Services